The Oasis of Bukhara

Volume 3

Arts and Archaeology of the Islamic World

Edited by

Margaret Graves (*Brown University*)
Marcus Milwright (*University of Victoria*)
Mariam Rosser-Owen (*Victoria and Albert Museum*)

VOLUME 21

The titles published in this series are listed at *brill.com/aaiw*

The Oasis of Bukhara

Volume 3: Material Culture, Socio-territorial Features, Archaeozoology and Archaeometry

Edited by

Rocco Rante

BRILL

LEIDEN | BOSTON

Cover illustration: Archaeological site studied by the Franco-Uzbek archaeological mission in the Bukhara oasis (MAFOUB). Musée du Louvre and Institute of Archeology of Samarkand. Aerial photo by kite. Copyright: Thomas Sagory / du-ciel.com, MAFOUB.

The Library of Congress Cataloging-in-Publication Data is available online at https://catalog.loc.gov
LC record available at https://lccn.loc.gov/2019009567

Typeface for the Latin, Greek, and Cyrillic scripts: "Brill". See and download: brill.com/brill-typeface.

ISSN 2213-3844
ISBN 978-90-04-50707-4 (hardback)
ISBN 978-90-04-69399-9 (e-book)
DOI 10.1163/9789004693999

Copyright 2024 by Rocco Rante. Published by Koninklijke Brill BV, Leiden, The Netherlands.
Koninklijke Brill BV incorporates the imprints Brill, Brill Nijhoff, Brill Schöningh, Brill Fink, Brill mentis, Brill Wageningen Academic, Vandenhoeck & Ruprecht, Böhlau and V&R unipress.
Koninklijke Brill BV reserves the right to protect this publication against unauthorized use. Requests for re-use and/or translations must be addressed to Koninklijke Brill BV via brill.com or copyright.com.

This book is printed on acid-free paper and produced in a sustainable manner.

To Lavinia and Antonio

Contents

Foreword IX
Preface X
List of Figures XI
List of Tables XVIII
Notes on Contributors XX

Introduction 1
   Rocco Rante

1 Settlements and Social Features within the Oasis of Bukhara 5
   Rocco Rante, Abdisabur Raimkulov and Fabrizio Crusco

2 Vardana and the Villages of Obavija
   Territorial Definition of a High Medieval District in the Bukhara Oasis 25
   Silvia Pozzi

3 The Bukhara Archaeological Expedition
   The History of Research in Paykend 43
   Andrey V. Omelchenko and Djamal Mirzaakhmedov
   Translated from Russian by Rocco Rante

4 Pottery 94
   Gabriele Puschnigg and Jacopo Bruno

5 Petrographic and Chemical Analyses of Ceramics from the Oasis of Bukhara 236
   Yvan Coquinot and Nathalie Gandolfo

6 Physico-chemical Analyses of Ceramics from Bukhara and Paykend 249
   Anne Bouquillon, Christel Doublet and Nathalie Gandolfo

7 Decorated Glazed Ceramics from Bukhara (15th–16th Centuries) 266
   Djamal Mirzaakhmedov
   Translated from Russian by Rocco Rante

8 Glassmaking in the Urban Centres of Uzbekistan in the 9th–15th Centuries 278
   Djamal Mirzaakhmedov
   Translated from Russian by Rocco Rante

9 Glass in the Bukhara Oasis, Uzbekistan 304
   Yoko Shindo (1960–2018), Takako Hosokawa, Tamako Takeda, Toshiyasu Shinmen and Ayano Endo

10 Animal Remains in the Oasis of Bukhara: Preliminary Results 364
    Decruyenaere Delphine, Rocco Rante, Manon Vuillien and Marjan Mashkour

11 Radiocarbon Dating in the Oasis of Bukhara 371
    Pascale Richardin and Rocco Rante

12 Luminescence Dating of Archaeological Sites from the Oasis of Bukhara 382
    Antoine Zink, Elisa Porto and Rocco Rante

Conclusion 405

General Bibliography 409
Index 423

Foreword

This third volume is the culmination of a magnificent series publishing research on the ten years of excavations by Rocco Rante and his teams in the oasis of Bukhara. For a museum, this work devoted mainly to material culture is undoubtedly rich, since it offers the study of perfectly contextualised object typologies. Thanks to an international team, the variety of materials and the richness of the products resulting from these years of excavations make this volume, we hope, a reference for the study of Central Asian objects in late antiquity and early Islam. The information from the numerous scientific examinations of the ceramics and the complete study of the glasses by our Japanese colleagues provide novel research on Central Asia. In addition, radiocarbon-dating studies have provided important interpretations. Finally, this work also sheds light on particular sites in the oasis by looking at historical excavations. In particular, we find the contributions of our colleague Silvia Pozzi, on the excavations carried out on the site of Vardana about ten years ago by the West Sogdian Archaeological expedition, and the decisive excavations carried out by our Russian colleagues at Paykend to be valuable.

May this work find the deserved echo among archaeologists and all researchers interested in the material culture of this region of Central Asia.

Dr. Yannick Lintz
President-Director of the Guimet Museum, Paris

Preface

After ten years as director of the Islamic Art collection at the Louvre Abu Dhabi, I was appointed director of the Islamic Art Department at the Louvre Museum in July 2023. Since the beginning, I had the opportunity to discover the several years of activities led by Rocco Rante in Uzbekistan, specifically in the Bukhara Oasis. Paleo-environmental and climatic studies – also linked to water resources – field excavations, surveys, studies on material culture, and several interdisciplinary activities such as the socio-archaeological and archaeo-economic, open new horizons and offer unpublished data useful for the scientific community.

Fifteen years and more than twenty seasons of field-work gave and still give to this research program scientific consistency and weight. Since 2019, the publication of the first volume of *The Oasis of Bukhara* also gave gratitude and visibility to this long-time work. The second volume of the same Bukhara Oasis series is a co-written book in which authors experimented and proposed new points of view, apt to revisit and complete this historical framework or even suggest new paths of research.

The third volume is the accomplishment of this collection, which is thought to give as complete as possible knowledge of the region, although not final of course, because the Archaeological Mission of the Louvre Museum is continuing the activities. This book is the result of years of interdisciplinary activities, historical and archaeological, with a focus on material culture. The long articles consecrated to the pottery and glass are full of new data, able to revisit a part of the culture of this region. The partnership with the Centre of Restauration and Research of the French Museum (C2RMF) shows the intense studies and operations conducted by different specialized teams. We can read articles on thermoluminescence, petrography, radiocarbon, and archeozoology, which will offer new data, knowledge, and perspectives for future generations.

Dr. Souraya Noujaim
Director of the Islamic Art Department
Musée du Louvre

Figures

1.1	General map of Western Central Asia 6	2.17	Sites registered after the cartographic analysis and sites analysed thanks to surveys 40
1.2	Hydrographic of the Oasis of Bukhara, SRTM Map 7	2.18	Heatmap and siteless areas 40
1.3	Hydrographic of the Oasis of Bukhara 7	2.19	Territorial extension of Obavija and sites dated to the Early Medieval Period 42
1.4	Historical hydrography of the Oasis of Bukhara, SRTM Map 8	3.1	Map, historical regions of Central Asia. Bukhara Oasis, schematic map 44
1.5	Tripartite sites and hydrography of the Oasis of Bukhara 9	3.2	Paykend city-site, plan with the excavation areas. Citadel and area to the north, aerial photography 46
1.6	Tripartite and bipartite sites and the hydrography of the Oasis of Bukhara 10	3.3	Paykend, citadel. Excavations in the central part of the city-site 47
1.7	Tripartite, bipartite, and unique tepe sites and the hydrography of the oasis of Bukhara 12	3.4	G.L. Semenov, the head of Bukhara Archaeological Expedition from the Hermitage Museum in 1981–2006; plan of the city-site with the excavation areas, 1985; plan of the northern part of the citadel, excavations before 1994 49
1.8	Paykend, fortress on the northern side 13		
1.9	Uch Kulakh 13		
1.10	Single tepe clusters within the oasis 15		
1.11	Clusters of single tepe between 3,000 and 4,000 m^2 17		
1.12	Clusters of single tepe between 5,000 and 7,000 m^2 17	3.5	Citadel: (a) remains of the north-eastern tower of the Hellenistic period; (b) remains of the smithy, 3rd century BCE; (c) forge-fire; (d) anvil 50
1.13	Clusters of single tepe around 1 ha 18		
1.14	Social and economic distribution clusters 20	3.6	(a) The stratigraphic trench in the north-western corner of the citadel; (b) Blacksmith's forge, floor no. 9; (c) Floor nos. 10–11; (d) Archaeological sectional drawing 51
1.15	Distribution by size of main sites within the oasis 22		
2.1	Oasis of Bukhara, localisation of the area of research (area of interest, AOI) 26		
2.2	Reconstruction of the premodern water supply and the marshy areas 27	3.7	(a) Citadel, fortifications: north-eastern corner; (b) North-western corner, additional entrance to the fortress between tower nos. 1 and 2, the end of the 3rd–4th centuries CE; (c) Towers, western entrance to the fortress, the end of the 4th–5th centuries CE 52
2.3	Archaeological site of Vardana 28		
2.4	Citadel of Vardana 28		
2.5	Topographical plan of the site 29		
2.6	Citadel of Vardana, late antique structures buried under the infilling of pebbles and sand 30	3.8	Table of the periodisation of artifacts from Paykend (4th–2nd centuries BCE) 59
2.7	Citadel of Vardana, late antique gallery buried under the infilling of pebbles and sand 31	3.9	Table of the periodisation of artifacts from Paykend (end of the 2nd century BCE to the beginning of the 2nd century CE) 60
2.8	Citadel of Vardana, plan of the early medieval palace 32		
2.9	Citadel of Vardana, hypothetical reconstruction of the early medieval palace 32	3.10	Artifacts from sacrificial pits (βόθροι) and favissa in the southern part of the citadel, 1st–2nd centuries CE 61
2.10	Citadel of Vardāna, early medieval structures, east sector 32	3.11	(a) Fire temple on the citadel of Paykend; (b) Courtyard of the fire temple, view from north-west; (c) "Palace", view from the north-east (2001); (d) "Palace", view from the south (2019) 64
2.11	Citadel of Vardana, mural paintings discovered in the eastern sector 33		
2.12	Citadel of Vardana, reconstruction of the hall decorated with mural paintings 33	3.12	(a) "Service room" between the fire temple and the "palace"; (b) Goblet and hand-made caldron; (c) Copper torch from the detail of ancient furniture 65
2.13	Citadel of Vardana, early medieval palace, eastern sector, mud brick platforms 33		
2.14	Citadel of Vardana, early medieval palace (eastern sector), storage area 33	3.13	"Corridor with high *sufa* benches", level 4, the end of the 3rd–4th centuries CE; Water pipe under floor (Larisa Yu. Kulakova) 66
2.15	Findings from the storage area 34		
2.16	Schematic map of the Bukhara Oasis according to Shishkin 37	3.14	Rooms of the garrison barracks, the end of the 3rd to the first third of the 4th centuries CE 67

3.15	Administrative quarter (2016); Area in front of the citadel (2018)　68	3.36	(a) Bukhara Archaeological Expedition: Grigory L. Semenov and Igor K. Malkiel, the 1980s; (b) The 1980s; (c) Near the building of the future Paykend Museum; (d) At the opening of the southern city gate　89
3.16	(a) Mural paintings from the citadel of Paykend: "Burned corridor" in the south of the citadel, 6th–7th centuries CE; (b) "Corridor with high *sufa* benches", the end of the 3rd–4th centuries CE; (c) Courtyard of the fire temple, upper cultural layers　69	3.37	(a) Bukhara Archaeological Expedition's field work, 2010–19; (b) Architectural measurements; (c) Clearing of fragments of mural painting; (d) Drawing of mural painting; (e) Clearing fragments of ganch *mihrab*, Raisa A. Kazimirova and Dilmurad O. Kholov　90
3.17	Table of the periodisation of ceramics from Paykend, end of 3rd to beginning of the 4th centuries CE　70	3.38	(a) Bukhara Archaeological Expedition's field laboratory work, 2010–19; (b) Djamal Mirzaakhmedov; (c) Clearing of iron weapons; (d) Sorting of copper coins from the hoard of 4,500 pieces (2013); (e) Drawing pottery; (f and g) Restoration of the ganch panel from the southern suburb mosque, Raisa A. Kazimirova and Olga S. Viktorova　91
3.18	Artifacts from Paykend from the end of 3rd to the beginning 5th centuries CE　71		
3.19	1 – Impress of a ring on a lid; 2–9 – bullae. 1–3 – barracks; 4–5 – courtyard of the fire temple; 6–9 – the "burned room" (corridor) in the south of the citadel　72		
3.20	(a) Towers of the southern fortification wall of shahrestan 1; (b) Tower no. 2; (c and d) Towers of shahrestan 2 (photos from 2010 and 1939)　73	3.39	(a) The opening of the reconstructed Paykend Museum; (b) A tour of the Paykend Museum; (c) Rooms of the museum　92
3.21	Shahrestan 1, the westward view　74	4.1	Fabric A　99
3.22	(a) Shahrestan 1, the eastward view; (b) Three-room dwelling unit in house no. 8; (c) House no. 8a (a "little hotel"), axonometry; (d) House no. 1, axonometry; (e) House no. 1, living rooms with podiums and hearths　75	4.2	Fabric A2　99
		4.3	Fabric A6　100
		4.4	Fabric E　100
		4.5	Fabric F　101
		4.6	Fabric I　101
3.23	Clay frieze decorated with moulded floral motifs from house no. 1 in shahrestan 1　76	4.7	Fabric CW1　102
		4.8	Fabric CW2　102
3.24	Terracotta figurines and decorations on pottery　77	4.9	Fabric CW7　103
3.25	Table of the periodisation of ceramics from Paykend from the second half of the 8th century　78	4.10	Bukhara, trench A. Assemblage from US162　105
		4.11	Bukhara, trench A. Plate　105
3.26	(a) Underground bases of columns in the mosque, 10th century; (b) Minaret　79	4.12	Bukhara, trench A. Lustre ware imitation　105
		4.13	Bukhara, trench A. Examples of pottery from 3rd-century BCE deposits　106
3.27	(a) Streets of Paykend: "A", between citadel and shahrestan 1; (b) "A", between shahrestan 1 and shahrestan 2, and southern entrance to the city; (c) "No. 2" in the south of the city　80	4.14	Bukhara, trench A. Small goblet with traces of red slip on the lower body profile　106
		4.15	Iskijkat, trench A. Examples of pottery from deposits from 3rd/2nd–1st centuries BCE　108
3.28	(a) Shahrestan 2: the westward view; (b) The eastward view　81	4.16	Iskijkat, trench A. Examples of pottery from deposits from 3rd/2nd–1st centuries BCE　109
3.29	Shahrestan 2, ganch (plaster) panel from courtyard of house no. 9 in shahrestan 1　82	4.17	Iskijkat, trench A. Examples of pottery from deposits from 1st century BCE–1st century CE　110
3.30	Kalybs (ceramic forms) from the 10th century　82	4.18	Iskijkat, trench A. Open shapes from deposits from 2nd–3rd centuries CE　111
3.31	Glazed pottery from Paykend　83		
3.32	1–7, 9 – Bronze and brass objects from the 10th century from Paykend; 8 – silver with turquoise　84	4.19	Iskijkat, trench A. Examples of pottery from deposits from 2nd–3rd centuries CE　112
3.33	(a) Southern suburb: the north-westward view; (b) The winter mosque; (c) Fragments of ganch (plaster) panel of a *mihrab* in the mosque (destruction layers); (d) Upper part of the ganch panel after reconstruction; (e) Lower part of the ganch panel *in situ*　85	4.20	Iskijkat, trench A. Examples of pottery from deposits from 4th century CE　113
		4.21	Iskijkat, trench A. Examples of pottery from deposits from 7th–9th centuries CE　114
		4.22	Iskijkat, trench A. Examples of pottery from deposits from 10th–12th centuries CE　115
3.34	Ostraka from Paykend　87		
3.35	Coins from Paykend　88		

FIGURES

4.23 Iskijkat, trench A. Handle from deposits from 10th–12th centuries CE 115
4.24 Iskijkat, trench B. Selected fragments from deposits from 1st century BCE to 1st century CE 116
4.25 Kakishtuvan, trench A. Examples of pottery from deposits from 1st century CE 117
4.26 Kakishtuvan, trench A. Examples of pottery from deposits from 1st century CE 117
4.27 Kakishtuvan, trench A. Examples of pottery from deposits from 2nd–3rd centuries CE 118
4.28 Kakishtuvan, trench A. Examples of pottery from deposits from 3rd–4th centuries CE 118
4.29 Kakishtuvan, trench A. Slip-painted jug and marked base 118
4.30 Kakishtuvan, trench A. Examples of pottery from deposits from 5th–6th centuries CE 119
4.31 Paykend, trench B. Examples of pottery from deposits from 5th–6th centuries CE 121
4.32 Paykend, trench B. Examples of pottery from deposits from 7th–9th centuries CE 122
4.33 Paykend, trench B. Examples of pottery from deposits from 10th–12th centuries CE 123
4.34 Paykend, trench B. Examples of pottery from deposits from 10th–12th centuries CE 124
4.35 Ramitan, trench A. Wheel-made and mould-made "plates" from US148 126
4.36 Ramitan, trench A. Wheel-made and mould-made "plates" from US148 127
4.37 Ramitan, trench A. Examples of open shapes from deposits from 3rd–4th centuries CE 128
4.38 Ramitan, trench A. Examples of closed shapes and bases from deposits from 3rd–4th centuries CE 129
4.39 Ramitan, trench A. Examples of diagnostic fragments from US131 131
4.40 Ramitan, trench C. Examples of pottery from deposits from 2nd–3rd centuries CE 132
4.41 Ramitan, trench C. Examples of pottery from deposits from 3rd–4th centuries CE 133
4.42 Ramitan, trench C. Examples of hand-made pottery from deposits from 3rd–4th centuries CE 134
4.43 Ramitan, trench C. Examples of pottery from deposits from 5th–6th centuries CE 134
4.44 Ramitan, trench C. Bowl with perforated base 135
4.45 Ramitan, trench C. Vessels and fragments from US530 and US531 135
4.46 Ramitan, trench C. Closed shapes from US530 136
4.47 Ramitan, trench D. Examples of pottery from deposits contemporary or pre-dating 6th century CE 138
4.48 Ramitan, trench D. Examples of pottery from deposits post-dating 6th century CE 139
4.49 Ramitan, trench D. Examples of pottery from US609 140
4.50 Ramitan, trench D. Examples of pottery from US604 141
4.51 Ramitan, trench F. Examples of pottery from US1063 142
4.52 Ramitan, trench G. Examples of pottery from deposits from 5th–6th centuries CE 144
4.53 Ramitan, trench G. Examples of pottery from deposits from 6th–8th centuries CE 145
4.54 Ramitan, trench G. Examples of pottery from deposits from 13th–14th centuries CE 146
4.55 Site 250, trench A. Examples of pottery from deposits from 1st century CE 147
4.56 Site 250, trench A. Examples of pottery from deposits from 2nd–3rd centuries CE 148
4.57 Site 250, trench A. Examples of open shapes from pit fill US156 149
4.58 Site 250, trench A. Examples of closed shapes from pit fill US156 150
4.59 Site 250, trench A. Examples of pottery from pit fill US114 151
4.60 Pottery volume by phase 153
4.61 Pottery volume by phase 154
4.62 Distribution of basic forms across phases 154
4.63 Distribution of rim diameters in open forms 155
4.64 Distribution of rim diameters in closed forms 155
4.65 Histogram of rim diameters for shape group R006 156
4.66 R007: distribution of rim diameters across phases 157
4.67 R20 and related shapes: distribution of rim diameters 159
4.68 Mould-made "plates"; Ramitan, trench A, US140 160
4.69 R41 and related shapes: distribution of rim diameters 161
4.70 Ramitan, trench C. Examples of coarse ware from deposits from 2nd–3rd and 3rd–4th centuries CE 163
4.71 Site 250, trench A. Example of a near-complete cooking ware pot from US156 163
4.72 Shape distribution among coarse-ware fabrics (the proportion of shapes is based on rim eves) 163
4.73 Proportion of fine and coarse wares across shape groups 163
4.74 Iskijkat, trench A. Example of hand-shaped storage vessel fragment 165
4.75 Bukhara Oasis, examples of storage jars R62 and related shapes 165
4.76 Ramitan, individual jars from late pre-Islamic contexts 167
4.77 Ramitan, trench F. Examples of lids from US1063 168

4.78	Coarse wares and lids: distribution of rim diameters 168	5.1	Al_2O_3 vs $(MgO + K_2O)$ diagram of ceramic fabrics from all the sherds studied 241
4.79	Bukhara Oasis. Slip-painted sherds from the MAFOUB excavations 170	5.2	Al_2O_3 vs $(MgO + K_2O)$ diagram of ceramic pastes from all the sherds studied 241
4.80	Bukhara Oasis. Other slip painted motifs 171	5.3a–c	Extracts from geological maps and synthetic geological sections of the Bukhara Oasis 245
4.81	Bukhara Oasis, slip-coated open vessels 171	6.1a–f	BUXA 162/1; BUXA 162/9; Dep.B.317; Dep.B.76; Dep.B.74; Dep.B.316 250
4.82	Bukhara Oasis, slip-coated close vessels 172	6.2	BUXA 162/1 Face 1 (sample 2): Optical microscope photographs of the cross-section 253
4.83	Bukhara Oasis, coccio-pesto technique 174	6.3	BUXA 162/1 Face 1 (sample 3): Optical microscope photographs of the cross-section 253
4.84	Bukhara Oasis, *badrab*s 175	6.4	BUXA 162/1 Face 1 (sample 2): SEM backscattered electron image of the cross-section 253
4.85	Bukhara Oasis, chronological distribution of R001 and related shapes 228	6.5	BUXA 162/1 Face 1 (sample 2): SEM backscattered electron image of the cross-section 253
4.86	Bukhara Oasis, chronological distribution of R006 and related shapes 228	6.6	Dep.B.317 (sample 6): Optical microscope photographs of the cross-section 255
4.87	Bukhara Oasis, chronological distribution of R007 and related shapes 229	6.7	Dep.B.76 (sample 9): Optical microscope photographs of the cross-section 255
4.88	Bukhara Oasis, chronological distribution of R010 and related shapes 229	6.8	Dep.B.317 (sample 4): Optical microscope photographs of the cross-section 255
4.89	Bukhara Oasis, chronological distribution of R020 and related shapes 229	6.9	Dep.B.74 (sample 7): Optical microscope photographs of the cross-section 255
4.90	Bukhara Oasis, chronological distribution of R038 and related shapes 230	6.10	Dep.B.316, face 1 (sample 10) – Optical microscope photographs of weathered area (porous and yellowish aspect) 256
4.91	Bukhara Oasis, chronological distribution of R041 and related shapes 230	6.11	Dep.B.316, face 1 (sample 10) – SEM backscattered electron image – The vitreous phase is completely weathered (porous and yellowish aspect) 256
4.92	Bukhara Oasis, chronological distribution of R045 and related shapes 230	6.12	Dep.B.316, face 2 (sample 11) – Optical microscope photographs of the cross-section – The white glaze appears very porous and altered 256
4.93	Bukhara Oasis, chronological distribution of R047 and related shapes 230	6.13	Dep.B.316, face 1 (sample 10) – SEM backscattered electron image – The white glaze appears weathered. The well-preserved upper zone corresponds to the dark blue glaze 256
4.94	Bukhara Oasis, chronological distribution of R055 and related shapes 231		
4.95	Bukhara Oasis, chronological distribution of R075 and related shapes 231	6.14	Dep.B.317, face 2 – Detail of the turquoise decoration 257
4.96	Bukhara Oasis, chronological distribution of R069 and related shapes 231	6.15	Dep.B.317, face 2 (sample 5) – Optical microscope photographs of the cross-section showing the coloration in the mass of the turquoise glaze 257
4.97	Bukhara Oasis, chronological distribution of R079 231		
4.98	Bukhara Oasis, chronological distribution of R076 and related shapes 232	6.16	Dep.B.317, face 2 (sample 5) – SEM backscattered electron image of the glaze – White microcrystals: cassiterite 257
4.99	Bukhara Oasis, chronological distribution of R062 and related shapes 232	6.17	Dep.B.317, face 2 (sample 5) – SEM backscattered electron image of the interface – grey crystals contain Si, Ca, Mg. In white: cassiterite 257
4.100	Bukhara Oasis, chronological distribution of R061 and related shapes 233		
4.101	Bukhara Oasis, chronological distribution of R088 and related shapes 233	6.18	Dep.B.316, face 2 257
4.102	Bukhara Oasis, complete or near-complete vessels, fragmentary chronological scheme of assemblages of contemporaneous vessel forms, 5th to 6th centuries CE 233	6.19	Dep.B.316, face 2 – Optical microscope photographs of the cross-section 257
4.103	Bukhara Oasis, complete or near-complete vessels, fragmentary chronological scheme of assemblages of contemporaneous vessel forms, 9th to 11th centuries CE 234		

6.20 Dep.B.316, face 2 (sample 11) – SEM backscattered electron image of the cross-section – The white glaze appears very porous and altered – the blue glaze is better preserved   258

6.21 Dep.B.316, face 2 (sample 11) – SEM backscattered electron image – Detail of the blue area. In white, Co-enriched unfused pigments; dark grey grain = alkaline feldspar   258

6.22 Dep.B.316, face 1 – detail of the dark spots on the surface   258

6.23 Dep.B.316, face 1 (sample 10): Optical microscope photographs of the cross-section in a dark area   258

6.24 Dep B. 316, face 1 (sample 10) – stratigraphical section observed with Scanning Electron Microscope   258

6.25 Dep.B.74, face 1 – Lustre ceramic sherd   258

6.26 Dep.B.74, face 1 – Stratigraphy of the lustred area   259

6.27 Dep.B.74, face 1 – Image of the lustre surface under diffuse light   259

6.28 Dep.B.74, face 1 – same area, but the surface is tilted to detect the specular reflected light and the metallic shine   259

6.29 Dep B. 74 – RBS spectra details of the lustred and not lustred sherds   260

6.30 Dep.B.74, face 2 – Elemental map of element Cu obtained by XRF   260

6.31 Dep.B.74, face 2   260

6.32a–c BUXA 162/1, face 2; a) Overall observation of the décor; b) detail of the "lustre"; c) image of the stratigraphy   261

6.33 BUXA 162/1, face 1 – Optical microscope photographs of the cross-section through the "lustre decoration"   261

6.34 BUXA 162/1, face 1 – SEM backscattered electron image – Detail of the pinkish layer with Cr-rich grains   261

6.35 BUXA 162/1, face 1 – SEM backscattered electron image of the cross-section – stratigraphic section through the "lustre decoration"   261

6.36 BUXA 162/1, face 1 – EDS Elemental map of elements Cr, Mg, Fe   262

6.37 Dep.B.316, face 2 (sample 11) – SEM backscattered electron image – Details of cobalt rich pigments. The grains appearing in white contain high amounts of Fe, Co, Mn, Ni, Cu   263

6.38 Dep.B.316, face 2 (sample 11) – SEM backscattered electron image-id – The grain appearing in white consists mainly of Fe (and O). The grey crystals forming the reaction crown are made up of Si, Mg, ca, Fe, Co and Mn   263

7.1 Bowl with white slip and transparent glaze, Bukhara   267

7.2 Bowl with white slip and transparent glaze, Bukhara   267

7.3 Bowl with white slip and transparent glaze, Bukhara   268

7.4 Dish with white slip and transparent glaze, Bukhara   268

7.5 Incense-burner with white slip and transparent glaze, Bukhara   269

7.6 Bowl with white slip and transparent glaze, geometrical decorations, Bukhara   271

7.7 Bowl with white slip and transparent glaze, Bukhara   271

7.8 Bowl with white slip and transparent glaze, polychrome ornamentation, Bukhara   271

7.9 Bowl with white slip and transparent glaze, polychrome ornamentation, Bukhara   271

7.10 Bowl with white slip and transparent glaze, polychrome ornamentation, Bukhara   272

7.11 Bowl with white slip and transparent glaze, polychrome ornamentation, Bukhara   272

7.12 Bowl with white slip and transparent glaze, polychrome ornamentation, Bukhara   272

7.13 Bowl with white slip and transparent glaze, polychrome ornamentation, Bukhara   272

7.14 Bowl with white slip and transparent glaze, polychrome ornamentation, Bukhara   273

7.15 Bowl fragment with white slip and transparent glaze, Chinese imitation of decorative motifs, Bukhara   273

7.16 Bowl fragment with white slip and transparent glaze, Bukhara   274

7.17 Bowl fragment with white slip and transparent glaze, Bukhara   274

7.18 Bowl fragment with white slip and transparent glaze, Bukhara   274

7.19 Bowl fragment with white slip and transparent glaze, Chinese imitation of decorative motifs, Bukhara   275

7.20 Bowl fragment with white slip and transparent glaze, figurative motifs, Bukhara   275

7.21 Bowl fragment with white slip and transparent glaze, figurative motifs, Bukhara   276

7.22 Bowl fragment with white slip and transparent glaze, zoomorphic motifs, Bukhara   276

7.23 Bowl fragment with white slip and transparent glaze, zoomorphic motifs, Bukhara   277

7.24 Bowl fragment with white slip and transparent glaze, zoomorphic motifs in a Chinese manner, Bukhara   277

8.1 Paykend, shahrestan, "pharmacy"   280

8.2	Paykend, shahrestan, glass fragments of pharmaceutical tools 280	9.8	Paykend, trench B&J. Fragments of glass vessels 313
8.3	Paykend, shahrestan, alembics 281	9.9	Paykend, trench F&C. Fragments of glass vessels 314
8.4	Paykend, shahrestan, alembics 282	9.10	Paykend, trench H. Fragments of glass vessels 315
8.5	*Maqamat* of al-Harīrī, Bibliothèque Nationale de France in Paris 282	9.11	Paykend, trench H. Fragments of cupping vessels 316
8.6	*Maqamat* of al-Harīrī, Institute of Oriental Studies in St. Petersburg 283	9.12	Paykend, Trench E. Fragments of glass vessels and glass cullet and slags 317
8.7	Bukhara, shahrestan, alembics 284	9.13	Three colour groups of glass materials 318
8.8	Paykend, shahrestan 2, alembics 285	9.14	Natural coloured glass 318
8.9	Paykend, shahrestan 2, set of glassware 286	9.15	Olive-green glass 318
8.10	Paykend, shahrestan 2, bulbous vessel 286	9.16	Decolourised colourless glass 319
8.11	Tashkent, old city, retort 287	9.17	Coloured glass 319
8.12	Tashkent, old city, small size flask 288	9.18	RIm pattern glass 320
8.13	Tashkent, old city, flasks 288	9.19	Base pattern 320
8.14	Binkat, decanter 289	9.20	Handle pattern 321
8.15	Akhsiket, pharmaceutical set 290	9.21	Thread decoration glass from trench H 321
8.16	Afrasiab, dishes 291	9.22	Thread decoration glass from trench A 321
8.17	Afrasiab, small flasks 291	9.23	Thread decoration glass from trench B 322
8.18	Bukhara, small flasks 292	9.24	Thread decoration glass from trench F 322
8.19	Afrasiab, jugs with flared rims 292	9.25	Moulded decoration glass from trench B 323
8.20	Afrasiab, jugs with high necks 292	9.26	Moulded decoration glass from trench B 323
8.21	Afrasiab, hygienic tools 293	9.27	Pinched decoration glass from trench B 323
8.22	Bukhara, glass mercury vessels 293	9.28	Facet-cut decoration glass from trench B 323
8.23	Afrasiab, cups for medical purposes 294	9.29	Artifacts excavated by the Uzbek mission 325
8.24	Termez, medallions 294	9.30	Artifacts excavated by the Uzbek mission 325
8.25	Paykend, shahrestan 1, cup set 294	9.31	Fragment of small cup 326
8.26	Maverannahr, circular objects 295	9.32	Fragment of bottle 326
8.27	Bukhara, table vessels 295	9.33	Fragment of large pot 326
8.28	Kuva, vessel 296	9.34	Handle 326
8.29	Kuva, vessels 297	9.35	Cupping vessel 327
8.30	Kuva, transparent, yellowish-greenish and yellowish vessels 297	9.36	Fragment of window pane 327
8.31	Kuva, vessels 298	9.37	Plan of Ramitan 329
8.32	Kuva, decanter and vase-like vessel 299	9.38	Ramitan, trench D&F. Fragments of glass vessels 330
8.33	Kuva, bowl, jug-shaped vessel and wine glass 299	9.39	Ramitan, trench G & Site250, trench A. Fragments of glass vessels 331
8.34	Kuva, flask, bulb-shaped form 300	9.40	Plan of Iskijkat 332
8.35	Afrasiab, bowl with ornamentation 300	9.41	Iskijkat, trench A&B & Kakishtuvan, trench A. Fragments of glass vessels 333
8.36	Maverannahr, bowls 301	9.42	Plan of Kakishtuvan 334
8.37	Maverannahr, cups 301	9.43	Bukhara, trench A. Fragments of glass vessels with cut decoration 335
8.38	Maverannahr, vessels 302	9.44	Bukhara, trench A. Fragments of glass vessels with decoration 336
9.1	Plan of Paykend 306	9.45	Bukhara, trench A. Fragments of glass vessels 337
9.2	Paykend, trench A&D. Fragments of glass vessels 307	9.46	Bukhara, trench A. Fragments of glass vessels & Paykend, Bangles 338
9.3	Paykend, trench B. Fragments of glass vessels with decoration 308	9.47	Plots of MgO vs. K_2O concentrations in all the samples 346
9.4	Paykend, trench B. Fragments of glass vessels with decoration 309	9.48	Plots of Na_2O vs. CaO concentrations in all the samples 347
9.5	Paykend, trench B. Fragments of glass vessels 310		
9.6	Paykend, trench B. Fragments of glass vessels 311		
9.7	Paykend, trench B. Fragments of glass vessels 312		

9.49	XRF spectra of blue glass (Py003) 347		11.3	Calibrated dates of the samples from Iskijkat (trenches A and B) 380
9.50	XRF spectra of blue glass (Py005) 347		11.4	Calibrated dates of the samples from Kakishtuvan (trench A) 380
9.51	XRF spectra of blue glass (Py001) 347		11.5	Calibrated dates of the samples from site 250 (trench A) 380
9.52	XRF spectra of black glass (Py008) 347		11.6	Calibrated dates of the samples from Bukhara (trench A) 381
9.53	XRF spectra of olive-green glass (Py009) 349		12.1	Mean measured dose rate as a function of the sites and field campaign 384
9.54	Plots of Al_2O_3 vs. Fe_2O_3 concentrations in the colourless glass and the naturally coloured glass 349		12.2	Variation of the measured dose with the position of the thorium peaks on the spectrometer 384
9.55	Plots of SiO_2 vs. Al_2O_3 concentrations in the colourless glass and the naturally coloured glass 349		12.3	Dose rate measurement around the north-east tower 385
9.56	Plots of K_2O vs. MgO concentrations in the colourless glass and the naturally coloured glass 349		12.4	Paykend, shahrestan 1, trench A 390
9.57	Plots of CaO vs. Na_2O concentrations in the colourless glass and the naturally coloured glass 349		12.5	Paykend citadel trench D 391
9.58	Plots of MnO vs. Fe_2O_3 concentrations in the colourless glass and the naturally coloured glass 349		12.6a	Ages of the sherds from Paykend: radial plot 392
			12.6b	Ages of the sherds from Paykend: finite mixture model (five components) 392
9.59	Classification of the glass-production materials and glass products by chemical composition 351		12.7	Age model for Paykend. For each age, two distributions have been plotted 392
10.1	Percentage of NR by chantier and period 374		12.8a	Age of the sherds from Ramitan: radial plot 393
10.2	Traces of rodent, small ruminant metatarsal, citadel, 10th century CE, Iskijkat 365		12.8b	Age of the sherds from Ramitan: finite mixture model (four components) 393
10.3	Metacarpals illustrating the similarity of small ruminant bones 366		12.9	Age model Ramitan 393
10.4	Metatarsals illustrating the similarity of small ruminant bones 367		12.10a	Ages of the sherds from Iskijkat: radial plot 398
10.5a	Sogdian musicians on a Bactrian camel, glazed earthenware, Tang Dynasty 368		12.10b	Ages of the sherds from Iskijkat: finite mixture model (four components) 398
10.5b	Right Calcaneum, *Camelus* sp., shahrestan, 7th–8th centuries CE, Iskijkat 368		12.11	Age model Iskijkat 399
10.6	Tarso-metatarsus, *Gallus gallus domesticus*, shahrestan, 1st century CE, Iskijkat 369		12.12	Summary of the chronologies of the different sites 399
10.7a	Pre-cut raw material, shahrestan, 1st century CE, Iskijkat 369		12.13	Brickyard 400
10.7b	Polished cow's mandible, *Bos* sp. citadel, 2nd–3rd centuries CE, Iskijkat 374		12.14	Rammed earth (*paksha*) house 400
			12.15	Making mud brick 401
11.1	Calibrated dates of the samples from Ramitan (trench A, C, F, G and D) 377		12.16	Chronogram 401
			12.17	Tower A 402
11.2	Calibrated dates of the samples from Paykend (trench E) 379		12.18	East wall 404

Tables

4.1 Sherd count 97
4.2 Sherd weight (gram) 97
4.3 Rim eves (estimated vessel equivalents) 98
4.4 Fabric A 98
4.5 Fabric A2 99
4.6 Fabric A6 100
4.7 Fabric E 100
4.8 Fabric F 101
4.9 Fabric I 101
4.10 Fabric CW1 102
4.11 Fabric CW3 103
4.12 Fabric CW7 103
4.13 Chronological coverage of the processed material for each trench in century slots based on the dates of the stratigraphic units 152
4.14 Pottery volume by phase 153
4.15 Pottery volume by phase 153
4.16 Distribution of basic forms across phases 154
5.1 Photographs of the fronts and backs of the studied sherds 236
5.2 Compositions in % by mass of oxides, for the major elements, of the pastes of the sherds studied that were obtained by X-ray fluorescence spectrometry 239
5.3 242
5.4 246
5.5 Photographs of the sherds prepared in section taken with a binocular magnifying glass 246
5.6 Photographs taken by optical microscopy under polarized light and analyzed 247
5.7 Photographs taken by optical microscopy under unanalyzed polarized light 248
6.1 List of samples 251
6.2 Chemical composition of the clay fabrics – PIXE data expressed in oxide weight % 252
6.3 Chemical composition of white slips – EDS data expressed in oxide weight % 252
6.4 Chemical composition of high lead glazes – EDS data expressed in oxide weight % and corresponding to the average of three analyzed areas – Standard deviation in italics 254
6.5 Chemical composition of high lead-alkali glazes – EDS data expressed in oxide weight % and corresponding to the average of three analyzed areas – Standard deviation 254
6.6 Sherd BUXA 162/1 – Composition of Cr-rich grains in the pinkish layer (EDS data expressed in atomic percentages) 262
6.7 Comparison of the chemical analyses of the clay bodies of Susa ceramics with those of the two imported sherds – PIXE data expressed in oxide weight % 263
6.8 Chemical analyses of the clay bodies of Paykend ceramics studied by E. Porto in 2012 and of four sherds belonging to our corpus – EDS data expressed in oxide weight % 264
6.9 Chemical analyses of white tin-opacified glazes from Susa, Samarra and Fustat compared with Dep.B.76 – EDS data expressed in oxide weight % 265
9.1 Unearthed glass by district and classification 324
9.2 List of analytical samples from the Bukhara Oasis 341
9.3 Classification of analytical samples 342
9.4 Chemical composition by ICP-OES (wt%) 345
9.5 Average chemical compositions of glass samples excavated from the Bukhara Oasis (wt%) 346
9.6 Average chemical compositions of the colourless glass and naturally coloured glass (wt%) 349
9.7 Average chemical compositions of the clustering groups (wt%) 351
9.8 List of objects unearthed from Paykend 1 354
9.9 List of objects unearthed from Paykend 2 355
9.10 List of objects unearthed from Paykend 3 356
9.11 List of objects unearthed from Paykend 4 357
9.12 List of objects unearthed from Paykend 5 358
9.13 List of objects unearthed from Paykend 6 359
9.14 List of objects unearthed from Ramitan and Site 250 360
9.15 List of objects unearthed from Iskijkat and Kakisutuvan 361
9.16 List of objects unearthed from Bukhara 1 362
9.17 List of objects unearthed from Bukhara 2 363
11.1 Radiocarbon ages and calibrated dates of the samples from Ramitan (trench A, C, F, G and D) 372
11.2 Radiocarbon ages and calibrated dates of the samples from Paykend (trench E) 376
11.3 Radiocarbon ages and calibrated dates of the samples from Iskijkat (trenches A and B) 378
11.4 Radiocarbon ages and calibrated dates of the samples from Kakishtuvan (trench A) 379
11.5 Radiocarbon ages and calibrated dates of the samples from site 250 (trench A) 380
11.6 Radiocarbon ages and calibrated dates of the samples from Bukhara (trench A) 381
12.1a Paykend, luminescence analysis 387
12.1b Paykend, dosimetry analysis 388

12.2	Distribution of the sherds of the different levels according to the Paykend groups 389	12.5b	Dosimetry analysis 397
12.3a	Luminescence analysis 394	12.6	Distribution of the sherds of the different levels according to the Iskijkat groups 399
12.3b	Dosimetry analysis 394	12.7	Finite mixture model of ages 403
12.4	Distribution of the sherds of the different levels according to the Romitan groups 396	12.8a	Luminescence analysis 403
12.5a	Luminescence analysis 397	12.8b	Dosimetry analysis 403

Notes on Contributors

Anne Bouquillon
ingénieur de recherche, Centre de recherche et de restauration des musées de France

Jacopo Bruno
archaeologist-ceramologist, Institute of Iranian Studies, Austrian Academy of Sciences

Yvan Coquinot
ingénieur géologue, Centre de recherche et de restauration des musées de France

Fabrizio Crusco
archaeologist, freelance, specialist on Central Asia, National Geographic

Delphine Decruyenaere
Ph.D. candidate, National Museum of Natural History, Paris. Lecturer, Department of History and Cultural Heritage, Silk Road University of Tourism and Cultural Heritage, Samarkand

Christel Doublet
ingénieur d'études, Centre de recherche et de restauration des musées de France

Ayano Endo
University of Nottingham

Nathalie Gandolfo
assistant ingénieur, Centre de recherche et de restauration des musées de France

Takako Hosokawa
Independent Researcher, responsible for the Glass Team, French-Uzbek Archaeological Mission in the Oasis of Bukhara

Marjan Mashkour
directrice de recherche, CNRS, Musée d'histoire naturelle, Paris

Djamal Mirzaakhmedov
archaeologist, Institute of Archaeology of Samarkand

Andrey Omelchenko
archaeologist, Hermitage Museum

Elisa Porto
ingénieur d'études, Centre de recherche et de restauration des musées de France

Silvia Pozzi
co-directeur archaeological mission at Vardanzeh

Gabriele Puschnigg
archaeologist-ceramologist, Institute of Iranian Studies, Austrian Academy of Sciences

Abdisabur Raimkulov
Institute of Archaeology of Samarkand

Rocco Rante
archaeologist, Louvre Museum, professeur des universités, Sorbonne-Panthéon

Pascale Richardin
ingénieur-chercheur, Centre de recherche et de restauration des musées de France

Yoko Shindo
former director of the Glass Expedition in the oasis of Bukhara

Toshiyasu Shinmen
Tokyo Gakugei University

Tamako Takeda
Yokohama Museum of Eurasian Cultures

Manon Vuillien
post-doctorante, CNRS

Antoine Zink
ingénieur de recherche, Centre de recherche et de restauration des musées de France

Introduction

This volume is the third of a trilogy dedicated to the oasis of Bukhara. The first volume focused on archaeological discoveries within the oasis, reexploring some parts of the history of this region of Central Asia, the second presented a pluridisciplinary project centred around an in-depth historical study reconsidering and highlighting the region's global Islamic history, and this volume completes the trilogy by presenting a wide overview of scientific activities.

This volume is a collection of all the activities we conducted in the oasis of Bukhara within the framework of the research program MAFOUB (Mission Archéologique Franco-Ouzbèke dans l'Oasis de Bukhara, www.mafoub.com),[1] as well as some other activities conducted by colleagues working in the same area. It is thus dedicated to different studies on the oasis of Bukhara that support, confirm and complete the archaeological work, thus rendering the results more robust.

The aims of this program and the new knowledge it has produced provide useful tools for a better and more complete understanding of the population and depopulation dynamics in the region (Rante and Mirzaakhmedov 2019).

It was not possible to publish all of the studies closely linked to the archaeological discoveries in the first volume. And so, it was not commercial intentions but motivations linked to the general organisation and schedule of the different authors that they are published together in this third volume.

Several previous studies have focused on the geomorphological evolution of the region, and they have been published in an article (Fouache et al. 2016) where the authors brought to light the different scenarios that have caused the transformation of the Zerafshan delta since the Middle Pleistocene. From this epoch and continuing until circa the Neolithic, the northern branches of the Zerafshan began a slow process of desiccation; however, this phenomenon did not completely erase the presence of water. Beginning in the Upper Pleistocene-Neolithic, the reappearance of a slightly humid and stationary climate generated the formation of lacustrine zones, probably seasonally, thus rendering human settlements possible, such as the ones that have been identified north of the oasis and westward.

Those who have doubts about the human occupations around paleo-lakes, along the ending parts of channels or along any channels in which the water flow is weaker, will be surprised knowing that the surveys leaded by the joint French-Uzbek Archeological Mission in the south (Kashka Darya delta) and the western areas of the oasis brought to light clear traces of Kel'teminar cultures, as well as modelled ceramic sherds datable to the Bronze Age (material still un published but consultable in the archives of the archaeological mission).[2] These areas are scattered and often covered by aeolian phenomena, probably the reason of the difficulty to identify them.

Even during the climatic fluctuations between the Late Pleistocene-Neolithic and the Bronze Age, this phenomenon of desiccation was relentless. The Bronze Age was also when several western canals dried up, as well as when the desiccation of the farthest western branches of the Kashka Darya, flowing east-west and probably reaching the Oxus, occurred. It is possible that by the 4th century BCE that catastrophic event had completely changed the landscape. The delta had previously been oriented towards the north, and from that period onwards it was oriented towards the south-west. This geomorphological dynamic rendered the oasis's ground more adaptable to a sedentary life.

Those who still have doubts about these discoveries, they perhaps did not understand the methodology, which is however well explained in some previous articles and book (Fouache et al. 2016; Rante et al. 2016; Rante and Mirzaakhmedov 2019). The gomorphological study of such a huge area should be observed from a wider view perspective. The phenomena of drought in our planet directly or indirectly linked to territorial changes, as in the oasis of Bukhara, cannot be seen as a moment or a time fixed and immobile. These phenomena can change along periods. Any serious specialist in these cases observes the tendency of a territory looking at the current studies and analyses in order to dispose of a as wide as possible fan of data and compare them.

In the case of the oasis of Bukhara, especially the western area, also called Bash tepe area, but which in this case is much larger than the small sites of "Bash tepe organisation", any serious specialist cannot imagine that the dynamic of channel dessication is not available if during the 1st century AD there are some occupations. *In primis* because since the Bronze Age people was able to dig canals, also reusing old channel following the slopes

---

1 MAFOUB was created in 2009, and its purpose is to conduct a global study of the region that corresponds with the Zerafshan delta.

2 I would like to thank Frédérique Brunet who helped me identify these cultures, which are not my specialty.

of the riverbed. *In secundis* because this area was an area consecrated to the defense of the oasis, and for this reason re-employed several times even if suffering channel dessication phenomena. *In terzis*, the water table in this zone could have been played a role in the occupation or re-occupation.[3] Our hypothesis is that this transformation is linked to periodic phenomena of thaw of permaphrost in Pamir responsible of big landslides generating dams destinated to explose creating huge and exceptional floods which, once invaded the delta of the Zerafshan, can generate changes on the water network.[4]

The earliest occupations within the oasis proper have been dated to the 3rd century BCE. The data on material culture show they belonged to Scythian groups. According to the archaeological evidence dated to this epoch (Rante 2016; Rante and Mirzaakhmedov 2019), these populations settled all along the main channel of the Zerafshan, but the densest settlements were in the western areas of the oasis. After this, a progression of new populations occupied the area, as shown from the study of pottery and other materials.[5] The analysis of these cultural changes revealed six cultural phases when settlements continued to develop within the oasis, and then a phase of depopulation started around the 13th–14th centuries CE.

Although some articles on the social and territorial features of the oasis are presented at the beginning of this volume, by and large it is mostly concerned with material culture, as well as archaeozoology and different archaeometric studies that address the technological details of the material and chronology.

---

[3] This metholdology has already been employed in Afghanistan, where no one expressed any doubt: see Fouache et al. for an exhaustive bibliography of this program.

[4] In this field of study, we should remain humble, and at the same time propose hypotheses recognising and observing these phenomena. Hoping, for the umptheenth time, that who had doubts can definitely focus rather on other more serious problematics, such as the ethics of archaeology.

[5] This dynamic of population is also dynamised by the opening of the route directly joining Merv to Bukhara, which should have been opened, or at least densly roamed after the 3rd century CE. This hypothesis is suppoted by different solid data: the presence of a site, as mentioned in Rante and Mirzaakhmedov (2019: 117), which is in the middle between the Oxus and Paykend, which present a pottery assemblage datable to the early centuries CE and which the only site of the micro-oasis of Qaraqöl, at the state of researches; the presence of sites along a path studied by Paul Wordsworth (2015, also in Rante and Mirzaakhmedov 2019: 117); the progressive decrease of the route through Bactra since the region was not more political stable; the huge demographical and economical development at that time of the oasis. The existence of fortified sites along the Oxus in one or the other river of the Oxus is explained by their military function and not as stopover along a caravan route.

The volume begins with an article that studies the social features associated with the settlements, which in the first volume, and to some extent in the second, have been categorised by their topographical typology. Here, after considering these topographical features, other aspects of the sites are studied. The intent of this analysis is to better define the function of the different settlements and highlight their social and economic dynamics. Thus, the settlements' distribution within the oasis and the connections between them are important points developed in this article. Although the main categories of tripartite and bipartite sites can be defined, it is hard to identify the real function of the single tepe, even more so during the pre-Islamic periods. In order to identify the characteristics of this category, the written sources at our disposal and the archaeological evidence are also analysed in this article.

The first part of this volume is dedicated to the territory and settlements. Silvia Pozzi's article on Vardana (Vardanzeh) looks at the landscape around this site, a large territory that is administratively referred to as Obavija. The research presented in the article aims to identify the geographical limits, the settlement distribution and the territorial development strategies of this early medieval district in the northern outskirts of the Bukhara Oasis, which included Vardana. The research examines archaeological data obtained through territorial reconnaissance and written sources, as well as geographic and topographical data. The territorial elements studied here concern the key role of water resources, which were necessary for the profitable agricultural development of the district. And this analysis will be useful as a comparative model for conducting similar studies of the other districts of the oasis.

Focusing further on territorial recognition, Andrey Omelchenko and Djamal K. Mirzaakhmedov look at the major site of Paykend, on the one hand highlighting the several decades of excavations conducted by the Hermitage Museum, and on the other hand addressing the major discoveries that cover a wide chronological and cultural spectrum extending from the end of the 4th century and the beginning of the 3rd century BCE up until the medieval Islamic period. Although an exhaustive presentation of the site was published in *Buxarskii Oazis i evo sosedi v drevnosti i srednevekove* in 2015, this article highlights the most recent discoveries.

The second part of this volume contains broad studies of two material cultures: pottery and glass. It opens with Gabriele Puschnigg and Jacopo Bruno's article, which presents the study of the ceramics brought to light in different sites throughout the oasis by the Franco-Uzbek Archaeological Mission (MAFOUB). The data presented are a scientific reference for a comprehensive study of the ceramic from this vast region and reflect major typo-chronological features and technological variations of the pottery within the oasis. The chronological depth of the material as well as its spatial distribution allow us to gain important insights into the dynamics of economic and cultural development, which still have not been subject to a comprehensive and systematic study. As archaeological work is still ongoing, the pottery analysis continues and this data is therefore not exhaustive or conclusive.

The study of the pottery continues with an exploration of the petrographic and surface analyses conducted at the Centre de Recherche et Restauration des Musées de France by Yvan Coquinot and Nathalie Gandolfo. The objective of this program was to study the pottery's geological aspects, the type and structure of the clays used, the components of the fabrics and the sources of the materials used for manufacturing. The ceramics studied come from two archaeological sites in the Bukhara Oasis: Iskijkat (29 sherds) and Vardanzeh (8 sherds) (37 sherds in total). All the ceramic sherds come from stratigraphical contexts. The results show a vast homogeneity of the fabrics, which is not surprising, and the coarse material has been grouped into subcategories, making it possible to categorise the ceramics.

While the petrographic analyses looked at the broad issues of the clay's features and the morphology of the fabrics in order to categorise the entire ceramic piece, the article by Anne Bouquillon, Christel Doublet and Nathalie Gandolfo, all members of the Centre de Recherche et Restauration des Musées de France, focuses on a specific material from a specific chronological period: glazed ceramics from the Islamic period. The study shows what types of analyses could be broadly implemented to answer to the general issues raised by the MAFOUB project's research, specifically concerning the importation of ceramics and their surface treatments. The study has been conducted on an extremely small number of sherds, but it is representative enough to answer to questions related to importation and surface treatment. Six fragments have been selected from two different archaeological sites within the oasis: Paykend and Bukhara. The analysed fragments offer a partial view of the production of glazed ceramics in the Bukhara Oasis in the 9th and 10th centuries, and one importation has been confirmed through comparisons with chemical analyses from Mesopotamia and Nishapur. Other results have been useful for better determining the ancient technique employed to produce the so-called "Ishkornaja" ceramics, a probable imitation of blue-cobalt productions (DEP B/74).

The next article focuses on pottery during the 15th and 16th centuries. Djamal Mirzaakhmedov portrays the Timurid period and the following century as an intense artistic time when pottery, architecture, architectural decoration, jewellry and book art prospered, the technologies used to produce them reached high levels of advancement and artistry. Within this framework, the 15th–16th-century glazed ceramic dishes from Bukhara testify to the process of syncretisation that local craftsmen engaged in during this period. This last chapter dedicated to ceramics looks at a historical period in the oasis that was characterised by a heavy depopulation of the settlements, a huge exodus corresponding to the new occupation of territories around or farther from the old ones.

The discussion of glass begins with another article by Djamal Mirzaakhmedov, who has dedicated much of his career to the study of this material. The article focuses on glasses from Bukhara during the 15th and 16th centuries, but the author also dedicates large sections of the article to discussions about glass in Uzbekistan's oases in general. Moreover, the author points out the different functions attributed to this material in various contexts, primarily focusing on pharmaceutical and medical uses. The "pharmaceutic building" excavated at Paykend is taken as a reference to show how this discipline and technology developed during the medieval period.

Like with the ceramic material, glass has also been analysed using archaeometric methods and technologies. Directed by Yoko Shindo, the Japanese team of Takako Hosokawa, Tamako Takeda, Toshiyasu Shinmen and Ayano Endo attempted to evaluate glass from the Bukhara Oasis within the broader historical context of Islamic glass, and they examine glass artifacts from Paykend, Ramitan, Iskijkat, Kakishtuvan, site 250 and Bukhara. The approach they used combines the methodologies of archaeology, glass typology and chemical analysis, and they specifically focus on Paykend, the site where the largest amount of glassware was found.

An article by Delphine Decruyenaere, Rocco Rante, Manon Vuillien and Marjan Mashkour looks at the preliminary results of the archeozoological activity conducted by D. Decruyenaere and presents a case study of the settlement of Iskijkat. This analysis takes into consideration the remains of bones brought to light during excavations and enhances our understanding of the subsistence economy and animal resource management in urban and rural contexts. Although the full study will concern all excavated sites of the oasis, this preliminary essay focuses solely on Iskijkat, one of the most important sites and one which shows a complete stratigraphical sequence. Moreover, the site is situated along the "Silk Road" that crosses the oasis; therefore, this study also provides information on animals used for transport, such as camels.

Two articles discussing radiocarbon and thermoluminescence analyses end the volume and these articles are the rich foundation on which our scientific data and historical interpretations and analyses are built. Pascale Richardin, from the Centre de Recherche et Restauration des Musées de France, and Rocco Rante spent several years analysing a huge quantity of organic materials, a small portion of which was analysed by the USA Beta Analytic laboratory. The resulting qualitative data are grouped by excavation and site for the sake of clarity and accessibility. Chronological segments can be directly observed through the graphs and some useful physico-chemical elements are described.

The same high degree of engagement characterises the article on thermoluminescence, in which Antoine Zink, Elisa Porto, also members of the Centre de Recherche et Restauration des Musées de France, and Rocco Rante analyse a huge quantity of non-organic material, mostly ceramic sherds and baked bricks. The methods they employ, which had already been used and refined in Nishapur (Iran) (Rante and Collinet 2013), have been used to not only define chronological spans but also to observe the different chrono-typological sequences of the pottery in the ceramic ateliers of Paykend. This article has also been the opportunity to test new methods linked to the analysis of mudbrick, an organic material for which the process of analysis is different and more complicated. Although the results are not yet conclusive, the method has been tested, proving its validity.

The studies published in this volume complete the framework presented in volumes 1 and 2. This volume provides the reader with the tools and context for fully apprehending the foundations of the research presented in the previous two volumes.

I would strongly like to thank all of the authors for their work. I wish to thank in particular the members of the Center of Research and Restauration of the French Museums. Many thanks in particular to Anne Bouquillon who fought against the unpredictable problems until the last night before the last issue.

CHAPTER 1

Settlements and Social Features within the Oasis of Bukhara

Rocco Rante, Abdisabur Raimkulov and Fabrizio Crusco

1   Introduction

In order to develop archaeological research in Central Asia, in 2009 the Louvre Museum, in collaboration with the Archaeological Institute of Samarkand and the Academy of Sciences of Tashkent, started a research program (Franco-Uzbek Archaeological Mission in the Bukhara Oasis, MAFOUB) to study the Bukhara region. This geographic area was chosen in relation to a larger study that covers the entire region of "Greater Khorasan", including eastern Iran, western Afghanistan and Turkmenistan. In this context, the Bukhara Oasis is the geographic entity closest to this vast region, which it is linked to from several points of view.

In general, this program's objective is to study this region's territorial and historical complexity by investigating its human occupations from antiquity to the Islamic period. Therefore, the research program focuses on the dynamics of occupation within this vast region by studying the evolution of human behaviour, as well as the urban and cultural evolution. In this broad context, one major interest is to reconsider urban environments since the post-Alexandrine era through the prism of the relationships between these urban entities and cities in western and eastern Iran. Therefore, this program aims to study and identify the factors that gave rise to a variety of cultural developments between antiquity and the Islamic era. It is also interested in a detailed study of local production and importation in order to conduct an in-depth investigation into the dynamics of trade between the eastern Mediterranean and the east.

The research program consists of several axes of study that revolve around archaeological activities. Archaeological excavation is therefore accompanied by various scientific operations, with the aim of constructing and/or supplementing the historical and cultural framework of the region. Among these activities, the study of human settlements occupies a fundamental place.[1] This topic has been treated from every possible angle as far as human occupation is concerned. An extensive topographical mapping of the settlements has been conducted, accompanied by accurate surveys, and through this, certain elements date the occupations and allow us to place them chronologically. Settlement categories have been identified in order to permit easier, correct characterisation and a more detailed study of their socio-economic features and relations.

Among these categories, settlements with two and three urban entities were identified and considered urban sites because they consisted of a citadel and lower cities, or villages, with or without suburbs (Rante and Mirzaakhmedov 2019). The third entity was simply presented as a site characterised by a single tepe ("unique tepe"), which in the first volume has been identified based exclusively on its topographical features. In fact, it has been mentioned as a category corresponding to different sorts of sites, including residences, kurgans, mills and any other smaller entity associated with the occupation of the territory. But knowledge about the single tepe and its function within the oasis is crucial for understanding the global organisation of the region in socio-political and economic terms. What are the main characteristics of these sites? What size are they, and what is their distribution within the oasis? What is their function in the middle of such a dense urban agglomeration?

This article will thus try to further develop this still scarcely known social picture. It will first consider several aspects of the topography of these sites. Then, it will look at their distribution within the oasis – this is the most important part of the analysis. Taken together, this information, in addition to the still scant scientific literature on this topic, will provide us with new features to use in our attempts to construct a social framework through which to determine the social and economic dynamics of the oasis.

2   Geographic Setting

The oases of Bukhara and Qaraqöl are located in the south-eastern part of Uzbekistan (fig. 1.1).

Covering approximately 5,100 km², this territory is bounded to the north by the Kyzyl Kum (red desert) and to the south by the Kara Kum (black desert). To the west flows the Amu Darya River, with a south/north course.

---

[1] For an exhaustive description and discussion of this topic, see Rante and Mirzaakhmedov 2019.

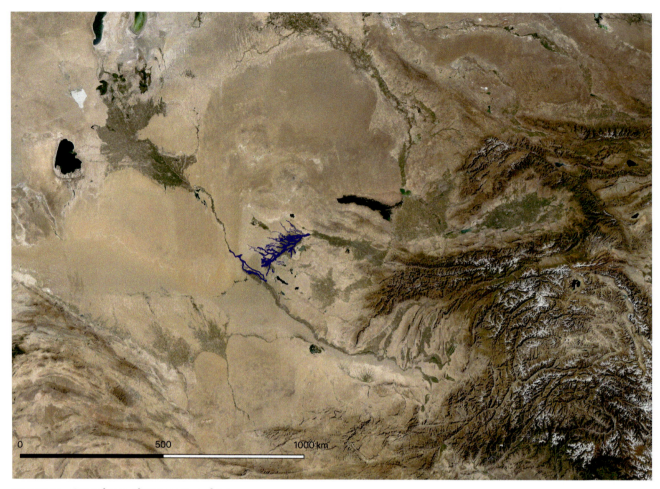

FIGURE 1.1   General map of Western Central Asia
©WORLD IMAGERY 2019; RANTE 2019

The Zerafshan River, with a drainage basin of 143,000 km², originates 741 km upstream from the Alai Mountains and the Zerafshan glacier in Tajikistan. The water from the Zerafshan River is the only source of water for agriculture and human activities. Until the 1960s, the Bukhara Oasis's only source of water for irrigation was from the Zerafshan River. The area studied corresponds to alluvial plains (fig. 1.2), with an average altitude of 260 m in the east and 200 m in the west. The Bukhara Oasis has an arid, cold desert climate.

As far as the hydrographic network is concerned, the oasis of Bukhara is in the endorheic delta of the Zerafshan River, implying a dense network of different sized watercourses. It is difficult to have a precise idea of the ancient network setting, since this region and its water resources have been subjected to continual transformation since the Middle Pleistocene. The geomorphologic study completed in collaboration with Eric Fouache (Fouache et al. 2016) created a map of the oasis's natural water network, avoiding all recent and modern canals. The map (figure 1.3) shows a hydrographic network that only traces the natural watercourses and contains hints of the other watercourses, which have disappeared today due to various transformations of the network. The current water network within the oasis does not reflect the authentic ancient setting.

Another water network has been drawn that corresponds to an old Russian map dated to 1893 (printed in 1923).[2] The GIS-supported vectorialisation of the watercourses (fig. 1.4) shows how dense the water network was at the end of the 19th century (Rante and Mirzaakhmedov 2019: fig. 6). Later, during the Soviet Union era, another precise map was created (Rante and Mirzaakhmedov 2019: fig. 7) that corresponds more accurately to the present day.

For our purposes, as will be shown later, the latter map is useless because it inacuritely presents the ancient territory and thus misrepresents the human occupations. Reconstructions conducted through GIS support have

---

2 This map has been found in the Staatsbibliothek of Munich. Its arrival at the library should be dated to the 1926.

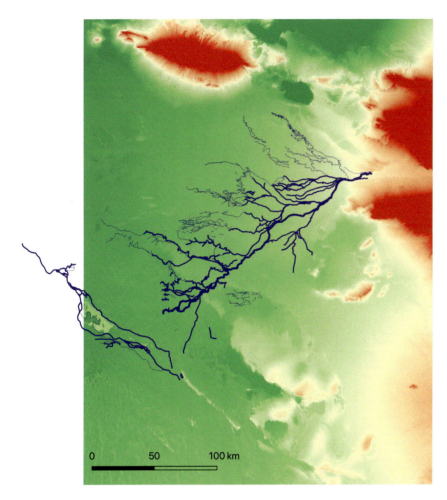

FIGURE 1.2
Hydrographic of the Oasis of Bukhara, SRTM Map
© RANTE 2019

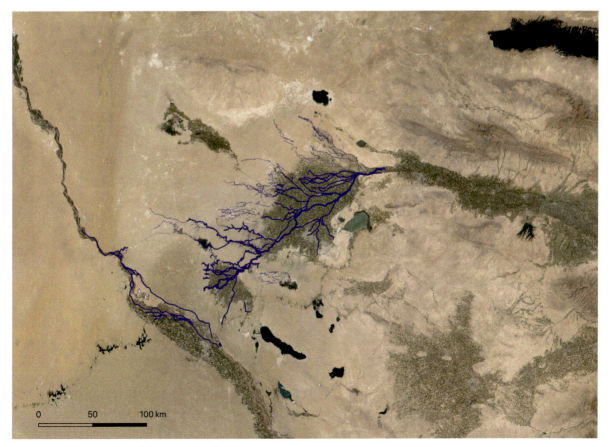

FIGURE 1.3 Hydrographic of the Oasis of Bukhara
© WORLD IMAGERY 2019; RANTE 2019

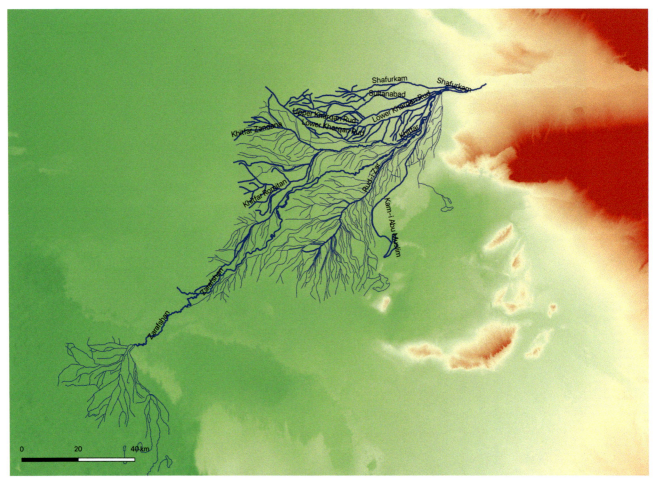

FIGURE 1.4   Historical hydrography of the oasis of Bukhara, SRTM Map
©WORLD IMAGERY 2019; RANTE 2019

shown it is hard to connected the 1893 hydrographic network to the ancient settlements. Therefore, the former geomorphological map is better suited for our objective, and the 1893 one is used to complete the general framework.

3 Settlements within the Oasis

In the first volume of *The Oasis of Bukhara* (Rante and Mirzaakhmedov 2019: 27–29) the 1,040 settlements within the oasis and the surrounding areas were categorised. Among the diverse settlements present in this territory, our study concentrated on the tripartite and bipartite sites in particular and did not reveal any precise or detailed characteristics of the third category, called "unique tepe".[3] It only mentioned that they might correspond with kurgans, caravanserais, residences, mills, forts or open sites and might have been used as production areas, ceramic distribution zones or for other kinds of human occupation. Indeed, this description was too general to convey even an approximate idea of their structure and function within the oasis. This article is an attempt to clarify this category and contextualise the sites within a dense network of urban and rural settlements. For this purpose, it is more appropriate to first outline the characteristics of the former settlements and then turn to the specific features of the unique tepe.

3.1 Tripartite Sites

A tripartite site is a settlement that consists of a citadel (the political centre), a shahrestan (the village) and a suburb, the *rabad* of the Islamic period (Tskitishvili 1971). Archaeological evidence brought to light that in the same period, although there was only one citadel, it was possible to have two (more than two have not yet been identified within the oasis) shahrestans and more than one suburb, which are divided into several mounds, as is the

---

3 Here "unique" is not used in the sense of "inimitable" or "exceptional" but as "individual" or "isolated", or better still "single".

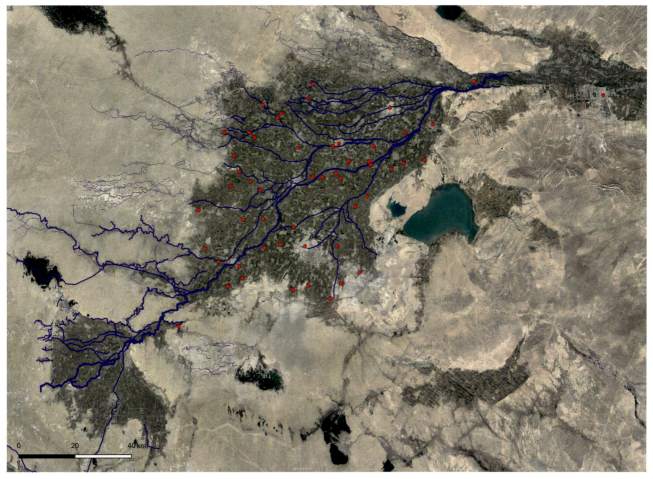

FIGURE 1.5 Tripartite sites and hydrography of the oasis of Bukhara
© RANTE 2019; WORLD IMAGERY 2019

case with Paykend, Ramitan, Ramish tepe and site 560, as well as several others.

Within the oasis, 53 tripartite sites have been identified (fig. 1.5). Their surface span ranges from a minimum of 3 ha to a maximum of approximately 45 ha, with only two exceptions recorded in the 10th century: Paykend, which reached an area of 82.5 ha (67 ha for the urban space and the rest considered as areas for caravans or non-residents) in that period, and Bukhara, which reached an area of 1,000 ha.[4] Some of these complex urban entities, most probably the large ones, appear to hold the record for longevity: founded as early as the 3rd century BCE and occupied until circa the 15th century. According to our recent researches on cities and urbanization (Rante, Schwarz and Tronca 2022: 6–28), tripartite sites, however, were not founded as tripartite sites. They were first unfortified country agglomerations, consisting of a political centre with a village at the foot, and only from the 5th century onwards did suburbs rise up all around this former urban agglomeration.

Their geographical distribution within the oasis seems clear and can be divided into three main areas. Tripartite settlements are observed primarily along the main rivers, along the main roads and at the western borders of the oasis. This organisation gives us some indication why the earliest occupations arose the distribution along watercourses and roads does not need any further commentary, being quite common in many other settlements. However, the concentration in the western limit of the oasis needs some clarification. It has been observed by this project that every tripartite site along the western border of the oasis was strongly fortified, indicating the need to protect the irrigated space from populations coming from the steppe territories. It is thus highly probable that this

---

4 The entire area Bukhara encompasses is a surprise. It has been calculated through satellite images and GIS support on the basis of the plans published by Beleniskij et al. 1973: fig. 94 II. Since it is difficult to precisely delimit the area from a sketch produced without any satellite or topographical maps, the area can vary from 550 ha (the area corresponding to the ancient urban settlements visible on satellite images) to 1,000 ha (the area corresponding to Beleniskij's 1973 map).

portion of the oasis was one of the earliest occupied areas, and from the beginning it was a place that needed to be defended. This likely occurred while sites were settling along the main watercourses, those along the roads were probably founded later.

The function of the tripartite sites as epicentres of a system of smaller villages and other structures all around is already clear in the early 1st century CE, that is, since the moment of the intense occupation and foundation of other settlements corresponding to "city-states". But this was much more the case in the 4th–5th centuries, when suburbs appeared and added more structure to their location and their function. These suburban entities became *de facto* places for inhabitants and for the production and sale of different goods. From this period on, the tripartite sites were the main towns to produce, sell and buy staple goods, not only to their own inhabitants but also to the other smaller sites around them.

There was certainly a hierarchy among tripartite sites. The larger and more developed ones, such as Ramitan, Bukhara, Vobkent, Vardana and some others, assumed a more central and larger political role than the others. The size of the settlements is an element that clearly shows the whole development of a site, and it possibly also indicates its supremacy; the construction and richness of the main buildings also played a role. Among these characteristics, one in particular often attracts our attention: mural paintings. Although the presence of mural paintings and iconographies decorating the halls of dwellings certainly played a social role, this feature alone is not a guarantee of political centrality, because mural paintings were quite common in the main buildings of the different settlements – tripartite as well bipartite and unique tepe.

3.2 *Bipartite Sites*

A bipartite site consists of a citadel and shahrestan. In this case, the citadel is mostly a more or less large fortified building encircled by a more or less dense agglomeration of houses and farms, the shahrestan.

Within the oasis, 291 bipartite sites have been identified (fig. 1.6). Their surface range extends from a minimum of 5,000 m² to a maximum of circa 10 ha. The chronological

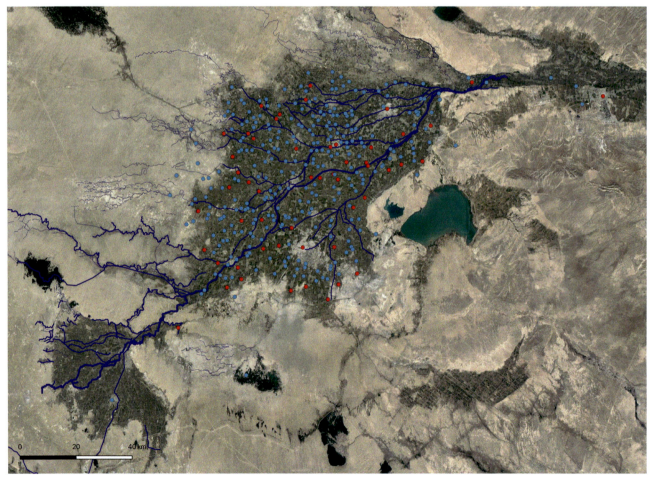

FIGURE 1.6 Tripartite and bipartite sites and the hydrography of the oasis of Bukhara
© RANTE 2019; WORLD IMAGERY 2019

range of this settlement category is harder to fix because of the high number of sites. Nevertheless, archaeological evidence and observations made in the field give us fairly solid data, indicating an origin between the 1st and the 3rd centuries CE. Obviously, further research will modify and identify this chronological span with more precision. The results presented here, however, are also supported by strong changes in material culture observed in the excavations, thus confirming the arrival of foreign populations within the oasis and showing how older traditions were modified or combined with new ones. Later, while other more central sites expanded into tripartite sites, these remained as bipartite sites, thus contributing to the socio-economic system previously mentioned.

The geographic distribution of these sites within the oasis is homogenous. It seems that generally they continued to organise along watercourses rather than along roads, although there are some examples south of Bukhara that follow the southern limit of the oasis.

Although some of them were heavily dependent on the main caravan roads, as is the case with the unique bipartite site found within the micro-oasis of Qaraqöl, site 1045, which welcomed caravans coming from the Oxus and then reached the border of the oasis through the Khorasan Road, others engaged in agricultural and/or manufacturing activities, thereby engendering and developing the socio-economic dynamic in each city-state system as well as between different city-states.

As far as the social structure is concerned, the main fortified building would have been occupied by a property lord, probably the *khwēsht*, the head of a village, rather than the *framānδār (prm'nd'r)*, administrator and tax collector (Livshits, 1962: 154),[5] or the *arspan ('rspn)*, mainly referring to a "postmaster" (Livshits 1962: 104–106, Nov. 2; 177, B-17; 153–54, B-18; Grenet and de la Vaissière 2002: 166–67) or more generally to an *āzatkār*, noble. The shahrestan was likely inhabited by mostly *kārekār*, merchants (*khwākar*) and other high classes – in my opinion they favoured the main sites more so than the rural ones (Grenet 2020: 7–8).

3.3 *Unique Tepe*

Among the main sites (tripartites) and the smaller or rural ones (bipartites), there is a category I called "unique tepe", and at the beginning, I only considered their simply

---

5 I would like to thank Frantz Grenet for some important details about the figure of the *framānδār (prm'nd'r)* who, based on the Mount Mugh documents, seems to not have been numerous and was responsible for a vast territory. Thus, this figure possibly directly depended on a higher figure: the *khuv* of Bukhara? Or of Sogdiana?

topography: they consisted of only one tepe. As previously mentioned, these mounds have been only partially observed in the field, archaeological interests focusing on more extended and structured sites. But once the social and economic network within the oasis was established, their importance within the global system became clear.

But the identification of this category of site presents more problems than the previous sites. Because of their smaller extension, they were often destroyed in the past for different reasons, or they were transformed into cemeteries. For these reasons, although the same research protocol was employed for this category as for the previous ones, this did not prevent an error in the calculation of the total number of these sites.

Unique tepe, as previously mentioned, is a category of different sorts of structures, identifiable with residences, fortified or not, kurgans, farms, isolated religious apparatus etc. This categorisation can only be further qualified through excavations, which are not yet the aim of MAFOUB. However, some specific categories, such as kurgans or current cemeteries, can be excluded. For the study presented here, I decided to ignore the group of unique tepe outside the oasis, such as Bash tepe located by the western, currently desert, part of the oasis.

There are 319 unique tepe that have been recorded (fig. 1.7), out of which 22 are most certainly isolated fortresses located mainly along watercourses, roads and near main settlements. For example, this is the case with Paykend and fortress 0120 (fig. 1.8). Speculations about their chronology are not possible here. Nevertheless, the mounds that have already been observed through surveys or were studied by other expeditions, for example Uch Kulakh (Silvi-Antonini and Mirzaakhmedov 2009), do not show any that were founded earlier than the 1st–3rd centuries CE – the one exception is the Bash tepe cluster.

3.3.1   Uch Kulakh (Site 0064)

Uch Kulakh is a good example of a site that illustrates this category's characteristics. Although at its base the whole tepe covers an area of circa 1.5 ha, its upper area is 6,400 m². The mound rises 8 m high above the plain (fig. 1.9).

The excavation of the mound brought to light two main entities: a central fortress ("castello") and an agglomeration of houses all around it. According to the excavation data (Silvi-Antonini and Mirzaakhmedov 2009: 47–74), the former structure covered an area of circa 2,170 m², and the castle and its southern fortification have been identified, and they are separated by a corridor. It is protected by strong ramparts, covered with vertical slots for archers. All around it – at the moment only its western part and

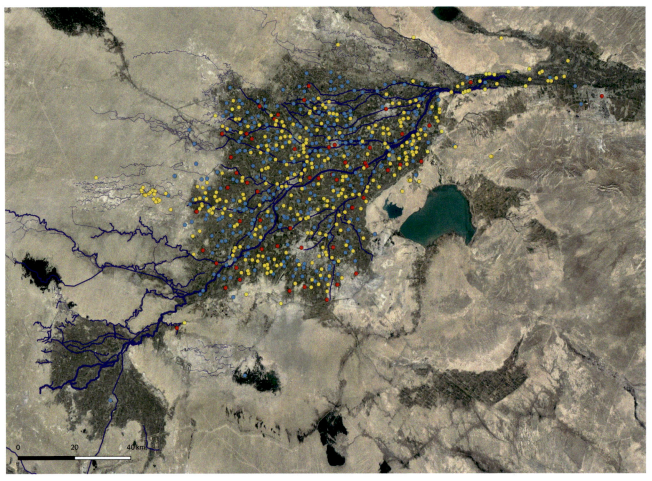

FIGURE 1.7 Tripartite, bipartite, and unique tepe sites and the hydrography of the oasis of Bukhara
© RANTE 2019; WORLD IMAGERY 2019

a small portion of its eastern part have been excavated – an agglomeration of houses rose up, probably connected with the central castle. Actually, it cannot be considered a village or a shahrestan, because it is not really separated by a well-defined citadel and is structurally connected with the central fortified area. This organisation, common within the oasis, is close to the one at Paykend. The Paykend citadel consists of the royal apparatus, a temple and residences that are concentrated on the western part (Omelchenko 2012: fig. 5). Outside the ramparts, towards the north, other agglomerations of residences have been excavated (Omelchenko et al. 2014), also likely connected with the citadel. There are also several other examples; Ramitan and Iskijkat, among others, also present a similar configuration (Rante and Mirzaakhmedov 2019: 145–83, 231–39).

The excavation at Uch Kulakh clearly shows that a large portion of each unique tepe consisted of a central fortified residence, also called a "castle", which generally covered an area of several thousand square metres, encircled by dwellings directly connected with the main structure. Considering this characteristic, it is possible that every settlement within the oasis developed in this way: fortified residence and habitats all around, sometime included within the ramparts, then some settlements built a shahrestan (village), while others continued with suburbs and so on. Ramitan and Paykend, the best known archaeologically speaking, perfectly explain this dynamic. Ramitan, after its early beginning as an unwalled agglomeration of buildings, developed into a fortified square-shaped city covering an area of circa 1.3 ha in the early 1st century CE. Already in this period, it is reasonable to imagine a central main fortified building encircled by smaller unwalled buildings directly linked to it. Only two centuries later, and certainly for demographic, military and political reasons, its extension did not likely modify the inner social and political organisation. At that time, the layout would correspond with that of Uch Kulakh, as with that of many other sites. Thus, between the 1st and the 3rd centuries CE urban entities began to develop on their own. However, having followed a similar early urban development does not mean that all sites were socially

FIGURE 1.8   Paykend, fortress on the northern side
© RANTE 2018

FIGURE 1.9   Uch Kulakh
© RILIEVI SRL 2014

and politically or militarily the same – far from this. The main sites, which developed further, already maintained power within the oasis.

3.3.2 Some Additional Unique Tepe within the Oasis

In the same area as Uch Kulakh, which from at least the first centuries CE depended on Varakhsha (Shishkin 1963), other unique tepes have been identified that have not yet been excavated. The closest example to Uch Kulakh is site 0219, Chandir tepe, identified as a "tepe deprived of [a] village" (Silvi-Antonini and Mirzaakhmedov 2009: 200, fig. IV.24). It covers an area close to that of Uch Kulakh, approximatively 6,500 m², and like Chandir tepe, it consists of an upper quadrangular zone, castle and a small southern lower part, which might correspond with the residential agglomeration linked to the central fortress. Site 0200, Bezymjannoe tepe (Silvi-Antonini and Mirzaakhmedov 2009: 200, fig. IV.27) is also near the previous ones. Its area is approximately 4,600 m², and it seems to consist of an upper part, probably the castle, and a residential agglomeration all around it. Site 0065 (Silvi-Antonini and Mirzaakhmedov 2009: 200, fig. IV.19) also belongs to this category.

Indeed, other similar unique tepe are distributed elsewhere within the oasis. In the north-western part, for example, sites 0321 and 0327 present a morphology similar to Uch Kulakh, with an upper castle and a residential agglomeration all around, which also cannot be properly considered a village. In the eastern part of the oasis, site 0552, although smaller than the previous ones, also belongs to this category, and not far eastward, site 0753 belongs to it as well. At the southern frontier of the oasis, south of Bukhara, site 0101, although larger than the previous ones – approximately 1 ha – also presents the same features as the previously mentioned sites.

The abovementioned unique tepe are only a small sample of this category, which spreads across every zone of the oasis. The intent here is not to examine the morphologies of the 319 sites in depth but rather to present different types of sites within this category. Their location within the oasis is a crucial factor for understanding how they are distributed within this network and linked to the other main sites – both tripartite and bipartite ones.

4 Distribution of Unique Tepe within the Oasis

The intent of this section is to establish the distribution of the unique tepe in order to determine their locations and links with watercourses, main roads, main sites and other precise areas in the oasis. The study of the distribution can therefore help us to identify clusters and their connections with the other abovementioned elements. This procedure is essential for understanding where they concentrated and finally why they concentrated there. After this, their particular distribution in that zone and their morphology can help us determine their specific function.

If one looks at the map (fig. 1.10) where every site is labelled, one sees that the unique tepe (yellow points) are primarily concentrated within the main oasis. Two areas appear to be outside the limits of the oasis proper, the western area, also called the Bash tepe cluster, and the north-eastern area, along the Zerafshan, westward from Karmana (0104).

The Bash tepe cluster contains over a dozen small tepe, covering an area smaller than 0.5 ha and dated between the Bronze-Early/Iron Age and the 1st century CE (Stark et al. 2019: 161, 248), in which other tepe were already roughly dated to the Bronze Age (Cerasuolo 2009: 207; see also Mukhamedjanov 1990). New discoveries attesting to the foundation of this site during that period do not refute the geomorphological data recently brought to light by the French-Uzbek Mission (Fouache et al. 2016), which has proven this area's tendency towards desertification. Moreover, the fact that this cluster was "a border fortress" (Stark et al. 2019: 245) highlights its peripherical location and thus its geomorphological position between irrigated and desert lands, further confirming a climatic tendency towards dryness. Moreover, this does not exclude the idea that this fortress cluster was already located in a semi-arid area, where life followed the rhythms of the seasonal rising of the water table, as might be the case in Kum Sultan south of Bukhara. All these reasons, but especially its brief existence, led us to treat this cluster separately. The north-eastern cluster is located in the irrigated lands just before the delta formation and has not yet been excavated. It belongs to a zone that is well-connected to the main oasis.

Looking at the same map in fig. 1.10, other clearly defined clusters can been observed. Except for those previously mentioned (the yellow ellipses), the red ellipses highlight the main clusters with a high concentration of unique tepe. The westernmost ones are concentrated in an area where several tripartite sites rise up, such as Ramitan (0074), Varakhsha (0069), Ramish tepe (0059) and Sivanj (0231), and the Khitfar Ramitan watercourse passes through this area, separating Ramitan and Sivanj on the northern side and Varakhsha and Ramish tepe on the southern side. Although in this specific study I am not

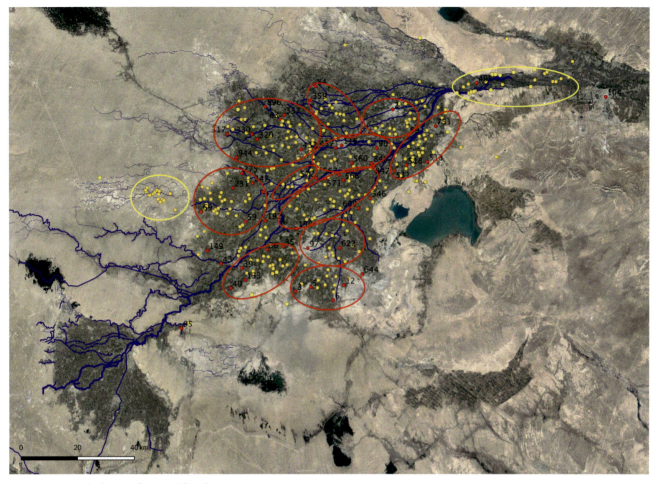

FIGURE 1.10 Single tepe clusters within the oasis
© RANTE 2019

precisely defining what connects unique tepe with tripartite sites, it is interesting to note that every unique tepe can be connected to a tripartite site within a radius under 7 km.[6] The same trend is observable across the whole oasis. This western area is also traversed by a main road leading towards Khorezm, although only the unique tepe closer to Varakhsha can really be linked to it; the others are too scattered across the whole area.

A further cluster has been identified southward, in the green portion between the Zerafshan and the southern limit of the oasis. This last cluster of unique tepe is also included in, and thus connected to, an area where several tripartite sites play the role of main towns, such as sites 0039, 0133, 0036 and 0035. In contrast with the previous ones, they are homogenously distributed along the main Khorasan Road, and every tepe is located at a distance of less than 1.5 km from the road.

At the south-eastern corner of the oasis, an additional cluster is included in a zone between Bukhara and several tripartite sites along the southern limit of the irrigated space. These unique tepe were probably connected with sites 0003, 0005, 0006 or 0012, and probably also with Bukhara, at least its southern unique tepe (from west to east), drawing a half circle that outlines the modern urban limits of the city. Each one, moreover, is located along a 19th-century road extending from Bukhara towards the south, probably reaching the network leading to the oasis of Karshi. Did their markets develop along the borders of the main city, which is where they are located today?

Another main cluster is located in the north-eastern zone of the oasis, between the eastern limit and the Zerafshan. Here, four main tripartite sites (Tavovis 0751, 0513, 0518 and 0531) are where the socio-economic activities were concentrated, thus connecting many other unique tepe, as well as bipartite sites, but the significant

---

6   Regarding this analysis see Rante and Trionfetti 2021 for a new archaeo-economic method to seek connections between cities and their distribution; See Rante, Schwarz and Tronca 2022 for a global analysis on social networks.

feature of this area is the distribution of the unique tepe. They are in fact organised in an oblong shape that follows the main ancient road in the direction leading away from Bukhara and eastward to Samarkand. Some of them also follow the ancient Kam-i Abu Muslim, which keeps it natural course until site 0518, where is assumes an artificial course southward, tracing the limit of the oasis.

The area located on the opposite side of the Zerafshan, and north of the main Khitfar watercourse, has another smaller cluster, and it is organised around the main sites of Gijduvan (0002) and Marzangon tepe (0089). And some southern sites also seem to be located along smaller roads leading from Gijduvan to the south of the oasis. Moreover, looking at the 19th-century hydrographic network, they appear to have been located along the small watercourses flowing to the south.

Further to the west, a smaller cluster is organised south-east of three main sites, Vardana (0084), Vobkent (0116) and Gulyamata (0359). I would like to add Khadicha Bibi tepa to this short list of main sites. It is a bipartite site that was identified by Silvia Pozzi[7] and does not include any main towns; it is interesting because it was the largest tepe in the area and for this reason was probably also socio-economically influential. It is difficult to observe the distribution of these sites along the watercourses since some parts of this last portion of the various branches of the Sultanabad and Shafirkam are artificial.

A cluster further along can be observed in the north-western part of the oasis. It is an important cluster where the network of unique tepe and bipartite sites is very dense. The Khitfar Zandana, flowing east-west until the site of Kakishtuvan, passes by this area and thus shapes the rhythm of life in it. The upper zone is organised around the main tripartite sites of Zandana (0083) and site 0357, as well as site 0896 along the boundary of the area, while the lower zone is organised around the main tripartite site 0432 and Kaththa (0320).

In the centre of the oasis, two unique tepe clusters face each other on opposite sides of the Zerafshan. The north-western one is distributed along the watercourses of the Khitfar Ramitan and the Tarab. These unique tepe are mainly connected with Ramitan and site 0572. Although a further and more detailed explanation of this cluster remains difficult, it should be noted that unique tepe observed inside it cover an area between 2,000 m^2 and 3,000 m^2, which could be attributed to farms directly connected with both main watercourses. The second and larger cluster is distributed within the area between the southern side of the Zerafshan and the Rud-i Zar, the watercourse flowing to Bukhara. It is spread all over this vast area, and its network is organised around sites 0566, 0567, 0571 and 0190. Moreover, if one looks at the 1893 map (Rante and Mirzaakhmedov 2019: fig. 6), the distribution seems to be concentrated in two main zones, following two main roads, in the middle of which swampy zones are marked on the map, and they probably also existed in these ancient periods.

Two other clusters are identifiable: the first in the area between the Khitfar and the Zerafshan and the second around Bukhara. Since the 7th century, but in the 9th century in particular, the Bukharan province has absorbed the whole area between the Zerafshan and the southern limit of the oasis.

Within the oasis, the size of unique tepe covers a range between 1,000 m^2 and 1 ha, except for a few that are either smaller or larger. Among these, however, the most representative sizes are 3,000 m^2 and 4,000 m^2. Sites whose sizes are between 5,000 m^2 and 7,000 m^2 are less representative, and those between 8,000 and 9,000 m^2 are very scarce – only 28 sites. In contrast, numerous unique tepe are 1 ha.

In this context, it is interesting to look at the size distribution within the oasis.[8] When looking at the different-sized clusters it is interesting to observe that the unique tepe covering an area smaller than 3,000 m^2 are mainly concentrated along watercourses and in the Bash tepe area, a zone characterised by military problems. The most numerous unique tepe, whose areas are between 3,000 and 4,000 m^2 (fig. 1.11), are mostly distributed along the main roads, such as Khorasan Road, west of Bukhara and around Tavovis, as well as around Khorezm Road where it crosses the area of Varakhsha, although these are smaller. A few of these sites are also distributed along watercourses, but they are too scattered for us to have a precise idea of their function. The group of sites with a size between 5,000 and 7,000 m^2 (fig. 1.12) is primarily concentrated in the areas of Ramitan and Sivanj, Vardana and Gulyamata, and south of Gijduvan. Lastly, it is also interesting to observe that sites of circa 1 ha (fig. 1.13) are concentrated in two main areas: Varakhsha/Sivanj and Zandana/Kaththa/0432.

---

7 See fig. 2.19 in her article published in this volume.

8 Size distribution here concerns the geographic size of settlements, not the population, which implies a different methodology: see Rante and Trionfetti 2021: 581–96.

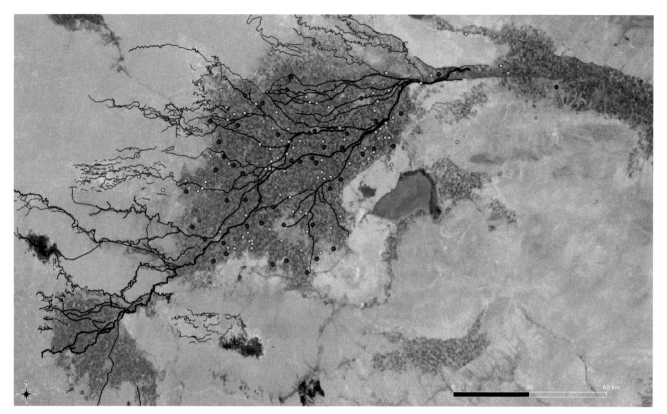

FIGURE 1.11   Clusters of single tepe between 3,000 and 4,000 m²
© RANTE 2019

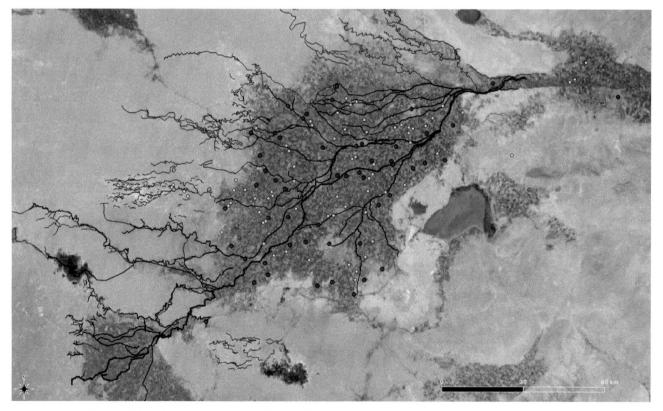

FIGURE 1.12   Clusters of single tepe between 5,000 and 7,000 m²
© RANTE 2019

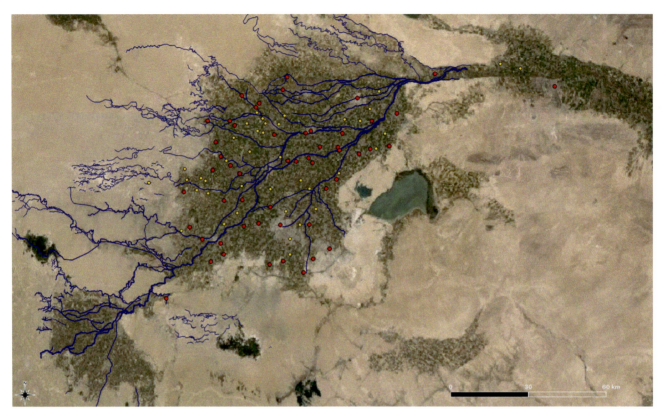

FIGURE 1.13 Clusters of single tepe around 1 ha
© RANTE 2019

5 What Do Written Sources Say?

It is difficult to find precise information about Sogdian urbanisation in the pre-Islamic periods. *Ancient Letters* and documents from Mount Mugh certainly provide a vast panorama of historical and socio-economic data, but little information, and none with any detail, is found about this topic. Nevertheless, in these sources there are some interesting elements that give a little more information.

In this section, no Islamic sources will be taken into consideration, except for the sake of comparison, because here the interest is the earlier organisation of this settlement network, thus before the Islamic re-organisation, which in the Bukhara Oasis took place during the Samanid Emirate. Moreover, at the end of the medieval Islamic period, as observed in archaeological fieldwork, some sites were abandoned, a phenomenon that pollutes the analysis, modifying the organisation of the site, not only in geographical terms but also in social and economic ones.

As far as the administrative and political framework is concerned, document A9 of the Mount Mugh documents (Livshits 1962: 91–104)[9] tells us about different figures dating to the first half of the 8th century CE, such as "nobles" (*āzatkār*), "merchants" (*khwākar*) and "workmen" (*kārekār*). Although for the term "merchants" the category seems to be etymologically well defined, the etymologies of the other two include several other administrative charges: *āzatkār* indicates persons with a "free condition" (Henning 1948: 606, n. 9), thus probably including several classes; *kārekār* indicates different sorts of professions, including farmers and peasants (al-Ṭabarī, 1879–1901: 2: 1444–45) (Smirnova 1970). These categories, and the management of society in general, were overseen by the community (*nāf*).[10] At the same time, in Sogdiana the *nāf* coexisted with a "lord", of whom there is clear mention since the 2nd–3rd centuries CE, as shown in the Kultobe inscriptions (Podushkin et al. 2007: 1029), at least for main cities such as Samarkand, Kesh, Nakhshab and Nok-Methan.

As far as the administrative and political apparati of oases is concerned, the relationships and boundaries between the "lord" (*khuv/ekhshedh*), who most probably resided in the main city, and the different landowners settling in or around the main city or main cities are not yet well determined. However, it is highly probable that, as

---

9 Among others, see also Grenet and de la Vaissière 2002: 171–79.

10 Regarding the *nāf*, see among others Shenkar 2020, who analysed the word and its implidcation in this ancient society.

postulated by Mukhamedjanov (1994: 280), *āzat* owned lands and villages and were the chief retainers of the local or provincial rulers.

If we accept that since the early 3rd century CE the "lord" settled in main cities of Samarkand or Kesh, as the Kultobe inscriptions show, then this could also hold true for the oasis of Bukhara, although it has not yet been proven that Bukhara was the capital city corresponding to Nok-methan, literally "Nouvelle Residence".[11] Whatever else Bukhara was or was not, since the 3rd century CE it was the main city of the oasis, or if in accordance with recent archaeological discoveries (Rante and Mirzaakhmedov 2019) Ramitan and Bukhara shared importance within the oasis since ancient times, it can be suggested that several *khuv* settled in one region, corresponding with each other as some documents post-721 CE[12] show.

Document Nov. 6 from the Mount Mugh archive shows monetary sums for an unknown authority given by someone responsible for irrigation and someone responsible for a canal (Livshits 1962: 185–88). These taxes were both for 8 *drachms*. These taxes were probably related to a small or medium-sized canal. It is possible that the sum was first delivered to the *khwēsht* or directly sent to the *khuv*.[13]

It should also be noted that in the Islamic period it is possible that the tax organisation for water management was similar. In fact, Ibn Ḥauqal (10th century) attests that the organisation of watercourses, whether natural or artificial, was in the hands of an important functionary, who charged employees with the responsibility of maintaining the watercourses and dams (Ibn Hawqal 1964: 476).

In the periods before and after the beginning of the Islamic period, the management of watercourses was one of the main tasks of the ruler, since agriculture and its management was a primary concern. The fact that districts in charge of the maintenance of watercourses and dams were exempt from taxes demonstrates the importance of water management and agriculture.

In the same Mount Mugh archive, document B-4 (Livshits 1962: 53–63), also dated before the enthronement of Dewashtich, concerns rent for three mills and canals (Livshits 1962: 57, 59) given to the same Dewashtich, *khuv* of Pindjikent, which was 460 *kafch* of flour each year (3,680 kg). In this countryside context, it is clear that this tax was given directly to the *khuv* Dewashtich. Perhaps mills were considered the realm's direct property? Since they were important, it is quite possible that mills in particular were under the direct management of the lord.

As for the oasis of Chach, coins were issued by different small local rulers who assumed the Sogdian title *xwβ* (de la Vaissière 2005: 113), "lord" according to Livshits's translation (2015: 233–34). This evidence confirms *de facto* that several lords shared land and water within a region. This is much more compelling in reference to the oasis of Bukhara, located in the delta of the Zerafshan, a territory where congenial sharing also guaranteed political stability. In fact, it is likely that in this region there were struggles between city-states over the appropriation of watercourses.

6   Social and Political Aspects within the Oasis of Bukhara

The peculiar geomorphology of the oasis of Bukhara implies strict and rigorous watercourse management, probably more than for the other oases of Sogdiana. There are two explanations for this phenomenon: the transformation of the young geological substrate, which has only permitted human occupation since around the middle of the 1st century BCE (earlier settlements are only found around the current oasis); the specific management of the numerous watercourses spreading out as a delta, and considering that they are affected by all upstream events, rigorous management is required. It is not astonishing to note that beginning in the Samanid period, all the main Bukharan "empires" the Shaybanids (Roemer 1986: 120) and the 20th-century Bukharan Emirate (Kügelgen 2009) expanded the territory to the east, to the Zerafshan's source in the Alai Mountains, in order to control the river upstream.

The territory of the oasis of Bukhara was therefore organised based on its geomorphology. And this obviously led to the oasis's rigorous administrative organisation.

During the earliest occupations of the oasis, and continuing until the 1st century BCE, settlements were distributed and organised based on specific needs, defenses and water resources, but the following centuries saw the organisation shift around the main sites, which thereby became city-states.[14] This phenomenon started sometime in the

---

11 Concerning this argument which still remain debated, see Sims-Williams 2007 and Schwarz 2022, who doesn't make the same analysis, but both are interesting. New archaeological discoveries will be needed to finally have the answer.

12 For this purpose, it is more useful to look at these documents before the enthronement of Dewashtich, the social and political setting corresponding more to our situation.

13 Silvia Pozzi proposes a further organisation, see her contribution in this volume, chapter 2.

14 Concerning the origin if the city-state, for a general background see Hansen 2006; more specifically, see also Di Cosmo 2000; Ilyasov 2006; and Shenkar 2020.

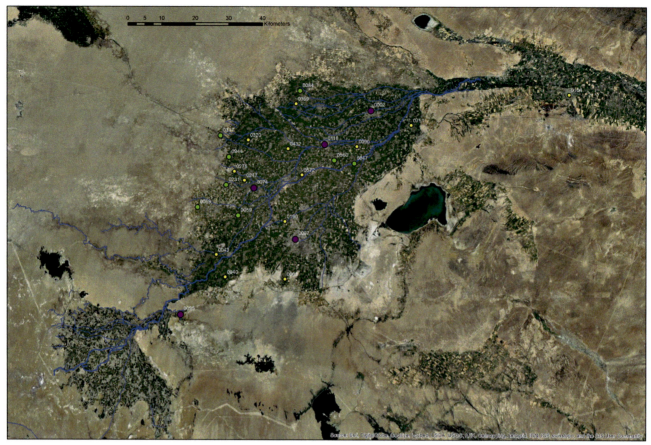

FIGURE 1.15   Distribution by size of main sites within the oasis
© RANTE 2019

tion of these main sites (26) is organised following three main landscape features: along the main watercourses; for the most part along the western and northern limits of the oasis; and along the main caravan roads. Sometimes sites share more of these characteristics, such as Varakhsha (0069) and Kakishtuvan (0317), which rose up at the starting point of the irrigated space and along the two roads leading to the oasis of Khorezm, or Bukhara (0097), which is located along the Khorasan Road and at the end of one of the most important watercourses, the Rud-i Zar.

It is difficult to precisely explain this phenomenon – single tepe→unique tepe or bipartite site→tripartite site – which looks like an evolution but is based instead on other principles. In fact, the different transformations and evolutions – single tepe→bipartite site or bipartite site→tripartite site as village→city – are not limited to the dynamic small group→big group but also correspond to the formation of groups with new relations and different *modi vivendi*. In my opinion, two macro factors have to be taken into consideration: the agrarian and the commercial. While the former continued to regulate the system, people and basic economy between the 1st and the 3rd centuries CE, after the arrival of new populations, the latter generated the formation of city-states and thus new relations between different social groups. In this context, while it is possible that the "urbanisation" of the bipartite site (thereby becoming a tripartite site) can be explained through the division of work in different groups – merchants (*khwākar*), warriors (*chakar*) and different sorts of workmen (*kārekār*), which also included farmers – it is not the same for the evolution from the single tepe to the bipartite site. Neither phenomena were linked to any agrarian decrease; on the contrary, the increase of agricultural fields and work was not an obstacle to urban development.[19]

As far as the socio-political structure is concerned, the bipartite sites were the settlements whose growth was thanks to political and economic support and activities. Considering that the village underlying the main residence

---

19   Later, in the Islamic period, the case of Bukhara is interesting to observe because its large province – but not limited to it – was marked by a depopulation of small and medium-sized sites, and these populations then settled in the capital of the oasis, and also the capital of a very large emirate, the Samanids. In this case, the phenomenon implies better work opportunities and a wide range of services provided by the new metropolis.

of a bipartite site developed quite rapidly, as shown by Rante and Mirzaakhmedov (2019), it is reasonable to think that this kind of settlement also rapidly acquired its socio-political *status* within the city-state property. It is therefore possible that the bipartite sites were ruled by figures close to the *khuv*, or to the *khuv*'s interests, who settled in the tripartite site. Given the abovementioned elements, it is reasonable to suggest that this figure was a *khwēsht*, perhaps a *framānδār*, or more generally an *āzatkār*. Their distribution within the oasis was driven by agricultural and hydrological needs and in order to manage and control these systems.

Although the origin of the unique tepe was the same as the bipartite sites, they "lost" the dynamics that led to the constitution of a bipartite structure. The reasons for this were probably due to economic factors, which generated the growth of fortified residences encircled by dwellings that functioned to control and administrate the lands all around, for their own interests as well as for those of the *khuv*. Some of them were probably directly linked to the lord settling in the tripartite site or another one settling close by in the bipartite site, himself dependent on the latter. According to their wide-ranging extension, some unique tepe were isolated buildings, caravanserais, mills or fortresses, etc. Whatever their specific function, they had active socio-economic links with the other sites.

As previously mentioned, Uch Kulakh was not only an isolated fortified residence, but it was also encircled by houses inhabited by people gravitating around the residence and the lord who settled there. In the global distribution of these unique tepe within the oasis, almost half of them (43%) covered an expanse between 3,000 and 4,000 m², mostly concentrated along the main roads and watercourses. They can be attributed to isolated residences (the palace of Ramitan covering an area of 4,500 m²) or caravanserais (the caravanserai of Paykend covering an area of 3,000 m²). Those covering an area of 5,000–7,000 ha, mostly distributed in the area of south Vardana, Sivanj/Ramitan and south Gijduvan, also belong to this category of residential rural places, with the exception that they did not have any caravanserai-related functions. Especially in areas of major settlement concentration, south of Gijduvan and Sivanj, one can observe a clear majority of unique tepe rather than bipartite sites. Unique tepe covering an area up to 1 ha, like Uch Kulakh and other similar single tepe, as previously mentioned, are mostly concentrated in the area of Varakhsha/Sivanj and Kaththa/0432/Zandana.

According to the richness and quality of the findings brought to light at Uch Kulakh (Silvi Antonini 2009), as well as at other excavated single tepe – including the strength of the fortifications, mural paintings and the quality and richness of the ceramics – one can suggest that these residential places were ruled by a figure related to the *āzatkār*, probably a subjacent administrative figure. In comparison, other tripartite and bipartite sites were primarily linked to the management of irrigation and were responsible for watercourses or a canal and the land. It is also possible that they were the secondary residences of lords or other high state figures living in the main sites or buildings corresponding to their politico-administrative functions.

Fortresses kept a specific morphology, such as Bash tepe, covering an area of 2,500 m² (Stark 2019: 222), or site 0120 near Paykend, probably dating to the Islamic period, covering circa 625 m².

7 Conclusion

Although the social and economic aspects of the oasis of Bukhara during the Islamic period are better known from written sources, those near the beginning of our era are still not very well known. This is the case not only because of the scarce written documentation from this epoch but also because of the scarce archaeological data.

The main written sources taken into consideration for these epochs are the documents of Mount Mugh, the *Ancient Letters* and the Kultobe inscriptions. Considering that Islamic written sources appear after the period we are concerned with and gloss over other issues, they have only been considered for the sake of comparison.

Written sources and modern studies, which have already commented on them and interpreted them, provide little but nevertheless useful information about social and political life during these epochs; however, they do so without any specific references to the settlement distributions within the territory or their relationships. For example, one suggested or attested that the *khuv* headed a city, but no further information is provided to help us locate it or to establish his relationship with other *khuv*(s), and thus with other settlements, in order to concretely determine the social and economic background within a territory, in this case the oasis. For this, solid archaeological data are needed, as wide as possible, in order to connect settlements, their different functions and attempt to identify their political and social structure.

MAFOUB brought to light new data regarding the settlements in the oasis, their distribution, their size and population and their relationships in order to reconstruct its social, political and economic framework.

The data acquired show that the oasis was divided into many city-states – the socio-political and economic micro-systems ruling over large territories that averaged approximate 65 ha – consisting of settlements of different morphologies and thus representing different social and economic conditions within the oasis. The genesis of these sites should have been similar, although it is difficult to obtain clear data about the earliest occupations of all settlements. The tripartite sites were at the centre of this system and were ruled by a *khuv*, belonging, like the others, to the *nāf*. The tripartite site was therefore at the head of a large territory, but it did not rule directly over this area. Bipartite sites and a small number of unique tepe insured the direct rule of fields, and especially watercourses, both natural and artificial. It is also possible that ruling over a natural watercourse guaranteed a higher status among the other sites. These rural sites with specific functions might have been ruled by a *khwēsht* or a *framānδār*, although this last figure could have also settled on a "second class" tripartite site, depending if a main one was close by. This framework is completed by the remains of unique tepe, which can be defined as residences, caravanserais, fortresses and any other building attached to fields and watercourses, such as farms, mills etc. A large portion of them most probably corresponded to residences ruled by an *āzatkār*, who was in charge of field exploitation and irrigation control, as well as being responsible for the watercourses for the *khuv*. It is also possible that some of them were assigned to secondary royal residences, which in any case always had functions linked to the lands and the water.

CHAPTER 2

Vardana and the Villages of Obavija

Territorial Definition of a High Medieval District in the Bukhara Oasis

Silvia Pozzi

1 Introduction

Starting towards the end of the 4th and the beginning of the 5th century CE, the oasis of Bukhara experienced renewed demographic growth and intense construction activity that significantly changed the landscape.[1] During this period, which lasted until the arrival of the Arabs (8th century CE), also known as the Early Middle Ages, the oasis appears to have been fragmented into many independent political entities, or districts, each one managing a portion of the territory using a network of villages under it. To date, knowledge about these early medieval districts mainly comes from written sources describing historical events (Frye 1954; Hinds 1990), while the finds within the territory are less in-depth: apart from the location of the capitals, little is known about their actual territorial extension or the internal settlement organisation.

This chapter looks at a district of Bukhara that was active in the early medieval period and known in written sources as the "villages of Obavija" (Frye 1954: 32). Vardana was this area's main city and became one of the most politically important areas in the oasis between the 7th and 8th centuries after the reigning sovereign Vardān Khudāh overtook the dynasty of the Bukhār Khudāh, becoming the staunchest opponent of the Arab enemy who was advancing in the region (see below). The goal of this study, which presents doctoral research carried out by the author,[2] is to return to the reconstruction of the territorial limits of this district and verify the influence geo-environmental characteristics had on the development of this area.

2 Methodology

This study uses an archaeological and territorial research methodology managed in a GIS environment, and it compares different types of data, such as written sources, topographic maps (historical and recent), satellite images and digital terrain models (digital elevation models, DEM), as well as archaeological data derived from past and present archaeological surveys carried out in the area of interest (AOI) of the research. After thoroughly analysing the written sources, significant elements were extrapolated and subsequently compared with archaeological and geo-environmental data from the area under investigation. Additional GIS analysis features, such as the Distribution Map and Viewshed Analysis, were used to manage the acquired data.

3 Geographic Definition

The AOI, equal to about 400 km², follows one of the northernmost edges of the Bukhara Oasis and corresponds to the agricultural area associated with the administrative district of Shafirkhan, also marginally affecting the districts of Gijduvan, Peshku and Vobkent (fig. 2.1).[3] To the north and west, this area is bordered by the Kyzyl Kum desert, while to the south it is contained by the Abdullakhon collecting channel, once a secondary branch of the Vabkendarya (ancient Au Khitfar), one of the main right-side effluents of the Zerafshan. Today, the water network of the Shāpurkām, also a right-side effluent of the Zerafshan, is the main source of irrigation in the districts of Shafirkhan and Gijduvan, as well as parts of Vobkent (Abdullaev 2004). The district is currently also irrigated by the Sultanabad and Pirmast, all right-side effluents of the

---

[1] For an updated study of the population and settlement evolution of the Bukhara Oasis, see Rante and Mirzaakhmedov 2019.

[2] The doctoral thesis (not published), entitled "Vardāna and the Obavija Feud: Dynamics of Settlement Development along the Northern Border of the Bukhāra Oasis during the Early Middle Ages", was defended at the University of Naples "l'Orientale" in the academic year 2017–18. The tutor was Prof. Bruno Genito (University of Naples "l'Orientale") and the co-tutor was Dr. Simone Mantellini (University of Bologna, alma mater Studiorum, University of Bologna), to whom my heartfelt thanks go.

[3] It was decided to include part of the districts of Gijduvan, Peshku and Vobkent in the area of interest (AOI) in order to have a large territorial margin with which to detect any areas of settlement unevenness with respect to the main core constituted by the territory of Shafirkhan.

FIGURE 2.1
Oasis of Bukhara, localisation of the area of research (area of interest, AOI). Modern cities (in black), main archaeological sites (in red). Background image: Landsat 7, 2000, EPP157R032_7F20010821
LANDSAT IMAGE COURTESY OF THE US GEOLOGICAL SURVEY

Zerafshan, which in turn branches into dozens of secondary channels.

In order to have a better hydrographic picture for comparing the distribution of the archaeological sites with the descriptions in written sources, it was decided to reconstruct the premodern water network structure of this area. This was achieved by superimposing topographic[4] maps and satellite[5] photos datable to different periods within the GIS. A Russian map dated to 1923, prior to the water interventions that started a few decades later under the Soviet government, proved particularly useful for identifying the branches of the rivers in the area under investigation. The river tracks taken from the maps were compared with data obtained from a geographic study of the Bukhara region that was carried out at the end of the 1800s by the Russian general N.F. Sitnjakovskij (1900). This work describes the major and minor canals of the area under investigation, as well as the main branches and the villages irrigated by each

canal. Both the Shāpurkām and Sultanabad split at one point into two channels: the northern branch of the Shāpurkām was called Kunya Shāpurkām and the southern one Yanghi Shāpurkām, while the northern branch of the Sultanabad was called Yanghi Sultanabad and the southern one Kunya Sultanabad. After analysing the data it would seem that in the district of Shafirkhan several minor canals of the Shāpurkām and Sultanabad connected to each other, forming a densely branching water system just south of Vardanzeh (fig. 2.2).

The 1923 map also reported the presence of some uncultivated areas inside the oasis, characterised by topographic elements referred to as clayey, very saline soils (solonchak) that were sometimes marshy – highly unsuited for agriculture – on which white saline efflorescence could form (Gintzburger 2003: 37). Two of these areas, both approximately 8 km², were located north of Gijduvan between the upper reaches of the Shāpurkām and the Sultanabad. A third area, approximately 3 km², was located further west, between the Yanghi Shāpurkām and the Sultanabad. Another area, approximately 10 km² wide, was located between the Sultanabad and the Pirmast, while the largest area corresponded with the Abdullakhon collector and extended for over 25 km² towards the desert.

Within the CORONA satellite images taken in the 1960s, white areas can be seen that precisely correspond with the solonchak areas reported in the 1923 map, suggesting the presence of saline efflorescence typical of these soils. In the northernmost solonchak areas, the satellite photos clearly showed the sinuous path of paleo canals,

---

4 Military topographic map 1960–72 (USSR ca. 1970); military topographic map 1948–72 (USSR 1977); military topographic map 1981–84 (USSR 1986); military topographic map 1983–84 (USSR 1989); agricultural topographic map (USSR, 1960–70?); agricultural topographic map 1987–89 (USSR 1990); military topographic map 1983 (USSR 1988); military topographic map 1958–59 (USSR 1964); geographic map (USSR 1923); geographic map (Russia, circa 1900).
5 Panchromatic photos CORONA 1965, 1967 (United States Geological Survey); WorldView-2 2013–15 (Digital Globe Foundation); Google Earth Pro 2016; Bing 2017; Landsat 2000–2001 (United States Geological Survey).

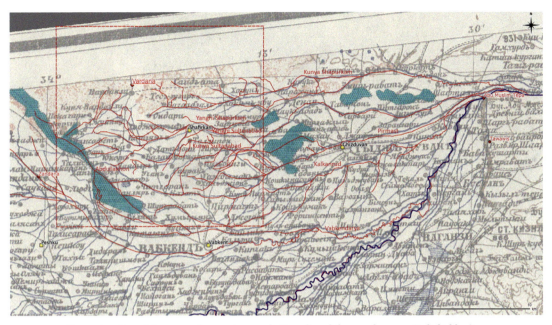

FIGURE 2.2 Reconstruction of the premodern water supply (in red) and the marshy areas (in light blue)
BACKGROUND IMAGE: SOVIET MAP DATING TO 1923, P.VII.L.3

suggesting that in ancient times, these areas were rarely cultivated. Over the years, all the solonchak areas inside the oasis have been reclaimed, and today they are cultivated, although solonchak areas still remain outside the northern limits of the oasis.

4 Historical and Archaeological Framework

The district of Obavija, a centre of activity until the Arab advance into the region, seems to have had a population surge between the 4th and 5th centuries CE.[6] According to the legend of the foundation of the capital city of Vardana mentioned by al-Narshakhī (Frye 1954: 7, 10, 16, 31–32, 45), a Sasanid prince named Shāpūr found refuge at the court of the Bukhār Khudāh after escaping from his father Kisra. One day soon after being welcomed to Bukhara, Shāpūr went to what would later become the Obavija district on a hunting trip. This uncultivated area that was used for grazing animals impressed the prince so much that he decided to ask the Bukhār Khudāh for it as a fiefdom. His request was granted and a large canal was dug, which was named Shāpurkām. The prince built the castle and the village of Vardana, as well as many other villages, and the district adopted the name "Obavija villages" and remained in the hands of the descendants of Shāpūr until the conquest of Qutayba b. Muslim (ibid.: 31–32). When describing Vardana, al-Narshakhī makes it clear that this village was among the most important ones in Bukhara, even older than the capital itself, and for a long time it was the seat of a royal dynasty.

The excavations currently underway in Vardana, carried out as part of the Swiss-Uzbek West Sogdian Archaeological Expedition (WSAE) project,[7] are helping to clarify the oldest phases of its occupation. The site (40° 9′50.97″ N, 64° 26′16.80″ E) is located 7 km north-west of today's Shafirkhan within a vast preserved archaeological area, which extends across an area of approximately 140 ha (fig. 2.3). The actual site extends for about 8 ha and is dominated by a citadel (108 × 66 m at the base, 0.85 ha), which stands out since it is 16 m[8] above the surrounding countryside, and several sections of the ancient walls are

---

6 The chronological data derive from the study of the ceramic material collected during the archaeological reconnaissance carried out by the author as part of the doctoral research as well as from previous reconnaissance carried out in the area, both published (Genito et al. 2003) and unpublished (reconnaissance carried out in 1980 by the Institute of Archaeology of the Samarkand Academy of Sciences; survey carried out in 2014 by Mirzaakhmedov).

7 The project, which began in 2009 and is still ongoing, arose from a collaboration between the Swiss The Society for the Exploration of EurAsia and the Institute of Archaeology of Samarkand. On the excavations of Vardana, see Mirzaakhmedov et al. 2013, 2016a, 2016b, 2016c, 2019; Wells 2014a, 2014b, 2016; Pozzi et al. 2019.

8 The topographic maps indicate a height of 22 m, which may have been calculated taking the height of the moat into consideration.

FIGURE 2.3 Archaeological site of Vardana. Background image: WV-2, 2013–15
SATELLITE IMAGE COURTESY OF THE DIGITAL GLOBE FOUNDATION

FIGURE 2.4 Citadel of Vardana: main entrance to the site, located on the southern side (upper image); second entrance on the eastern side (below)
© SOCIETY FOR THE EXPLORATION OF EURASIA

FIGURE 2.5 Topographical plan of the site. S. Mirzaakhmedov on O. Cerasuolo topography
© SOCIETY FOR THE EXPLORATION OF EURASIA

still visible today (figs. 2.4 and 2.5). An irregularly shaped forepart that has deep traces of erosion is located on the south side of the citadel and protrudes about 15 m from the outer profile of the southern walls, while the remains of an entrance to the citadel are located on the east side. The ruins of the lower city extend 50 m south of the citadel and are separated from it by two deep depressions. The first part of the lower city (shahrestan), immediately south of the citadel, is rectangular in shape (122 × 150 m, 2 ha), while the second more irregularly shaped populated area (370 × 236 m, 4.8 ha) extends south of the former and forms a continuum with it.

In recent years, excavations have focused mainly on the citadel, while a stratigraphic survey is currently underway in only the lower part of the site. Recent C^{14} analyses, carried out on a sample from this test,[9] date the first phase of this area's occupation from the 2nd century BCE to the

---

9 The stratigraphic test carried out in 2017 reached virgin soil. This and the other C^{14} analyses performed on materials from the

FIGURE 2.6 Citadel of Vardana, late antique structures buried under the infilling of pebbles and sand
© SOCIETY FOR THE EXPLORATION OF EURASIA

1st century CE. In the citadel, the oldest phase that has been analysed and dated using C^{14} analysis dates back to the 1st–4th century CE (late antique phase), but we have good reason to believe that this phase is placed on top of previous structures that have not been excavated yet, perhaps contemporary with the documented occupation outside the citadel. The structures identified to the late antique period consist of some rooms and a system of tunnels still under study (figs. 2.6 and 2.7).

Between the end of the 4th and the beginning of the 5th century CE the citadel began to undergo important renovations and was equipped with a thicker external curtain wall and a palatial structure built above the late antique structures and was sealed by a filling of pebbles and sand that is about 3 m high. The new building

---

Vardana excavation were performed at the University of Salento's CEDAD laboratory.

has a well-defined rectangular plan (internal measures 70 × 34 m) and is organised into three sectors, conventionally defined as the west sector, central sector and east sector (figs. 2.8 and 2.9).

The characteristic element is a corridor about 4 m wide, which encloses these three sectors running along the entire perimeter of the building. The west sector was a residential area encircled on all four sides by a corridor that gave access to some rooms. The central sector, separated from the west sector by a wall, was probably connected with a large external empty courtyard onto which three rooms opened on the north side. The southern area of the central sector has not been excavated, but it is likely that it provided access to the palace. An imposing wall divided the central sector from the eastern one, which initially housed the audience rooms. The most important room found at the time had an elongated shape and was oriented north-south, while another elongated room was located west of the first (fig. 2.10).

The general function attributed to this area of the building is based on the presence of mural paintings, found both *in situ* and in the filling of these rooms (fig. 2.11).

All the walls in the main hall, as well as the north side of the contiguous room, had to be painted. The base of the walls (preserved to a height of 30 cm) was decorated with alternating bands of white, red and traces of geometric patterns in black, subsequently covered by a *sufa* built along the room's walls (fig. 2.12).

The upper part of the walls was decorated in a different way, as suggested by traces of white and blue paint and fragments depicting stylised vegetable volutes on a red or ochre background.

At some point between the 7th and 8th centuries CE this sector changes function, shifting from a reception hall to a food storage area: The walls were stripped of paint and the paintings. Baked brick platforms, oriented east-west and separated from each other, raised the walking surface and made it level (fig. 2.13).

Small storage rooms, separated by thin partition walls, were built above the platforms (fig. 2.14). Inside the rooms, large quantities of storage pottery were found intact: jars, pitchers, kitchen and tableware and iron utensils (fig. 2.15).

Other areas of the building also underwent significant changes from the original layout, resulting in a division of spaces. The floor of the western, northern and eastern segments of the corridor surrounding the building

FIGURE 2.7 Citadel of Vardana, late antique gallery buried under the infilling of pebbles and sand
© SOCIETY FOR THE EXPLORATION OF EURASIA

was raised, and the space was divided into several rooms, some of which have *sufa*.

This spatial reorganisation occurred during the period of the Arab advance into the region, which began in 674 CE. Written sources focus on a ruler of Turkish origin, Vardān Khudāh, who is placed in Vardana during this period. Al-Narshakhī says that towards the end of the 7th century CE, Bukhara's political situation had become unstable and that at some point Vardān Khudāh usurped the throne of the Bukhār Khudāh and took control of the region (Frye 1954: 10). Obavija's political leadership is also indirectly confirmed by al-Ṭabarī (d. 923), who speaks of the clashes between Vardān Khudāh and Qutayba b. Muslim between 708 and 709 and on two occasions refers to Vardān Khudāh as the "king of Bukhāra" (Hinds 1990: 147, 150). In fact, Vardān Khudāh represented the last major obstacle to the conquest of the region, and al-Narshakhī reports that "Qutayba had to fight many battles against him" (Frye 1954: 10, 45). In this unstable historical context, the reorganisation of the building, which even led to the elimination of the reception rooms located in the eastern sector, may have been due to war preparations or preparing for a siege, for which it was necessary to utilise the space to store food reserves and perhaps also soldiers, especially in the rooms created in the external corridor. The occupation of the eastern sector ended after a vast fire, perhaps attributable to the Arab conquest of Vardana, the traces of which are evident in the charred wood in the storage rooms, blackened pottery and numerous burnt organic finds (see fig. 2.15).

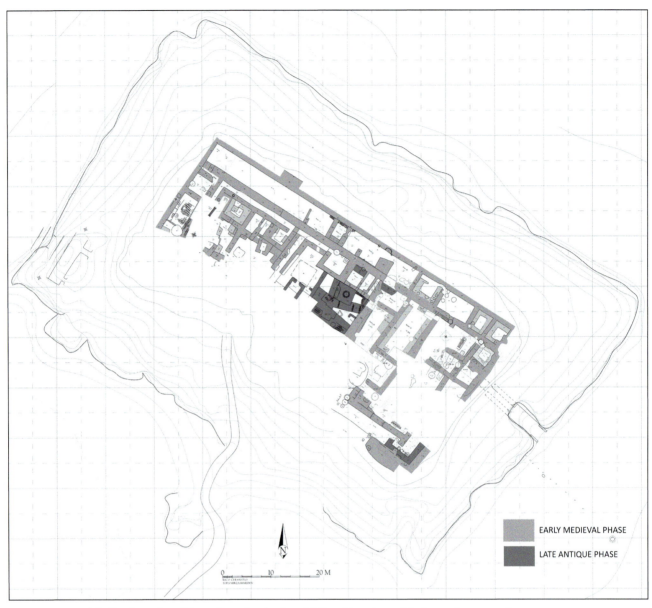

FIGURE 2.8 Citadel of Vardana, plan of the early medieval palace. S. Mirzaakhmedov and O. Cerasuolo topography
© SOCIETY FOR THE EXPLORATION OF EURASIA

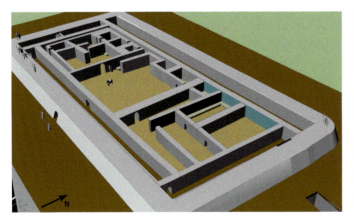

FIGURE 2.9 Citadel of Vardana, hypothetical reconstruction of the early medieval palace. S. Pozzi
© SOCIETY FOR THE EXPLORATION OF EURASIA

FIGURE 2.10 Citadel of Vardana, early medieval structures, east sector (on right side)
© SOCIETY FOR THE EXPLORATION OF EURASIA

FIGURE 2.11 Citadel of Vardana, mural paintings discovered in the eastern sector
© SOCIETY FOR THE EXPLORATION OF EURASIA

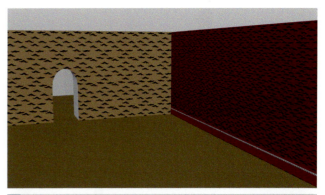

FIGURE 2.12 Citadel of Vardana, reconstruction of the hall decorated with mural paintings. First phase (on top): hall without *sufa*; second phase (below): hall with *sufa*. S. Pozzi
© SOCIETY FOR THE EXPLORATION OF EURASIA

FIGURE 2.13 Citadel of Vardana, early medieval palace, eastern sector, mud brick platforms
© SOCIETY FOR THE EXPLORATION OF EURASIA

FIGURE 2.14 Citadel of Vardana, early medieval palace (eastern sector), storage area
© SOCIETY FOR THE EXPLORATION OF EURASIA

FIGURE 2.15 Findings from the storage area: 1. ovoid jar decorated with fingermark impressions and stripes of coloured paint; 2. jug with spout, decorated with stripes of coloured paint; 3. globular pot decorated with red paint and an incised symbol (tamgha); 4. shears used for sheep shearing; 5. globular jar decorated with incisions; 6. dish with base decorated with knife cuts; 7. lentils seeds; 8. millstone

5 Written Sources and Geo-environmental Data

The analysis of a selection of Sogdian, Islamic and Chinese written sources connected with the geo-environmental data of the territory under investigation allowed us to make some general observations about the extension and territorial organisation of the Sogdian districts in the early medieval period, as well as the location of Obavija in particular.

The main Sogdian reference is legal documents and letters found in the well-known archive of Dewashtich in Mount Mugh, located in the Upper Zerafshan Valley.[10] The archive was useful for framing the management of water resources and defining some figures within the Sogdian ruling class in the years preceding the Arab conquest. Among the Arabic and Persian Islamic sources that talk about the Maverannahr and the oasis of Bukhara, we focused on the works of two of the greatest Arab geographers and travellers, al-Iṣṭakhrī (d. 957) and Ibn Ḥauqal (d. 988). Both visited the region in the second half of the 10th century CE, and to them we owe the *Kitāb al-Masālik al-mamālik*[11] (Book of Lands and Realms) and the *Kitāb Surat al-Arḍ*[12] (The Configuration of the Earth) respectively. We also analysed the *Aḥsan al-taqāsīm fī maʿrifat al-aqālīm* (The Best Division for the Knowledge of the Regions, Collins 1994: 240, 249–51), written by al-Muqaddasī (*c.*985) at the end of the 10th century CE.

Other elements related to the territorial definition of Obavija were obtained from the historical descriptions of the clashes that took place between locals and the Arabs in the first century of the conquest of the region, when the still unstable Arab power allowed the previous political and social organisations to remain. The chronicles analysed here are the *Tarīkh al-rusul wa-l-mulūk* (The Story of the Prophets and Kings, Morony 1987: 178–79; Hinds 1990: 146–52) by al-Ṭabarī and the *Tarīkh-i Bukhārā* (The Story of Bukhara) by al-Narshakhī (d. 959), the historian born in Narshak, a village not far from Vardana. This latter historical chronicle is dedicated entirely to Bukhara and its hinterland, was presented to the Samanid sovereign Ibn Nasr in 943 CE, and has come down to us in a Persian version from the 12th century CE, in the process of which the original text has been summarised and reworked several times (Frye 1954).[13]

Finally, among the Chinese sources that deal with the Sogdiana, some passages relating to Bukhara were selected from the *Si-Yu-Ki* (Buddhist Record of the Western World, Beal 1884: 34–35), written by the Chinese pilgrim and traveller Xuanzang (d. 664), and the biography *The Life of Hiuen-Tsiang* by Shaman Hwui Li (Beal 1914: 46). These texts provided some information useful for defining the possible territorial extension of early medieval districts in the oasis of Bukhara.

5.1 General Characteristics of the Early Medieval Districts

By reading the descriptions written by medieval travellers in the Maverannahr we can get an idea of what the landscape must have looked like in the Early Middle Ages. In fact, we know that medieval Sogdiana was divided into administrative districts, called rustaq, many of which had incorporated the ancient early medieval districts within them (Barthold 2007: 92–93). Water networks are one element that in some cases can indicate the area associated with each rustaq. From the descriptions of Ibn Ḥauqal we learn that several districts in the Samarkand region were associated with an effluent (arik) of the Zerafshan, from which secondary channels branched off and irrigated the individual villages within the territory (Ibn Hawqal 1964: 476). When speaking about the size of a district, the author always provides the length but does not always provide the width, suggesting that the extension of a district was probably calculated using the length of the canal along which it developed. A single village or hamlet could also be irrigated by more than one canal (ibid.: 476), a circumstance also confirmed by al-Narshakhī, who recalls that Varakhsha was the largest village in Bukhara and was irrigated by 12 canals. (Frye 1954: 17). On the other hand, some districts were irrigated solely by means of seasonal streams and rainwater, as in the case of Yarkath (in the region of Samarkand), which despite this enjoyed large pastures (Ibn Hawqal 1964: 478; Collins 1994: 249).

The fact that in the medieval period, water management was an important activity for the "state" is confirmed by a passage where Ibn Ḥauqal recalls that the person responsible for the distribution of water in the Samarkand region was a prominent official and head of employees who maintained the individual channels and made sure they were functioning properly (Ibn Hawqal 1964: 476). Another passage (ibidem) supporting this theory states

---

10 The archive, found in 1932, contains documents in Sogdian, Arabic, Turkish and Chinese, which were published for the first time in 1934 in *Sogdijskij sbornik*. They have recently been revised by Livshits 2015. See also Grenet and de la Vaissière 2002.

11 Consulted in Ritter's German translation 1845: 129–30. Thanks to Dr. Ashraf Hassan and Dr. Francesco Grosso for having respectively identified and translated from Arabic some passages relating to Vardana from the edition of de Goeje 1927: 310.

12 Consulted in the French translation by Kramers and Wiet, Ibn Hawqal 1964: 444–45, 463–71. There is also an English translation of Ouseley 1800, which however may not refer to Ibn Ḥauqal but rather to al-Iṣṭakhrī.

13 There is also a more recent critical edition in Russian, Kamoliddin 2011.

that near Waraghsar[14] (in the region of Samarkand), a well-known place whose name means "the head of the dam" (Mantellini 2015: 3), there was a district that was exempt from paying land taxes because much of the population was in charge of dam maintenance.[15]

We can hypothesize that a similar water management structure was also in place in the early medieval Sogdiana. Both the early medieval *dihqān*s (lords) and the new class of *dihqān*s formed during the Abbasid period were interested in sustaining agricultural production, which was entirely dependent upon efficient water management. Some passages found in the archives of Mount Mugh confirm this theory, thereby also confirming the connection between the length of the main canals and the extension of the districts. In document Nov. 6 (*Sogdijskij sbornik* 1934: 167–70), a type of account book that recorded the monetary transactions carried out when Dewashtich still ruled Penjikent, the sums listed as paid were probably written down by an irrigation worker, as well as the manager of the irrigation canal. Although the beneficiary of these payments is not specified, it is clear that the water network was well organised and managed by a "superior" authority, which ruled over an area as long as the length of a canal. Since the taxes paid by the canal manager (8 drachmas) in the Nov. 6 document were the same amounts as the taxes paid by those who irrigated the fields, we can hypothesize that the social standing of these two figures was similar and that it was a modest-sized canal, perhaps serving a single village.

Another example is the legal contract B-4 from Mount Mugh (*Sogdijskij sbornik* 1934: 44–52), which establishes the terms for renting three water mills belonging to the royal court that were all located along the same canal. This document presents further evidence that the channels and structures connected to them were all managed by a single authority. In the case of the mills, considering the production of assets through their use, the rent was paid in kind, while the irrigation operator and the canal manager received monetary compensation.

5.2 Vardana and the District of Obavija

Due to the Sughd (Zerafshan) River running through it, the Bukhara region is described by medieval authors as a populous and lush land, praised for the presence of numerous rivers and for its important agricultural production (Ibn Hawqal 1964: 466), corn and fruit trees in particular (Ouseley 1800: 249). A raw earth wall known as Kampirak, the "old lady" (Frye 1954: 33), enclosed most of the region. According to Ibn Ḥauqal (Ouseley 1800: 245, 249; Ibn Hawqal 1964: 467) and al-Muqaddasī (Collins 1994: 240), the territory within the wall was densely occupied and contained villages and districts; there were no vacant lands, hills or desert areas. Ibn Ḥauqal relates that every fortified city in the Bukhara region, with the exception of Paykend, had a rustaq (with or without fortifications) made up of a number of villages (Ouseley 1800: 250). Most of the sites had an economy based on agriculture and owned a certain amount of land (Ibn Hawqal 1964: 469), which was both cultivated and left to pasture. On the other hand, some villages specialised in handicrafts, such as the production of fabrics, while others owed their fortune to their location on the Shah Rah (Frye 1954: 13), the royal road that connected Bukhara and Samarkand.

The names of several rustaqs from the Bukhara region are given by both al-Iṣṭakhrī and Ibn Ḥauqal, and thanks to them we also know that some rustaqs were found outside the walls.[16] In some cases, the names of the rustaqs coincided with those of the main canals that crossed them, while in others there were no districts bearing that name, as was the case with the Shāpurkām canal. Strangely, al-Narshakhī, who devotes an entire chapter to the description of the canals of Bukhara, does not refer to the location of the canals in relation to the Kampirak (Frye 1954: 31–32), and he also rarely speaks about districts,[17] mentioning rather the villages and cities, and even in this case without making any distinction between the villages located inside or outside the walls.

The position of Vardana in relation to the Kampirak is still debated today, since only a few sections of the wall have been preserved. Several scholars have examined written sources and the preserved sections of the wall, putting forward proposals for the reconstruction of the northern portion of the ancient route. According to Adylov and Babaev (2011: 38, figs. 1–2), the Kampirak passed north of the upper and middle course of the Shāpurkām but avoided the terminal part of the river, which is where Vardana was located. Adylov and Mirzaakhmedov (2001: 157) also believe that the Obavija district is identical to the medieval rustaq of Shabakhash, which according to al-Iṣṭakhrī was located outside the walls. Archaeological research carried out by S. Stark (Stark and Mirzaakhmedov 2015) highlighted the presence of some preserved segments of the Kampirak in different parts of

---

14 On the topic, see also Mantellini 2015a and related bibliography.
15 Also, according to al-Narshakhī, in Bukhara there must have been some dams whose construction was attributed to one of the judges of Bukhara, Saʿīd ibn Khalaf al-Balkhī, elected in 828 CE (Frye 1954: 5).
16 For the list of districts enunciated by Iṣṭakhrī, see Barthold 2007: 116; for those enunciated by Ibn Ḥauqal, see Ibn Hawqal 1964: 466.
17 Al-Narshakhī speaks of districts on two occasions: in the first case he refers to Vardana (Frye 1954: 10), in the second he speaks of districts in general, without specifying which ones (ibid: 10 and 15).

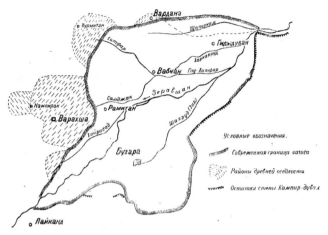

FIGURE 2.16 Schematic map of the Bukhara Oasis according to Shishkin (1940: fig. 11)

the oasis, but none have been identified south of Vardana, where numerous tepas still stand today. In reality, even north of Vardana there is no trace of the Kampirak, except for a short stretch north-west of the site and an elongated embankment identified north-east of Gijduvan, a location about 20 km south-east of Vardana. The real archaeological nature of this unexcavated embankment is, however, called into question by the same scholar, according to whom this evidence could also have originated during the excavation and cleaning of the Dzhalvan canal, which is located a little further south (ibid: 87).

The schematic map of the Bukhara Oasis attached to the report of the archaeological activities conducted by V.A. Shishkin in 1937 (Shishkin 1940: 4, fig. 1) suggests another possibility, one that in our opinion is the most credible (fig. 2.16). This map indicates that some segments of the Kampirak, as well as the ancient and "modern" limits of the oasis, have been reconstructed. According to this scholar, the northern limit of the ancient oasis was located north of Vardana and then turned east, passing north of Gijduvan, into the area currently under cultivation. More specifically, this border was located south of the upper and middle course of the Shāpurkām, which flowed just north of Gijduvan. The northern border of the ancient oasis can therefore be traced to the lands south of the modern limit and not to the north, where it has currently been looked for.

The hypothesis that the area north of Gijduvan could have been outside the ancient oasis in the past is supported by the 1923 Soviet topographic map, in which vast marshy areas are reported in the area to the north and west of Gijduvan. If we consider that according to Islamic sources, there were no uncultivated lands inside the walls, the ancient wall layout could in fact correspond to the limits of the ancient oasis traced by Shishkin. It seems reasonable to think that not only did the wall contain cultivated lands, leaving desert and uncultivated lands outside, but that it also included areas where there were other forms of occupation, given the presence of rustaq inside and outside the walls. We can hypothesize that the rustaqs outside the walls coincided with uncultivated areas, which were used for grazing livestock or for hunting. The fact that no traces of the wall remain inside the modern oasis can possibly be attributed to the fertilisation techniques practiced in the 1800s, which included, among other things, the use of earth dug from hills to improve the productivity of the fields (Sitnjakovskij 1900: 152). If it is true that the Kampirak passed within the current oasis, the building material may have been continuously reused since the 1800s, when these lands were already partially cultivated.

The presence of marshy areas close to the middle and upper reaches of the Shāpurkām brings to mind the uncultivated area where, according to al-Narshakhī, Obavija would have been built. It is possible that originally, similar environmental conditions also characterised the terminal part of the river and that the "reclamation of Shapur" only affected this area, since the presence of two rivers connected to each other, the Shāpurkām and the Sultanabad, guaranteed a greater and more stable water supply. Agricultural development along the upper reaches of these rivers would certainly require a greater effort to reclaim water and conduct ordinary maintenance. The seasonal floods made the settlement of the upper reaches of the rivers dangerous and directed the occupation towards the terminal portions, which were stabler and safer. An example of this is the Ishtikhan canal, located in the region of Samarkand: Ibn Ḥauqal says that the river was unusable for 4 farsakhs (26–30 km) from its origin, that is to say, in its initial stretch (Ibn Hawqal 1964: 475–76).

Carefully rereading the passage where Ibn Ḥauqal describes the rivers that supplied the localities and districts of Bukhara, there are details that support the inclusion of Vardana and the lower reaches of the Shāpurkām within the Kampirak. Speaking of the Sughd (Zerafshan) River, Ibn Ḥauqal tells us that "[…] divisé en plusieurs branches dans le territorie de Bukhara, hors de la cité, avant la muraille extérieure, vers la région de Tawawis et jusqu'à l'entrée de la villas. Ces cours d'eau se répandent dans les villages et les terrains cultivés compris a l'intérieur de la muraille, et de ces irrigations dépend la fertié des villages de la banlieue de Bukhara. Le canal appelé Shafari-Kam, issue du fleuve, arrose les villages jusqu'à Wardana et procure aux habitants l'eau potable" (Ibn Hawqal 1964: 466–67). Al-Iṣṭakhrī also begins the channel list with the Shāpurkām and confirms that the Sughd River branched into several channels outside the outer walls (De Goeje 1927: 310). Until now it has always been assumed that the Zerafshan branched into multiple effluents inside the walls, but this passage suggests that the Zerafshan was divided into several channels outside the wall. However, Ibn Ḥauqal tells us that the canals he mentioned irrigated the villages located within the walls, and Shāpurkām is the first one he mentions. A plausible explanation for reconciling these two seemingly conflicting descriptions is to consider the possibility that the initial stretch of the effluents of the Zerafshan flowed outside the walls and that only at a certain point did they enter the walls.

Trying to further circumscribe the district of Obavija, the passage where al-Ṭabarī describes the battle of the lower Kharqāna, fought between Qutayba b. Muslim and Vardān Khudāh in 709 CE, is significant. The district of the lower Kharqāna was located within the Kampirak and to the right (and therefore to the east) of Vardana (Hinds 1990: 147). This place has been identified as Gijduvan (Barthold 2007: 120; Adylov and Babaev 2011: 46) and was therefore the district closest to the eastern border of Obavija.

The southern border of Obavija is also easy to locate and is found in the area north of Vobkent and north-east of ancient Zandāna, a town located about 13 km south-west of Vardana. Zandāna is always described in the sources as a village and is never associated with any of the rustaqs; however, numerous mentions in written sources suggest it was important, probably linked to the still disputed local production of zandaniji fabric. Therefore, it is probable that in the early medieval period Zandāna was the centre of a district, which perhaps in the Middle Ages was incorporated into the Nadjdjar-Khitfar rustaq (Ibn Hawqal 1964: 466). From the analysis of the right effluents of the Zerafshan flowing south of Vardāna, it appears that Zandāna and nearby Vobkent were served by the canal al-Narshakhī called Au Khitfar and Ibn Ḥauqal and al-Iṣṭakhrī called Nadjar Khitfar, today's Vabkendarya (Mukhamedjanov 1978: 30; Adylov and Babaev 2011: 45). As we have seen from the analysis of the Mount Mugh documents, the fact that some villages shared the same water network probably implied a common political organisation that regulated the maintenance and cleaning of the canals. Given these premises, it is possible to exclude the lands irrigated by the Vabkendarya from the settlement sphere of Obavija, which, as already pointed out, was instead irrigated by the Shāpurkām.

5.3 Vardana in Chinese Sources?

While the Arab sources clearly describe the village of Vardana and its historical events, its identification in Chinese sources is more controversial. Xuanzang, describing Bukhara, lists the kingdoms that were part of it, and according to some scholars, one of them can be identified as Vardana. Entering the territory of Bukhara from Samarkand, Xuanzang recounts that the westernmost kingdom was Ho-Han, identifiable with Kharghana, an ancient town north of Karmina (today's Navoi) (Beal 1884: 34–35). Proceeding 400 li[18] to the west of Ho-han one arrived at Pu-ho, identifiable with Bukhara (ibid) and then, advancing further west for another 400 li one would arrive at the kingdom of Fa-ti. Hwui-li's biography reports the same realms but assigns a different distance between Pu-ho and Fa-ti, one equal to 100 li (Beal 1914: 46).

The first scholar to propose identifying Fa-ti with Vardana was J. Marquart (1898: 62). By verifying the linear distance between Pu-ho and Fa-ti on the basis of Hwui-li's biography, he demonstrates how this coincides with the real distance between Bukhara and Vardana, which is about 50 km. E. Chavannes (1903: 134) and P. Pelliot (1905: 449) also accept the association, and more recently, this hypothesis has also been taken up by A. Naymark (2001: 209–10), M. Compareti (2003) and R. Xinjiang and L. Feng (2016: 298). However, it should be emphasised that the identification of Fa-ti with Vardana has found the strongest support by looking at the political role Vardana held rather than linguistic reasons. W. Tomaschek (1877: 109) and S. Beal (1884: 35) had a different hypothesis and identified Fa-ti with Betik, a locality not far from today's Farabr (Turkmenistan).

Fat-ti cannot be conclusively identified with Vardana: in fact, Xuanzang says that Fa-ti was west of Bukhara and that proceeding 500 li south-west of Fa-ti you reach Chorasmia (Beal 1884: 34; 1914: 46). Although A. Naymark insists that "Vardāna is situated to the north of Bukhara, but in the western part of the Bukharan oasis, i.e. to the west of the 'realm of Buhe'" (Naymark 2001: 209), geographically speaking this location is located north of Bukhara, and in my opinion, it cannot be related to the western part of the oasis in any way.

Fa-ti was nevertheless one of the kingdoms that made up the territory of Bukhara in the Early Middle Ages. It is therefore interesting to expand on the information provided by Xuanzang for a general understanding of the early medieval districts. When describing Fa-ti, the Chinese pilgrim limits himself to saying that this kingdom had a "circumference" (circuit in Beal 1884: 35) of 400 li. In ancient times the Chinese li was used as a unit of both linear and surface measurement, so Fa-ti could have had

---

18 The size of the Chinese *li* varied according to the dynasties and was quantified between 300 and 500 metres (Borovkova 1989: 5, n. 1; Beleniskij et al. 1973: 6). In the pre-Qin period, 1 li was equivalent to 300 bu = 0.54 km (1 bu = 2 yards = 0.0018 km) (Calculations based on tables 16–17 in Wilkinson 2000: 234–46).

a perimeter of about 216 km or an area of 216 km². Based on research carried out within the territory of Bukhara, a district with a perimeter of 216 km would cover a very large area, almost as large as the entire oasis, while an area of 216 km² covers a more modest area, for example, equal to the southern part of the current Shafirkhan district. Reading "circuit" as an area and not a perimeter is therefore, at least in this context, the most appropriate description for a district located in the territory of Bukhara.

6 Data Analysis

In order to identify the archaeological sites of the Early Middle Ages that belonged to the Obavija district and verify the hypothesis of its location obtained from the analysis of the written sources, the archaeological sites that had already been surveyed were first identified and georeferenced within the GIS. All the potential archaeological sites reported in the cartography were then mapped, including not only those that fell within the AOI but also those that were located along some effluents on the right side of the Zerafshan, since they were taken into consideration during the analysis of written sources. The potential archaeological evidence (both preserved and destroyed) located within the AOI that has not yet been surveyed was finally subjected to survey,[19] thus integrating the preliminary data that was extracted remotely (fig. 2.17).

The distribution of georeferenced archaeological sites was evaluated using the Concentration Map, a GIS tool, through which it was possible to obtain an immediate display of any concentrations (clusters) of points, constituted in this case by our sites, and of areas with a low concentration of sites or no sites (siteless areas). The analysis, applied to all sites in the northern area of the oasis, highlighted a cluster in the southern area of the district of Shafirkhan, which also bordered on the districts of Peshku and Vobkent (fig. 2.18). The cluster appeared bordered, to the north-east, east and south by some siteless areas of different sizes, while on the western and northern fronts it was demarcated by the ecological-environmental boundary of the steppes. The largest siteless area, located to the north and east of the cluster, extended as far as Gijduvan and intercepted a large area of solonchaks west of this centre. To the north of this siteless area very few sites were reported, and as mentioned above, those that were reported were mainly located in areas that corresponded with the middle course of the Shāpurkām and Sultanabad.[20] The siteless areas to the south and south-west of the cluster, smaller in size than those to the north-east, separated the cluster from a more densely occupied southern area marked by the Abdullakhon canal.

It is clear that the district of Obavija should be looked for in the cluster of sites south of Vardana. By applying a chronological filter relating to data from the Early Medieval Period,[21] some unique distribution characteristics emerge regarding the sites and the route of the ancient water network. Most of the cluster sites were located in areas that correspond with the lower course of the Sultanabad and the Yanghi Shāpurkām, while only a few were located along the Kunya Shāpurkām. There were also only a few sites identified along the upper course of the Pirmast, while there was a greater number along its terminal portion. If we consider that according to al-Narshakhī the Shāpurkām canal that Shapur wanted built irrigated a "vast domain" (Frye 1954: 32), it is difficult to locate it in the lands lapped by the Kunya Shāpurkām, along which there are very few archaeological sites, or in the lands served only by the Yanghi Shāpurkām, along which the archaeological sites are slightly more numerous but not a number that could be considered a "vast domain".

Finally, I verified whether the extension of the territory of Obavija I reconstructed was compatible with the inter-visibility relations between the various early medieval sites in the district. On a theoretical level, a given centre's zone of political influence is considered more effective if it has visual control of the territory (Dytchkovwskyj, Aagesen, and Costopoulos 2005: 2). This verification was carried out by applying Viewshed Analysis, another GIS tool, which allows you to calculate the field of observation

---

19 The field verification of potential archaeological sites, carried out by the author as part of the doctoral research, involved 94 locations, previously identified remotely through the cross-analysis of topographic maps and satellite photos. As is known, the reference cartography, made mainly during the Soviet period, reports the presence of archaeological sites through the specific topographical symbology of tepa or the trigonometric point on tepa (see US Department of the Army: 1958). In addition to this symbolism, the survey also evaluated the symbols of modern and low-relief cemeteries. We thus detected the presence of archaeological sites characterised by a relief (tepe) and areas characterised by off-site activities, identified in correspondence with some modern flat cemeteries.

20 It is interesting to note that the low density of sites in the area north of Gijduvan was also noticed by Shishkin during his 1937 reconnaissance (Shishkin 1940: 40).

21 Although aware of the limitations from dating a site using only the outcropping pottery, the sites subject to reconnaissance have been dated according to this criterion. In the case of sites now destroyed or in which no outcropping pottery or datable fragments had been found, the criterion of the bipartite plan was relied upon, which would constitute, according to some scholars (Mukhamedjanov et al. 1990: 162), a typical settlement typology of the Early Medieval Period.

FIGURE 2.17 Sites registered after the cartographic analysis (in white) and sites analysed thanks to the data of previous surveys and of the new surveys realised during the PhD research of the author. Background image: Landsat 7 del 2000, EPP157R032_7F20010821
LANDSAT IMAGE COURTESY OF THE US GEOLOGICAL SURVEY

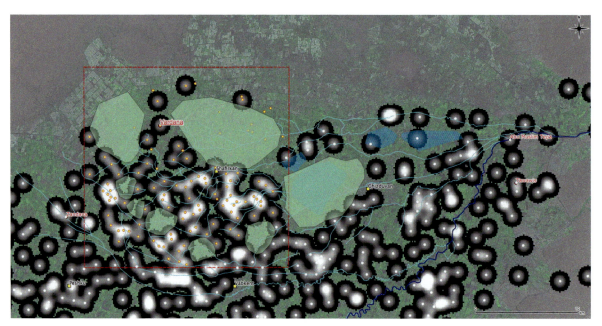

FIGURE 2.18 Heatmap and siteless areas (in green). Background image: Landsat 7 del 2000, EPP157R032_7F20010821
LANDSAT IMAGE COURTESY OF THE US GEOLOGICAL SURVEY

according to the position and horizon of a site, as well as taking the morphological characteristics of the environment into consideration (Forte 2002: 96). Using a digital model of the terrain at 30 m,[22] it was verified that from

---

22 For this analysis, Globalmapper software and a DEM of the type STRM1N40E064V3 (2000) were used. The radius was set as 20 km and the height of the observer and receiver as 1.60 m.

Vardana there was a good visual control of the surrounding territory up to 6 km. Beyond this limit, visibility was less effective but could reach 15 km, thus also including part of the siteless areas south of the cluster. On the other hand, there was no optimal control of the eastern and south-eastern sites in the cluster. Having identified the presence of a site that could constitute a focal point within the territory (Khadicha Bibi tepa) through the typological and hierarchical[23] study of the Obavija settlements, I also applied Viewshed Analysis to this site. The results showed that from Khadicha Bibi tepa it was possible to control the eastern and south-eastern part of the cluster. Total visual control of the territory was therefore guaranteed by the localities of Vardana and Khadicha Bibi tepa, which was clearly visible between them.

7 Results

The distribution of the sites within the territory confirms what was hypothesized based on an analysis of the written sources, namely that the heart of the district of Obavija was located south of Vardana, in the area irrigated by the Shāpurkām-Sultanabad system. Some peripheral sites located along the Kunya Sultanabad and the Pirmast were also part of Obavija. In light of the data collected, it is possible to argue that the strategy that dictated the settlement of the population, and therefore the extension of the lands ruled by Obavija, was to settle down where land could be irrigated using water from several rivers. This was necessary in an area bordering the steppes, which means it was exposed to desertification and a greater effort was required to wrest the arable land from the desert. Instead, the upper and middle course area of these rivers was avoided, as they required more effort to reclaim and maintain. The data related to the foundation of Vardana that was reported by al-Narshakhī, according to whom Obavija would have developed following the excavation of the Shāpurkām canal by the Sasanid prince Shapur, should therefore be framed not so much as the excavation of a new canal but rather as arranging the terminal portion of the Shāpurkām and implementing a water network formed by this river and the Sultanabad.

As for the possible boundaries, it is believed that the district was bordered on the western, northern and eastern fronts by the Kampirak, leaving the marshes located west of Gijduvan and the area relating to the upper and middle courses of the Shāpurkām and Sultanabad outside of it (fig. 2.19). As no trace of this wall remains along the entire north-eastern strip of the Bukhara Oasis, it has been hypothesized that the border fell where arable land gave way to steppes and deserts. Based on the "Home Range Theory" (Powell 2000: 65), the limit was placed about 2.5 km away from the outermost sites of the cluster. Starting from the value of 2 km, equivalent to the distance between the cultivated land and the reference villages (Chisholm 1968: 43–49), we also considered the possibility that wagons or grazing livestock were used, thus increasing the start value by 500 m (Cadeddu 2012: 250). The value of 2.5 km was applied to the outermost sites of the Obavija group in order to establish the relevant hypothetical area.

In the area north of Vardana, the path of the Kampirak roughly corresponded with a tepa that is now destroyed, and therefore undated, but we do know it was located 2.3 km from Vardana along the road that led north. We know that the Kampirak had entrances and guarded forts (Frye 1954: 34), and given the location of this site along a road coming out of the oasis, it could be the remains of an entrance. Moving towards the east, the theoretical limit would include the terminal part of the Shāpurkām (Kunya and Yanghi Shāpurkām) inside it and then continue southwards. The wall would pass just before the Sultanabad bifurcation, leaving the marshy area west of Gijduvan outside it. Corresponding with the terminal part of the Pirmast included in the wall, the Kampirak had to bend towards the east, and it is here in fact that siteless areas begin, and they delimit the cluster of sites to the south and separate it from the Vabkendarya.[24] R. Bonzani theorises that in ancient times areas without sites were political-territorial borders (1992: 211–13, 219). According to this scholar, in state-like societies characterised by a capital of considerable size compared to the rest of the settlements and by a precise internal hierarchy, the borders would be well defined and made up of large uninhabited areas. Furthermore, in these political situations, there would not be groups of sites but rather they would be dispersed throughout the territory, a situation that also characterises the distribution of the sites in Obavija.

According to a hypothesis already advanced about Sogdiana along the Middle Zerafshan Valley (Mantellini 2017: 170), the coexistence of populated areas and siteless areas could also reflect a mixed economy based on different strategies of land exploitation. Even today, uncultivated areas and marshes are used for hunting or for collecting reeds, rushes and other plant material that can be used both as building material and as food for livestock. In the case of Obavija, the southern siteless areas could be linked to the need to draw economic benefits from those areas where for various reasons irrigated agriculture was difficult or impossible. The excavations conducted in Vardanzeh have returned finds that confirm the existence of subsistence strategies linked to both agriculture and

---

23   The typological and hierarchical study of the Obavija sites was carried out during doctoral research and has not yet been published.

24   Topographic maps from the early 1900s indicate an area of marshes and solonchaks in the Abdullakhon canal area. Given the presence of ancient sites, it is likely that this particular soil condition is relatively recent.

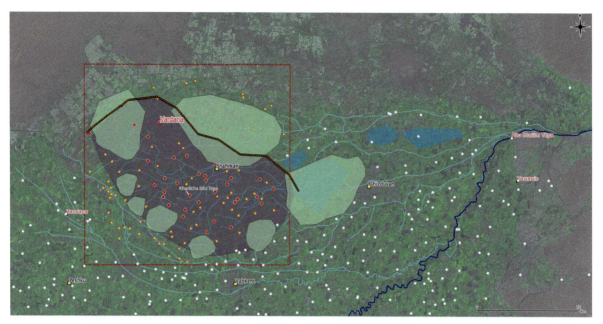

FIGURE 2.19   Territorial extension of Obavija (in violet) and sites dated to the Early Medieval Period, attributed to Obavija (in red). Siteless areas (areas in green); marshy areas (areas in light blue) and hypothetical path of Kampirak wall. Background image: Landsat 7 del 2000, EPP157R032_7F20010821
LANDSAT IMAGE COURTESY OF THE US GEOLOGICAL SURVEY

pastoralism: millstones, pestles, lentil seeds (lens culinaris, var. Microcorpe) and barley (Hordeum vulgare, var. vulgare),[25] as well as shears used for cutting sheep's wool (see fig. 2.15).

The western border of Obavija was also delimited by Kampir Duwal, as confirmed by the presence of a site identified in a more secluded position than the cluster and perhaps used to control the western border of the territory. The total area hypothetically attributable to the political sphere of Obavija, also taking the southern siteless areas into consideration, would be around 190 km². The dimensions appear to be slightly smaller but still compatible with those attributed to Fat-ti (216 km²), one of the principalities of Bukhara indicated in Chinese sources.

8   Final Reflections

In light of what has been studied in depth here, it is possible to argue that the early medieval Sogdiana districts' area of political-territorial relevance was generally associated with the paths of important rivers that flowed through them. Although for us the waterways are an important factor in the identification of these districts, the settlement characteristics found in Obavija demonstrate that this trend was not a hard and fast rule; there were adaptations, mainly dictated by the physical characteristics of each territory but also by the political weight held by the dominant centre.

The territorial expansion of Obavija – whose uniqueness, compared to other districts of Bukhara, was that it was located on the outskirts of the oasis – would have been modulated in such a way as to make the most of the natural resources available, which in this case had some weak areas. The Shāpurkām, mentioned by written sources, was in fact negatively influenced by the proximity of arid lands and solonchak areas located along the middle and upper courses of the river. In my opinion, this was alleviated by concentrating the settlements along the lower course of this river and another river, the Sultanabad, which together would have guaranteed more capillaries and a more consistent water supply, considering that more water networks would ensure a "reserve" of water, should one be running low. Finally, the presence of siteless areas within the borders of Obavija suggest economic advantages could also be gained from areas that were perhaps less productive from an agricultural point of view by using them for alternative activities, such as pastoralism, with the certainty of them remaining protected inside of the Kampirak. We must imagine that control of several waterways and a vast territory was an exception, since situations like this could only be managed by a politically strong capital, and Vardana, as written sources and archaeological findings show, was certainly one of them.

---

25   Thanks to Dr. R.N. Spengler (Max Planck Institute for the Science of Human History) for the interpretation of paleobotanical materials.

CHAPTER 3

The Bukhara Archaeological Expedition

The History of Research in Paykend

Andrey V. Omelchenko and Djamal Mirzaakhmedov

Translated from Russian by Rocco Rante

1 Introduction

Paykend is an ancient city located on the south-western border of the Bukhara region near the lower Zerafshan River. Its emergence and flourishing were due to its geography: the settlement was located a two-day caravan journey away from the capital city Bukhara along the main road connecting the area between the Amu Darya and Syr Darya rivers, that is, connecting Transoxiana (Maverannahr) with Traxiane (Khorasan). To the south of Paykend, Amul-Farab was a two-day caravan trip – it was the most important crossing on the Amu Darya River. Here, the northern (Black Sea and Volga regions and Khorezm) and eastern (China, East Turkestan, Fergana, Chach (Tashkent) and Samarkand Sogd) roads converged. From here one branch went to the south-west, through Merv to Iran and the Near East, and another one went along the Amu Darya to the south-east, to the lands of Tokharistan and on to India (fig. 3.1 top).[1]

Paykend (Baykand, Bi) is mentioned in medieval Chinese, Arab and Persian written sources, in particular by authors between the late 9th century and early 11th century. The *History of Bukhara* by al-Narshakhī mentions Paykend, which was "older than Bukhara" and well fortified, thus it received the name shahristan-i Roin (Copper City). In his history of Iranian rulers named Shah-name, Ferdowsi mentioned that Feridun (Traetaon), the epic king of Ariana and Turan, built one of the most ancient fire temples in Paykend. According to the legendary chronology, this occurred around 800 BCE. Later, the city became one of the residences of the rulers of Bukhara – the Bukhār Khudāhs (Frye 1954).

Two works with the same title, *The Book of Roads and Kingdoms*, by the geographers Ibn Khordadbeh and al-Iṣṭakhrī and Ibn Ḥauqal referred to Paykend. Qudama Ibn Ja'far, who was an official at the Abbasid court, wrote about Paykend in the *Book of the Land Tax*, as did the scientist and theologian al-Ṭabarī in his *History of the Prophets and Kings*. The geographer-traveller al-Muqaddasī also spoke about Paykend. He personally visited most of the regions and created a logical system for describing them in the book *The Best Divisions in the Knowledge of the Regions*.[2]

In ancient times, the Paykend Upland was a watershed between the beds of the lower reaches of the Zerafshan[3] and Kashkadarya rivers. A vast lake lay to the south of the city, which was called Bargini-Farah (large reservoir), or Dengiz (sea) according to al-Narshakhī, Bahr al-Bukhara (Bukhara sea) on Ibn Ḥauqal's map and Mavza-i Baykand (Lake at Paykend) in the anonymous 10th-century *Hudud al-Alam* (Mukhamedjanov, Adylov, Mirzaakhmedov, and Semenov 1988: 19–20). Even in the Early Middle Ages, the area around the city was rich in fish and game who inhabited the riparian woodland (*tugai*).

As the geological and hydrographic observations of the area around Paykend show,[4] in ancient times its territory contained several branches of the Zerafshan (later they were channels). In medieval times, two of the main city streets passed along them: between the citadel and shahrestan 1, and between shahrestans 1 and 2. For this reason there a large number of stone tools used by Neolithic Keltiminar hunters and fishermen,[5] as well as flint arrowheads from tribes during the Zamanbaba Bronze Age, who were the first farmers in the lower reaches of the Zerafshan (Sayfullayev 2007: 49–52, figs. 112–14). There are some bronze Saka-type arrowheads from the 7th–5th

---

1 This map is a hypothesis of the possible routes crossing Paykend and the Bukhara oasis, as a hypothesis is the reconstitution of the Kampir duwal surrounding the whole oasis.
2 Regarding the historical sources on Paykend, as well as a studies of the oasis, see Mukhamedjanov, Adylov, Mirzaakhmedov, and Semenov 1988; Lo Muzio, 2009; Rante, Schwarz, and Tronca 2022.
3 This channel of the Sogda River started in Bukhara and was called Nakhri-Zar (Mukhamedjanov, Adylov, Mirzaakhmedov, and Semenov 1988: 16).
4 Regarding geomorphology of the region, see Fouache et al. 2016.
5 It is believed that the lower stream of the Zerafshan was one of the core places the Keltiminar culture arose (Bryune 2014: 59).

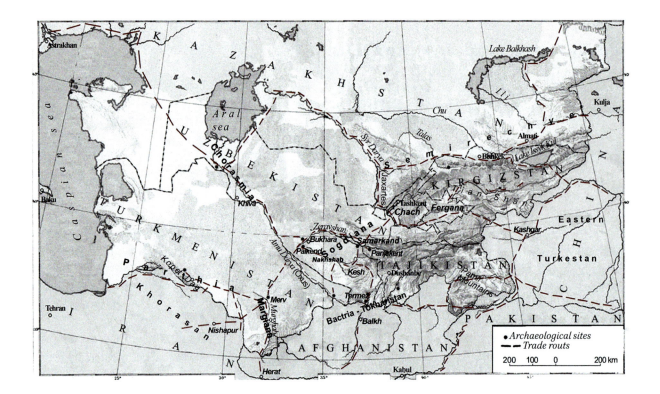
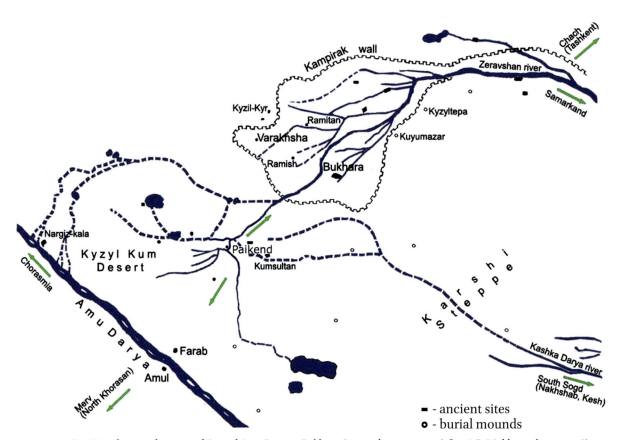

FIGURE 3.1 Top: Map, historical regions of Central Asia. Bottom: Bukhara Oasis, schematic map (after A.R. Mukhamedjanov, 1978)

centuries BCE in the cultural layers and constructions of later eras.

Paykend was located outside of Kampir Duwal – the defensive wall that had surrounded the Bukhara Oasis since at least the 5th century CE. However, Paykend was the main, well-fortified point when approaching the core of the region from the south (fig. 3.1 bottom).

Mentions of Paykend in Arabic and Persian sources provoked interest among European researchers in the 19th century. Thus, V. Tomaschek (1877) and J. Markwart (1938) believed that one of the residences of the kings of the Hephthalites, known in Chinese sources as Pa-ti-yan, was located in Paykend. Paykend is also associated with a story retold by al-Narshakhī (apparently from the last quarter of the 6th century) about the struggle between the usurper King Abrui and the *dihqan*s (grand people) of the city,[6] who were helped by the Turkic Hagan.

According to historical sources (Beleniskij, Bentovich, and Bolshakov 1973: 150), merchants from Paykend took an active part in intermediary trade between China and Iran. It is hypothesised that in the 7th century Paykend turned into a "merchant republic", which was unique in Central Asia. Also during this time, the final shape of the city was defined: the total area within the walls is approximately 18.5 ha – the citadel is 0.9 ha, the area in front of it is 0.6 ha, shahrestan 1 is 11 ha and shahrestan 2 is 6 ha (fig. 3.2: 1). There were also some early medieval residential buildings in the suburbs.

Because of its proximity to Northern Khorasan (Merv) and because it was wealthy, Paykend became one of the first targets of Arab raids on Maverannahr, the earliest of which, according to al-Ṭabarī, took place in 674. He and al-Narshakhī wrote that in 705/706 Paykend strongly resisted the beginning of a new phase of the Arab conquest of Central Asia led by Qutayba b. Muslim. For the uprising that followed the capture of the city, it was devastated, and the surviving inhabitants were enslaved. According to al-Ṭabarī: "[…] rich booty was captured, similar to which they (the Arabs) caught in Khorasan before" (1879–1901: 1189). According to Narshakhi (Frye 1954), however, Paykend was soon rebuilt by the townspeople, who were ransomed by their fellow countrymen.

The caliphate's subjugation of Central Asia, as well as the process of Islamisation, took almost 150 years. According to al-Narshakhī (Frye 1954), until the middle of the 9th century in Paykend vicinity there were numerous rabats – fortified gathering places for ghazi – for fighters who defended the area against the raids of non-Muslim Turks. In the first half of the 10th century the suburbs covered an area of up to 70 ha[7] of dispersed buildings.

According to Narshakhi (Frye 1954), beginning at the end of the 10th century, most residents of Paykend gradually abandoned the city due to the lack of water: the lower streams of the Zerafshan had dried up. But some people (including craftsmen) continued to live in the old structures outside the city (*rabat*s) (Rante and Mirzaakhmedov 2019: 229). In the first quarter of the 12th century, the Qarakhanid ruler Arslan Khan attempted to bring life back to the oasis. But construction of a canal was unsuccessful (Frye 1954).

Between the 15th and 17th centuries some small parts of the city-site were periodically settled, but after this period and up to the time of the excavations at the beginning of the 20th century, Paykend was completely deserted and covered by sand, thus representing an interesting archaeological site (Mukhamedjanov et al. 1988).

In 1896, the ruins of Paykend were visited by a topographer, a member of the Turkestan Circle of Archaeology Lovers, N.F. Sitnyakovsky, who made the first schematic plan of the city/site. In 1903, the American geologist R. Pumpelly, one of the pioneers of the archaeological study of the southern part of Central Asia, visited it. But a key player in this research was the Oriental School of St. Petersburg. In the early stages, the famous V.V. Bartold did much for the first steps of the archaeological study of Paykend. From 1913–14 L.A. Zimin, his student, a graduate of the Faculty of Oriental Languages at St. Petersburg University and secretary of the Turkestan Circle of Archaeology Lovers, carried out the first excavations (fig. 3.3 top).

In 1939–40 Paykend was studied by the Zerafshan expedition of the Hermitage, the Institute of the History of Material Culture, and the Uzbekistan Committee for the Protection of Antiquities and Art. M.M. Dyakonov, V.A. Shishkin, V.N. Kesaev, S.K. Kabanov, N.P. Kiparisova and others took part in the excavations under the overall leadership of A.Yu. Yakubovsky. A new plan of Paykend and its surroundings was made; the stratigraphy of the citadel (fig. 3.3 bottom) and shahrestan 1 were studied, and excavations of a large medieval building in the area of shahrestan 2 began. World War 2 interrupted Paykend's research for a long time. In 1954 and 1956 a team from the Institute of History and Archaeology of Uzbekistan (G.V. Shishkina, S.N. Yurenev, D.G. Zil'per and H. Duke) explored

---

6   In this case, apparently it was about the hereditary representatives of the most prosperous urban families (patricians) – merchants and owners of urban real estate – rather than the Central Asian feudal lords, called *dihqan*s in the Middle Ages.

7   According to data from the French (Louvre Museum)-Uzbek (Institute of Archaeology) expedition, it was 82.5 ha (Rante and Mirzaakhmedov 2019: 207).

FIGURE 3.2 Top: Paykend city-site, plan with the excavation areas (drawing by Bukhara Archaeological Expedition, BAE). Bottom: Citadel and area to the north, aerial photography: (1) fire temple; (2) external yard of the fire temple; (3) "palace"; (4) administrative quarter; (5) garrison barracks; (6) southern entrance to the citadel; (7) northern entrance to the citadel, the end of the 3rd–4th centuries CE; (8) western entrance to the citadel, 5th century CE; (9) mosque; (10) minaret; (11) area in front of the citadel

FIGURE 3.3 Top: Paykend, citadel (photo by Zerafshan Archaeological Expedition, 1939–40). Bottom: Excavations in the central part of the city-site (photo by L.A. Zimin, 1914)

the territory to the north-east of the city. There, Badasiya castle and a necropolis were partly excavated, in which were discovered nauses with ossuaries (Mukhamedjanov, Adylov, Mirzaakhmedov, and Semenov 1988: 5–6).

Archaeological research directly on the territory of Paykend was resumed 40 years later, in 1981, by the Bukhara archaeological expedition. In the 1980s it worked under the overall direction of Abdulahad Rakhimzhanovich Mukhamedjanov (1931–2006). In the 1990s, on the Uzbek side it was headed by Djamal Kamalovich Mirzaakhmedov. The Hermitage's expedition was led by Grigory L'vovich Semenov[8] (1950–2007), who came to Uzbekistan with extensive field experience in the excavations of Penjikent, the famous early medieval city in Eastern Sogd (fig. 3.4). Between 1983 and 1985 an archaeological group from the State Museum of Oriental Art (Moscow) under the leadership of Alexander Ilich Naymark took part in the work.

The first years of the expedition were difficult: there was not enough funding, there were difficulties with water, the archaeological base and transport, and dust storms were frequent at the site. Despite this, significant field research has been carried out with interesting results. The outcome of the first stages was the collective monograph *Paykend Site* (Mukhamedjanov, Adylov, Mirzaakhmedov, and Semenov 1988: 5–6).

From the very beginning, an essential part of excavations at Bukhara was the study of the city's fortifications (fig. 3.4). G.L. Semenov addressed the issue due to scientific interests and published articles and monographs (Semenov 1996b). The construction history of the Paykend citadel has number of phases. G.L. Semenov attributed the earliest walls to the 3rd–4th centuries CE, and in the northwestern sector, they were reinforced by three rectangular towers (one corner) that were 8–8.5 m wide. The entrances to the towers were from the so-called archer's corridor. As recent excavations have shown, it apparently ran around the perimeter of the late antique fortress. Archaeological layers were found under these structures as well. Materials from a trench in the eastern part of the citadel[9] showed that habitation of the area began at least during the end of the 4th century BCE. The fortress took its final shape in the 5th century CE, when the northeastern sector was decorated with tower ledges that had loopholes (Mukhamedjanov, Adylov, Mirzaakhmedov, and Semenov 1988: 148–54). Later, fortification walls were reconstructed and thickened (excavations by S.N. Makeev and B. Abdullaev).

In the 1980s and 1990s, the Zoroastrian fire temple was explored in the north of the citadel, (fig. 3.11a). Since at least the 4th century CE it was a monumental structure with two rising sanctuaries (7 × 5.3 and 6.9 × 5.5 m) and corridors along the perimeter. Square podiums for the sacred fire were in the centre of each sanctuary. The sanctuaries were connected by staircases and had an internal courtyard (Semenov 1996d: 171–78; Semenov 1996c: figs. 10–14), which had a four-column iwan. Traces of earlier structures were observed in the platform under the fire temple.

According to the general layout (cella on three sides in the corridor), the Paykend temple belongs to a type that had been common since Parthian times (Litvinsky and Pichikyan 2000: 205; Suleimanov 2000: 250). Periods[10] 3–5 (of six) also show comparisons with other fire temples in the Iranian world. The temple was vertically divided into terraces connected by stairs. This and other elements were combined in such a way as to make difficult to view the rooms with altars from the adjacent courtyard. The iwan had an even number of columns. Since Period 4, alabaster and burnt bricks were widely used in the interior, which is not typical for ancient and early medieval architecture in Central Asia north of the Amu Darya. At the same time, the Paykend complex had two sanctuaries[11] that are unusual for temples in Transoxiana, but we see this feature in Iran, for example, in the Sasanian temple of the royal fire, Adur Gushnasp, in Takht-i Suleiman[12] (Stronach 1985: 624, figs. 3, 9).

Seals (inserts) of semiprecious stones, clay imprints of seals or bullae (fig. 3.19: 4, 5) and a fragment of a wall painting resembling synchronous samples from Tokharistan (fig. 3.16c) were also found in the temple complex.

An "administrative" quarter, divided into blocks of ordinary buildings by a street and alleys, was excavated to the west of the fire temple in the late 1980s. According to G.L. Semenov (1996a: 44–45), in this part of the citadel there were warehouses and housing for servants of the fire temple. Coins produced for the ruler of Asbar and some imitations discovered here date the complex to the

---

8   Subsequently, he was the head of the Oriental Department of the State Hermitage.
9   Sh.T. Adylov worked here. Archaeologists I.O. Babanov and L.N. Sergienko also took part in excavations in various parts of the citadel.
10 The chronology of Paykend has been divided into "Periods" during our excavations (Mukhamedjanov et al 1988).
11 Perhaps one room was a *chortaq* (the main sanctuary) and the second was an *ateshgah* (where the fire was constantly maintained), and they could change functions, which is associated with the periodic erection and destruction of partitions in bypass corridors.
12 Even the sizes of these parts of the Iranian and Paykend temples coincide.

FIGURE 3.4 G.L. Semenov, the head of Bukhara Archaeological Expedition from the Hermitage Museum in 1981–2006; plan of the city-site with the excavation areas, 1985; plan of the northern part of the citadel, excavations before 1994
DRAWINGS BY BAE

FIGURE 3.5 Citadel: (a) remains of the north-eastern tower of the Hellenistic period under fortification walls of the 3rd–4th centuries CE; (b) remains of the smithy, 3rd century BCE; (c) forge fire; (d) anvil

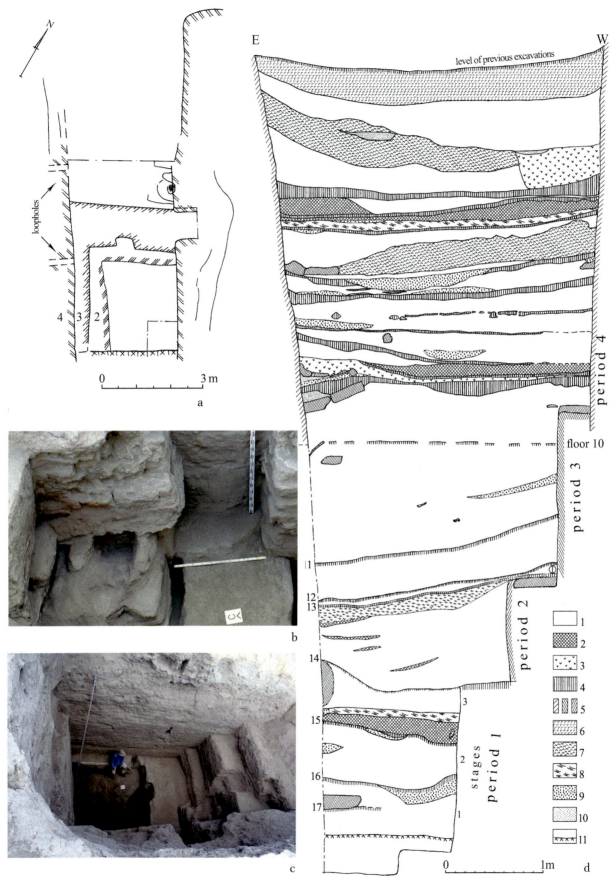

FIGURE 3.6 (a) The stratigraphic trench in the north-western corner of the citadel. Plan of the excavation; (b) Blacksmith's forge, floor no. 9; (c) Floor nos. 10–11 (Andrey V. Omelchenko); (d) Archaeological sectional drawing

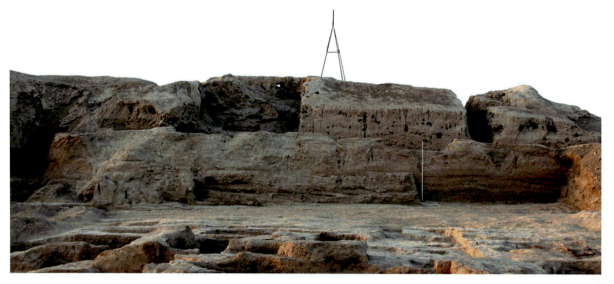

FIGURE 3.7 (a) Citadel, fortifications: north-eastern corner; (b) North-western corner, additional entrance to the fortress between tower nos. 1 and 2, the end of the 3rd–4th centuries CE; (c) Towers, western entrance to the fortress, the end of the 4th–5th centuries CE

6th–7th centuries.[13] Curiously, in the upper layers of the north-western tower a large burnt and ruled brick for a game similar to modern backgammon was found.

Another monumental structure was studied in the eastern part of the citadel next to the fire temple (excavations of I.K. Malkiel', A.V. Bekhter and others). This building (56 × 16 m) included two halls (6.5 × 5 m and 7.5 × 7.9 m) and a large courtyard adjacent to the south (fig. 3.11c). An iwan in front of the halls included two rows of columns. Two floors were covered with tiles, and the lower one had traces of a big fire. The entrance to the complex was located on the western wall. In a corridor there was a well and a *tazar* (drain) line with clay pipes (*kubur*s) enclosed in a vaulted "box" of burnt bricks (Semenov, Mirzaakhmedov et al. 2003: figs. 2–3).

The layout of the Paykend building, especially its main part, is similar to throne rooms in the early medieval palace complexes of Central Asia, for example, in Penjikent, Shahrestan and Varakhsha (Khmelnitsky 2000: figs. 181, 184, 191). However, due to the lack of clearly dated material as well as the reuse of early structures in the following periods, the exact time of its construction remains a controversial issue. At the last stage, at the beginning of the 12th century, the palace of Arslan Khan was constructed within the framework of old structures. In the western part of the courtyard, an iwan with columns on octagonal bases (1.15–1.4 m in diameter) and several rooms were added (Semenov, Mirzaakhmedov et al. 2000: 58–59; Semenov, Mirzaakhmedov et al. 2002: 13–16, figs. 4–5; Semenov, Mirzaakhmedov et al. 2005: 25–28, figs. 58–60).

Two circumstances should be noted when studying Paykend's architecture (Mukhamedjanov et al. 1988). First, there was a shortage of good natural resources for adobe construction, so old buildings were often dismantled to the foundation and their clay was reused for new structures. Second, the widespread use of burnt bricks from the 4th to the 10th century occurred here more than in other regions of Central Asia. The presence of water and wood in the vicinity contributed to this. However, when the city was finally abandoned, burnt bricks from its buildings became a valuable resource and, later on, began to be "mined" for sale, especially in the 15th–18th centuries. There is a famous saying that "half of Bukhara is built of Paykend bricks". In this regard, all the medieval objects excavated up to now in Paykend contain traces of such activities in the form of trenches, imprints of former brickwork, destroyed upper parts of wells, etc. The citadel and its monumental structures in particular were badly damaged. The pavement in the southern part of the "palace" was completely removed, and the adjacent so-called southern "archer's" corridor was destroyed by treasure hunters to a depth of 5–6 m and filled with sand.

Sometimes, the researchers made important discoveries. These excavations (in the south of the citadel) were carried out by Shukhrat Teshibaevich Adylov, who had been present since the beginning of the Bukhara expedition. In the south-eastern section of the citadel, in a corridor, a rare fragment of a Paykend wall painting with a scene of worship was discovered *in situ* (fig. 3.16a). A treasure of Bukhār Khudāh drachms was hidden nearby. In the western part of this corridor, damaged by fire, nine bullae were found, most likely sealing documents (fig. 3.19: 6–9). Here, a treasure of weapons was also discovered under a floor of burnt bricks. It included iron swords, daggers, spears and arrowheads, bone lining for bows, remnants of a shield and bronze belt linings, etc. According to the archaeological context, these finds date back to the 7th–early 8th centuries, but the weapons had parallels among materials used by Sarmatian tribes during the first centuries BCE. Researchers believe that the treasure was kept as a relic and was hidden at the time of the Arabs' assault on Paykend in 705/706 (Semenov and Adylov 2006).

In the south-west of the citadel the remains of a 10th-century mosque were discovered in the early 2000s (excavations of B. Abdullaev). It is possible that al-Muqaddasī mentioned it as having the most beautiful *mihrab* in Maverannahr. Only the lower parts of the mosque's walls and the square basement of the columns remained (fig. 3.26a).

To the north of the citadel, the base of the minaret was discovered (by A.V. Bekhter). An adobe monolith 4.7 m in diameter was in its core. Two circular brickworks, one 7 and the other 11 m in diameter, surrounded the central part of the minaret (fig. 3.26b). The latter size makes it one of the largest minarets in Central Asia (assuming it was completed).

The area located north of the citadel was explored by archaeologists from the State Museum of Oriental Art in 1983–85. The construction of the fortress wall, equipped with a shooting corridor, was attributed to the Kushano-Sasanid period. The power of the fortifications was given by the bedrock that formed their base.

Early medieval households from the third construction period were discovered in the north-east and north-west corners of the area. The living rooms had a plan typical for Paykend during this period: *sufas* (benches) around

---

13   The well-known specialist in the field of Transoxiana numismatics, Evgeny Vladislavovich Zeimal' (1932–98), carried out the identification of ancient and early medieval coins from Paykend for many years.

the perimeter and a central podium for fire. Remnants of structures from the two upper periods were found everywhere, too, but they are not well-preserved. There, furnaces for the production of glass were identified. They might be connected with the construction of the palace on the citadel or with other buildings at the beginning of the 12th century.

The fortifications of the shahrestans have been studied from the beginning of the Bukhara expedition's work. The towers of shahrestan 2 have been uniquely preserved and are visible at large distances from the city (fig. 3.20d). The fortress walls of shahrestan 1 do not seem to have had towers. Excavations by G.L. Semenov in the 1980s and 1990s found only one bastion in the south-western corner, which, as further work showed, defended the southern gates of the city after it expanded its area (Semenov 1996b: 116–18). A stratigraphic study of the earliest construction period inside of the fortifications walls of shahrestan 1 found ceramics from the 5th–early 6th centuries CE.[14] In the last stages of the city's development, the fortification walls fall into decline, and their massive brickwork was used as clay "quarries" for ceramics production. One pottery kiln was constructed in the walls in the south-eastern corner of shahrestan 1 (excavated by I.A. Arzhantseva).

An extensive study of the street network was carried out in Paykend as well. It was found that the shahrestans were divided by main streets and T-shaped alleys into standard blocks (fig. 3.27c).

Between the citadel and shahrestan 1 a 3.5–4.5 m wide street appeared for more than 130 m. It had a central "carriageway" and sidewalks made from burnt bricks (fig. 3.27a). A well (or a sump) of burnt bricks, about 3 m. in diameter, was made at the intersection of the street and one of the alleys (no. 4) (Semenov, Mirzaakhmedov et al. 2005: 14–16; Torgoev, Mirzaakhmedov et al. 2011: 31, fig. 117). All four lanes that surrounded the residential quarter in the north-western corner of shahrestan 1 were also excavated. Their width varied from 0.8 to 1.7 m; some had significant differences in levels at the ends (Semenov, Mirzaakhmedov et al. 2000: 28–30).

The north-western residential quarter (84 × 22–25 m) in shahrestan 1 is the most studied in the city-site (figs. 3.21 and 3.22). In 1981, a stratigraphic trench found five main construction periods (Mukhamedjanov, Adylov, Mirzaakhmedov, and Semenov 1988: 38–41). In 1989–90 the first houses were opened (work by Emilia F. Wulfert). The quarter was excavated every season from 1998 to 2018. The work was carried out under the overall coordination of G.L. Semenov (the archaeologists were N.M. Omarov, P.B. Lurje, A.I. Torgoev[15] and N.Zh. Saparov). Houses from the end of the 8th to the early 11th centuries were completely opened.[16] There were ten houses in the period between the 6th and 8th centuries, and half of them were excavated completely (Saparov and Torgoev 2013: 66). The quarter was divided into two parts by a thick main wall almost to the eastern edge, where the largest of those studied, "House 1", was located (Semenov 2006: 555–69).

House no. 1, with a total area of 370 m^2, included 12 rooms, connected through a long corridor (fig. 3.22d). There was a large hall (60 m^2) with four columns supporting the ceilings, a smaller hall, separate sleeping rooms with *sufas* along the perimeter and a fire place over a special podium in the centre (figs. 3.22b and 3.22e)[17] and utility rooms, including a kitchen. The interior of the hall was decorated with bas-reliefs of carved, painted clay with geometric and floral ornaments (palmette, grapevines) and anthropomorphic themes (fig. 3.23).

Later, the house was twice divided into four parts,[18] which researchers associate with the fragmentation of a large patriarchal family. Other early medieval households usually repeat the layout of House 1 but in a reduced form. It is possible that the separate rooms facing the streets, as in Penjikent, were rented shops. A small quarter mosque was built in the 10th century (or in the second half of the 9th century) in the south-eastern corner of the quarter (Semenov 2006: 559–60, 565).

The wealth and distant trade ties of Paykend's people are evident in some finds from the residential quarter: hoards of coins, including Chinese (Kai-yuan tun-bao) and local denominations imitating them (figs. 3.35 and 3.29–36), a Chinese mirror, a crossbow bolt and coral

---

14 It is believed that these were 4th-century CE houses (Rante and Mirzaakhmedov 2019: 208). But these dates, which we theorise on the basis of carbon dating, stand in stark contrast with the character of the material culture. We know the material complexes from the end of the 3rd to the beginning 5th centuries CE well due to excavations in the citadel that brought to light coins with good data.

15 The head of the Bukhara expedition 2007–10.

16 The buildings of the uppermost period are heavily eroded; the plans of some houses had been reconstructed. Houses on the eastern and western edges of the quarter were studied down to the natural ground (the thickness of cultural layers is more than 4.5 m).

17 A similar layout, for example in Penjikent, was called the "Bukhara guest's room".

18 Soon, the northern household (1a) burnt down, as well as the adjacent one (2a). G.L. Semenov suggested that the fire was related to Qutayba b. Muslim taking Paykend in 706. Now, based on coin finds, there is another view: the fire occurred later, after 759 (Saparov and Torgoev 2013: 71).

beads. A potter's wheel, terracotta figurines and fragments of vessels with Sogdian ink inscriptions, one of which had the name "Kidara", which is known from historical sources[19] (fig. 3.34: 7), were also found.

The fortifications of shahrestan 2 were the best preserved: even at the beginning of the last century, judging from the reports of L.A. Zimin, the fortification walls rose more than 6 m above the level of the plain (fig. 3.20d). G.L. Semenov identified three main periods in the development of the fortification of this part of the city. The first walls with towers were erected on the base of the levelled conglomerate of the Paykend plateau. The towers are rectangular (fig. 3.20c), about 11 m high, located at a distance of 56–70 m from each other, and were equipped with three rows of slit-like loopholes arranged in a fan-like and chequered manner (the middle row was false). Thus, archers could shoot straight as well as along the walls (behind curtains). The inner part of the towers (mainly 4 × 5 m) had two floors. In three towers, secret gates for a sudden attack were found. Later, all loopholes were closed with *pakhsa*, and the fortress could be defended from the top of the towers. Finally, towards the beginning of the 9th century, the fortifications of shahrestan 2 lost their function (Semenov 1996b: 119–35).

As in other parts of the city/site, the first study conducted in shahrestan 2 was a stratigraphic one (excavations of Sh.T. Adylov in 1981 and I.K. Malkiel' in 1999). A trench in the north-western sector, 70 m south-west of tower no. 2, detected a street. It functioned from the beginning of the settlement on the territory of shahrestan 2, between the 6th and beginning of the 7th century (?), until its abandonment in the first third of the 11th century. The width of the street varied from 1.75 to 2.25 m at different times (Mukhamedjanov, Adylov, Mirzaakhmedov, and Semenov 1988: 41–44; Semenov, Mirzaakhmedov et al. 2000: 52–55, figs. 124–26).

The most important consequence of incorporating Sogd into Islamic civilisation was the dissemination of knowledge based on a unified written and scientific language, Arabic. This is reflected in particular in the field of medicine – unique evidence was revealed in the excavations at Paykend. On the border of shahrestans 1 and 2, a multiroom pharmacy-clinic was discovered (excavations by V.I. Kesaev and then by G.L. Semenov). A *tabib* (doctor) worked here at the end of the 8th century; this is the earliest evidence in Transoxiana. In two rooms a set of ceramics and glassware were found. Special jars with a long nose – alembics used both for distillation and for bloodletting. Ostracons found here had Arabic inscriptions in ink with names and an exact date: 30 June 790/12 Safar 174 (fig. 3.34: 8). Researchers believed this was a voucher for a doctor, the first one found in Maverannahr (Mukhamedjanov and Semenov 1984).

In the 9th and 10th centuries Paykend was an important transit point on the way to Khorasan, as well as a large trade and craft centre. In medieval times, this activity usually concentrated near the main city gate, proven by excavations in Paykend. Here, the south gateway was laid out in the form of a S-shaped labyrinth between the towers of shahrestan 1 and 2. Studies (excavations by I.K. Malkiel') showed that the double gate was 2.7 m wide (figs. 3.27: 2; 3.36: 4). The street ("A") near the gate probably had a ceiling as well (Semenov, Mirzaakhmedov et al. 2004: 30–32, 52, figs. 46, 106).

Only street "A" led from the gates into the city along the western wall of shahrestan 1. It went towards the pharmacy and then to the northern city gates (fig. 3.27b). Excavations in the south-eastern sector of shahrestan 2 revealed a network of streets (excavations by S.N. Makeev and I.K. Malkiel'), dividing the area of the city into equal sections that are each 35–37 m wide. Routes were connected only by "T"-shaped junctions (fig. 3.27c) (Semenov, Mirzaakhmedov et al. 2000: 58–59; Semenov, Mirzaakhmedov et al. 2004: 30–32, 52, fig. 46; Semenov, Mirzaakhmedov et al. 2005: 25–28, figs. 58–60).

The width of street "A" (4–6 m) confirms that it was one of the main city avenues. The street was studied by stratigraphic excavations until the natural soil (depth of 4 m). There were 25 main street layers, the thickness of which decreased in the upper part. Half of them were connected with road maintenance, with pottery fragments, pieces of bedrock and clay coatings. In turn, the lower layers (until the end of the 8th century) were thick – up to 50 cm. They had humus deposits, which apparently indicate the great role cattle breeding played in Paykend's economy in the Early Middle Ages (Semenov, Mirzaakhmedov et al. 2005: 131–33; Omelchenko and Kholov 2018: 51–53, figs. 131–34).

A line of clay *tazar* (drain) line pipes (*kuburs*), enclosed in a vaulted "box" of burnt bricks, was made under street "A" in the 10th century. It directed the water away from the city gates. Ground-penetrating radar studies in 2015 showed that underground there were water pipelines (Torgoev, Mirzaakhmedov et al. 2009: 12, figs. 28–36; Torgoev, Mirzaakhmedov et al. 2011: 31–33, figs. 122–29).

A small bazaar with stores and handicraft workshops was built along street "A" near the western face of the

---

[19] The reading of the Sogdian inscriptions from the excavations in Paykend is by P.B. Lurie, to whom we express our sincerest thanks.

fortification wall of shahrestan 1 no earlier than the 9th century. The wide sidewalk served as a *sufa* as well. Here, goods were displayed or customers waited or rested. The rooms facing the street had iwans (excavations of A.I. Torgoev and N.Zh. Saparov).

There were also bakers' shops with stoves (*tandoors*). They served as small canteens where food could be bought and taken home to eat. Two workshops for repairing soapstone boilers, and one that belonged to a bone-carver, were opened nearby. Three shops were related to medicine – alembics and a glass vessel for rose water were found there (Torgoev 2008). One workshop was a smithy (Torgoev, Mirzaakhmedov et al. 2009: 13–16, fig. 44). Thanks to a coin hoard hidden under the floor beams, it was possible to establish the date of the fire: the third quarter of the 10th century.

A water supply system was constructed after the fire. It included a deep well, water wheel that animals probably rotated, a basin to collect water and water lines of clay pipes (*kuburs*), which moved in different paths. This worked until the beginning of the second third of the 11th century, when this part of the city was finally abandoned (Semenov, Mirzaakhmedov et al. 2005: 28–33, fig. 60; Semenov, Mirzaakhmedov et al. 2006: 21–34, fig. 43; Semenov et al. 2007: 23–31, 43, figs. 60–70; Torgoev et al. 2008: 13–15, fig. 28).

Shops with stoves and a jeweller's (?) workshop were on the street near the already abandoned pharmacy in the 10th and early 11th centuries (Semenov et al. 2005: 48).

The first residential complex opened by the Bukhara expedition in shahrestan 2 was a 9th–10th–century house near northern tower no. 2 (excavations 1982–83). It was medium in size (75 m^2) and included five rooms. One was for living; the others were for grain processing and bread baking. After the Arab conquest, special sections for sanitation and accommodations appeared in all houses; and a new system of heating appeared as well (Mukhamedjanov, Adylov, Mirzaakhmedov, and Semenov 1988: 70–74).

Large-scale excavations of the residential quarter in shahrestan 2 were carried out under the leadership of Igor Karlovich Malkiel' in the 1990s and early 2000s. Two houses were excavated completely and two partially in the north-western sector. There was a street (2.1 m wide) and an alley as well. A very important find in the second lower stratigraphic horizon was the Chinese coin Kai-yuan tong-bao, which makes it possible to date the beginning of a residential development in shahrestan 2 no earlier than the end of the 6th century (Semenov, Mirzaakhmedov et al. 2000: 55).

The most extensive research in shahrestan 2 was carried out in the residential quarter between the southern fortification wall and street "1". Fourteen houses built between the 10th century and the first third of the 11th century were excavated at the length of 130 m, near tower nos. 8 and 10 (fig. 3.28). Those that were further from the city gate were of a similar layout and size (17–18 × 5 m). Thus, we can assume that this was the general building-development plan that existed for shahrestan 2.

The housing scheme was standard: (three to eight) rooms were connected by a common corridor leading to the exit. Living rooms (with *sufas*) were placed as away from the entrance as possible. In rich houses, a special small room was built to pray in. Kitchens and utility rooms were situated either in the central part of the house or closer to the exit. Typically, there was a small hallway behind an entrance.

It was possible to determine who the inhabitants of the houses were two times. One of them (no. 8) was occupied by a master ceramist. In a back bedroom in a wooden chest he kept various *kalyb*s – moulds for stamping intricate ornaments on ceramics – stamps and blanks (fig. 3.30: 1–6). Nearby there were two vessels filled with clay and small crushed stones. Pottery was sold in a shop, which was part of the house but had a separate exit and a small storeroom.

The neighboring dwelling belonged to a person who specialized in processing metal. In his house (no. 7), iron tools were found: a saw that cuts metal, a chisel and punches. Finished products were also found (Semenov, Mirzaakhmedov et al. 2001: 68–79, 84–86).

The dwelling house (no. 3) (17 × 10 m), which occupied two plots of land, is an example of a large household. It contained 14 rooms, which were grouped into two blocks with separate exits to the street. One of the rooms was a prayer room, as evidenced by a *mihrab* niche decorated with a plaster (*ganch*) panel of carved vegetative-geometric patterns.

There was a public well near the house. It was built during the last stage of the city's life – at the end of the 10th or the beginning of the 11th century, when the lack of water in Paykend was acutely felt.[20] The city's inhabitants constantly dug the well deeper due to fall of groundwater level, finally reaching down to 17 m deep (Semenov, Mirzaakhmedov et al. 2000: 60–74, figs. 135, 175).

The house (no. 9) located opposite tower no. 9 included 17 rooms, had four entrances and was even larger than the others (26.5 × 17 m). It formed several blocks: residential, guest, kitchen, warehouse, all connected with two courtyards with an area of 60 m^2 (central) and 75 m^2 (corner).

---

20 The absence of bathrooms, which were common until the middle of the 10th century, in this period's houses confirms this.

Their floors were covered with burnt bricks, and the walls of the larger courtyard were decorated with carved and painted plaster panels. An inscription was placed within the composition of the vegetative-geometric ornament. It was written in "blossoming" Kufic script: "The kingdom (belongs) to Allah, the greatness (belongs) to Allah" (fig. 3.29) (Semenov, Mirzaakhmedov et al. 2002: 51–72, figs. 57, 98–103; Semenov, Mirzaakhmedov et al. 2003: 73–75, figs. 116–18). It is believed that the building might have belonged to a city or district administrator, and the large corner courtyard was a mosque. Bronze pyxis and a brass lamp with two spouts, which were found here (fig. 3.32: 3) (Semenov, Mirzaakhmedov et al. 2002: 76, fig. 115), confirm the uniqueness of the building as well.

It seems the entire part to the east, from house no. 8 on, was for public needs. So the next house, no. 10, with a total area of almost 450 m², included several three-room sections that were typical for caravanserai buildings to the east of the city. There, the entrance to the house from the side of the street is unusually wide – more than 3.5 m. There was a long room with special *sufas* (0.75 m high) near the fortification wall. They were presumably used for unloading the goods from pack animals. All of this indicates that house no. 9 was a small hotel for merchants who could afford to stay inside the city not far from the south gate (Semenov, Mirzaakhmedov et al. 2002: 52–61, 87, figs. 58, 59).

The same functions were performed by house no. 11, which had a total area of 262.5 m². The central place in it was occupied by the courtyard, around which there were residential and utility (kitchen block) rooms. As in house no. 10, a narrow couloir with *sufas* in the middle for storing goods was adjoined to the fortification wall (Semenov, Mirzaakhmedov et al. 2004: 52–61, 87, figs. 47, 59).

Excavations of the quarters in shahrestans 1 and 2 have yielded a rich archaeological complex that reflects various aspects of the lives of the townspeople in Paykend during the Samanid and early Qarakhanid periods. There are various unglazed ceramics that are often decorated with stamped ornaments. Paykend's "trademark" was dishes covered with a dense dark green glaze (fig. 3.31: 1–5). Less common are vessels covered with a transparent lead glaze, with engraved ornamentation, and others with a white background and dark brown epigraphic vegetal ornamentation or strict Kufic script. Here is a remarkable example of an inscription applied to a small pot: "Eat (from it) to your health!" (fig. 3.31: 6). Another vessel from the citadel had a didactic inscription: "Generosity is a feature of the righteous man" (fig. 3.31: 7) (Semenov, Mirzaakhmedov et al. 2002: 36, fig. 43; Semenov, Mirzaakhmedov et al. 2006: 11, fig. 14).

The excavations of Paykend testify to the literacy of its inhabitants: sherds of vessels with Arabic inscriptions made in ink, fragments of *kalamdans* (pen cases) and inkpots were found in both shahrestans (fig. 3.34: 8–12).

Medicinal, hygienic and well-being needs required an increase in the production of glass. Craftsmen made tableware, perfumery and pharmaceutical utensils, as well as special-purpose items: mugs, jugs, decanters, jars and cups, inkwells, *tuvaks* and *sumaks*, bottles, flasks, alembics and window glass.

Copper and brass were used to make cauldrons, jugs, lamps, pyxis, vessels for making cosmetics (*usmadjushaks*), scales, forks, spoons and keys, as well as thimbles, bells, buckles, belt overlay and ornaments (fig. 3.32). Iron was used to make weapons and tools: household knives, fire steels, sickles, mattocks, horseshoes and door details such as bolts, locks, keys, nails and many others.

The products by Paykend's jewellers are represented by beads of various forms made from "black amber" or jet (gemstone), chalcedony, agate, coral, bone, glass of different colours, *kashin* (stonepast) and also carnelian – a favorite in the Middle Ages. Bronze and silver rings had inlays of semiprecious stones.

The high level of Paykend's trade, both local and international, especially during the medieval period, is confirmed by numerous finds of coins, including hoards: fals and dirhams from all the dynasties that ruled Maverannahr starting from the time of the Arab caliphate's conquest[21] (fig. 3.35: 40–49).

As was the case across the east, handicrafts and trade in Maverannahr in the medieval period occurred in suburbs. But a specific feature of Paykend, one that was mention by Arab and Persian authors, were the 1,000 fortresses (*rabats*) for ghazis (warriors) in its vicinity. However, the topographic survey conducted the 1930s and aerial photography from the 1980s showed some monumental buildings. Most of them were to the east of the city/site, on the opposite side of the Zerafshan channel at the beginning of the ancient road from Paykend to Bukhara. Between 1981 and 1987 rabat no. 1 (77 × 77 m), which had been inhabited since the end of the 8th century, was fully studied (excavations conducted under the direction of D.K. Mirzaakhmedov).

The layout of the building was well thought out: the rooms were located around a square courtyard all along

---

21 Coin finds from Paykend during the Islamic period were identified by the famous specialist in Central Asian medieval numismatics, Boris Dmitrievich Kochnev (1940–2002), and now continue to be identified his student, A.Kh. Atakhodjaev, from the Institute of Archaeology of Uzbekistan. We express our sincere gratitude to him.

the perimeter of the outer walls. Three-room individual sections are clearly identified, and they were divided by one-room sections that served as warehouses or kitchens. There were large raised platforms in the centre of the courtyard, presumably for unloading the goods from pack animals. Two entrances to the building were located on opposite walls on the same axis. Thus, all indicate that this was a caravanserai, perhaps the earliest of those excavated in Maverannahr (Mukhamedjanov, Adylov, Mirzaakhmedov, and Semenov 1988: 116, 117, 145–47). In turn, the layout and character of the interiors of several rooms indicate there were two special sections: a Zoroastrian chapel in the north-western corner and a mosque at the southern gate of the building (Khmel'nitskiy 1996: 180–82).

Since 2004, the Bukhara expedition has been excavating the so-called southern suburb – a complex of structures (125 × 20 m) located 70 m south of the city gate (excavations by N.D. Sobirov, A.I. Torgoev and A.V. Kulish). Apparently, a large trading square lay between it and the city wall (fig. 3.33a). Initially, the building served as a caravanserai. In addition to traditional three-room and one-room sections, the building included storage facilities, stables, a bathhouse and a mosque. At the last stage of the city's life, when the population was displaced from the city due to the lack of water, residents concentrated in its suburbs; the rooms of the caravanserai were rebuilt as permanent accommodations for the poor. Kilns for stoneware appeared on the edge of the quarter. A large number of terracotta figurines of zebu-like bulls, associated with fertility, were discovered in one of them. They were connected with the celebration of Navruz, the local New Year, and indicate that the ancient beliefs and folk tradition of the Sogdians continued to live on in the Islamic era (Torgoev, Mirzaakhmedov et al. 2009: 24, fig. 58).

In general, at the beginning of the 2010s, about 12% of the Paykend area was excavated inside the walls on the upper building horizon (9th–11th centuries). Thus, in a fairly short period of time, Paykend, along with Penjikent, Samarkand and Termez, became one of the most well-studied medieval Central Asian cities. All this was made possible through the work of a close-knit team (fig. 3.36), which includes not only archaeologists but also architects (L.Yu. Kulakova, E.P. Buklaeva, I.V. Kuznetsov, I.O. Gurov, S.D. Mirzaakhmedov, A.V. Kulish and others), artists (I.I. Suikanen, A.E. Manevsky and S.A. Malkiel') and restorers (V.A.Fominykh, A.Yu. Stepanov, E.P. Stepanova, O.L. Semenova, R.A. Kazimirova, O.N. Viktorova and D.O. Kholov).

2   New Discoveries and Perspectives

Nevertheless, a number of issues, especially concerning the ancient history of Paykend, were left unresolved. In 2011, an international conference dedicated to the 30th anniversary of the Bukhara expedition was held in Paykend and Bukhara. During this time, a research program investigating the early stages of Paykend's development was launched. The main efforts focus on the excavation of the lower layers of the citadel, the area in front of it and shahrestan 1. The main task is creating the timeline of the development of local (Bukhara) material culture across all periods (figs. 3.8–10, 17–19, 25, 30–32, 34, 35).

The *Ark-kuhendiz* (citadel) of Paykend had significantly thick cultural layers. For this reason, research has focused primarily in the sectors where construction levels have already been opened to a considerable depth.[22]

The earliest materials related to the first stage of permanent settlement in the site were obtained in the north of the citadel, in the areas adjacent to outside and inside the fortification wall (studies by A.V. Omelchenko, E.N. Sobirov, V.V. Mokroborodov and R.M. Toyirov). Excavations were brought up to the natural ground in the north-western corner of the ark, in the so-called archer's corridor (depth 14.4 m from the benchmark) (figs. 3.6a–d). Here, in the lowest layers, the period of habitation was before the defenses. The pottery assemblage in these layers (Paykend-1, last quarter of the 4th century to the beginning of the 3rd century BCE) were in the late Achaemenid "cylinder-conical" tradition (fig. 3.8). However, new influences associated with Central Asia's integration into the Hellenistic world are visible in the tableware (Omelchenko 2019: 203–25; Omelchenko and Mokroborodov, forthcoming). Thus, the old idea of the first permanent settlement in territory of Paykend's citadel is confirmed. It also corresponds with the hypothesis that army's violent suppression of the Alexander the Great's troops in Sogdiana (Adilov 2006 et al. Adilov 2012 et al.) as well asgeomorphologic changes in the 4th century BCE in the Zerafshan valley (Rante, Fouache, and Mirzaakhmedov 2016: 441–46) facilitated farmers resettling in the Bukhara Oasis.

The first monumental buildings in Paykend are naturally associated with the Zoroastrian sanctuary in the north-east of the ancient citadel. Yerkurgan (Sulejmanov 2000: 88–101) and Uzunkir (Sangirtepa) in the valley of the river and Kashkadarya, as well as Koktepe (Rapin and Isamiddinov 2013: 124–31), in the Middle Zerafshan

---

22   The citadel excavations are proceeding under the direction of A.V. Omelchenko, coleader of the Bukhara expedition since 2011.

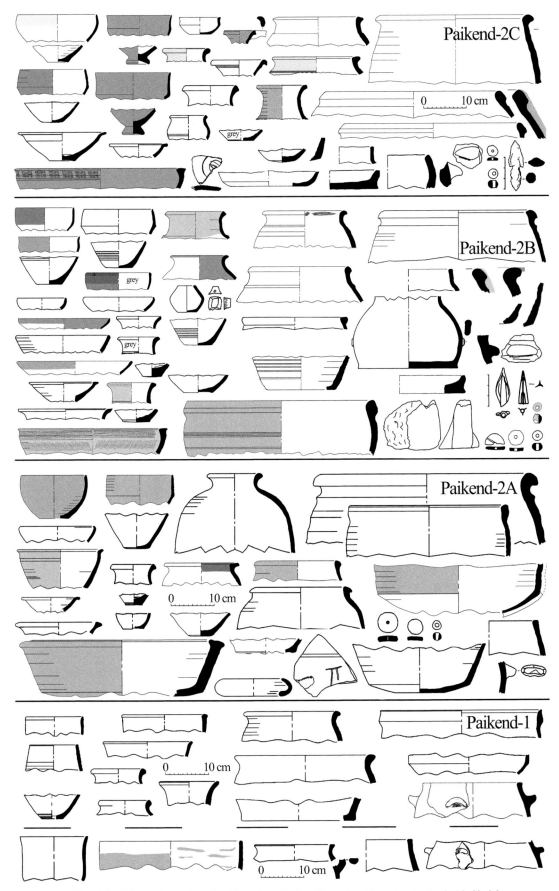

FIGURE 3.8 The table of the periodisation of artifacts from Paykend from the 4th century to the first half of the 2nd century BCE

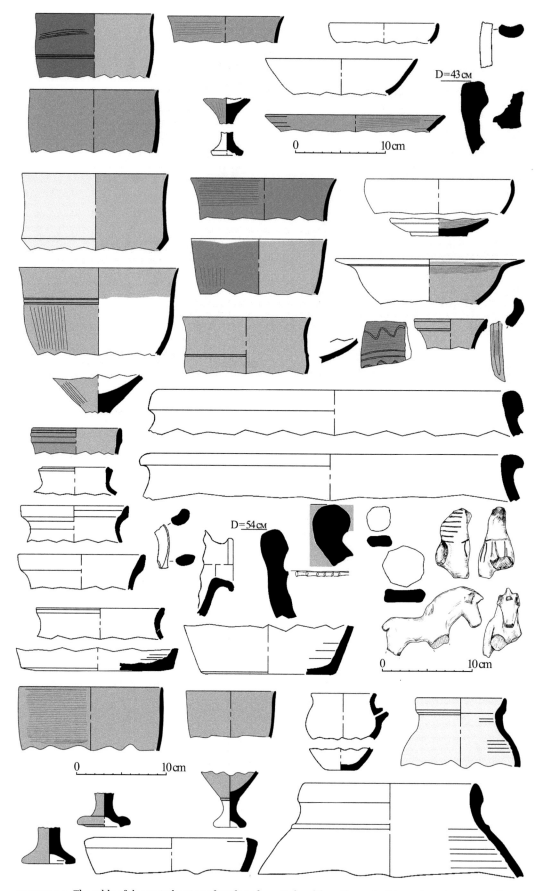

FIGURE 3.9 The table of the periodisation of artifacts from Paykend from the end of the 2nd century BCE to the beginning of the 2nd century CE

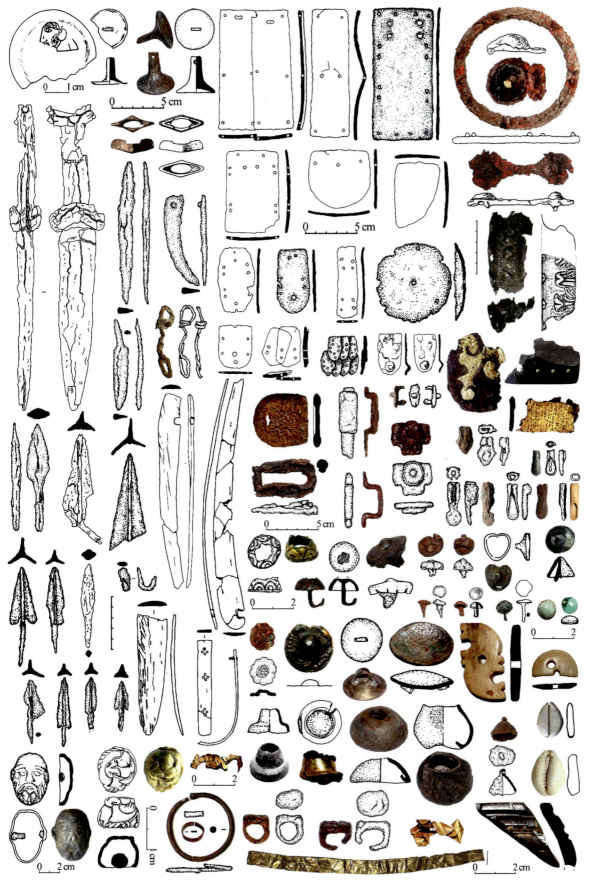

FIGURE 3.10 Artifacts from sacrificial pits (βόθροι) and favissa in the southern part of the citadel, 1st century to the beginning of the 2nd century CE

demonstrate the emergence of urban centres near temples in Sogd. It is interesting that legendary sources mention an ancient Zoroastrian tradition in Paykend. This was due to its proximity to Iran.

To the south of the sanctuaries, in the courtyard of the fire temple,[23] a platform that had several constructive levels was found. At the northern edge of the temple, under the archer's corridor, a series of pits were studied. The earliest ones were carved in ground soil. They did not have household purposes and, presumably, were used for Zoroastrian rites.

At the north-eastern corner of the temple, under the massif of the walls from the 3rd–4th centuries CE (fig. 3.7a), the remains of the earliest fortifications of the citadel, from the beginning of the 3rd century BCE, were found. There was a platform made of flat, convex rectangular adobe, a tower 4.5 m wide (fig. 3.5a) and a section of a wall with a slit-like loophole made of large square adobe and pakhsa. Surveys in 2019 to the west of the tower (work of E.N. Sobirov) discovered the remains of frame-and-pillar structures, as well as a smithy from the middle of the 3rd century BCE (fig. 3.5b–d). There were a forge, a special adobe table for smithing and big jar (*hum*) for water.[24] Remains of the walls dating back to this time were also found in the north-western corner of the citadel (excavations of A.V. Omelchenko and V.V. Mokroborodov). Pottery assemblages from the beginning of the 3rd to the first half of the 2nd century BCE (Paykend-2A, B, C) (fig. 3.8) had a characteristic Central Asian "Hellenised" appearance (Omelchenko 2019: figs. 10, 11; Omelchenko and Mokroborodov, forthcoming).

The antiquities of the next, "Kangju", chronological horizon (second half of the 2nd century BCE to the 2nd century CE) are found here as well, both inside and outside the northern wall. They were at the bottom of the ditch near the western wall, which later became a street between the citadel and shahrestan 1 (fig. 3.37a) (Mirzaakhmedov, Omelchenko et al. 2016: 39, fig. 92). Changes in the archaeological complex are obvious and are reflected in the ceramics (goblets appeared in particular), terracotta (figurines of horsemen) (fig. 3.9) and numerous weapons (fig. 3.10). Similar innovations were noted in Bactria after its conquest by nomads and the formation of domains under the control of nomadic dynasties.

The range and number of items related to military affairs expanded significantly after new excavations in the southern archer's corridor of the citadel and the adjacent sector of the "palace" (excavations by A.V. Omelchenko and I.N. Sobirov). At first, the objects were found at the level that correlated with the first "treasure" from the "room with the painting" (i.e., the early medieval context)[25] (Mirzaakhmedov, Omelchenko et al. 2013: figs. 61, 62; Mirzaakhmedov, Omelchenko et al. 2016: fig. 47; Omelchenko, Kholov, Gorin and Sobirov, 2018: 9–14, figs. 26–30). However, most of them came from the special pits (βόθροι) in the lowest and earliest horizon in the area. This was supplemented by finds from a large (storage?) room in the southern sector of the "palace". Some of them were in the mudbrick box (*favissa*), while others were on the floor, apparently having fallen when carried. There were fragments of swords, daggers with volute-like and bar-shaped finals, knives, spears, three-bladed arrowheads and a quiver's hook, bone laths of a bow, parts of gorytos, armour plates and a shield boss (fig. 3.10).

Some artifacts were decorated with gold foil appliqués. Parts of belts, such as rivets, brackets, pendants, buttons, buckles, inserts etc. made from bone, shell (cowrie), silver, copper, iron and turquoise, are numerous. Of particular interest are a copper *phalera* similar to a cup with an ornament of acanthus leaves. A gold buckle (button?) with the image of a curled-up griffin was perhaps part of a scabbard. One fragment of a belt buckle was made of horn or steatite and decorated with gold nails.[26] Interestingly, an image was scratched on one of the cone-shaped bronze finals of the sword or dagger. It looks like the portrait on coins of King Hirkod, the founder of one of the domains in post-Hellenistic Sogdiana.

Some of the things from the pits might be related to equipment for a heavily armed rider, such as those shown on the famous Orlat belt plates in Samarkand Sogd. According to one version, they depict Kangju warriors (Pugachenkova 1989: 144, 153–54).

The rite of concealing of worn-out temple offerings in Paykend is similar to those in the Temple of Oxus in Bactria (Litvinsky 2001). The objects have parallels in the Xiongnu-Sarmatian, Saka and Tokhars (Eastern Sarmatians) complexes of the Eurasian steppe and in the vast territories from Han China, Afghanistan[27] and Central

---

23   This is the so-called external courtyard, to the south of the iwan and in front of the sanctuaries. It was excavated by I.K. Malkiel', A.V. Bekhter, N.D. Sobirov, T.G. Emelianenko and A.V. Omelchenko.

24   Olga A. Papakhristu, a leading expert in the iron and steel industry of Central Asia, believes that it is a forge for the manufacture of weapons.

25   There were many finds of iron knives and armour plates, as well as some copper tacks and two earrings (?) with inserts of turquoise and a bone belt plate.

26   A fragmented buckle of the same type was found by A.I. Naymark in the upper layers of the northern archer's corridor of the citadel.

27   Tillya Tepe.

Asia[28] to Altai, the South Urals and the Northern Black Sea region (Omelchenko 2020).

Semifinished products and remnants of metal-working were found along with weapons.

Great changes in the construction history and material culture of Paykend took place in the late 3rd–early 4th centuries. New investigations in the inner courtyard of the fire temple (excavations by S. Khujamov, G.P. Ivanov and A.V. Omelchenko) found that in the previous period, before the early medieval period, there was an iwan (portico) as well, but from another plan. It had two rows of wooden hexagonal columns. Stairs went up to the cella of the temple on both sides of the courtyard. There was a square adobe table (3.17 × 2.85 m, 27–41 cm high) coated with alabaster (*ganch*) (fig. 3.11b) in the middle part of the iwan. It was surrounded by *sufas*, coated with burnt bricks, some of which had *tamga* signs. These remains, as well as finds of traces of metals,[29] are associated with a passage in the "Chronology" of al-Bīrūnī. It describes Bukhara magicians who gathered in Paykend to celebrate the autumn holiday, Nak-h-Agam.

A room with a hearth was opened to the east of the courtyard (research by S. Khuzhamov and A.V. Kulish in 2019). Perhaps it was for temple servants (fig. 3.12a). Ceramics (figs. 3.12b and 3.12c) and a unique copper torch (total length 41 cm) with the remains of a wooden handle was found here. It was made from a reused antique furniture leg (fig. 3.12d).

The south-western sector of the citadel was added in the late 3rd–early 4th centuries CE. Excavations, which have been ongoing since 2005 (B. Abdullaev, A.I. Torgoev, A.N. Gorin, D.O. Kholov and A.V. Omelchenko), opened the garrison barracks of the fortress (fig. 3.14). It presents a complex of corridor with a comb-type layout that was built in a short period of time.[30] Every third room in the chain of chambers was a warehouse. The defense of the fortress in the sector was at least three-tiered: through the rooms' loopholes, through a parapet of valgang above them and through a parapet over the corridor.[31]

Finds from the barracks differ sharply from the previous ones (fig. 3.17).[32] It contains elements of the so-called Kushan-Sasanid complex (Omelchenko 2013: 116–17), which became widespread in the former lands of the Kushan state after their capture by the Sasanids (Zavyalov 2008: 194). Fundamental changes took place in coinage: in the territory of the Bukhara Oasis, from Varakhsha and Paykend (fig. 3.35: 4–12), copper imitations of Great Kushan coins and issues by Sasanid governors (rulers) were in circulation (Naymark 1995: 36–37, 46). The finds of bone pins with figured tops, spindle whorls made of marbled limestone and fragments of glass vessels are also indicative of this (fig. 3.18). At the same time, the influence of the Syr Darya seminomadic tribes is obvious.

In 2015–19 the south entrance to the citadel was investigated. It was divided into a labyrinth, protected by walls with slot-like loopholes (excavations by N.D. Sobirov), and the so-called corridor with high *sufas* (excavations by A.V. Omelchenko). The latter (0.9 m high) were convenient for unloading luggage from pack animals (fig. 3.13 left). Here, a second large fragment (40 × 45 cm) of a Paykend wall painting was found. There were images of three figures standing or walking shoulder to shoulder (fig. 3.16b). One has an object such as a torch or incense burner in his hand, the other holds a rod (mace?) and the third has his palm forward (Omelchenko 2016: fig. 19, 5). Along the central axis of the corridor (open to a length of 15 m), a *kubur* (clay pipe) line ran under the floor (fig. 3.13 right). Perhaps it is the oldest example of a drainage system using pipes in Sogd (Omelchenko, Kholov, Gorin, and Sobirov, 2018: 5–9, figs. 6–16).

Another entrance to the citadel (1.4 m wide) was unexpectedly discovered in the northwestern corner of the citadel (fig. 3.7b), between towers 1 and 2 (excavations by R.M. Toyirov). The gates were double and used in the administrative quarter near the fire temple.

After a not very long period of functioning as barracks, it was abandoned. Signs of desolation – washaways, sand deposits and the destruction of the adobe masonry – are obviously.

In summary, the new fortress (citadel) of Paykend was built as a stronghold for the Sasanid troops in the Bukhara

---

28 There are complexes from mounds in the north-east of the Bukhara and Samarkand oases, burial grounds in the Beshkent valley in Bactria, as well as monuments from the Middle Syrdarya and Khorezm during the 1st century BCE to the 1st–2nd centuries CE.

29 More than 20 unbroken daggers and knives were found on the floors and in the ash from the fire temple altars. In the external courtyard there were fragments of limited types of ceramics: bowls (or goblets), cauldrons, braziers and less often jugs. One hundred and ninety-nine unbroken small cups of a specific form were stacked and hidden in the corridor of the sanctuary, and one was near the stairs. Large numbers of wild (mainly boar) and domestic animal bones were found as well (Omelchenko 2013: 108).

30 The same layout was featured in the south-eastern section of the archer's corridor, which was partitioned into compartments with access to the common corridor.

31 This was reconstructed based on the holes from the floor beams in the walls and the remains of the fallen ceilings with big jars (*hum*s) from the second floor.

32 For example, tagora vases with twisted handles, which are not found in other regions of Sogdiana, appeared in the new pottery assemblage.

FIGURE 3.11 (a) Fire temple on the citadel of Paykend, plan, stages 3–4; (b) Courtyard of the fire temple, view from north-west; (c) "Palace", view from the north-east (2001); (d) "Palace", view from the south (2019)

FIGURE 3.12 (a) "Service room" between the fire temple and the "palace" (b) Goblet and hand-made caldron; (c) Copper torch from the detail of ancient furniture

FIGURE 3.13　Left: "Corridor with high *sufa* benches", level 4, the end of the 3rd–4th centuries CE: Clearing of fragments of mural painting (Dilmurad O. Kholov); right: Water pipe under floor (Larisa Yu. Kulakova)

FIGURE 3.14   Rooms of the garrison barracks, the end of the 3rd to the first third of the 4th centuries CE
DMITRY V. SADOFEEV

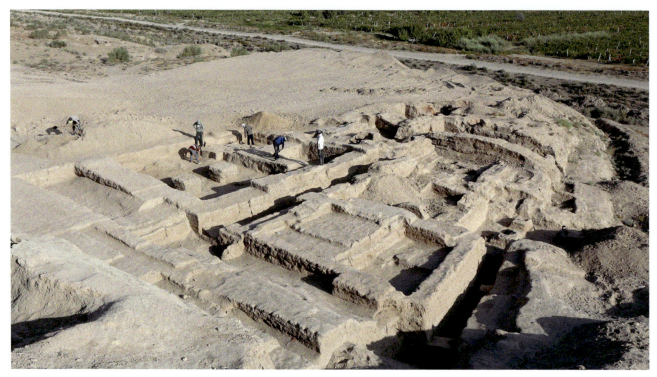

FIGURE 3.15 Top: Administrative quarter (2016); Bottom: Area in front of the citadel (2018)
ELBEK N. SOBIROV

FIGURE 3.16 (a) Mural paintings from the citadel of Paykend: "Burned corridor" in the south of the citadel, 6th–7th centuries CE; (b) "Corridor with high *sufa* benches", the end of the 3rd–4th centuries CE (drawing by Larisa Yu. Kulakova); (c) Courtyard of the fire temple, upper cultural layers

Oasis. This took place between the end of the 3rd and the beginning of the 4th century, when Shāpūr I expanded his empire "to the borders of Chach" (Tashkent Oasis). The fortress's decline might be explained by the movement of the Xionites (White Huns) to Transoxiana, who pushed the Iranian kings to the south (Omelchenko 2016: 85, 86).

Apparently, at the end of the 4th century the citadel underwent large-scale reconstruction. The barrack rooms were filled up with sands, covered with adobe brickwork and turned into a massive stylobate. The archer's corridor became fortification walls. And loopholes were left only in critical points, in particular at the southern entrance to the fortress, which had stayed in its previous position. The north-western gate was closed, a new entrance to the administrative quarter (2 m wide) was built in the western fortress wall (fig. 3.7c). Two towers (7 × 5 m) with slit-like loopholes arranged in a chequered manner were built to protect it (excavations by D.O. Kholov).

Part of the administrative quarter was also excavated and dated At the end of the 4th century and beginning of the 5th century CE (A.N. Gorin, A.V. Omelchenko and G.P. Ivanov). Nine rooms were connected by the covered streets "A" and "B" (figs. 3.2 and 3.15 top). As in the early medieval period, they apparently were inhabited by fire-temple servants, and they also stored supplies. The most interesting finds are the copper coin of Shapur I (the first archaeological find in Transoxiana), which became an ornament (fig. 3.35: 9), a coin minted in Khorezm (fig. 3.35: 13), a large faceted rock crystal bead and a semifinished glass product.[33]

Excavations at the area to the north of Paykend's citadel were resumed after a 25-year hiatus (figs. 3.2 and 3.15 bottom). Significant research is being carried out in its south-eastern corner (excavation no. 2, studies by E.N. Sobirov). A gate leading from the street into the quarter was found in the eastern wall. But the main street was the "military" highway passing directly by the fortress wall of the citadel. Its original width with sidewalks was about 10 m.

In the north-western corner of the site, excavations of the 1980s were brought to ground soil. The estimated

---

33 A terracotta figurine of the "Bukhara goddess" has the same chronology but was found in another place (fig. 3.24, 3).

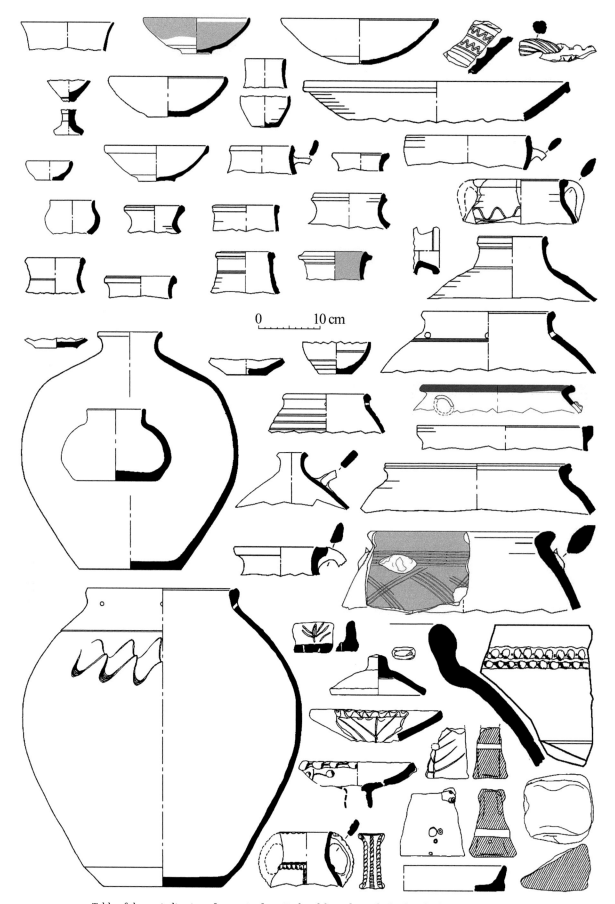

FIGURE 3.17   Table of the periodisation of ceramics from Paykend from the end of 3rd to the beginning of the 4th centuries CE

FIGURE 3.18 Artifacts from Paykend from the end of 3rd to the beginning 5th centuries CE. 1, 2, 3, 5–9, 11, 13, 14, 17–19, 21–25, 26–29 – barracks; 10, 12, 15, 16, 20, 25 – administrative quarter; 4 – area in front of the citadel, under fortification walls. 1, 2 – arrowheads; 3 – belt buckle; 4 – balance; 5 – button; 6–9, 12–14 – spindle whorls; 10 – chip; 15 – fragment of comb; 16–19 – hairpins; 20–28 – beads; 29 – earring; 1, 2 – iron; 3, 5 – silver; 4 – bronze, 6, 7 – marbleised limestone; 8–10 – clay; 11, 21, 23–26, 28 – glass; 12–19 – bone; 20 – rock crystal; 22 – agate (?); 27 – coral; 29 – silver and turquoise

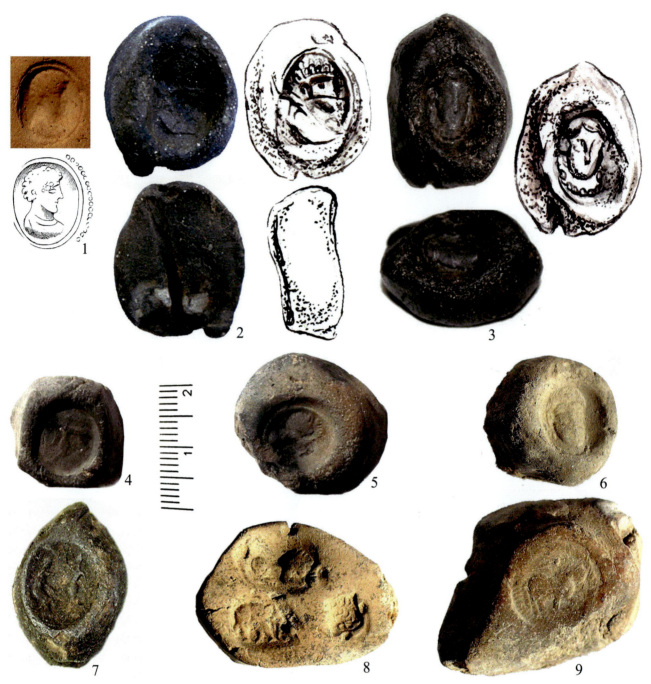

FIGURE 3.19   1 – Impress of a ring on a lid; 2–9 – bullae. 1–3 – barracks; 4–5 – courtyard of the fire temple; 6–9 – the "burned room" (corridor) in the south of the citadel

FIGURE 3.20 (a) Towers on the southern fortification wall of shahrestan 1; (b) Tower no. 2; (c and d) Towers of shahrestan 2 (photos from 2010 and 1939)

FIGURE 3.21   Shahrestan 1, the westward view

FIGURE 3.22 (a) Shahrestan 1, the eastward view; (b) Three-room dwelling unit in house no. 8; (c) House no. 8a (a "little hotel"), axonometry (drawing by A.V. Kulish); (d) House no. 1, axonometry (after G.L. Semenov, 2006); (e) House no. 1, living rooms with podiums and hearths

FIGURE 3.23   Clay frieze decorated with moulded floral motifs from house no. 1 in shahrestan 1

western fortification wall was not found, but the time of the initial stage of permanent occupation of the area was confirmed – between the end of the 4th century and the beginning of the 5th century CE. Thus, the area in front of the citadel is actually the earliest shahrestan in Paykend. It was formed when the territory of the administrative quarter on the citadel was no longer sufficient for all residents and so it grew beyond the wall of the fortress. Under the northern wall of the area, a unique find was made – shoulder scales of the late Roman type (fig. 3.18: 4). A terracotta figurine of a Zoroastrian deity – Verethragna or Srosh (fig. 3.24: 4) was found in the western sector.

Most of the structures discovered by new excavations in the area date to the early medieval era. There were mainly dwelling buildings in the quarters (figs. 3.2: 11; 3.15 bottom). Some of them had large halls with central pillars to support ceilings. Along with numerous copper coins, three Sasanid silver drachmas of Bahram V and Jamasp were found in the area. A humcha (large pitcher) with the Sogdian inscription "Vagivande" was found in one of the rooms (fig. 3.34: 1).

The history and time of construction of the palace in the citadel are debatable. New excavations (fig. 3.11d), apparently, date it to the second half of the 8th century

FIGURE 3.24 Terracotta figurines and decorations on pottery: 1, 4–7 – shahrestan 1; 2 – south suburb; 3 – citadel, area of the barracks, upper level

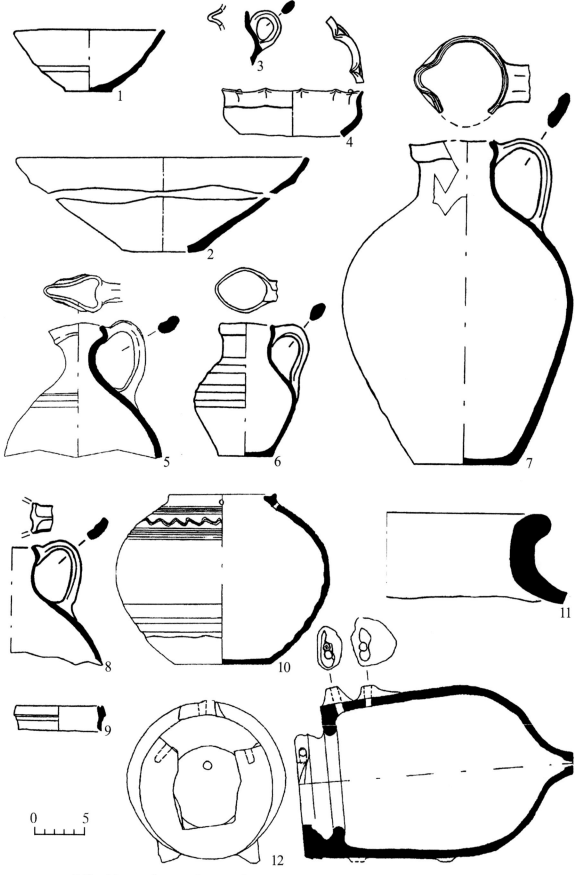

FIGURE 3.25   Table of the periodisation of ceramics from Paykend from the second half of the 8th century (after Saparov and Torgoev 2013)

FIGURE 3.26 (a) Underground bases of columns in the mosque, 10th century; (b) Minaret

FIGURE 3.27 (a) Streets of Paykend: "A", between the citadel and shahrestan 1; (b) "A", between shahrestan 1 and shahrestan 2, and southern entrance to the city; (c) "No. 2" in the south of the city
STANISLAV N. MAKEEV

FIGURE 3.28   (a) Shahrestan 2: the westward view; (b) The eastward view

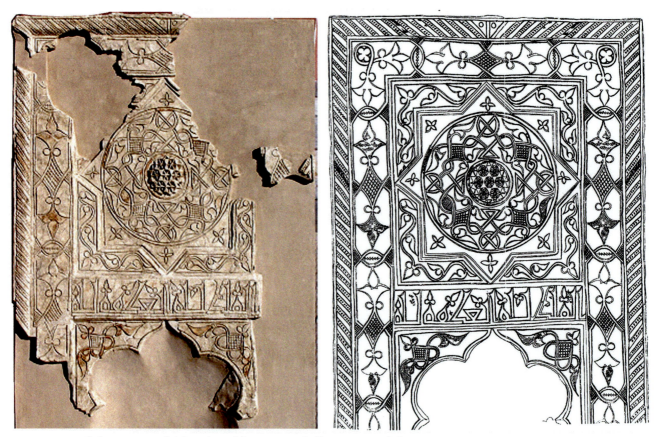

FIGURE 3.29   Shahrestan 2, ganch (plaster) panel from courtyard of house no. 9 in shahrestan 1
DRAWING BY ELENA P. STEPANOVA

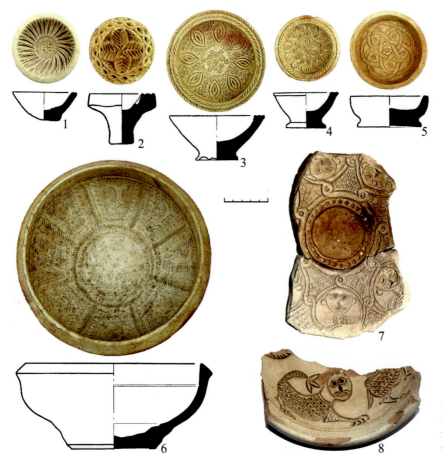

FIGURE 3.30
Kalybs (ceramic forms) from the 10th century:
1–6 – shahrestan 2, the dwelling house no. 8;
7–8 – shahrestan 2, city dump

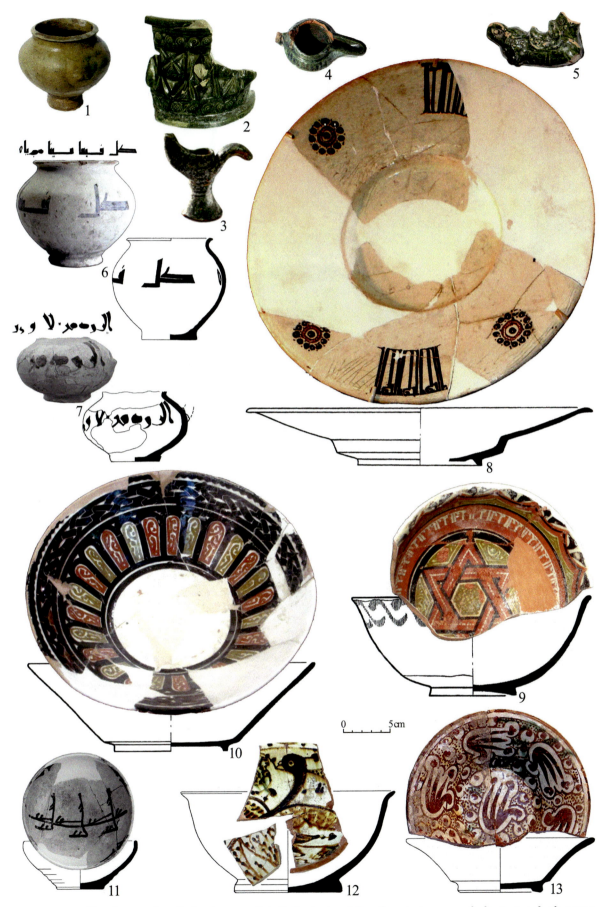

FIGURE 3.31   Glazed pottery from Paykend: 1–11 – 10th to the beginning of the 11th centuries; 12–13 – the beginning of 12th century

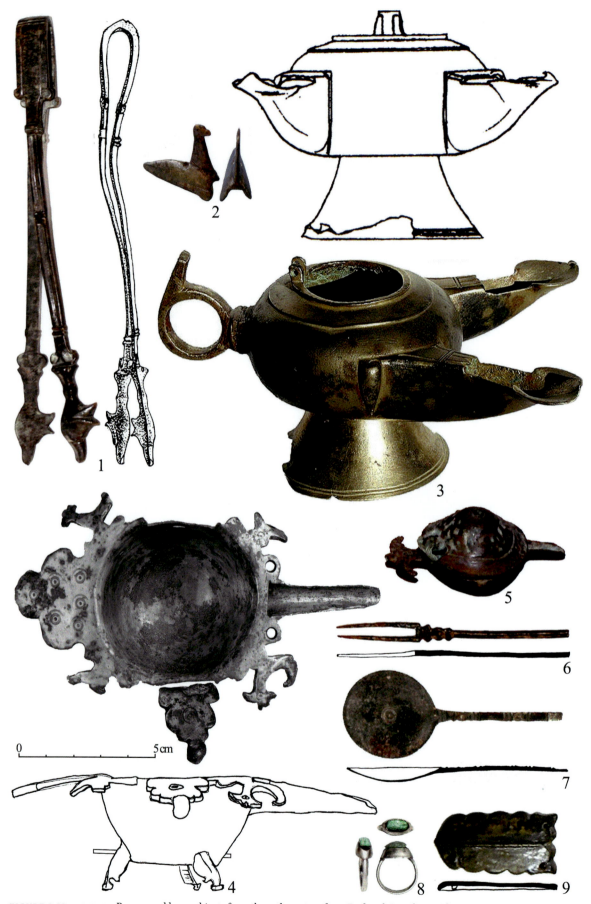

FIGURE 3.32 1–7, 9 – Bronze and brass objects from the 10th century from Paykend; 8 – silver with turquoise

FIGURE 3.33 (a) Southern suburb: the north-westward view; (b) The winter mosque; (c) Fragments of ganch (plaster) panel of a *mihrab* in the mosque (destruction layers); (d) Upper part of the ganch panel after reconstruction; (e) Lower part of the ganch panel *in situ*

(the proposition of A.V. Kulish). Perhaps the original function of the "palace" was as another temple for the city's entire Zoroastrian community.[34]

In 2015, ground-penetrating radar research was carried out in different sectors in all parts of the city/site (work by V.V. Andryushchenko). In particular, this showed that the administrative quarter extended to the 10th-century mosque in the south-western sector of the citadel. On its southern edge, radar survey showed a large structure with massive bases for columns. The 2019 excavations fully confirmed this. A ceramic assemblage from the late 7th to early 8th centuries was obtained from the levels of the adobe bases. One fragment was an ostracon with a Sogdian inscription (fig. 3.34: 3).

The underground structures of the mosque were studied as well. Remnants of a large building with pillar (an early mosque?) were found. Two ostraca were also found here. They had inscriptions the "Ahmad" and "Abu-Rahman" (fig. 3.34: 10, 11), made by an early Arab duct (style) (Mirzaakhmedov, Omelchenko et al. 2013: fig. 66, 4, 5). A treasure of 15 Bukhār Khudāh drachmas (imitations of the Sasanian Bahram V) was in the filling between the bases of the columns. They look like the coins in the "room with the painting" and date back to the beginning of the 8th century. (Baratova and Omelchenko 2013: 340–41).

The towers of the first southern fortification wall of shahrestan 1 became one of the most important discoveries of the expedition's latest years (excavations by E.N. Sobirov, A.I. Torgoev, N.D. Sobirov and S. Khuzhamov). As noted earlier, they were not visible in the relief, because they were "hidden" by late constructions. The towers (5.5–6 × 5.5 m wide) are sub-oval in shape, without internal rooms, and were built of pakhsa blocks and located at a distance of 12.5–13.5 m from each other (figs. 3.20a and 3.20b). The early fortress wall was made of adobe bricks and was 3 m wide. Then, as a result of periodic build-ups, they reached a thickness 8.5 m. The towers' form looks like towers in Sasanid Iran. In the body of the first fortification wall and towers only Kushan-Sasanid coins were found. Early medieval coins were in "shirts" (extensions) of the wall (Sobirov 2018: 49–50, figs. 127–29, 159, 7–13).

New studies of the western and eastern sectors of the residential quarter on shahrestan 1 were undertaken. In the west, in house no. 1, a 10th-century well was discovered (excavations by A.I. Torgoev). It is very interesting that before the construction of the house, there was a dugout with a *sufa* bench. The facility was part of a pottery workshop. According to the pottery and the coin of King Mavak found there (fig. 3.35: 16), this period is dated between the 5th century and the first half of the 6th century (Torgoev 2018: 41–42, figs. 102, 103). A treasure of almost 4,500 copper coins was found in the neighboring house, no 2. It is the largest one from the Early Middle Ages in the Bukhara Oasis. It dated back to the second quarter of the 8th century and mainly included local coinage; the main type is a king in a tiara on one side with a walking horse on the reverse side. Some coins from other domains in Central Asia (Samarkand, Kesh, Chach, Otrar, Khorezm), as well as early caliphate coins were present (fig. 3.35: 23–26, 39, 41, 42) (Torgoev, Mirzaakhmedov, and Kulish 2014). The distinctive pottery assemblage was identified (fig. 3.25) (Saparov and Torgoev 2013).

Excavations in the western sector of the residential quarter showed that starting at least from the middle of the 8th century, public buildings were located here. There was a canteen (*tandoor-khona*) and a hotel with a warehouse (Saparov and Omelchenko 2017). The latter was a four-room section, not typical for Paykend residential buildings. It had a kitchen at the entrance, a room for drinking wine and games and two sleeping rooms (figs. 3.22a and 3.22b). A large number of coins[35] and finds are unusual for a residential house. There was a cross made of stone, pieces of bitumen and lead, etc.

In one of the *tandoor* hearths in the canteen, located on the other side of the quarter, seven dirhams dated to the 8th century were brought to light in the 1980s (fig. 3.35: 44, 45).[36] Apparently, this was part of a sale because a receipt was found next to the coins. It had an inscription about selling a batch of furs for 5,000 coins (fig. 3.34: 9) (Kuleshov and Saparov 2016). In the same area, but in the layers of the previous building's horizon, a treasury of 29 copper coins of King Asbar was found (fig. 3.35: 17, 18) (Mirzaakhmedov, Omelchenko et al. 2016: figs. 116, 125–27).

Another unexpected discovery in the west of the quarter was a street under the earliest buildings. It ran parallel to the western fortification wall of shahrestan 1 and included a 2 m carriageway and sidewalks 0.6 and 0.9 m wide (Saparov 2018: 48, fig. 120).

The study of the southern suburb outside the Paykend walled city gate has been completed (fig. 3.33a). Excavations show that the entrance to the original caravanserai,

---

34   In the second half of the 1970s to the early 1980s. In the 8th century, the Bukhara Oasis was one of the areas where the Mukanna movement was present; a time when, according to al-Narshakhī, "[…] from the villages of Bukhara, many became disbelievers and openly showed disbelief" (al-Narshakhī 2011: 67).

35   The latest is the fals minted in 759/760.

36   The latest was minted in 782/783. The coins were identified by Vyach. S. Kuleshov.

FIGURE 3.34 Ostraka from Paykend: 1–7 – Sogdian; 8–12 – Arabic inscriptions

FIGURE 3.35 Coins from Paykend: 1–3, 14, 15, 27, 28, 44, 45 – silver; the rest are copper

FIGURE 3.36 (a) Bukhara Archaeological Expedition: Grigory L. Semenov and Igor K. Malkiel, the 1980s; (b) The 1980s; (c) Near the building of the future Paykend Museum (from left to right: Svenlana A. Malkiel, Larisa Yu. Kulakova, Tamara I. Zeimal, Shukhrat T. Adylov, Golib N. Kurbanov, Grigory L. Semenov, Robert V. Almeev); (d) At the opening of the southern city gate

FIGURE 3.37 (a) Bukhara Archaeological Expedition's field work, 2010–19: Aleksey N. Gorin and Dmitry V. Sadofeev; (b) Architectural measurements, Larisa Yu. Kulakova, Asan I. Torgoev, Ruslan M. Toirov; (c) Clearing of fragments of mural painting, Dilmurad O. Kholov; (d) Drawing of mural painting, Larisa Yu. Kulakova; (e) Clearing fragments of ganch *mihrab*, Raisa A. Kazimirova and Dilmurad O. Kholov

FIGURE 3.38 (a) Bukhara Archaeological Expedition's field laboratory work, 2010–19: Architects Larisa Yu. Kulakova and Siroj D. Mirzaakhmedov; (b) Djamal Mirzaakhmedov; (c) Clearing of iron weapons, Olga L. Semenova; (d) Sorting of copper coins from the hoard of 4,500 pieces (2013), Aleksey V. Kulish and Asan I. Torgoev; (e) Drawing pottery, Nazbergen J. Saparov and Asan I. Torgoev; (f and g) Restoration of the ganch panel from the southern suburb mosque, Raisa A. Kazimirova and Olga S. Viktorova

FIGURE 3.39 (a) The opening of the reconstructed Paykend Museum at the conference devoted to the 30th anniversary of the Bukhara Archaeological Expedition, the speaker is Robert V. Almeev (2011); (b) A tour of the Paykend Museum, director Normamat D. Sobirov; (c) Rooms of the museum

and later to the residential area, was issued by a *pischtak* (research by A.V. Kulish). There was a bath and laundry complex to the right of it. Later, apparently due to a lack of water, it changed its function. The winter mosque was built here (fig. 33b). It had a *mihrab* decorated with a carved and painted plaster panel (fig. 33c–e). A treasure of coins was found at the western end of the caravanserai, under the surrounding wall (excavations by S. Khuzhamov). It allows us to date the caravanserai to between the first half and the middle of the 9th century (Kulish and Khuzhamov 2019).

Thus, over the past decade, the Bukhara archaeological expedition team has done a lot of work related to the study of the history of Paykend (figs. 3.37 and 3.38). A number of previous archaeological objects with finalized excavations were preserved, some will be further investigated. The main work is now being carried out on the citadel and the area to the north of it. In the first case, it is necessary to establish the boundaries of the fortresses of the Hellenistic and "Kangju" periods, as well as to find out what the "palace" was and what the early medieval and late antique buildings were in the west of the fortress. The main southern entrance to the fortress from the early periods is awaiting excavation as well. We hope that research of the area in front of the citadel will help answer the questions about whether it was protected by a wall from all sides and how it was built.

Every season archaeological artifacts from the excavations are added the collection of the Bukhara State Architectural and Art Museum-Reserve and its branch – the Museum of the History of Paykend (Normamat D. Sobirov is the director). It was opened near the city/site in 2002 thanks to the efforts of G.L. Semenov and the former director of the Bukhara Museum, R.V. Almeev (fig. 3.39). Some exhibits, primarily those of iron weapons, artistic ceramics and carved plaster, would honour any large collection of antiquities. The Museum of the History of Paykend serves as an important local cultural centre, visited by both residents and foreign guests.

Research conducted by the Bukhara archaeological expedition in the Paykend city/site continues to this day. They bring to light new, interesting findings, thus expanding our knowledge of the history and culture of the Bukhara Oasis and Central Asia in general.

Abbreviation

MBAE *Materiali Bukharskoj Archeologičeskoj Expedizii.* Issues 1–14. Raskopki v Paykend e (2000–2005); Otchet o Raskopkah v Paykend e (2006–2018). [*Materials of Bukhara archaeological expedition.* Issues 1–14. Excavations in Paykend (2000–2005); Report on excavations in Paykend (2006–2018).] St. Petersburg: Publishing House of the State Hermitage Museum.

CHAPTER 4

Pottery

Gabriele Puschnigg and Jacopo Bruno

1 Introduction

This chapter presents an initial overview of the ceramic material found in the sites explored during the course of the MAFOUB project in the Bukhara Oasis. The archaeological work is still ongoing, as is the pottery analysis, so our assessments are preliminary but nonetheless present major typo-chronological features and technological variations of the pottery within the oasis. The chronological depth of the material as well as its spatial distribution allow us to gain important insights into the dynamics of economic and cultural development that have not been systematically studied yet.

For more than a decade the MAFOUB project conducted field work, including surveys and excavations, in the central and southern parts of the oasis (Rante and Mirzaakhmedov 2019). The surveys and excavations produced a large amount of ceramic material. Over this extended period, several teams worked on discrete parts of and individual topics related to this collection. Assemblages from surveys and the excavation of the "pottery quarter" at Paykend (trench E) were studied by a group of specialists from the National Centre for Scientific Research (CNRS) (Rante and Mirzaakhmedov 2019: 216). The goal of our study was to examine assemblages from the excavations of the private house in Paykend and other excavations in the oasis, including the Bukhara citadel, Kakishtuvan, Iskijkat, Ramitan and site 250. Apart from the authors of this report, our group included Anahita Mittertrainer (2016) and was supported in the field by Samara Broglia de Moura (2016), Anne-Salomé Daure (2017), Nolwenn Gilbert (2018) and Valentina Bruccoleri (2019).[1] In addition, Faith Vardy assisted our team as the draftsperson.

Along with our investigation a series of scientific analyses were initiated, which form part of a separate chapter (see Coquinot and Gandolfo in this volume). Due to this dynamic project structure, with major work still in progress, our research cannot reach the same depth across all fields but will focus on those areas and themes where our investigations are the furthest advanced. Our main aim is to outline the breadth and potential of the ceramic assemblage and to present specific aspects that shed light on chronological, technological and cultural developments in more detail.

Along with the chapter in this volume, a collection of digital resources is being developed (https://www.oeaw.ac.at/en/ifi/blog/detail/material-tales-from-the-land-behind-bukhara).

1.1 Research History
Previous research on the pottery in the oasis unfolded in conjunction with field projects and excavations, primarily out of the need for chronological assessments. The archaeological exploration of the Bukhara Oasis intensified over the course of the 20th century (Rante and Mirzaakhmedov 2019: 8). In the context of our study, earlier research at the city of Bukhara, Paykend and, to a lesser extent, Ramitan are of particular relevance.

1.1.1 Bukhara
The city of Bukhara was subject to extensive study, particularly its historical role and significance and its magnificent architecture (Rante and Mirzaakhmedov 2019: 252). With regard to ceramic studies, two publications are of special interest here. Mukhamedjanov, Mirzaakhmedov and Adylov (1982) established the periodisation of the pottery from the lower stratigraphic levels of various excavations at Bukhara, using data from trenches near the Madrese Mir-i-Arab and the domed Bazar of Toki-Tel'pak-Furushon in particular. This article is an important reference on early pottery in the area, although typological and technological developments are not represented in full due to the lack of assemblages large enough to reflect contemporary repertoires. Material from the Islamic period is discussed in Nekrasova's publication on the citadel of Bukhara (Nekrasova 1999).

1.1.2 Paykend
Paykend is one of the most intensely studied sites in the oasis (see also chapter 3 in this volume). Archaeological explorations, including surveys and initial excavations, had already begun in the second decade of the 20th century (Zimin 1915a and 1915b; Rante and Mirzaakhmedov 2019:8). During the 1930s, field work

---

1 We are also very grateful for the continued local assistance with washing the pottery.

continued under Shishkin (1940), and a first account of the pottery was published in 1949 (Rante and Mirzaakhmedov 2019). In the 1980s, excavations intensified and are still ongoing (Mukhamedjanov et al. 1988; Rante and Mirzaakhmedov 2019: 195–96; Mirzaakhmedov 2000; Semenov and Mirzaakhmedov 2007). The chronological range of the field work covers the entire development of the city, from the earliest levels up to the Islamic period, and pottery reports and ceramic studies are published on a regular basis (Semenov and Mirzaakhmedov 2007; Mirzaakhmedov and Omelchenko 2018; Omelchenko 2019). These publications provide important comparisons for our study, specifically regarding vessel forms and the overview of the chronological recurrence of pottery types. Together with the data from the MAFOUB excavations of the kiln sites, trench E at Paykend (Guionova 2013) provides a wealth of reference material for this study.

1.1.3 Ramitan

In 1972 a stratigraphic sounding was excavated by Suleimanov at the southern foot of the highest citadel in the middle of the square-shaped, fortified city (Suleimanov 1984; Rante and Mirzaakhmedov 2019: 267). Suleimanov illustrated a brief pottery sequence in his report based on his stratigraphic trench (Suleimanov 1984: 124), which represents the only ceramic material published from this site so far.

1.1.4 Iskijkat, Kakishtuvan and Site 250

These three sites are not documented in any previous publications, and no regular excavations were conducted there before the MAFOUB explorations.

Aside from individual site reports or specially themed articles, the comprehensive comparative study published by Koshelenko in the mid-1980s remains a highly useful companion for gaining an overview of the materials collected, earlier assessments and previous publications on material from within the boundaries of the oasis and its adjacent territories (Koshelenko 1985).

1.2 *Methodology*

Our work on the pottery began in 2016, after the MAFOUB program had already been running for several years. As a considerable part of the archaeological fieldwork had already been completed by this time, we had to adjust our research and tailor it to the existing research strategies and procedures undertaken by the ongoing excavations. The MAFOUB project aims to understand the long-term transformation of settlement patterns in the oasis in conjunction with changes to its water systems and the cultural developments that influenced life in the settlements and that are mirrored in the archaeological finds. In line with the enormous scale of this program, a large number of sites have been explored archaeologically, some for the first time. Excavations focused on six sites, including Iskijkat, Kakishtuvan, Paykend, Ramitan, site 250 and Bukhara. Initially, these sites were explored stratigraphically to understand their occupational histories. The stratigraphic investigations were conducted in the form of artificial trenches (mostly 5 × 5 m) passing through the entire depositional sequence of the sites. For an independent chronological assessment, charcoal samples were collected from the various levels for dating, which led to a series of C^{14} dates revealing refined chronological data for the development of settlements in the oasis.

Open area excavations, particularly at Paykend and Ramitan, aimed to clarify specific architectural developments, individual structures or urban quarters and focused on certain chronological periods.

The strategy for the ceramic study required an equally discerning approach.

All excavations progressed in single stratigraphic units, but the boundaries of the stratigraphic trenches did not cover the spatial extent of these units. As a consequence, archaeological deposits and structural features were sometimes partial. And this created a situation where we have parts of pottery assemblages – their actual proportions are undeterminable – and do not know how much of the original material we have and what part is missing. Accordingly, most of the pottery assemblages from the stratigraphic soundings are incomplete, leading to a severe truncation of the research potential of the collected pottery.

Excavations of individual structures, on the other hand, produced complete assemblages, which reflect the character of the deposit and facilitate more comprehensive analyses of the pottery assemblages.

Ceramic studies dealing with questions about chronological and cultural developments largely rely on comparing assemblages throughout the different phases of occupation within one excavation and/or across various excavations and sites, and comparison is most effective when conducted using fully quantified material in particular considering the fragmented state of the pottery. This method is, however, only applicable if complete assemblages are considered. For now, our data from complete assemblages is not large enough to merit a full quantitative statistical analysis. In the general evaluation of chronological variations, we use some quantitative comparisons for large vessel groups concerning their rim diameters and ware distribution in relation to the overall data. These descriptive statistics only refer to our sample assemblage.

TABLE 4.3 Rim eves (estimated vessel equivalents)

	Bukhara	Iskijkat	Kakishtuvan	Paykend	Ramitan	Site 250
Ch A	1.48	9.49	2.05		9.58	13.96
Ch B				9.47		
Ch C					9.79	
Ch D					4.39	
Ch F					6.50	
Ch G					7.15	
Total	**1.48**	**9.49**	**2.05**	**9.47**	**37.41**	**13.96**

2 Pottery Fabrics

At the start of our study, we differentiated between various fabric groups[2] according to colour variations in the break and distinct appearances of texture and inclusions. These differentiations proved to be partially unsubstantiated when it came to their petrographic composition (see Coquinot and Gandolfo in this volume), and we subsequently simplified our classification system. In contrast to the scientific fabric analysis, the aim of our grouping is to define easily recognisable features, which are subject to technological and chronological variations. Changes in the colouring of fabrics thus potentially indicate variations in the firing temperature and help to identify long-term developments in the oasis's ceramic industry. Differences in temper are also highly significant, but in some cases, they are not easily recognised in the field due to the lack of specialist equipment and expertise. For this reason, the combination of the fabric classification developed in the field and the results of chemical and petrographic analyses are all the more important. The scientific analyses are ongoing and further modifications to our system are likely to be implemented in the future.

Our current classification system[3] relies on criteria that can be identified by eye and the help of a 10× magnifying lens. These criteria include colour[4] (cores and margins of the fresh break and surfaces), hardness, characteristics of the fracture, type of inclusions and surface treatments. Nine main groups are currently recorded, encompassing six fine-ware and three coarse-ware groups. A few representative sherds were chosen for each fabric group, which were then stored and serve as a reference collection for our work.

2.1 Fine-ware Groups

Concerning fine ware, since no substantial petrographic variations have been detected to date, we mainly took into account the gradual change in colour related to firing conditions or temperature and observations concerning the texture of the fabric.

Fabric A
Classification: fine ware.
Reference sherds: Ia368/18 (a); Ib615/2 (b); RomD2009/7 (c); RomC554/2 (d).

Hard body, rough fracture and irregular texture. Sometimes smooth fracture and fine texture. Mainly fine to medium mineral inclusions. Inclusions are mostly white opaque (calcite?), moderately dense and of medium size. Dark opaque inclusions (sandy grits) are sparse. Low frequency of medium voids. The colour of the surfaces and breaks is usually red to reddish brown.

TABLE 4.4 Fabric A

Colour			Inclusions			
Colour	Red	Reddish brown		1	2	3
Core	2.5YR5/8	5YR6/4	Colour	White	Buff, grey, black	Voids
Margin	2.5YR5/8	5YR6/4				
Surface	2.5YR6/6	5YR6/6				
			Frequency	Moderate	Sparse	Sparse
			Size	0.5–2.0 mm	≤0.5 mm	≤0.5 mm
			Sorting	Fair	Good	Fair
			Shape	Sub-angular	Sub-angular	Rounded
			ID	Calcite	Sand	Air holes

---

2 Here, we follow the definition of "fabric" provided by Orton and Hughes (2013: 71) to describe the characteristics related to the clay matrix, inclusions, firing temperature and kiln atmosphere.
3 Orton and Hughes 2013: 71–89, 275–85. See also Priestman 2018.
4 Colour defined according to the "Munsell Soil Charts" (Rice 1987: 339–43; Orton and Hughes 2013: 73–74, 277).

POTTERY

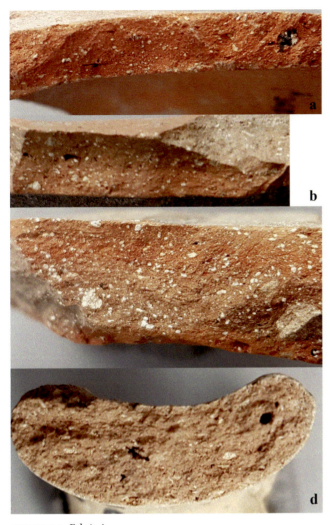

FIGURE 4.1 Fabric A
PHOTOS MAFOUB

FIGURE 4.2 Fabric A2
PHOTOS MAFOUB

TABLE 4.5 Fabric A2

Colour			Inclusions			
Colour	Red	Reddish yellow		1	2	3
Core	2.5YR4/8	5YR6/6	Colour	White	Transparent, dark	Voids
Margin	2.5YR4/8	5YR6/6				
Surface	2.5YR6/6	5YR6/5				
			Frequency	Sparse	Sparse	Sparse
			Size	≤5 mm	≤0.25 mm	0.5–2.0 mm
			Sorting	Good	Good	Fair
			Shape	Sub-angular	Sub-angular	Rounded
			ID	Calcite	Sand	Air holes

Comment: fine to medium porous fabric; mainly distinguished by the presence of white calcareous inclusions and by the red, reddish-brown colour of the break.

Fabric A2
Classification: fine ware.
Reference sherds: Ib614/1 (a); RomC550/7 (b); RomC550/6 (c).

Hard body, rough fracture and irregular texture. Sometimes very hard body, smooth fracture and fine texture. Mainly fine mineral inclusions. Sparse medium-size white opaque inclusions (calcite?), very fine transparent brilliant inclusions (mica?) and rare fine dark inclusions (sand?). Low frequency of medium voids. The colour of the surfaces and breaks is usually red to reddish yellow.

Comment: less numerous white inclusions and pores than A; white opaque and sandy inclusions; fracture smoother and finer than A.

Fabric A6
Classification: fine ware.
Reference sherds: Ib615/1 (a); RomC554/5 (b).

Hard body (sporadically very hard body), rough to smooth fracture and fine texture. Mainly fine mineral inclusions. Sparse fine white opaque inclusions (calcite?) and fine to very fine transparent brilliant inclusions (mica/sandy grits?). Low frequency of medium voids. The colour of the surfaces and breaks is usually reddish yellow. Sometimes a pale slip (self-slip) appears on the surface.

FIGURE 4.3 Fabric A6
PHOTOS MAFOUB

TABLE 4.6 Fabric A6

Colour		Inclusions			
Colour	Reddish yellow		1	2	3
Core	5YR6/6	Colour	White	Transparent	Voids
Margin	5YR6/6				
Surface	5YR6/6				
		Frequency	Sparse	Sparse	Sparse
		Size	≤5 mm	≤0.25 mm	≥0.5 mm
		Sorting	Good	Good	Fair
		Shape	Sub-angular	Flat	Rounded
		ID	Calcite	Sandy grits	Air holes

Comment: smoother fracture and finer texture than A2; more compact and homogeneous appearance; clear presence of sandy grits.

Fabric E
Classification: fine ware.
Reference sherds: RomD609/62 (a); RomD609/92 (b).

Hard body, rough fracture and fine texture with small, closely spaced irregularities. Inclusions not recognisable by eye, probably very fine mineral inclusions (sandy appearance of the fracture). Low frequency of fine to medium voids. Whitish to pinkish colour of surfaces and breaks.

FIGURE 4.4 Fabric E
PHOTOS MAFOUB

TABLE 4.7 Fabric E

Colour		Inclusions	
Colour	Very pale brown		1
Core	7.5YR8/2	Colour	Voids
Margin	7.5YR8/2		
Surface	7.5YR8/2		
		Frequency	Sparse
		Size	≤5 mm
		Sorting	Good
		Shape	Sub-rounded
		ID	Air holes

Comment: mainly distinguished by the colour and sandy appearance of the fracture.

Fabric F
Classification: fine ware.
Reference sherds: RomD609/17 (a); RomD609/42 (b).

Hard to very hard body, quite smooth fracture and texture. Sparse fine to very fine sandy inclusions and pores. Usually reddish yellow surfaces and breaks. Sometimes pale slip (self-slip) on the surface.

POTTERY

FIGURE 4.5 Fabric F
PHOTOS MAFOUB

TABLE 4.8 Fabric F

Colour		Inclusions		
Colour	Pink		1	2
Core	7.5YR8/4	Colour	White, red, black	Voids
Margin	7.5YR8/4			
Surface	10YR8/4			
		Frequency	Sparse	Moderate
		Size	≤2.5 mm	≤2.5 mm
		Sorting	Good	Good
		Shape	Sub-angular	Rounded
		ID	Sandy grits	Air holes

Comment: mainly distinguished by colour, hardness, texture and sandy inclusions; the inclusions stand out against the background of a compact texture when the fracture is observed with a magnifying glass.

Fabric I

Classification: fine ware.
Reference sherds: RomD604/4 (a); RomD609/67 (b).

Hard body, rough fracture and fine texture. Inclusions not recognisable by eye, probably very fine mineral inclusions (sandy appearance of the fracture). Low frequency of fine to medium voids. Pinkish colour of surfaces and breaks. Glazed surfaces.

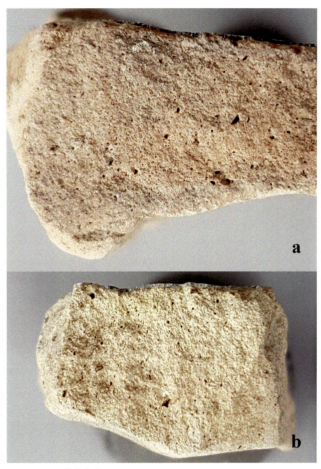

FIGURE 4.6 Fabric I
PHOTOS MAFOUB

TABLE 4.9 Fabric I

Colour		Inclusions	
Colour	Very pale brown		1
Core	10YR8/4	Colour	Void
Margin	10YR8/4		
Surface	10YR8/4		
		Frequency	Sparse
		Size	≤5 mm
		Sorting	Good
		Shape	Sub-rounded
		ID	Air holes

Comment: the glazed version of E.

2.2 Coarse-ware Groups

Regarding coarse wares, we distinguished between marked differences in texture and the appearance of temper, although our groupings are preliminary and are most likely subject to further modifications once scientific analyses and re-evaluation are completed. Some alterations to the original system can be traced in the individual comments.

Fabric CW1
Classification: coarse ware.
Reference sherds: RomG1939/13 (a); RomG1952/28 (b); RomG1952/24 (c); RomD613/41 (d).

Soft to hard body, hackly fracture, and irregular and coarse texture. Moderate coarse to very coarse temper and pores: sandy grits (quartz?), pebbles and white opaque inclusions (calcite?).

The colour of the surfaces and breaks is usually red to reddish brown. Sometimes a darker core (grey; GLEY 5/N) and margins. Frequently, traces of black soot on the surfaces.

TABLE 4.10 Fabric CW1

Colour		Inclusions			
			1	2	3
Core	2.5YR4/2	Colour	White	White, black, red	Voids
Margin	2.5YR6/6				
surface	7.5YR8/3				
		Frequency	Moderate	Moderate	moderate
		Size	≥1 mm	≥1 mm	≥1 mm
		Sorting	Poor	Poor	Poor
		Shape	Sub-angular	Angular	Rounded
		ID	Calcite	Sandy grits and pebbles	Air holes

Comment: defined primarily by the presence of pebbles and inclusion of sandy grits. CW2 merged with CW1.

Fabric CW3
Classification: coarse ware.
Reference sherds: RomC546/1 (a); RomC550/9 (b); RomC554/11 (c).

Soft to hard body, hackly and sometimes laminated fracture. Very brittle texture. Moderately coarse to very coarse temper and poorly sorted inclusions and pores: pebbles/sandy grits, grog (?), calcareous white inclusions (secondary calcite in the pores?) and traces of organic temper (straw?).

FIGURE 4.7 Fabric CW1
PHOTOS MAFOUB

FIGURE 4.8 Fabric CW2
PHOTOS MAFOUB

The colour of the surfaces and breaks is usually brown or pale brown. Sometimes a darker core (grey or dark grey; 10YR4/1–7.5YR4/1) and margins. Frequently, traces of black soot on the surfaces.

TABLE 4.11   Fabric CW3

Colour			Inclusions			
	Light brown	Pale brown		1	2	3
Core	7.5YR7/6	10YR6/3	Colour	White	White, black, red	Voids
Margin	7.5YR7/6	7.5YR5/6				
Surface	7.5YR8/4	7.5YR8/3				
			Frequency	Moderate	Moderate	Moderate
			Size	≥1 mm	≥1 mm	≥1 mm
			Sorting	Poor	Very poor	Poor
			Shape	Sub-angular	Angular	Rounded and flat
			ID	Calcite	Sandy grits (and grog?)	Air holes (and straw?)

Comment: CW3, CW4 and CW5 were merged into one group: very coarse and brittle fabric with various coarse inclusions.

Fabric CW7
Classification: coarse ware.
Reference sherds: RomC522/6 (a); RomC515/17 (b); RomC515/6 (c).

Body quite hard, coarse fracture and irregular to hackly texture. Mainly coarse mineral inclusions/temper (sandy grits and pebbles) and white opaque fine inclusions (calcite?). The colour of the surfaces and breaks is usually grey to greyish brown. The surfaces are often covered with dark soot.

FIGURE 4.9   Fabric CW7
PHOTOS MAFOUB

TABLE 4.12   Fabric CW7

Colour		Inclusions			
	Grey		1	2	3
Core	10YR5/1	Colour	White	White, red, black	Voids
Margin	10YR5/1				
Surface	10YR5/3				
		Frequency	Sparse	Sparse	Moderate
		Size	≤5 mm	≥1 mm	≥1 mm
		Sorting	Good	Poor	Poor
		Shape	Rounded	Angular/sub-angular	Rounded
		ID	Calcite	Sandy grits and pebbles	Air holes

Comment: CW6 was merged with CW7.

2.3   *Preliminary Observations*

Definitions of the fine-ware groups primarily rely on differentiations in colouring and texture, so there are hardly any clear-cut boundaries between groups. Specifically, as far as the colouring is concerned, ceramic sherds occasionally display ambivalent characteristics and could be assigned to either of two similar, adjacent tones. Sustained changes in fabric colour occur over a long period of time and are often gradual leading to an overlap between certain fabric groups. Fabric A6 is thus often close in appearance to fabric F. A progressive development might be traced from

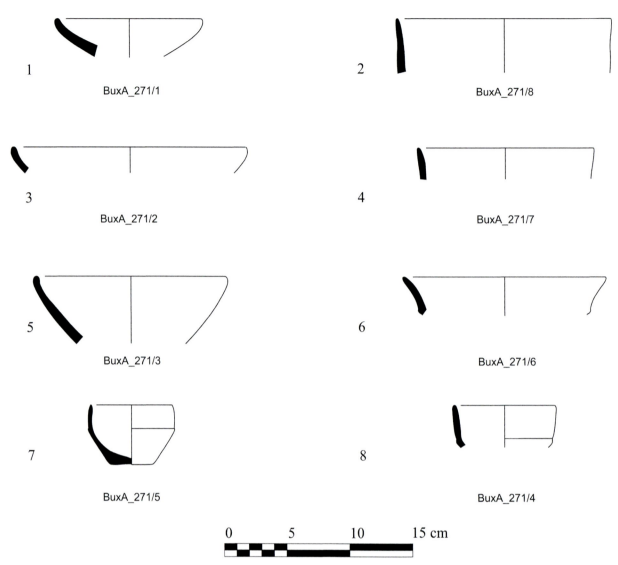

FIGURE 4.13 Bukhara, trench A. Examples of pottery from 3rd-century BCE deposits
DRAWINGS JACOPO BRUNO

FIGURE 4.14 Bukhara, trench A. Small goblet with traces of red slip on the lower body profile
PHOTO MAFOUB

3.2 *Iskijkat*

The site occupies a mound in the central part of the oasis near the modern village of Pushemon (Rante and Mirzaakhmedov 2019: 231–32). Two stratigraphic trenches were opened at Iskijkat. The first one, trench A, is located in a central elevated part and enabled us to explore the complete stratigraphic sequence of the settlement (Rante and Mirzaakhmedov 2019: 234). This trench reached layers that were dated by C^{14} to the 3rd to 2nd centuries BCE, which together with the evidence from the Bukhara citadel reveals the earliest securely dated occupation within the oasis so far (Rante and Mirzaakhmedov 2019: 234). Throughout its individual stratigraphic units, trench A reflected various cycles of occupation and destruction, growing more substantial and significant in the phase between the 1st century BCE and the 3rd century CE (Rante and Mirzaakhmedov 2019: 234). Later occupational phases appear to be less dense, though frequent constructional changes were documented in the upper levels throughout the 7th to 9th centuries and up to the abandonment of the site in the Timurid period (Rante and Mirzaakhmedov 2019: 234–36).

A second trench, trench B, targeted the boundary of the shahrestan, which against original expectations was not secured by a rampart (Rante and Mirzaakhmedov 2019: 236). Consequently, trench B progressed as a step trench along the slope of the mound (Rante and Mirzaakhmedov 2019: 237, fig. 204). At its deepest levels, deposits in trench B showed parallels with the earliest occupational traces of trench A, suggesting a considerably large settlement area at this initial stage (Rante and Mirzaakhmedov 2019: 236). The occupational cycles generally followed a pattern similar to trench A and end in the Islamic period (Rante and Mirzaakhmedov 2019: 238).

Material from the deepest occupational levels from Iskijkat (trench A) and Bukhara (trench A) provide insight into the earliest pottery production and repertoires of the oasis. Due to the limited volume of the assemblages, however, our assessments have to remain preliminary for now.

Trench A

As stated above, our time restrictions did not allow us to process all the material. Following the approach devised for our pottery study, we prioritised assemblages from deposits that were scientifically dated or were adjacent to securely dated stratigraphic units. Altogether 22 assemblages were recorded. Pottery from the earliest deposits in this trench provided evidence for this initial phase in the ceramic production and use within the Bukhara Oasis. On the other hand, the quality of this evidence is inconsistent, as it only represents a small section of the contemporary repertoire. Overall, the material is considerably fragmented, and no complete vessels could be reconstructed, although individual specimens show major parts of the vessel profiles. Moreover, some of the shapes are well-known (Filanovich 1983, 33 fig. 8; Lyonnet 2000, 80 figs. 1–3), so that the extant parts can easily be associated with specific pottery types. The earliest assemblages (US392 and US384) contain specimens of goblets with a foot, necked jars, and hand-made storage jars, as well as coarse-ware vessels, which unfortunately were only present in body sherds. Some of the fragments showed lines of dark slip paint, while others were entirely covered with a thin black slip. Carinated goblets and associated base shapes were missing from the later assemblages. Pottery sequences from stratigraphic soundings are not easy to understand since the outlook on the chronological development of structures and materials is so narrow. Layers and structural elements are revealed only in random parts and often their function or architectural dynamics cannot be comprehensively interpreted. Without this background information, however, it is difficult in some instances to assess the chronological relationship of different ware groups or vessel types independently, specifically since the fragmented material often shows traces of wear. Some of the ceramic shapes found in contexts scientifically dated to the 7th century CE and later might thus belong to the ceramic production of the 3rd or 4th century CE.

Trench B

Only six assemblages from the early occupation levels of trench B were studied for a brief comparison with material from trench A. The respective deposits were dated with C^{14} to the 1st century CE (Rante and Mirzaakhmedov 2019: 238). In general, the assemblages are similar to those of trench A, deriving from occupational activities, albeit from secondary contexts. Ceramics from this trench reflected a composition of tableware, storage vessels and coarse ware similar to that of the corresponding levels in trench A. Some tableware fragments, specifically closed forms, were covered with black or occasionally brown slip. In one instance, red slip was applied to part of the vessel.

3.2.1 Iskijkat, Trench A

Phase scientifically dated	Date inferred through stratigraphic position in relation to scientifically dated deposits	Assemblage related to phase
C^{14}, 3rd/2nd–1st centuries BCE		US392
C^{14}, 3rd/2nd–1st centuries BCE		US384
	1st century BCE–1st century CE	US378
	1st century BCE–1st century CE	US377
	1st century BCE–1st century CE	US375
C^{14}, 2nd–3rd centuries CE		US371
C^{14}, 2nd–3rd centuries CE		US370
C^{14}, 2nd–3rd centuries CE		US368
C^{14}, 2nd–3rd centuries CE		US354
	4th century CE	US341
	4th century CE	US338

(cont.)

Phase scientifically dated	Date inferred through stratigraphic position in relation to scientifically dated deposits	Assemblage related to phase
	4th century CE	US336
	7th–9th centuries CE	US312
	7th–9th centuries CE	US321
	7th–9th centuries CE	US316
	7th–9th centuries CE	US304
	7th–9th centuries CE	US296
	10th century CE	US292
C¹⁴, 11th–12th centuries CE		US265
C¹⁴, 11th–12th centuries CE		US253
	13th–early 14th centuries CE	US216
TL, 13th–early 14th centuries CE		US225

3.2.1.1 3rd/2nd–1st Centuries BCE

Material from the earliest deposits at Iskijkat, trench A, display a variety of different pottery traditions. Most of the pottery was highly fragmented, although some pieces, such as the upper part of a goblet (fig. 4.15.1), were better preserved than others. It is thus possible that the ceramic forms were originally produced at different periods and do not reflect a contemporary repertoire.

As the goblet is missing its base, it is not possible to determine the associated shape, although fragments and the complete specimen of a foot shape (figs. 4.16.2–3) were also found in these early deposits. Aside from the goblet, open forms were not present in these early assemblages. Closed forms, on the other hand, are more diverse. Necked vessels show an everted, thickened rim (figs. 4.15.2–3). One larger jar, probably for storage, is neckless with a broad groove on the rim top, probably to fit a lid (fig. 4.15.4).

Surface treatments range from incised lines to trickling patterns of slip paint or a slip coating of substantial vessel parts or entire surfaces (figs. 4.16.5–7). Incised decoration includes horizontal straight or wavy lines and individual arrangements resembling a hash (figs. 4.16.4 and 4.16.6).

Fabrics fall into fine and coarse wares. Fine wares are fired to a reddish (2.5YR5/8) or rose (5YR6/6) colouring.

Rim shapes: R018, R035, R037, R039.
Base shapes: BA01, BA09.
Surface treatments: red wash, dark/black slip, trickling slip paint, incised decoration.
Fabric groups: A, A6; CW3.

3.2.1.2 1st Century BCE–1st Century CE

Assemblages from deposits dated within this time period also show the distinct pottery traditions of the previous phase, but differences are noticeable in the variety of vessel forms. Goblets were not encountered in these levels,

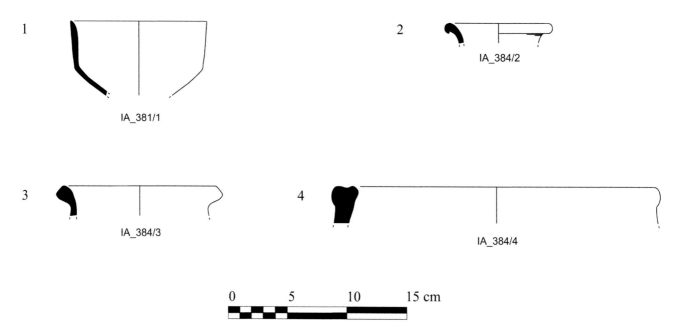

FIGURE 4.15 Iskijkat, trench A. Examples of pottery from deposits from the 3rd/2nd–1st centuries BCE
DRAWINGS FAITH VARDY

FIGURE 4.16 Iskijkat, trench A. Examples of pottery from deposits from the 3rd/2nd–1st centuries BCE
PHOTOS MAFOUB

although such observations need to be evaluated with care, since some fragments of small open forms (e.g., fig. 4.17.2) might have broken above the potential carination. Small open forms include shallow bowls and deeper varieties (figs. 4.17.1 and 4.17.3). Jar shapes occurred in tableware, such as a neckless jar with a thickened rim, and in cooking ware, including a whole-mouth jar (fig. 4.17.8). The necked jars with everted rims continued to be part of the material in these deposits. Vessel bases generally appear to be flat (figs. 4.17.5–6).

Surface treatments were similar to the pottery from the previous levels. Many fragments and rims were covered with black, sometimes purple, shiny slip, but there were occasional sherds covered with red slip, too. Jar bases and body sherds often displayed patterns of drizzling slip paint.

One specimen showed vertical burnishing (fig. 4.17.2). Incised decoration only occurred in the form of individual horizontal lines.

Fabrics largely continued in the same range as previously, without any further evidence for coarse ware fabric CW3. Fine wares mostly showed reddish fabrics (2.5YR5/8, 5YR6/6). The exterior surface of vessels was occasionally of a light creamy tone (7.5YR8/3), which most probably derives from the wet finishing of the surface (self-slip) and does not involve the coating of the vessel. Coarse-ware fabrics were similar to the fine wares, only with a much coarser temper.

Rim shapes: R001, R004, R007, R035, R038, R056, R064, R065, R066.
Base shapes: BA04, BA05.
Surface treatments: red wash, red slip, dark/black slip, dark/purple shining slip, trickling slip paint, incised decoration, burnished decoration.
Fabric groups: A, A6; CW1.

3.2.1.3 2nd–3rd Centuries CE

Excavated deposits from this period brought to light a number of rich pottery assemblages. These still broadly reflect the different composite elements observed in the preceding levels, although some changes and innovations are noticeable.

Concerning ceramic shapes, new types of medium open forms occurred. In particular, medium-sized bowls with a waisted profile appeared in the assemblages (figs. 4.18.1–7), and bowls with upright rims also featured occasionally (fig. 4.18.10). Some open forms might have also served as lids (fig. 4.18.9). The necked jars with everted rims, by contrast, decrease sharply. A single specimen of a coarser shape was recorded (fig. 4.19.3). The shape of jars with narrow necks seems to change gradually. Jars show short or longer necks and thickened rims (figs. 4.19.4 and 4.19.6). There is also a variety of neckless jars with externally thickened rims (fig. 4.19.5), some of them lid-seated. Similar jars were already observed in the preceding assemblages. For the first time the shape of a flask (gourd) occurred in this phase. The specimen was relatively large, with a rim diameter of 20 to 21 cm (fig. 4.19.7). Such forms are not frequent but are widespread throughout Central Asia. In the Bukhara Oasis, similar flasks are documented from Kyzylkyr-1 and Setalak 2 (Filanovich 1983: 33, fig. 8.16; 41; 59, fig. 19.15–16, 28). Chronologically, the deposits where the MAFOUB flasks occur all dated to the 2nd to 3rd and 4th centuries CE (see the Catalogue), roughly corresponding with the dates proposed for the Kyzylkyr and Setalak sites (Filanovich 1983: 112–15).

Most vessels apparently had flat bases, some slightly recessed and some with protruding profiles. One fragment of a pedestal base or foot was also recorded.

Surface treatments continued in the same fashion as with pottery from the preceding levels, including slip coating, trickling slip-painted patterns, and simple incised lines. However, slip-coated vessels displayed a larger colour variety. Open forms in particular showed a change in the slip's colouring. This relates to variations in the firing atmosphere due to the different locations inside the kiln where the pottery and bowls were stacked. Vessels coated with red slip were less frequent. Body and base fragments of different sized jars were often decorated with trickling slip paint.

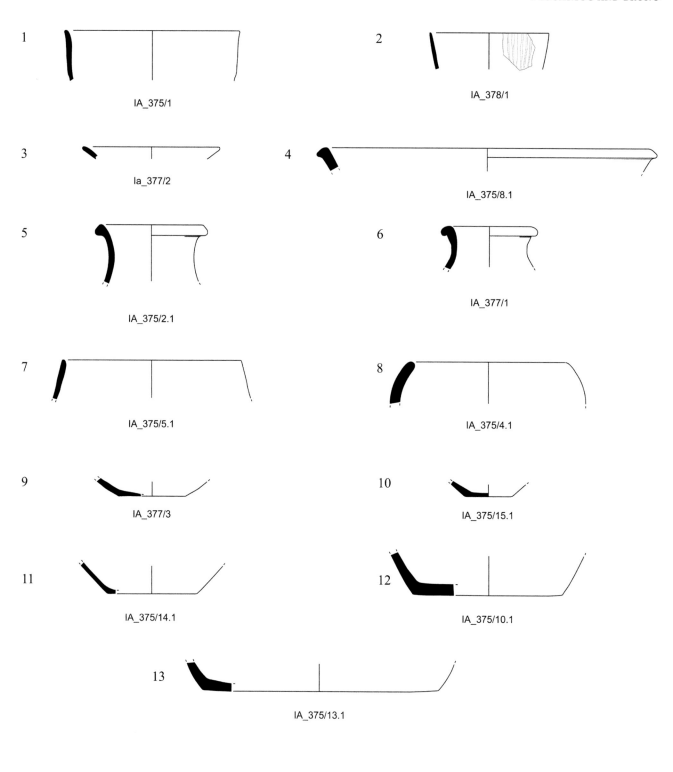

FIGURE 4.17 Iskijkat, trench A. Examples of pottery from deposits from 1st century BCE–1st century CE
DRAWINGS FAITH VARDY AND JACOPO BRUNO

Among the fabrics, reddish colours (5YR6/6) on the body still predominated. Some vessels showed a light surface colour. Coarse wares were mostly hand-made, occasionally showing some very coarse temper.

Rim shapes: R006, R008, R009, R010, R033, R034, R036, R040, R041, R041.1, R042, R043, R060, R075, R079.

Base shapes: BA01, BA04, BA05, BA07, BA09.1, BA10, BA11.
Surface treatment: red wash, red slip, dark/black slip, dark/purple slip, dark red to black coating, brown coating, grey coating; trickling slip-painted patterns, incised decoration, scratch marks.
Fabric groups: A, A6, E, F; CW1, CW3.

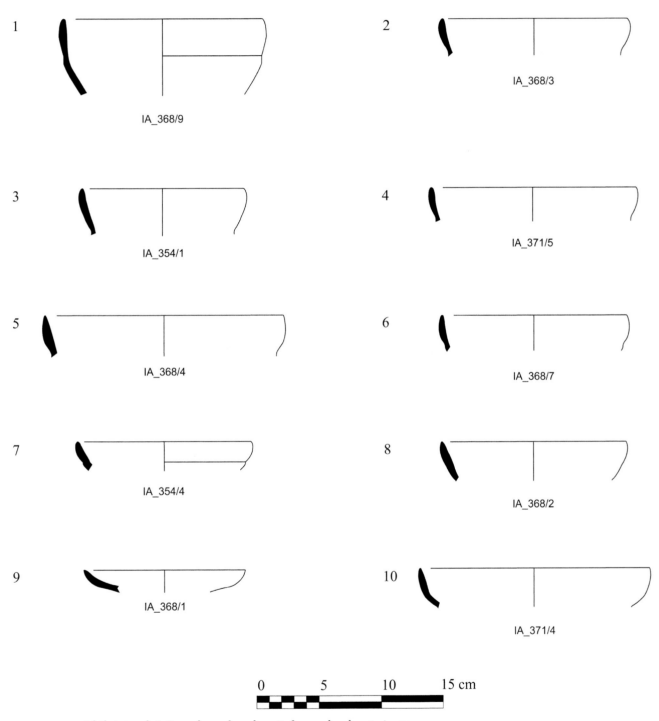

FIGURE 4.18 Iskijkat, trench A. Open shapes from deposits from 2nd–3rd centuries CE
DRAWINGS JACOPO BRUNO

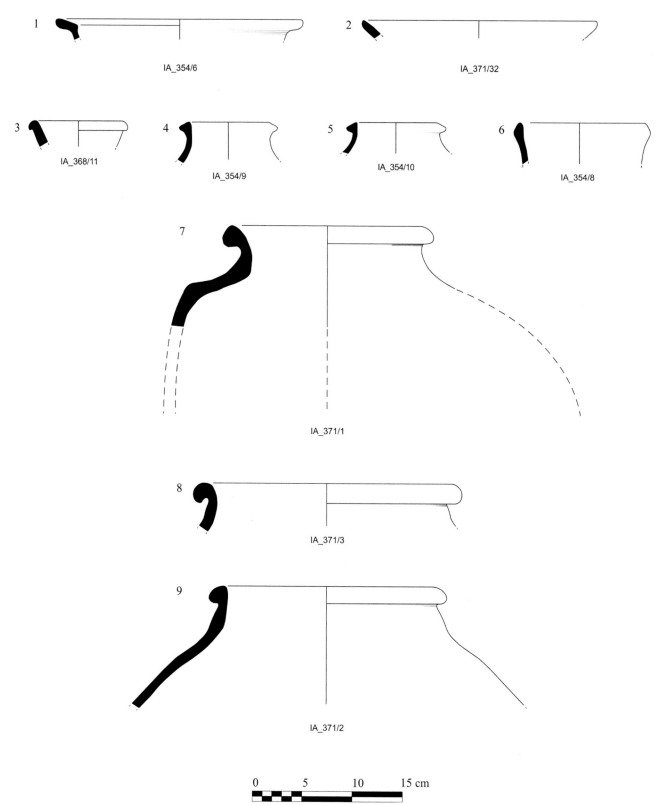

FIGURE 4.19   Iskijkat, trench A. Examples of pottery from deposits from 2nd–3rd centuries CE
DRAWINGS FAITH VARDY

3.2.1.4 4th Century CE

Few assemblages fall into this date range. The general impression is that little changes in the pottery production or that most of the ceramic fragments are residual and belong to previous periods.

The only shape not previously documented is a shallow hand-made coarse-ware dish or pan (fig. 4.20.5).

Most other ceramic shapes are already known. Some of the fragments from medium-sized open bowls might have broken just above a possible carination.

Surface treatments and fabric range also remain largely unchanged.

Rim shapes: R006, R008, R010, R037, R041, R041.1.
Base shapes: BA04, BA05, BA08.
Surface treatments: dark brown slip, red slip, black slip, slip-painted decoration, incised lines.
Fabric groups: A, A2, A6, F; CW1, CW3.

3.2.1.5 7th–9th Centuries CE

Material from deposits from the 7th to 9th centuries CE is more substantial and shows a number of vessel shapes not recorded in earlier phases at Iskijkat, some of which may nonetheless be residual. Apart from various bowls with flaring straight walls, a new goblet shape with a curving profile

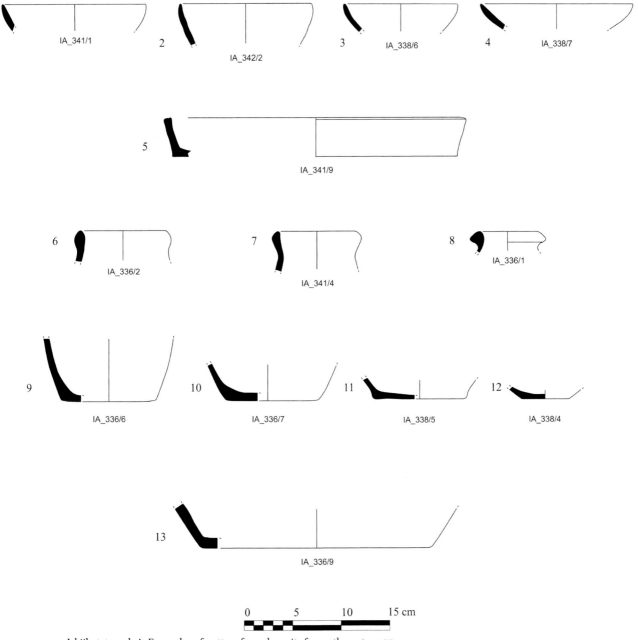

FIGURE 4.20 Iskijkat, trench A. Examples of pottery from deposits from 4th century CE
DRAWINGS FAITH VARDY

Phase scientifically dated	Date inferred through stratigraphic position in relation to scientifically dated deposits	Assemblage related to phase
C^{14}, 1st century CE		US609
C^{14}, 1st century CE		US610
C^{14}, 1st century CE		US613
C^{14}, 1st century CE		US614
C^{14}, 1st century CE		US615
C^{14}, 1st century CE		US616

All the assemblages are from deposits dated between the 1st century BCE and the 1st century CE.

3.2.2.1 1st Century BCE–1st Century CE

Pottery shapes and surface treatments (fig. 4.24) closely correspond with the ceramic evidence from contemporary layers of trench A (cf. figs. 4.17 and 4.18). Necked jars are covered with dark or black slip. One body sherd illustrates a partly slip-coated vessel.

As diagnostic sherds are not yet recorded in detail, but only photographed, no summary list on shape codes, surface treatments or fabrics is provided here.

FIGURE 4.24
Iskijkat, trench B. Selected fragments from deposits from the 1st century BCE to the 1st century CE
PHOTOS MAFOUB

3.3 Kakishtuvan

Excavations at Kakishtuvan were limited to a single stratigraphic trench, trench A, located at the citadel, and this was used to explore the site's stratigraphic sequence (Rante and Mirzaakhmedov 2019: 240). The occupational sequence begins in the 1st century CE and continues until early Islamic times (Rante and Mirzaakhmedov 2019: 242–45). Assemblages from trench A were only selectively processed, covering 18 deposits from the 1st to the 6th century CE. Chronological changes in surface treatments and shape roughly correspond with observations from other sites.

3.3.1 Kakishtuvan, Trench A

Assemblages from this trench were generally small, providing only a truncated picture of the variety of pottery used at this site over time.

Phase scientifically dated	Date inferred through stratigraphic position in relation to scientifically dated deposits	Assemblage related to phase
	1st century CE	US301
	1st century CE	US302
	2nd–3rd centuries CE	US291
	2nd–3rd centuries CE	US292
	2nd–3rd centuries CE	US296
	2nd–3rd centuries CE	US297
C^{14}, 2nd–3rd centuries CE		US299
C^{14}, 2nd–3rd centuries CE		US300
	3rd–4th centuries CE	US263
	3rd–4th centuries CE	US267
	3rd–4th centuries CE	US285
	3rd–4th centuries CE	US286
	3rd–4th centuries CE	US287
	5th century CE	US227
	5th century CE	US229
	6th century CE	US172
	6th century CE	US173
	6th century CE	US174

3.3.1.1 1st Century CE

The sparse collection of pottery from deposits dated to this period contained only a few diagnostic sherds (figs. 4.25.1–2). Nevertheless, they illustrate a range of wares and surface treatments similar to material from contemporary deposits from Iskijkat. The rim fragment of an open form covered with slip shows a change in colouring, from black around the rim to reddish brown on the body (fig. 4.26.1). This typically results from the way, in which such open forms are stacked inside the kiln during the firing process. Other fragments were covered with black or red slip, and the body sherd of a storage vessel displays the well-known trickling pattern of slip paint (fig. 4.26.3). Interestingly, one of the assemblages contains part of a handle with a bean-shaped section (fig. 4.25.2). Vessel forms with handles appear to be comparatively scant in early deposits

FIGURE 4.25 Kakishtuvan, trench A. Examples of pottery from deposits from 1st century CE
DRAWINGS JACOPO BRUNO

at other sites in the oasis, such as in Iskijkat or Ramitan, though this might still be related to the relatively small volume of material from deposits dating from the 1st century CE. The handle fragment shows a light cream surface, which derives from the finishing of the vessel and subsequent firing process rather than a separately applied slip (fig. 4.26.4).

Fine-ware fabrics show a reddish colour (5YR6/6). One coarse-ware fabric was found.[7]

Rim shapes: R026.
Handle shape: H01SC01.
Surface treatments: red slip, black slip, pale brown slip, trickling patterns of slip paint.
Fabric groups: A, A6; CW3.

FIGURE 4.26 Kakishtuvan, trench A. Examples of pottery from deposits from 1st century CE
PHOTOS MAFOUB

---

7 Again, coarse-ware fabrics require some re-examination once their petrographic analyses are completed.

3.3.1.2 *2nd–3rd Centuries CE*

Assemblages related to this period are a bit more substantial in volume, but there are still only a few fragments that are diagnostic and indicative of vessel shapes. Apart from open forms analogous to the previous period (figs. 4.27.1–2), the rim fragment of a necked jar with an everted rim and the rim and neck of a flask[8] or bottle shape illustrate some closed forms (figs. 4.27.3–4).

The body sherd of a coarse-ware vessel shows traces of what appears most probably to be a ledge handle. Surface treatments remain much the same as in the previous period. One specimen displayed a horizontal groove.

Fabric groups also largely continued as in the previous period.

Rim shape: R006, R026, R035, R053.
Surface treatments: red slip, black slip, pale brown slip, trickling patterns of slip paint, horizontal groove.
Fabric groups: A, A6; CW3.

3.3.1.3 *3rd–4th Centuries CE*

Material is equally scant from this period's deposits. One open and one closed form, a jug, are documented in the assemblages (figs. 4.28.1–2). The jug shows the same type of handle shape as that from the 1st-century CE deposits (fig. 4.28.1 and fig. 4.29.1; cf. also fig. 25.2).

Fragments of vessel bases show a flat shape.

---

8 Flasks are comparatively rare shapes in the MAFOUB assemblages. The body profile of R053 is not preserved. It is possible, however, that the form was similar to R033, which represents a flask with an asymmetric body form – one side is flat, while the other is rounded (see Catalogue).

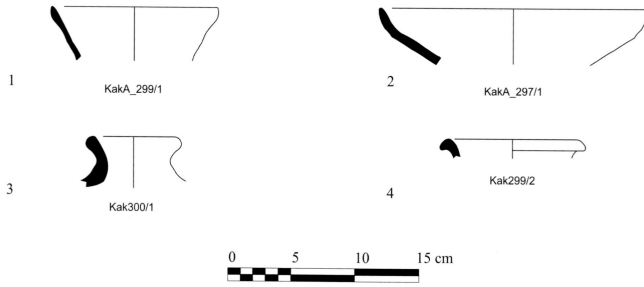

FIGURE 4.27   Kakishtuvan, trench A. Examples of pottery from deposits from 2nd–3rd centuries CE
DRAWINGS JACOPO BRUNO

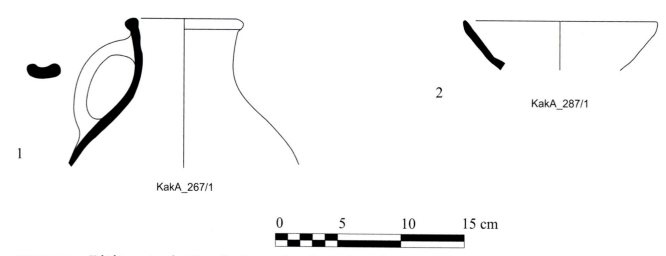

FIGURE 4.28   Kakishtuvan, trench A. Examples of pottery from deposits from 3rd–4th centuries CE
DRAWINGS JACOPO BRUNO

Decorative patterns and surface treatments include a variety of slips that are reddish, pale brown (fig. 4.29.1) and brown to black, as well as slip paint in combination with some hash-shaped incised patterns, probably a mark (fig. 4.29.2). The slips indicate a greater variation in colouring than in the previous phases.

Apart from the usual reddish colour (5YR6/6), fine-ware fabrics now include more pale brown to cream tones (7.5YR8/2). Coarse wares appear to be made of the same fabric as fine wares, just with a coarser temper.

FIGURE 4.29   Kakishtuvan, trench A. Slip-painted jug and marked base
PHOTOS MAFOUB

Rim shape: R025, R051.
Base shape: BA04.
Handle shape: H01SC01.
Surface treatments: reddish, pale brown and brown slip, trickling pattern of slip paint, incised decoration.
Fabric groups: A, A6; CW1.

3.3.1.4 5th–6th Centuries CE

Assemblages associated with this period are again few and small, so we combine both centuries here.

The material from our collection illustrates both old and new elements (figs. 4.30.1–4). Due to the sparsity of the pottery and the lack of complete assemblages, it is difficult to assess whether the shapes that appear to be new in this phase are contemporary with the deposits in which they were found or whether they were already in use earlier but merely by chance were missing from assemblages of the previous phases.

Only closed vessel forms are represented, which is most certainly related to the small amount of material. Rim fragments derive from necked vessels, and one of them, a jug (fig. 4.30.2), has the identical shape as one from the previous periods, though the handle section differs and shows an irregular oval instead of a bean shape. Two sherds illustrate various forms of storage jars (figs. 4.30.3–4). Base shapes are again flat.

Surface treatments include slip coatings in black, red, or brownish tones. Sometimes the slip appears to be very thin, so it could possibly be described as a wash. The strong abrasion on some fragments, however, hampers any strict definition. Trickling patterns of slip paint are still present on storage jar fragments, although in a very pale version.

Light brown to beige fired fabrics dominate the assemblages, although storage jar fragments still show the red colour from previous phases. Coarse wares are again a coarsely tempered version of the fine wares.

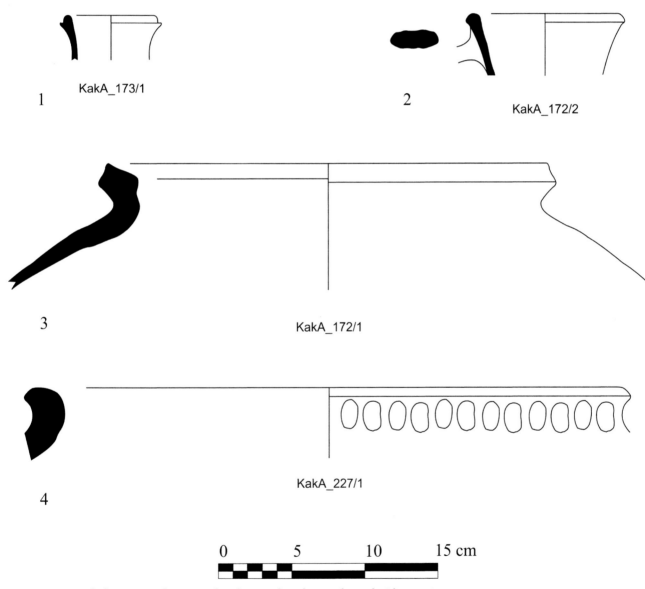

FIGURE 4.30 Kakishtuvan, trench A. Examples of pottery from deposits from 5th–6th centuries CE
DRAWINGS JACOPO BRUNO

Rim shape: R045, R050, R051.
Base shape: BA04, BA05.
Handle shape: H01SC04.
Surface treatment: red wash, pale brown to dark brown slip, trickling pattern of slip paint, horizontal rib or ridge.
Fabric Groups: A, A6, F; CW1.

3.4 *Paykend*

Assemblages from Paykend relate to excavations of the private dwelling, trench B, situated in shahrestan 1. This domestic structure covered a long occupational sequence beginning in the late 4th century CE and lasting into the 12th century CE (Rante and Mirzaakhmedov 2019: 208–14). The phases represented in the processed ceramic assemblages start with phase 2 and reach phase 7. Material associated with the 7th–9th-century and 10th–12th-century contexts are particularly well represented. Aside from Ramitan G, trench B in Paykend provided the largest volume of complete assemblages from the recent excavations. They were related to various types of deposits, such as infillings, make-up layers and surfaces. Based on their archaeological properties, these deposits resembled those from Ramitan G, but on average they contained more pottery. All 17 processed assemblages provided diagnostic fragments, of which the rim sherds amounted to 9.47 eves. This difference in ceramic volume by deposit between Paykend B and Ramitan G might relate to variations in the formation of the individual consecutive phases, as well as the distinct functions of the buildings and/or differences in the social status of the occupants. The trench B dwelling seems to represent a wealthy household (Rante and Mirzaakhmedov 2019: 208).

Paykend is one of the most extensively explored sites in the oasis. Separate from activities of other international teams around the urban architecture, MAFOUB opened an area of the potters' workshops, trench E, which functioned from the transition of the 8th to 9th centuries CE onwards (Rante and Mirzaakhmedov 2019: 226). A sequence of potter's wheels, kilns and waste pits were excavated that extend into the 14th to 15th centuries CE (Rante and Mirzaakhmedov 2019: 226). The ceramics from these kiln sites have been examined in separated studies (Guionova et al. 2013; Guionova, Dieulefet, and Mangiaracina 2014) and affords us with a rich pool of comparative material, facilitating a thorough typological and chronological evaluation.

3.4.1 Paykend, Trench B

Phase scientifically dated	Date inferred through stratigraphic position in relation to scientifically dated deposits	Assemblage related to stratigraphic phase	Corresponding architectural phase
	5th century CE	US5189	Phase 2
	5th century CE	US5199	Phase 2
	5th–6th centuries CE	US5188	Phase 2
	6th century CE	US5177	Phase 3
	8th century CE	US5104	Phase 3
	8th century CE	US5165	Phase 3
	8th century CE	US5170	Phase 3
	7th–8th centuries CE	US5251	Phase 4
	8th–9th centuries CE	US5156	Phase 4
	8th–9th centuries CE	US5157	Phase 4
	10th century CE	US3852	Phase 5
	10th century CE	US5112	Phase 5
	10th century CE	US5130	Phase 5
	10th–11th centuries CE	US1632	Phase 6
	10th–11th centuries CE	US1635	Phase 6
	10th–11th centuries CE	US1685	Phase 6
	10th century CE	US698	Phase 7

3.4.1.1 *5th–6th Centuries CE*

The ceramic material is related to phase 2 and the beginning of phase 3 at the dwelling excavated in trench B and corresponds to the occupation during the pre-Islamic period[9] (Rante and Mirzaakhmedov 2019: 208). The selected contexts (US5177, US5188, US5189, US5199) yielded a few types of rim shapes that were only related to closed vessel forms. These are hole-mouth jars (see Catalogue R069.1, R069.2; figs. 4.31.1–2) with externally thickened, collared and lid-seated rims and jugs or jars with short necks and externally thickened (R103; fig. 4.31.5) or moulded rims (R045; figs. 4.31.3–4). One of the hole-mouth jars shows traces of dark sediment or soot on the inner surface and therefore might have been used as a cooking vessel. Moreover, similar traces appear on the breaks, which are probably related to post-depositional effects. Bases are generally flat (BA004; figs. 4.31.6–9) with a rough and sometimes sandy bottom. The very worn and abraded fragment of a foot (fig. 4.31.10) was found in US5188. Handles fall into two

---

9 Unfortunately, no material from phase 1 was processed during the mission.

main types: rod (H03) and strap (H01). Surfaces treatments and embellishments are almost absent in the assemblages and are mainly restricted to incised decoration.

The pottery is predominantly made of fine-ware fabrics fired to reddish yellow (5YR6/6) and beige (7.5YR8/4) tones.

Rim shapes: R045, R069.1, R069.2, R103.
Base shapes: BA04.
Handle shapes: H01SC04, H01SC05, H01SC06, H03SC03, H03SC04.
Surface treatments: horizontal and wavy incised lines and grooves, red wash.
Fabric groups: A6, F.

3.4.1.2   7th–9th Centuries CE

Assemblages associated with this period belong to phases 3 and 4 of the dwelling (US5104, US5156, US5157, US5165, US5170, US5251), which correspond to the transition between the pre-Islamic and Islamic occupation of the area (Rante and Mirzaakhmedov 2019: 208). As in the preceding period, most of the vessels are related to closed shapes, mainly jugs and jars, with only a few sherds from open forms. The hole-mouth jar with a lid-seated rim is identical in shape and incised decoration to a corresponding specimen in one of the previous phases (R069.2; fig. 4.32.2). One of the fragments belonged to a small, solid, flat lid (R061.1; fig. 4.32.7). The sherd of a large storage jar (R062; fig. 4.32.1) shows a short neck with a row of

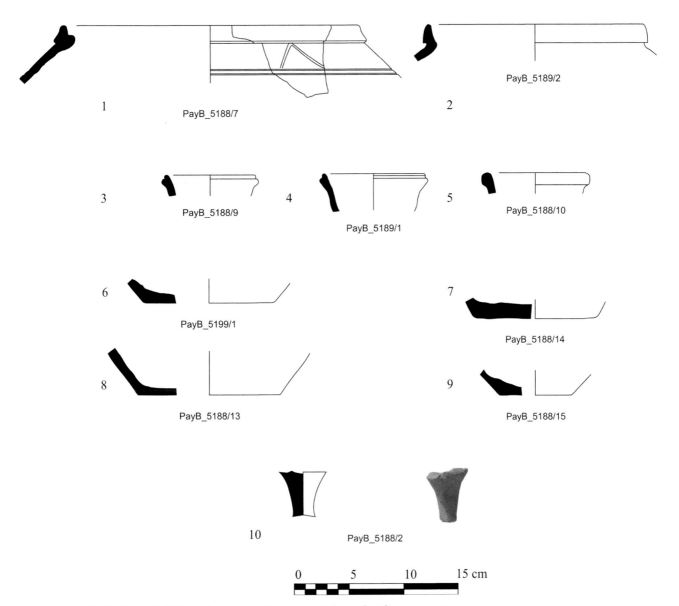

FIGURE 4.31   Paykend, trench B. Examples of pottery from deposits from 5th–6th centuries CE
DRAWINGS JACOPO BRUNO

impressions and an upright rim with traces of slip-painted decoration. Fragments of open shapes (figs. 4.32.8–9) represent two different types of bowls or cups with straight flaring walls and simple (R001) or slightly everted (R001.1) rims. Both forms are well attested elsewhere in the oasis. Flat bases with a rough and sandy bottom occur frequently in the assemblages. Many body sherds show lightly incised horizontal lines, which probably reflect traces of the process of shaping or finishing the vessel on the potter's wheel, while deep horizontal or wavy incised lines are used as decoration, mainly on vessels' necks and shoulders.

The fabrics are identical to those of the previous period, mostly fired to a reddish colour, with only one specimen of coarse ware.

Rim shapes: R001, R001.1, R028, R041.1, R041.2, R043, R051, R061.1, R062, R069.2, R079, R098.
Base shapes: BA04, BA05, BA15.
Handle shapes: H01SC06.
Surface treatments: horizontal and wavy grooves, trickling pattern of slip paint.
Fabric groups: A, A6, E, F; CW1.

3.4.1.3 10th–12th Centuries CE

Material associated with this period, phases 5 to 7 of the Islamic dwelling, is quite rich (US698, US1632, US1635, US1685, US3852, US5112, US5130) (Rante and Mirzaakhmedov 2019: 211–14). Some characteristics from previous phases persevere, while many others, especially

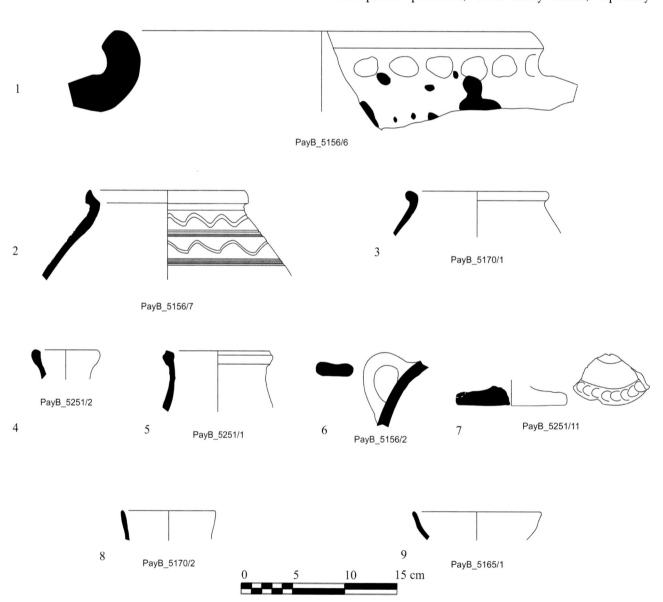

FIGURE 4.32   Paykend, trench B. Examples of pottery from deposits from 7th–9th centuries CE
DRAWINGS JACOPO BRUNO

POTTERY 123

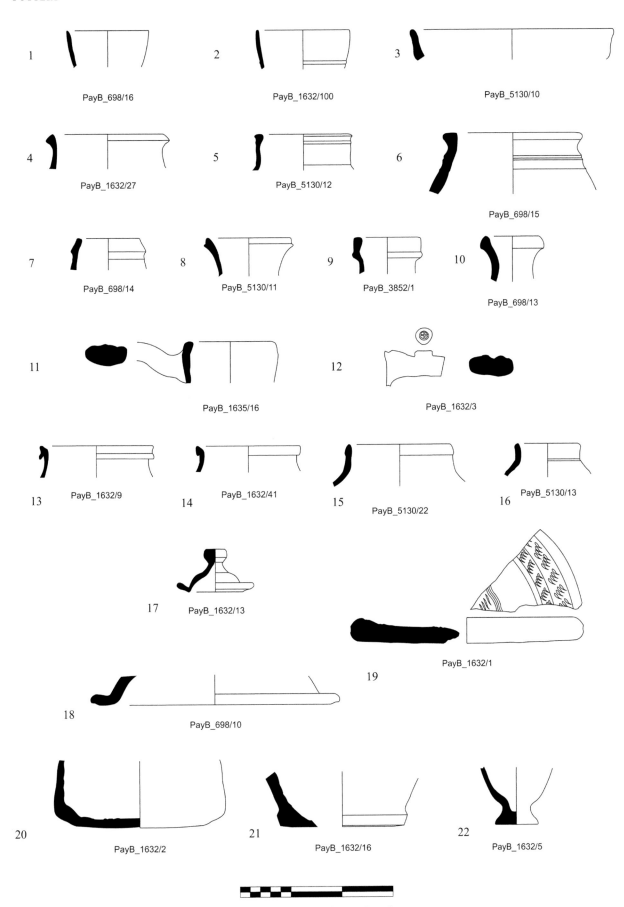

FIGURE 4.33   Paykend, trench B. Examples of pottery from deposits from 10th–12th centuries CE
DRAWINGS JACOPO BRUNO

new vessel forms and new surface treatments, appear for the first time during this period. As for the shapes, there are some that were already attested in the deposits from the 7th to 9th (R001, R028, R041.1, R041.2, R051, R061.1) and 5th to 6th centuries CE (R045), but many others are new. These innovations mainly concern closed shapes, medium and small jars and jugs (figs. 4.33.1–22), while open forms are restricted to a few common types of bowls (figs. 4.33.1 and 4.33.3). Related to these new vessel forms, different types of bases developed, which are not attested previously (figs. 4.33.20–22). Other novel elements include flat and domed lid shapes (R061, R061.1, R088, R088.1; figs. 4.33.17–19). Lids were already attested in the assemblages from the 7th to 9th centuries CE (R061.1) but now appear to grow more common and increasingly elaborate in shape and decoration. Furthermore, while some are still wheel-made or shaped by hand, there are also mould-made specimens (cf. fig. 4.34.7). Handles are mostly similar to those from previous periods, with rod and strap handles vertically attached to the necks and shoulders of the vessels, but a new shape of handle formed by two parallel rods with a circular section, (fig. 4.33.12; see also Catalogue) a thumb-stop knob and applied decoration appear in these assemblages. Fresh elements also emerge in surface treatments, which are generally more widespread in this period. The use of horizontal and wavy incised lines continues from the previous phases, but now many closed shapes are decorated with more complex combed and stamped patterns, especially on vessels' necks and shoulders (figs. 4.34.4–5). Furthermore, polychrome and monochrome glazed-ware specimens appear that were not previously attested in the contexts of trench B. A few body sherds show traces of abraded coating with a green to yellow glaze. Slightly more often, polychrome ware occurs mostly with fragments of bowls (R001, R007, R007.1, R011), showing black and red motifs on a white background under clear glaze (figs. 4.34.1–3).

The fabrics used in the production of the pottery only slightly vary from the preceding phases. New elements in this regard include fabrics I and CW7.

Rim shapes: R001, R007, R007.1, R011, R028, R031, R038, R040.1, R041.1, R041.2, R042, R044, R045, R051, R055, R060, R061, R061.1, R070, R075, R076, R077, R080, R083, R088, R088.1, R093, R099.
Base shapes: BA04, BA05, BA07, BA08, BA09.3, BA11, BA12, BA16, BA17.
Handle shapes: H01SC03, H01SC04, H03SC04, H03SC05, H04SC02.

Surface treatments: glaze, horizontal and wavy grooves, slip paint, combed decoration, moulded decoration, applied decoration, stamped decoration.
Fabric groups: A, A2, A6, E, F, I; CW1, CW7.

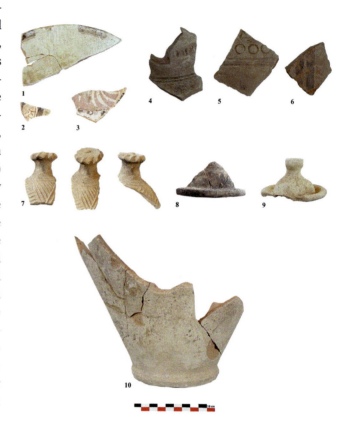

FIGURE 4.34   Paykend, trench B. Examples of pottery from deposits from 10th–12th centuries CE
PHOTOS MAFOUB

3.5 Ramitan

The urban site of Ramitan was subject to comprehensive archaeological explorations under MAFOUB. Three stratigraphic soundings were opened in different parts of the town, including the citadel, trench A, the shahrestan, trench C, and the western suburb, trench F (Rante and Mirzaakhmedov 2019: 150). Apart from these stratigraphic trenches, distinct architectural complexes and areas within the city were examined through further excavations. These focused on the citadel and its palace, trench D (Rante and Mirzaakhmedov 2019: 158–74), and fortifications, trenches B and E (Rante and Mirzaakhmedov 2019: 174–83), as well as parts of structures that appear to have served commercial functions in the suburb, trench G (Rante and Mirzaakhmedov 2019: 183–92). Of these excavations, those of the palace, trench D, and the commercial quarter, trench G, produced complete assemblages, although many were either secondary and thus chronologically mixed or very small. Specifically, assemblages from Ramitan G either contained mostly storage jar fragments or were so small that no significant amount of tableware was represented. Nevertheless, they help to elucidate a few specific habits in the city's building tradition and use of materials. On the other hand, the stratigraphic soundings provided largely incomplete assemblages that were not fully quantified but served as a reference collection for understanding typological and technological developments over time. While initial phases of the palace and the commercial quarter dated to the 3rd to 4th centuries CE and 5th to 6th centuries CE respectively, the stratigraphic sounding on the square citadel, trench A, showed an earlier architectural phase at Ramitan that dated to the 1st century CE[10] (Rante and Mirzaakhmedov 2019: 226).

A comparatively large proportion of the excavated material was processed and recorded, affording us with a strong basis for comparative studies. Trenches A and C provide insight into the earlier pottery repertoires, beginning with deposits from the 1st and 2nd centuries CE, while excavations in trenches D and G included later material, up to the 13th and 14th centuries CE. Early material from the stratigraphic soundings is thus chronologically comparable to that of Iskijkat, while the pottery from later levels, specifically the 5th century onwards, better corresponds with Paykend and site 250.

3.5.1 Ramitan, Trench A

Deposits from trench A are associated with the constructional sequence and development of the city's earliest rampart and parts of its towers (Rante and Mirzaakhmedov 2019: 150–51). Overall, 16 assemblages were processed from trench A. Again, these generally derived from secondary deposits, though in some instances specific functional aspects might have been preserved, which due to the truncated nature of the evidence unfortunately cannot be completely clarified. One specific context was especially rich in large open forms (some of these shapes could have also served as lids, see 4.4.2.2.1) that so far have not occurred in any of the other excavations. Different assemblages, however, show parallels with corresponding occupational levels at other sites.

---

10   According to the excavators, the earliest human occupation of the area of Ramitan took place around the 3rd–2nd centuries BCE, as showed by TL analysis on some fragments found out of context (Rante and Mirzaakhmedov 2019: 62–65, 156).

Phase scientifically dated	Date inferred through stratigraphic position in relation to scientifically dated deposits	Assemblage related to stratigraphic phase
	1st–early 3rd centuries CE	US148
	1st–early 3rd centuries CE	US153
	1st–early 3rd centuries CE	US147
	1st–early 3rd centuries CE	US150
		US151
	1st–early 3rd centuries CE	US154
	1st–early 3rd centuries CE	US163
	3rd century CE	US126=131
	3rd century CE	US133
	3rd century CE	US134
		US140
		US144
	3rd century CE	US202
	3rd–4th centuries CE	US204
	3rd–4th centuries CE	US128
	3rd–4th centuries CE	US130

3.5.1.1 *1st–early 3rd Centuries CE*

One large assemblage (US148) dominates the collection of ceramics recorded from deposits dated to this period. A considerable amount (2.77 rim eves) of large open bowls and basins occurred in US148 (fig. 4.35). The basins range from over 30 to 45 cm in rim diameter and most have a rough exterior surface, which sometimes looks as if the vessel was coated with a sandy slip on the outside or put on a sand surface for drying. Some show a rather careless shaping process and are probably made from moulds (figs. 4.36 and 4.68). This density of open forms in one deposit is striking and might reflect a specific function associated with the original assemblage. Basins of this type have not been recorded elsewhere in the MAFOUB excavations so far. US144 also contained a number of these basins (0.70 rim eves). Aside from the large open forms, assemblages included a number of neckless jars with upright, simple or externally thickened rims, or with everted dropping rims. Base shapes are mainly flat or slightly recessed, especially in open forms.

Few of the vessel fragments show a pale slip (10YR8/3) on the surface. A small group of fragments is decorated with trickling patterns of slip paint.

Few coarse wares occurred in the assemblages, two of them appear to be coarsely tempered versions of the usual fine-ware fabrics.

Rim shapes: R020, R021, R022, R023, R024, R041.1, R047, R055, R056, R058.
Base shapes: BA01, BA04.
Surface treatments: pale slip, trickling pattern of slip paint.
Fabric groups: A, F; CW1, other require further analysis.

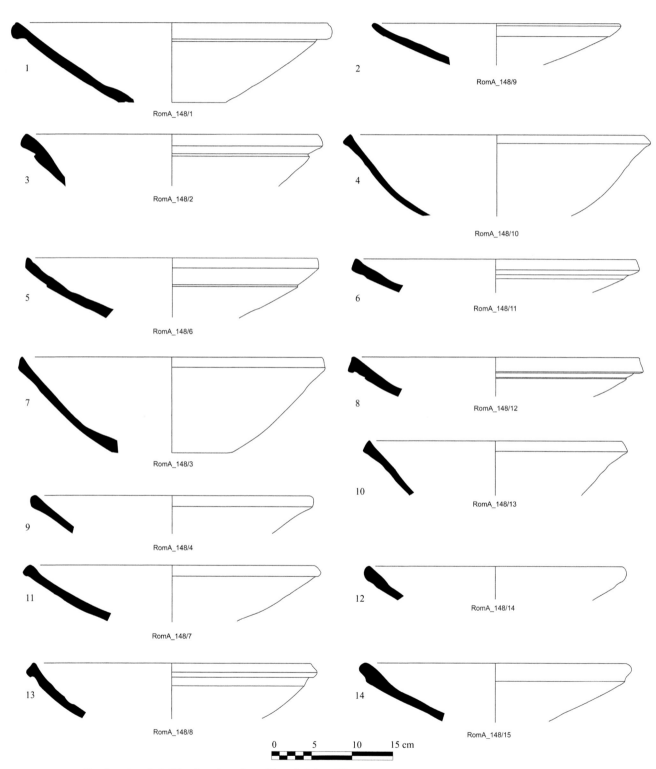

FIGURE 4.35 Ramitan, trench A. Wheel-made and mould-made "plates" from US148
DRAWINGS JACOPO BRUNO

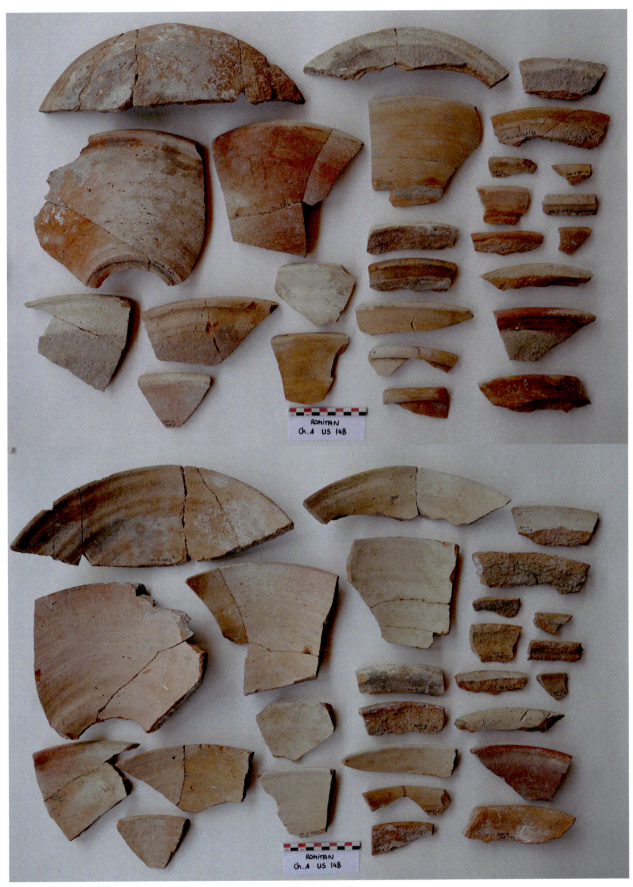

FIGURE 4.36 Ramitan, trench A. Wheel-made and mould-made "plates" from US148
PHOTOS MAFOUB

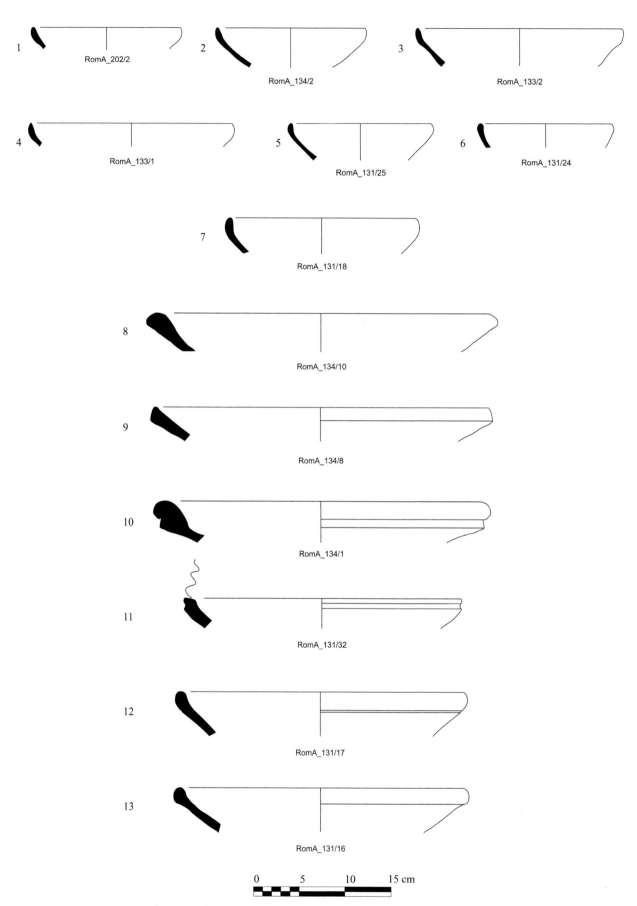

FIGURE 4.37 Ramitan, trench A. Examples of open shapes from deposits from 3rd–4th centuries CE
DRAWINGS JACOPO BRUNO

3.5.1.2 3rd–4th Centuries CE

Deposits from this period yielded a greater variety of vessel shapes. Unfortunately, the large assemblage of US131=US126 proved to be contaminated, containing a fragment of glazed pottery (fig. 4.39).

Assemblages of deposits from the 3rd to 4th centuries CE contained a variety of medium-sized bowl shapes (figs. 4.37.1–7). Their body profile is either rounded with an upright simple rim or flared with a collared rim. Fragments of larger bowls and basins were also found (figs. 4.37.8–13), some of which occurred in the preceding levels, as well. Among the closed forms, one rim shape in particular (figs. 4.38.1 and 4.38.4) belongs to the same type (R051) found in contemporary deposits at Kakishtuvan. A fragment of a large storage jar shows an upright rim with a row of impressions underneath (fig. 4.38.10). A smaller

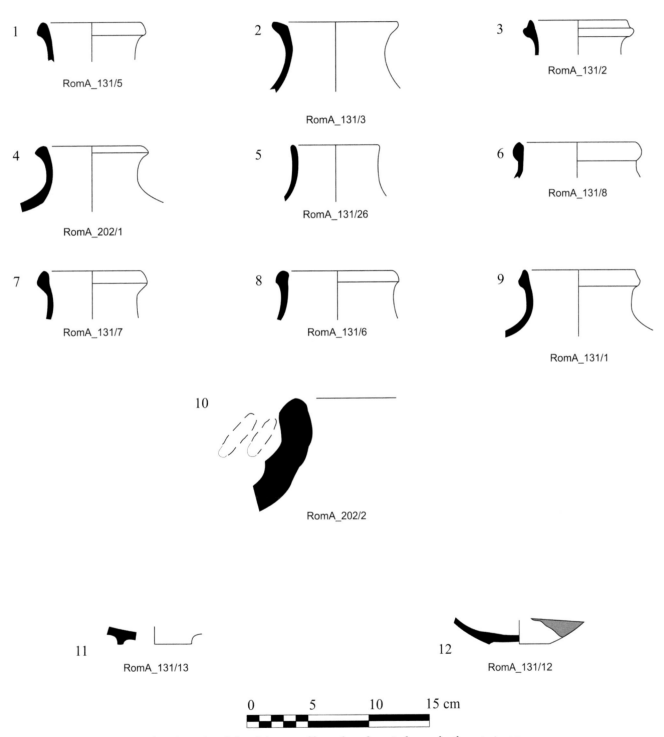

FIGURE 4.38   Ramitan, trench A. Examples of closed shapes and bases from deposits from 3rd–4th centuries CE
DRAWINGS JACOPO BRUNO

coarse-ware jar with an upright simple rim is equally decorated with a row of impressions. Traces of blackening indicate its use as a cooking pot. Base shapes are predominantly flat and recessed (figs. 4.38.12) or show a low ring base (fig. 4.38.11). One handle fragment with a bean-shaped section corresponds well with similar types from earlier levels at Kakishtuvan.

Surface treatments consist of pale slip, red slip, patterns of trickling slip paint, horizontal incised lines and impressed decoration.

Pottery fabrics are red but also light brown. A number of coarse wares were also recorded but require further examination.

Rim shapes: R006, R006.2, R020, R021, R051, R052, R055.
Base shapes: BA01, BA02, BA04, BA05.
Handle shapes: H01SC01, H01SC03.
Surface treatments: pale slip, red slip, patterns of trickling slip paint, incised and impressed decoration.
Fabric groups: A, F; CW requiring further analysis.

3.5.2   Ramitan, Trench C

Assemblages from Ramitan, trench C, set in slightly later in the chronology than deposits from trench A, which enables us to crosscheck potential patterns of material reuse in addition to long-term chronological transformations. This is particularly relevant in regard to the excavations of the citadel and palace complex, trench D, and the shahrestan, trench G.

Ceramics from trench C generally showed an even mix of tablewares and coarse wares, as well as some storage vessels. All 41 assemblages were processed. They contained a number of near-complete vessels or vessel profiles, which contributed substantially to the understanding of the typological diversity and development in the oasis as reflected in our collection.

Phase scientifically dated	Date inferred through stratigraphic position in relation to scientifically dated deposits	Assemblage related to stratigraphic phase
C¹⁴, 2nd–3rd centuries CE		US554
		US555
C¹⁴, 2nd–3rd centuries CE		US556
C¹⁴, 2nd–3rd centuries CE		US557
	2nd–3rd centuries CE	US551
	2nd–4th centuries CE	US552
	2nd–3rd centuries CE	US553
	3rd–4th centuries CE	US540
	3rd–4th centuries CE	US541
	3rd–4th centuries CE	US542
	3rd–4th centuries CE	US543
	3rd–4th centuries CE	US544
	3rd–4th centuries CE	US546
	3rd–4th centuries CE	US548
	3rd–4th centuries CE	US549
	3rd–4th centuries CE	US550
	4th century CE	US532
	4th century CE	US534
	4th century CE	US535
C¹⁴, early 4th century CE		US536=US537
	4th century CE	US538
	4th century CE	US539
	5th–6th centuries CE	US511
	5th–6th centuries CE	US512
	5th–6th centuries CE	US513
	5th–6th centuries CE	US514
	5th–6th centuries CE	US515
	5th–6th centuries CE	US516
	5th–6th centuries CE	US517
	5th–6th centuries CE	US521
	5th–6th centuries CE	US522
	5th–6th centuries CE	US525
	5th–6th centuries CE	US528
	5th–6th centuries CE	US530
	5th–6th centuries CE	US531
	7th–9th centuries CE	US503
	7th–9th centuries CE	US504
	7th–9th centuries CE	US505
	7th–9th centuries CE	US507
	7th–9th centuries CE	US509
		US501
		US500

POTTERY 131

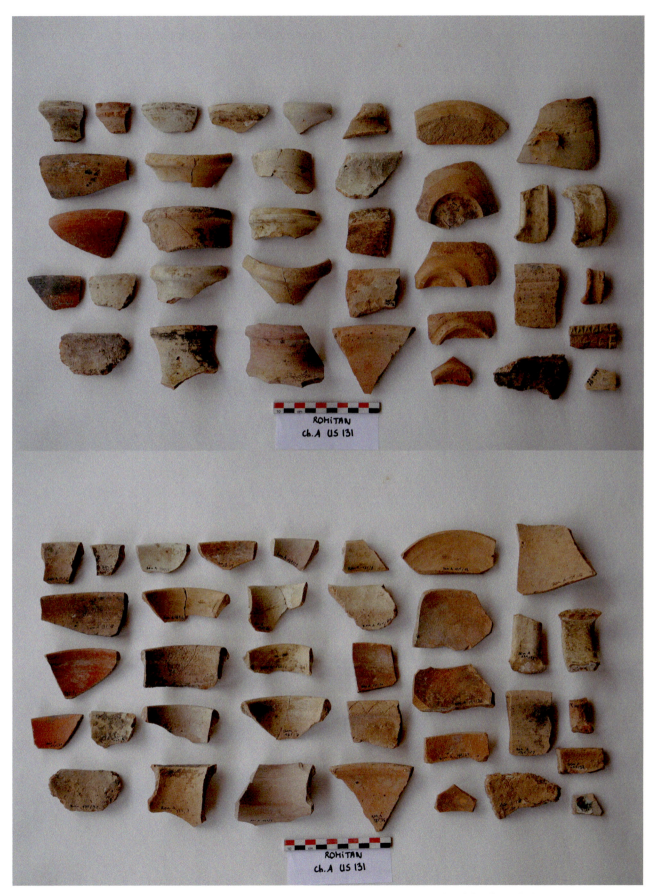

FIGURE 4.39 Ramitan, trench A. Examples of diagnostic fragments from US131. The intrusive glazed sherd is at the bottom right
PHOTOS MAFOUB

3.5.2.1 2nd–3rd Centuries CE

Deposits from this period contained a limited variety of shapes, which mainly consist of rounded bowls and coarse-ware vessels (fig. 4.40.5). The bowl shapes are mostly slip-coated and correspond to those of roughly contemporary levels at Kakishtuvan, trench A, and Ramitan, trench A. Coarse-ware rim fragments all belong to a single shape, R055, a simple jar with an upright or slightly everted rim (see 4.4.2.2.2). These jars are hand-shaped and are also found in slightly earlier as well as contemporary phases in Ramitan, trench A (see 4.3.5.1). Jugs or other closed vessel forms are reflected in a number of handle and/or base fragments and also in wall fragments with incised decoration (fig. 4.40.6).

Rim shapes: R006, R006.2, R055.
Base shapes: BA04, BA13.
Handles: H01SC01.
Surface treatments: red, black, dark brown, light cream slip; patterns of trickling slip-paint; incised wavy decoration.
Fabric groups: A, A2, A6, F, E; CW1, CW3 and other not yet classified coarse wares.[11]

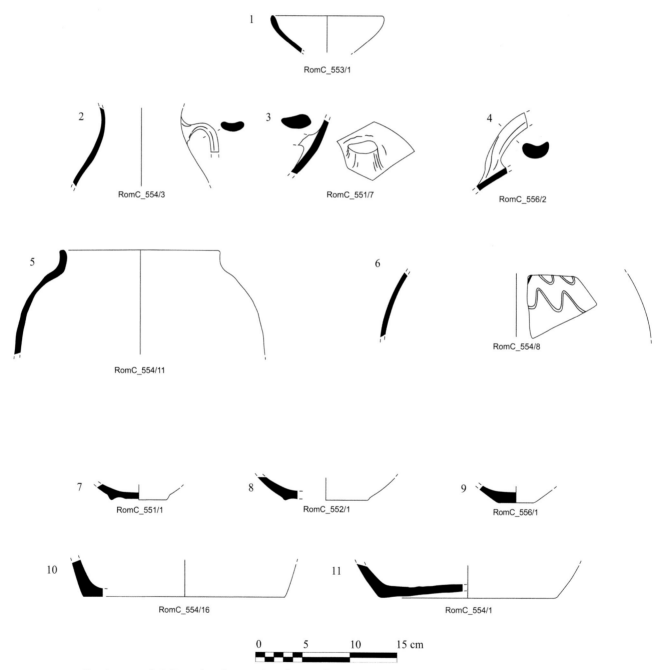

FIGURE 4.40 Ramitan, trench C. Examples of pottery from deposits from 2nd–3rd centuries CE
DRAWINGS FAITH VARDY

---

11 These fabrics were sampled and are subject to ongoing scientific analyses.

3.5.2.2 3rd–4th Centuries CE

Assemblages from this phase are still characterised by rounded bowl shapes, some of them showing the versions with upright rims that dominated earlier contexts. Jars or jug shapes as well as flasks are better represented in these deposits than in the preceding phase (cf. fig. 4.40). Two fine-ware fragments stand out from the rest, as they are hand-shaped, adding an interesting feature to the ceramic material of this phase (figs. 4.41.7 and 4.41.10). One seems to be a narrow neck with a burnished surface (fig. 4.42.1), while the other one is a pedestal base (fig. 4.42.3). Unfortunately, the remains of the respective vessels are not preserved. The hand-shaped high foot resembles specimens found at Paykend during excavations of the shahrestan (Semenov and Mirzaakhmedov 2007: 88, figs. 36.15, 36.19; 89 fig. 37.2). These pedestal bases belonged to incense burners, which were found in chronologically later, 6th to 7th centuries CE, contexts (Semenov and Mirzaakhmedov 2007: 42–43). Deposits from Ramitan, trench C, also yielded a number of interesting coarse-ware jars (figs. 4.41.4 and 4.41.9). The vessels were shaped by hand, and one specimen (fig. 4.41.9) has a vertical lug-handle and is decorated with a raised cordon with impressions. Similar coarse-ware vessels occurred in deposits from the eastern part of the sanctuary at Paykend, which were dated to the 4th and 5th centuries CE (Semenov and Mirzaakhmedov 2007: 41, 62 figs. 10.1–2).

Rim Shapes: R006, R006.2, R007, R008, R041, R047, R053, R054, R075, R079, R094, R097.
Base shapes: BA04, BA05, BA08, BA11, BA14.
Surface treatments: red wash, red and brown slip, patterns of trickling slip paint; horizontal incised lines, applied bands with thumb impressions; burnishing.
Fabric groups: A, A2, A6, F; CW3.

3.5.2.3 5th–6th Centuries CE

Assemblages from deposits dated to the 5th and 6th centuries show a mix of shapes recorded in earlier phases and those with no previous occurrence. Two open forms are of interest here (figs. 4.43.1–2). One of them, R094 (fig. 4.43.2), seems to be the fragment of a flared bowl or

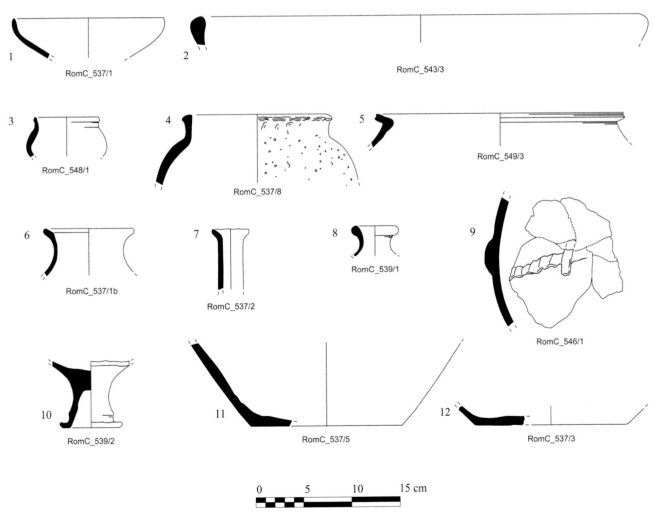

FIGURE 4.41 Ramitan, trench C. Examples of pottery from deposits from 3rd–4th centuries CE
DRAWINGS FAITH VARDY

FIGURE 4.42 Ramitan, trench C. Examples of hand-made pottery from deposits from 3rd–4th centuries CE
PHOTOS MAFOUB

a conical lid with an externally bevelled rim. The other shape, R085, is preserved in its complete profile and shows a perforated base (fig. 4.43.1). Clearly, the vessel was perforated before firing and probably served as a funnel or filter (fig. 4.44.1–2). Recent excavations at the site of Vardana brought to light an analogous shape of a filter bowl (Pozzi, Mirzaakhmedov, and Sultanova 2019: 236, fig. 7.5). The corresponding ceramic assemblage at Vardana is dated to the 7th and 8th centuries CE, slightly later than the stratigraphic context at Ramitan C (Pozzi, Mirzaakhmedov, and Sultanova 2019: 237). One of the jar shapes, R047, has an analogy in one of the coarse-ware vessels from the preceding phase (fig. 4.42.2). Interestingly, the present specimen is made of a fine fabric, although it was still shaped by hand. Some of the early shapes present in the assemblages, for example R006, might be residual.

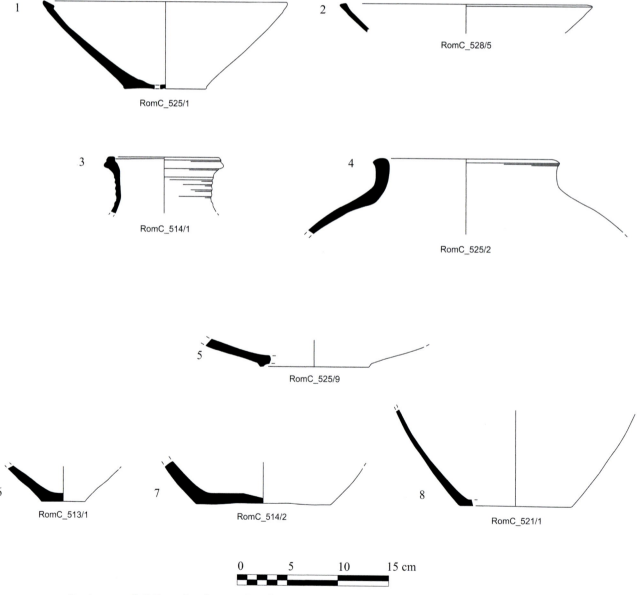

FIGURE 4.43 Ramitan, trench C. Examples of pottery from deposits from 5th–6th centuries CE
DRAWINGS FAITH VARDY

POTTERY

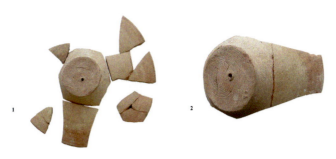

FIGURE 4.44 Ramitan, trench C. Bowl with perforated base
PHOTOS MAFOUB

Rim Shapes: R006, R007, R010, R041.2, R045, R047, R062.1, R084, R085, R093, R094.
Base shapes: BA01, BA04, BA05, BA07, BA13, BA16.
Surface treatments: dark/black slip, red slip red-orange slip, red wash, slip-painted decoration, horizontal rib.
Fabric groups: A, A2, A6, E, F; CW1, CW7.

US 530 (pit fill) and US531 (floor)
The stratigraphic unit US530 represents a small pit within a well-defined floor (US531). The pit fill contained a large number of chicken bones but only two near-complete vessels (Rante and Mirzaakhmedov 2019: 152). The excavator dated the phase this deposit is part of to the 5th and 6th

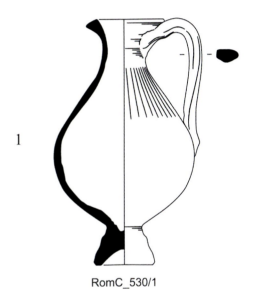

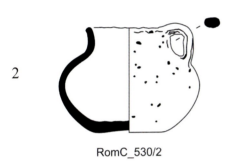

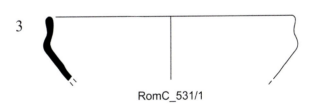

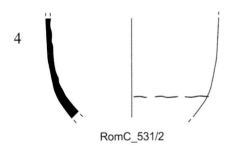

FIGURE 4.45 Ramitan, trench C. Vessels and fragments from US530 and US531
DRAWINGS FAITH VARDY

FIGURE 4.46 Ramitan, trench C. Closed shapes from US530
PHOTOS MAFOUB

centuries based on his impression of the pottery (Rante and Mirzaakhmedov 2019: 152).

In order to avoid circular arguments, we consider these two assemblages separately.

The two vessels found in pit US530 include a fine tableware jug with a high foot and burnished surface (figs. 4.45.1 and 4.46.1) and a small coarse-ware jar (figs. 4.45.2 and 4.46.2). The coarse-ware jar belongs to Ro55, is formed by hand and shows traces of blackening on the surface, indicating it was used for cooking. Ro55 is well-documented as a coarse-ware shape from the 1st century CE onwards (see 4.4.2.2.2). This ceramic type exists in various sizes and apparently remained in production for a considerable period of time. From its rim diameter and size, the jar belongs to the smaller version of Ro55.

However, the jug is a unique piece within the MAFOUB assemblages to date. Its rim is only preserved around the handle attachment but is likely to have been pinched or modelled to a trefoil-shaped opening. Burnished surfaces are poorly represented in the assemblages processed so far. Trefoil-mouthed jugs burnished in a similar fashion from the 4th and 5th centuries CE are also known elsewhere in Central Asia (Puschnigg 2006: 129–31, pl. 7).

The assemblage from US531 is relatively modest, which corresponds to US531's interpretation as a floor. Diagnostics comprise a few wall fragments, one bowl rim and a peculiar vessel base (figs. 4.45.3–4). The shape of the bowl is distinct and also occurred in previous excavations at Paykend, where it was dated to the 6th and 7th centuries CE (Mukhamedjanov, Mirzaakhmedov, and Adylov 1984: 100, fig. 1.12).

3.5.2.4 7th–9th Centuries

Material from these levels is comparatively sparse and highly fragmented. Two larger assemblages (US503 and US505) contained porcelain sherds, suggesting they are contaminated and leaving little reliably assessable pottery from this period in trench C. Diagnostic shapes include neckless jars or jugs with short necks and flat bases. All occurred in earlier levels, and it is possible that these few fragments are residual.

Rim shapes: R041.1, R041.2.
Base shape: BA04.
Fabric groups: A6, F; CW to be further analysed.

3.5.3 Ramitan, Trench D

Concerning the palace complex excavations, our work concentrated on material from the southern building, including the antechamber (room D), square room (room E) and the western room (room F). Two assemblages each were processed from the room with the rectangular fireplace (US2030 and US2037) and an adjacent room interpreted as an antechamber (US2039 and US2046) (Rante and Mirzaakhmedov 2019: 163–70, fig. 158). Additional material derived from partially recovered infills (US2009 and US2028) of adjacent structures. Except for the ceramic fragments from US2030, a thick ashy layer on top of the rectangular fireplace or possible private altar (Rante and Mirzaakhmedov 2019: 165), the pottery is linked to infills or make-up layers in rooms. A few assemblages from the southern enclosure of the square room (US3050, US3051, US3053 and US3057) were also studied (Rante and Mirzaakhmedov 2019: 165).

All these assemblages are modest in size, containing only low numbers of diagnostic fragments, which were generally abraded and worn. Here, the material is brought into correlation with selected C^{14}-dated layers and falls into one group contemporary with and pre-dating the mid-6th century date and another group post-dating this horizon.

Furthermore, we examined the infill of a silo structure in room G in the northern building. In contrast to deposits from the southern building, the infill (US609) and a layer sealing this infill (US604), both post-dating the use of the silo, yielded rich assemblages.

The silo testifies to the post-destruction use of this area, and the silo itself functioned over two construction phases (Rante and Mirzaakhmedov 2019: 171). Its infill shows a mix of various elements reflecting different depositional histories. Thus, parts of the pottery fragments were completely burnt, while others were covered with sinter. The material is also chronologically diverse, including fragments of the later Islamic pottery tradition.

Phase scientifically dated	Date inferred through stratigraphic position in relation to scientifically dated deposits	Assemblage related to stratigraphic phase
		US604
		US609
		US615
		US2009
		US2028
C^{14}, mid-6th century CE		US2030
		US2037
		US2039
		US2046
		US3051
		US3053
		US3057
		US3050

3.5.3.1 6th Century CE and Earlier Phases

One of the scientifically dated contexts is the ashy layer (US2030) covering the rectangular fireplace in the southern building. Charcoal samples of this layer were dated to the mid-6th century CE. Only six diagnostic sherds were recovered from US2030. Firing groups and surface treatments, including red wash or slip and a low horizontal rib with nail impressions, correspond to the characteristics of the pottery from the first half to the middle of the 1st millennium CE (fig. 4.47). Few fragments were also contained in US2037, which was excavated in the same room as US2030. All the sherds are plain, but the attachment of a strap handle with a single finger imprint suggests that the material reflects a slightly later phase than that of US2030. The partially excavated infill of US2009 shows material that reflects pottery traditions from earlier centuries (figs. 4.47.3–5). Fragments almost exclusively derive from large storage vessels and parts of them show slip-painted decoration in a style that is documented in the oasis from the earliest occupation deposits (see 4.4.3.1). Analogous storage jar rims are found also at Ramitan, trench A, in a deposit dated to the 3rd century CE, and at other sites in the oasis (see 4.4.2.2.3).

Rim shapes: R052, R062.1, R062.2, two fragments are too small for shape identification.
Base shapes: BA016.
Handles: H01SC01.
Surface treatment: dark slip, red wash, slip-painted decoration, row of impressions.
Fabric groups: A, F.

3.5.3.2 Post-6th Century CE

All other assemblages belong to this later group. Most contain glazed material and vessel forms that undoubtedly point to Islamic ceramic traditions.

Again, the contexts from the southern building were rather modest in volume but in parts contained highly diagnostic fragments of sgraffito ware (US2039/3) or combed decorations (US3051/3) (figs. 4.48.1–2). Assemblages processed from the southern building generally included storage vessels and tableware. No cooking- or coarse-ware vessels were recovered.

The contexts related to the silo structure in the northern building of the palace complex were considerably larger and richer in pottery shapes. The silo infill (US609) clearly shows that different parts of the material were subject to distinct processes before ending up in the same assemblage. Some of the fragments are extensively blackened, indicating they were exposed to fire. Shapes predominantly belong to closed forms (figs. 4.49.1–4). Coarse wares are also present in this infill.

Fragments from the overlying context US604 seem even more abraded than those from the infill. In contrast to the previous assemblages, US604 included a number of fragments from large open bowls or plates, many of these with glazed decoration (see fig. 4.50). Numerous fragments show monochrome glazes, but a few display polychrome patterns, including the base of a plate as well as individual rim and body sherds. Other than the infill (US609), this layer (US604) only contained a single coarse-ware fragment. Some of the unglazed material from the silo infill relates to the late pre-Islamic or transitional (pre-Islamic to Islamic period) ceramic tradition. The pottery from layer US604 in general relates to Islamic types.

Rim shapes: R006 (glazed), R006.2, R015, R031, R031.1, R032, R041, R041.1, R045.1, R046, R047, R048, R055, R067, R068, R069, R070, R071.
Base shapes: BA004, BA013, BA018.

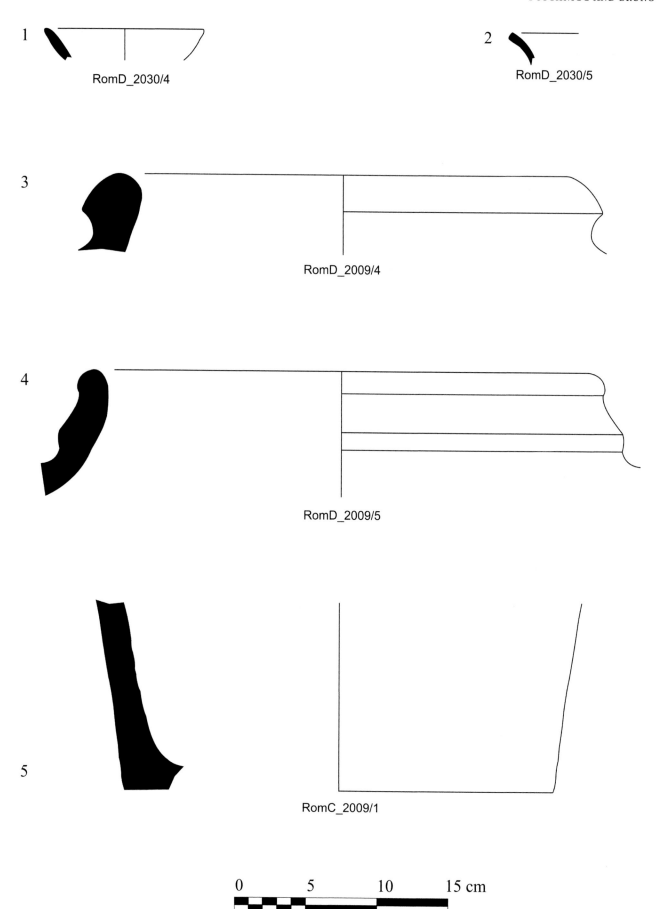

FIGURE 4.47 Ramitan, trench D. Examples of pottery from deposits contemporary or pre-dating 6th century CE
DRAWINGS JACOPO BRUNO

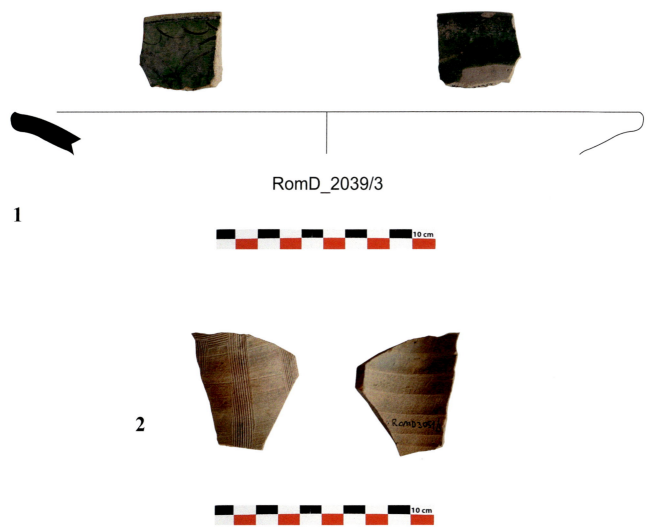

FIGURE 4.48　Ramitan, trench D. Examples of pottery from deposits post-dating 6th century CE. 1. Rom D 2039/3; 2. Rom D 3051/3
PHOTOS MAFOUB

Handles: H01SC01, H01SC04, H03SC04.
Surface treatment: dark/black slip, red wash, glaze, horizontal and wavy incised decoration, combed decoration, horizontal ribs.
Fabrics: A, E, F, H, I; CW1, CW3, CW7.

3.5.4　Ramitan, Trench F

Our study of the material from trench F has only started, and so far, one large assemblage (US1063) of mostly utilitarian pottery was recorded. This assemblage and its associated deposit are part of a phase of sparse occupation, which according to C^{14} dating belonged to the 9th to 11th centuries CE (chapter 11 in this volume; Rante and Mirzaakhmedov 2019: 156). Despite the secondary nature of the deposit and its weak occupational context, the assemblage contained a number of well-preserved pottery forms.

Phase scientifically dated	Date inferred through stratigraphic position in relation to scientifically dated deposits	Assemblage related to stratigraphic phase
	9th–11th centuries CE	US1063
		US1064
		US1084

Of the three deposits recorded so far from trench F only US1063 contained pottery vessels, the two others yielding only ceramic pipes.

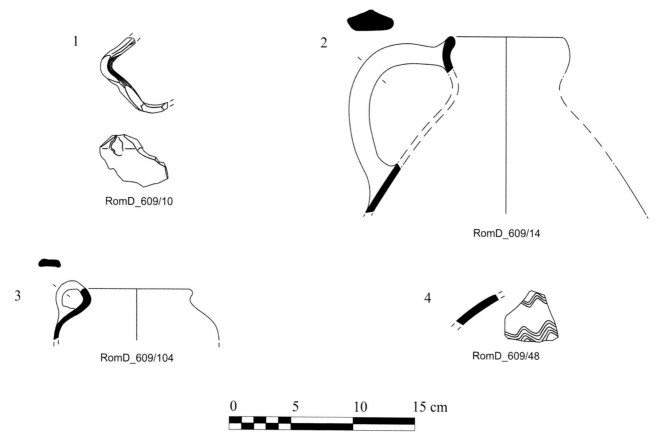

FIGURE 4.49   Ramitan, trench D. Examples of pottery from US609
DRAWINGS FAITH VARDY

3.5.4.1   *9th–11th Centuries CE*
The assemblage retrieved from US1063 offered a rich collection of early Islamic pottery shapes, some of them in a near-complete state (figs. 4.51 and 4.77). Aside from some bowl shapes and many jars, as well as jugs, this layer proved to be particularly rich in lid forms (fig. 4.51.2, see also 4.4.2.2.4). The near-complete specimen of a special flask (R087; fig. 4.51.1) is of great interest, as it represents a highly diagnostic early Islamic vessel form. One analogous specimen occurred in previous excavations of the Paykend citadel (Mukhamedjanov, Mirzaakhmedov, and Adylov 1984: 97, 100 fig. 1.20). Context US1063 also contained part of a spouted glazed lamp and numerous tanour fragments.

Rim shapes: R004, R005, R007, R045, R046, R050.1, R061, R061.1, R062.2, R066, R071, R075, R088, R090, R091.
Base shapes: BA004, BA008, BA012, BA013, BA018.
Handle: H01SC04.
Surface treatment: black slip, red slip, pale brown slip, red wash, slip-painted decoration, glaze, incised decoration, combed decoration, impressed decoration, moulded decoration, applied decoration.

Fabric groups: A, A2, A6, E, F, I, fritware; CW1, CW7 and CW to be further analysed.

3.5.5   Ramitan, Trench G
Excavations in this area targeted a section of a suburban habitat and revealed several consecutive phases of a mud-brick structure, which appears to have served commercial or artisanal purposes (Rante and Mirzaakhmedov 2019: 183–92). According to charcoal samples dated through C^{14}, occupation in this area began in the 5th century CE (chapter 2 in this volume; Rante and Mirzaakhmedov 2019: 183) and continued until the 14th century CE (Rante and Mirzaakhmedov 2019: 192).

Trench G provided the highest number of complete assemblages in Ramitan. These derived from consecutive occupational activities, including make-up layers and floor levels as well as infillings of fireplaces and pits. Unfortunately, many assemblages were very small and fragmented, leaving insufficient material for a thorough comparative study. Of the 33 processed assemblages, seven did not contain any diagnostic fragments. The remaining 26 assemblages yielded pottery that only amounts to 7.15

POTTERY 141

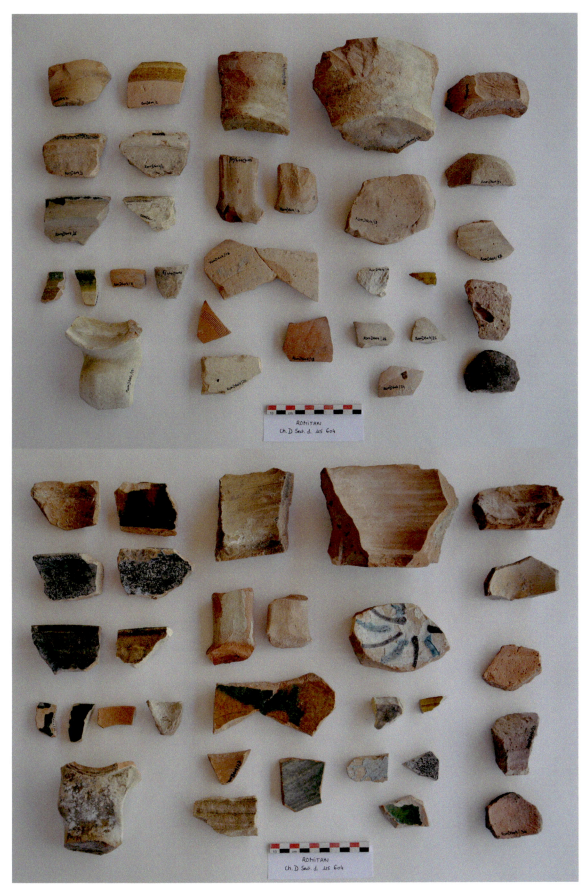

FIGURE 4.50 Ramitan, trench D. Examples of pottery from US604
PHOTOS MAFOUB

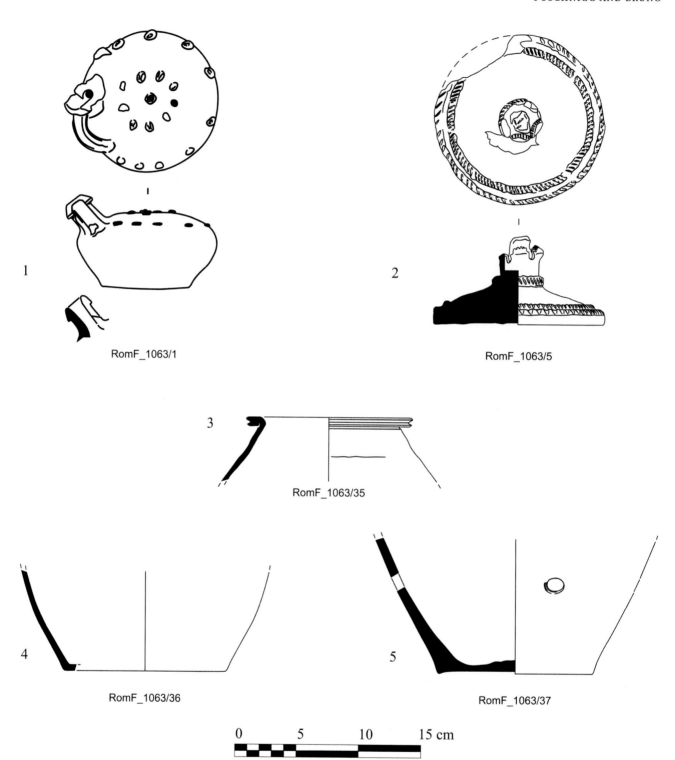

FIGURE 4.51 Ramitan, trench F. Examples of pottery from US1063
DRAWINGS FAITH VARDY

rim eves (the estimated equivalent of just over seven vessels). On the other hand, they allowed us to reconstruct some interesting patterns of material reuse at this site, such as the use of ceramic fragments as floor pavement. We are thus able to assess in detail what kind of material was selected to serve a secondary function.

Phase scientifically dated	Date inferred through stratigraphic position in relation to scientifically dated deposits	Assemblage related to stratigraphic phase	Corresponding architectural phase
	5th–6th centuries CE	US1710	Phase 2
	5th–6th centuries CE	US1725	Phase 2
	5th–6th centuries CE	US1735	Phase 2
C14, 5th–6th centuries CE		US1739	Phase 1
C14, 5th–6th centuries CE		US1741	Phase 1
	5th–6th centuries CE	US1750	Phase 1
C14, 5th–6th century CE		US1922	Phase 1
	5th–6th centuries CE	US1936	Phase 2
	5th–6th centuries CE	US1945	Phase 2
C14, 5th–6th century CE		US1946	Phase 1
	5th–6th centuries CE	US1948	Phase 1
	5th–6th centuries CE	US1952	Phase 1
C14, 5th–6th centuries CE		US1953	Phase 1
C14, 5th–6th centuries CE		US1955	Phase 1
C14, 5th–6th centuries CE		US1958	Phase 1
	5th–6th centuries CE	US6051	Phase 1
	5th–6th centuries CE	US6055	Phase 2
	5th–6th centuries CE	US1716	Phase 3
	6th–8th centuries CE	US1939	Phase 4
	6th–8th centuries CE	US6043	Phase 4
	13th century CE	US1681	Phase 5
	13th century CE	US1895	Phase 5
	13th century CE	US1896	Phase 5
	13th–14th centuries CE	US1667	Phase 7
	13th–14th centuries CE	US1841	
	13th–14th centuries CE	US1843	Phase 7
		US1940	
		US6000	
		US6004	
		US6008	
		US6009	
		US6010	
		US6026	

3.5.5.1 5th–6th Centuries CE

Many of the deposits dated to this period contained little material and no diagnostic sherds. Larger assemblages revealed predominantly storage jar fragments and a few other closed forms. The rim of a jug resembles the rim shape of later water jugs (R076), though its diameter is slightly larger than usual, and the neck is funnel-shaped. The body shape is not preserved. One fragment shows the upper part of a conical lid. The lid knob is structured with impressions (fig. 4.52.3). Among the decorations, the motif on a large storage jar fragment, showing white circular patterns on a dark or black background, differs from the usual slip-painted ware. Analogous fragments of this white-on-dark pattern occurred in phase 7 deposits in trench G (cf. fig. 4.54, rim fragment in the middle register, upper left section), and in other sites, including Iskijkat, trench A, US321 (see also 4.4.3.1). Most sherds in the assemblages of this phase are worn and abraded.

Rim shapes: R041.2, R048, R050.1, R051, R060.1, R062, R062.1, R062.3, R076, R084.
Base shapes: BA004.
Handle: H01SC05.
Surface treatments: red wash, slip-painted decoration, incised decoration.
Fabric groups: A, A2, A6, F; CW1, CW3.

3.5.5.2 6th–8th Centuries CE

This period is represented by only two assemblages (US1939 and US6043), and the variety in ceramic types is accordingly poor (fig. 4.53).

Only one rim shape occurred in the deposits, a jar rim (R075), which is also found in other MAFOUB trenches (see Catalogue) and which in its coarse-ware version is diagnostic for the transitional time between the pre-Islamic and early Islamic periods.

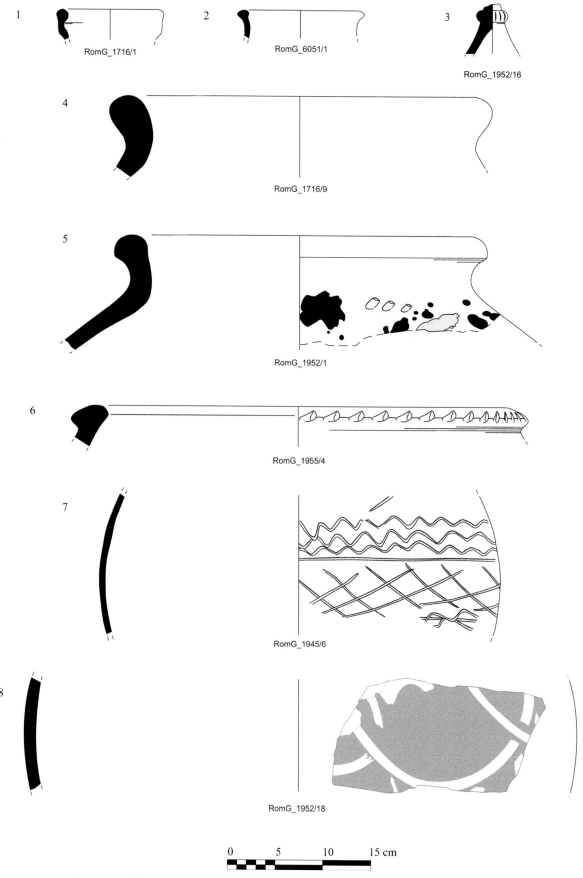

FIGURE 4.52   Ramitan, trench G. Examples of pottery from deposits from 5th–6th centuries CE
DRAWINGS FAITH VARDY

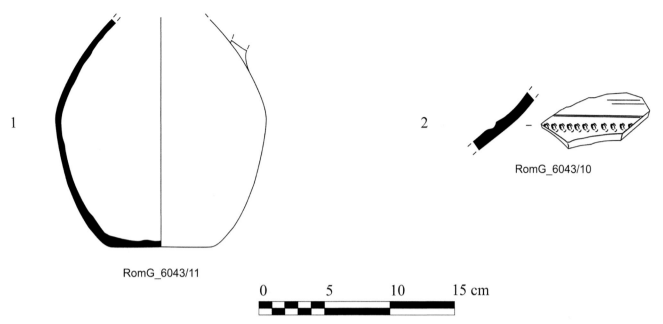

FIGURE 4.53   Ramitan, trench G. Examples of pottery from deposits from 6th–8th centuries CE
DRAWINGS FAITH VARDY

Rim shape: R075.
Base shapes: BA004, BA013.
Surface treatments: red slip, slip-painted decorations, impressed decoration.
Fabric groups: A, A6, E, F; CW1, CW7.

3.5.5.3   13th–14th Centuries CE

Most prominent among the assemblages associated with this phase is the rich collection of fragments reused as a pavement in a "coccio-pesto" technique during the last phase of occupation in trench G, when the building had obviously transformed, and room functions had changed (Rante and Mirzaakhmedov 2019: 192). The majority of the pottery employed for this purpose derives from large and thick-walled storage vessels, many of them characteristically decorated with slip-paint (fig. 4.54). One fragment shows a white design on a dark background (fig. 4.54, rim fragment, upper left section). This inverted concept is also documented in phase 3 (cf. fig. 4.52.8). A few sherds derive from other vessels, probably jugs, with combed patterns on the vessel body (fig. 4.52.7). Other assemblages recorded from this phase are again small and contribute less material to our collection. They usually contain small and abraded fragments. In one case, the shape of a rim fragment is analogous to the funnel or filter bowl found in Ramitan, trench C, and also has a similar rim diameter. However, since the base is not preserved, we cannot ascertain if this vessel served the same purpose.

Reused as part of a *badrab*, a number of storage jars were recovered from this phase in almost complete states. Usually, the base was chiselled out to form a large hole (fig. 4.84.4), but this was often the only part missing from the original jar (see 4.4.2.2.3 and 4.5.3).

Rim shape: R038, R041.1, R062, R062.1, R062.3, R085.
Base shape: BA004.
Handle: H01SC04, H03SC04.
Surface treatments: slip-painted decorations, impressed decoration, combed decoration.
Fabric groups: A, A6, E, F, I; CW to be further analysed.

3.6   Site 250

This small urban site was investigated by a single stratigraphic sounding, trench A (Rante and Mirzaakhmedov 2019: 249). Its earliest occupation dates back to the 1st century CE, and activities and urban development continued into the 10th century CE (Rante and Mirzaakhmedov 2019: 249). Pottery from trench A is significant for the early Islamic period, as the fill of a pit provided a number of near-complete pottery shapes as well as reconstructable vessel profiles. This is an ideal case, as we get a better understanding of the vessel repertoire and the contemporaneity of a group of shapes from it. Earlier phases at the site yielded smaller assemblages, although these, too, help us to evaluate the variety of shapes and styles across time. The processing of the material has not been

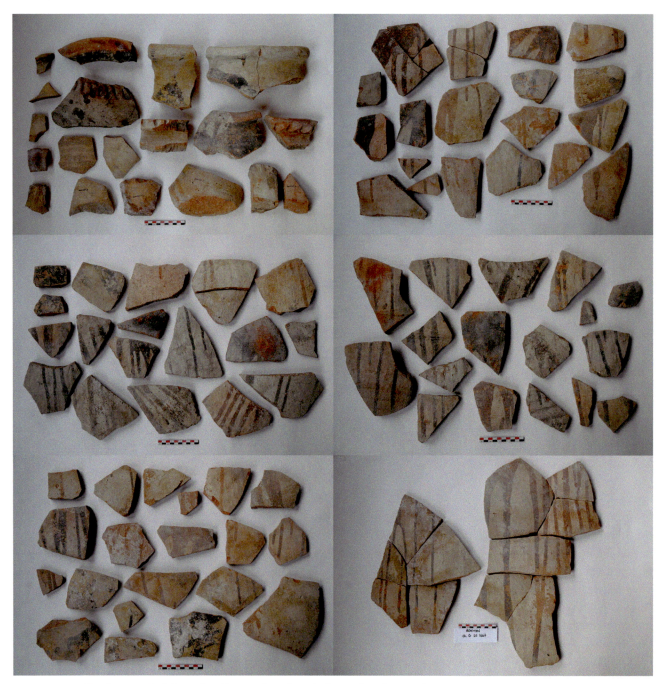

FIGURE 4.54   Ramitan, trench G. Examples of pottery from deposits from 13th–14th centuries CE

3.6.1 Site 250, Trench A

Phase scientifically dated	Date inferred through stratigraphic position in relation to scientifically dated deposits	Assemblage related to stratigraphic phase
	1st century CE	US226
	1st century CE	US227
	1st century CE	US228
	1st century CE	US230
C^{14}, 1st century CE		US231
	2nd–3rd centuries CE	US221
	2nd–3rd centuries CE	US222
	10th–11th centuries CE	US114
		US125
		US173
		US174
		US183
		US185
		US187
	9th–10th centuries CE	US156

3.6.1.1 1st Century CE

Assemblages from the earliest occupation level at site 250 contain a number of open forms, jars and storage vessels. The rim of a goblet with red slip relates to material from the last centuries BCE at Iskijkat, trench A, and Bukhara, trench A. Apart from the usual rounded bowls, one specimen with a waisted profile (R027; fig. 4.55.2) is noticeable, as it is distinct from the type (R010) found in subsequent phases across many sites in the oasis (see 4.4.2.2.1). Interestingly, this new shape has occurred only once in the MAFOUB assemblages so far. It seems very close to a shape that was widespread and popular during the Kushan and Kushano-Sasanian periods across Bactria and also in the early Sasanian period in Margiana (Puschnigg 2006: 132–34). The piece from site 250 is covered with dark slip, which corresponds to many tableware forms associated with this phase. Only two wall fragments of coarse-ware vessels were recorded from this phase.

Rim shapes: R001, R006.2, R018, R027, R041.1, R047, R062, R102.
Base shape: BA004.
Surface treatments: black slip, dark grey/black slip, dark brown slip, red slip, red wash.
Fabric groups: require further examination, only a basic distinction between fine and coarse wares were recorded.

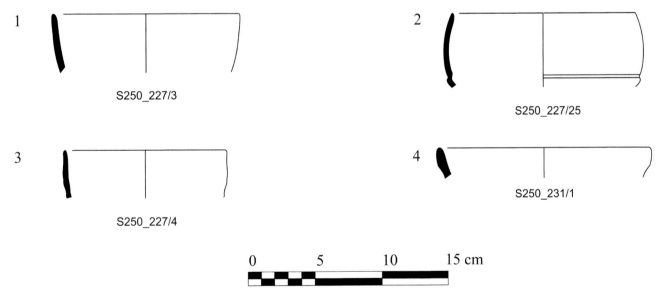

FIGURE 4.55 Site 250, trench A. Examples of pottery from deposits from 1st century CE
DRAWINGS JACOPO BRUNO

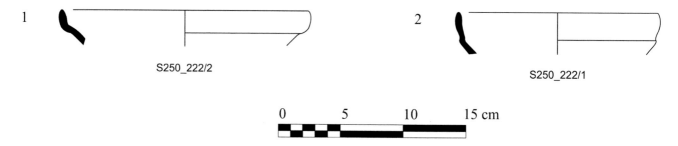

FIGURE 4.56 Site 250, trench A. Examples of pottery from deposits from 2nd–3rd centuries CE
DRAWINGS JACOPO BRUNO

3.6.1.2 2nd–3rd Centuries CE

Two assemblages associated with this period were processed. They featured a number of shapes well documented in other excavations of the MAFOUB archaeological program, where they belonged to similar chronological phases (fig. 4.56).

Aside from the tableware bowls and jars, many wall sherds of storage jars were noted.

Rim shapes: R006.2, R010, R041.1, R045.
Base shape: BA004.
Surface treatments: red slip, black slip, red wash, slip-painted decoration, incised decoration.
Fabric groups: require further examination, only fineware fabrics.

3.6.1.3 Pit Fills Associated with the 9th–10th and 10th–11th Centuries CE

The infill of a pit, US156, provided the largest assemblage of site 250. However, ceramics recovered from this pit fill show distinct degrees of completeness, suggesting different depositional histories; some vessels are almost fully preserved, while others only occur in small fragments. Apart from plain-ware jugs, jars and lids, the assemblage contained a substantial quantity of coarse wares and glazed material, including the fragment of a lamp. Not all the pottery is contemporaneous, though, and the state of preservation is not the only hint in this regard. Some specimens, such as the complete profile of a bowl with an upright rim and red slip (R006.1; fig. 4.57.14) testify to the style and repertoire of the late pre-Islamic phase, while others, for instance the semi-complete bowl with white glaze (R012; fig. 4.57.15), reflect the ceramic design and quality that correspond to the time of the pit's formation. Most interesting are the coarse wares, which are also partly preserved as complete vessel profiles (R075; fig. 4.58.5–10). Some of these coarse-ware vessels are clearly shaped on the wheel and show a relatively thin vessel wall (see fig. 4.71); however, other coarse-ware jars in the same assemblage are hand-made and have a rather coarse appearance. A number of jars (figs. 4.58.17–18) and a lid with slip-painted decoration form an intriguing group that shows a distinct fashion.

Pit US114 (fig. 4.59), which is dated slightly later, yielded a much smaller assemblage than US156. Many sherds showed a greenish tinge on the surfaces, indicating that they were water-logged for some time. Aside from a number of mostly glazed bowl rims, the pit fill also contained fragments of a jug, which joined together with sherds from US125 to form a near-complete vessel profile (fig. 4.59.5). Only a few coarse-ware shapes were found in the assemblage.

Rim shapes: R005, R006, R006.1, R007, R007.1, R011, R012, R030, R038, R047, R048, R061, R062, R075, R075.1, R076, R077, R078, R079, R080, R082, R083, R088, R100.
Base shapes: BA003, BA004, BA006, BA013, BA018, BA019.
Handles: H01SC04, H01SC05, H03SC04.
Surface treatments: red slip, red wash, slip-painted decoration, glaze, horizontal rib, incised decoration, impressed decoration, combed decoration, moulded decoration.
Fabric groups:[12] E, F; CW1, CW7.

3.7 Concluding Comment

The description of the individual site assemblages by phase provided single snapshots of various elements of the ceramic repertoire. In light of the secondary nature of some deposits, it is not easy to assess their potential contemporaneity.

Some features appear to be consistent across different sites over a certain time period. Among these are the use

---

12   Fragments from US156 are not yet fabric typed, only a basic distinction between fine and coarse wares is recorded.

POTTERY

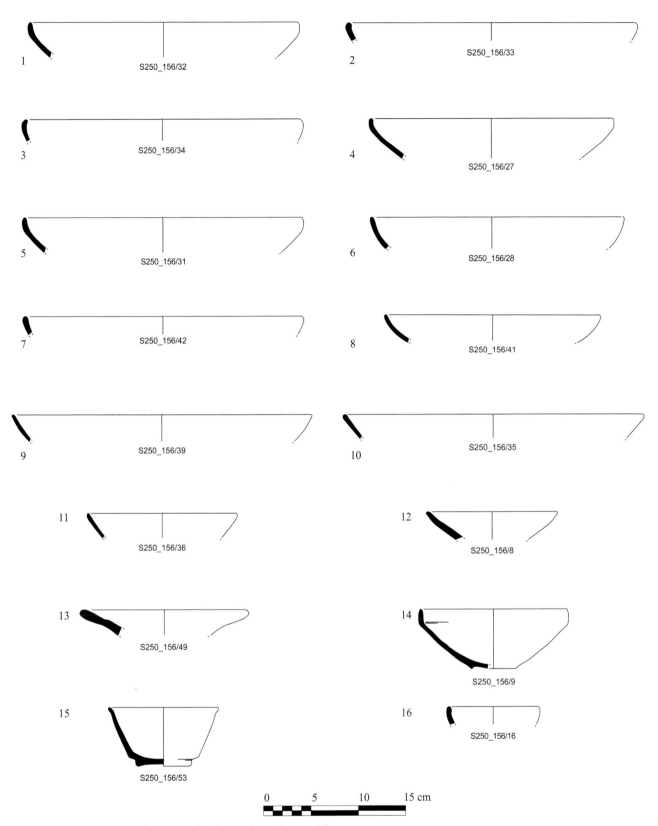

FIGURE 4.57 Site 250, trench A. Examples of open shapes from pit fill US156
DRAWINGS FAITH VARDY

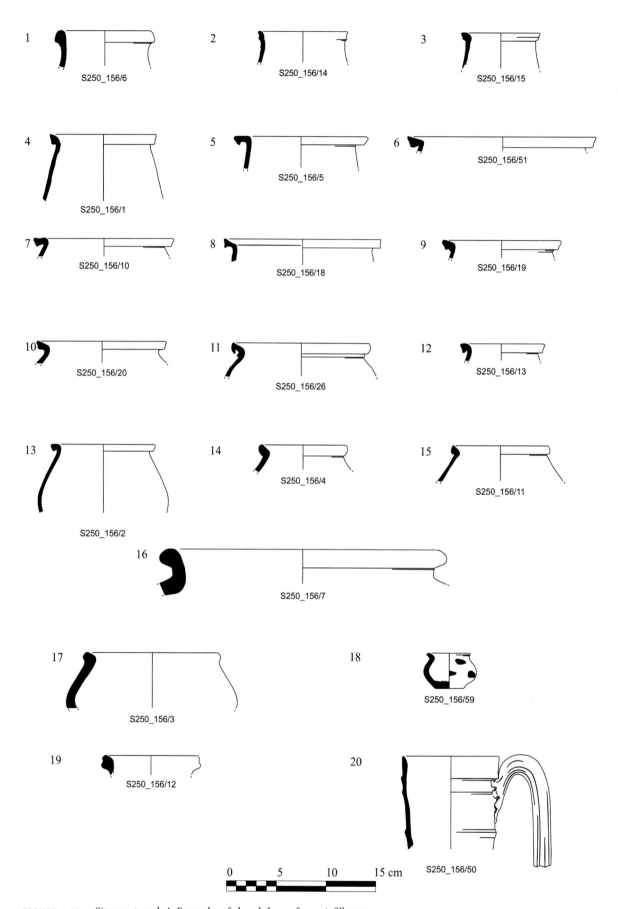

FIGURE 4.58 Site 250, trench A. Examples of closed shapes from pit fill US156
DRAWINGS FAITH VARDY

POTTERY 151

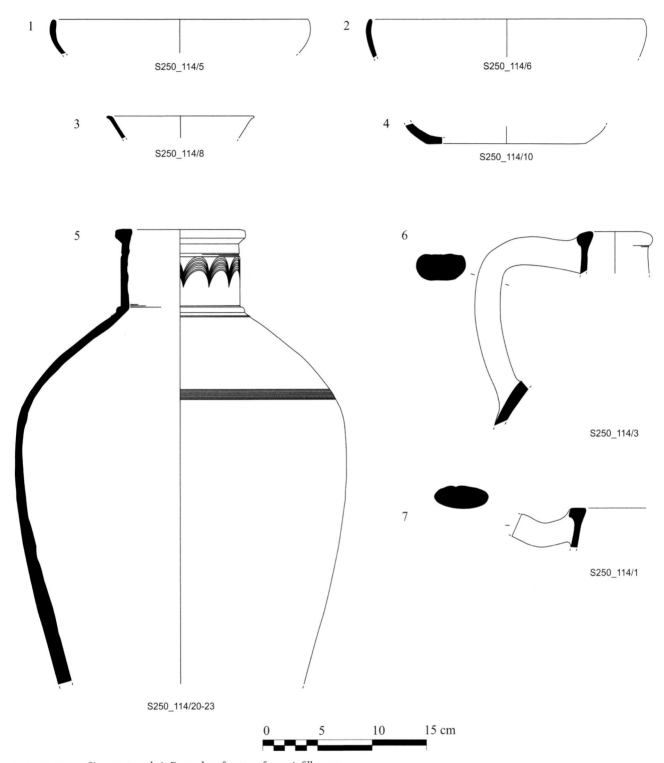

FIGURE 4.59   Site 250, trench A. Examples of pottery from pit fill US114
DRAWINGS FAITH VARDY

of red and black slips for coating tableware vessels and the application of slip-painted decorations on containers of various sizes from the earliest phases of occupation. Certain vessel shapes, including some of the rounded bowls and jugs with everted and thickened rims, are fairly regular items in assemblages after the 1st century BCE.

Others provide only random observations of traits that are difficult to relate to the broader pottery development. These include some of the unusual slip-painted wares or cooking vessels, which are only sparsely present. As a consequence, we are currently unable to provide a systematic sequence of pottery repertoires including tableware, coarse- or cooking-ware and ceramic containers. On the whole, this limits our understanding of the continuous development of design fashions and production technologies, specifically since changes might not occur synchronously across the entire repertoire.

4   Chronological Patterns: the General Perspective

In the second and more analytical part of our study we explore our recorded data systematically concerning common long-term trends across the oasis. Exploring the potential pottery sequence through quantitative assemblage comparison or statistical means was not possible because of the incomplete recovery of most stratigraphic units. Instead, we are trying to highlight those aspects of change that are most palpable in the material and assess them against the grid of scientific dates and the stratigraphic evidence. At the same time, we focus on a number of well-represented shapes, studying their correlations with specific surface treatments or decorative features and types of ware. This provides a glimpse into long-term continuities as well as short-lived fashions and allows us to observe functional consistencies.

First, however, we need to evaluate our data and determine the scope of our examination. Which aspects of the ceramic production are best represented and where are potential flaws that might inhibit further interpretation?

4.1   Assemblages and Phasing

A synopsis of the chronological coverage of the assemblages processed from the various MAFOUB excavations is given in table 4.13. For the sake of clarity, the table shows the periods represented in century units.

For an initial chronological overview, we attempt to integrate the phasing established for each site into a coherent sequence. This endeavour is not straightforward, since in different excavations, time brackets given for the

TABLE 4.13   Chronological coverage of the processed material for each trench in century slots based on the dates of the stratigraphic units

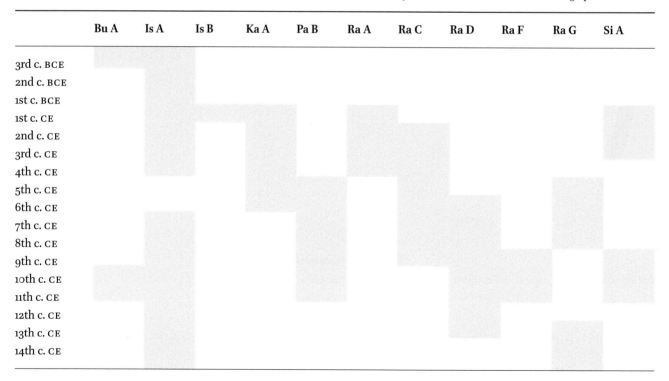

Legend: Bu A = Bukhara, trench A; Is A = Iskijkat, trench A; Is B = Iskijkat, trench B; Ka A = Kakishtuvan, trench A; Pa B = Paykend, trench B; Ra C = Ramitan, trench C; Ra D = Ramitan, trench D; Ra F = Ramitan, trench F; Ra G = Ramitan, trench G; Si A = site 250, trench A

date of a context or phase vary. Thus, the dates of phases are given as 1st to early 3rd centuries CE in some cases and 2nd to 3rd centuries CE or 3rd to 4th centuries CE in others, to provide just a few examples. As the phases do not fall within "natural" intervals, we explored different groupings in various degrees of magnitude, from relatively narrow to broad, in order to define appropriate chronological macro-phases against which the relative sequence of material culture can be compared.

4.1.1 Volume by Phase

At the outset, we assess how much pottery, in terms of diagnostic material, our data contain for each phase group. We begin with a relatively narrow chronological spacing (table 4.14).

The table illustrates how many diagnostic fragments were recorded for each phase group and how much this adds up to in terms of estimated vessel equivalents (eves). Regarding the eves, we focus on rim eves here (see 4.1.2.). The counts of rim diameters specify how many rim sherds were recorded with measurements. Occasionally, fragments are too small and damaged to give a reading for rim diameters and cannot be properly assessed as to the percentage which the extant rim part represents in relation to the complete rim (100% of the rim preserved = 1,00 rim eves). The measures of the rim eves indicate an estimate of how many vessels the recorded rim sherds represent.

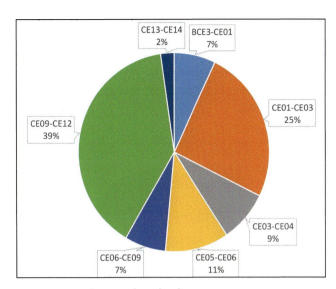

FIGURE 4.60   Pottery volume by phase

Occasionally, rim fragments are broken in a way that facilitates reading the diameter and percentage value of the preserved rim, but the actual sherd is still too small to identify which vessel shape it belongs to or even whether it is an open or closed form. Table 4.15 shows how many of the rim fragments had their shape identified in relation to the total number of recorded and measured rims, which is given in table 4.14 (count of rim diameter and sum of rim eves).

TABLE 4.14   Pottery volume by phase

Phase group	Diagnostics*	Count R Dia	Sum R eves
BCE3–CE01	202	35	4.31
CE01–CE03	541	132	15.27
CE03–CE04	193	41	5.14
CE05–CE06	316	55	6.56
CE06–CE09	221	44	4.21
CE09–CE12	719	161	23.85
CE13–CE14	140	10	1.38
Total	2,332	478	60.72**

*   This figure refers to all recorded diagnostics, not only rim and base fragments but also handles, neck-shoulder junctions and decorated body sherds.
** The sum of rim eves diverges from that obtained by adding up the rim eves recorded for the individual MAFOUB excavations so far (table 4.3) since some of the deposits were not assigned to a specific phase and could not be considered here.

The pottery volume contributed by each phase to the overall assemblage is depicted in Fig. 4.60.

TABLE 4.15   Pottery volume by phase

	Count R Dia	Count R Dia %	R eves	R eves %
BCE3–CE01	32	91.4%	4.11	95.4%
CE01–CE03	121	91.7%	14.70	96.3%
CE03–CE04	32	78%	4.8	93.4%
CE05–CE06	44	80%	6.21	94.7%
CE06–CE09	36	81.8%	3.83	91%
CE09–CE12	117	72.7%	19.43	81.5%
CE13–CE14	9	90%	1.35	97.8%

The volume of the recorded data grouped by phase demonstrates that some chronological periods are better represented, containing more material, than others. In order to improve the validity of a broad comparative view of ceramic assemblages across time, we amalgamate the seven phase groups listed in Tables 4.14 and 4.15 into three large and more evenly spread macro-phases. These roughly reflect the period from the earliest occupation levels up to late antiquity (3rd century BCE to 3rd century CE), followed by the late antique to early medieval phase (3rd century CE to 9th century CE), and finally the Islamic period (9th century CE to 14th century CE). The distribution of pottery volume by phase seems now more balanced without blurring major chronological developments (fig. 4.61).

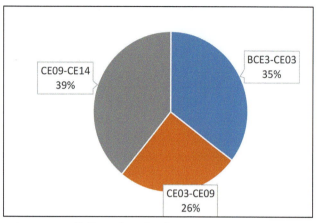

FIGURE 4.61   Pottery volume by phase

4.2 Chronological Variations in the MAFOUB Assemblages

In this section, we highlight the main chronological variations in the assemblages that are observable through time in relation to potential modifications in the vessel repertoires. To begin, we explore general trends and characteristics noticeable in the overall ceramic assemblage.

4.2.1 General Patterns

All identified rim fragments were assigned to one of these broad categories: open or closed vessel forms and lid shapes. The latter comprises all forms that could scarcely be used for any other function, in contrast to some of the shapes suitable as either a bowl or a lid. Our evidence was then summarised according to the macro-phases determined above (fig. 4.62).

Figure 4.62 illustrates proportional variations of basic vessel forms, open and closed, and lid forms across the three macro-phases. The percentage values are based on rim eves, which are shown in the data table below the chart.

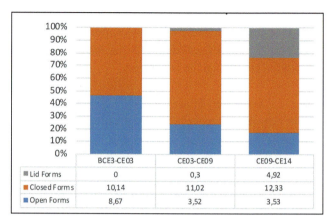

FIGURE 4.62   Distribution of basic forms across phases

Across the phases a steady decrease in open forms is reflected in the data. Even if we assumed that some open forms were partially also used as lids, this overall trend still persists, as indicated in table 4.16. As the portion of incomplete assemblages is large, we do not know how representative this observation is in connection to the original situation in the past. For this reason, we await further evidence to corroborate our findings. Similar tendencies showing a drop in open vessel forms are also documented for the ceramic evidence from Merv, Turkmenistan, between the last centuries BCE and the 6th to 7th centuries CE (Puschnigg 2019: 336–37).

Regarding the variations in size within the main vessel groups, the distribution of rim diameters clearly indicates preferences among open and closed forms (figs. 4.63 and 4.64).

Figure 4.63 shows the most common size range for each of the basic form groups. No chronological distinction is made in this chart, as our data are not sufficient for further subdivisions and refinements.

TABLE 4.16   Distribution of basic forms across phases

	BCE3–CE03	CE03–CE09	CE09–CE14
Lid forms	0% (0 eves)	2% (0.3 eves)	23.7% (4.92 eves)
Closed forms	53.9% (10.14 eves)	74.3% (11.02 eves)	59.3% (12.33 eves)
Open forms	27.8% (5.22 eves)	23% (3.42 eves)	17% (3.53 eves)
Open forms/lids	18.3% (3.45 eves)	0.7% (0.1 eves)	0% (0 eves)
Total	100% (18.81 eves)	100% (14.84 eves)	100% (20.78 eves)

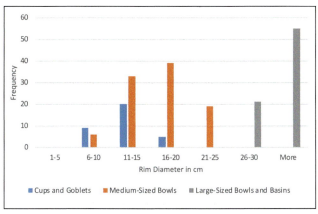

FIGURE 4.63   Distribution of rim diameters in open forms

In Fig. 4.64, closed vessel forms reflect a more marked distinction in the distribution of rim diameters. Most striking is the concentration of necked jars around the 6 to 10 cm diameter range. Vessels in this diameter range include not only most of the tableware jugs but also large water jugs dated to the early Islamic period. Neckless jars are less numerous, although they comprise most cooking pots as well as jars for other forms of food processing or intermediate storage. Any further analysis regarding possible chronological variations in the size of certain vessel groups is not yet feasible. More research on this is planned once the processing of all excavated material is complete.

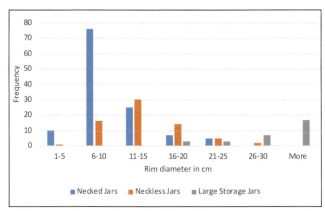

FIGURE 4.64   Distribution of rim diameters in closed forms

4.2.2   Vessel Shapes

In this second step, we examine a number of individual vessel shapes within the recorded material that proved significant. Our selection is based on number of recurrences of the single shape codes across the different sites and phases and on the total sum of rim eves. As often happens with archaeological assemblages, many shapes occur only once, which makes it difficult to understand their position both chronologically as well as functionally (within the repertoire, etc.). Some forms show a chronologically coherent distribution, while others at first sight appear to straddle the complete sequence. Occasionally, this concerns shapes with an almost ubiquitous and relatively indistinct profile, such as rounded bowls with simple rims. These occur in early and late versions. In other cases, the long chronological distribution reflects patterns of redeposition and deliberate reuse of certain vessel types, specifically storage jars, for purposes other than their original one. Our discussion is roughly structured into vessel groups, open and closed, as well as special forms, including lids, lamps and other individual shapes. Reference will also be made to the distinction between coarse or cooking wares and fine wares.

4.2.2.1   Open Vessel Forms

Shape code R001. Bowl or cup with flaring wall and simple rim and related shapes (R001.1, R005, R012, R030, R091).

This shape code designates open vessel forms, which most probably represent cups, or even goblets, and straight-walled bowls. Most fragments only show the upper part of the vessel, so its complete profile is not yet known, which might also account for the heterogeneous structure of this group. The distribution of rim shape R001 across the chronological range and its diverse spread of rim diameters and decorative patterns suggest that the shape in its current definition still comprises different vessel types. The early specimens are likely to belong to some form of goblet, in some cases the original vessel may have been carinated and the break of the extant fragment occurred above the carination. One of these sherds showed vertical burnishing. More often, however, this rim shape was found in later contexts. One of the fragments from the later contexts (find no. PAYB1632/47) is covered with a white glaze, demonstrating that the vessel was produced in the early Islamic period. Fragments of shape R001 from the later and late pre-Islamic and early Islamic contexts are mostly plain, and it is therefore difficult to assess whether some of these sherds are residual and belong to earlier periods. Such differentiations are always challenging when it comes to fragmented pottery, but as more material is being processed, we hope to be able to further clarify the definition of this shape code in the future.

Rim shape R001.1 is morphologically close to the previous shape, although the chronological distribution from the later pre-Islamic to Islamic levels is slightly less diverse. One specimen shows a red slip. The rim shape most probably belongs to a cup or deep bowl. A shallow version of this represents shape code R005.

Other cup shapes show a distinctly everted (R012, R030) or collared (R091) rim. So far, specimens of these rim shapes are all glazed and appear to be more or less contemporary with the glazed fragment (PAYB1632/47) of R001.

Shape code R006. Bowl, rounded, with upright thickened rim, and related shapes (R006.1, R006.2).

R006 exemplifies a medium-sized bowl shape. The form is well-defined and has a relatively concise chronological profile, primarily occurring in contexts from the 2nd to the 4th centuries CE. Individual fragments were also recorded from later 5th to 6th centuries' contexts and specifically from the large heterogeneous pit fill at site 250 (US156). These late occurrences belong to the early Islamic pottery production and are distinguished from the remainder of R006 by their larger rim diameter (29–30 cm) and glazed decoration. Many of the specimens from the first half of the first millennium CE are covered with slip, from red to dark brown and black in colour, some of them showing the characteristic change of tone around the rim area. The bowl appears to be standard inventory of this period and features in the relevant levels across most of the studied sites, including Iskijkat, Kakishtuvan, Ramitan and site 250. Analogous shapes are also presented in recent excavations of the Hermitage Museum in Paykend citadel (Semenov and Mirzaakhmedov 2007: 13–14, 74, figs. 22.1–3).

R006.1 shows a slightly different bowl profile, with an upright rim and a carination at about three-quarters of the vessel height. The complete vessel contour with a low ring base is preserved on a specimen, originally covered with red slip, from the mixed assemblage from site 250 (US156). So far, we have only recorded one example of this variant, but similar bowls feature in the scientific literature of previous and ongoing work in the oasis (Stark and Mirzaakhmedov 2015: 88, 91, fig. 15.4; Silvi Antonini 2009: 146, fig. 3, Type B; Koshelenko 1985: 423, pl. 135; Mukhamedjanov, Mirzaakhmedov, and Adylov 1982: 92, fig. 3.28). In the literature, this type is dated variously between the 3rd/4th–5th centuries CE (Stark and Mirzaakhmedov 2015: 93; Koshelenko 1985: 287, 423; Mukhamedjanov, Mirzaakhmedov, and Adylov 1982: 96) and 6th–7th centuries CE (Silvi Antonini 2009: 163). At Paykend, excavations of structure VIII-7 in the domestic quarter brought to light a particularly rich assemblage of near-complete vessels of this type (Semenov and Mirzaakhmedov 2007: 42, 91, fig. 39. 1–10, 92, figs. 40.1–2, 96, figs. 44.1–6). Semenov and Mirzaakhmedov regard this type of bowl as part of the early medieval pottery repertoire in the oasis, predating the early 8th century CE (Semenov and Mirzaakhmedov 2007: 18–19, 42).

Another shape, R006.2, represents a bowl with a more flared wall profile and an upright thickened rim. Specimens of R006.2 frequently showed traces of slip coating of various shades of red. Occurrences of this shape to date show a chronological profile similar to that of R006 (see Catalogue). One fragment occurred in a context of site 250 dated to the 1st century CE (US231). Material previously excavated in the oasis and more recent evidence found by other projects, however, indicate a different chronological frame for this shape. A similar shape from Ramish is illustrated for the 3rd-to-2nd–centuries BCE phase of the Bukhara Oasis in Koshelenko's compilation (Ayaktepinskii Etap, Ramish 2) (Koshelenko 1985: 422, pl. 134). Similarly, a comparable bowl shape was published by the Hermitage Museum from more recent excavations in Paykend (Omelchenko 2019: 213, fig. 7.8). Omelchenko attributes this find to his phase Paykend 2B, for which he suggests a dating of the 3rd century BCE (Omelchenko 2019: 220–21, figs. 10–11). In contrast, Mirzaakhmedov dated the context of specimens found in excavations at the citadel of Paykend to the 4th and 5th centuries CE (Semenov and Mirzaakhmedov 2007: 13–14, 73, fig. 21.5, 74, fig. 22.4). It is possible that shape R006.2 or a similar version appears in the repertoire of the oasis earlier and that some of the fragments recorded from the MAFOUB excavations are residual fragments in chronologically later contexts. Conversely, it is also possible that this type of bowl shape – with variations – continued to be used into the early centuries of the Common Era.

Despite minor variabilities detectable between earlier and later – Islamic – versions, the group of bowl shapes around R006 appears to be generally coherent as far as size, decoration and stratigraphic distribution is concerned (see Fig. 4.65 and Catalogue).

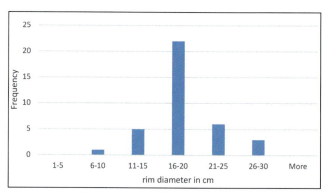

FIGURE 4.65   Histogram of rim diameters for shape group R006

Shape code R007. Bowl, rounded with upright or slightly inturned, simple rim, and related shapes (R007.1, R011).

Due to the high fragmentation of the ceramic material, combined with the relatively unspecific morphological criteria of this bowl shape, the recorded observations of R007 comprise a number of distinct types of rounded bowls with simple rims. Any further differentiation between these bowl types, however, requires the preservation of a larger proportion of the vessel profile. With more material being processed and comparative studies underway, it might be possible to distinguish different variants of R007 in the future.

Considering the bowl shape R007 in its current broad definition, it spreads across all investigated sites and occurs throughout different chronological phases with fluctuating popularity. Rounded bowls with simple upright or inturned rims appeared in the earliest occupational contexts dated to the 3rd century BCE (see Catalogue). Following this early phase of occurrence, which lasts until the 3rd to 4th centuries CE, the shape features prominently again in early Islamic occupation levels. Most of the specimens from these later 9th–11th-century contexts are glazed, demonstrating a relatively close chronological relationship between this pottery and its stratigraphic position, despite the largely secondary nature of the contexts. Fragments from the mixed assemblage of site 250 (US156) mostly show glazed decoration, thus indicating a late production date. Early versions of R007 in turn occasionally exhibit traces of slip, although there are also plain fragments. Rim diameters are more broadly spread in this shape group than in R006 (see fig. 4.66). Most of the bowls from earlier contexts have a rim diameter between 11 and 20 cm, while early Islamic productions are between 21 and 30 cm wide. This divide, which is tentatively suggested by our data, will require reconsideration as new material is being processed and since recent work by the Hermitage Museum at Paykend produced, among other things, a number of bowls with large diameters from the early occupation levels of the city (Omelchenko 2019: 217). These bowls may partly correspond to our shape code R007, although the illustrated specimens would primarily fall under different shape codes within our system.

Rounded bowls are often illustrated in archaeological publications on work in the oasis, including Paykend (Omelchenko 2019: 210, figs 5.15–16, 213, figs. 7.37–38, 214, figs. 8.32–33; Semenov and Mirzaakhmedov 2007: 13–14, 74, fig. 22.5), Bashtepe (Stark et al. 2016: 237, fig. 29.6, 240) and Ramish, phases 2 and 5 (Koshelenko 1985: 422, pl. 134, 423, 135). In the chronological ceramic sequence of Mukhamedjanov, Mirzaakhmedov and Adylov, they occur in phases 1, 3, 4 and 6 (Mukhamedjanov, Mirzaakhmedov, and Adylov 1982: 82, fig. 1.17 (Bukhara I), 87, fig. 2.14 (Bukhara III), 9 (Bukhara IV), 92, fig. 3.16 (Bukhara VI)). One example of the later versions of R007 is presented in the excavations of shahrestan 2 in Paykend (Semenov and Mirzaakhmedov 2007: 136, fig. 84.1). The bowl is glazed and has a rim diameter of about 23 cm.

Shape R008, which differs from R007 only in its pointed rim, is related to the round bowl. The few specimens documented for this rim code occurred in contexts of the 2nd to 4th centuries CE. Some fragments were covered with slip.

Shape R007.1 designates a version of R007 with generally thinner walls. So far, this type is only recorded in later contexts, and most specimens of R007.1 have glazed decorations.

A shape similar to these fine bowls is rim code R011, a bowl with straight flaring walls and simple rims. All fragments to date occurred in late Islamic contexts (see Catalogue), and most of them were glazed.

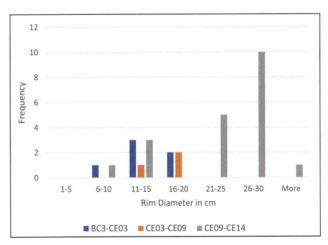

FIGURE 4.66   R007: distribution of rim diameters across phases

Shape code R010. Bowl with waisted profile and upright, slightly thickened rim, and related shape (R027).

Fragments of bowl shape R010 occurred in assemblages at three sites: Iskijkat, Ramitan and site 250. Excavations at Iskijkat produced the largest proportion of this type. Specimens are often slip-coated. Black or shades of dark aubergine seem to be the preferred colours, but there are also dark red tones. Some fragments show a colour change between red and black. The distribution of rim diameters indicates that the bowl size commonly varies between 14 cm and 17 cm diameters. Records of bowl R010 reflect a well-defined pottery type with a relatively concise chronological distribution. Contexts where R010 occurred are dated primarily to the 2nd and 3rd centuries CE, and also to the 4th century CE and the 5th to 6th centuries CE. The specimen from the context of the 5th–6th century at Ramitan is plain and distinct in its colouring. It may thus represent a later version of the bowl.

Bowl shapes comparable to R010 are found at Kyzylkyr in levels attributed to the periods Kyzylkyr 1 and 2 (Filanovich 1983: 33, figs. 8.23–24, 28; 50, figs. 16.34–35, 40), as well as at Setalak 1 and 2 (Filanovich 1983: 59, figs. 19.8–9, 30; 100, fig. 37.8, 70). Kyzylkyr and Setalak are dated between the 3rd and 4th–5th centuries CE (Filanovich 1983: 36, 120). Some of the bowls from the rich deposit found in Paykend's shahrestan also show a waisted body profile (Semenov and Mirzaakhmedov 2007: 91, fig. 39.15, 92, fig. 40.3, 96, fig. 44.8). To judge from the illustrations and descriptions of these specimens, they are plain and appear to be closer to the fragment from Ramitan. This would also correlate with the later date of both deposits.

Vessel shapes of various types with waisted profile are widespread in Central Asia before the Islamic period. The Bukhara Oasis fits well into this framework.

Shape R027 represents a comparatively fine version of a waisted bowl profile. Only one fragment testifies to this type. It is coated with a dark/black slip. The archaeological context where this piece was found belongs to the earliest phase of occupation at site 250, which is C^{14}-dated to the 1st century CE. No immediate parallel is illustrated in the scholarship on the oasis, but a similar bowl shape is published for the site of Bulakbashi in the Koshrabad district of the Miankalya region west of Samarkand (Pugachenkova 1989: 117, fig. 51). Pugachenkova compares the pottery of Bulakbashi to that of the Kaunchi 1 period and dates it very generally to antiquity (Pugachenkova 1989: 116, 199 no. 2). The bowl form R027 differs from the better documented R010. More data is needed to fully understand shape R027 and its chronological distribution.

Shape code R020. Large shallow plate with a recess below the rim, and related shapes (R021, R022, R023).

Alternatively, this shape could have served as a domed lid. The plate commonly has a large diameter, over 30 cm, and a coarse appearance. Most specimens show a rough, sandy exterior surface. Recesses and/or horizontal ridges below the rim suggest that this shape is mould-made. Unfortunately, no complete profile has been preserved, leaving an incomplete interpretation of this shape for now. Interestingly, so far shape R020 has occurred exclusively in assemblages from Ramitan A, which indicates a special function associated with this type at this site and/or a special archaeological situation. More than 77% of the total rim eves of R020 were concentrated in two contexts (US148 and US144). US148 counted for 12 occurrences of this shape. Both contexts appear to represent rich make-up layers to either side of the rampart exposed in trench A (Broglia de Moura 2013: 31–32; Rante and Mirzaakhmedov 2019: 151). The chronological spread of R020 is limited to a period between the 1st and 3rd centuries CE (Rante and Mirzaakhmedov 2019: 251). Due to the specific peculiarities of their surface structure and manufacturing traces, no parallels are readily identifiable in the literature. This might, however, be related as much to the style and scale of published ceramic drawings as to the potential absence of this specific shape from available archaeological publications.

Related bowl shapes mostly overlap with R020 when they occur.

R021 is a large, rounded bowl with a slightly everted, thickened and externally bevelled rim. Some of the better-preserved vessel profiles suggest that this form had a flat base. The exterior surface of R021 is plain. Most specimens have a rim diameter well over 30 cm, with one exception, which is 25 cm in diameter. Mukhamedjanov, Mirzaakhmedov and Adylov describe similar vessels in their chronological study of the phase Bukhara 4 and compare them to lid shapes from Afrasiab, although they state that the Bukhara specimens might have been used as bowls (Mukhamedjanov, Mirzaakhmedov, and Adylov 1982: 87, figs. 2.34–35, 90). In this chronological study, the phase Bukhara 4 is dated to the 2nd to 3rd centuries CE (Mukhamedjanov, Mirzaakhmedov, and Adylov 1982: 95). Shape R021 appears to be generally deeper than R020 but could have served both as a lid and as a bowl.

R022 represents a large flaring bowl with an externally thickened and dropping rim (see Catalogue). This shape has so far occurred only two times, both in the context of Ramitan A (US144 and US148), again overlapping with the strong presence of shape R020. In contrast to R020, this form is slightly deeper and shows a flared, not rounded, profile. As with R020 and R021, the appearance of the vessels is rather coarse, and they might have served as basins as well as some kind of lid.

The last shape in this group, R023, is a large flaring bowl with a thickened rim. Again, this form features in the same assemblages as the previous ones, although it is the only one of these large bowl shapes that also occurs in trench C at Ramitan. Mukhamedjanov, Mirzaakhmedov and Adylov illustrate similar shapes for their phases Bukhara 5 and 6 (Mukhamedjanov, Mirzaakhmedov, and Adylov 1982: 92, fig. 3.27 (Bukhara V), fig. 3.36 (Bukhara

VI), 93–94). For Bukhara 5 the authors suggest that the relevant shape might have served as a matrix to form the base of large storage vessels (Mukhamedjanov, Mirzaakhmedov, and Adylov 1982: 93). Most of the larger storage jars, however, have wall profiles too steep to fit in these bowls, or their flat bases exceed the diameter of the central flat part of the supposed matrix. Still, the relatively standardised size (see fig. 4.67) and coarse execution of these open forms indicates a specific pattern of use. More data might facilitate a precise understanding of R020 and its related shapes.

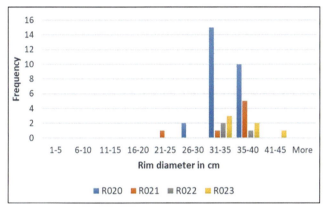

FIGURE 4.67   R20 and related shapes: distribution of rim diameters

4.2.2.2   Closed Vessel Forms

Shape code R038. Jar or jug with externally thickened and bevelled rim, and related shapes (R035, R051).

R038 represents a widespread form of necked jar or jug that appears throughout Central Asia from the Hellenistic period onwards (Puschnigg and Houal 2019: 125–26, fig. 3). Due to the generally high fragmentation of the material, it is difficult to reconstruct the complete vessel shape, but the evidence published from various sites suggests that analogous rim shapes were used for neck jars, amphora-shaped vessels and jugs (Lyonnet 2012: 151, fig. 5.6, 8; 162 figs. 9.3–4; Puschnigg and Houal 2019: 126, fig. 3). The shape occurs at various MAFOUB excavation sites, although observations are not numerous in total (see Catalogue). The chronological spread of the jar or jug rim covers much of the entire occupational history. Despite the fragmentary state of the material, rim sherds from later deposits cannot be regarded as only residual, since they also show lighter fabric and firing groups, which are typical for the later chronological periods. Some fragments show a slip or wash, although many are plain.

R035, a jar or jug with an everted, externally thickened and slightly dropping rim, occurred rarely and was confined to deposits between the 3rd century BCE and 3rd century CE. All fragments so far were slip-coated.

Shape R051, a jar or jug with a slightly everted, externally thickened rim differs from R038 only in its more roundish rim profile. R051 is equally widespread across sites, but again the fragments are not numerous and cover a long chronological span (see Catalogue).

All three rim shapes show a relatively narrow range of rim diameters between 8 and 12 cm. This group of necked jars or jugs often features in ceramic chronologies of the Bukhara Oasis (Koshelenko 1985: 422, pl. 134 (Ramish II–III), 423, pl. 135 (Ramish IV–VI); Mukhamedjanov, Mirzaakhmedov, and Adylov 1982: 82, fig. 1.11 (Bukhara I), fig. 1.12 (Bukhara II), 87, fig. 2.5 (Bukhara III), 92, fig. 3.34 (Bukhara V)). Jars or jugs with similar rim profiles also occurred in excavations at the Bukhara citadel (Mukhamedjanov 1983: 63, fig. 2.A), at Kyzylkyr and Setalak (Filanovich 1983: 50, figs. 16.19–20; 100, fig. 37.75), and more recently at Paykend (Omelchenko 2019: 210, fig. 5.17, 46; 212, fig. 6.16, 24; 213, figs. 7.16–17, 47) and Bashtepe (Stark et al. 2016: 238, fig. 30.3). The dating suggestions generally run from the 3rd century BCE to the 4th–5th centuries CE (Mukhamedjanov, Mirzaakhmedov, and Adylov 1982: 95; Filanovich 1983: 120; Mukhamedjanov 1983: 60; Omelchenko 2019: 220, figs. 10, 221; Stark et al. 2016: 240–42). A date of the 4th to 5th centuries CE or slightly later is also proposed for analogous shapes from the east part of the sanctuary at the Paykend citadel (Semenov and Mirzaakhmedov 2007: 8, 10–11, 63, figs. 11.6–7).

Shape code R041. Jar or jug with a short neck and slightly everted, externally thickened and internally hollowed rim, and related shapes (R041.1, R041.2).

These rim shapes designate a closed short-necked or neckless form, which appears to be comparatively popular throughout the oasis, occurring at almost every site. The specimens recorded so far did not show any handles, although this might be due to the fragments' states of preservation. Most rim sherds show a plain surface, while surface slips are scarcely observed.

R041 appears specifically in deposits from the 2nd and 4th centuries CE, but later occurrences in early Islamic contexts suggest that this shape might encompass two chronologically distinct versions. The range of rim diameters, between 6 and 10 cm, is relatively narrow. The shape is well documented in previous excavations at the oasis.

In comparison, R041.1 covers a much broader range of rim diameters (see also fig. 4.69). Again, there is a strong showing in deposits from the 1st to 4th centuries CE, while

FIGURE 4.68 Mould-made "plates"; Ramitan, trench A, US140
PHOTO MAFOUB

a number of fragments also occur in contexts from the 7th to 10th centuries CE. Not all of these rim sherds appear to be residual, some of them show fabric and firing groups that suggest a later manufacturing date than the first half of the first millennium CE.

Observations of shape R041.2 on the other hand so far do not exceed a rim diameter of 12 cm (see Fig. 4.69). The shape differs from R041 in its pronounced thickening and profiling of the rim. The structure and concept of both, however, are analogous and facilitate covering the vessel with either lids or cloth/fabric, an aspect that qualifies them as intermediate storage vessels. Rim shape R041.2 occurs in contexts dated to the 3rd century CE but also features in deposits from the 5th to 6th centuries, which distinguishes this variant from the other two. Fragments were equally found in contexts dated up to the 10th century. Again, records of R041.2 are too few at the moment to reliably assess the production period or use of this type, but in its principle form it apparently covered a substantial time span.

The rim sherd from a jar comparable to the R041/R041.2 group from Paykend, trench B (US1637), shows a decorated lip corresponding to patterns characteristic for the early Islamic period (Semenov and Mirzaakhmedov 2007: 131, fig. 79.8).

Analogous rim shapes are illustrated for Kyzylkyr and Setalak (Filanovich 1983: 50, fig. 16.32; 100, figs. 37.13, 37, 50, 73), for Ganchtepa (Mirzaakhmedov et al. 2013: 107, fig. 7.10) and for excavations at the Paykend citadel (Semenov and Mirzaakhmedov 2007: 74, fig. 22.7). In Koshelenko's compilation of the ceramic development in the Bukhara Oasis, rim shapes R041 and R041.2 feature in phases Ramish 5 and 6 (Koshelenko 1985: 423, pl. 135 (Phases Ramish V and VI)). The suggested dates of these analogies largely range from the 3rd to the 5th centuries CE (Filanovich 1983: 120; Semenov and Mirzaakhmedov 2007: 12–14; Mirzaakhmedov et al. 2013: 106–107).

Fragments of rim shape R041.1 appear early in the published pottery sequences of Bukhara and Paykend and are dated to the last centuries BCE (Mukhamedjanov, Mirzaakhmedov, and Adylov 1982: 82, fig. 1.20 (Bukhara II); Omelchenko 2019: 210, fig. 5.20). The specimen from Paykend is slip-coated. In our present data, this form appears slightly later (see Catalogue).

R041.1 in its basic structure also shows similarities with rim profiles of large storage vessels from an early period onwards (Mukhamedjanov, Mirzaakhmedov, and Adylov 1982: 82, figs. 1.5–6).

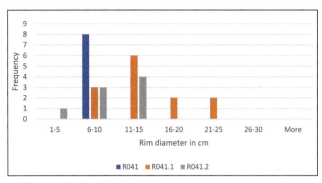

FIGURE 4.69   R41 and related shapes: distribution of rim diameters

Shape code R045. Jar or jug with short neck and externally thickened and moulded rim, and related shapes (R045.1, R070).

The jar or jug occurs at a number of MAFOUB excavations. Most specimens show a rim diameter between 8 and 11 cm, with the exception of a single fragment, which has a diameter of 6 cm. None of the fragments recorded so far had a handle attachment, but this could equally be due to the variable state of preservation. It is also possible that some of the specimens actually belong to a form of pitcher, as suggested by some of the published material (Semenov and Mirzaakhmedov 2007: 73, fig. 21.15). Rim sherds of this type were mostly found in deposits from the 2nd and 3rd to the 6th centuries CE. Two fragments in later contexts, 8th–9th and 9th–11th centuries CE, might be residual. Specimens are generally plain or show a light self-slip.

Similar rim shapes are well documented for the Paykend citadel (Semenov and Mirzaakhmedov 2007: 73 fig. 21. 14–16) and shahrestan 1, where a particularly rich assemblage was found (Semenov and Mirzaakhmedov 2007: 86, fig. 34.1; 93, figs. 41.1–6, 10; 97, figs. 45.2–10: 101, figs. 49.5–8). These parallels suggest that at least some of the vessels were jugs. The material is regarded as representative of the early medieval pottery repertoire of Paykend (Semenov and Mirzaakhmedov 2007: 18–19, 42).

R045.1, a jar or jug with a short neck and an everted, externally thickened and almost straight-edged rim was only recorded twice so far. Both specimens are glazed on the inside and around the rim but vary considerably in rim diameter. They derive from different sections of Ramitan, trench D. Their archaeological contexts (US609, infill of a silo, and US3053) appear to be chronologically ambiguous (Rante and Mirzaakhmedov 2019: 171–72). No immediate parallels are found in the literature, and it is still unclear how these glazed variants relate chronologically or functionally to the jars and jugs of R045.

A few R045 specimens are explicitly identifiable as jugs with pinched or trefoil-mouthed rims. Archaeological contexts where these fragments occurred are mostly dated to the early Islamic period (see Catalogue). There is a possibility that some of the specimens attributed to R045 could actually be pitchers with a pinched rim, although the extant rim part makes any unequivocal identification unfeasible. Pitchers or trefoil-mouthed jugs, however, were already part of the pottery repertoire of the oasis (Semenov and Mirzaakhmedov 2007: 14, 73, fig. 21.15).

Shape code R047. Jar, short necked with externally thickened and dropping rim, and related shapes (R046, R048).

R047 rim sherds are not very numerous in the records and, so far, occurred only at Ramitan and site 250. The shape is plain, and two of the specimens show a coarse fabric. One of these coarse-ware jars, a pot from Ramitan C, is hand-made and partly blackened, suggesting it was used for cooking. The other coarse-ware fragment, a jar from site 250 US156, a heterogeneous pit fill, is completely burnt, but the high number of coarse-ware fragments and semi-complete pots that clearly show traces of use as cooking vessels makes it plausible that this was also the case for the second R047 coarse-ware rim. Rim diameters range from 11 to 17 cm. No specific distinction is noticeable between common and coarse wares in this respect. The shape generally occurred in deposits dated between the 1st and 6th centuries CE.

Similar jar shapes feature in the scientific literature on the oasis from the earliest occupation levels (Koshelenko 1985: 422, pl. 134 (Ramish II), 423, pl. 135 (Ramish IV and VI); Omelchenko 2019: 209–10, fig. 5.36, 212, fig. 6.5, 25). Analogous jar rims are also illustrated for the Kyzylkyr and Setalak occupation phases, which are dated from the 3rd to 6th centuries CE (Filanovich 1983: 50, fig. 16.8, 100, fig. 37.28). A specimen of a similar or slightly later date is documented from Ganchtepa (Mirzaakhmedov et al. 2016: 225, fig. 10.14).

Only three specimens of jar rim R046 have been recorded so far. This jar with a short neck has an externally thickened and bevelled or straight-edged rim. One fragment derives from an earlier, 2nd–3rd-century context, while the other two occurred in early Islamic deposits (see Catalogue). All pieces are made from fine fabrics; two are slip-coated. The rim sherd from the early assemblage shows traces of a dark slip, which would correspond to the surface appearance of pottery from this period, while one of the rims from an early Islamic context has remnants of a red coating. For now, it is impossible to discern whether any distinctive features could help to subdivide R046 into separate coherent types. Similar rim shapes appear in the scientific literature on the Bukhara Oasis at various points along the chronological spectrum (Omelchenko 2019: 218, fig. 9.18; Mirzaakhmedov et al. 2013: 107, fig. 7.7; Semenov and Mirzaakhmedov 2007: 10–11; 63, fig. 11.8; 64, fig. 12.3; Filanovich 1983: 50, fig. 16.6; Mukhamedjanov, Mirzaakhmedov, and Adylov 1982: 92, fig. 3.20 (Bukhara VI)).

Rim shape R048 distinguishes itself from the other two forms through a more everted rim, which is also externally thickened. According to our records, this jar was often produced in coarse-ware fabrics, and one fragment is also blackened, testifying to the use of this jar for cooking. Rim diameters range between 9 and 21 cm and illustrate substantial variations in size for this jar type. Both the largest and smallest rim diameters are related to coarse-ware vessels. R048 appears in deposits from the 5th to 6th centuries and later. Similar shapes are illustrated for the domestic quarter of Paykend, shahrestan 1 (Semenov and Mirzaakhmedov 2007: 87, fig. 35.4; 100, fig. 48.5). The suggested date for these analogies – early medieval (Semenov and Mirzaakhmedov 2007: 19) – roughly corresponds to our preliminary findings but does not add further precision to our chronological assessment.

Shape code R055. Jar, neckless and globular, with upright or slightly everted simple rim, and related shape (R055.1).

R055 designates a basic jar shape with a substantial variation in rim diameters. The majority of fragments have a coarse fabric, and individual sherds show traces of blackening, which suggests this type of vessel was used in food preparation and cooking. Many of the vessels were clearly hand-made. Two specimens show a handle (see one example in fig. 4.46.2), which may have been a standard feature. So far, R055 jar rims have only featured in assemblages at Ramitan and Paykend. Relevant deposits were dated from the first centuries CE up to the early Islamic period (see Catalogue). No pattern is noticeable in ware, size or state of preservation across this considerable chronological range, and it is possible that such basic shapes related to food preparation persist largely unchanged.

In the oasis, comparable jar shapes are documented for Kyzylkyr and Setalak (Filanovich 1983: 33, fig. 8.13; 50, fig. 16.36; 100, fig. 37.23) as well as for Ganchtepa (Mirzaakhmedov et al. 2016: 225, fig. 10.1). These analogies are dated to a similar time span as the MAFOUB material, between the 1st and 8th centuries CE (Mirzaakhmedov et al. 2016: 225).

Despite some specimens of this shape being produced in fine ware, R055 constitutes the most popular coarse- and/or cooking-ware shape in the assemblages studied here.

Shape code R075. Jar, neckless, with everted, right-angled and externally thickened rim and lid-seated, and related shapes (R075.1 and R078).

Jars of this type are generally geographically and chronologically widespread. The shape is documented at four of the excavated MAFOUB sites so far, occurring in assemblages from the 1st century BCE to the 11th century CE. Interestingly, the early specimens of R075 are fine-ware vessels, while all the coarse-ware jars are recorded in assemblages from the transition from pre-Islamic to Islamic times or from the early Islamic period. Fine-ware versions are, however, still present in the late assemblages suggesting that there is no clear distinction according to ware (see also fig. 4.73). It is important to note that these observations are still preliminary, as the R075 coarse-ware specimens are only documented in four assemblages, with a marked concentration in two of them (Ramitan F US1063 and site 250 US156). Analogies to R075 were recorded at various sites in the Bukhara Oasis, including Ganchtepa (Mirzaakhmedov et al. 2016: 225, fig. 10.15) and Setalak 1 (Filanovich 1983: 90, figs. 37.34–35, 80), in assemblages dated between the 4th and the 8th centuries CE.

R075.1 differs from R075 only in its slimmer body profile (see Catalogue). A single occurrence is recorded so far.

R078 (see Catalogue) is also close to the original shape, presenting a version with an almost hooked rim profile. Similar to R075, there are fine- and coarse-ware fragments.

Both R075.1 and R078 were found in early Islamic assemblages.

Together with shape group R047, R048 and R055, jar shape R075 constitutes one of the most prominent coarse-ware types (fig. 4.72). At the same time, it should be stressed that none of these shapes are limited to coarse-ware fabrics (fig. 4.73).

FIGURE 4.71 Site 250, trench A. Example of a near-complete cooking ware pot from US156
PHOTO MAFOUB

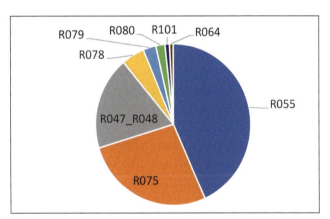

FIGURE 4.72 Shape distribution among coarse-ware fabrics (the proportion of shapes is based on rim eves)

FIGURE 4.70 Ramitan, trench C. Examples of coarse ware from deposits from 2nd–3rd and 3rd–4th centuries CE
PHOTOS MAFOUB

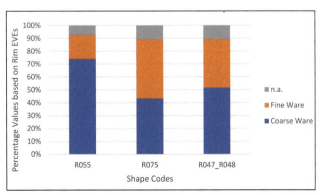

FIGURE 4.73 Proportion of fine and coarse wares across shape groups

Figure 4.73 shows the proportion of fine and coarse wares across the three shape groups that feature most prominently among coarse-ware fabrics. The unidentified fragments will be re-examined during the upcoming field seasons. Even if these should prove to be coarse wares, the overall picture will not change.

Shape code R069. Hole-mouth jar with externally thickened, straight-edged and lid-seated rim, and related shapes (R069.1 and R069.2).

The overall shape of R069 is clearly related to R075 but represents a separate pottery type with a distinct function. Specimens of R069 and related shapes are produced in fine-ware fabrics and usually show incised decoration on the vessel shoulder. One fragment has a perforation below the rim. Considering similar jars from excavations of shahrestan 1 in Paykend, both the decorative scheme and perforations seem to be a regular feature of later versions of this shape (Semenov and Mirzaakhmedov 2007: 86, fig. 34.4; 94, fig. 42.9; 98, figs. 46.1–2). Jar R069 appears in assemblages from the 2nd and 3rd centuries CE up to the 8th to 9th centuries CE. Its full chronological range is not yet clear, as this shape has relatively sparse recurrences in all three varieties (see Catalogue). Many parallels are documented from the oasis, though, such as at Kyzylkyr 2 (Filanovich 1983: 50, fig. 16.7) and Setalak 2 (Filanovich 1983: 59, fig. 19.6). Later specimens from Vardana show rich incised decorations analogous to some of the MAFOUB fragments (Pozzi, Mirzaakhmedov, and Sultanova 2019: 236, fig. 7.8). Chronologically, these comparisons correspond to the late pre-Islamic occurrences recorded in our data.

Shape code R079. Jar, biconical and neckless, with everted, right-angled rim, and often with slip-painted decoration.

This jar shape exists in various sizes ranging from small to medium. Most prominent are the slip-decorated specimens (see also 4.4.3.1), which all occurred in a single assemblage and form a distinct group. Other fragments were labelled with this shape code based on vessel profile similarities, although the shape definition might be adapted in the future when more data becomes available. The small version of R079 with slip-painted decoration is hand-shaped, while the larger vessels are wheel-thrown. The shape is generally very simple. Slip-painted ware occurs in the assemblages of the MAFOUB excavations from the earliest periods (see 4.4.3.1), but the specific dotted patterns are found on jars from an early Islamic context (site 250 US156). Vessel shapes and patterns show parallels with ceramics from Khorezm (Bolelov 2000: 30, fig. 1) and Chach (Levina 1971: 118–20, fig. 35.14, figs. 36.10–11).

Shape code R076. Jug with slightly flaring neck, collared rim and ovoid body, slightly projecting flat base and strap handle reaching from just below the rim to the vessel body near its maximum diameter, and related shapes (R071 and R077).

R076 and its related shapes constitute a group of vessels that reached their greatest prominence in the early Islamic period and were most probably used as water jugs. The necks and bodies of these jugs are often decorated with incised, combed or impressed motifs (cf. fig. 4.59.5). One jug rim occurred in a context from the 5th to 6th centuries (Ramitan G US1958). At 10 cm it has the largest rim diameter of all the jugs in this group and might constitute an early version of this type.

4.2.2.3 Large Containers/Storage Jars

Shape code R062. Storage jar, large, with short neck and almost upright or slightly everted, thickened rim, and related shapes (R062.1, R062.2, R062.3, R062.4 and R052, R050).

Storage jars of this type are generally large but vary in size between roughly 60 cm and about 1m in height and 20 cm to 46 cm in rim diameter. Specimens are usually thick-walled (>1.2 cm).

Large storage jars are a vessel group that is difficult to assess chronologically within the Bukhara Oasis, as the vessels apparently formed prime objects for reuse in various functions (see 4.5.3). Accordingly, none of the near-complete specimens were found in their original contexts. Rim fragments, wall sherds or parts of bases occasionally cropped up in the excavated assemblages, usually in varied states of preservation, some still quite crisp, while others so worn that they betray a longer cycle of redepositing. Consequently, archaeological contexts that contained fragments of R062 cover a large chronological span, reaching from the 1st to the 14th century CE. Most storage jars of this type generally appear to be shaped from coils. Potentially later specimens might have been shaped on the wheel, although they do not appear to be wheel-thrown. Decorative schemes include trickling patterns of slip-paint and rows of impressions around the rim or shoulder area. One specimen from Ramitan, trench G, US1952 showed a mark on the shoulder in the shape of three parallel indents (fig. 4.75.2). Marks on storage vessels are well documented within the Bukhara Oasis and other areas in Sogdia and are thought to be related to taxation or indicative of customer and artisan/workshop relations (Marshak 2012: 145–46; Pozzi, Mirzaakhmedov and Sultanova 2019: 237–38). Only this one example is recorded from the MAFOUB excavations so far. The archaeological context of the rim fragment belongs to the first phase of the architectural structure of Ramitan G and is dated to the 5th and 6th centuries CE (Rante and Mirzaakhmedov 2019: 187, fig. 177A).

In the literature, storage jar rims similar to Ro62 appear from the last century BCE, although large container vessels are part of the repertoire from the outset (Mukhamedjanov, Mirzaakhmedov, and Adylov 1982: 87, fig. 2.3 (Bukhara 3) and 2–3 (Bukhara 4)). Body sherds of large hand-shaped storage vessels occurred in the early assemblages of Iskijkat A (US384; fig. 4.74) dated to the 3rd and 2nd centuries BCE, although the associated rim shapes are unknown. Jars similar to Ro62 are also part of the assemblages at Kyzylkyr 2 (Filanovich 1983: 50, fig. 16.5). The semi-complete specimen (Ramitan G US6026) was found reused in a *badrab* and is comparable to a jar from the site of Vardana in the oasis, which is dated to the 7th and 8th centuries CE (Pozzi, Mirzaakhmedov, and Sultanova 2019: 235–37, fig. 7.10). However, the vessel from Vardana has a smaller rim diameter. Ro62 contributes the largest proportion of our recorded data.

The related shapes illustrate the variety of these storage jars.

archaeological contexts cover a date range from the 5th and 6th to the 13th and 14th centuries CE.

Ro62.2 can be regarded as another version of the neckless storage jar. Our data on this shape so far is too sparse (see Catalogue) for further interpretations. One fragment showed a row of impressions.

Ro62.3 represents a form with short neck. In contrast to Ro62, the rim profile is squared with a straight edge. All records of this shape derive from Ramitan trench G. One fragment occurred in a context associated with phase 1 of the structure and dated to the 5th to 6th centuries CE, while another fragment was reused for pavement in a much later context, dated to the 13th to 14th centuries. The semi-complete specimen of Ro62.3 was found as part of a *badrab* construction.

Ro62.4 shows a thickened rim with bevelled edge. This variant again has a short neck and is decorated with a row of impressions. One semi-complete specimen derives from a *badrab* excavated at site 250.

FIGURE 4.74   Iskijkat, trench A. Example of hand-shaped storage vessel fragment
PHOTOS MAFOUB

Ro62.1 is documented from various trenches at Ramitan (see Catalogue). Only the rim part is preserved, reflecting a neckless jar with an externally thickened and rounded rim. Fragments show traces of red wash or slip-painted decoration and rows of impressions on the rim. Again, the original time of manufacturing and use of this shape is difficult to assess, as all the sherds were residual or reused. Neckless storage jars appear in the Bukhara Oasis in the earliest assemblages (Mukhamedjanov, Mirzaakhmedov, and Adylov 1982: 82, fig. 1.3 (Bukhara-1); Omelchenko 2019: 220–21, fig. 10 (Paikend IIA)), though it is difficult to assess morphological similarities due to the poor state of preservation of the MAFOUB specimens. The associated

FIGURE 4.75   Bukhara Oasis, examples of storage jars R62 and related shapes: (1) Site 250, trench A, US125; (2) Ramitan, trench G, US1952
PHOTOS MAFOUB

R052 shows the upright rim of a neckless storage jar. A ridge below the rim is decorated with regular impressions. This form only occurred twice in assemblages so far. To judge from the worn state, the fragments were residual. The shape is quite distinct, though, and is illustrated in other sites in the oasis, including Kyzylkyr 1, Setalak 1 and 2 and Bukhara, all of these dated to the 3rd–5th centuries CE (Filanovich 1983: 33, fig. 8.4, 6, 59, fig. 19.14, 32, 90, fig. 37.26, 29, 58–59; Mukhamedjanov, Mirzaakhmedov, and Adylov 1982: 92, fig. 3.6 (Bukhara 5)).

Storage vessels in the shape of whole-mouth jars with externally thickened rims, either flat-topped (R060) or rounded with regular indentations (R060.1), are attested as well, although data on this type is insufficient at this stage to go into further detail.

Individual jars from late pre-Islamic contexts (Ramitan F US1103 and Ramitan G US1866B, Fig. 4.76) show a more elaborate rim and slightly thinner walls (approximately 0.8–1.3 cm). One of the jars has an internally bevelled rim, the other a lid-seated one.

Similarly, R050 represents a neckless storage jar with an everted, squared and lid-seated rim. A variety with a short neck (R050.1) is also attested. Both types first occurred in contexts dated to the 5th and 6th centuries CE (see Catalogue).

Overall, a distinction in manufacturing technique is noticeable in the various storage jars, which might concern both size and chronological developments in the shaping technique of the vessels. While the large thick-walled specimens are coil-built and show corresponding traces on the inner and outer surfaces of wall fragments, the slightly more delicate and smaller vessels are shaped on the wheel and display respective marks on the interior surface. The earliest wall fragments are good examples of coil-built vessels, but some of the near-complete vessels still show the surface irregularities characteristic of hand-shaped vessels. It is thus difficult to determine an exact time horizon for an enduring change in shaping technology for both coil-building and wheel-shaping, and they might have been used simultaneously, perhaps in different workshops.

The lid-seated rim structure raises the question of the types of lids employed to cover these containers. Answers to this question have to remain partially hypothetical due to the lack of adequate evidence. For the large and sturdy jars, stone lids might have been an option, and relevant stone fragments were found in some contexts. Other materials could have equally been used on the jars, including pottery lids or possibly wood (?). Most rim structures would also allow for a textile cover to be strung around the rim.

4.2.2.4 *Special Forms*
Lids:
Shape code R061. Lid, flat with straight edge, and related shape (R61.1).

Lids repeatedly formed a part of assemblages in the MAFOUB excavations. Flat lids in the shape of R061 have occurred at all excavated sites so far, with the exception of Iskijkat. Their chronological distribution suggests that this type of lid emerged at the beginning of the Islamic period. In this regard, further lid shapes might still appear at Iskijkat when more pottery from Islamic period contexts is processed in the future. Specimens of R61 show various combed, mould-stamped or incised concentric decorations, which again point to an Islamic date (figs. 4.77.1 and 4.77.3). Several fragments were blackened around the rim, suggesting they were, at least partly, used on cooking pots. However, the lids are made of a different fabric, which is often porous and slightly grainier than fabric A, with occasional coarse inclusions, but is less densely tempered than CW1. Flat lids similar to R061 occurred in assemblages from pits related to MAFOUB excavations of the kiln area at Paykend, sector E (Rante and Mirzaakhmedov 2019: 224–25; Guionova et al. 2013: 87–88, pls. 4.3–4). Guionova assumes that the flat lids could have been used to cover tanours (Guionova 2013: 88). Fragments from tanours from context Ramitan F SU1063, however, are much larger in diameter (c.40–60 cm) than most of the lids. A single R061 specimen showed a diameter of 38 cm. This might have potentially been used to cover a tanour. Aside from the MAFOUB excavations, analogous lids were also found by the Russian-Uzbek team during field work in the Paykend suburb (Semenov and Mirzaakhmedov 2007: 160, figs. 108.7–8).

Unlike R061, a flat lid of even thickness, the related shape R061.1 is a massive lid with a flat bottom and triangular (conical) section. Specimens of R061.1 reflect rich and varied decoration, which seems to be characteristic of this type (figs. 4.77.2 and 4.77.4–5). At least some of these lids appear to have been moulded. Fragments recorded so far were concentrated in two sites, Ramitan, trench F, and Paykend, trench B. Chronologically, the form seems to be contemporary with R061. Again, a number of specimens show a blackened underside, which points to their use in cooking.

POTTERY

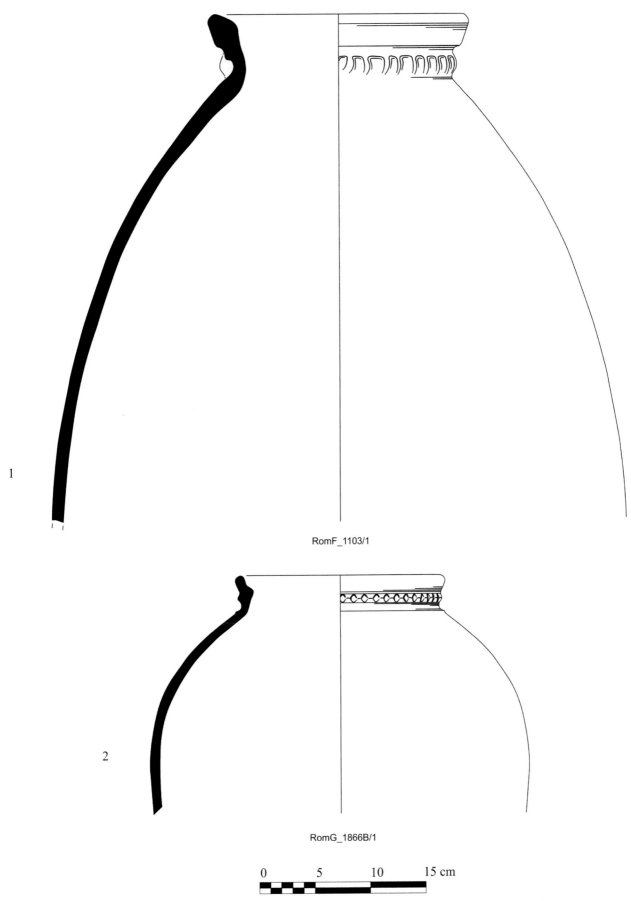

FIGURE 4.76 Ramitan, individual jars from late pre-Islamic contexts: (1) Ramitan, trench F, US1103; (2) Ramitan, trench G, US1866B
DRAWINGS FAITH VARDY

Shape code R088. Lid, domed with everted, flat and almost straight-cut edge, and related shapes (R088.1)

These lid shapes constitute the second popular group of lids in the MAFOUB assemblages. Manufacturing traces on specimens indicate that this form was mould-made (see fig. 4.34.7). Fragments also show a rich decorative pattern. Their chronological spread largely mirrors that of R061 and R061.1 and seems confined to the early Islamic period (see Catalogue). Both shape groups have a high rate of co-occurrences in the assemblages of Paykend B, Ramitan F and site 250. The use of R088 might have been more diverse than that of R061 and R061.1, as only the fragment from Paykend (PayB1632/4) displays traces of soot around the rim. Lids of shape R088 are made with fine-ware fabrics, including fabric/firing groups A and F. A rich assemblage of analogous lids was part of the material from the MAFOUB excavations of Paykend sector E, the pottery kilns (Rante and Mirzaakhmedov 2019: 224–25; Guionova et al. 2013: 83, 86, pl. 6.2) Interestingly, many of these analogous lids are plain. Parallels from the Russian-Uzbek excavations of the Paykend suburb, by contrast, show rich decorations (Semenov and Mirzaakhmedov 2007: 161, figs. 109.4–7).

One further lid shape, R082 (see Catalogue), deserves mention here, although it only occurred once in the assemblages. This singular piece represents an interesting example, as it is part of the assemblage of a large pit (US156) at site 250 and shows slip-painted decoration similar to the jars of shape R079 in the same assemblage. US156 also accounts for a large proportion of lid shape R088 and also fragments of R061. The slip-painted lid sets itself apart from the other lid shapes in its appearance and decorative scheme. It was probably used on jars of analogous decoration.

Our evidence for dedicated lid shapes is predominantly related to the end of the pre-Islamic period and the initial centuries of Islamic rule. Filanovich mentions conical lids from the sites Kyzylkyr 2 and Setalak 2 in the Bukhara Oasis, which she dated mainly to the 4th and 5th centuries (Filanovich 1983: 50, fig. 16.39; 52–53; 58–60, figs. 19.11, 18; 120). The lid-knob recorded from US1952 in Ramitan G could correspond to these specimens. R009 (see Catalogue) also shows a profile that appears to be more suitable for a lid than a dish. This shape only occurred once in a 2nd–3rd-centuries context. No further analogies are recorded from the pre-Islamic contexts of the MAFOUB excavations to date, although this may change as more material is being processed.

FIGURE 4.77   Ramitan, trench F. Examples of lids from US1063
PHOTOS MAFOUB

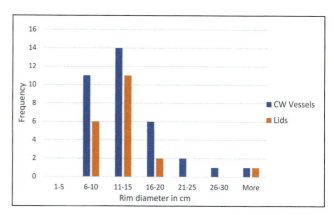

FIGURE 4.78   Coarse wares and lids: distribution of rim diameters

4.3   *Variations in Surface Treatments*

Ceramic assemblages of the Bukhara Oasis show an interesting mix of vessel shapes, surface treatments and decorative styles from antiquity to the early Islamic period. Individual decorative patterns and techniques appear to be restricted to certain parts of the repertoire, and their decorative schemes change over time.

In this section, we selected the most significant techniques and decorative patterns within the pottery assemblages, and they allow us to follow the diachronic variations in the use of surface treatments in the oasis's repertoire.

As already demonstrated for the vessel forms, some of the discussed surface treatments show a chronologically consistent distribution, while others seem to appear throughout the whole sequence. In those cases, the long chronological distribution could reflect a continuity in the use of this particular treatment through time, or it could imply patterns of re-deposition and the reuse of vessels with certain surface treatments and decorative elements in contexts later than their original one.

4.3.1   Slip Paint

The use of clay slips for decorating ceramic vessels with a trickling pattern is a well-known technique throughout the Bukhara Oasis, specifically in pre-Islamic times (Bruno and Puschnigg, 2022). Once the vessels have dried to the "leather-hard" stage, a watery slip is poured on the shoulder and trickles down the external surface. During the firing process, the slip assumes a reddish or brownish colour of different shades, mostly depending on the kiln temperature and atmosphere, as well as the composition of the slip, that creates a sharp contrast with the light or cream-coloured background of the vessel's surface.

The trickling pattern of slip paint is usually found on large storage jars (such as R062, R062.1, R062.4) and less frequently on other closed shapes, such as jar or jugs (R051) and small pots. According to the data collected so far, this kind of decoration seems to be introduced in the Bukhara Oasis at an early stage in its occupational history. The first evidence of this technique in our assemblages derives from Iskijkat, trench A, where sherds of storage jars with slip-painted decorations appear in contexts dated to the 3rd–1st centuries BCE (US384) and to a period between the 1st century BCE and the 1st century CE (US375). Roughly at the same time, we find this technique on pottery from Kakishtuvan (US301, 1st century CE) and Ramitan (trench A, US148, 1st to early 3rd century CE). In the following phases, during the 2nd–3rd centuries and the 3rd–4th centuries CE, the use of slip-painted decoration seems to have increased, and relevant sherds occur at various sites across the oasis.

During the 5th–6th centuries CE, the technique is still well attested in the archaeological contexts, although the number of specimens slightly decreases through time, and by the 7th–9th centuries CE slip-painted decoration is rarely found in the assemblages, as attested by the later deposits in Iskijkat, site 250, Paykend, trench B, and Ramitan, trench G. Nevertheless, many sherds, as well as near-complete storage jars with slip-painted decoration occurred in some of these later contexts, albeit as residual or reused elements. Some specimens are badly abraded due to their long depositional histories, suggesting an earlier date of manufacturing, while others are still in a relatively good condition, illustrating the reuse of this type of vessel for constructions and installations (see 4.5.3).

According to our data, the decorative pattern shows only minor modifications through time. These modifications concern the quality of the slip and variations in colour, ranging from a dark brown, almost black, to a reddish-brown depending on differences in firing conditions. Earlier designs of slip-painted decoration tendentially show relatively thick, dark slip around the upper part of the vessel running down the walls and against a contrasting light background, while the slip applied to later specimens generally appears to be thinner and of a watery consistency. Almost all the fragments and vessels with slip-painted decoration belong to the same fabrics (group A), which is widespread in the pre-Islamic layers of the oasis (see 4.2.1).

The data that emerged from the recent excavations attest to the diffusion of the slip-painted decoration across the main sites of the oasis from their early occupation levels onwards. This pattern of distribution is consistent with the results of previous excavations in the Bukhara Oasis, as reflected in the ceramic sequence of Ramish (Sulejmanov and Urakov 1977: 58; Shishkina, Sulejmanov, and Koshelenko 1985: pls. 134–35), where black streaks on vessels appear in layers dated to the 1st–2nd centuries CE (Shishkina, Sulejmanov, and Koshelenko 1985: 286–87) and increase in frequency during the 2nd–3rd centuries and 3rd–4th centuries CE (Sulejmanov and Urakov 1977: 64; Shishkina, Sulejmanov, and Koshelenko 1985: 287). The same process seems to be reflected in the ceramic sequence of Bukhara (Mukhamedjanov, Mirzaakhmedov, and Adylov 1982: 91). Following the MAFOUB excavations, we can now ascertain that the first evidence for this decorative technique appears in the Bukhara Oasis in an earlier phase than what commonly attributed, as testified by the specimens from Iskijkat, which were found in contexts C^{14}-dated to the 3rd–1st centuries BCE and the 1st century BCE to the 1st century CE. These fragments demonstrate that this technique was already used at this early time in the heart of the oasis.

Patterns of trickling slip paint is a well-known type of decoration in the Kaunchi-period assemblages in ancient Chach (Tashkent Oasis), where they constitute a dominant trait of the pottery production of the phases Kaunchi 1 and 2 (Buryakov und Koshelenko 1985: pls. 146–48), which are dated from the 2nd century BCE to the 2nd century CE and from the 2nd to 4th centuries CE, respectively (Buryakov and Koshelenko 1985: pls. 146–48). The slip-painted vessels found in the early levels at the sites of the Bukhara Oasis should then be considered to be contemporary with those of the Tashkent Oasis. This correlation in decorative techniques is further reflected in individual shapes found in the Bukhara Oasis, which correspond to those from ancient Chach. Previous studies found that during the 2nd and 3rd centuries CE the number of vessel forms similar to those in the Kaunchi-period Tashkent Oasis appear to

FIGURE 4.79   Bukhara Oasis. Slip-painted sherds from the MAFOUB excavations
PHOTOS MAFOUB

increase (Mukhamedjanov, Mirzaakhmedov and Adylov 1982: 90, 95–96).[13]

13   The use of slip-painted decoration for medium-sized closed shapes is well attested at Samarkand in the pre-Islamic period (Lyonnet 2013: 277). In terms of the use of slip paint, pottery excavated from rubbish pits dated to the second half of the 5th and 6th centuries show close similarities to the ceramic material found in the Bukhara Oasis (Lebedeva 1990: fig. 1. 25–34). According to Lebedeva (Lebedeva 1990: 163) this assemblage is of a mixed character, also showing elements of the Kaunchi pottery tradition. For the Bukhara Oasis, the ceramic repertoire appears to be equally mixed (Mukhamedjanov, Mirzaakhmedov, and Adylov 1982: 96–97). In the Kattakurgan district of the Samarkand region, between Samarkand and Bukhara, jugs and

Slip paint is also used to produce a wider range of colour contrasting motifs (fig. 4.80), although most again occur on closed shapes.[14] A pattern of intersecting semi-circles (fig. 4.80.1) is depicted on two fragments of storage vessels found in Ramitan (trench G, US 1952) and Iskijkat (trench A, US321), respectively. In opposition to

jars with a similar type of slip-painted decoration were found (Pugachenkova 1989: 30–32, fig. 9).

14   As occurrences of these types of decoration are very rare so far, we do not fully understand their spatial or chronological distribution within the Bukhara Oasis. Still, these fragments show that there was more variety in the use of slip as a decorative feature than initially expected.

the trickling patterns associated with the Kaunchi tradition, the light-coloured circular elements contrast with the dark background of the surface. This variety in colour effects testifies to the advanced competence in controlling the firing process and a generally high standard of artisanship in the ceramic production of the oasis at the time. In both cases, the stratigraphic context of these sherds is later than the main evidence of trickling patterns of slip paint that are dated to the 2nd–3rd centuries CE. At Ramitan, trench G, the context (US1952) is assigned to the 5th–6th centuries CE, while at Iskijkat, trench A, the stratigraphic position of the context (US321) points to the 7th–9th centuries CE phase. Due to the well-known reason of material reuse and the fragmentary state of the pottery, it is difficult to assess the period of manufacturing of these two pieces, though it seems plausible to assume that they are contemporary with part of the Kaunchi-style slip-painted vessels.

Another slip-painted pattern occurs on two vessels found at site 250 (US156; figs. 4.80.2–3). The first specimen (fig. 4.80.3) is a small hand-shaped jar with individual dark brown dots or horizontally oriented brush strokes of slip paint on the cream-coloured background of the external surface and a streak of the same slip around the rim. The second specimen, a fragment of a bigger and wheel-thrown jar (fig. 4.80.2), shows a slightly different pattern with vertically oriented brush strokes of red-coloured slip paint on the vessel shoulder. Both were found during the excavation of a deep pit related to the 9th–10th centuries CE phase of the settlement. A further fragment of what might be a lid shows a similar pattern (cf. 4.4.2.2.4, R082). Analogous jar shapes, with parts that also have dotted patterns, occur chronologically earlier in the Kaunchi tradition of ancient Chach (Levina 1971: 118–20, fig. 35.14, figs. 36.10–11) and the Kangju period of Khorezm (Vishnevskaya 2001: 132, figs. 3.1–2). Still, later versions of such decorative motifs are also attested at the site of Kanka in the Tashkent Oasis (Brusenko and Galieva 1982: 126, figs. 2.1, 7, 11, 15).

4.3.2 Slip-Coated Vessels

The coating of tableware vessels or medium-sized jars predominantly occurs in the assemblages of the pre-Islamic levels. Due to the fragmented state of most of the specimens, it is often difficult to assess how much of the vessel surfaces were covered by slip. Sometimes the horizontal boundary of the slip-coated area is clearly visible on the surfaces (fig. 4.82.6). Slip-coated vessels often belong to open shapes, while closed forms are also attested, albeit less frequently (fig. 4.82). The slip is usually of good quality, ranging from red (fig. 4.81.2) to reddish-brown and black (fig. 4.81.3) tones, mostly without any traces of burnishing. In open shapes, the upper part of the rim is often of a darker colour (figs. 4.81.4–5), probably due to stacking the vessels inside the kiln for firing.

Slip-coated vessels are widespread throughout the oasis, and fragments with this surface treatment were found in the lower levels of almost all the trenches opened by MAFOUB. Some of the earliest specimens with this treatment, such as a small goblet with traces of a very abraded red slip (fig. 4.81.1), were found in Bukhara, trench A, in a context related to the earliest occupation of the site and dated to the 3rd century BCE (US271), as well as in Iskijkat (trench A, US384, US392), where fragments with a red and black coating were found in contexts dated to the 3rd–1st centuries BCE together with the first specimens of slip-painted decoration. Later on, and mostly during the first centuries of our era, the fragments of slip-coated vessels increase in number, and red, brown or black slips appear on many open shapes (fig. 4.81), especially on rounded bowls with upright, thickened rim (R006, R006.1, R006.2). The chronological distribution of slip-coated vessels is the same across all the MAFOUB excavations, peaking around the 2nd–3rd centuries CE and the 3rd–4th

FIGURE 4.81   Bukhara Oasis, slip-coated open vessels: (1) Bukhara, trench A, US271; (2) Ramitan, trench A, US131; (3) Ramitan, trench C, US557; (4) Kakishtuvan, trench A, US302; (5) Kakishtuvan, trench A, US297
DRAWINGS JACOPO BRUNO; PHOTOS MAFOUB

FIGURE 4.80   Bukhara Oasis. Other slip painted motifs: (1) Ramitan, trench G, US1952; (2–4) site 250, trench A, US156
DRAWINGS FAITH VARDY; PHOTOS MAFOUB

FIGURE 4.82 Bukhara Oasis, slip-coated close vessels: (1) Iskijkat, trench A, US375; (2) Iskijkat, trench A, US375; (3) Iskijkat, trench B, US614; (4) Iskijkat, trench A, US371; (5) Iskijkat, trench B, US610; (6) Iskijkat, trench B, US616
PHOTOS MAFOUB

centuries CE, while in later complexes a sharp decline is noticeable, and the rare specimens of slip-coated vessels are probably residual.

4.3.3 Glazed Ware

The quantity of glazed material in our collection is quite restricted since we initially focused on pre-Islamic assemblages. In total we recorded approximately 210 glazed sherds so far, mostly body sherds and rim fragments of open shapes. The first specimens appear in contexts related to 7th–9th century CE phase, reflecting the introduction of this technique in the oasis that is commonly dated to the end of the 8th century and the beginning of the 9th century CE (Shishkina 1979: 21–24; Silvi Antonini 2009: 171). Both monochrome and polychrome glazed wares are documented in the assemblages. Most of the specimens were found in contexts related to the 10th–12th centuries and are consistent with the typical assemblages of this period, as attested elsewhere in the oasis (Mirzaakhmedov and Pozzi 2019: 250–53). Many of them show the characteristic black, or black and red, motifs on white background under clear glaze that are typical of the 10th–11th-century production.

5 Conclusion: Ceramics from the Bukhara Oasis – the Current Perspective

Our evidence from the six different sites sampled in the MAFOUB excavations draws a rich and multi-layered image of the ceramic production and use in the oasis across the centuries. The current findings are certainly preliminary in many aspects, but a number of observations are highly significant and reflect the situation succinctly.

On the whole, it is important to note that developments, both technological and in design, do not occur simultaneously in all the different parts of the pottery repertoire. Developments are thus not strictly linear and cannot unambiguously be divided into "before" and "after". Divisions are not only reflecting purely chronological processes but also functional variations.

5.1 Variations in the Vessel Repertoire

Repertoires are conventionally separated into vessel groups catering to distinct functions, such as tableware, containers and coarse or cooking ware. These are potentially subject to various rates of change and transformation.

We cannot reconstruct all the stages of development along the entire chronological scale, but a rough outline is projected here according to the various functions and activities involved.

Drinking: relevant vessel forms include goblets and deep bowls. Goblets are part of the vessel repertoire from the earliest occupation levels. Often, their base is shaped like a foot, but there are also flat-based versions. Footed goblets are not frequent elements in the assemblages but span the chronological sequence from the beginning until the later pre-Islamic phase; subsequently, they disappear. During this long period of production and use, footed goblets show a variety of different body profiles, volumes and vessel heights. The development appears to be broadly consistent with other Sogdian sites, including Erkurgan and Samarkand (Koshelenko 1985: 418, pl. 130, 420–21, pls. 132–33).

In contrast to the footed vessels, the evidence for goblets with flat or ring bases are limited within the MAFOUB assemblage, although this could be entirely accidental. Some of these shapes might also overlap with deep bowls with a similar rim diameter, which could have served the same purpose. Goblets had vanished by the advent of the Islamic period. Instead, we find deep bowls, sometimes with everted rims, which resemble modern tea bowls in shape and could have been used for drinking.

At this point in time, other materials, such as glass, would have started to play an increasing role in the vessel repertoires as well. Many points are still unknown, but we may generally assume that some vessel forms served multiple functions, similar to modern Central Asian dinnerware.

Eating: medium-sized bowls are the obvious choice in this regard. The medium-sized bowls occur, with different variations of shape, throughout the chronological sequence of the oasis. The relationship between medium-sized and large bowls is not clear yet. Most of the large open forms in our data have the appearance of basins and might have been used in food preparation as well as for serving food. In early Islamic deposits, large shallow bowls or plates emerge, which generally show a refined quality. During the late pre-Islamic phase new shallow forms appear in the repertoire, giving rise to the impression that large shallow plates are now a more prominent part of the tableware repertoire. Our data in this regard might be incomplete, though, as excavations of early occupation levels at Paykend showed that large and relatively shallow bowls were already in use at the time. More material is needed to evaluate potential changes in the repertoire of open forms across the entire chronological sequence.

Storing: vessels for storing food show a variety of sizes. Large jars for longer-term storage first occur in our data from the early centuries CE. Apart from differentiations in rim shape, the form remains largely unchanged for centuries, including the typical slip-painted decoration. Jars of the late pre-Islamic and early Islamic phase show a finer shaped rim and are smaller in size. Larger storage facilities, for instance such as the silo, might have partly fulfilled the purpose of the large jars. We do not yet have enough evidence to redraw the entire development of the large storage vessels. Smaller containers are present from the beginning and might have been used in different places in the household. Some of the neckless jars show perforation below the rim, which could have allowed air inside the jar even when covered. The exact use of such vessels is as yet unclear, but they are fairly widespread across Central Asia.

Cooking: cooking pots vary considerable in size. Smaller pots often have a rod handle. Most of the larger specimens are not fully preserved, although some body sherds show lug-handles attached to the vessel wall. Potential correlations between vessel forms and certain fabrics are unknown at the moment and further research, specifically scientific analyses, is needed to draw any conclusions. Later specimens are lid-seated and many of the dedicated lids show traces of soot around the edge, suggesting that they were used to cover pots during the cooking process. For the earlier pots, no obvious covers were identified. This does not necessarily mean that lids were not commonly used in cooking, and again more material is needed to evaluate the situation.

Fragments of low, pan-shaped coarse-ware forms were also recorded. These vessels are, however, rare in our data. In the literature, they are often referred to as braziers (Semenov and Mirzaakhmedov 2007: 8, 62, fig. 10.3), though their function might have varied and possibly included food preparation. The shape is again well documented throughout Central Asia, but it generally seems to be scarce within assemblages.

Aside from the cooking vessels, a number of tanour fragments occurred in deposits from the 5th to 6th centuries CE onwards. Our observations are still too fragmentary to draw any conclusions regarding their chronological development or potential changes in shape or size.

5.2 Variations in Technology

Manufacturing techniques mostly include shaping by hand, shaping on the wheel, throwing on the wheel and the use of moulds. As initially stated, these techniques are not strictly consecutive in a chronological sense, but to some degree depend on the type of vessel, the ware and the fabric. A detailed study of how specific vessel types are shaped is still needed, but a brief survey will suffice for now.

Many pottery vessels from the earliest levels onwards are wheel-thrown. Some of the shallow forms, such as R020, are most probably shaped with the help of a mould. Early coarse wares generally appear to be hand-shaped, while some of the later cooking pots are clearly produced with the help of the potter's wheel. It is still unclear whether this change in vessel shaping correlates in any way with the use and preparation of a specific clay fabric. At the same time, a number of hand-shaped fine-ware vessels occur sporadically throughout the chronological sequence. More data and more detailed analysis are required to assess whether these exceptions relate to vessels made for specific purposes. We mentioned the example of incense burners, but the spectrum appears to be broader. Some shapes betray a distinct style, such as the small jar in pit US156, though the use of slip-painted decoration is part of the ceramic production in the oasis from the outset. Various strains of manufacturing techniques appear to co-exist over various phases in the ceramic development.

Changes in firing technology are more linear, it seems. The fabrics and colouring of the ceramic surfaces indicate

FIGURE 4.83 Bukhara Oasis, coccio-pesto technique: (1) Paykend, shahrestan 1, Islamic dwelling; (2) Ramitan, trench G, US1820; (3) Ramitan, trench G, US1667
PHOTOS MAFOUB

a gradual increase in firing temperature. Glazed pottery only appears after the introduction of Islamic rule, as is generally the case in Central Asia. The early Islamic ceramic repertoire certainly reflects substantial changes, including greater variations in applied and moulded decoration. Still, some of the older traditions, such as the slip-painted wares, persist for some time.

Another innovation that appears in our data in the Islamic phase is lamps, which are usually glazed. No specific lamp shape was identified from earlier contexts. We need to look in more detail at traces of reuse, which might indicate if certain vessel parts might have been reused as lamps. At the moment we have no clear evidence for this.

5.3   Patterns of Reuse

Occasionally, excavations revealed distinct types of material reuse, which provide a glimpse into the economic management of resources at the time. Most obvious in this regard are the sewage facilities or *badrab*s (fig. 4.84), which consist of old vessels stacked together to obtain some form of waste pipe. These constructions belong to the early Islamic period and rely on large storage vessels and water jugs. Occasionally, ceramic pipes are also found. The vessels have their bases chiselled out to facilitate unhindered passage. Some of the storage vessels involved belong to preceding phases, which blurs the exact chronological assessment of these jars.

Another form of material reuse is reflected in a number of buildings, again from the Islamic period, which show either floor pavement or wall tiling using large ceramic sherds (fig. 4.83). Here, large storage jars appear to provide the bulk of material as well.

In both cases, *badrab* and pavement or tiling, the vessels or pottery fragments used are not always contemporary and might derive from several preceding phases. Such practises remind us, however, that many interventions occur in the course of the stratigraphic build-up that affect the expected order. The careful evaluation of site formation processes in conjunction with the study of the ceramic material thus becomes all the more indispensable.

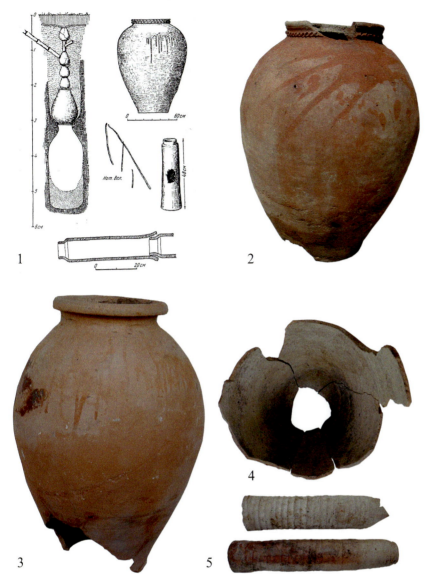

FIGURE 4.84
Bukhara Oasis, *badrab*s: (1) *badrab* (after Shishkin 1963: 113, fig. 53); (2) khum from *badrab* in Ramitan, trench G, US1866b; (3) khum from *badrab* in Ramitan, trench G, US6026; (4) khum from *badrab* in site 250, trench A, US125; (5) pipes from *badrab* in Ramitan, trench G, US6026
PHOTOS MAFOUB

Finally, the deliberate crushing of old vessels to produce temper for coarse wares is a less obvious form of material reuse. It is practised from the early phases of occupation in the oasis, as documented in the petrographic analysis. How much material is lost in this process is not yet clear, as samples are too small at the moment.

5.4 *Outlook*

In light of this open-ended study, our immediate aim is to complete the processing and recording of the remaining material and continue to accompany MAFOUB's ongoing fieldwork. As our understanding of the ceramic tradition within the Bukhara Oasis grows, we seek to further integrate our findings with other ongoing projects to explore concordances as well as potential differences relating to the various approaches and perspectives applied.

Moreover, we will link our evidence concerning pottery development with research on other materials, specifically glass and metals, as these industries directly affect the technological potential of ceramic production. This is of particular interest concerning the emergence of glazed wares and the refinement of cooking vessels, which appear in the early Islamic period. Still, interactions between different industries certainly occurred throughout the history of this region, and we need to consider all the various materials suitable to serve functions complementary to those of ceramic vessels if we want to understand the management of resources through time. Pottery is but one aspect of the rich material culture of Bukhara and its oasis.

6 Catalogue

All drawings in the catalogue are by F. Vardy and J. Bruno.

6.1 *Base Shapes*

Shape code	Total number of occurrences	Total sum of eves	Sites	Chronology of archaeological contexts
BA001	12	3.67	Iskijkat A Ramitan A, C	CE01–03, CE02–03, CE03, CE03–04, CE05–06
			Low ring base with simple, recessed base	
BA002	2	0.30	Ramitan A, C	CE03
			Ring base, ring profile almost right angled with smooth transition to vessel body	

Shape code	Total number of occurrences	Total sum of eves	Sites	Chronology of archaeological contexts
BA003	6	1.45	Iskijkat A Ramitan D Site 250 A	CE04–10, CE11–12
		Ring base or low ring foot with clear edgy foot profile		
BA004	142	24.41	Iskijkat A Kakishtuvan A Paykend B Ramitan A, C, D, F Site 250 A	BCE01–CE01, CE01, CE01–03, CE02–03, CE03–04, CE04, CE05, CE05–06, CE06, CE07–09, CE08–09, CE04–10, CE09–11, CE10, CE10–11, CE11–12, CE13–14
		Flat base, thick walled		

Shape code	Total number of occurrences	Total sum of eves	Sites	Chronology of archaeological contexts
BA005	31	4,69	Iskijkat A Kakishtuvan A Paykend B Ramitan A, C	BCE01–CE01, CE02–03, CE03, CE03–04, CE04, CE05, CE05–06, CE06, CE07–09, CE08–09, CE09, CE10
		Flat base, thin walled		
BA006	2	1.35	Bukhara A Site 250 A	CE04–10
		Ring base, ring profile acute angled		

Shape code	Total number of occurrences	Total sum of eves	Sites	Chronology of archaeological contexts
BA007	6	0.90	Iskijkat A Paykend B Ramitan C	CE02–03, CE05–06, CE07–09, CE10
		Flat base with slightly projecting profile, thick walled		
BA008	6	1.28	Iskijkat A Paykend B Ramitan C, F	CE03–04, CE04, CE09–10, CE10
		Flat base with slightly projecting profile, thin walled		
BA009	4	1.00	Iskijkat A Paykend B	BCE03–01, CE05–06
		Foot		

Shape code	Total number of occurrences	Total sum of eves	Sites	Chronology of archaeological contexts
BA009.1	1	0.22	Iskijkat A	CE02–03

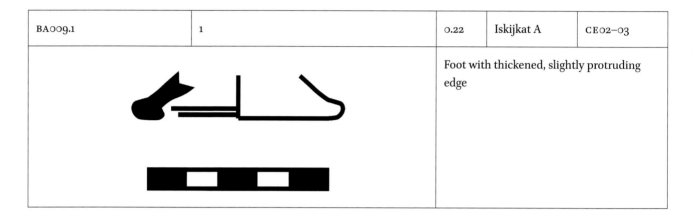

Foot with thickened, slightly protruding edge

BA009.2	1	0.30	Ramitan C	CE03–04

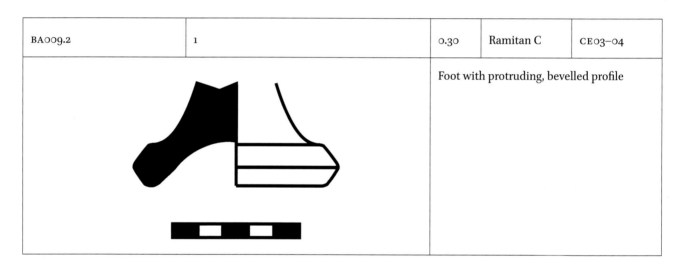

Foot with protruding, bevelled profile

BA009.3	1	1.00	Paykend B	CE10

Solid conical foot or pedestal

Shape code	Total number of occurrences	Total sum of eves	Sites	Chronology of archaeological contexts
BA010	1	0.20	Iskijkat A	CE02–03
		Flat base, obtuse angled, with clubbed edge		
BA011	6	1.73	Iskijkat A Paykend B Ramitan C Site 250 A	CE02–03, CE03–04, CE10, CE10–11
		Flat base with splayed profile		
BA012	15	4.48	Paykend B Ramitan C, D, F	CE07–09, CE08–09, CE09–11, CE10
		Flat base, obtuse angled, with protruding, bevelled edge		

Shape code	Total number of occurrences	Total sum of eves	Sites	Chronology of archaeological contexts
BA013	7	2.72	Ramitan C, D, F Site 250 A	CE02–03, CE05–06, CE04–10, CE09–11
		Flat base, recessed		
BA014	1	0.35	Ramitan C	CE04
		High foot or pedestal base, conical, hollow with protruding edge		
BA015	1	0.40	Paykend B	CE08–09
		Solid cylindrical pedestal		

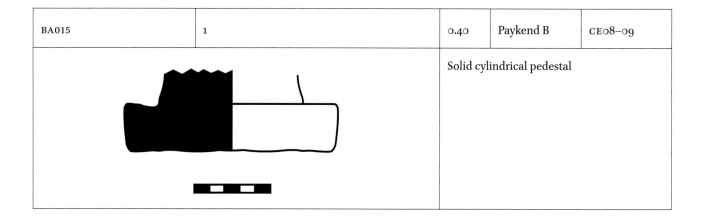

Shape code	Total number of occurrences	Total sum of eves	Sites	Chronology of archaeological contexts
BA016	8	1.58	Paykend B, Ramitan C, D	CE05–06, CE10
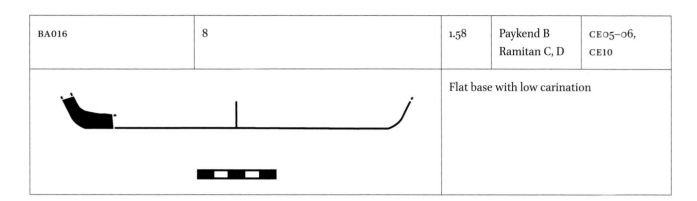		Flat base with low carination		
BA017	1	1.00	Paykend B	CE10
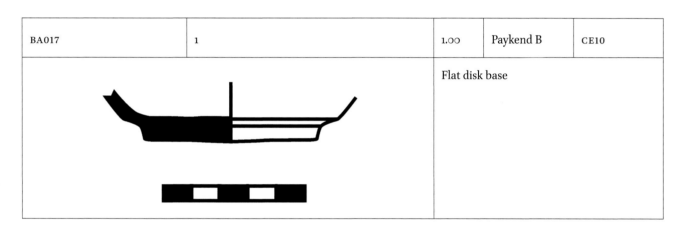		Flat disk base		
BA018	5	1.84	Ramitan D, F, Site 250 A	CE04–10, CE09–11
		Concave base with straight edge		

Shape code	Total number of occurrences	Total sum of eves	Sites	Chronology of archaeological contexts
BA019	2	0.80	Site 250 A	CE04–10
		Flat base, obtuse-angled, with projecting rounded profile		

6.2 *Rim Shapes*

Shape code	Total number of occurrences	Total sum of eves	Sites	Chronology of archaeological contexts
R001	11	0.82	Iskijkat A Paykend B Site 250 A	BCE01–CE01, CE01, CE02–03, CE07–09, CE10
		Bowl or cup with straight flaring wall and simple rim		

Shape code	Total number of occurrences	Total sum of eves	Sites	Chronology of archaeological contexts
R001.1	4	0.18	Iskijkat A Paykend B	CE05–06, CE07–09, CE11–12
			Bowl or cup with flaring wall and slightly everted, simple rim	
R002	4	0.25	Bukhara A Iskijkat A	BCE03, CE07–09
			Bowl or goblet with straight vertical walls and simple rim	
R003	1	0.05	Iskijkat A	CE07–09
			Bowl, shallow, with broad flat base and straight flaring walls and simple rim	

Shape code	Total number of occurrences	Total sum of eves	Sites	Chronology of archaeological contexts
R004	3	0.18	Bukhara A Iskijkat A Ramitan F	BCE01–CE01, CE09–11
		Bowl or lid, shallow, with straight flaring walls and simple rim		
R005	2	0.15	Ramitan F Site 250 A	CE09–10, CE09–11
		Bowl with straight flaring walls and slightly upward-bent rim		
R006	26	1.98	Iskijkat A Kakishtuvan A Ramitan A, C Site 250 A	CE02–03, CE03, CE03–04, CE04, CE05–06, CE09–10
		Bowl, rounded with upright thickened rim		

Shape code	Total number of occurrences	Total sum of eves	Sites	Chronology of archaeological contexts
R006.1	1	0.05	Site 250 A	CE09–10

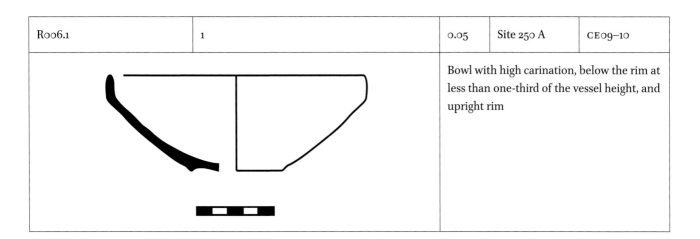

				Bowl with high carination, below the rim at less than one-third of the vessel height, and upright rim

R006.2	13	0.92	Ramitan A, C, D Site 250 A	CE01, CE02–03, CE03, CE03–04

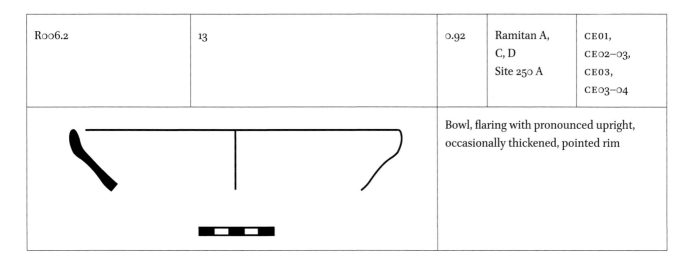

Bowl, flaring with pronounced upright, occasionally thickened, pointed rim

Shape code	Total number of occurrences	Total sum of eves	Sites	Chronology of archaeological contexts
R007	32	1.68	Bukhara A Iskijkat A Paykend B Ramitan A, C, F, G Site 250 A	BCE03, BCE01–CE01, CE03, CE03–04, CE05–06, CE09–10, CE09, CE09–11, CE10, CE10–11
		Bowl, rounded with upright or slightly inturned, simple rim		
R007.1	4	0.06	Paykend B Site 250 A	CE09–10, CE10
		Bowl, shallow, rounded with upright or simple rim and very fine, thin walls		
R008	5	0.35	Iskijkat A Ramitan C	CE02–03, CE04
		Bowl, rounded with pointed rim		

Shape code	Total number of occurrences	Total sum of eves	Sites	Chronology of archaeological contexts
R009	1	0.08	Iskijkat A	CE02–03
	Bowl or lid, shallow with upright, pointed rim			
R010	16	1.15	Iskijkat A Ramitan C Site 250 A	CE02–03, CE04, CE05–06
	Bowl with waisted profile and upright, simple rim			
R011	12	0.83	Bukhara A Paykend B Ramitan C Site 250 A	CE07–09, CE09, CE09–10, CE10
	Bowl with straight flaring walls and simple rim			

Shape code	Total number of occurrences	Total sum of eves	Sites	Chronology of archaeological contexts
R012	1	0.60	Site 250 A	CE09–10
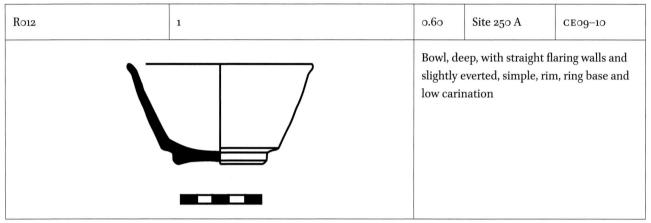		Bowl, deep, with straight flaring walls and slightly everted, simple, rim, ring base and low carination		
R013	1	n.a.	Iskijkat A	CE07–09
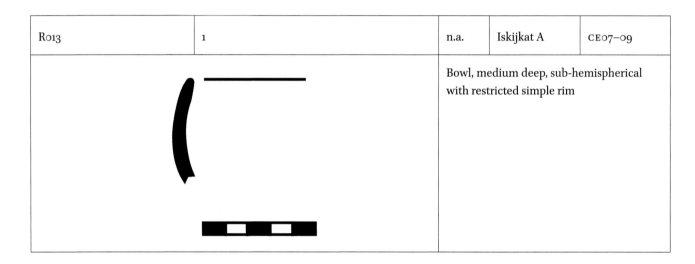		Bowl, medium deep, sub-hemispherical with restricted simple rim		
R014	1	0.05	Iskijkat A	CE07–09
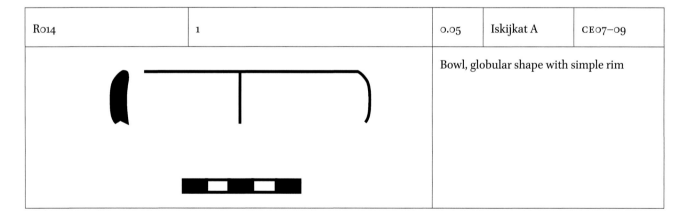		Bowl, globular shape with simple rim		

Shape code	Total number of occurrences	Total sum of eves	Sites	Chronology of archaeological contexts
R015	1	0.10	Ramitan D	n.a.

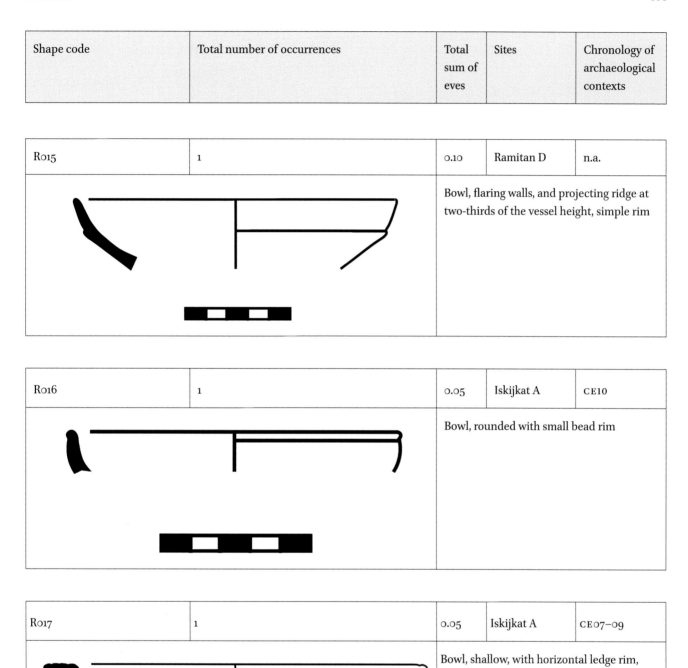

R015: Bowl, flaring walls, and projecting ridge at two-thirds of the vessel height, simple rim

R016 | 1 | | 0.05 | Iskijkat A | CE10

R016: Bowl, rounded with small bead rim

R017 | 1 | | 0.05 | Iskijkat A | CE07–09

R017: Bowl, shallow, with horizontal ledge rim, rilled on top

Shape code	Total number of occurrences	Total sum of eves	Sites	Chronology of archaeological contexts
R018	2	0.50	Iskijkat A, Site 250 A	BCE03–01, CE01
		Goblet with carinated wall and upright vertical rim		
R019	3	0.28	Bukhara A, Iskijkat A	BCE03, CE07–09
		Goblet with outcurving rim, horizontal incised lines or horizontal rib around the middle height of the body		
R020	29	3.32	Ramitan A	CE01–03, CE03
		Plate or lid (or mould?), large, shallow, domed, with a recess below the rim		

Shape code	Total number of occurrences	Total sum of eves	Sites	Chronology of archaeological contexts
R021	10	1.20	Ramitan A	CE01–03, CE03
R022	5	0.25	Ramitan A	CE01–03
R023	8	0.50	Ramitan A, C	CE01–03, CE03, CE03–04

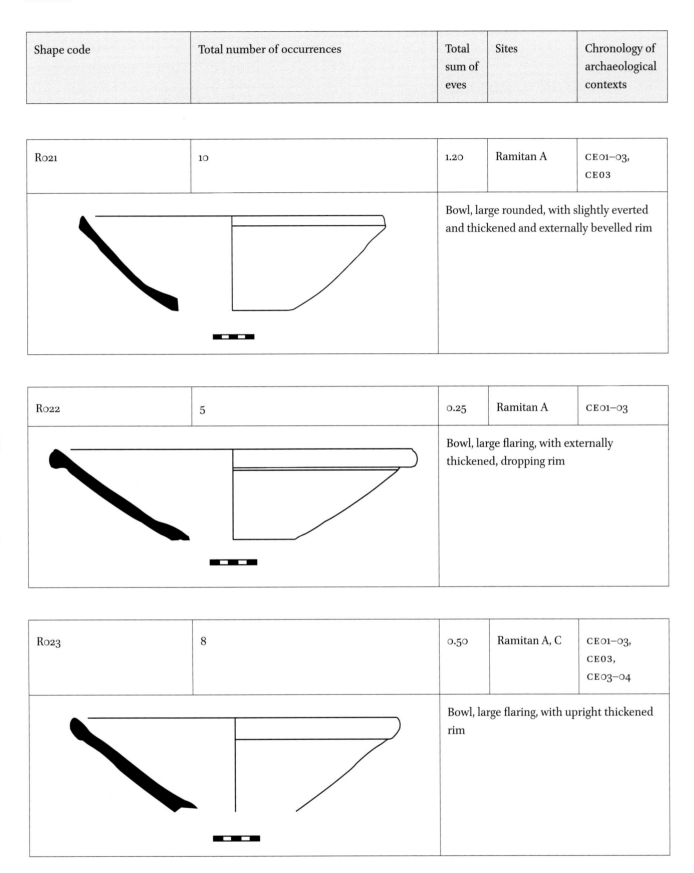

R021: Bowl, large rounded, with slightly everted and thickened and externally bevelled rim

R022: Bowl, large flaring, with externally thickened, dropping rim

R023: Bowl, large flaring, with upright thickened rim

Shape code	Total number of occurrences	Total sum of eves	Sites	Chronology of archaeological contexts
R024	1	0.10	Ramitan A	CE01–03

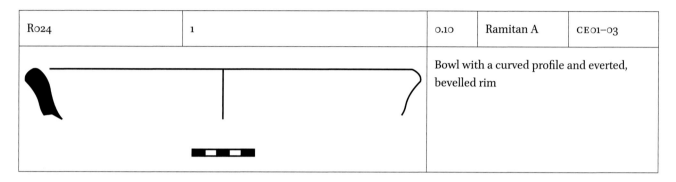

Bowl with a curved profile and everted, bevelled rim

Shape code	Total number of occurrences	Total sum of eves	Sites	Chronology of archaeological contexts
R025	1	0.18	Kakishtuvan A	CE03–04

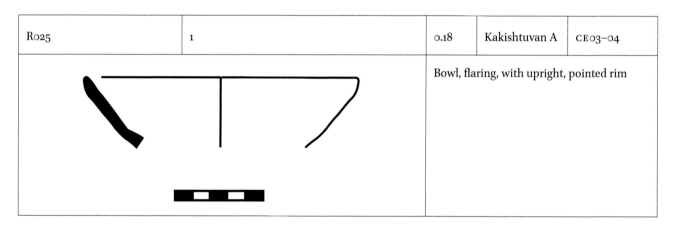

Bowl, flaring, with upright, pointed rim

Shape code	Total number of occurrences	Total sum of eves	Sites	Chronology of archaeological contexts
R026	3	0.31	Kakishtuvan A, Ramitan A	CE01, CE02–03, CE03

Bowl or beaker with steep flaring walls and externally thickened, pointed rim

Shape code	Total number of occurrences	Total sum of eves	Sites	Chronology of archaeological contexts
R027	1	0.15	Site 250 A	CE01
		Bowl with waisted profile and slightly restricted rim		
R028	4	0.20	Paykend B, Ramitan C	CE05–06, CE08–09
		Bowl with waisted profile and short, upright and externally slightly thickened rim		
R029	2	0.27	Bukhara A	BCE03
		Goblet, miniature size, with carinated wall and vertical, simple rim		

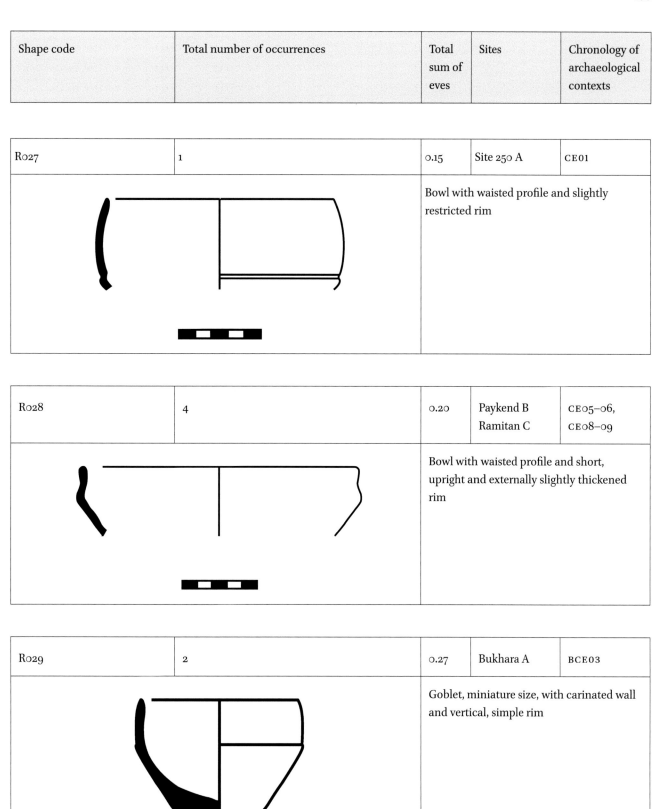

Shape code	Total number of occurrences	Total sum of eves	Sites	Chronology of archaeological contexts
R030	1	0.07	Site 250 A	CE10–11
		Bowl, deep with flaring wall and everted rim		
R031	2	0.05	Paykend B Ramitan D	CE09
		Bowl or plate, large, with externally thickened dropping rim and a ridge below the rim		
R031.1	2	0.10	Ramitan D	n.a.
		Bowl or plate with bevelled rim and ridge below the rim		
R032	1	0.05	Ramitan D	n.a.
		Bowl or plate, large, with thickened and dropping rim		

Shape code	Total number of occurrences	Total sum of eves	Sites	Chronology of archaeological contexts
Ro33	3	0.78	Iskijkat A	CE02–03
		Gourd, jar or flask with one rounded and one flat side, a short neck and externally thickened rim		
Ro34	1	0.12	Iskijkat A	CE02–03
		Gourd (?), jar or flask with hooked rim		
Ro35	3	0.58	Iskijkat A, Kakishtuvan A	BCE03–01, BCE01–CE01, CE02–03
		Jar or jug with everted, externally thickened and slightly dropping rim and short neck		

Shape code	Total number of occurrences	Total sum of eves	Sites	Chronology of archaeological contexts
R036	1	0.15	Iskijkat A	CE02–03
	Jar or jug with flaring neck and externally thickened rim			
R037	2	0.23	Iskijkat A	BCE03–01, CE04
	Jar with short conical neck or neckless and with everted, externally thickened and bevelled rim			
R038	6	1.18	Iskijkat A, Paykend B, Ramitan A, G, Site 250 A	BCE01–CE01, CE03, CE09–10, CE10, CE13–14
	Jar or jug with externally thickened and bevelled rim			

Shape code	Total number of occurrences	Total sum of eves	Sites	Chronology of archaeological contexts
R039	2	0.12	Iskijkat A, Ramitan C	BCE03–01, n.a.

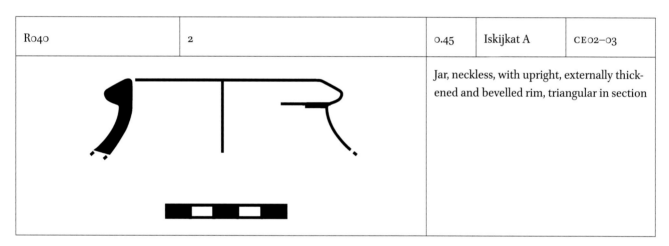

Jar, large, with conical neck and externally thickened upright rim, grooved on top

R040	2	0.45	Iskijkat A	CE02–03

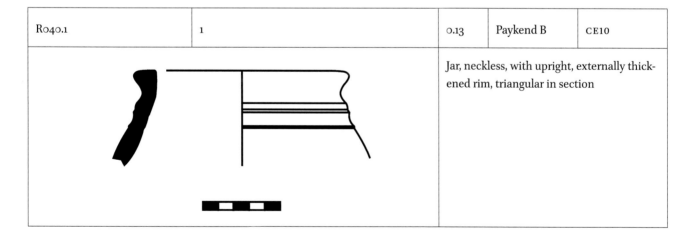

Jar, neckless, with upright, externally thickened and bevelled rim, triangular in section

R040.1	1	0.13	Paykend B	CE10

Jar, neckless, with upright, externally thickened rim, triangular in section

Shape code	Total number of occurrences	Total sum of eves	Sites	Chronology of archaeological contexts
R041	9	1.52	Iskijkat A Ramitan A, D Site 250 A	CE02–03, CE03, CE04, CE10–11
		Jar or jug with short neck and slightly everted and externally thickened rim, internally hollowed out		
R041.1	14	1.54	Iskijkat A Paykend B Ramitan A, C, D, G Site 250 A	CE01, CE01–03, CE02–03, CE03, CE04, CE07–09, CE08–09, CE10, CE13
		Jar or jug, neckless, with upright, externally thickened rim		

Shape code	Total number of occurrences	Total sum of eves	Sites	Chronology of archaeological contexts
R041.2	9	1.90	Paykend B, Ramitan A, C, G, Site 250 A	CE01, CE03, CE03–04, CE05, CE05–06, CE07–09, CE10
	Jar or jug, with short concave neck and slightly everted, externally thickened and bevelled rim			
R042	2	0.11	Iskijkat A, Paykend B	CE02–03, CE10
	Bowl, large, with everted, almost horizontal rim			
R043	2	0.32	Iskijkat A, Paykend B	CE02–03, CE05
	Jug with everted, thickened and internally bevelled rim			

Shape code	Total number of occurrences	Total sum of eves	Sites	Chronology of archaeological contexts
R044	3	0.41	Iskijkat A, Paykend B	CE07–09, CE10
	Jar with conical or slightly inturned and externally squared rim			
R045	12	1.41	Kakishtuvan A, Paykend B, Ramitan A, C, F, G, Site 250 A	CE02–03, CE03, CE05–06, CE06, CE09–11
	Jar or jug with short neck and externally thickened and moulded rim			
R045.1	2	0.35	Ramitan D	n.a.
	Jar or jug with short neck and everted, externally thickened, almost straight-edged rim			

Shape code	Total number of occurrences	Total sum of eves	Sites	Chronology of archaeological contexts
R046	3	0.63	Ramitan D, F	CE09–11
		Jar, short necked, with externally thickened and bevelled or straight-edged rim		
R047	6	1.22	Ramitan A, C, D Site 250 A	CE01, CE01–03, CE04, CE05–06, CE09–10
		Jar, short necked with externally thickened and dropping rim		
R048	6	0.68	Ramitan C, D, G Site 250 A	CE05–06, CE09–10
		Jar, short necked, with everted, externally thickened rim		

Shape code	Total number of occurrences	Total sum of eves	Sites	Chronology of archaeological contexts
R050	1	0.04	Kakishtuvan A	CE06

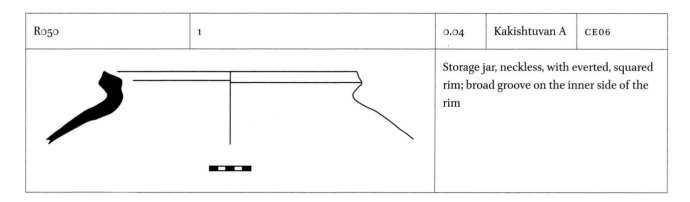

Storage jar, neckless, with everted, squared rim; broad groove on the inner side of the rim

Shape code	Total number of occurrences	Total sum of eves	Sites	Chronology of archaeological contexts
R050.1	2	0.20	Ramitan F, G	CE05–06, CE09–11

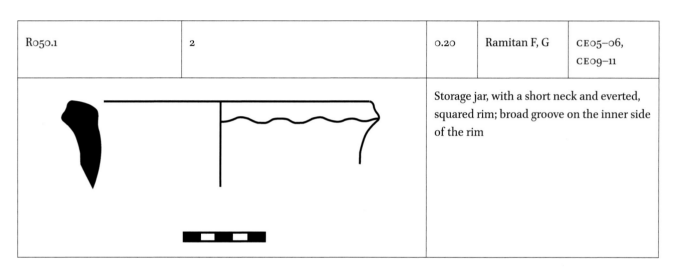

Storage jar, with a short neck and everted, squared rim; broad groove on the inner side of the rim

Shape code	Total number of occurrences	Total sum of eves	Sites	Chronology of archaeological contexts
R051	6	0.83	Kakishtuvan A, Paykend B, Ramitan A, G	CE03, CE03–04, CE05–06, CE06, CE08–09

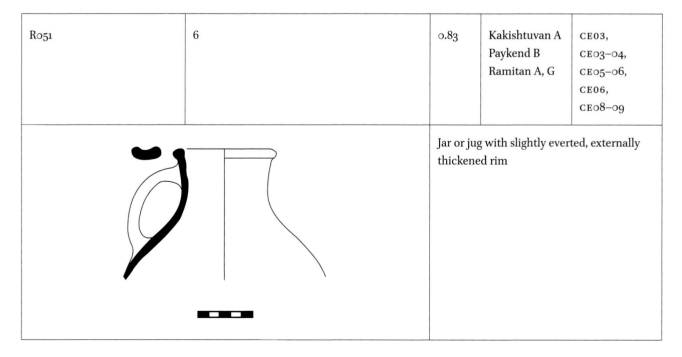

Jar or jug with slightly everted, externally thickened rim

Shape code	Total number of occurrences	Total sum of eves	Sites	Chronology of archaeological contexts
R052	2	0.15	Ramitan A, D	CE03
		Storage jar, neckless, with upright, collared rim; this rim type is often decorated with rows of imprints		
R053	2	2.00	Kakishtuvan A, Ramitan C	CE02–03, CE04
		Flask or jug (?), with slightly everted, externally thickened and rounded rim		
R054	2	0.30	Ramitan A, C	CE03, CE04
		Jar or jug with slightly everted, internally bevelled rim		

Shape code	Total number of occurrences	Total sum of eves	Sites	Chronology of archaeological contexts
Ro55	16	2.93	Paykend B Ramitan A, C, D	CE01–03, CE02–03, CE03, CE05–06, CE07–09, CE08–09, CE10
		Jar, neckless and globular, with upright or slightly everted simple rim		
Ro55.1	1	0.15	Ramitan C	CE03–04
		Jar, globular, with a short neck and triangular rim		
Ro56	3	0.30	Iskijkat A Ramitan A	BCE01–CE01, CE01–03, CE03
		Jar or jug (?) with slightly everted, almost upright, simple rim		

POTTERY 207

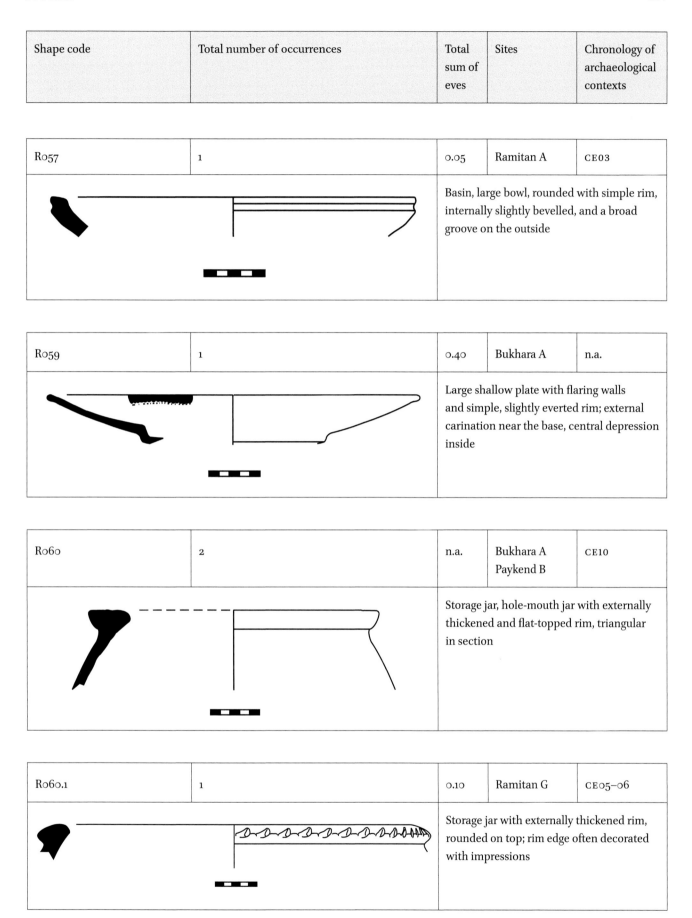

Shape code	Total number of occurrences	Total sum of eves	Sites	Chronology of archaeological contexts
R057	1	0.05	Ramitan A	CE03
		Basin, large bowl, rounded with simple rim, internally slightly bevelled, and a broad groove on the outside		
R059	1	0.40	Bukhara A	n.a.
		Large shallow plate with flaring walls and simple, slightly everted rim; external carination near the base, central depression inside		
R060	2	n.a.	Bukhara A Paykend B	CE10
		Storage jar, hole-mouth jar with externally thickened and flat-topped rim, triangular in section		
R060.1	1	0.10	Ramitan G	CE05–06
		Storage jar with externally thickened rim, rounded on top; rim edge often decorated with impressions		

Shape code	Total number of occurrences	Total sum of eves	Sites	Chronology of archaeological contexts
R061	5	0.51	Bukhara A Paykend B Ramitan F Site 250 A	CE09–10, CE09–11, CE10
		Flat lid with straight edge		
R061.1	6	3.05	Paykend B Ramitan F	CE07–08, CE09–11, CE10–11
		Flat lid with a knob		

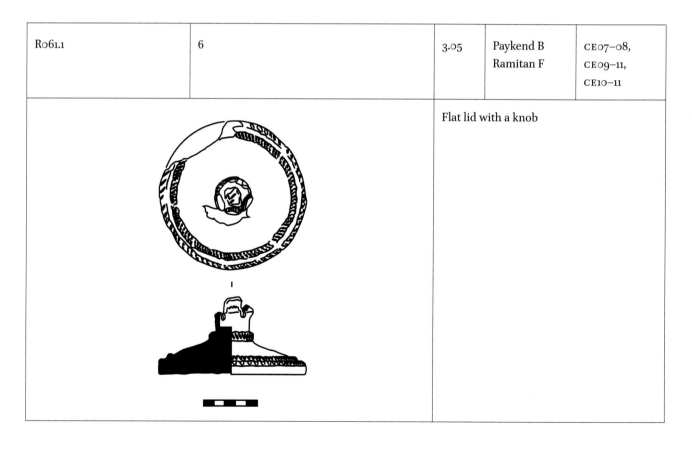

Shape code	Total number of occurrences	Total sum of eves	Sites	Chronology of archaeological contexts
Ro62	10	2.00	Paykend B Ramitan C, G Site 250 A	CE01, CE05–06, CE07–10, CE08–09, CE09–10, CE13–14

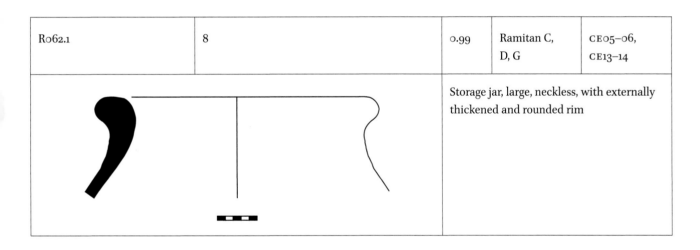

Storage jar, large, with short neck and almost upright or slightly everted, thickened rim

Ro62.1	8	0.99	Ramitan C, D, G	CE05–06, CE13–14

Storage jar, large, neckless, with externally thickened and rounded rim

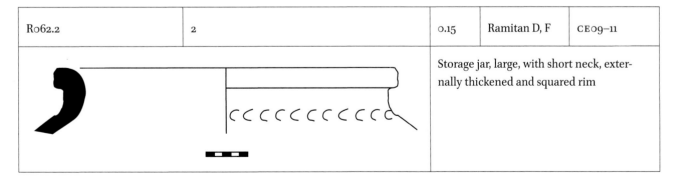

Ro62.2	2	0.15	Ramitan D, F	CE09–11

Storage jar, large, with short neck, externally thickened and squared rim

Shape code	Total number of occurrences	Total sum of eves	Sites	Chronology of archaeological contexts
Ro62.3	3	1.30	Ramitan G	CE05–06, CE13–14

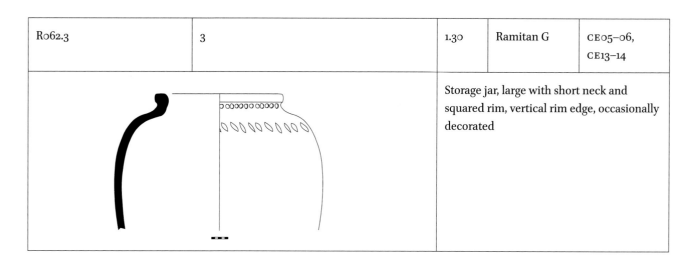

Storage jar, large with short neck and squared rim, vertical rim edge, occasionally decorated

Ro62.4	1	1.00	Site 250 A	n.a.

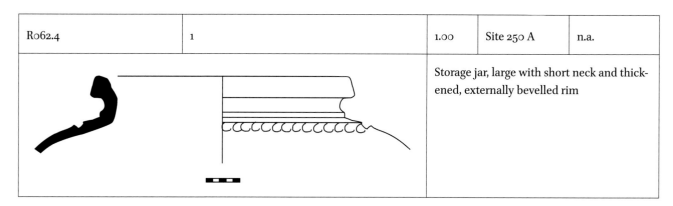

Storage jar, large with short neck and thickened, externally bevelled rim

Ro63	1	n.a.	Iskijkat A	CE11–12

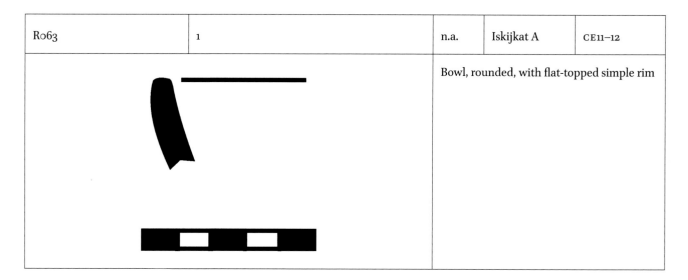

Bowl, rounded, with flat-topped simple rim

Shape code	Total number of occurrences	Total sum of eves	Sites	Chronology of archaeological contexts
Ro64	1	0.04	Iskijkat A	BCE01–CE01
		Jar, hole-mouth, with simple rim		
Ro65	1	0.03	Iskijkat A	BCE01–CE01
		Goblet or jar (?), hole-mouth, with simple upright rim		
Ro66	3	0.19	Iskijkat A, Ramitan C, F	BCE01–CE01, CE07–09, CE09–11
		Bowl or plate, large, with externally thickened and bevelled rim		

Shape code	Total number of occurrences	Total sum of eves	Sites	Chronology of archaeological contexts
R071	5	1.00	Ramitan D, F	CE09–11
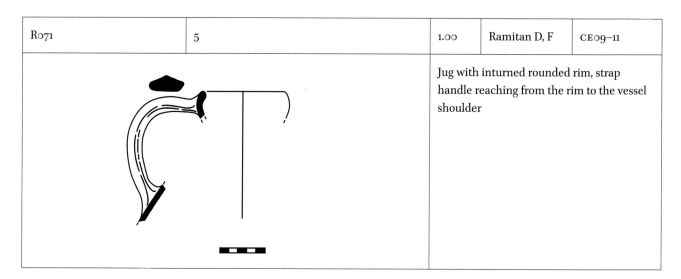			Jug with inturned rounded rim, strap handle reaching from the rim to the vessel shoulder	
R072	3	0.09	Ramitan C, D	CE07–09
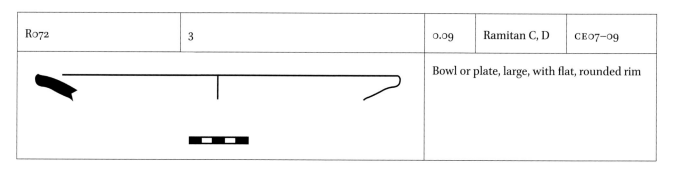			Bowl or plate, large, with flat, rounded rim	
R074	2	0.24	Ramitan G	CE05–06
			Jar or jug with flaring neck and externally thickened, flat-topped and almost straight-edged, slightly dropping rim	

Shape code	Total number of occurrences	Total sum of eves	Sites	Chronology of archaeological contexts
R075	19	3.23	Iskijkat A Paykend B Ramitan C, F, G Site 250 A	BCE01–CE01, CE03–04, CE07–10, CE09–10, CE09–11, CE10
			Jar, neckless, with everted, right-angled and externally thickened rim; lid-seated	
R075.1	1	0.05	Site 250 A	CE09–10
			Jar or jug with conical neck and everted, thickened and grooved rim	

Shape code	Total number of occurrences	Total sum of eves	Sites	Chronology of archaeological contexts
R076	6	1.50	Iskijkat A Paykend B Ramitan G Site 250 A	CE05–06, CE07–09, CE09–10, CE10, CE10–11

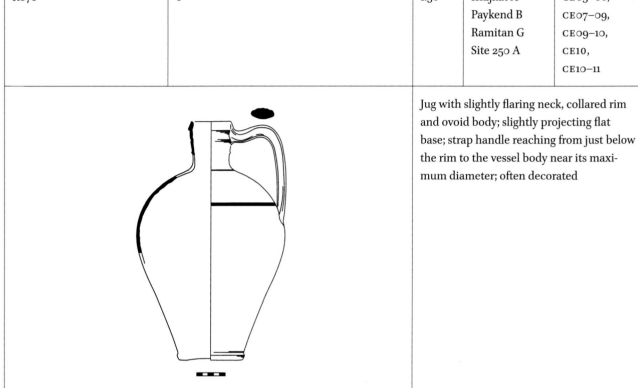

Jug with slightly flaring neck, collared rim and ovoid body; slightly projecting flat base; strap handle reaching from just below the rim to the vessel body near its maximum diameter; often decorated

| R077 | 4 | 1.06 | Paykend B
Site 250 A | CE10,
CE10–11 |

Jug with conical neck and slightly inturned, externally thickened rim; strap handle reaching from the rim to the vessel body near its maximum diameter

POTTERY 217

Shape code	Total number of occurrences	Total sum of eves	Sites	Chronology of archaeological contexts
R078	4	0.45	Ramitan C Site 250 A	CE09–10
		Jar, rounded and neckless, with almost hooked, thickened rim		
R079	5	1.53	Iskijkat A Paykend B Site 250 A	CE02–03, CE05–06, CE09–10
		Jar, biconical, neckless, with everted, right-angled rim		
R080	2	0.28	Paykend B Site 250 A	CE09, CE09–10
		Jar or jug with slightly everted rim; rim edge divided by a broad groove		

Shape code	Total number of occurrences	Total sum of eves	Sites	Chronology of archaeological contexts
Ro82	1	0.15	Site 250 A	CE09–10
		Bowl or lid with flat, simple rim, relatively thick-walled		
Ro83	7	0.76	Paykend B, Site 250 A	CE09–10, CE10
		Jar or jug with slightly flaring neck and simple rim, neck profiled through horizontal steps, thin-walled		
Ro84	3	0.30	Ramitan C, G	CE05–06, CE07–10
		Jar or jug with collared, internally thickened rim		

Shape code	Total number of occurrences	Total sum of eves	Sites	Chronology of archaeological contexts
R085	3	0.35	Ramitan C, G	CE05–06, CE13–14
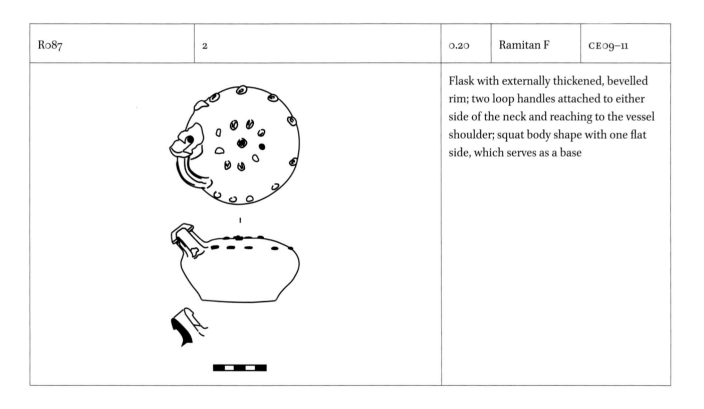		Bowl with flared profile and internally thickened and bevelled rim		
R087	2	0.20	Ramitan F	CE09–11
		Flask with externally thickened, bevelled rim; two loop handles attached to either side of the neck and reaching to the vessel shoulder; squat body shape with one flat side, which serves as a base		

Shape code	Total number of occurrences	Total sum of eves	Sites	Chronology of archaeological contexts
R088	14	1.82	Paykend B Ramitan C, F Site 250 A	CE07–09, CE09–10, CE09–11, CE10

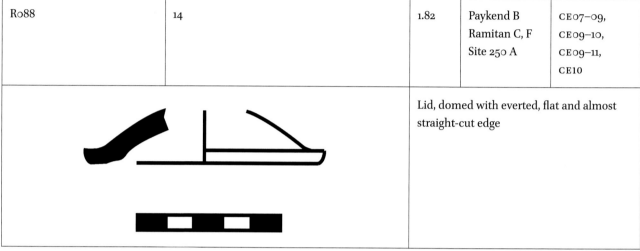

Lid, domed with everted, flat and almost straight-cut edge

R088.1	1	1.00	Paykend B	CE10

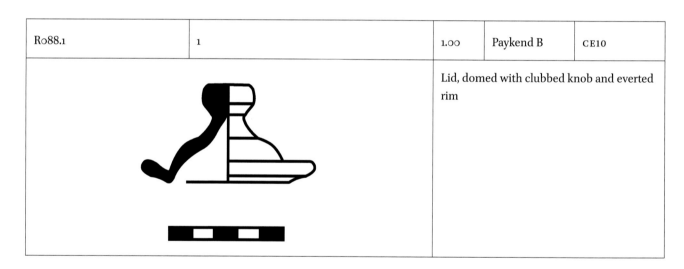

Lid, domed with clubbed knob and everted rim

R090	1	0.05	Ramitan F	CE09–11

Jar with inturned collared rim, impressed decoration below the rim

Shape code	Total number of occurrences	Total sum of eves	Sites	Chronology of archaeological contexts
R091	1	0.07	Ramitan F	CE09–11
		Bowl, deep, with internally thickened and bevelled rim and a horizontal groove inside just below the rim		
R093	2	0.29	Paykend B Ramitan C	CE05–06, CE10
		Jug with flared neck and externally thickened and grooved rim		
R094	2	0.10	Ramitan C	CE04, CE05–06
		Bowl with flat, slightly thickened and externally bevelled rim		

Shape code	Total number of occurrences	Total sum of eves	Sites	Chronology of archaeological contexts
R095	2	0.30	Ramitan C Site 250 A	CE05–06
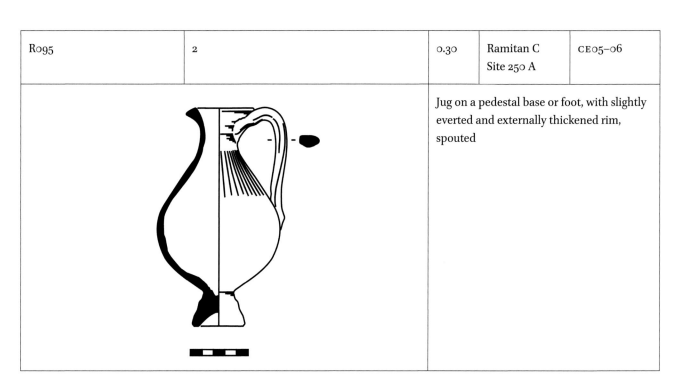			Jug on a pedestal base or foot, with slightly everted and externally thickened rim, spouted	
R097	1	1.00	Ramitan C	CE04
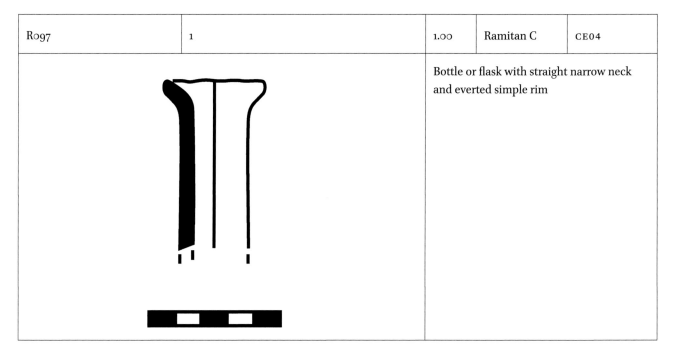			Bottle or flask with straight narrow neck and everted simple rim	

POTTERY 223

Shape code	Total number of occurrences	Total sum of eves	Sites	Chronology of archaeological contexts
R098	1	0.07	Paykend B	CE08–09
		Jar with a short neck, upright flattened and thickened rim with two grooves on the top		
R099	3	0.51	Paykend B	CE10
		Jar or jug with straight neck and triangular rim with a flat top		
R100	1	1.00	Site 250 A	CE09–10
		Jug with narrow neck and everted, straight-edged rim		

Shape code	Total number of occurrences	Total sum of eves	Sites	Chronology of archaeological contexts
R101	2	0.05	Iskijkat A	CE04
		Pan or tray with upright, externally bevelled rim		
R102	1	0.1	Site 250 A	CE01
		Jar, neckless, with slightly everted rounded rim		
R103	1	0.05	Paykend B	CE05–06
		Jar or jug, flared neck, externally thickened rim		

POTTERY 225

6.3 *Handle Shapes*

Shape code	Total number of occurrences	Sites	Chronology of archaeological contexts
H01SC01	6	Kakishtuvan A Ramitan A, C	CE01, CE02–03, CE03, CE03–04
		Loop-, side-, vertical-, strap handle with a bean-shaped section	
H01SC03	3	Ramitan A Paykend B	CE03, CE10–11
		Loop-, side-, vertical-, strap handle with a rectangular/sub-rectangular section	
H01SC04	2	Iskijkat A Ramitan F, G Paykend B Site 250 A	CE09–10, CE09–11, CE11–12
		Loop-, side-, vertical-, strap handle with an oval/sub-oval section	

Shape code	Total number of occurrences	Total sum of eves	Sites	Chronology of archaeological contexts
H01SC05	5		Ramitan C, G Paykend B Site 250 A	CE05–06, CE10–11

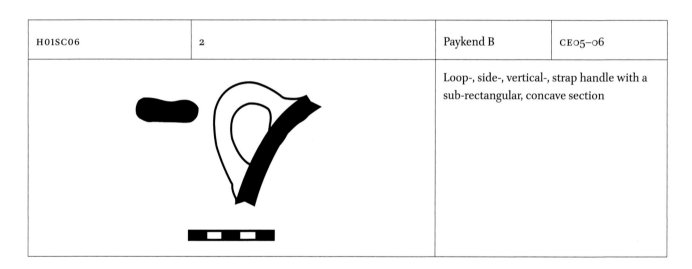

Loop-, side-, vertical-, strap handle with a trapezoidal/sub-trapezoidal section

H01SC06	2		Paykend B	CE05–06

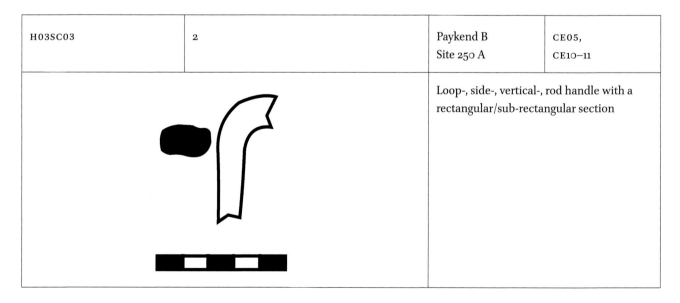

Loop-, side-, vertical-, strap handle with a sub-rectangular, concave section

H03SC03	2		Paykend B Site 250 A	CE05, CE10–11

Loop-, side-, vertical-, rod handle with a rectangular/sub-rectangular section

Shape code	Total number of occurrences	Total sum of eves	Sites	Chronology of archaeological contexts
H03SC04	13		Ramitan D, G Paykend B Site 250 A	CE05–06, CE09–10, CE10–11
			Loop-, side-, vertical-, rod handle with an oval/sub-oval section	
H03SC05	5		Paykend B Site 250 A	CE09–10, CE10–11
			Loop-, side-, vertical-, rod handle with a trapezoidal/sub-trapezoidal section	
H04SC02	3		Paykend B	CE10, CE10–11
			Loop-, side-, vertical-, double rods handle with circular/sub-circular sections	

Addendum: Classifications and Chronologies

For much of the archaeologically investigated periods ceramics remain the backbone of chronological assessments and sometimes the only available evidence for dating. This results in the common desire to have for reference a chrono-typological tabulation, some sort of quick guide for comparative dating. From the distribution of pottery volume by chronological phase that we illustrated above (Table 4.14), it becomes clear that two phases, 1st to 3rd centuries CE and 9th to 12th centuries CE are represented by much larger assemblages, both in terms of counts of diagnostics and rim eves, than the remainder. This means that the material basis for identifying material related to these chronological phases is much more reliable than for the others. The larger the volume of ceramics found in each phase, the clearer becomes the distinction between vessels more contemporary to this phase and those of earlier manufacturing date. Additionally, the correlation of our material with site formation processes is important for any chronological assessment. The general rule is, the more complete the vessel, the less often it was redeposited and the closer it is in date to the formation of its archaeological context. Individual complete vessels thus provide glimpses on assemblages of a known date. Such incidences so far occurred more often in contexts of Islamic date with single exceptions of late pre-Islamic date.

The following charts provide a condensed view of a still fragmentary chronological sequence of vessel assemblages as reflected in our evidence to date that is being continuously amended and will grow more complete throughout our future publications. The sequence is twofold, showing on the one hand the chronological spread and development of specific vessel families (potential pottery types), and single complete forms as part of a contemporaneous vessel assemblage reflecting the characteristics of the pottery design of a specific phase. Vessel families illustrate the diachronic presence of vessels serving specific functions in the assemblage and best reflect the developments in design or surface treatments or technologies. These chronological differentiations within the individual families are in the process of being validated and refined and will result in a better understanding of changes within assemblages through time.

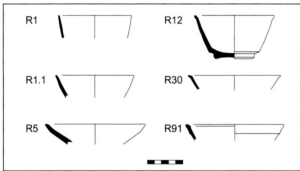 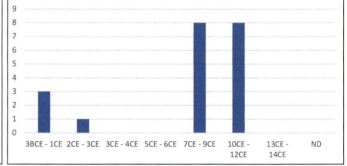

FIGURE 4.85   Bukhara Oasis, chronological distribution of R001 and related shapes (R001.1, R005, R012, R030, and R091)

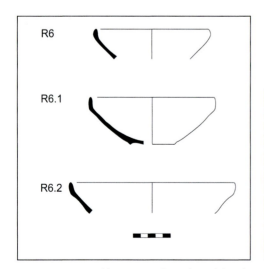 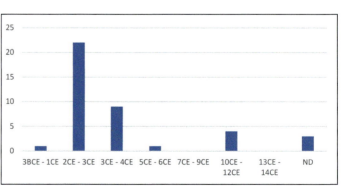

FIGURE 4.86   Bukhara Oasis, chronological distribution of R006 and related shapes (R006.1, R006.2)

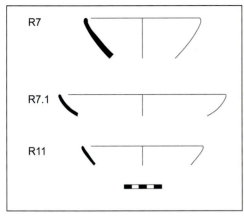
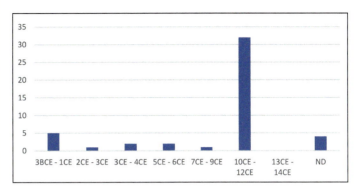

FIGURE 4.87   Bukhara Oasis, chronological distribution of R007 and related shapes (R007.1, R011)

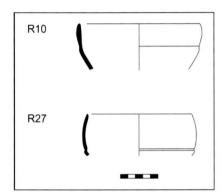
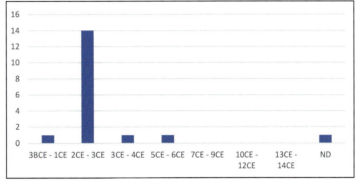

FIGURE 4.88   Bukhara Oasis, chronological distribution of R010 and related shapes (R027)

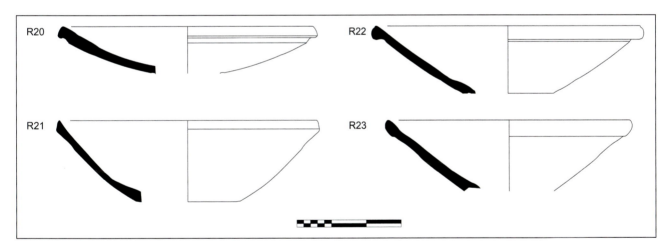
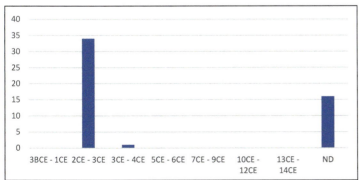

FIGURE 4.89   Bukhara Oasis, chronological distribution of R020 and related shapes (R021, R022, R023)

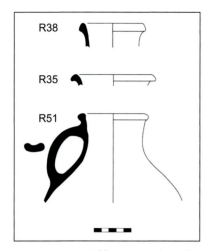
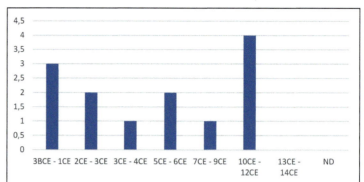

FIGURE 4.90   Bukhara Oasis, chronological distribution of R038 and related shapes (R035, R051)

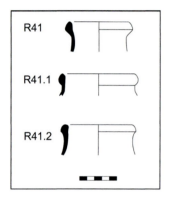
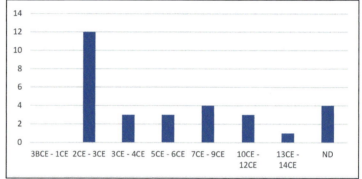

FIGURE 4.91   Bukhara Oasis, chronological distribution of R041 and related shapes (R041.1, R041.2)

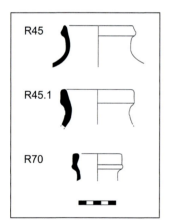
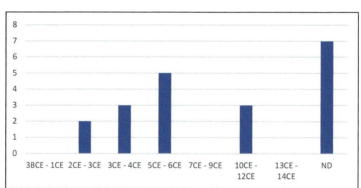

FIGURE 4.92   Bukhara Oasis, chronological distribution of R045 and related shapes (R045.1, R070)

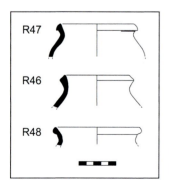
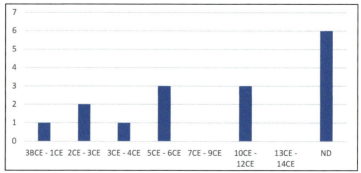

FIGURE 4.93   Bukhara Oasis, chronological distribution of R047 and related shapes (R046, R048)

POTTERY

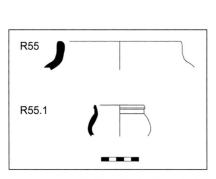 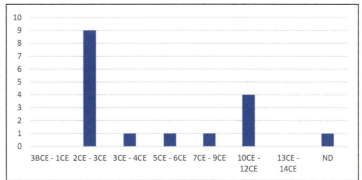

FIGURE 4.94 Bukhara Oasis, chronological distribution of R055 and related shapes (R055.1)

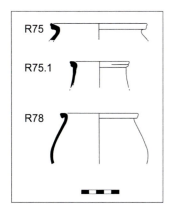 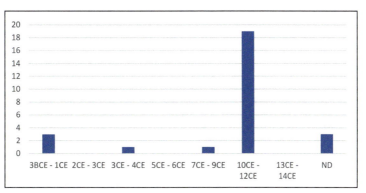

FIGURE 4.95 Bukhara Oasis, chronological distribution of R075 and related shapes (R075.1, R078)

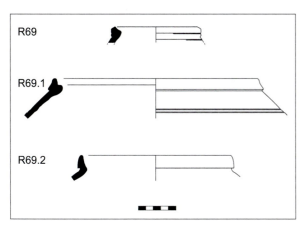 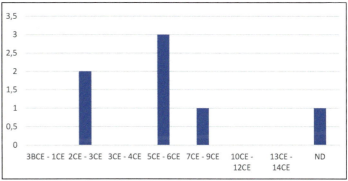

FIGURE 4.96 Bukhara Oasis, chronological distribution of R069 and related shapes (R069.1, R069.2)

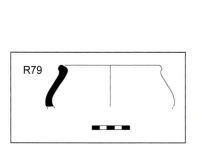 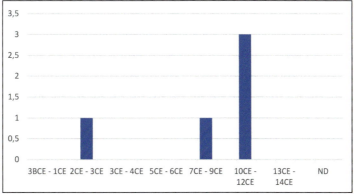

FIGURE 4.97 Bukhara Oasis, chronological distribution of R079

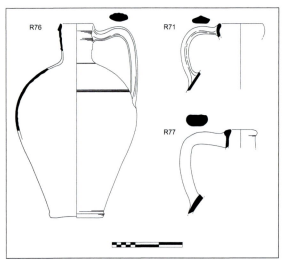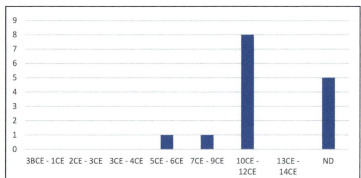

FIGURE 4.98 Bukhara Oasis, chronological distribution of R076 and related shapes (R071, R077)

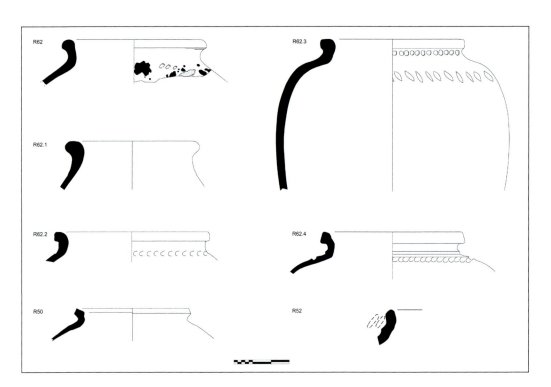

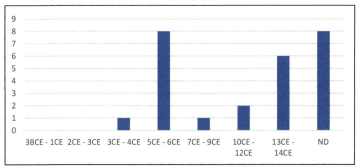

FIGURE 4.99 Bukhara Oasis, chronological distribution of R062 and related shapes (R062.1, R062.2, R062.3, R062.4, R052 and R050)

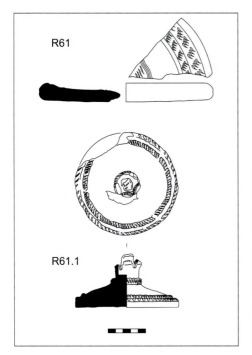
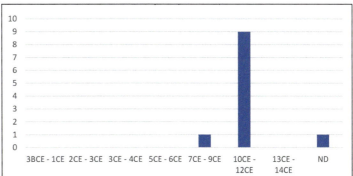

FIGURE 4.100   Bukhara Oasis, chronological distribution of R061 and related shapes (R061.1)

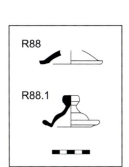
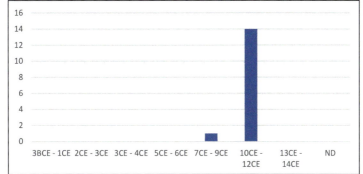

FIGURE 4.101   Bukhara Oasis, chronological distribution of R088 and related shapes (R088.1)

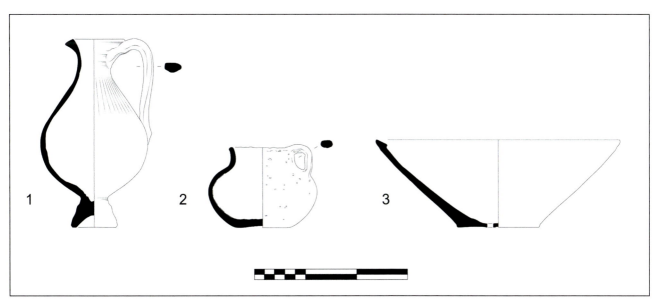

FIGURE 4.102   Bukhara Oasis, complete or near-complete vessels, fragmentary chronological scheme of assemblages of contemporaneous vessel forms, 5th to 6th centuries CE, Ramitan C: (1) table ware jug, (2) cooking ware handled jar, (3) plain ware funnel
DRAWINGS FAITH VARDY

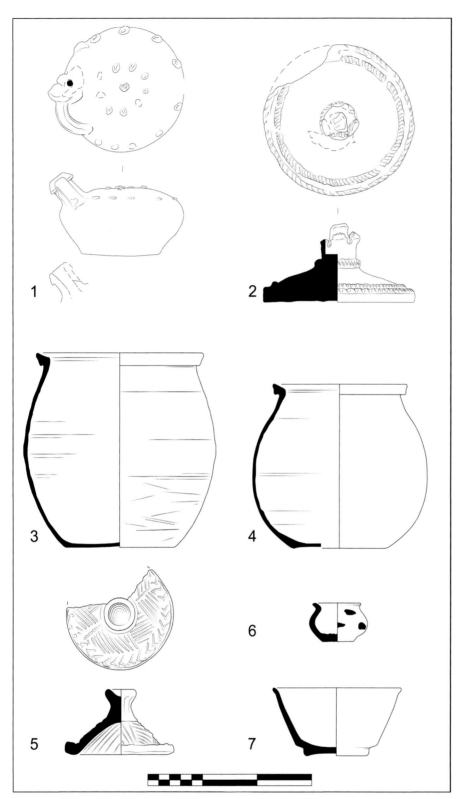

FIGURE 4.103   Bukhara Oasis, complete or near-complete vessels, fragmentary chronological scheme of assemblages of contemporaneous vessel forms, 9th to 11th centuries CE, Ramitan, trench F: (1) plain ware flask, (2) lid with impressed decoration; Site 250, trench A: (3–4) lid-seated jars, (5) mould-made lid, (6) slip-painted miniature jar, (7) table ware bowl with monochrome glaze
DRAWINGS FAITH VARDY

Acknowledgments

The study of excavated materials always depends on the support and cooperation of all institutions and persons involved. In this respect, we would like to thank the Institute of Archaeology of Samarkand and the Academy of Sciences at Tashkent for enabling this research. We are equally grateful for the continuous friendly and open collaboration with the MAFOUB field team under its head, Rocco Rante. Our particular thanks extend to the Institute of Iranian Studies at the Austrian Academy of Sciences and its director Florian Schwarz, who facilitated and supported our post-excavation work and all necessary travel.

Meeting fellow researchers and specialists during the various seasons at Bukhara was a great pleasure and privilege and allowed us to benefit from their knowledge and expertise in our work.

CHAPTER 5

Petrographic and Chemical Analyses of Ceramics from the Oasis of Bukhara

Yvan Coquinot and Nathalie Gandolfo

1 Introduction

This study is part of the Franco-Uzbek Archaeological Mission in the Bukhara Oasis (MAFOUB), which has been led by the Louvre since 2009 and is directed by Dr. Rocco Rante. In general, the objective of this program is to study this region's territorial and historical complexity through the investigation of human occupations from antiquity to the Islamic period. The research program consists of several axes of study, of which the study of material culture occupies an important place (Rante and Mirzaakhmedov 2019). In this context, ceramics have been the object of numerous archaeometry analyses. As the study focused on a vast region, the interest in the geological aspects, the type and structure of clays, the components of the fabrics and the sources of materials used for manufacturing became a priority. This is the reason why a petrographic study on some selected sherds has been conducted.

2 Studied Material

The ceramics studied come from two archaeological sites located in the oasis of Bukhara, Iskijkat and Vardana (37 sherds in total): 29 ceramic sherds were collected at Iskijkat and 8 sherds were collected at Vardana. All ceramic sherds come from a stratigraphical context.

For the 29 sherds from Iskijkat, 15 groups of fabrics have been distinguished by archaeologists in the field: from A1 to A6 (6 fabrics), B, C, CW1 to CW5 (5 fabrics), D and F.

For the 8 sherds from Vardana, no fabric distinction was made (the front and back photographs of each sherd are shown in table 5.1). Annexes (tables 5.5 to 5.7) present the chronological framework for the sherds coming from the site of Iskijkat that are dated over a period spreading from the 2nd century BCE to the 4th century CE. Vardana does not yet present this type of chronological sequence.

TABLE 5.1 Photographs of the fronts and backs of the studied sherds

Iskijkat fabric A1

IA352/5 A1 IA370/23 A1 IA370/26 A1

Iskijkat fabric A2 **Iskijkat fabric A3**

IA354/58 IA370/22 IA375/2

Iskijkat fabric A4

IA371/17 IA371/23 IA378/4

TABLE 5.1 Photographs of the fronts and backs of the studied sherds (*cont.*)

Skijkat fabric A5
IA370/5

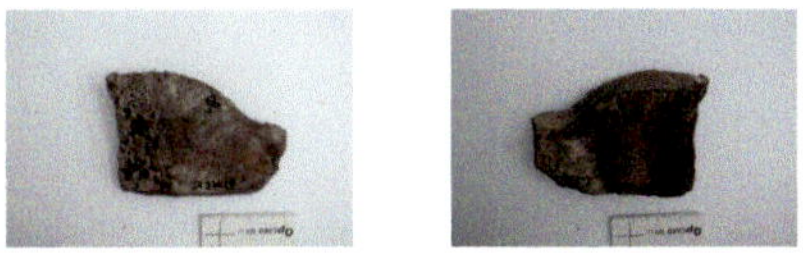

IA377/6

Skijkat fabric A6
IA341/2

IA368/34

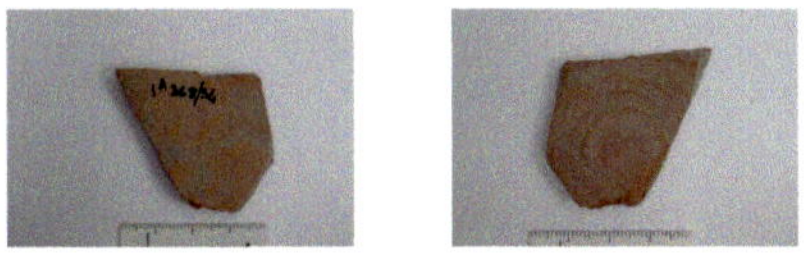

IA384/15

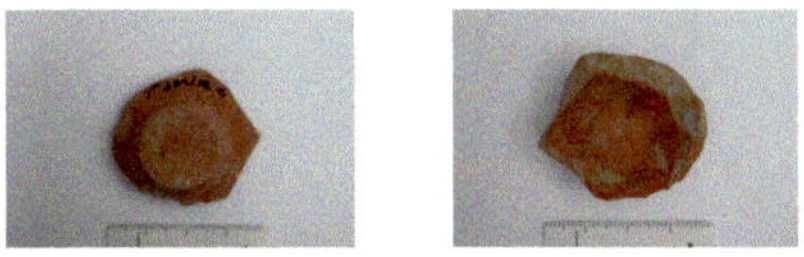

Iskijkat fabric B
IA375/8

Iskijkat fabric C
IA370/4

IA377/5

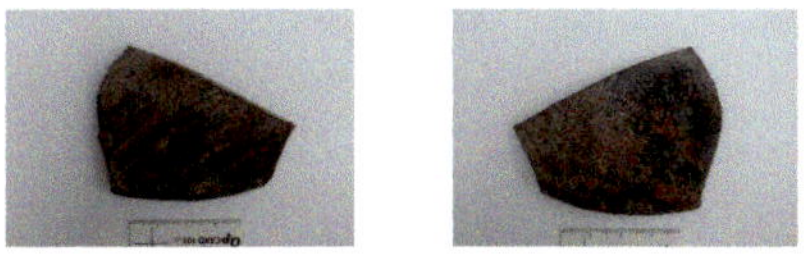

Iskijkat fabric CW1
IA370/1

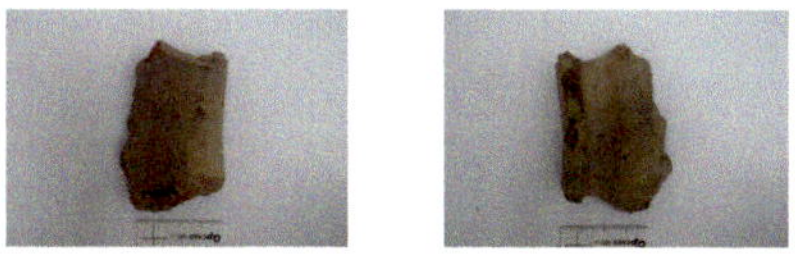

IA371/34

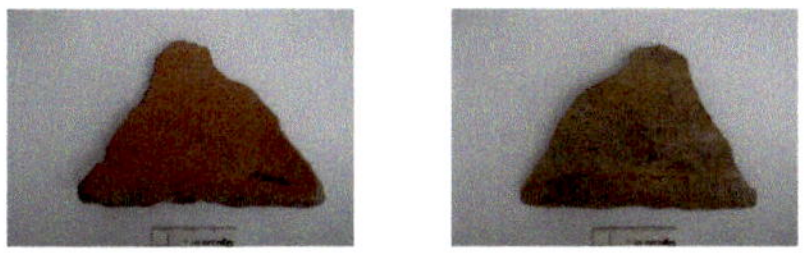

Iskijkat CW2
IA341/9

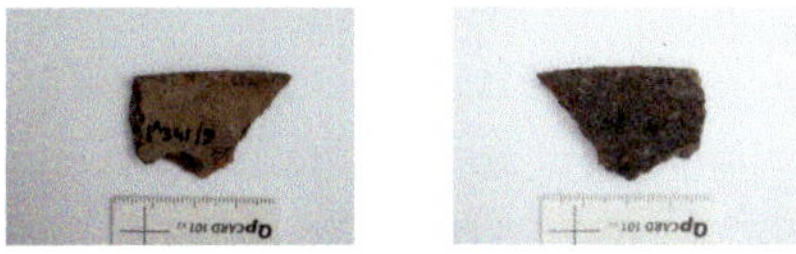

IA370/13

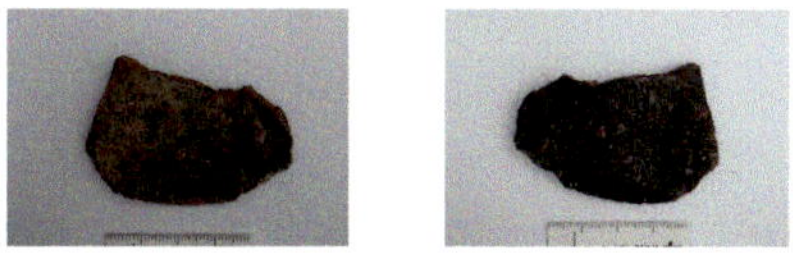

Iskijkat CW3
IA358/151

IA370/16

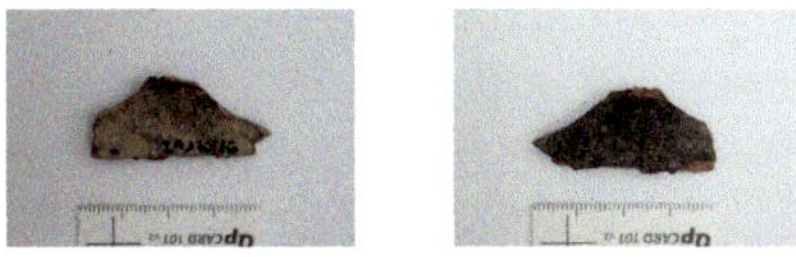

Iskijkat CW4
IA370/20

Iskijkat CW5
IA384/16

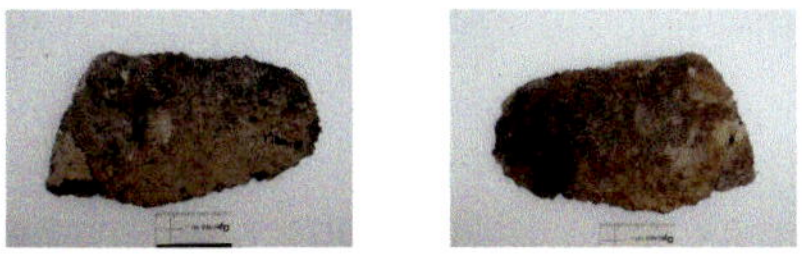

Iskijkat fabric D
IA384/8

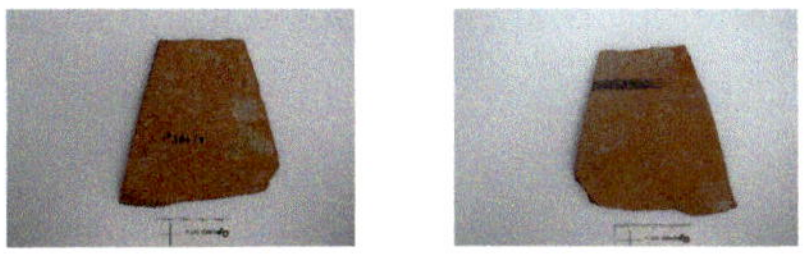

Iskijkat fabric F
IA354/15

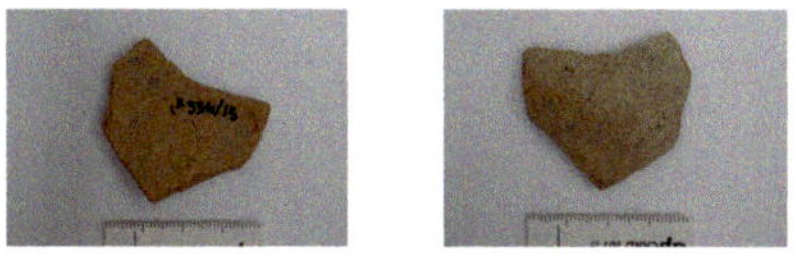

IA354/59

IA354/64

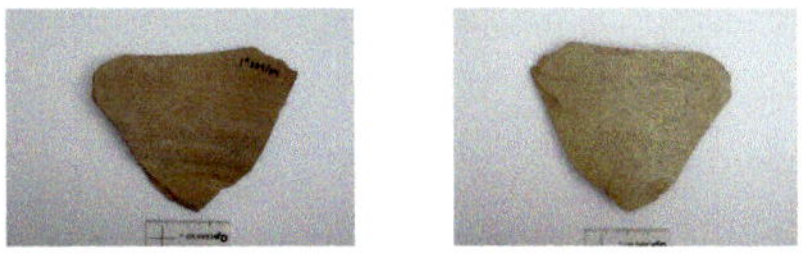

TABLE 5.1   Photographs of the fronts and backs of the studied sherds (*cont.*)

Vardanzeh

KV15-492-3-6A   KV15-557-6B   KV15-605-28-6

KV15-605-49-6   KV15-605-52-26   KV16-713-30

KV16-822-6   KV16-822-29-1

3   Methodology

Once photographed, the sherds were sampled; the size of the sherd was chosen according to the texture of the fabric, i.e., around 8 mm² for fine-to-medium fabric and around 1.5 cm² for medium-to-coarse fabric. They were then plunged in an epoxy resin and polished. Binocular observations were first made on them. Then, 37 thin sections were produced and observed under optical microscopy, in polarised light, with crossed polarisers and with a single polariser. This method of examination was used to identify the mineralogical and lithological nature of the silty and sandy fraction of the grains, corresponding to the degreaser added by the potter and to grains of a size between 20 μm and 2 mm initially present in the silty sediment. It is also a question of characterising the petrofabric of the clay. The objectives of these observations:

1. Establish "petrographic groups" based on the nature of the grains of the silty and sandy particle-size fractions and the textures of the fabric (grain size and morphology, particle size classification, etc.), which may be related to a specific production locality or a given period; the different fabrics distinguished with the naked eye will be compared with the petrographic characteristics and the elementary chemical composition of the fabric.
2. Compare the nature of the silty and sandy grains with the geological context of the site in order to see if the ceramics correspond to local production or might be imported from another site.

Finally, elementary chemical analyses were carried out with a portable X-ray fluorescence spectrometry device on the sawn edges of the sherds.

4   Analytical Conditions

4.1   *Petrography*

The petrographic observations were made with an Olympus BH2 polarising microscope, under light known as "non-analysed polarised" (LPNA = only the polariser under the sample is present) and under so-called "polarised and analysed" light (LPA = the polariser placed under the sample and the one placed above are at 90°).

4.2   *X-ray Fluorescence Spectrometry*

The analyses were carried out with the portable Thermo Scientific© model Niton xl3t GOLDD + model under helium flow to detect and quantify the Mg when it exceeds 0.5% by mass. X-rays are emitted by a silver anode. The analyses were carried out with a 3 mm spot, in "mining" mode, with acquisition of 4 spectra in sequence according to the conditions:

spectrum 1 ("Main range"): 30 seconds at 40kV and 50μA;
spectrum 2 ("Low range"): 30 seconds at 20kV and 100μA;
spectrum 3 ("High range"): 30 seconds at 50kV and 40μA;
spectrum 4 ("Light range"): 30 seconds at 6.4kV and 200μA.

These analyses give quantitative results but are less sensitive than other methods, like PIXE or ICP. They were made under the same conditions for all the samples and are therefore comparable. However, several factors influence the accuracy of the results: roughness and surface flatness (not always perfect), the thickness of the sample and its geometry (curved or flat sherd). This technique is also not very efficient for the quantification of trace elements present at less than 0.01%. In this report, only the results for the major and minor elements are reported in table 5.2.

5 Results

5.1 Chemical Composition

The results of the X-ray fluorescence analyses are presented below.

TABLE 5.2 Compositions in % by mass of oxides, for the major elements, of the pastes of the sherds studied that were obtained by X-ray fluorescence spectrometry

Ceramics of Iskijkat		MgO $\varepsilon=\pm0.30$	Al_2O_3 $\varepsilon=\pm0.30$	SiO_2 $\varepsilon=\pm0.40$	K_2O $\varepsilon=\pm0.10$	CaO $\varepsilon=\pm0.10$	TiO_2 $\varepsilon=\pm0.04$	MnO $\varepsilon=\pm0.02$	Fe_2O_3 $\varepsilon=\pm0.20$
1530	Ia 370/23 A1	3,00	13,82	59,88	4,32	11,08	0,73	0,00	7,06
1390	Ia352/5 A1	2,80	14,70	64,80	4,39	4,73	0,92	0,05	8,04
1393	Ia370/26 A1	2,84	16,75	67,20	4,59	1,97	0,82	0,00	6,14
1394	Ia370/26 A1	2,96	16,03	69,18	4,09	1,97	0,70	0,00	5,23
1396	Ia354/58 A2	3,28	14,96	66,12	4,76	3,16	0,81	0,05	7,09
1398	Ia370/22 A2	3,61	17,73	63,72	3,89	4,78	0,76	0,00	5,78
1531	Ia370/22 A2	2,49	15,38	62,60	4,68	5,81	0,96	0,05	7,78
1532	Ia375/2 A3	4,23	14,49	61,26	3,76	8,17	0,81	0,04	7,38
1400	Ia375/2 A3	3,90	13,72	60,73	3,91	8,79	0,91	0,05	7,75
1401	Ia371/17 A4	3,38	14,21	63,78	4,14	7,99	0,68	0,00	5,80
1402	Ia371/17 A4	3,46	13,86	62,66	4,14	9,84	0,62	0,00	5,62
1403	Ia371/23 A4	2,57	16,45	66,36	4,73	2,19	0,89	0,02	6,69
1533	Ia378/4 A4	2,56	14,44	67,18	4,37	2,91	0,94	0,03	7,58
1406	Ia370/5 A5	3,55	15,45	58,45	4,43	9,99	0,79	0,00	7,24
1534	Ia370/5 A5	4,11	16,07	59,71	4,61	7,17	0,84	0,05	7,29
1408	Ia377/6 A5	1,85	14,54	66,93	5,30	2,17	0,98	0,00	8,38
1535	Ia377/6 A5	2,88	16,35	66,24	4,54	1,66	0,87	0,03	7,35
1409	Ia341/2 A6	2,54	13,19	65,12	4,51	6,91	0,79	0,03	6,96
1536	Ia341/2 A6	3,14	14,80	63,09	4,25	6,90	0,77	0,07	6,86
1412	Ia368/34 A6	3,16	12,95	65,23	4,68	5,10	0,89	0,06	8,06
1537	Ia368/34 A6	4,32	14,93	64,13	4,20	4,49	0,76	0,09	7,13
1418	Ia384/15 A6	1,23	14,76	69,67	4,77	1,48	1,10	0,05	6,95
1539	Ia384/15 A6	1,80	16,57	69,37	4,20	1,15	0,95	0,00	6,05
1419	Ia375/8 B	2,22	13,88	67,26	4,70	1,88	1,05	0,00	9,00
1421	Ia370/4 C	1,78	13,80	68,42	5,08	0,93	1,05	0,00	8,74
1422	Ia370/4 C	2,53	14,84	67,64	4,48	1,43	0,86	0,00	8,20
1423	Ia375/5 C	3,27	17,01	66,91	3,99	1,49	0,79	0,00	6,36
1424	Ia370/1 CW1	4,55	15,33	63,40	5,18	4,95	0,71	0,00	6,05
1540	Ia370/1 CW1	2,96	11,87	67,52	5,10	5,00	0,69	0,00	6,70
1425	Ia371/34 CW1	3,72	16,11	64,90	3,98	4,26	0,78	0,00	6,53
1541	Ia371/34 CW1	3,10	14,90	65,05	4,43	4,11	0,88	0,04	7,65
1426	Ia341/9 CW2	2,65	16,77	69,66	4,42	0,38	0,95	0,00	4,92

TABLE 5.2 Compositions in % by mass of oxides (cont.)

		MgO	Al$_2$O$_3$	SiO$_2$	K$_2$O	CaO	TiO$_2$	MnO	Fe$_2$O$_3$
Ceramics of Iskijkat		ε=±0.30	ε=±0.30	ε=±0.40	ε=±0.10	ε=±0.10	ε=±0.04	ε=±0.02	ε=±0.20
1427	Ia370/13 CW2	2,76	14,86	65,21	4,25	4,86	0,94	0,00	7,03
1428	Ia368/151 CW3	3,34	17,31	68,71	3,18	1,17	0,94	0,00	5,23
1542	IA368/151 CW3	2,13	14,88	70,09	3,92	1,45	1,15	0,00	6,56
1429	Ia370/16 CW3	2,91	16,51	68,03	3,79	2,28	0,84	0,00	5,61
1430	Ia370/20 CW4	1,74	13,73	70,53	4,96	0,80	1,22	0,00	6,99
1431	Ia384/16 CW5	2,53	16,17	70,40	3,43	1,40	0,81	0,00	5,24
1432	Ia384/8 D	2,70	14,78	65,32	4,47	4,31	0,93	0,00	7,39
1543	Ia384/8 D	2,61	15,83	65,58	4,42	3,39	0,98	0,00	7,43
1435	Ia354/15 F	3,69	13,22	65,75	2,91	8,86	0,60	0,00	4,91
1544	Ia354/15 F	2,83	13,53	62,71	3,57	10,19	0,78	0,06	6,35
1436	Ia354/59 F	3,15	12,11	59,61	2,95	14,53	0,79	0,10	6,78
1545	Ia354/59 F	3,14	13,73	59,01	2,97	13,97	0,80	0,06	6,54
1437	Ia354/64 F	3,92	14,10	61,78	2,94	11,81	0,62	0,00	4,91
1546	Ia 354/64 F	3,86	14,66	54,93	3,30	15,63	0,77	0,10	6,84
Ceramics of Vardanzeh									
1438	KV15 492-3-6-A	1,54	13,10	66,60	3,86	6,88	0,86	0,00	6,95
1439	KV15-557-6B	3,90	16,83	64,35	3,87	4,26	0,69	0,00	6,12
1440	KV15615-28-69	1,63	11,79	66,63	3,52	10,22	0,68	0,00	5,71
1445	KV15-605-49-6	1,06	11,01	68,61	3,72	9,26	0,68	0,00	6,21
1446	KV15-605-52-24	1,57	13,34	69,21	3,79	1,11	1,26	0,00	9,92
1449	KV16-713-30-6D	1,78	10,97	67,37	3,89	8,37	1,02	0,05	6,68
1450	KV16-822-6	2,00	10,67	67,17	3,53	9,58	0,75	0,00	6,31
1451	KV16-822-29-1	3,36	12,55	55,52	5,50	13,85	0,85	0,19	8,36

For each site, the compositions of the fabrics are relatively homogeneous for all of the chemical elements except calcium (between 0.3% and 15.6%). As the petrographic observations clearly show, this heterogeneity of the calcium contents is explained by the presence of calcitic grains in more or less significant proportions. Thus, when no grain of calcite is present in a clay, the calcium content is very low.

The compositions are not correlated with petrofabrics. However, the "F-type" sherds all have very close and also very high calcium values and seem to be grouped together in figure 5.2, which presents the variations of calcium as a function of magnesium. But we do not have enough samples for this to be confirmed. The clay matrix can also be more or less rich in calcium. Caution is needed because during the deposit of the sherds, secondary calcite (from the deposit) may have crystallised in the pores of the sample. This phenomenon could indeed be observed by optical microscopy in certain samples.

Concerning Vardana, the magnesium contents are relatively homogeneous (between 1% and 2%) except for two samples: KV15-557-6B and KV16-822-29. Six sherds from Vardana differ significantly from the Iskijkat samples due to their Mg, Al and K content (see figures 5.2 and 5.3). For potassium we also observe very similar values for the Vardana group, around 3.5–3.9% (except for KV16-822-29, where K$_2$O is slightly higher: 5.5%). This is why the choice was made to draw a diagram %Al$_2$O$_3$ vs %MgO + %K$_2$O (fig. 5.2). Thus, despite the small percentage variations for these chemical elements, six Vardana sherds are clearly distinguished from all of the Iskijkat ones. This means that the silts used for the studied pottery at the two sites had a slightly different composition.

Two of the ceramics samples from Vardana (KV15-557-6B and KV16-822-29-1) have a composition that significantly differs from the others from the same site, but both are similar to the ceramics from Iskiskat. This difference is mainly due to the percentage of MgO, which is greater

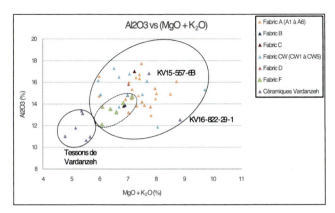

FIGURE 5.1 Al_2O_3 vs $(MgO + K_2O)$ diagram of ceramic fabrics from all the sherds studied

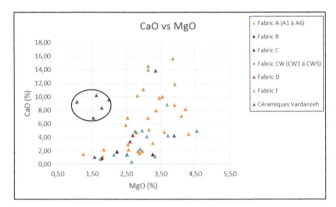

FIGURE 5.2 Al_2O_3 vs $(MgO + K_2O)$ diagram of ceramic pastes from all the sherds studied

in the fabric from Iskijkat. Magnesium is very interesting because, since little or none is found in the sandy fraction, it is therefore a significant characteristic of the nature of the clay fraction.

It is, however, not possible to say if both ceramics are imports or if they were shaped with a silt of the same kind as that of Iskijkat.

Inside the cloud of points corresponding to the analyses of the Iskijkat sherds, we do not see the appearance of groups that can correspond to the different fabrics that could be distinguished before the study. However, the samples from factory F seem to be grouped together.

5.2   Petrographic Examinations

The 37 thin sections of sherds were observed and photographed under a binocular microscope, under optical microscopy under polarised light and under polarised light and then analysed. The photography plates are presented in the annexes (tables 5.4–5.9).

The first information we acquired from microscopic examination is texture. In our case, it corresponds to the distribution and concentration of quartz grains, the major mineral in our samples.

Almost all the samples have a fine to medium texture. Six samples have a texture described as "coarse" due to the presence of chamotte grains of a size greater than 400 μm. We observe this type of grain both in the CW factory group (Ia341 / 9 CW2, Ia370 / 16 CW3, Ia370 / 20 CW4, Ia384 / 16 CW5) and in the KV factory group (KV16-713-30, KV16-822-6).

It is not possible to establish groups of petrofacies based on textural characteristics exclusively because of a certain homogeneity. In addition, they are generally linked to the processing of the fabric, often a function of the typology and the function of the pottery or the heterogeneity of the raw clay material. The latter therefore do not constitute criteria for distinguishing different places of production. However, these differences in texture may allow us to distinguish subgroups of petrofacies.

Petrographic observations have also made it possible to identify several types of grains based on their mineralogical and lithological nature (as a fragment of rock). For each sample, table 5.2 presents the different types of grains in the silty and sandy particle size fraction, sometimes with a visual evaluation of the quantities.

The nature of the grains allows us to gain valuable information about the geological context, the scale of the sedimentation basin (Bukhara Oasis) and the source areas of the sediments deposited in the oasis (Zerafshan watershed).

We generally observe a certain homogeneity in terms of the nature of the inclusions present in all of the fabrics, which reflects the same geological context. Despite everything, some variations have allowed us to identify the following petrographic groupings.

5.2.1   Sherds from Iskijkat

The majority of sherds from Iskijkat belong to petrographic group A. The main characteristics of this group are the presence of:

1. a majority of polycrystalline quartz of metamorphic origin corresponding to micro quartzite or meta chert mixed with monocrystalline quartz and some feldspars;
2. the matrix is often micaceous (a parameter that is not always easy to observe if the micas are of too small dimensions or if the matrix is too dark).

Subgroups can be differentiated according to the texture and some differences in the nature of the grains and their relative importance depending on the clay matrix:

A1: characterised by the presence of the mineral species listed above. A sherd (Ia352 / 5A1) presents characteristics close to group B3 established for certain samples from the Varadanzeh site;

TABLE 5.3

	fabric	pétro fabric	Quartz mono-cristallin	Quartz poly-cristallin	Quartz ext ond	Feldspaths Feldspath plagioclase	Feldspaths Feldspath Potassique/ perthite	Calcite Grains de calcite (m/s)	Calcite calcite matricielle	Calcite Cc pedoge
Céramiques Iskijkat										
Ia 352/5 A1	A1	A1	++	(+)	n.o.	+	(+)	cc 2dre?		(+)6
Ia 370/23 A1	A1	A1	++	(+)	+	+	(+)	cc 2dre?		+
Ia 370/26 A1	A1	A1	+(+)	(+)	+	+	(+)			+ (f)
Ia 354/58 A2	A2	A1	+++	+	+	+	+	cc 2dre (+)		
Ia 370/22 A2	A2	A1	+	(+)	n.o.	(+)2	(+)2	+ (= μfossile ?)		(+)?
Ia375/2 A3	A3	A1	+	(+)2	+	(+)2	(+)1	+=cc 2dre ; s(+)		(+)1
Ia371/17 A4	A4	A1	++	(+)	+	(+)				++**(f)
Ia 371/23 A4	A4	A1	++	(+)	+	(+)	(+)			++**(f)
Ia 378/4 A4	A4	A1	++	(+)	+	+	(+)	+		
Ia 370/5 A5	A5	A1	+		n.o.	(+)1	(+)			+++
Ia 377/6 A5	A5	A1	++	(+)	+	(+)7	(+)3			
Ia 341/2 A6	A6	A1	+++	(+)	+	(+)	+(+)	(+)m+s	?	+
Ia 384/15 A6	A6	A1	++	+	+	(+)	(+)			
Ia 368/34 A6	A6	A2	+++		+	(+)3	(+)2			
Ia375/8 B	B	A1	+	(+)	+	(+)2	(+)2	+		(+)?
Ia370/4 C	C	A1	+(+)		+	(+)3	+			
Ia 377/5 C	C	A1	++		+	+	(+)	cc 2dre		
Ia 384/8 D	D	A1	+++	(+)	+	(+)5	(+)2	(+)		+
Ia 354/15 F	F	A3	+	++	+	+	(+)	+		
Ia 354/59 F	F	A3	+	++	+	+	(+)	+		
Ia 354/64 F	F	A3	+(+)	(+)	+	(+)	(+)	+		
Ia370/1 CW1	CW1	A1	+	(+)	+	(+)2	(+)2	+		(+)?
Ia371/34 CW1	CW1	A1	+	(+)	+	(+)3	(+)2	+		(+)?
Ia 341/9 CW2	CW2	B	+		n.o.	(+)				
Ia370/13 CW2	CW2	A1	+	(+)	+	(+)				
Ia 358/151 CW3	CW3	A5	+	(+)	n.o.					
Ia 370/16 CW3	CW3	A1	++		n.o.	(+)3		cc 2dre(3)		
Ia370/20 CW4	CW4	A6	+	(+)2	n.o	(+)				
Ia 384/16 CW5	CW5	A4	+++	(+)	+	+				
Céramiques Vardanzeh										
KV15-492-3-6A		C1	++++	+	+	+	+	+		
KV15-557-6B		C2	++	(+)	+	(+)	+	+	+	+
KV15-605-28-6		C1	++++		+	+	+	+	+	
KV15-605-49-6		C1	++++		+	+	+	+ =m	+?	
KV15-605-52-24		D	+		n.o.	(+)1				
KV16-713-30-6D		C1	++++	+	+	+	+		++	
KV16-822-6		C1	++++	+	+	+	+		++	
KV16-822-29-1		C3	+		n.o.	(+)2	(+)3	+		(+)

								fgt roches				
fossile	Oxyde de fer	Muscovite	Biotite	Epidote	Amphibole(A) /pyroxene(P)	apatite	pelite/ siltite	fgt schiste ou μquartzite	meta chert	gres ferru	fgt γ	chamotte	fgt fibre veg
		(+)	(+)1	(+)2	(+)8			+					
		(+)	(+)4	(+)3	(+)2			+	(+)				
		(+)	(+)4	(+)1				+(+)	+				
		+	(+)2			(+)1		(+)1	+	(+)1			
(+)		(+)	(+)2					(+)					
				(+)1									
		+(micro-baquettes)	(+)3	(+)2	(+)1			(+)					
		+(microba-guettes)	(+)2	(+)3	(+)1			+					
		+			(+)1			+					
(+)1		(+)2						(+)2	(+)2		(+)1		
		(+)8		(+)1	(+)			+	(+)				
(+)		(+)6	(+)2		(+)8			+					
		+	(+)5	(+)1				(+)					
		(+)8		(+)2			(+)3	+					
(+)		(+)	(+)2					(+)					
		(+)						(+)					
		+	(+)1	(+)1	(+)1	(+)		+					
		(+)6			(+)6			+	+		(+)1		
								++	+		(+)1		
								++	+		(+)1		
		(+)2	(+)1	(+)1				++	+				
(+)		(+)	(+)2	(+)1				(+)					
(+)		(+)		(+)1				(+)					
(+)1												++	
		(+)						(+)?					
		(+)						(+)					+++
		+		(+)2			(+)					+	
		+						(+)3				(+)3	
								+				+++	
		(+)	(+)3	(+)2	(+)8			+					
		+	(+)1	(+)1	A(+)1;P(+)1			(+)	+				
(+)					(+)2			(+)					
				(+)2				(+)	+				
		+						+					
		(+)			(+)2			++	++			(+)	
		(+)			(+)2			++	++			(+)	
(+)1		+	(+)					(+)	(+)				

The ceramics from the two sites are distinct due to their chemical composition and certain petrographic characteristics. However, two ceramics from Vardana (KV15-557-6B and KV16-822-29-1, from the petrofabrics C2 and C3 respectively) are chemically close to the Iskijkat selection, if we consider more precisely the chemical element magnesium (characteristic of clay matter). However, it is not possible to know if these differences constitute signatures for the two sites or if they can be observed at the same site because of the probable heterogeneity of the silts of the sedimentary basin of Bukhara.

Annexes

TABLE 5.4

Fabric	n. shard	Chronology
CW1	IA370/1	2–3 S. AD
	IA371/34	
CW2	IA370/13	2–3 S. AD
	IA341/9	4 S. AD
CW3	IA368/151	2–3 S. AD
	IA370/16	
CW4	IA370/20	2–3 S. AD

TABLE 5.4 (cont.)

Fabric	n. shard	Chronology
CW5	IA384/16	2–1 S. BC
A1	370/23	2–3 S. AD
	370/26	3–4 AD
	352/5	
A2	370/22	2–3 S. AD
	354/58	3–4 S. AD
A3		1 S. AD
A4	378/4	1 S. BC–1 S. AD
	371/17	2–3 S. AD
	371/23	
A5	377/6	1 S. BC–1 S. AD
	370/5	2–3 S. AD
A6	384/15	2–1 BC
	368/34	2–3 S. AD
	341/2	4 S. AD
B	375/8	1 S. BC–1 S. AD
C	377/5	1 S. BC–1 S. AD
	370/4	2–3 S. AD
D	384/8	2–1 BC
F	354/59	2–3 S. AD
	354/15	
	354/64	

TABLE 5.5 Photographs of the sherds prepared in section taken with a binocular magnifying glass

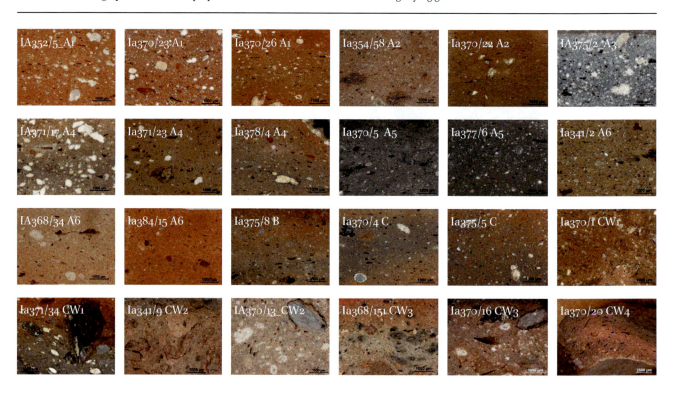

TABLE 5.5   Photographs of the sherds prepared in section taken with a binocular magnifying glass (*cont.*)

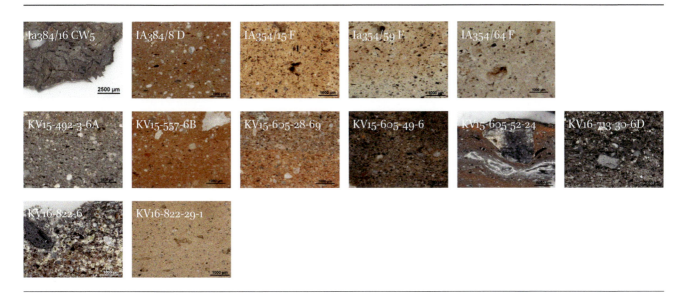

TABLE 5.6   Photographs taken by optical microscopy under polarized light and analyzed

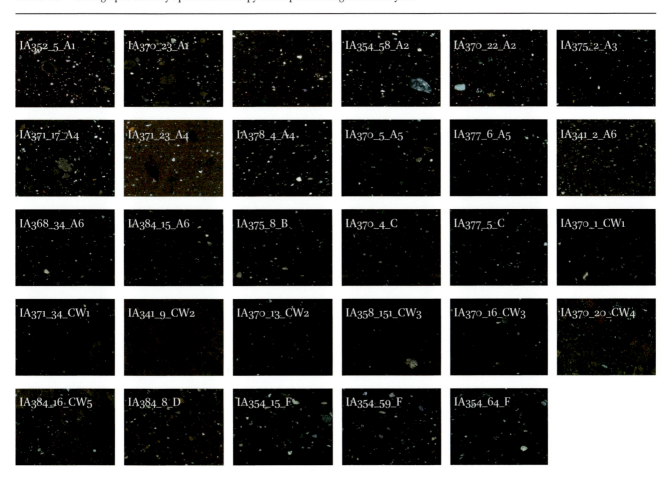

TABLE 5.6 Photographs taken by optical microscopy under polarized light and analyzed (*cont.*)

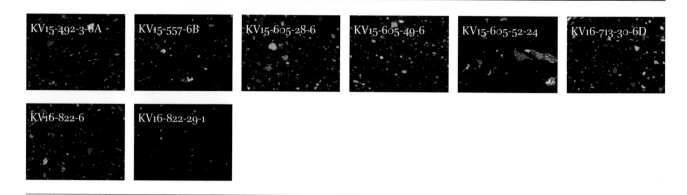

TABLE 5.7 Photographs taken by optical microscopy under unanalyzed polarized light

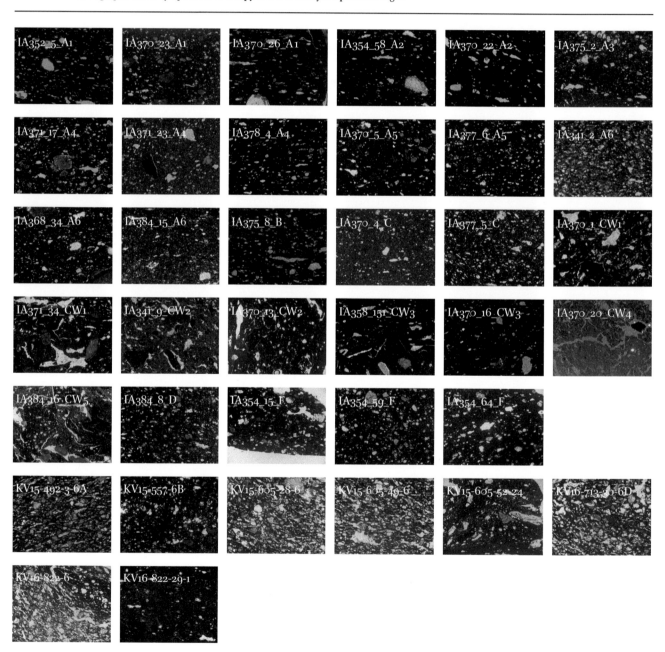

CHAPTER 6

Physico-chemical Analyses of Ceramics from Bukhara and Paykend

Anne Bouquillon, Christel Doublet and Nathalie Gandolfo

1 Archaeological and Historical Context

The study presented here is an exploratory approach conducted on an extremely small number of sherds.[1] Its main purpose is to show what types of analyses can be broadly implemented to answer to the general issues raised by the research developed by the MAFOUB project.

The six fragments selected by R. Rante come from two major sites in the Bukhara and Paykend oases (Rante and Mirzaakhmedov 2019). Between the end of the 8th and the 10th century, these cities underwent intense cultural development, conferring them with the *status* of the richest cities of the oasis, one due to its function as the capital, Bukhara, and the other, Paykend, due to its strategic political, military and commercial location along the road to Khorasan.

The excavation carried out in the centre of the citadel of Bukhara has given us rich and original material that has a well-defined stratigraphic context. In the layers dated to the 10th–11th centuries, two sherds were selected from among the rich material discovered in these Samanid princely residences (Gangler et al. 2004: 44). These two pieces (BUXA 162/1 and BUXA 162/9) were chosen to provide elements that could answer questions about local production technologies and local imitations of imported luxury productions (here lustres specifically).

The fragments from Paykend (Dep.B. 317, Dep.B. 316, Dep.B. 74 and Dep.B. 76) were found in a rich context, in a filling layer of the settlement dump excavated in shahrestan 1. In the 9th–10th centuries, this residence, framed by ditch-streets in an orthogonal plan that consisted of three domestic areas: a kitchen-workshop area and services, an area used mainly for rest and receiving guest, and an outdoor courtyard. These areas were in use until the 10th century, when they were transformed into a large dump area, where we found large quantities of ceramics, coins, iron instruments and other objects related to everyday life. The analyses of the four sherds should help us: 1. highlight and trace the origins of some of the types of imported ceramics; and 2. describe some technical characteristics of the two examples of locally produced ceramic called Ishkornaïa, of which some examples were found in a small dump by furnace 915 in the pottery quarter (Rante and Mirzaakhmedov 2019: fig. 195).

2 Material and Methods

The fragments are specific to local production (BUXA 162/1, BUXA 162/9, Dep.B.317, Dep.B.76) or are clearly high-quality imports, namely lustre ceramics (Dep.B.74) or pieces covered with white and dark blue glazes (Dep.B.316). All the fragments are glazed on the external face and only sometimes on the inner face.

A sample of clay body, in the form of powder (50 mg), was taken using a tungsten carbide drill bit on each fragment. Millimetric scales of glaze were sampled with a scalpel (table 6.1).

The analytical protocols are those usually used at the C2RMF to study glazed ceramics: PIXE (particle-induced X-ray emission) for elemental chemical analysis of the clay bodies and characterisation of the blue pigment in the glazes, RBS (Rutherford Backscattering Spectrometry) for studying lustre, SEM-EDX (Scanning Electron Microscopy–Energy Dispersive Spectrometry) for chemical analysis of all the glazes and observation of their microstructures. 2D X-ray fluorescence was used occasionally to study the lustre.

PIXE

Some of the powder collected during the sampling of clay fabrics was used to form pellets that are 6mm in diameter using a mould supporting a pressure of 4T for one minute. No binder was added. The pellets were glued onto a plexiglass plate with double-sided adhesive and then analysed using PIXE, which provides precise, quantitative basic chemical information. The analyses were carried out using the configuration of the AGLAE accelerator available since 2012: three SDD detectors dedicated to the detection of high energy X-rays (> 3keV) and another detector optimised for low energy X-rays (1–10keV) (Pichon et al. 2014: 27–31). There are only a few differences with the one set up during the AGLAE update in February 2018. Each analysis was carried out by scanning an area of $500 \times 500\ \mu m^2$

---

[1] All three authors are from Centre de recherche et de restauration des musées de France (C2RMF), Palais du Louvre, Porte des Lions, 14 quai François Mitterrand, F-75001 Paris.

FIGURES 6.1A–F
a. BUXA 162/1, Boukhara chantier A (front and back);
b. BUXA 162/9, Boukhara chantier A (front and back);
c. Dep.B.317, Paykend chantier B (front and back);
d. Dep.B.76, Paykend chantier B (front and back);
e. Dep.B.74, Paykend chantier B (front and back);
f. Dep.B.316, Paykend chantier B (front and back)

TABLE 6.1 List of samples

N° fragment	Production place	N° sample	Face	Description
BUXA 162/1	local	Ech 1	Face 1	Colourless glaze / greenish decor / white slip
		Ech 2	Face 1	White glaze / white slip
BUXA 162/9	local	Ech 3	Face 1	White glaze / white slip
DEP.B. 317	local ?	Ech 4	Face 1	White glaze
		Ech 5	Face 2	Green-blue glaze
		Ech 6	Face 2	White glaze
DEP.B. 76	local?	Ech 9	Face 1	White glaze
DEP B / 74	imported?	Ech 8	Face 1	Lustre white glaze
		Ech 7	Face 2	White glaze
DEP.B.316	imported?	Ech 10	Face 1	Black / white layer
		Ech 11	Face 2	Blue / white layer

with a beam of 50 μm in diameter in order to minimise the influence of the heterogeneity of the material. A helium flow (2l / min) was maintained on both the proton and X-ray path to reduce the effects of energy loss and absorption. The compositions were obtained using a 3MeV proton beam, and the concentrations of major, minor and trace elements were determined using Traupixe (Pichon et al. 2010) and Gupixwin (Campbell et al. 2010). Each series of results is validated by the systematic analysis of the geological standard DrN of the Center for Petrographic and Geochemical Research (CRPG) of Nancy.

For the analysis of the glazes, the measurements were carried out directly on the fragments in the least altered areas. The standards used are BGIRA 3 and BGIRA 4, Brill C.

RBS

The lustre was studied on the AGLAE accelerator using RBS directly on the fragment. The RBS detector is positioned at an angle of 130° in relation to the incident proton beam. The spectra were calibrated using silica standards covered with a thin layer of gold (1.5 μm).

The processing of point-in-time RBS data was carried out with SIMNRA v 6.5 software. SIMNRA simulates the RBS spectrum of a theoretical target with a stratigraphy chosen by the user. Each layer is defined by its thickness given in TFU (Thin Film Unit, with 1 TFU = 1015 at / cm^2) and its composition given in atomic percentages. Each layer is assumed to be homogeneous during the calculation. This spectrum is then visually compared to the experimental spectrum. The theoretical target is manually modified in order to obtain a satisfactory correspondence between the spectrum simulated by the software and the experimental spectrum.

MEB and MEB-EDS

In order to obtain complete stratigraphic information about the materials and the microstructure of the glazes and slips, a millimetre scale is taken with a scalpel. It is placed in a block of polyester resin and sliced perpendicular to the surface of the sample in order to highlight the entire succession of layers, from the surface decoration to the clay fabric. It is then polished using diamond powders with decreasing particle sizes (from 6 μm to ¼ μm). Before observation, the sample is made conductive by depositing a thin layer of carbon. A FEI XL30CP scanning electron microscope (SEM) is used in a high vacuum, and it is connected to an Oxford Aztec Energy Dispersive Spectrometry (EDS) analysis system associated with an SDD X-Max detector with an active surface of 50mm^2. The images are taken at an electron acceleration voltage of 10kV and the analyses are performed at 15kV. All quantitative analytical data (with hidden witnesses) presented below correspond to the average of 3 zones. The results are given in the form of oxide percentages unless otherwise indicated.

2D X-ray Fluorescence

Two-dimensional X-ray fluorescence mapping was performed using the C2RMF laboratory's X-ray analysis system. It is constituted of an X-ray tube (Moxtek) with a molybdenum anode with a maximum power of 40 watts. The analyses were carried out at a voltage of 45 kV and an intensity of 800 μA. The Röntec Peltier-cooled X-flash detector is positioned at 45°. Acquisitions are made directly on the sherd, without contact; the source and the detector must be positioned at a distance between 0.5 and 6 cm from the studied surface. The collimator at the outlet of the X-ray source was chosen to obtain a beam with a diameter of 200 μm. The entire analysis head is placed on a table system motorised in X and Y and programmable. The scanned area was 20 × 35 mm², the size of the pixel was 200 μm and the counting time per pixel was 150 ms, for a total scan time of approximately 45 minutes.

The results obtained indicate the presence of the elements in a volume defined by the size of the pixel and the depth that can be analysed by this technique (20–100 μm). The set of pixels forms a data image. By using the Pymca software and selecting the energy zone corresponding to the chemical element of interest, it is possible to obtain a map of the elemental distribution of that element over the area under study.

3 Analysis Results

3.1 Fabrics

The six sherds are characterized by very fine clay fabrics. On the basis of chemical analyses, two distinct groups can be identified (table 6.2).

The first corresponds to a set of three sherds (Dep 76, 162.1 and 162.9), whose fabric contains about 12% CaO, 3.7% MgO and more than 55% SiO_2; the average alumina (Al_2O_3) and iron (Fe_2O_3) contents reach 15.5% and 6.5% respectively. Potassium (K_2O) and sodium (Na_2O) correspond to approximately 4% of the total composition, potassium being more abundant. These three sherds represent, according to ceramologists, the local production of the oasis.

The second group (Dep 74 and Dep 316) differs markedly from the previous one by an increase in magnesium and calcium contents (7% MgO and around 20% CaO). The aluminum, silicon, sodium and potassium contents are lower, and the fabric is lighter.

The next sherd (Dep 317) is a slightly more complex case: at first glance, it can be attached to the first group, despite significant differences in magnesium (5,5% MgO) and aluminium (only 13% Al2O3) contents.

3.2 Slips

They are found on only two sherds (DEP 162.1 and 162.9), where a white layer of 100 micrometres clearly separates the reddish fabric from the glaze (figs. 6.2 and 6.3).

This slip, of 100 micrometres thick, makes it possible to hide the red colour of the fabric and to obtain a good quality white background, which can bring out a coloured decoration. In both cases, the white slip is very siliceous (table 6.3), and its porosity is clear (figs. 6.4 and 6.5). It consists of almost 70% silica, 10–15% alumina, 3% potassium (K_2O) and almost 15% lead oxide. It undoubtedly is composed of a mixture of crushed grains of sand and potassium white clay (illite?). The presence of lead can be explained either by the presence of crushed lead-glass (or by the addition of lead oxides only, which would act as flux) in the initial mixture, or by the diffusion of this element from the glaze into the slip during firing. Several observations

TABLE 6.2 Chemical composition of the clay fabrics – PIXE data expressed in oxide weight %

Sherd	Na_2O	MgO	Al_2O_3	SiO_2	P_2O_5	SO_3	Cl	K_2O	CaO	TiO_2	MnO	Fe_2O_3	PbO
Dep 76	2,14	3,75	15,42	55,82	0,13	0,42	0,18	2,18	12,46	0,66	0,12	6,58	0,13
162.1	1,10	3,77	16,28	55,73	0,24	0,08	0,10	3,44	11,37	0,70	0,11	6,73	0,35
162.9	1,15	3,81	15,51	54,34	0,17	0,25	0,07	2,84	14,23	0,69	0,12	6,81	0,01
Dep 317	1,21	5,54	13,17	58,92	0,33	0,09	0,07	2,40	12,24	0,67	0,08	5,18	0,10
Dep 74	1,79	7,03	12,87	48,84	0,18	0,13	0,21	1,07	18,82	0,73	0,14	7,93	0,25
Dep 316	1,29	7,45	13,06	48,59	0,13	0,12	0,06	1,17	19,23	0,74	0,16	7,93	0,06

TABLE 6.3 Chemical composition of white slips – EDS data expressed in oxide weight %

		Na_2O	MgO	Al_2O_3	SiO_2	P_2O_5	K_2O	CaO	TiO_2	Fe_2O_3	PbO
BUXA162/1	face 1	0,41	0,62	11,51	69,89	0	2,95	0,46	0,17	0	14,00
BUXA162/1	face 2	0,35	0,67	10,00	68,13	0,63	2,82	0,94	0,4	0,37	15,68
BUXA162/9		0,66	0,91	15,10	64,91	0	4,06	0,97	0,44	0,30	12,65

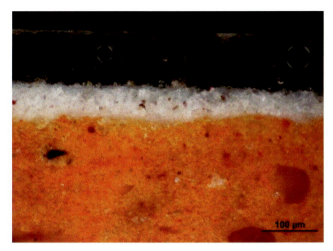

FIGURE 6.2 BUXA 162/1 Face 1 (sample 2): Optical microscope photographs of the cross-section
©C2RMF

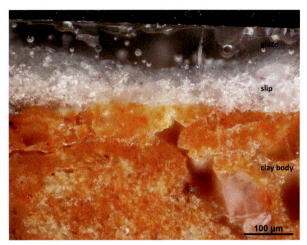

FIGURE 6.3 BUXA 162/1 Face 1 (sample 3): Optical microscope photographs of the cross-section
©C2RMF

FIGURE 6.4 BUXA 162/1 Face 1 (sample 2): SEM backscattered electron image of the cross-section (*scale = 100 μm*)
©C2RMF

FIGURE 6.5 BUXA 162/1 Face 1 (sample 2): SEM backscattered electron image of the cross-section (*scale = 250 μm*)
©C2RMF

allow us to decide between these two hypotheses: there does not seem to be a lead gradient within the slip; the interfaces are crisp; no greater vitrification is observed in the slip in the vicinity of the glaze, except perhaps in the first microns (see fig. 6.5); and the lead concentrations drop suddenly at the interface between the slip and the clay fabric. All these indications point to the deliberate addition of lead, either in the form of oxides or crushed glass, to the slip mixture to obtain a good cohesion of the various constituents of the slip during firing and perhaps also to intensify the resemblance to a white glaze opacified with tin.

If the slips' compositions on the internal and external faces of the BUX A 162/1 sherd are similar, it will be a slightly different from the other sherd, especially in terms of silica, alumina and alkalis. The basic recipes are the same, but the sand/clay proportions have changed.

3.3 Glazes

All six samples analyzed are covered with a glaze containing significant quantities of Pb. Depending on the proportions, two groups can be distinguished: glazes with a high lead content (over 50% PbO), and those in which lead is associated with higher amount of alkaline elements.

3.3.1 High-lead Transparent Glazes

Two sherds are taken into consideration (162/1 and 162/9). The glazes are perfectly homogeneous, without bubbles and with few inclusions. Their thickness is around 100μm (figs. 6.2 and 6.3). They contain more than 50% lead oxides (PbO) and have the same compositions on their internal and external faces. Despite these similar general characteristics, the glazes of the two sherds show clear differences: that of sherd 162.9 is depleted in lead, but more aluminous and potassic than the two glazes of sherd 162.1. It is probably due to different recipes, but this composition could also result from an interaction with the components of the underlying slip. Indeed, research by Roisine et al. (2018) shows that during firing, aluminum can migrate quite easily into a lead glaze, as can potassium, modifying the composition of the initial mixture. At the moment, we do not have enough data to be able to make a correct assessment of the dispersion of glaze compositions in this type of production.

3.3.2 White Lead-Alkali Glazes

All are opacified with cassiterite (SnO_2), whose proportions vary from 5 to 9% (table 6.5). The glazes, depending on whether they are placed on the internal or external face of the sherd, vary in thickness, but they are always placed directly on the clay body, without an intermediate slip (figs. 6.6–6.9).

Note that the glaze of Dep. 316 is deeply weathered so that we can only present qualitative results. For the others, two observations are important: 1. the PbO / SnO_2 ratio varies greatly (from 1 to 7), not only from one sample to another but also from one side to the other of the same sherd (table 6.5). The DEP B. 317 sherd has, on the face bearing the green decoration, a white glaze (ech.6) that is lead-enriched (40% PbO) and in which sodium

TABLE 6.4 Chemical composition of high lead glazes – EDS data expressed in oxide weight % and corresponding to the average of three analyzed areas – Standard deviation in italics

	N° ech.	Colour	Na_2O	MgO	Al_2O_3	SiO_2	K_2O	CaO	TiO_2	Fe_2O_3	PbO
BUXA162/1 Boukhara Chantier A (above decorative motif)	Ech 1	colourless	0,14	0,21	1,27	30,67	0,40	0,87	0,08	0,29	66,07
			0,01	*0,01*	*0,16*	*0,25*	*0,09*	*0,06*	*0,08*	*0,02*	*0,33*
BUXA162/1 Boukhara Chantier A	Ech 2	colourless	0,29	0,23	1,31	31,00	0,83	0,89		0,16	65,25
			0,04	*0,03*	*0,16*	*0,29*	*0,06*	*0,07*		*0,03*	*0,57*
BUXA162/9 Boukhara Chantier A	Ech 3	colourless	0,33	0,35	5,12	43,67	1,55	0,76		0,24	48,00
			0,02	*0,02*	*0,12*	*0,10*	*0,06*	*0,08*		*0,13*	*0,24*

TABLE 6.5 Chemical composition of high lead-alkali glazes – EDS data expressed in oxide weight % and corresponding to the average of three analyzed areas – Standard deviation in italics

	N° ech.	Colour	Na_2O	MgO	Al_2O_3	SiO_2	P_2O_5	SO_3	Cl	K_2O	CaO	TiO_2	MnO	Fe_2O_3	CoO	CuO	SnO_2	PbO	PbO/SnO_2
DEP.B.317 Chantier B	Smp 4	White	1.40	2.01	4.35	46.46	0.22	0	0	2.01	5.25	0.12	0	1.22			9.05	27.9	3.1
			0.01	*0.18*	*0.42*	*2.65*	*0.05*	*0*	*0*	*0.16*	*0.72*	*0.11*	*0*	*0.35*			*1.04*	*3.22*	
	Smp 5	Green	2.10	1.30	2.66	38.51	0.16	0	0	1.69	4.12	0.09	0	0.47		3.14	5.44	40.31	7.4
			0.05	*0.16*	*0.07*	*0.46*	*0.05*	*0*	*0*	*0.06*	*0.2*	*0.08*	*0*	*0.12*		*0.19*	*0.57*	*0.97*	
	Smp 6	White	2.53	1.25	3.04	41.91	0.22	0	0	2.02	3.82	0.06	0.03	0.40			5.36	39.35	7.3
			0.1	*0.02*	*0.13*	*0.16*	*0.03*	*0*	*0*	*0.08*	*0.18*	*0.06*	*0.05*	*0.06*			*0.62*	*0.4*	
DEP.B.76	Smp 9	White	5.18	2.49	2.86	57.72	0.11	0.05	0.37	4.17	5.81	0.11	0.12	0.91			8.71	11.38	1.3
			0.12	*0.17*	*0.48*	*0.95*	*0.02*	*0.09*	*0.06*	*0.14*	*0.25*	*0.03*	*0.02*	*0.18*			*0.86*	*0.28*	
DEP.B.74 Paykend dépôt chantier B	Smp 8	White	5.7	2.45	2.44	56.44	0.03	0.03	0.35	4.12	5.43	0.03	0.12	0.65			9.29	12.93	1.4
			0.06	*0.11*	*0.23*	*0.31*	*0.06*	*0.05*	*0.04*	*0.04*	*0.39*	*0.05*	*0.01*	*0.15*			*0.32*	*0.26*	
	Smp 7	White	3.19	1.42	4.13	46.09	0.02	0	0.08	3.67	2.95	0.08	0.09	0.58			7.95	29.76	3.7
			0.14	*0.08*	*0.53*	*2.3*	*0.04*	*0*	*0.06*	*0.42*	*0.32*	*0.1*	*0.12*	*0.06*			*1.55*	*1.98*	
DEP.316 Chantier B	Smp 10	White	totally altered – contains SiO_2 and a little Na_2O, MgO, Al_2O_3, K_2O, CaO, SnO_2, PbO																
	Smp 11	White	totally altered – contains SiO_2, PbO, SnO_2 and a little Na_2O, MgO, Al_2O_3, K_2O, CaO																
		Blue	6.81	2.08	3,5	58.1	0.21	0	0.3	4.63	4.18	0.18	0.26	5.53	0.68	0.57	0.23	12.77	
			0.13	*0.18*	*0.96*	*0.16*	*0.05*	*0*	*0*	*0.39*	*0.27*	*0*	*0.04*	*0.65*	*0.02*	*0.15*	*0.06*	*1.21*	

FIGURE 6.6 Dep.B.317 (sample 6): Optical microscope photographs of the cross-section
©C2RMF

FIGURE 6.7 Dep.B.76 (sample 9): Optical microscope photographs of the cross-section
©C2RMF

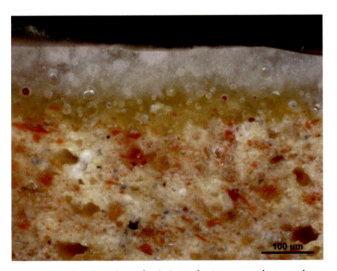

FIGURE 6.8 Dep.B.317 (sample 4): Optical microscope photographs of the cross-section
©C2RMF

FIGURE 6.9 Dep.B.74 (sample 7): Optical microscope photographs of the cross-section
©C2RMF

and potassium do not exceed 2%. On the other hand, the composition of the white glaze on its internal face (sample 4) shows a less marked lead character (28% PbO vs. 40% PbO); the decrease in lead is compensated for by the presence of higher amounts of alumina and alkalis ($Na_2O + K_2O$, sometimes exceeding 10%). This composition is comparable to one of the glazes from Dep.B. 74 found at Paykend (table 6.5). 2. The other lead-alkali glazes (Dep.B. 74, Dep.B. 76 and Dep.B. 317) are very similar (12% PbO, 55% SiO_2, 9% SnO_2).

The white glaze of sample Dep.B.316 is characterised by an extremely advanced state of alteration of the vitreous phase (figs. 6.10–13). There is a high silica content (more than 75% SiO_2), which indicates the start of the a leaching of the fluxing elements (Na_2O, K_2O and even PbO). These characteristics are typical of weathered glass (Davison 2003). In the leached layer, only unmelted silica grains and a few cassiterite microcrystals persist. Their presence is interesting and should be considered an index of the initial composition. In fact, during weathering phenomena, cassiterite, which is not sensitive to leaching processes, is concentrated in the weathering film. Detecting less than 5% here reveals that originally the glaze must have been very weakly stanniferous (probably less than 5% SnO_2), and the opacity or perhaps rather the opalescence of the glaze would be obtained thanks to the inclusions of silica as much as cassiterite. In the current state of the analyses, we therefore assume that it was a

FIGURE 6.10   Dep.B.316, face 1 (sample 10) – Optical microscope photographs of weathered area (porous and yellowish aspect)
©C2RMF

FIGURE 6.11   Dep.B.316, face 1 (sample 10) – SEM backscattered electron image – The vitreous phase is completely weathered (porous and yellowish aspect)
©C2RMF

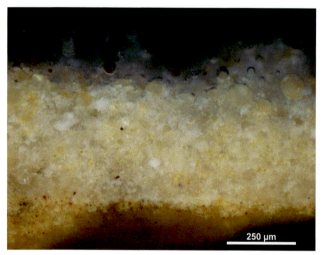

FIGURE 6.12   Dep.B.316, face 2 (sample 11) – Optical microscope photographs of the cross-section – The white glaze appears very porous and altered
©C2RMF

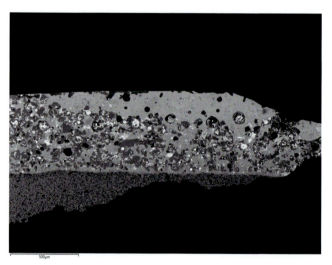

FIGURE 6.13   Dep.B.316, face 1 (sample 10) – SEM backscattered electron image – The white glaze appears weathered. The well-preserved upper zone corresponds to the dark blue glaze
©C2RMF

heterogeneous lead-alkali glass rich in quartz inclusions and slightly opacified by cassiterite.

3.3.3 Coloured Glazes

Among all the fragments, we studied only two coloured glazes: one turquoise (Dep.B. 317) and the other dark blue (Dep.B. 316). They are both lead-alkali glazes (table 6.5), without any other similarities. Indeed, the turquoise glaze is coloured by copper oxide, opacified by tin oxide and placed directly on the fabric (figs. 6.14 and 6.15). Comparisons between the compositions of the turquoise glaze (sample 5) and the white glaze, which adjoins the green areas (sample 6), show that the colouring oxide was simply added to the white mixture.

The glaze is fairly homogeneous, with few bubbles, and the cassiterite microcrystals are distributed heterogeneously. Note that at the interface, numerous magnesium and calcium silicate (diopside?) crystals appear in black on the photomicrograph (figs. 6.16 and 6.17).

The thin dark blue glaze (figs. 6.18–24), coloured with cobalt, is completely transparent. It is painted on an extremely altered underlying opaque or opalescent white glaze (see below). The blue areas are less altered, probably because of the presence of 2.5% alumina and 5% calcium

FIGURE 6.14 Dep.B.317, face 2 – Detail of the turquoise decoration
©C2RMF

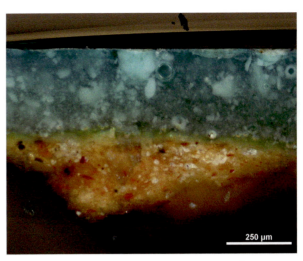

FIGURE 6.15 Dep.B.317, face 2 (sample 5) – Optical microscope photographs of the cross-section showing the coloration in the mass of the turquoise glaze
©C2RMF

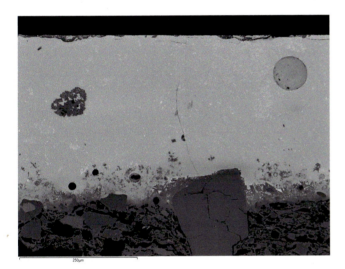

FIGURE 6.16 Dep.B.317, face 2 (sample 5) – SEM backscattered electron image of the glaze – White microcrystals: cassiterite
©C2RMF

FIGURE 6.17 Dep.B.317, face 2 (sample 5) – SEM backscattered electron image of the interface – grey crystals contain Si, Ca, Mg. In white: cassiterite
©C2RMF

FIGURE 6.18 Dep.B.316, face 2
©C2RMF

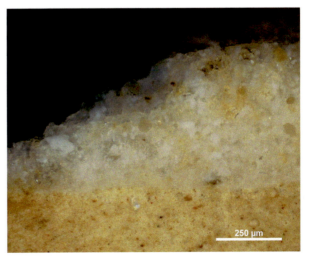

FIGURE 6.19 Dep.B.316, face 2 – Optical microscope photographs of the cross-section
©C2RMF

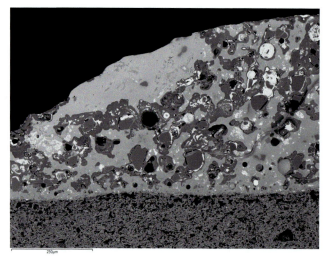

FIGURE 6.20 Dep.B.316, face 2 (sample 11) – SEM backscattered electron image of the cross-section – The white glaze appears very porous and altered – the blue glaze is better preserved
©C2RMF

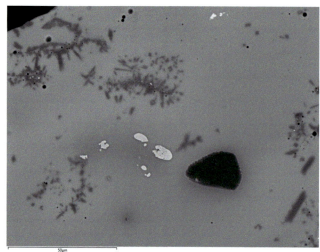

FIGURE 6.21 Dep.B.316, face 2 (sample 11) – SEM backscattered electron image – Detail of the blue area. In white, Co-enriched unfused pigments; dark grey grain = alkaline feldspar
©C2RMF

FIGURE 6.22 Dep.B.316, face 1 – detail of the dark spots on the surface
©C2RMF

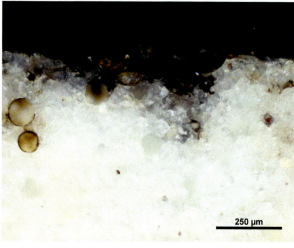

FIGURE 6.23 Dep.B.316, face 1 (sample 10): Optical microscope photographs of the cross-section in a dark area
©C2RMF

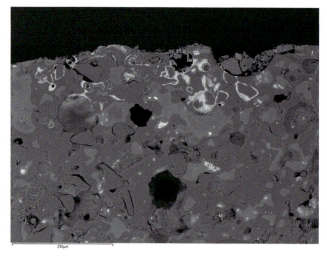

FIGURE 6.24 Dep B. 316, face 1 (sample 10) – stratigraphical section observed with Scanning Electron Microscope
©C2RMF

FIGURE 6.25 Dep.B.74, face 1 – Lustre ceramic sherd
©C2RMF

oxide. Note that other metallic elements are linked to cobalt: iron, manganese, nickel and copper (and maybe traces of zinc, which are only detected by PIXE).

The surfaces of sherd Dep.B.316 have a frequently speckled appearance (fig. 6.22). Surface analyses show that the spots consist of manganese, often associated with vanadium. On figure 6.24 the two elements (appearing in white) apparently concentrate in altered zones around the silica grains and bubbles. This could be a phenomenon related to the extreme surface weathering linked to the burial.

3.3.4 Lustre and Imitation of Lustre
Dep.B. 74

A single sherd, Dep.B.74, has a real lustre (figs. 6.25–28). The metallescent effect is clear (fig. 6.28) on the external surface. This is due to a thin layer of and/or silver nanoparticles on the surface.

The RBS spectrum seems to indicate a complex stratigraphy: a metal-free, lead-depleted outer layer, then the main layer containing silver and copper nanoparticles. It is not clear whether the copper and silver are concentrated in the same layer, or whether the copper nanoparticles are located just below the Ag-enriched layer (fig. 6.29). However, the interpretation is complicated by the high degree of alteration.

On the back of the sherd, the presence of a lustre was complicated to ascertain after a simple visual observation (fig. 6.30), but we were able to find the lustrous decoration, which had almost completely disappeared, by studying the distribution of copper detected by 2D X-ray fluorescence (fig. 6.31). As no silver was detected, we conclude that the lustre mixture was different from that found on the outer surface. However, another hypothesis could be proposed: the use of polychrome lustre. Such elaborate decorations have already been found in some Abbasid productions (Chabanne et al., 2008).

The lustre on each side of the sherd is placed on a white lead-alkaline glaze opacified by cassiterite microcrystals.

BUXA 162/1

The decoration of the BUXA 162/1 sherd is an imitation of lustre. It incorporates the codes of lustre decoration (small dots, triangles, etc.), all placed on a white background (figs. 6.32a–c), but no metallescent effect is observed, except, locally, some iridescence due to problems related to the surface deterioration of the glaze.

Copper or silver are not detected in the composition of the glaze in the brown-yellow areas. In fact, it is necessary to look for the origin of the colouring under the transparent glaze (fig. 6.33). A thin pink layer appears between

FIGURE 6.26 Dep.B.74, face 1 – Stratigraphy of the lustred area
©C2RMF

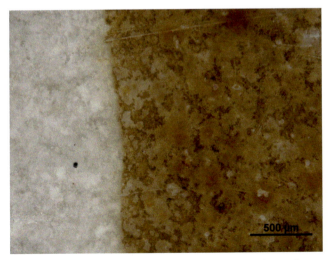

FIGURE 6.27 Dep.B.74, face 1 – Image of the lustre surface under diffuse light
©C2RMF

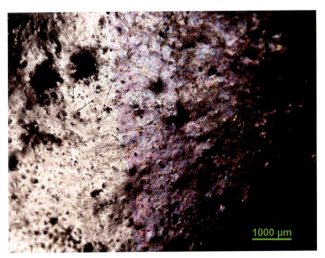

FIGURE 6.28 Dep.B.74, face 1 – same area, but the surface is tilted to detect the specular reflected light and the metallic shine
©C2RMF

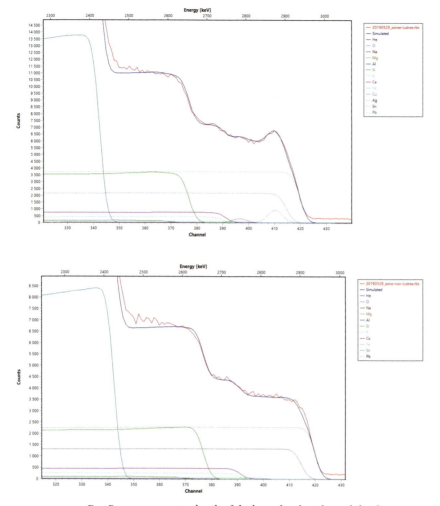

FIGURE 6.29   Dep B. 74 – RBS spectra details of the lustred and not lustred sherds
©C2RMF

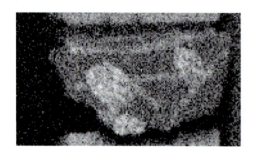

FIGURE 6.30   Dep.B.74, face 2 – Elemental map of element Cu obtained by XRF
©C2RMF

FIGURE 6.31   Dep.B.74, face 2
©C2RMF

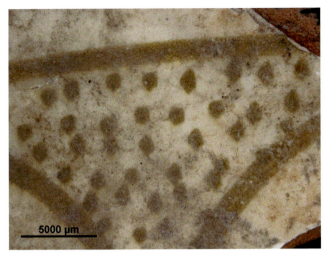

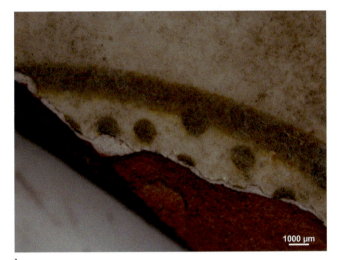

FIGURES 6.32A–C   BUXA 162/1, face 2; a) Overall observation of the décor; b) detail of the "lustre"; c) image of the stratigraphy
©C2RMF

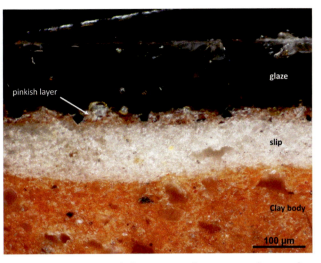

FIGURE 6.33   BUXA 162/1, face 1 – Optical microscope photographs of the cross-section through the "lustre decoration"
©C2RMF

FIGURE 6.34   BUXA 162/1, face 1 – SEM backscattered electron image – Detail of the pinkish layer with Cr-rich grains
©C2RMF

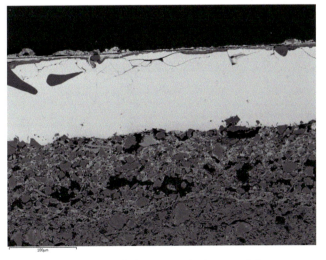

FIGURES 6.35   BUXA 162/1, face 1 – SEM backscattered electron image of the cross-section – stratigraphic section through the "lustre decoration"
©C2RMF

FIGURES 6.36 BUXA 162/1, face 1 – EDS Elemental map of elements Cr, Mg, Fe
©C2RMF

the white slip and the transparent lead glaze (fig. 6.33); this layer contains large dark grains (figs. 6.34 and 6.35) enriched in chromium, magnesium, iron and sometimes aluminum (fig. 6.36).

Only a few crystals could be analysed by MEB-EDX because most of them are extremely small. The compositions of the largest crystals are given in table 6.6. They are all rich in chromium, but their compositions vary between a pole rich in aluminum and iron (spectra 21 and 22) and a more magnesian weighted pole (spectra 12, 13 and 19). They are reminiscent of those chromites (spinels of formula $FeCr_2O_4$, sometimes containing Mn, Mg or Al) and magnesiochromites ($MgCr_2O_4$ containing highly variable proportions of Al and Mg), which constitute the magnesian pole of the series. In general, these types of spinels are found in the same deposits.

TABLE 6.6 Sherd BUXA 162/1 – Composition of Cr-rich grains in the pinkish layer (EDS data expressed in atomic percentages)

Spectrum	O	Mg	Al	Cr	Fe
Pt 12	52,72	15,21	0,92	27,61	3,54
Pt 13	54,83	14,83	5,53	21,96	2,85
Pt 19	54,65	13,47	10,20	17,85	3,83
Pt 21	59,28	3,79	10,22	14,34	12,37
Pt 22	57,56	0,96	8,53	18,22	14,73

4 Discussion

The results presented above show a diversity of techniques. Many questions arise but, in the absence of a larger corpus, and especially the lack of reference material for local productions, the discussions cannot be more detailed at the moment.

We chose to separate the imported productions (the lustre sherd and the sherd with cobalt blue and white decor) from the other four pieces – according to archaeologists at least three of them were produced in local workshops.

4.1 *Imported Productions*

The two imported sherds (Dep.B. 74 and Dep.B. 316) have stylistic characteristics that encourage archaeologists to propose a Mesopotamian origin for each of the two productions. During the time period that interests us here (9th–10th centuries), Abbasid ceramics were indeed widely distributed. They are characterised by distinct, homogeneous fabric, marked in particular by a high magnesian character. At the C2RMF we analysed nearly 50 works from the Louvre Museum to use as references (see table 6.7).

The correspondence between the compositions of the fabric from the Susa group and the two imported sherds is excellent, as it is with Mesopotamian sherds discovered in Nishapur (Bouquillon et al. 2013: 76). The same is true for the decoration techniques (lustres or blue decorations) and the pigment compositions.

The decorations are placed on a white lead-alkaline glaze opacified with tin oxide. This background glaze can have different compositions on the front and back of the same sherd, as we highlighted during the study of the Abbasid productions from Susa (unpublished data from Bouquillon, forthcoming). At that time, at least in Iran and Iraq, the first tin-opaque glazes appeared, notably in Susa, Samarra (Mason and Tite 1997). A recent article by Matin, Tite and Watson (2018) proposes that they appear in the 8th century in the Egyptian sites of Alexandria and Fustat as well as other sites in the Levant, Al Mina, among others.

The cobalt used to make the blue decoration on the two imported sherds is associated with iron, with a fairly high copper, nickel and manganese content. There is no arsenic (figs. 6.37 and 6.38).

TABLE 6.7   Comparison of the chemical analyses of the clay bodies of Susa ceramics with those of the two imported sherds – PIXE data expressed in oxide weight %

		Na₂O	MgO	Al₂O₃	SiO₂	P₂O₅	SO₃	Cl	K₂O	CaO	TiO₂	MnO	Fe₂O₃
SUSE	Moyenne	1,76	6,75	12,75	47,4	0,15	1,38	0,55	1,5	19,3	0,68	0,13	7,58
(43 pieces)	écart-type	1,39	0,85	0,84	2,9	0,12	2,21	1,22	0,57	2,28	0,19	0,02	0,62
DEP 74		1,79	7,03	12,87	48,84	0,18	0,13	0,21	1,05	18,82	0,73	0,14	7,93
DEP 316		1,29	7,45	13,06	48,59	0,13	0,12	0,06	1,17	19,23	0,74	0,16	7,93

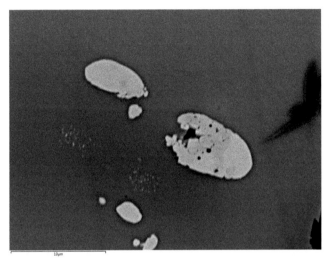

FIGURE 6.37   Dep.B.316, face 2 (sample 11) – SEM backscattered electron image – Details of cobalt rich pigments. The grains appearing in white contain high amounts of Fe, Co, Mn, Ni, Cu
©C2RMF

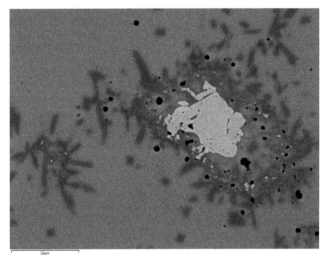

FIGURE 6.38   Dep.B.316, face 2 (sample 11) – SEM backscattered electron image-id – The grain appearing in white consists mainly of Fe (and O). The grey crystals forming the reaction crown are made up of Si, Mg, ca, Fe, Co and Mn
©C2RMF

This association is confirmed by analysis of the incompletely melted colour grains (figs. 6.37 and 6.38). Although the high degree of alteration of the glazes does not allow us to conclude with certainty about the origin of the cobalt pigment, it is interesting to note the similarities with the cobalt pigments used in Abbasid production.

This information corroborates the hypothesis that ceramics from the Mesopotamian world were imported to the oasis of Bukhara, probably even before the 10th century according to the typology and the dating of the stratigraphic levels in which the sherds were found.

4.2   Local Productions (?)

The four remaining sherds (two from Paykend and two from Bukhara) show similarities, both in the colour of the paste and in their chemical composition. They are much closer to the chemical characteristics of a set of ceramics of Paykend analysed by E. Porto after the 2012 excavation campaign (table 6.8). This would be consistent with local production, at least for BUXA 162/1, BUXA 162/9, Dep.B.76.

However, sherd Dep.B.317 stands out slightly from the others because of its magnesian character.

4.3   The Multiple Decor Techniques

The small number of sherds studied does not allow us to present a statistical map of the types of decorations, but it is quite interesting and very promising to show the diversity of technologies implemented by the potters in the oasis; they either imitated prestigious imported works or created their own style.

4.3.1   Imitations of Metallic Lustres

The sherd Dep.B.74 that we analysed corresponds to shiny ceramics found in the Abbasid sites of Susa and Samarra in Mesopotamia.

It is very interesting to see that the potters in the Bukhara Oasis tried to reproduce this type of decoration using an entirely innovative technique (sherd BUXA 162/9). They used a white slip, which imitates the opaque white glaze of Mesopotamian productions. Then, they painted the

TABLE 6.8 Chemical analyses of the clay bodies of Paykend ceramics studied by E. Porto in 2012 and of four sherds belonging to our corpus – EDS data expressed in oxide weight %

	Na$_2$O	MgO	Al$_2$O$_3$	SiO$_2$	P$_2$O$_5$	SO$_3$	Cl	K$_2$O	CaO	TiO$_2$	MnO	Fe$_2$O$_3$
558-8 Paykend	1,54	3,70	13,92	55,01	0,00	2,39	0,45	3,96	12,26	0,69	0,09	5,99
557-1 Paykend	0,94	3,13	15,32	57,90	0,04	3,26	0,08	3,49	9,07	0,64	0,08	6,04
560-2 Paykend	1,23	3,33	16,37	59,05	0,37	0,29	0,33	3,94	7,75	0,70	0,07	6,55
768-2 Paykend	1,15	3,48	15,31	55,36	0,05	0,14	0,24	2,98	13,82	0,69	0,10	6,68
Surf foot Paykend	1,31	3,67	16,52	55,49	0,05	0,22	0,11	3,09	11,95	0,70	0,10	6,78
Surf sherd Paykend	1,07	3,96	15,84	54,71	0,00	3,68	0,04	3,50	9,97	0,76	0,09	6,38
Pay2012-4622-1	1,68	3,72	16,23	52,15	0,19	0,12	0,20	3,42	14,84	0,67	0,11	6,67
Pay2012-4622-2	1,59	5,51	13,57	53,96	0,27	0,24	0,29	2,69	15,29	0,60	0,04	5,75
Pay2012-4622-4	1,58	4,12	16,29	53,15	0,20	0,27	0,22	3,45	12,85	0,69	0,12	7,06
Pay2012-18-1	1,09	4,15	15,79	53,49	0,19	0,06	0,00	3,79	13,41	0,79	0,16	7,09
Pay2012 18 2	0,91	3,33	15,08	51,75	0,35	0,14	0,00	3,65	16,27	0,76	0,18	7,49
PAY2012-18-3	1,25	3,23	16,65	56,05	0,39	0,00	0,02	3,79	10,39	0,73	0,14	7,27
PAY2012-7a	1,82	5,07	15,89	52,89	0,19	0,04	0,04	2,07	14,03	0,68	0,10	6,93
Dep.B.76	2,14	3,75	15,42	55,82	0,13	0,42	0,18	2,18	12,46	0,66	0,12	6,58
BUXA 162/1	1,10	3,77	16,28	55,73	0,24	0,08	0,10	3,44	11,37	0,70	0,11	6,73
BUXA 162/9	1,15	3,81	15,51	54,34	0,17	0,25	0,07	2,84	14,23	0,69	0,12	6,81
Dep.B.317	1,21	5,54	13,17	58,90	0,33	0,10	0,10	2,40	12,20	0,67	0,08	5,18

decorative motifs at the interface between the glaze and the slip with a material rich in chromium crystals. This thin layer appears as a very dark purplish red in the stratigraphic section observed under the light microscope (figs. 6.32 and 6.33). In order to obtain a very shiny surface, a high-lead glaze was applied (fig. 6.35). The lead content of over 60% explains the slightly yellow hue of the white areas and the more orange colour of the 'false lustre'. Brongniart (1877) confirms the importance of the lead, which intensifies the yellow colour due to the chrome and brings it closer to the actual colour of the lustre they were trying to imitate. We do not often highlight the use of chromium at that time; in Western productions, this element marks very late chronologies, in particular in the 19th century. However, in Central Asia, or in Nishapur or India (Bouquillon, Coquinot, and Doublet 2013: 115; Gulmini et al. 2013: 581–82), the use of chromium-based pigments in the 10th century CE is known. An example is the yellow (sample 70) and black glazes of certain shahrestan ceramics. These results, obtained in 2013 by Bouquillon et al. have since been confirmed by Parviz Holakooeia et al. (2019). Therefore, these Iranian regions had knowledge of the colouring potential of this chemical element that potters have at their disposal.

Chromium was also detected in productions from the 11th–12th centuries in southern Afghanistan. Ceramists used a similar technique: above a white slip, a thin layer of grains rich in chromium (chromite and magnesiochromite) is deposited under a transparent glaze containing more than 60% lead oxide; the resulting colour is described as light brown (Gulmini et al. 2013).

4.3.2 Obtaining a White Glaze

The potters in the oasis, whether in Paykend or Bukhara, implemented various technologies. We observe at least two different types of white décor, depending on the colour of the clay body.

Indeed, when the clay fabric is red (DEP 162/1 and 162/9), it was necessary to mask this annoying underlying colour: the potter therefore used a thick, dense slip containing numerous grains of finely ground quartz, lead and clay. The gloss was obtained using a high lead and perfectly transparent glaze on the surface. The high lead content explains the slightly yellowish hue, which appears more clearly when we compare the local sherds with the imported productions. In their article devoted to Ishkornaïa, Guionova and Bouquet (2017: 772) indicate that no form discovered in Paykend, Sogdiane or Chach shows a slip under the glaze, but examples of this technique are found in Tajikistan (Siméon 2009: 89–90). Perhaps this technique was used by a small group of craftsmen in Bukhara who specialised in the imitation of lustres?

TABLE 6.9 Chemical analyses of white tin-opacified glazes from Susa, Samarra and Fustat compared with Dep.B.76 – EDS data expressed in oxide weight %

		Na_2O	MgO	Al_2O_3	SiO_2	K_2O	CaO	MnO	Fe_2O_3	SnO_2	PbO
Suse	MAX	8,26	3,62	3,82	73,3	5,51	7,8	0,66	1,04	12,8	8,65
	MIN	0,63	1,20	1,88	61,5	2,28	2,34	0,06	0,32	3,2	1,43
Samarra	MAX	3,92	3,11	2,14	76,3	6,32	5,26	0,41	0,9	15,3	7,74
	MIN	2,19	1,81	1,07	61,5	3,15	3,51	0,13	0,55	2,03	1,40
Fustat	MAX	4,17	3,14	2,03	75,2	6,4	6,66	0,67	0,99	9,22	9,43
	MIN	0,99	2,32	1,38	61,5	3,61	3,3	0,13	0,56	2,83	1,67
Dep.B.76		5,18	2,49	2,86	57,72	4,17	5,81	0,11	0,91	8,71	11,38

For the lighter fabrics (sherd Dep.B. 76), which were discovered at Paykend and which according to R. Rante also correspond to the local productions, the lead-alkaline glaze, opacified by tin oxide microcrystals, is placed directly on the paste. Guionova and Bouquet (2017) show that these clouded lead-alkaline glazes are quite frequent at the Paykend and Bukhara sites, thus confirming local production.

If we compare this white glaze with those of Mesopotamian lustre ceramics discovered in the regions of Susa, Samarra and Fustat (table 6.9), we can see strong similarities in the compositions. The proportions of the various constituents (especially silica and iron) of the DepB.76 glaze are slightly different, but we had already observed a high degree of variability in Abbasid glazes in the 9th and 10th centuries. It seems that there were no truly standardised recipes at that time. It should also be noted that the state of alteration is often important, which contributes to the impression of scattered values. If this ceramics were indeed produced locally, it is clear that the artisans of the Bukhara oasis had perfectly assimilated the technique of tin opacification.

In the particular case of sherd Dep.B.317, its white glaze is also lead-alkaline, placed directly on the paste, but the "recipes" are different: the sodium contents decrease and the lead character is much more marked. We do not have the same initial mixes. Being neither from a different chronology, nor imports, since this type of ceramic has indeed been found in the kilns in the potters' district in Paykend (Rante and Mirzaakhmedov 2019: 216–30), the hypothesis of an other local production should be favoured.

4.3.3 Turquoise Glaze

It is coloured with copper oxide, and the turquoise colour is obtained thanks to the presence of alkalis in the composition of the glaze. This is not a transparent coloured decoration placed on a layer of white glaze, as suggested by Guionova and Bouquet (2017), but an opaque glaze coloured in the mass. This observation is interesting, but it would be necessary to study other green/turquoise and white glazed ceramics discovered at Paykend (see fig. 3 of the article by Guionova and Bouquet) to assess the reproducibility of this technique and the importance of this know-how in the ceramic production of the oasis.

5 Conclusion

The analysed fragments offer a glimpse into the production of glazed ceramics in the Bukhara Oasis in the 9th and 10th centuries. It will be noted, for example, that no alkaline glazes typical of the region, the so-called Ishkornaïa glazes that are emblematic of the oasis, could be studied in the corpus.

However, we have already confirmed the importation of high quality Abbasid ceramics. We have been able to demonstrate the diversity of the craftsmen's skills, whether in creating complex polychrome decorations or in imitating lustre ceramics or in obtaining white glossy glazes. It is interesting to note that these typologies of ceramics which tried to imitate either white productions with cobalt blue décor or lustres did not last long.

This work, therefore, shows the full potential of a more developed archaeometric study of glazed ceramics that will have to be conducted in the future.

CHAPTER 7

Decorated Glazed Ceramics from Bukhara (15th–16th Centuries)

Djamal Mirzaakhmedov

Translated from Russian by Rocco Rante

The period between end of the 14th century and the 15th century is characterised by the creation of a giant Timurid superpower within Central Asia, and it united the majority of the developed countries in the Old East. The export of huge wealth and elite artisans to Samarkand, the capital of the empire, as well as to the largest cities in Maverannahr, contributed to an unprecedented rise in the economy, culture and art of the region. This period's heritage not only includes artistic and cultural monuments that are grand in character but also includes significant scientific achievements, including the emergence of the astronomical school of Ulugbek, which received recognition in the literary works of A. Navoi.

Despite the fact that a large number of written sources have come down to us from this period of history, the material culture of this time, which is the main indicator of the daily life and culture of the people, remains largely unexplored. First of all, it is necessary to emphasise that the economic growth and flourishing of culture in this era was largely due to the campaigns of Amir Timur, who exported tens of thousands of elite artisan elites along with material goods to Maverannahr. This served as the basis not only for significant construction and production activities but also for the flourishing of the mass production of an iconic handicraft: ceramics.

The Sheibanid Dynasty that replaced the Timurids, and Abdullakhan II in particular, continued active construction activities. After a long break, Bukhara was once again chosen as the capital and was completely rebuilt at the end of the 16th century – and today it retains this appearance. Material culture in this era continued the traditions of the previous century, and for ceramic production this meant that along with cobalt painting, polychrome compositions with black and blue colours were widely used.

Therefore, the complex of finds from the metropolis of Bukhara, which was the second most important urban centre of the Timurids, often compared to Samarkand, indicates the rise of culture and crafts in the region. Bukhara was also home to various Sufi brotherhoods that turned the city into the eastern Mecca of the Islamic world.

The bulk of the material presented here was obtained during archaeological research at shahrestan 1 in Bukhara in the 1970s and was connected with work on an excavation site 50 × 50 m north of the Miri Arab madrasah.

I want to begin by looking at the ceramics obtained from the garbage pit, which is an archaeological closed context datable to the 15th–16th centuries, because this gives us an idea of the common household tableware of townspeople and items that had special purposes. This find consists of two bowls (braid), a cup (bowl), a dish (*tabok*) and an aroma bowl.

The bowls (braid) have annular bottoms that are hemispherical at the bases and slightly wide towards the tops of the bowls' walls (figs. 7.1 and 7.2). White slip and transparent glaze cover their entire inner, and for the most part also the outer, surfaces. There is a rich polychrome ornamentation consisting of black, light blue and blue colours with swirling petal rosettes in the centre, and repeating plant, flower and berry compositions adorn the inner surface of the bowls. Outside, only standard common schematic motifs were applied in the form of concentric circles and plant shoots stylised in the form of a question mark (*Kultura i iskusstvo drevnego Uzbekistana* 1991: 2: fig. 757).

A single copy of a bowl was found, and it is made of soft, porous white *kashin* and is very light and decorated with cobalt painting (Culture and Art of Ancient Uzbekistan 1991: 2: fig. 761). It has an annular base and hemispherical walls with a pointed rim (fig. 7.3) and is covered with a transparent, colourless glaze up to the base of the pallet on the outer surface. The ornamental composition along the inner plane of the cup consists of a hexagonal rosette in the centre that is surrounded by eight oblique strokes and nets and wavy motifs at the edges. The outer plane contains a pattern filled with a continuous wriggling motif. The rosette in the centre resembles a six-star ornament to some extent, and the wavy motifs on the bottom of a dish date from the end of the second decade of the 15th century (Syharev 1948: fig. 2).

The single copy of the dish (*tabok*) in the find has a small circular base that is hemispherical at the base of the wall and has a wide rim bent outward (Culture and

FIGURE 7.1 Bowl with white slip and transparent glaze, Bukhara
© MIRZAAKHMEDOV 2020

FIGURE 7.2 Bowl with white slip and transparent glaze, Bukhara
© MIRZAAKHMEDOV 2020

Art of Ancient Uzbekistan 1991: 2: fig. 755). Based on the shape, the ornamental composition, which is overtop a white engobe and covered under a transparent glaze, is divided into three ribbon belts (fig. 7.4). In the centre of the dish there is a schematic arrangement of a flower with a repeating leaf shape and a continuous wriggling shoot motif along a steep curved part and a side bent outward. The outer surface of the dish, which was not intended for viewing, is decorated with two rows of meanders and repeating spiral and dash motifs are schematically painted with wide strokes. In general, the dish closely parallels Iranian samples (Watson 2004: Cat. Q. 23) and is an imitation of the more expensive, exquisite imported Chinese porcelain.

The incense-burner is made in the shape of a cup, on a profiled graceful stem-foot (fig. 7.5). Along the rim, its walls slightly dip 0.5 cm inward and completely overlap the reservoir of the vessel. It has a pea-sized hole at the edge. Under the transparent glaze, there is a stylised inscription in blooming kufi handwriting on the body. The rest of it is also covered with rich vegetative and geometric ornamentation in cobalt.

The functional purpose of similarly designed vessels from late antiquity and the Early Middle Ages that resemble this sample has not been concretely ascertained by the authors. Although it has been suggested that they were used by cults as "lamps – incense burners" (Smagulov 2015: 209). In our opinion, not all the forms of vessels presented by the author are "incense burners", some of them, the closest in time to us, have a "jug-shaped" form (Smagulov 2015: fig. 1: 5) and could have a different purpose. First of all, we note that no traces of combustion were detected when the vessel was opened, and no traces of combustion were noted on a vessel similar to ours (but without a leg) from Afrasiab that was made during the 10th–12th centuries.

It is well known that in the High and Late Middle Ages, some old traditions were disrupted or acquired new forms over the centuries due to the advent of Islam and a new way of life. Therefore, based on its small size, hollow cylindrical body and the single small hole from which liquid pours out poorly, one can assume it had one of two possible uses. First, as a container for vinegar, which in small doses could be added to food to improve its taste and arouse the appetite. Second, as an aromatic (i.e., a

FIGURE 7.3 Bowl with white slip and transparent glaze, Bukhara
© MIRZAAKHMEDOV 2020

FIGURE 7.4 Dish with white slip and transparent glaze, Bukhara
© MIRZAAKHMEDOV 2020

cosmetic vessel for fragrant rose water), which was used in everyday life by both women and men, and during ceremonial receptions and festivals, it would be used to spray rose water on the premises and incoming guests. Taking into account that prolonged use of acetic acid would gradually destroy the vessel and that its ceremonial use had practically lost its meaning at that time, the second use is the more likely one.

Previously, in the High Middle Ages, glass ceremonial aromas were common. They had a rounded body and a long tubular neck tapering toward the top with a graceful raised leg, similar to our sample, and we find direct parallels in neighbouring regions (Mirzaakhmedov, Adylov, and Matbabaev 2008: fig. 9: 6) and the countries of the Middle East (À l'ombre d'Avicenne 1996: ills. 118–23; Islamische kunst 1984: Glas, ill. 192) in miniature paintings and ethnographic materials (Maslenitsyna 1975: fig. 52). The rare examples found in 10th- to early 13th-century complexes are much closer to the ones from Bukhara. These examples are low, glazed ceramic vessels with the same cylindrical shape and the characteristic hole on the top, but without leg stands.

Thus, on the basis of the material we are looking at, the earlier examples that have an identical or similarly shaped reservoir can be related to earlier prototypes of the aroma dish that come from the ceramic complex in Bukhara.

Regarding other finds from the complex, let us first take a further look at the two bowls noted above. This epoch is characterised by the predominance of bowl shapes rather than dishes in tableware. This trend is observed to an even greater extent in the previous period (8th–14th centuries), but to my opinion it was only in the 15th century that the standards were set for the relationship between these two forms of tableware, depending on the number of family members as well as the frequency of the use of liquid versus solid forms of food. In comparison with samples from

FIGURE 7.5 Incense-burner with white slip and transparent glaze, Bukhara
© MIRZAAKHMEDOV 2020

Samarkand or ones made from Chinese porcelain from the same time period, the bowls' shapes are noteworthy due to the complete absence of or a weakly pronounced bending of the rims. In our opinion, the bending of the bowls' rims is an indicator of a traditionally established form of individual tableware that exists to this day and makes them easy to use for liquid foods. The implementation of such tendencies in cup forms already dates back to the 13th–14th centuries, when pronounced hemispherical walls and ring bottoms finally took shape. The ring bottoms were convenient, not only when placing bowls on *dastarkhan* but also when carrying hot soups that could burn one's hands.

Thus, in these bowls from the complex, the absence of a bend or the weakly pronounced bend of the rims indicates the tendency for ceramic forms in Bukhara to lag behind the development of similar products from the capital city of Samarkand (Pugachenkova 1948: ill. 1) as well as to lag behind those from other urban centres, like Tashkent (Mirzaakhmedov 1992: fig. 9–4), Shakhrukhiya (Mirzaakhmedov and Alimov 2006: figs. 9–10), Eski Turkestan (Smagulov 1992: figs. 1 and 3) and Nisa (Pugachenkova 1949: figs. 12 and 13).

The composition layout of the main ornamental load on the bowls tended to lag behind developments in the capital and other regional centres, and for this reason, a similar load on the bowls fell on their inner plane until the 15th century. External ornamentation was either completely absent or was carried out by the application of the simplest stylised, symbolic and repetitive motifs. Apparently this fashion was determined not only by the aesthetic norms of the High Middle Ages but also by the tableware requirements of the population, since tableware was one of the standard means of decorating ceremonial premises. That is, products richly decorated with polychrome paintings or epigraphic motifs containing inscriptions on the inner surface could be hung on walls or could decorate the shelves in mikhmankhan.

In 15th-century Samarkand, Tashkent and Turkestan bowls were are already beginning to undergo a gradual transition where the main ornamental composition was placed on the space from the inner to the outer plane of the dishes, leaving the inner surface white and therefore resembling as close as possible its hygienic, functional purpose (Mirzaakhmedov 1992: figs. 1–4; Smagulov 1992: figs. 3–4), that is, like on modern traditional dishes.

Turning to the innovative features of the dish obtained from the complex, it is necessary to note not only its new shape, with a wide oblique side bent outward, but also the monochrome ornamental decoration painted with cobalt. In the first case, as already noted above concerning the use of bowls for liquids, the dishes' shapes, with sides bent wide outward, were adapted for solid food. Secondly, the size of the dishes implies they were used in collective meals – not individual ones – for example, with family, friends and during collective festive and memorial events. Thirdly, the widespread use of monochrome tableware with cobalt painting in this era is a clear indicator that ceramic art conformed with the fashions of the era, which came from widely disseminated samples of Chinese porcelain.

But here, too, we continue to observe a lag in the development of the form as illustrated by the dish from the complex. The traditional production of dishes with a small bottom can be compared with similar products from Samarkand (Syharev 1948: fig. 3) or the porcelain from the Celestial Empire, where their new forms with bent outward sides are based on massive wide bases (Watson 2004: Cat. 1). The forms with bent outward sides correspond in their final stage to the formation of the dishes used today in everyday life – dishes of the lyagan type, exclusively adapted for the collective serving of thick forms of food.

The present examples with outwardly bent sides and small bottoms continued to be widely used in neighbouring regions (Smagulov 1992: fig. 5) and states (Golombek, Masson, and Bailey 1994: ch. 5, fig. 5.2), both in this era and subsequent eras (Mirzaakhmedov 1990: figs. 11–14). Therefore, it is necessary to connect them with the new dish-shaped forms (Mirzaakhmedov 1981: figs. 3–5).

And finally, another form we have a single sample of is a *kashin* cup made of a white porous silicate mass. The subtle execution of the ornamentation with cobalt and the lightness and the porosity of the mass testifies not only to its ceremonial use but also to the local nature of its manufacture. The authors attributed the bowl to Samarkand (Golombek, Masson, and Bailey 1994: plate 15). The exquisitely painted geometric motifs on the inside and twisting *islimi* on the outside are also found in Chinese porcelain and traditional locally glazed wares. The shape of the annular base and the hemispherical walls resemble modern samples of the bowl, with the exception of the rim that is bent outward. Thus, here too, we observe a lag in the development of the form, and as in the case of the bowls, there is no shift in the main load of the ornamental composition on the outer dishes.

To summarise the description of the materials from the complex: it should first be noted that in the era under study here, polychrome and monochrome ornamental compositions were mass-made with black, dark brown, blue and blue (cobalt) paints on the inner surface of the dishes, and the simplified repeating stylised motifs on the external surfaces are quite different from the examples of the so-called Timurid ceramic style that was characteristic during the heyday of the empire and was observed until the end of Ulugbek's rule. The machine bowl and the goblet-shaped ceramic aroma bowl can be classified as ceremonial dishes. Therefore, in general, the complex can be chronologically placed between the second half of the 15th century and the early 16th century and finds parallels in dishes from other regions of Central Asia.

Several other bowls, as well as a fragment from the bottom of a dish obtained from the same excavation, to the north of the Miri Arab madrasah, and as they are also from the period between the 15th and 16th centuries, resemble the materials from the complex that are described above. The overwhelming majority of them are ceramic bowls with the same form (figs. 7.6–14). In the first two (figs. 7.6–7), the monochrome ornamentation is completely in cobalt and includes plant and geometric motifs of varying complexity.

In the next seven (figs. 7.8–14), the ornamentation is polychrome and consists mainly of plant compositions made in dark brown, black, blue and blue paints on a white engobe. Its main load, as on the bowls from the complex, falls on the inner plane of the dishes and mainly contains petal rosettes in the centre, plant compositions of varying complexity along the walls and a narrow ribbon border with stylised repeating motifs along the edge of the rim. On the reverse side of these bowls, schematic, repeating motifs of strokes, circles, spirals or shoots inscribed in one or two ribbon stripes occupy most of the outer plane of the tableware.

Only on two bowls does the ornamentation stand out somewhat from the rest. The first one (fig. 7.13) has a centric character with motifs of twigs and pseudo-epigraphy along the walls, and the ornamentation of the second (fig. 7.14) imitates Chinese models and consists of a central motif of a life tree or symbolic gate and schematic eights wriggling in the abstract chaos, apparently symbolising abra motifs or the Chinese philosophical concept of balance – yin and yang.

The fragment of a small bottom of a dish with a petal rosette in the centre, surrounded by solid plant motifs painted with cobalt, imitating Chinese examples, can be attributed to the same group of bowls (fig. 7.15).

Thus, as already noted, the materials described above can also be dated within the time period between the second half of the 15th century and the 16th century. In general, the most characteristic examples of polychrome products have dark brown or black plant compositions in combination with blue motifs symbolising fruits, berries, flowers and petals. Both polychrome and monochromatic cobalt paintings completely rework Chinese symbols found on porcelain, which were very popular in the 15th century, using their own local, deeply traditional ornamental motifs. At the same time, the ceramists highlight their products as imitations of the Chinese style, for which they used monochrome cobalt painting, and for expensive ceremonial items they also used white *kashin*.

FIGURE 7.6 Bowl with white slip and transparent glaze, geometrical decorations, Bukhara
© MIRZAAKHMEDOV 2020

FIGURE 7.7 Bowl with white slip and transparent glaze, Bukhara
© MIRZAAKHMEDOV 2020

FIGURE 7.8 Bowl with white slip and transparent glaze, polychrome ornamentation, Bukhara
© MIRZAAKHMEDOV 2020

FIGURE 7.9 Bowl with white slip and transparent glaze, polychrome ornamentation, Bukhara
© MIRZAAKHMEDOV 2020

FIGURE 7.10 Bowl with white slip and transparent glaze, polychrome ornamentation, Bukhara
© MIRZAAKHMEDOV 2020

FIGURE 7.11 Bowl with white slip and transparent glaze, polychrome ornamentation, Bukhara
© MIRZAAKHMEDOV 2020

FIGURE 7.12 Bowl with white slip and transparent glaze, polychrome ornamentation, Bukhara
© MIRZAAKHMEDOV 2020

FIGURE 7.13 Bowl with white slip and transparent glaze, polychrome ornamentation, Bukhara
© MIRZAAKHMEDOV 2020

Decorated Glazed Ceramics from Bukhara

FIGURE 7.14 Bowl with white slip and transparent glaze, polychrome ornamentation, Bukhara
© MIRZAAKHMEDOV 2020

FIGURE 7.15 Bowl fragment with white slip and transparent glaze, Chinese imitation of decorative motifs, Bukhara
© MIRZAAKHMEDOV 2020

Although the following materials are fragments, based on the nature of the ornamental compositions, they can be attributed to a somewhat earlier stage of production (figs. 7.16–18). They were obtained from an excavation site 50 × 50 m north of the Mir Arab madrasah and from other points in the old shahrestan of Bukhara during various new construction work.

They are fragments of the bottoms of bowls and dishes, made from ceramic and using *kashin* sherds. The ornamentation is mostly monochrome, painted with cobalt in thick and light tones and less often with black paint, white engobes and transparent glazes.

The bottom compositions are outlined in circular lines and consist of very finely executed graceful, rising plant compositions. For the period under study, this ceramic style is usually called Timurid.

The compositions found on these fragments contain freely wriggling bushes, flowers, holly grasses and petal rosettes (figs. 7.16–18). On one of them (fig. 7.16), the wall ornamentation motif containing alternately rising blue and dark brown vertical lines, which are commonly found on bowls from the period under study, was partially preserved (Mirzaakhmedov and Alimov 2006: fig. 4). On others, the wall decoration has a white background (fig. 7.16: 2, 3; fig. 7.17: 1). At the same time, the last two fragments are made on a white soft *kashin* base with a slightly tinted, bluish transparent glaze (fig. 7.17).

The shapes of the plates are presented on a small annular bottom, and in the upper part there is a small side that gradually bends outward (fig. 7.18). The main part of the wide inner surface contains a composition of a realistic image of a branched tree surrounded by shrubs of holly grasses, berries and flowers. Along the abrupt bend of the walls and the side, repeating, schematically stylised plant elements are applied in the form of borders. On the outer surface, only the upper part of the walls is covered with glaze, with no decoration.

Despite the fragmentation of the preserved group, their exceptionally high decorative character should be noted, and they were produced as imitations of Chinese porcelain examples.

Some of the examples of dishes presented here are made of *kashin* and, for the most part, painted with cobalt paint, and as such are imitations of the more expensive Chinese porcelain. In the minds of contemporaries, porcelain represented higher quality standard tableware, and it indicates that local ceramics were entering into a wider international sphere.

FIGURE 7.16 Bowl fragment with white slip and transparent glaze, Bukhara
© MIRZAAKHMEDOV 2020

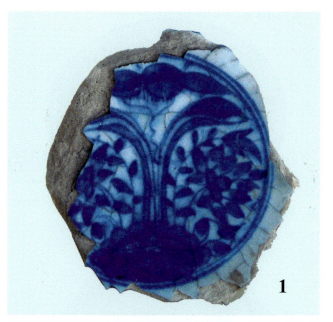

FIGURE 7.17 Bowl fragment with white slip and transparent glaze, Bukhara
© MIRZAAKHMEDOV 2020

FIGURE 7.18
Bowl fragment with white slip and transparent glaze, Bukhara
© MIRZAAKHMEDOV 2020

FIGURE 7.19 Bowl fragment with white slip and transparent glaze, Chinese imitation of decorative motifs, Bukhara
© MIRZAAKHMEDOV 2020

FIGURE 7.20 Bowl fragment with white slip and transparent glaze, figurative motifs, Bukhara
© MIRZAAKHMEDOV 2020

The production of these dishes can be attributed to the heyday of the Timurid state and dated between the first half and the middle of the 15th century.

Moving on to the description of the next group of items, it should be noted that all of them, with the exception of one ceramic piece (fig. 7.22), are fragments of the bottoms of bowls and dishes made on *kashin* mass.

Kashin is white and has varying degrees of density, but in most cases it is porous and soft. The high cost of the composition of the bases indicates the ceremonial character of their design, which consists of anthropomorphic, ornithomorphic and zoomorphic images.

Among the anthropomorphic subjects, the most interesting is the fragment depicting the figure of a rider galloping on a horse (fig. 7.19). The partially preserved face of the rider is rendered very schematically. On the rider's head there is something resembling a turban, and in his right hand there is a straight, narrow object like a whip. Judging from the slender legs of the horse, depicted mid-gallop, it can be assumed that this is a thoroughbred horse, possibly of Arab blood. The importance of the rider and the expensive breed of horse are also indicated by specially marked sultans on the chest and croup of the latter.

The entire scene is rendered on a partially preserved background based on traditional Chinese park scenes depicting a tussock of land with a bush of holly grasses and a tree branch, but demonstrating a typical local theme.

On the second fragment, there is a depiction of a character who, below the chest, has his hands slightly raised and spread apart, resembling a dancing man (fig. 7.20). His face is rendered very vaguely, and on his head there is a peaked cap that is shifted to the side. Perhaps this represents a scene from popular holiday festivities that would have performances by dancers and folk actors.

On the third fragment (fig. 7.21), there is an image of a stately man with one hand lowered and the other bent at the elbow and raised. He is wearing an object in the form of a rough, massive glove. The face is not traced and a turban-shaped headdress is on his head. Despite the general sketchiness, it can be assumed that the drawing conveys a noble character on a falconry, and the massive glove in his hand is for a bird.

In general, these anthropomorphic images are characterised by schematic, foggy or a complete absence of facial outlines. The glazes have a slightly bluish tint and are covered with a *tsek*. The nature of the images are varied,

FIGURE 7.21 Bowl fragment with white slip and transparent glaze, figurative motifs, Bukhara
© MIRZAAKHMEDOV 2020

typical for the local environment, but the surrounding landscape motifs have a certain Far Eastern flavour.

The next few fragments show ornithomorphic images (figs. 7.22–23). On the first base, a partial reproduction of a running bird with a tail who is surrounded by lush vegetation has been preserved (fig. 7.22: 1). The second, even smaller fragment from the thick-walled wide base of a dish shows a large bird's head (fig. 7.22: 2). Despite the insignificance of the surviving sample, one can confidently note the width of its base, which testifies to the appearance of wide dishes such as lyagans in Bukhara. On the third fragment, the upper part of an image of a bird of prey, masterfully rendered by a mature artist, has been preserved (fig. 7.23). It is undoubtedly located in its nest, since the nearby image of a chick's head has also been preserved on this fragment.

On the first two samples the monochrome cobalt painting is rendered in a more saturated colour, but on the last one it is a light blue colour, outlined with black paint to prevent blurring and enhance tonality. In the latter case,

FIGURE 7.22 Bowl fragment with white slip and transparent glaze, zoomorphic motifs, Bukhara
© MIRZAAKHMEDOV 2020

the glazes are slightly tinted with a bluish tone to give depth. On the last fragment with a zoomorphic plot, in a typical Chinese manner, there is an image of a monkey on the branches of a tree and surrounded by lush vegetation (fig. 7.24). This is a densely sintered, whitish, hard sherd, slightly tinted to add depth to the pattern with a bluish glaze that covered the outer surface up to the pallet, that has the remnants of a Chinese brand, partially preserved here, on the pallet, which may indicate that the dish was made from a lesser quality porcelain at one of the private Chinese factories.

Thus, in conclusion, it should be noted that glazed ceramic dishes from Bukhara, despite some lag in the

FIGURE 7.23 Bowl fragment with white slip and transparent glaze, zoomorphic motifs, Bukhara
© MIRZAAKHMEDOV 2020

development of forms, as well as in the nature of the arrangement of artistic compositions on the inner and outer planes of mass dishes, testify to the active accumulation and syncretisation of a highly artistic trend in Far Eastern ceramics process by local craftsmen.

Park and landscape compositions, as well as anthropomorphic and ornithomorphic motifs, extremely realistically rendered on ceremonial examples, are undoubtedly an indicator of the general rise of culture, art and crafts in all regions of Central Asia. The impeccable adaption and

FIGURE 7.24 Bowl fragment with white slip and transparent glaze, zoomorphic motifs in a Chinese manner, Bukhara
© MIRZAAKHMEDOV 2020

development of Far Eastern porcelain and Middle Eastern earthenware trends by ceramists and nakkosh artists indicate broad international economic and cultural contact, tolerance and the absence of conservative religious beliefs among the majority of the region's population.

CHAPTER 8

Glassmaking in the Urban Centres of Uzbekistan in the 9th–15th Centuries

Djamal Mirzaakhmedov

Translated from Russian by Rocco Rante

When identifying the medieval productions of Uzbekistan, it is necessary to rely on archaeological data and material from written sources, both of which clearly show that between the 9th and early 13th centuries a variety of industries developed within the region and became famous far beyond its borders. It is no coincidence that al-Iṣṭakhrī argued that the inhabitants of Maverannahr had everything in abundance and did not need any handicrafts imported from other countries, since they made everything they needed in abundance (Bartold 1963: 295).

Glassmaking occupied a significant place within the handicraft industries of medieval Central Asia. Its production was considered quite complex and was associated with the urban environment (Beleniskij, Bentovich, and Bolshakov 1973: 285). During the pre-Islamic period the manufacturing technology for glasswork was still imperfect, and the secrets of craftsmanship were passed down from generation to generation. The first known mention of its production is in the Chinese chronicle *Beishu*, where it is reported that "in 424, highly qualified glassmakers who arrived from the Yuezhi made multi-coloured glasses by melting rocks, which in their qualities were superior to products brought from Western countries" (Bichurin 1950: 321–22). In the subsequent period, the chronicle *Tangshu* reports that between 713 and 755 red- and emerald-coloured glass products, which were highly valued in the Celestial Empire, were regularly sent to China from Central Asia (Bichurin 1950: 321–22).

It is clear in these fragmentary pieces of data from the Chinese chronicles that Central Asia and the southern regions of Uzbekistan in particular not only might have been well-known centres of glassmaking but also the first to introduce its production to the Chinese empire.

Nevertheless, according to archaeological material, glass items, both in antiquity and in the Early Middle Ages, continued to be quite rare and expensive luxury items, which included small forms of perfumery.

The earliest glass finds from Uzbekistan's archaeological contexts come from Bronze Age burial monuments in Sogdiana and Khorezm. These are glass beads from the Zamanbaba burial ground, dating from the end of the 3rd to the first half of the 2nd centuries BCE, in the Bukhara Oasis (Kuzmina 1958: 30–31), as well as beads made out of a light blue paste from the Kokcha 3 burial ground in Khorezm, dating from the 13th to the 11th centuries BCE (Itina 1961: 86–89).

Of course, these finds were imported, but they are the first indisputable evidence of the region's contact with distant places. Much later, along with the continuing demand for glass jewellery, glassware also spread across the region.

So, according to the results of excavations in Afrasiab in 1947, A.I. Terenozhkin uncovered an elongated, teardrop-shaped vessel (bottle?) with an unpreserved rim in the in the Afrasiab-IV layers, which he dated between the 2nd century BCE and the 1st century CE (Terenozhkin 1950: 157, fig. 70.7, fig. 69.5). Based on the results of subsequent studies and using the ceramic material found with it, G.V. Shishkina concluded that it should be dated to the beginning of our era (Shishkina 1986: 18). A fragment of a spherical blue bottle was obtained from a pit in the Old Termez citadel in the Greco-Bactrian period layers (Abdullaev 1998: 129).

Of much greater interest are the glass finds obtained during the excavations of temple buildings 1 and 2 in the Toprak kala settlement – the ancient residence of the rulers of Khorezm. This contains, first of all, a huge amount of small green, blue, red and yellow glass beads (663 pieces), glass beads of various shapes (343 pieces) and numerous pieces of glassware. The latter contains a large group of fragments from the following: vessels with polished and engraved ornaments in transparent colourless or greenish and yellowish shades; thick- and thin-walled cups; glasses; bowls; rims; and the bodies of jugs. It also includes pieces of thin glass walls from goblets and fragments of mosaic glass, with ornamentation from applied threads and painting and covered with strong iridescence or patina, that date back to the period of late antiquity or the period of the great migration of peoples coming from the north-east from the 3rd to the beginning of the 6th centuries (Rante and Mirzaakhmedov 2019).

According to the results of studies conducted on a wide range of monuments from ancient Khorezm – Dzhanbas kala, Ayaz kala, Duman kala, Bazar kala, Berkut kala,

© DJAMAL MIRZAAKHMEDOV, 2024 | DOI:10.1163/9789004693999_010

Naringjan and Kavat kala – the same large number of finds were noted, including mainly glass beads of various sizes, shapes and colours from antiquity and the Early Middle Ages. They have a wide range of parallels with finds from sites in the Northern Black Sea region, the Caucasus, Eastern Europe and Siberia, and sometimes in Central Asia as well, in most cases indicating these finds were imports.

However, along with these beads, there were types that differed from the imported ones in a number of ways. The lack of parallels for some of them, at least according to Ptashnikova, indicates not only the presence of local Khorezm glass production but also trade in glass products (Ptashnikova 1952: 110–18). Based on the originality of the female and male jewellery found in Toprak Kala and the traces of the consistent industrial production of some types of beads, as well as fragments of dishes without any parallels, Trudnovskaya comes to the same conclusion (Trudnovskaya 1952: 130–31).

Thus, scholars researching antiquity note the emergence of a limited number of glass vessels. Basically, glass continued to be used to make jewellery, mainly beads. Glass acted as a substitute for precious stones and semi-precious stones, as well as for inlaid art pieces, and glass beads were widely used in both nomadic and sedentary agricultural environments (Abdurazakov, Bezborodov, and Zadneprovsky 1963: 82–83).

Further, some authors suggest the most probable origin of glass production in Central Asia was in the last centuries BCE, justifying this by the large number of finds and their widespread distribution, as well as the expansion of the range of glass products (Abdurazakov, Bezborodov, and Zadneprovsky 1963: 88).

In the next stage, the early medieval period between the 7th and early 8th centuries, we observe the emergence of new types of glass products in Tokharistan (Balalyk tepa) and Sogd (Afrasiab): small medallions with female deities reflecting the cult of the mother goddess and fertility (Al'baum 1960: fig. 53; Terenozhkin 1950: fig. 72.1). A.I. Terenozhkin further notes that up until the Muslim period, there are few glass finds.

At the site, a massive surge in its production can be traced back to the second half of the 8th century, when glassware became almost as common as pottery for Samarkand residents. The most common forms at that time were vessels blown into shapes with a relief pattern (Terenozhkin 1950: 167).

G.V. Shishkina, in her overview of glass from Afrasiab, agrees with this assessment: "The almost complete absence of glass items in Afrasiab among the finds in layers up to the middle of the 8th century can be explained, presumably, by the small volume of production associated with it's high cost and [the] low prevalence of glass in everyday life. Dated glass items in Afrasiab are known only from the end of the 8th century" (Shishkina 1986: 18). In a recent publication on glass from the Early Middle Ages, V.I. Raspopova also supports A.I. Terenozhkin's view and adds: "It seems to me that until this time it is impossible to talk about developed, independent Sogdian glassmaking. The great majority of glass products were imported. Glass vessels from Penjikent reflect Sogd's trade relations with the countries of the Near and Middle East" (Raspopova 2010: 4). And then Raspopova succinctly emphasises that "my acquaintance with glass vessels, not by publications but concretely, confirmed my opinion that glass vessels in Sogd in the 5th to the first third of the 8th century were not of local production, but imported" (Raspopova 2010: 6). Finally, summarising the above points, I.B. Bentovich notes that in the "6th–7th centuries in the cities of Central Asia, glass production existed, but not yet at a high level. The range of products is not very rich. Local glassmaking workshops mainly produced perfumes and, in very limited quantities, household dishes" (Beleniskij, Bentovich, and Bolshakov 1973: 69).

Thus, despite the brief analysis of the glass from antiquity and the Early Middle Ages, a unified picture of their use as luxury items emerges, since they mainly come from palace contexts and rich burials. They had a limited distribution, consisting mainly of jewellery and a small number of perfumery and dishware forms. Some generalising studies (Davidovich 1953 ; Mirzaakhmedov 2008) conclude that glass was only widespread starting from the end of the 8th to the beginning of the 9th centuries.

However, over the past decades, research on glass in the largest medieval urban centres of Uzbekistan has amended the above conclusions and adjusted theories about the nature and purpose of certain types of products. According to researchers, the discovery of the remains of a unique "pharmacy" in Paykend in 1983 laid the foundation for an in-depth study of one significant type of glassmaking in the Late Middle Ages (Mukhamedjanov and Semenov 1984: 35–39).

This type was found in the central part of the monument at the crossroads of the main streets connecting the two shahrestans of the city. Here, in the first of the three rooms of the "pharmacy" (fig. 8.1), 14 intact glass alembics and their greenish translucent glass fragments were brought to light, as well as a small copper quadrangular cup measuring 23 × 23 × 7 mm that had wax residue on the bottom (fig. 8.2).

Most of the alembics and their fragments were found crushed on the floor of the room and in a niche filled

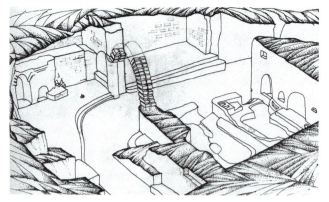

FIGURE 8.1 Paykend, shahrestan, "pharmacy"

FIGURE 8.2 Paykend, shahrestan, glass fragments of pharmaceutical tools

with pure white ash, and a few archaeologically intact ones were found in one of the pits (Mukhamedjanov and Semyonov 1984: 35–39). The alembics have a cylindrical shape, with a rounded base and a slightly thickened rim. There is a hollow glass tube inside. The surfaces of some alembics are smooth and shiny, while others are slightly matte. The diameters of their reservoirs range from 3.5 to 5.1 cm, the height from 4.5 to 8 cm and the spouts of the vessels have been preserved for a length ranging from 6 to 9 cm (Mukhamedjanov and Semenov 1988: 62–63).

Such vessels were widespread in Near and Middle Eastern countries between the 10th and early 13th centuries. The earliest samples come from Iran and date back to the 6th–8th centuries (Lamm 1935: 15).

The purpose of these vessels has been discussed elsewhere. Most researchers agree that they are a special chemical vessel and believe they were related to the distillation process.[1]

Given that in glass-like alembics during distillation the stem was directed upward rather than downward, other researchers believed that this type of alembic was intended for simpler operations, such as pouring mercury into other vessels (Abdurazakov, Bezborodov, and Zadneprovsky, 1963: 132) or pouring various expensive aromatic oils into receptacles (Dzhanpoladyan, 1965: 214–15).

According to one miniature from a 13th-century Baghdad school, in most cases the researchers did not take Lamm's earliest demonstration as serious (Lamm 1930: tabl. 1: 13, 14, 16).

A small quadrangular cup (23 × 23 × 7 mm) containing wax residue at the bottom that was found in the Paykend "pharmacy" helps us to further identify the range of activities that took place in this location (see fig. 8.2). According to written sources (Ibn Sina 1956: 396–97), in the Middle Ages wax was widely used for various handicrafts as well as in everyday life. But this small vessel with wax indicates a medical nature rather than an industrial one. In the eastern pharmacopoeia, wax (*mum*) was considered a cure for various diseases and had both internal and external uses.

Ibn Sīnā notes that wax is used on its own and in various mixtures: when taken orally – taken in the form of pills similar in size to millet grains – it helps to stop milk secretion in the breasts of a woman; and ten millet-sized pills placed in millet and rice gruel helps cure ulcers in the intestines (Ibn Sina 1956: 396–97). And the small volume of wax found in the "pharmacy" corresponds to written sources' descriptions of the use of limited amounts of wax on its own.

Thus, the materials found on the floors of the room, as well as a large *sufa* located there – where patients could be seen and medicine sold to them – indicate this is the remains of a "pharmacy" or a special room where a local doctor could receive patients. The dating of the "pharmacy" is fixed and based on other material found on the floor of the room: a large number of coins and a sherd with an early Arabic inscription with the date "*yawm al-sabt* 12 Safar 174" (Saturday, 30 June 790) indicate it was functioning at the end of the 8th century.

Regarding the function of the building, although scholars call it a "pharmacy", its functions are also associated with chemical activities, as well as being linked to medicine and alchemy (Mukhamedjanov and Semyonov 1988: 64).

Another hypothesis about glass-like alembics can be brought to light from their discovery in a *badrab* (a drainage system for dusty water) dated between the second half of the 10th and the early 11th centuries in Paykend. Here, along with other types of glassware, two alembics have been identified. The diameters of their rims are 5.5–6 cm, the heights are 5–6 cm and the remaining lengths of the

---

1 For a detailed explanation of the chemical process, see Amindzhanova 1961: 253; Papakhristu and Akhrarov 1981: 94; Atagaryiev 1980: 116; Sharakhimov 1973: 228.

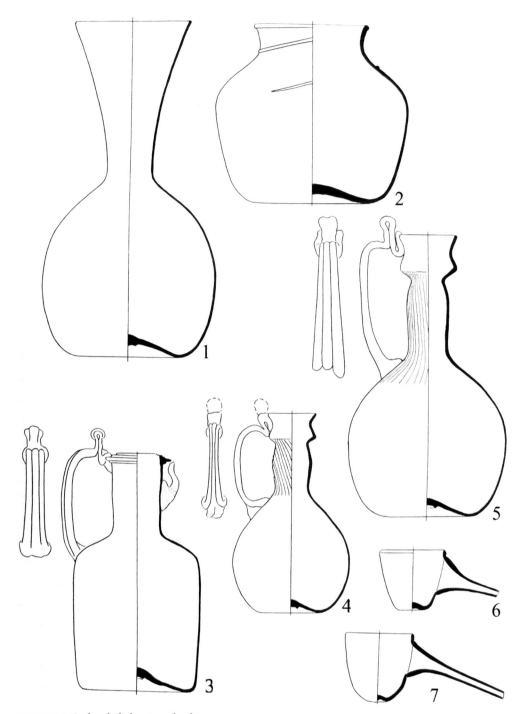

FIGURE 8.3 Paykend, shahrestan, alembics

spouts are 6–9 cm (fig. 8.3: 6 and 7). Researchers examining these types of vessels note that in addition to the glass-like variety, there was a second much less common variety that was of a larger size.

Glass alembics of this larger variety had wide, straight necks extending into flask-shaped reservoirs, thus creating receptacles with internal grooves (fig. 8.4).

The spouts of these vessels extend straight or downward, relative to the hemispherical base. Such a vessel was apparently convenient for condensing mercury and other substances from a vapour into a liquid. While settling and cooling, the evaporating vapours flowed down the walls into the groove and then down the spout and into a pre-installed vessel (Mirzaakhmedov, Adylov, and Mukhamedjanov 1990: 45).

According to R.M. Dzhanpoladyan (1965), who studied medieval Armenian manuscripts, these larger alembics correspond to vessels that alchemists used for distillation. The alembic was placed on a vessel containing the original substance, and its spout was connected to the receiving

FIGURE 8.4 Paykend, shahrestan, alembics

vessel. These devices were not only used in the laboratory but were also widely used in everyday life. Dzhanpoladyan also indicates that apparati for obtaining rose water were also arranged in a similar way.

Rose water was widely used in cosmetics and medicine and was also a popular trade item (Dzhanpoladyan 1965: 214). As for glass-like alembics, they are not suitable as a direct condenser: they have a relatively small reservoir, and there is no internal groove where condensed liquid can accumulate. The spouts of these vessels are not designed to drain mercury into other vessels. If their spouts were positioned in the same way as alembics of the second type, downward relative to the neck, only a small part of the condensed liquid could flow down the tube.

The noses of all glass alembics are directed upward relative to the neck. Proceeding from this, it can be argued that to obtain mercury, or similar heavy elements/chemicals, it was more convenient to use large alembics with a direct condensation process. This can be confirmed by M.E. Masson's discovery of a large glass alembic with a ceramic retort for distilling mercury in the Bukhara region; it is now stored in the Museum of the History of Uzbekistan in Tashkent (Amindzhanova 1961: 248).

In contrast to the large ones, the small alembics, which are found much more often among the archaeological material, apparently were more common. Proof that the latter were used as bloodletters is identified in later scholarship where, along with the alembics from Paykend, reference is made to a miniature from the 1237 Baghdad manuscript of the *Maqamat* of al-Harīrī, which is conserved in the Bibliothèque Nationale de France in Paris. The minature shows an audience in a medical lecture session, and behind the patient, who is sitting and whose back is bare, there are small alembics standing in a row on a shelf (fig. 8.5).

This is further corroborated in a miniature from a 1240 version of al-Harīrī's manuscript conserved at the Institute

FIGURE 8.5 *Maqamat* of al-Harīrī, Bibliothèque Nationale de France in Paris

of Oriental Studies in St. Petersburg (fig. 8.6). It also shows a session with a large audience, and the lecturer is putting an alembic on the bare back of a sitting patient (Semenov and Mirzaakhmedov 1996: 90–91).

Another historical source, *Treatise on Surgery and Instruments*, by a physician who lived at the turn of the 10th century (al-Zahrawi 1983: 211–16), talks about the use of blood-sucking cups and how to use them, and this helps us develop our ideas about the use of small alembics. The author notes that they were made of horns, wood, copper or glass and were intended to extract blood, not to bleed, as noted above.

They were used in two different ways: cuts were made on the skin and then they were applied to suction blood, or they were applied without cuts. Depending on the illness of the patient and the doctor's prescription, the alembics had different uses, designs and sizes. The difference in size is also explained by the age of the patients and the place on the body where they were applied, as well as to which veins they were attached (al-Zahrawi 1983: 211–16).

FIGURE 8.6 *Maqamat* of al-Harīrī, Institute of Oriental Studies in St. Petersburg

Interesting ethnographic material can be added the abovementioned sources. Currently, in the Paykend district (in the Karakul district of the Bukhara region), a traditional medicine practitioner continues to treat certain diseases by suctioning blood. The instrument for this procedure is a small horn from a bull (about 10 cm in length). Along with the natural opening at the top of the reservoir, a small through hole is drilled at the pointed tip of the horn. The bloodletting procedure consists of making small incisions on the patient, where the wide base of the horn is tightly attached, and then the suctioning can occur from the pointed end of the horn by sucking air from the reservoir of the instrument. The doctor, with the help of his tongue, covers the horn with a soft skin. As a result of the blood flowing into the reservoir, not only does the blood suction proceed much faster, but it also produces natural blood coagulation from the small incisions, and there is no need to repeat this procedure (Mirzaakhmedov, Adylov, and Mukhamedjanov 1990: 46–47).

Thus, the abovementioned material from archaeology, historical sources and ethnographic data clearly indicate that the small glass alembics were not used as chemistry instruments, as previously stated by most researchers, but as medical ones. Their long nose-like tubes directed upward were intended for doctors to suction out air and create blood flow into the reservoir. The different sizes indicate which part of the body the small alembics were attached to – large ones were usually used for the torso and smaller one for the head, neck and arms, and also for smaller patients.

In comparison to their metal, bone or wooden counterparts, according to archaeological evidence, small glass alembics were apparently widely used from the 9th to early 13th centuries, and their use is explained by the fact that their transparency made it possible to visually control the suction process, and they were more hygienic to use repeatedly. Also, it is necessary to take into account their relative inexpensiveness in comparison to metal and bone samples, as well as the fact that traditional oriental medicine used them to treat a wide range of diseases.

The simplicity of the procedure and the cheapness of glass alembics, as well as it being an easily controlled process, meant that in most cases it was a course of treatment or repeated procedure that could be carried out in the home or by quarter barbers who, according to medieval Persian prose and ethnographic studies of Bukhara, often engaged in similar operations for bloodletting, pulling teeth, and extracting thin long worms, "rishta" (D. medinensis), from the body.

The historical roots of the tradition of bloodletting, as well as its origin and importance within the western parts of the caliphate, are indicated by the special holidays dedicated to bloodletting in Baghdad that are noted in written sources (Metz 1966: 335, note 76). The operation was performed by a barber, who received approximately half a dirham for it in 912. Rich people kept their own barber (Metz 1966: 335, note 76). In the same context, it is necessary to consider the data from a 10th-century source, where wearing colourful clothes – befitting women and servants – is condemned. As a last resort, a man could wear them within the four walls of his house during the days he was treated with blood-sucking cups or during a binge (Metz 1966: 306).

The original complex of small alembics of various sizes was obtained from an excavation site (50 × 50m) located to the north of the Miri Arab madrasah in the ancient shahrestan of Bukhara city in 1978. Six intact alembics and fragments from more than eight small alembics were extracted from a small pit (55 × 43 cm) filled with pure greyish ash (fig. 8.7). The pit and the heavily destroyed cultural level related to it were excavated in the destroyed southern early medieval walls of the city's first shahrestan, which was once divided by the channels of the Shahrud (city river) that split from the Zerafshan into several independent delta channels.

The ceramic material obtained from the pit and adjacent to it consisted of small fragments of jug-like vessels. The nature of this material, as well as the absence of any fragments of glazed ceramics and the ash pit's location within the structure of an abandoned early medieval wall,

FIGURE 8.7 Bukhara, shahrestan, alembics

indicate the finds can be dated to around the beginning of the 9th century. On the basis of archaeologically intact specimens, the complex consisted mainly of large vessels and ones half the size of glass alembics; most were bluish and patina-covered, and less often they were made of greenish glass. The diameters of the large ones range from 5–5.5 cm, the height range is 5.5–6 cm and the length of the spouts reach 8.5 cm. The diameter of the small alembics is 3.5 cm and the height is 4.5 cm.

Along with the alembics, a large collection of highly corroded bronze fragments were also uncovered in the ash pit. A large piece of a rounded reservoir with a diameter of 5.5 cm, a flat base with a diameter of 3 cm and a broken spout (2 cm) that had a characteristic groove for draining liquids from the vessel has been preserved.

In general, this material and its context have interesting parallels with the "pharmacy" of Paykend. This concerns not only the discovery of alembics of various sizes, but also a bronze vessel, as well as a niche containing ash, which is where the alembic fragments were found, in the Paykend "pharmacy". These parallels are not accidental. Note that all the intact alembics and fragments in the complex from Bukhara were found in an ash layer. Let us now investigate why professional doctors kept this common tool, as well as copper vessels, in the ash pan.

Material from the Middle Ages, as well as broad ethnographic parallels I observed up to the present day, show that pure ash, which is alkaline, was widely used for washing clothes and bleaching fabrics, as well as in daily life for cleaning dishes and other utensils. In this era, medieval doctors sometimes used it as an antiseptic to clean their tools – destroying at least a significant amount of dangerous microorganisms – but more commonly used it as an aseptic. If water was added to the ash, then a more active disinfectant solution was obtained – a simple universal means of sterilising instruments (Mirzaakhmedov 2003: 5).

All this data and evidence suggests that by the end of the 8th and the early 9th centuries, traditional medicine in Maverannahr had clear ideas about the infectious nature of certain diseases. Based on our archaeological materials, we can state with confidence that the doctors knew that human blood could be a source of disease and that disease was carried by reusable medical instruments such as alembics and knives used to make incisions. To disinfect these instruments, according to our archaeological materials, special pits with ash were constructed in doctors' reception rooms.

The second find is from Bukhara: the remains of a bronze *usmadon* (cosmetic vessel), along with alembics, were found in an ash pan. Like in the first find from Paykend, these are relatively small forms. The bronze vessel from the Paykend "pharmacy" contained the remains of wax (*mum*), which allowed us determine it was used for scientific or medical purposes, while in the complex in Bukhara the bronze *usmadon* is a cosmetic device women used to collect *usma* juice for tinting their eyebrows. It was especially indispensable in the winter, when the leaves of the plant that were dried in the summer were placed in the *usmadon* reservoir, moistened with water and heated over fire (Mirzaakhmedov 1998: 117). And although according to ethnographic parallels, observed but still unpublished, this vessel's purpose is quite clear, nevertheless, finding it in a complex with alembics, as well as a similar vessel from the Paykend complex, cannot be accidental.

It seems to us that during the Early and Late Middle Ages *usmadon*s might have had a wider range of uses (Shirinov, Matbabaev, and Ivanov 1998: fig. 34; Kabanov 1956: fig. 19). Based on the materials found in Penjikent from the middle of the 8th century, Raspopova was of the opinion that they were used for pharmaceutical and cosmetic purposes (Raspopova 1980: 125, fig. 82: 7, 9). Wax (*mum*) could also be stored in them, and in winter it could be heated over the fire. We believe both vessels are linked based the fact that wax balls were softened in the mouth after sucking air out of the alembic reservoir, as we observed in ethnographic parallels.

Thus, both the alembics and the cups with wax that were used to suction blood could be disinfected; in the first case by being left in in ashes, and in the second, by heating the bronze vessels with wax over a fire.

Another archaeological achievement in recent years was the discovery of three shops at Paykend, in shahrestan 2,

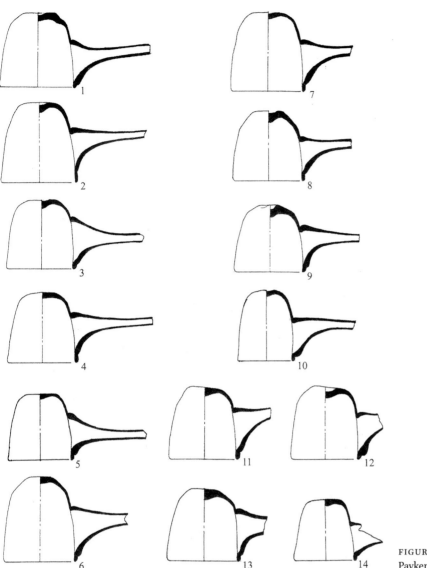

FIGURE 8.8
Paykend, shahrestan 2, alembics

along one of the central trade arteries leading to the southern gates, from which a large number of small alembics were extracted (Torgoev 2007: 24–29). The material was extracted from the floors of the rooms, and from the latrine and from a rectangular utility box dating back to the second half of the 10th to the early 11th centuries. In shop 5, eight archaeologically intact items and about 20 fragments were found, in shop 11 at least nine fragments, and in shop 12, 28 archaeologically intact items and more than 70 in a fragmentary state (fig. 8.8) (Torgoev 2007: 24–29). Moreover, in the last shop's complex fragments of a knife, which was possibly used to cut the skin, were found. These items included a small set of glassware – flasks, jugs, cups and vials – typically used for medicine or chemistry (fig. 8.9).

The most interesting forms in the last figure (fig. 8.9: 1, 2) include a glass bottle with embossed ornamentation that was made by blowing into a mould; this bottle was made to store aromatic liquids or ointments. Another rare type is a bulbous vessel with a small spherical base and a long, narrow cylindrical neck (fig. 8.10). Among the materials dated to the beginning of our era, such vessels are called *balsamaria*, which was a bottle for storing fragrant oil and was widely used in burial rituals (Kunina 1997: cat. 220, 221).

In 20th-century literature on chemistry, such forms are called volumetric flasks, and they are round-bottomed with a long, narrow cylindrical neck. They were used to dissolve substances, prepare solutions of certain concentrations, etc. Both items of course were also related to the doctor's shop, since the vessels were used for both perfumery and pharmaceutical purposes.

Thus, it should be taken into account that small alembics, albeit in small quantities, are ubiquitous in archaeological contexts from the 9th to early 13th centuries; in all regions of Maverannahr they were not only to the

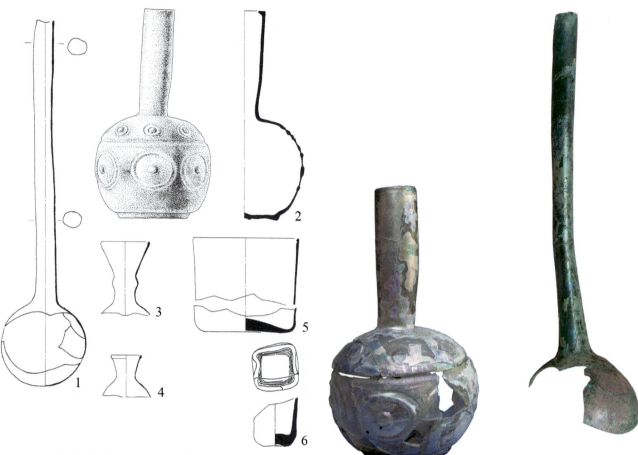

FIGURE 8.9   Paykend, shahrestan 2, set of glassware

FIGURE 8.10   Paykend, shahrestan 2, bulbous vessel

most common but also to the earliest type of glass medical instruments found in the second half of the 8th century. Even more interesting are the massive finds in the Bukhara Oasis, which in some cases include about a hundred specimens.

Today, we can confidently assert that not only the Paykend "pharmacy" but also the Bukhara complex and three shops from Paykend were undoubtedly local doctors' reception rooms. The widespread use of these rooms is also indicated by their location. The Paykend "pharmacy" is located at the crossroads of the main streets connecting shahrestans 1 and 2, and the next three shops are on the main street at the entrance to the city by the southern gate, where there was a bazaar outside the gates where villagers flocked with goods.

Thus, on the basis of the presented materials, we believe that the number of doctors' reception rooms in Bukhara and Paykend clearly indicate a significant rise in medical treatment within the oasis after the 10th century. Proceeding from this, it seems quite natural that an outstanding encyclopaedist and doctor such as Ibn Sīnā, whose knowledge – we are convinced – relied on familiarity with traditional folk medicine, would originate from Bukhara. And a century before Ibn Sīnā, the outstanding alchemist and physician al-Rāzī – who originated from the same region – not only identified such dangerous infectious diseases as measles and smallpox but also proposed an innovative method of treating the latter that is still used today: "vaccinations" (Karimov 1957: 32–33).

The next small group of glass vessels, which we briefly discussed above, are large alembics. The best-preserved copy of one is kept in the Museum of the History of Uzbekistan in Tashkent. It also comes from Bukhara and was found by M.E. Masson, together with a ceramic retort for distilling mercury (Aminjanova 1961: 248). It has an interesting feature: a solid round handle on the hemispherical top.

Determining what large glass alembics were used for is not controversial: authors agree that they were used to distil water and for various other preparations, as well as to capture mercury vapours. The process of distillation is described in late medieval Armenian manuscripts, where alembics are shown as part of a distillation apparatus fitted with an open tank on the wider neck of a retort that could be made of various materials, including glass (Janpoladyan 1965: 212–14).

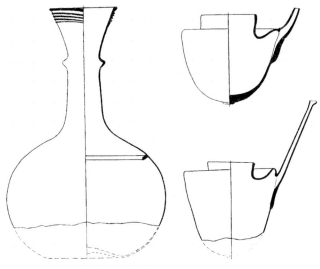

FIGURE 8.11   Tashkent, old city, retort

The retort containing the raw liquid was heated over a fire, and the rising vapours came into contact with the semicircular top of the alembic, cooled down and flowed into the groove and then through the tube into the receiver. Such devices had a wide spectrum of uses, not only in the alchemy, pharmacy and handicraft industries but also in everyday life – for obtaining pink water or rose oil, and even for restoring the colour of pearls (al-Biruni 1963: 121).

One interesting archaeological find was a discovery in the old city of Tashkent in 1985 on the border of the old shahrestan and the city's *rabad*: *badrab* (no. 5) and a complex of similar glass chemical vessels dating from the end of the 10th to the middle of the 11th centuries (Mirzaakhmedov, Ilyasova, and Adylov 1999: 243–45). It is a unique find because, along with two large glass alembics (i.e., nozzles), the find contained: two flasks (one large and one small), one large decanter and a whole set of small bottles made of transparent bluish glass. It turned out that the two large alembics fit very conveniently on the neck of the large retort flask (Mirzaakhmedov, Ilyasova, and Adylov 1999: fig. 3: 4, 5, 6).

Thus, this large retort, complete with attachments (i.e., the alembics), was used to heat and condense some liquids, for example mercury or distilled water (fig. 8.11). This is confirmed by the pieces of pure clay excavated in this *badrab*. The clay was hardened by the heat. Initially, we did not attach any importance to this, but after the discovery of a large flask without a bottom and large alembics – obtained from the *badrab* – that fit tightly onto the neck of the flask, it is now thought that this is a special type of clay noted in the written sources.

Al-Rāzī calles it the "clay of wisdom" and describes its manufacture in detail (Karimov 1957: 156, note 358). Al-Rāzī and Armenian sources recommended covering the bottoms of glass and ceramic vessels with it so that they would not burst in the fire, as well as using it to seal the edges of the devices placed on top of each other, making them fit tightly together during chemical operations (Kazanjyan 1955).

Let us briefly turn to the features of the retort flask where the distillation occurred. The body is wide, spherical and has a rim with a socket for the nozzle. The neck has a small expansion (i.e., groove), and along the shoulders, the so-called rib – a rigid rim formed by a slight inward indentation of the walls – contributed to the strength of the vessel.

Researchers believe that both the slight spherical expansion of the walls at the neck and the protrusion inside the walls along the shoulders served mainly for distillation, that is, for the convenience of decanting the liquid and leaving the sediment in the vessel. The protrusion along the shoulders was sediment's first obstacle, and the expanding neck on its neck was the second, once again indicating its purpose as a chemistry tool (Dzhanpoladyan 1965: 215–16). Both large alembics and large retort flasks are found in Bukhara, Tashkent and Samarkand (Shishkina 1986: fig. 6: 7), as well as in neighbouring states.

This chemical kit apparently included another flask, one of a smaller size (fig. 8.12: 1). Several similar small flasks were identified in adjacent *badrabs* 8 and 10 (fig. 8.13: 15,16). The walls of their bodies are almost spherical and have a characteristic circular expansion on their necks. We can also add that the grooves (i.e., necks) were intended to slow down the flow rate and thin the liquid stream when it was poured out. Similar grooves are still used in modern bottle production (Mirzaakhmedov, Ilyasova, and Adylov 1999: 241). This data once again indicates that the flasks were used for decantation, that is, decanting liquid while leaving residue or sediment in the vessel, and this indicates the chemical nature of their use.

Since the mouths of these flasks are small, it would not be possible to place alembics on them. Therefore, liquids were most likely mixed in them, although this does not exclude the possibility that they were placed over heat to produce a chemical reaction. And the flask from *badrab* 8 could have been used for processing as well as storing reagents, since the mouth of the vessel is clearly designed for a lid (fig. 8.13: 16).

Badrab 5 was the origin of the original set of chemical vessels from the late 10th to the first half of the 11th centuries discussed above, and other forms of glassware found there are also of interest because they belong to the home laboratory of a medieval pharmacist or alchemist from Binkat/Tashkent. They include a large decanter with

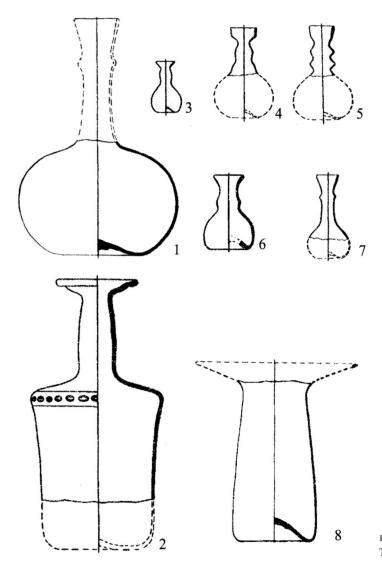

FIGURE 8.12 Tashkent, old city, small size flask

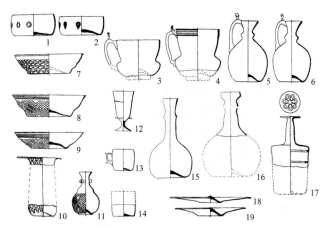

FIGURE 8.13 Tashkent, old city, flasks

a subcylindrical body slightly tapering toward the base, along the shoulders of which there is a circular pattern of dents (fig. 8.12: 2). A decanter identical in shape but smaller in size, dating from the 10th century, was discovered in nearby *badrab* 10 (fig. 8.13: 17). Unlike the previous

larger one, the glass blower along the top of the body has small narrow stripes that form two stiffening ribs.

Both decanters lack an expanding neck (i.e., a groove on their necks,) which most likely indicates their purpose was not so much for distilling as for storing liquids, and the narrow mouth and horizontally bent side is quite suitable for placing a cover on. Similar decanters were also common in other regions of Uzbekistan (fig. 8.14) (Mirzaakhmedov, Adylov, and Matbabaev 2008: fig. 5: 3), in Samarkand in particular (Aminjanova 1962: fig. 1: 14, 15; Almazova 1997: fig. 1: 17; Dzhanpoladyan 1965: fig. 4: 3).

The last group of vessels related to *badrab* 5 is a set of five small vials made of transparent blue and yellow glass, in general having similar shapes and sizes (fig. 8.12: 3–7). We believe that to some extent, they are related to the abovementioned set of chemical glassware. Such vessels were used to manufacture and store medicines, as well as perfumes, and they were used to mix various components in small doses.

FIGURE 8.14
Binkat, decanter

Nevertheless, although a simple form, on the neck of each of them there are one or two expanding necks, and the rims are intended for decantation. If we take into account their possible connection with the flask for heating liquids and the distillation process through large alembics, these vials could have been at the receiving end of the process.

Summing up the analysis of material from *badrab* 5, we note the exceptional case of the discovery of a set of chemical glassware, dated to the late 10th to the first half of the 11th centuries, that contains a large retort with large alembics. This find confirms the theory about the specific purpose of large and small alembics, and small fragments from the bottom of a retort with a solid layer of a special kind of clay confirm without a doubt that the vessel was used for thermal operations.

The small perfumery and pharmaceutical objects obtained from the same *badrab* that have special grooves on their necks were apparently used not only for pouring doses of, mixing or decanting the liquids contained in them but also as vessels that received the substances drained from the nose of the alembic. Some specially designated lids were clearly intended to plug these small vessels – to store quickly evaporating aromatic or unpleasant chemicals that would be dangerous if released into the air.

This set of vessels also indicates that the owner of the household, to one degree or another, was engaged in chemical operations related to pharmacology, perfumery or medicine.

In Uzbekistan closed archaeological contexts show many finds of small vials, flasks, decanters and other forms of glassware that had a definite medical, perfumery or chemical purpose. Researchers refer to them as perfumery and pharmaceutical objects. At the beginning of the last century, V.L. Vyatkin believed that a large amount of glassware was used in the pharmaceutical and perfumery trades. Sometimes many identical objects are found in one place, for example bottles (Vyatkin 1926: 62, figs. 72–75).

This is the case with a set of glassware from the early 11th century found in the Ark of Akhsiket. Here, along with fragments of decanters and small alembics, close to 50 bottles without any external decoration were found among fragments of pear-shaped, translucent light blue glass (Papakhristu and Akhrarov 1981: 93).

Given the large number of fragments of similar forms, Papakhristu and Akhrarov note that it is necessary to distinguish between products intended as perfume and those intended as medicine. Liquids with heavy and strong odours were placed in vessels with an appropriate design. Well-known and well-made bottles from Nisa, Abrlyg and Khulbuk were most likely intended for perfumery purposes. Vessels intended for medicine did not require such an elegant, decorative treatment. We believe that these vessels from the pit layer dated to the early 11th century were intended specifically for medicine (Papakhristu and Akhrarov 1981: 93–94).

Archaeological work in the following decades in the Ark of Akhsiket identified a find from the 10th–11th centuries that contained glass products from the *badrab* that were even more reminiscent of a pharmaceutical set (Anarbaev 2002: fig. 10). The defining feature of most of them is their bulbous shape: two large-sized ones and three small-sized ones, but all with expanding grooves on their necks for decantation (fig. 8.15). Another bottle with a glass strand attached along the neck is a similar type of vessel and used to store various tinctures, and it is commonly found in other contexts (Papakhristu and Akhrarov 1981: fig. 1: 16). All these vessels were made of light blue and light green transparent thin-walled glass.

Based on the materials found in Bukhara, Abdullaev comes to the same conclusion, "Glass products in the form of chemical vessels of light greenish-blue colour are predominantly transparent. Vessels with thin-walled profiling used in everyday life are painted in various colours – from light yellow, blue and light green to deep dark blue, green, violet and brown tones" (Abdullaev 1981: 57).

While in general agreeing with these researchers' claims about the possible purpose of these vessels, claims

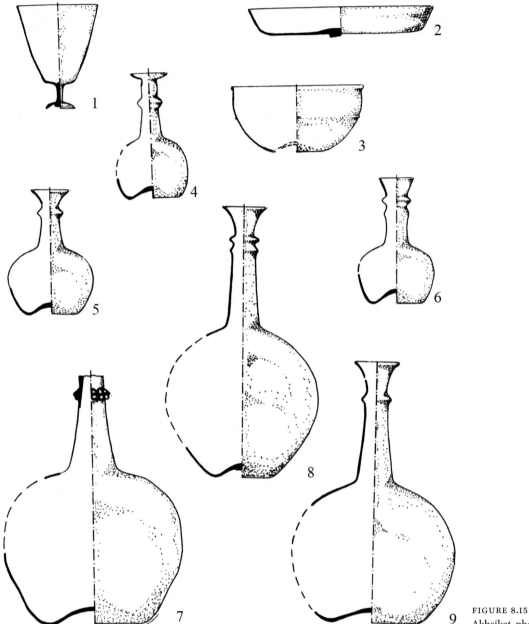

FIGURE 8.15
Akhsiket, pharmaceutical set

that are based on the nature of their external design, we also note that a clear requirement for glassware used for medical and pharmaceutical purposes was transparency, or at least the ability to observe the presence or absence of precipitation and the colour, quantity and other parameters of the drugs contained in the vessel.

In the section on glass in *Kitāb al-Jamāhir fī ma'rifat al-jawāhir* al-Bīrūnī notes: "From the vessels made of it, complete transparency is required, so that from the outside one can see what is inside them" (al-Biruni 1963: 208).

Al-Rāzī's opinion can be added here as well. In the alchemical part of *The Book of Secrets*, in a section devoted to the description of devices, he divides them into two groups: instruments for the manufacture of metals and instruments for other chemical operations with nonmetallic substances. Many of the devices in the second group should be "made of glass, which will be better, for such devices are not in the least erased or mixed with substances. Such mixing is very harmful, and glass devices (for this) are not dangerous and are good" (Amindzhanova 1961: 248).

Thus, the abovementioned data from historical sources, together with the archaeological material identified as early glass products, demonstrate several things: first, the beginning of their entry and spread into the life of the population from the end of the 8th century onwards.

FIGURE 8.16   Afrasiab, dishes

Second, the most popular form of glass medical products among the townspeople turned out to be bloodletting jars, followed by pharmaceutical and perfumery dishes.

The next stage, which became widespread in the Late Middle Ages, is the production of perfumery glassware. As noted above, finds were recorded in previous periods, but mainly in elite contexts, and they continued to remain quite rare and expensive luxury items, mainly imported.

In the 9th century, glass products began to appear in the daily life of the townspeople much more frequently. At end of the 8th and beginning of the 9th centuries, in some closed contexts in Afrasiab, the ratio of glass items to ceramic forms is about 25%. And for the middle of the 9th century, this ratio in the first closed complex reaches 35%, and in the second about 50%. Later, in the second half of the 9th through the 10th and 11th centuries, this trend becomes more stable, accounting for about half the vessels found (Shishkina 1986: 19, 23, 27). According to sources, in the cities, and in Bukhara in particular, there were whole quarters for glass-makers and "bottle-makers" (Beleniskij, Bentovich, and Bolshakov 1973: 285).

At the same time, along with other glass products, cosmetic – or, as researchers more often note, perfumery and pharmaceutical – dishes continue to increase steadily in closed contexts (fig. 8.16). This phenomenon, especially at the initial stage of the development of glassmaking, is explained by glass's entry into the lives of a broad spectrum of townspeople. The shapes of the perfumery and pharmaceutical vessels are largely identical, simple in design, small in size and mostly rounded and subcylindrical or subrectangular in shape. Although they are found more often than other types of glass products (Aminjanova 1962: 96, figs. 1–3) and have a variety of forms (Abdurazakov, Bezborodov, and Zadneprovsky 1963: 125–26, fig. 26), it is possible that the glassmakers did not make a clear distinction between perfumery and cosmetic and pharmaceutical vessels.

However, because they used museum material that was in general poorly developed and dated within a broad framework from the 9th to the early 13th centuries

FIGURE 8.17   Afrasiab, small flasks

(Aminjanova 1962: 90), researchers failed to construct a chronological scale of development, as well as changes in the form and purpose of the products. Meanwhile, by the 10th and 11th centuries, some master glassblowers had begun to create distinct vessels for perfumery and cosmetic purposes (Abdullaev 1981: fig. 1: 8, 9; Kabanov 1956: fig. 25).[2] Although, once again we stipulate that among ordinary townspeople, small flasks were most commonly used for cosmetic purposes (fig. 8.17). Thus, during archaeological work near the former Tashkent Road, east of the Museum of the History of the City of Samarkand, a small rounded flask with remnants of a pink blush at the bottom was found among some small glass fragments. Similar small flasks, simple in shape with remnants of pink blush, were observed in Bukhara (fig. 8.18).

The next large group of items in the archaeological contexts of medieval Maverannahr is glass tableware. Based on materials from Afrasiab, the earliest samples, dating from the end of the 8th to the early 9th centuries, are glasses with bell-shaped reservoirs on small unstable legs. The cylindrical jars and hemispherical bowls were shaped using the technique of blowing them into an ornamental shape. Samples of mugs, alembics, a bottle, a

---

2   See also *Terres secrètes de Samarcande* 1993: n. 316–19; *Islamishe kunst* 1984: nos. 1–5, 6–8.

FIGURE 8.18   Bukhara, small flasks

vial, a narrow neck of a flask-shaped vessel, etc. were also found (Shishkina 1986: fig. 1).

Based on materials from Afrasiab, G.V. Shishkina demonstrates how previous productions were improved and new forms emerged between the first half and the mid-9th century: glasses acquire thinner and more stable legs and false threads appear on their walls. Vessels with cord-shaped or multi-lobed circular linings on the necks, bottles with expanded mouths, as well as stiffening ribs along the body, spoons with twisted handles, and glasses and jars blown into cellular, ribbed and figured shapes have also been identified (Shishkina 1986: figs. 2–4).

At the end of the 9th and into the 10th century, other forms appear that were used in daily life: jugs with flared rims (fig. 8.19); discoid glasses for windows; flasks with high necks, shelves at the mouths designed to be closed with a cork and several swells or grooves for decantation; large bottles with bell necks, possibly used to heat substances with the help of large alembic nozzles; jugs with high necks (fig. 8.20); glass *tuvak* (sanitary pots placed in a baby's cradle) and other accessories for children's cradles, such as *sumak* (used to drain the baby's urine into a pot); and cosmetic bottles with a multifaceted or bumpy body (Shishkina 1986: figs. 5–9).

Between the second half of the 11th and the first half of the 12th century wine glasses were the most common item. And coloured (light red) window panes also began to appear during this time, apparently decorating window bars, *pandjara*, fragments of which are also found in Afrasiab and dated to this period. In the second part of the 12th and the early 13th centuries no significant changes in the development of glassmaking in Afrasiab are identified (Shishkina 1986: figs. 10, 11, 13).

The aforementioned find of glass tableware of various shapes, colours and ornaments, given their fragility, was mainly used during ceremonial occasions, when receiving guests, for celebrations or to decorate the shelves of the *mikhmankhana* (living room).

A somewhat smaller group of glass items in the contexts are for special purposes, including window panes of various colours inserted into lattices (*panjara*) (fig. 8.13: 18, 19). The appearance of glass panes, sometimes with different

FIGURE 8.19   Afrasiab, jugs with flared rims

FIGURE 8.20   Afrasiab, jugs with high necks

FIGURE 8.21   Afrasiab, hygienic tools

colours, marks a new stage of development in residential and public urban planning, a significant improvement in the quality of life among all strata of society and the improvement of the interiors of civil and monumental structures.

Other types of special-purpose items, such as accessories for a *beshik* (baby cradle), *tuvaki* and *sumaki* (baby potties), are also common during this time. The emergence of glass *tuvak*s and *sumak*s, which were more hygienic and convenient to use – and from the end of the 10th to the beginning of the 11th centuries, opaque *tuvak*s made of dark or black glass – is related to the cultural growth of a wide range of consumers and glassmakers (fig. 8.21).

The third type of special-purpose items that are often found in archaeological contexts are small glass inkpots of various shapes. The simplest of them had anywhere from one to five glass sides that were inserted into alabaster stands (Terenozhkin 1950: fig. 72: 3; Staviskiy 1960: 278–81). Talc-chlorite multi-hole inkpots were less common (Aminjanova 1962: fig. 3: 7).

Inkpots are undoubtedly an indicator of the population's literacy, its education and the cultural growth of society in general. And the presence of multi-hole inkwells means different colours of ink were used when writing. Thanks to medieval sources, we know that different colours of ink were used when writing letters of an official, joyful, sad or amorous nature. Undoubtedly, these divided inkpots might be related to this. Also, multi-celled glass inkpots with various colours of ink were used when writing manuscripts, which was a fairly common occupation for calligraphers, and later for educated people in general, during this era (Davidovich 1953, Aminjanova, M. 1962). Through material in museums we are familiar with items such as funnels, glass mercury vessels and *simobkuzacha* (vessels for storing and transporting mercury) (Aminjanova 1962: fig. 2: 9.28), of which an example with a massive body and broken neck has been found in Bukhara (fig. 8.22). There are also small glass drinking bowls from the 10th to 12th centuries that have an extended narrow

FIGURE 8.22   Bukhara, glass mercury vessels

nose for children (Kabanov 1955: fig. 26). This rare form includes a larger 10th-century drinking cup that has a spherical shape and is reminiscent of a modern teapot, but its spout is located on the side in relation to the handle (Sharakhimov 1973: fig. 1: 7). We believe that such cups had a medical nature, intended for sick people who were lying down (fig. 8.23).

Another rare find are pendants with stamped medallions/amulets depicting a female deity from Afrasiab and Balalyk Tepe and dated to the 7th and early 8th centuries (Terenozhkin 1950: fig. 72: 1; Al'baum 1960: fig. 53). This group includes medallions, but a little later in time, of the

FIGURE 8.23 Afrasiab, cups for medical purposes

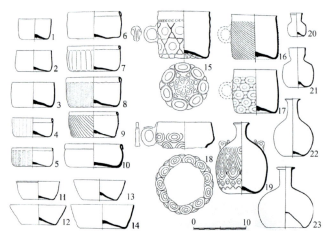

FIGURE 8.25 Paykend, shahrestan 1, cup set

FIGURE 8.24 Termez, medallions

type resembling samples originating from the palace complex of the 12th- to early 13-century Termez rulers. They are made of greenish or reddish glass, in most cases with images of various scenes of a hunting nature (fig. 8.24), with zoomorphic, ornithomorphic and epigraphic motifs, which, apparently, were also inserted into the window bars/*panjara* (window grill) (Zhukov 1945: 150–56).

Of particular importance for characterising glassmaking from the period under study are the sets from closed contexts, which allow one to get acquainted with the range of products used in the daily life of individual citizens at various stages of our history. These include a complex of glassware made in the *badrab* of shahrestan 1 in Paykend, the tableware of which dates back to the second half of the 10th century (Mirzaakhmedov, Adylov, Mukhamedjanov 1990: fig. 1, 2). The predominant cups in the set are of two shapes: cylindrical, jar-shaped cups with walls slightly bent inward (fig. 8.25: 1–10); and cups of a truncated conical configuration with walls diverging to the sides (fig. 8.25: 11–14).

A significant portion of the cups were made using the technique of blowing into a mould, and they have walls with oblique and vertical relief lines and are made of transparent glass, with greenish, bluish and yellowish shades.

Archaeological excavations in regions of Central Asia and neighbouring states show their prevalence in the 10th–12th centuries, although the term "bowl" would be acceptable for the larger vessels intended for the everyday consumption of liquid food and drinks. Our vessels are squatter, have a small capacity and are inconvenient for drinking. Similar vessels used for drinking were recorded in Dvin, Bukhara, Tashkent, Samarkand and nearby Kumushkent, but they are higher glass-like forms (Dzhanpoladyan 1969: fig. 6; Abdullaev 1981: fig. 1: 3; Mirzaakhmedov, Ilyasova, and Adylov 1999: fig. 2: 6; Shishkina 1986: fig. 1: 10, 11; fig. 4: 22, 24; Almazova 1997: fig. 1: 1, 12, 26, 27).

Considering the large number of such items in finds from the Paykend complex, as well as their uniformity and ceremonial and everyday forms, it can be assumed that these items had a wide range of uses, but first and foremost, they were apparently used for serving on *dastarkhan* (tablecloth). In Bukhara today, similar cups/bowls are served to guests. In such vessels, various seasonings and spices for hot food and delicacies are displayed: fried peas, pistachios, almond and apricot seeds, nuts, raisins, dried apricots and dozens of different types of confectioneries or sweets, such as halva and *nishalda* (a national sweet).

The smaller cups (fig. 8.25: 1–5) could also be used as salt shakers, pepper shakers or as perfume and pharmaceutical vessels for cosmetic charcoal, blush, whitening powder and medicinal ointments.

Cups with a truncated conical shape (fig. 8.25: 11–14), with walls expanding towards the top, were probably

FIGURE 8.26   Maverannahr, circular objects

more suitable for semi-liquid dairy (*kaymak*) or sweet (e.g. jams) products. Jam, *jaupazak* and *murabboi guli* were very popular in Bukhara. The first was made from mulberry or grape juice, the second, from a special variety of small May apples, and the third, from the petals of a specially grown variety of roses sold at a special bazaar (*bozori gul*). Jam made from carrots, melons, watermelon, quince, apricot, fig, etc. was also very popular in Bukhara (Mirzaakhmedov 1990).

The circular objects are represented in the complex with fragments from four vessels (fig. 8.25: 15–18). They are covered with rich relief ornaments. Most are cylindrical in shape and have a loop-shaped handle made of relatively transparent glass in greenish and bluish shades. On the first circular object, the patterns along the walls consist of repeating embossed stars with a border along the rim of spherical motifs, and along the bottom of a petal rosette surrounded by ellipses. The walls of the second circular object are decorated with oblique relief lines, and the walls of the third are decorated with repeating ellipsoidal motifs. The fourth one has a truncated conical-shaped walls, with an elbow bent into a tapering bottom, closely resembling metal circular objects of this type (Darkevich 1976: table 33). The ornamentation also consists of ellipsoidal motifs, possibly on a pallet, that concentrate around a rosette, as in the first instance.

Judging from the rich ornamentation, the circular objects had a ceremonial character and, apparently, were imitations of earlier metal prototypes, or possibly of crystal products that were beginning to receive wider distribution during this period (Hilal al-Sabi 1983: 69; Weimarn 1974: ill. 71.72). Similar samples in shape are also found in other regions of Maverannahr (fig. 8.26).

Glass mugs were a necessary part of the table sets. Apparently, guests were served not only various types of fruit juices (Hilal al-Sabi 1983: 69) but also *musallas*, *kumis*, *buza*, refreshing milk (*shabbat*, *ayran*, *cholob*) or sweet traditional ritual drinks – *sharbati* or *gulob*, serving them is mandatory in Bukhara today – in them. So, today any wedding in Bukhara necessarily began with

FIGURE 8.27   Bukhara, table vessels

serving a sweet drink with added aromatic substances (*gulob*) in bowls that were passed out on trays. *Sharbati* (sweet water) was served to the bride and groom after the marriage was signed (Mirzaakhmedov, Adylov, and Mukhamezhanov 1990).

Archaeological sealed contexts consist of three jugs, a jug-shaped decanter and a pot-shaped jar. The jugs are made of transparent light blue glass (fig. 8.3: 3–5). They have spherical and subcylindrical body shapes, necks with an oblique bend of the relief lines and a groove for decantation that widens at the mouth, as well as handles made of three inlaid cords – sticks with a tuft. In general, the profile of the jugs, especially those with a subcylindrical body shape and moulding along the rim imitating nozzles for installing lids, are made in imitation of metal forms (Voronina 1977: fig. 35, b) and are very interesting.

Despite the thinness of the body's walls, glass jugs were quite strong, but in everyday life they were inferior to metal and ceramic vessels, and apparently, they were more often used on special occasions – when receiving guests and on holidays – and on other days they were used to decorate the interiors of premises.

Only fragments of a jug-shaped vessel with a spherical body and a neck with a bell have survived (fig. 8.3: 1).

A pot-shaped jar (fig. 8.3: 2), often found among archaeological materials, also belongs among table vessels. It is also found in Bukhara (Abdullaev 1981: fig. 1: 1, 2). Judging from its shape and volume, which was about one litre, such vessels had a wide range of purposes and were apparently used for storing dried fruits, certain types of sweets or medicinal herbs (fig. 8.27).

It has been determined that vessels for perfumery purposes are represented by one large narrow-necked bottle with richly embossed ornamentation and two overhead loops for hanging (fig. 8.25: 19). The richness of the design, graceful loops for hanging by the neck or shoulders and narrow neck for the cork indicate that the bottle could have been used to store rose water.

On the next four bottles of various sizes, ornamentation was absent (fig. 8.25: 20–23), and it can be determined that they were used as perfumery and pharmaceutical vessels. Two larger ones, with narrow necks, were used for storing medicinal or aromatic preparations, and small vessels with wide necks were more convenient for blush, lipstick, mascara, rose oil or other ointments of a cosmetic or medicinal nature.

In addition to these vessels, there were several small alembics in the complex.

A set of glassware from a separate private household in Paykend, a town dweller who lived between the second half of the 10th and early 11th century, contains an assortment of tableware, many of which are richly decorated with relief ornamentation. Among them, cups, mugs and jugs stand out, and they, along with ceramic dishes, were intended to decorate the festive table and living room niches.

At the same time, the shapes of the cups, and especially the mugs, in terms of their sophistication, colour scheme and transparency, look preferable to their ceramic prototypes and, judging by the data from the sources, were in great demand among the upper strata of society (Sadyk-i-Kashkari 1992: 52). Proceeding from this, glass's external features were apparently inferior only to the bright forms of expensive metal products, as indicated by the individual samples of glass jugs made in imitation of them.

Along with tableware, sets of perfumery, pharmaceutical and medical vessels are richly presented in this glassware set, testifying to the widespread practices of women using cosmetics and of storing medicines at home.

The next interesting archaeological complex with glassware finds contained materials obtained from two nearby locations in the shahrestan of Kuva. The *badrab*s, located half a metre apart, were directly connected to one household and, judging from the ceramic materials originating from them, as well as from the premises' floors, date back to the 11th century (Mirzaakhmedov, Adylov, Matbabaev 2008: fig. 6–9).

Several archaeologically intact forms and fragments of glass products, the household utensils of a single Kuva

FIGURE 8.28   Kuva, vessel

family, come from *badrab* 6 and can be dated to a certain chronological period of time. The glass samples include a small spherical vessel of a greenish hue with a narrow neck, convenient for plugging and most likely intended for storing highly volatile, aromatic cosmetic drugs (fig. 8.28: 6).

The next small vessel had a jug-like shape, but in size and purpose it is closer to the samples of decorated glasses. It is made of greenish glass, has a wide rim and the body has bevelled corrugated walls (fig. 8.28: 7). Archaeologically, the form resembles a salad bowl and is made of blue glass and decorated with solar symbolism that has ribbed lines radiating from the bottom (fig. 8.28: 5). Like the previous vessel, this one was made using the blowing technique and rotating it into a mould.

The rest of the forms from *badrab* 6 are glasses and wine glasses made of transparent thin yellowish glass. They were divided according to their artistic embellishments: the simplest did not have any ornamentation (fig. 8.28: 1), and other had two or more circular glass threads overlapping along the upper part of the reservoir (fig. 8.28: 4). To especially refined specimens, overhead broken lines made of other glass colours were added along the base of the tank (fig. 8.28: 2,3) or a disc-shaped cone made of woven glass threads (fig. 8.28: 3).

In terms of the place of discovery and chronology, the ones closest to the last sample are glasses and wine glasses from the 11th century that also originate from archaeological excavations at Kuva (Akhrarov 1960: fig. 1.2). In general, we believe that the glasses and wine glasses, which constituted the majority of forms in the complex, were the most complex products in terms of their execution: they were assembled from several parts and ornamental motifs of a different, contrasting colour of glass were placed on them.

FIGURE 8.29 Kuva, vessels

FIGURE 8.30 Kuva, transparent, yellowish-greenish and yellowish vessels

They are one of the clearest indicators of the glassmakers' skilfulness.

One characteristic of the complex is that the ceramic and glass samples obtained in the *badrab* lead to opposite conclusions. So, on the ceramic ware of the previous period, the main type of ornamentation consisted of imitation of kufic calligraphy. Often only one stylised word – replete with meaning – is repeated on the dishes, taking up little space and leaving the vast majority of the inner and outer surfaces of the dishes free from any ornamentation.

The second indicator in the complex is the presence of a significant number of forms of various colourful glass products that are of a good quality.

Due to reduced quantities and a decrease in the artistry of some ceramic dishes, their presence on the shelves in the *mikhmankhana* (living room) was gradually replaced with elegant, highly artistic samples of glassware. Glasses and wine glasses stand out among them, from the simplest ones to exquisitely decorated ones with overlaid threads. Despite the varying degrees of complexity of their external design, which determines the price range of the object and the purchasing power of the population, the standard form and technique of decoration indicates they were manufactured by the same master. Based on ceramic materials, they are chronologically dated to the 11th century, suggesting a wide export to neighbouring regions (Mirzaakhmedov, Adylov, Matbabaev 2008: 194–95).

Badrab 7, located on one floor level and undoubtedly having a consistent filling pattern, turned out to be even richer. Here, along with glazed and unglazed ceramics, a large number of glass fragments were found, from which a number of original forms were assembled.

The largest number, six copies, are glass wine glasses. Of these, as in the previous set, four of them are the usual forms (fig. 8.29: 1, 2), without additional decoration. The glasses are transparent, yellowish-greenish and yellowish in colour (fig. 8.30).

The fifth specimen is the same, only with an addition in the form of a disc-shaped grooved expansion along the base of the tank (fig. 8.29: 3), most likely used for decantation. Of course, such graceful forms were intended for intoxicating drinks – most often wine – and there are often cases of precipitation at the bottom of the vessel. The sixth sample is more complicated, made of transparent glass with a yellowish-greenish tint (fig. 8.29: 4), and contrasting blue threads run across the tank. Below the body, a pseudo-epigraphic pattern is applied with a thicker blue patch cord, and a disc-shaped shield made of twisted glass threads is at the base of the tank.

In general, the sizes of the wine glasses vary: height within the range of 10–11.1 cm; diameters of the rims 6–7 cm; diameters of the bottoms 3.3–3.6 cm.

Along with the wine glasses, fragments were found in the set, and the shape of one glass was restored, which is of a larger size in comparison with the ones mentioned above. It is made of transparent glass that has a yellowish tint, with ornamentation of applied circular and S-shaped spirals of the base colour that alternate with zigzag broken lines made of contrasting blue glass (fig. 8.29: 5).

In contrast to the previous complex, here we find a new shape of the glass that has a larger volume, and the design of applied threads of contrasting blue glass is added to the ornamental compositions. Almost identical to it in shape, colour and ornamentation is another glass from Kuva that was obtained earlier (Akhrarov 1960: fig. 1). Although it is slightly larger in size, the colour scheme and repetition of S-shaped and zigzag motifs, noted in the form of the blooming flower below, certainly might indicate that they were made by the same master.

The new form in the complex is a graceful snifter made of yellow glass (fig. 8.29: 6). It has a spherical body set

FIGURE 8.31   Kuva, vessels

on a wide base and a long nose tapering towards the top (fig. 8.31). The ornamentation along the body consists of alternating S-shaped and zigzag overhead flagella of different thicknesses. At the base of the neck are two circular decorative rings made by wrapping the same threads.

The aromas contained rose water, which, as a rule, was used not only for personal purposes but also to spray guests and spray at different locations during holidays, celebrations, weddings, etc. Therefore, the aromas were of a cosmetic nature; they were ceremonial and were exhibited on the shelves of *mikhmankhana*. We found a typology with a similar shape, size and character of ornamentation among the 11th-century materials from the city of Akhsiket, located to the north of the capital centre of Fergana (Abdurazakov 1986: 1), and it is also widely present in finds from neighbouring regions (Shishkina 1986: fig. 11: 8; Islamische Kunst 1984: ills. 138, 190, 192, 197; *Iskusstvo islama* 1990: N64; Baypakov 1990: 137), and was in use until the Late Middle Ages (Maslenitsa 1975: no. 52).

They have late medieval parallels, where they are widely represented in more practical metal samples, and they are also well-known from images in miniature paintings. These paintings include a number of well-known scenes, such as the famous couple Layla and Majnun, where an aroma is used to spray someone who has fainted and restore them to consciousness (Grube 2013: figs. 2, 3, 5, 7, 8).

Based on medieval sources in Iran, it can be argued that in the era being studied here, industrial floriculture was distributed widely, and rich landowners mass produced numerous varieties of rose oil and rose water, which were used not only for perfumery and cosmetic purposes but also as medicinal ointments for various diseases (Petrushevsky 1960: S. 226–29). Flowers played a similar role, not only for decorative purposes but also for the manufacture of various medicines and perfumery items in Central Asia (Abduraimov 1966: 229–30).

Another find in the complex is a *tuvak* made of opaque black glass with the usual cylindrical shape and a rim bent outward (fig. 8.29: 8). It is made using the technique of blowing the shape and creating a pattern of rhombuses across the body. Fragments of another *tuvak*, practically identical in size, colour and character of design, was identified from the same 11th-century layers of the excavation of *badrab*s 6 and 7.

Based on the external design of the finds, including those in the neighbouring excavations at Kuva, and taking into account their specific purpose, it is noteworthy that the majority of this period's glass was opaque black glass, and it appears that this colour, standardisation of sizes and external design was a widespread cultural tradition.

The last archaeologically complete form in the complex is a flask-shaped bottle made of transparent greenish glass (fig. 8.29: 7). The body is spherical, with a tapering aperture and a rim turned outward. Taking the other mass finds of glasses and wine glasses from *badrab*s 6 and 7, it can quite confidently be claim that this vessel was used for storing and pouring various wine drinks, or possibly juices. Also, this special form of tableware, along with a glass, wine glasses and aroma bowls, apparently was not

FIGURE 8.32 Kuva, decanter and vase-like vessel

only a necessary part of the ceremonial tableware but also a good decoration and an irreplaceable addition to any set that traditionally decorated living room shelves. Therefore, it is frequently found throughout a wide geographical area in the studied era (Islamische Kunst 1984: ill. 10), and it may be indirect evidence of the appearance of such shelves inside residential rooms, at least since the 11th century. Beginning in the first third of the 14th century, similar shelves or *shahnishin* (richly decorated living room shelves), with expensive, beautiful dishes exhibited on them for decoration in some locations in Khorezm, in Central Asia, were mentioned by Ibn Baṭṭūṭa (Ibragimov 1988: 75).

Two additional glass forms that are of interest were obtained from the floors of the rooms in the same household (5b) at the 11th-century stratigraphic level, like in *badrab*s 6 and 7. The first is a large greenish glass decanter with a cylindrical body and an unfolded rim (fig. 8.32:1). To strengthen the walls, rigid ribs (a frame) protrude outward at the base and are inwardly concave at the shoulders.

The second specimen is represented by an incompletely preserved vase-like vessel made of yellow glass (fig. 8.32: 2), with ornamentation of repeated pairs of S-shaped and dotted patches along the body, as well as a contrasting blue ribbon strip along the rim.

The peculiarities of the decanter intended for storage and pouring various liquids, including wine, include the presence of stiffening ribs that strengthened the walls of the body. The second vessel is a new, original vase-like form for serving various sweets or dried fruits to the table. The presence of a contrasting blue ribbon strip along the rim and the original S-shaped spiral motif along the body brings it closer to the samples of a glass and aroma from *badrab* 7, indicating they were purchased as part of a glass table service from a Kuva master, with characteristic motif of the master's products.

FIGURE 8.33 Kuva, bowl, jug-shaped vessel and wine glass

Materials from *badrab*s 6 and 7 and related rooms of the 11th-century households complement each other and include some new forms of tableware, testifying to the growth of the range of tableware form and indicating the further improvement of the artistry and sophistication of Kuva glassmakers, which had reached the peak of its development by the 11th century.

To enhance and more robustly characterise this era's glassmaking, we will use materials from the third closed complex – *badrab* 17 from excavation 9, located in the southern part of the Kuva citadel. The handicrafts obtained here – glazed and non-glazed ceramics and glass products – have direct parallels with the above-described contexts from *badrab*s 6 and 7 from excavation 5b, and to a certain extent they supplement them.

Among the items obtained here, a planar form of bluish glass with low vertical walls stands out, what we conventionally call a salad bowl (fig. 8.33: 1). This form is quite rare. The diameter of its rim is 19 cm, and its height is 2.3 cm, and it may have been used to serve a wide range of sweets, from small sweets to various seeds, nuts, raisins, dried apricots, jida, berries, etc.

The next original form is a graceful handleless jug-shaped vessel with a hemispherical body and a wide neck (fig. 8.33: 2). The product is made of yellowish glass with overlaid spiral, broken and point motifs, similar in style to the aforementioned examples of the aroma holder, glass and vase. This piece was also created by the same master, as evidenced by the individual adhesion dots applied to

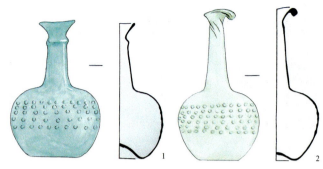

FIGURE 8.34   Kuva, flask, bulb-shaped form

contrast with the blue glass. Undoubtedly, a richly ornamented vessel would have had a more decorative use.

The last glass item from the third complex, a piece quite traditional for Kuva and dated to the 11th century, has the same shape as the wine glass (fig. 8.33: 3) and is yellowish in colour with a circular disc-shaped shield made of twisted glass threads at the base.

Glass products from *badrab* 3 once again show the expanding range of forms. These samples, the appearance of which reached a peak in the 11th century, undoubtedly replaced ceremonial ceramic dishes at the table and on the shelves decorating living rooms. During excavation (still unpublished), we observed such large sizes and a variety of shapes, colours and manufacturing elegance only in neighbouring regional capital centres, such as Akhsiket, Samarkand, Tashkent and Bukhara. Nevertheless, both according to our materials and ones from previous years, Kuva was among the largest producers and exporters of these products to the surrounding regions of Central Asia.

By the second half of the 12th to the early 13th centuries, in closed contexts in Kuva we observe a significant decrease in the number and a reduction in the range of glass products. This tendency includes two flask-shaped vessels obtained from the *badrab*s in the upper cultural level in excavation 5b at Kuva. A traditional blue glass flask from *badrab* 1 (fig. 8.34: 1) is small in size, and it is ornamented with several rows of small oval dents along the body, obtained in the process of blowing the vessel into the mould. The next bulb-shaped form of yellowish glass (fig. 8.34: 2) is close in size and ornamentation to the first. At the same time, for decorative purposes, the rim of the latter is slightly unfolded, creating oblique relief folds along the neck, and ends with a beak-shaped drain.

Among the ceramic and metal object found in an early 13th-century *badrab* at Samarkand (Afrasiab) was a single glass bowl-shaped vessel (fig. 8.35) with scaly relief ornamentation made from greenish glass blown into the shape (Mirzaakhmedov 2007: fig. 1: 4). Perhaps this is additional evidence of the reduced number of glass items in contexts from the second half of the 12th to the early 13th centuries.

FIGURE 8.35   Afrasiab, bowl with ornamentation

Thus, the presence of a significant number of glass products of different colours, shapes and purposes, demonstrate the unrivalled craftmanship the of glass blowers' products. We also believe that they were cheaper and, successfully competing with glazed ceramic dishes, began to oust *mehmankhana* from the shelves starting in the 11th century; the glazed ceramic dishes, in most cases, were already losing their artistic appeal.

On the basis of various closed contexts with ceramic and glass material from the 9th to early 13th centuries, we can conclude that if the height of glazed ceramics' popularity in Maverannahr falls on the 10th century, and since in the 11th century its gradual deterioration is observed, then glassmaking's peak and best achievements are recorded in the 11th century.

In this article we noted that the end of the 8th century was a key moment in the development of the economy, ideology and culture of the peoples of Central Asia. During this time it became part of the caliphate's new Afro-Eurasian empire.

This era was marked by the decrease of Zoroastrianism and the rise of Islam. The gradual disappearance of *dihqans* (lords) and the emergence of a new bureaucratic class forced the eviction of merchant aristocracies and *dihqans* from the urban centres, and the entry of new ethnic groups introduced new languages: Arabic and later Persian.

At the same time, Maverannahr's entry into the new economic space and the majority of educated people mastering Arabic, the language of science and culture, contributed to the latest scientific and technological achievements from the most developed western parts of the caliphate entering the region. Under the Abbasid caliphs, in the "House of Wisdom" in Baghdad, enormous work was carried out to collect and translate the most outstanding scholars and valuable ancient Greco-Roman

FIGURE 8.36   Maverannahr, bowls

FIGURE 8.37   Maverannahr, cups

writings into Arabic. These translations – in the form of manuscripts – as well as the migration of scientists, artisans and the educated classes spread far to the east.

Thus, we believe that some forms of glass production in Central Asia existed before these migrations, as evidenced by data from Chinese chronicles. But, in this era glassblowers began to migrate from the western parts of the empire and gradually introduce their products here.

According to archaeological material, this period is also marked by the appearance of the first baths, *badrab* and *tashnau* in the cities. Glassmaking and glazed ceramics are just part of this growth and point to the broader influence of the metropolis on the outskirts of the caliphate. In this region it was the impetus for a new cultural and industrial revolution, later called the Muslim Renaissance.

Our archaeological contexts show the entry and gradual transformation of glassmaking into one of the most significant, independent industries of medieval Maverannahr, and it is recorded from the end of the 8th century onwards.

We believe that the reason for its widespread introduction into the everyday life of the townspeople was due to the demand for medical care, more specifically, the treatment of a wide range of diseases using bloodletting cups, which were predominately made of glass. A little later, a much larger number pharmaceutical and chemical glassware forms, used in the manufacture and storage of drugs, appears.

Medical and pharmaceutical glassware – taking into account the chemical, physical, and hygienic advantages of glass in comparison with other materials, as well as its cheapness – was indispensable in the daily life of the common people. This propelled the development of glassmaking in Maverannahr and its widespread introduction into a number of other branches of handicraft production. This includes the appearance of the first samples of richly painted and glass-glazed ceramic tableware in large urban centres, as well as striking works of art to adorn the ceremonial halls of living rooms.

Perfumery dishes also become more common in this era, mainly consisting of small, richly decorated, coloured flasks and bottles that store blush, whitewash, rose oil and rose water, etc.

Starting in the second half of the 9th century and continuing in the 10th and 11th centuries, glassmaking reached such a scale that in closed archaeological contexts it is found in nearly equivalent as or even slightly larger proportions than ceramic samples. Richly decorated tableware was widespread: bowls (fig. 8.36), cups (fig. 8.37), vases, decanters, flasks, bottles, jugs, dishes (fig. 8.38), salad bowls, glasses, mugs, glasses and wine glasses; as well as vessels with special purposes, such as aroma bowls, inkpots, window glass, bracelets, *tuvak*s and *sumak*s. Less common are large alembics, glass sphero-conical vessels, spoons, medallions, funnels, rhytons and lids.

In closed archaeological contexts from the second half of the 9th to 12th centuries, along with richly ornamented coloured tableware, the presence of small alembics and other medical and pharmaceutical vessels continues to be recorded in many places. Along with the aforementioned presence of a large number of healers (*tabibs*) who had reception rooms in the cities, this may indicate the widespread introduction of medical knowledge to the population and, possibly, the presence of first-aid kits in homes. When children or older family members with a chronic disease were present in a household, the presence and storage, to one degree or another, of natural pharmaceuticals and medical devices apparently was mandatory.

FIGURE 8.38   Maverannahr, vessels

Thus, the glass material presented in this chapter confirms the data from historical sources describing the rise of the economy, culture and science, including medicine, between the 9th and early 13th centuries.

The Mongol invasion seems to have put an end to the development of glassmaking in Maverannahr, although no solid data are at our disposal to prove this. In most cases, artisans probably left and travelled elsewhere. The finds from the period between the 13th and 15th centuries are very fragmentary, and archaeological research in the late medieval cities of Uzbekistan is limited and has not yet yielded glass assemblages.

We note that in the closed contexts from the second half of the 12th century to the beginning of the 13th century, there are already significantly few glass products – including less variety as well as reduced quantities.

Glass undoubtedly played a huge role in the formation of the medical, pharmaceutical and chemical industries, as well as in the ceramic and other handicraft industries. It also occupied an important place within ceremonial tableware and adorned *mikhmankhana* shelves. But from the 12th to the beginning of the 13th centuries, in connection with the emerging economic crisis in the region and the increasing impoverishment of the population – clearly traced in the deterioration of the quality of ceramic products (Mirzaakhmedov 2008: 65–68) – the demand for glass, a fragile, less practical material in daily life, gradually declined.

Nevertheless, glassware was present in the wealthy houses of the aristocracy in limited quantities. This is indicated by the Chinese traveller Chang Chun's descriptions of Samarkand in the early years of the Mongol conquest (in the 1320s): "The city seemed rich to Chang Chun: everywhere copper vessels were visible, shining like gold, in addition, there was a lot of porcelain and glassware. They drank wine only from the latter" (Bartold 1965: 241). A century later, this is witnessed by Ibn Baṭṭūṭa when he passes through Khorezm, but in the form of imported Syrian goods: glass vessels, wooden spoons, grapes and amazing melons. He also describes the premise's rich decorations: beautiful carpets, walls upholstered with cloth and many niches, which each have silver vessels with gilding and Iraqi jugs (Ibragimov 1988: 75–76). Perhaps the latter could also have been made of glass. Dukan shops selling expensive ceremonial tableware, such as Chinese porcelain, ceramics and narrow-necked glass jugs of various colours, are also depicted in medieval book miniatures (*Miniatyuryi k proizvedeniyam Alishera Navoi* 1982: table 199). According to these miniatures, glass jugs were used for bottling wine drinks.

Also, although glass products were very beautiful and relatively cheap, in our opinion they nevertheless fell out of demand among the impoverished population of the region during the 12th century CE. In wealthy houses, it was replaced by more refined, coloured local and imported forms, as well as by Chinese porcelain. Metal vessels, which, according to scientific literature, by the 12th and early 13th centuries were also common, attained significant acclaim and refinement (Buryakov 1990: figs. 2–5; Beleniskij, Bentovich, and Bolshakov 1973: 287; Bartold 1965: 241).

From this point until the 15th century, the only realm where glassblowers continued to hone their craft was coloured window glass for the architectural monuments of Samarkand. Round, solid or cut glass panes of various colours – red, blue, green, yellow, violet, cherry and blue shades – were inserted into the window bars (*panjara*). They were found on many architectural monuments from the Timurid era – Gur Emir, Ishrat khan and Chinni khan (Davidovich 1953: 145–56) – as well as on a number of Shakhi Zinda mausoleums. It goes without saying that other architectural monuments from this era that have not been preserved were traditionally decorated with similar multicoloured glass-pane mosaics.

A handicraft closely related to glassmaking, irrigated architectural terracotta, was also widespread and used in limited quantities. Turquoise mosaic pieces were place on the monuments in Bukhara for the first time at the beginning of the 12th century (Kalyan Minaret, Vobkent Minaret, Magoki Attori Mosque). Then, from the 14th and 15th centuries on, this technique was often employed.

This article gives an overview of the glass production and glass typologies. These data depend on older excavations and previous studies. New data coming from recent and future archaeological excavations will give us further material to complete and revise this framework.

CHAPTER 9

Glass in the Bukhara Oasis, Uzbekistan

Yoko Shindo (1960–2018), Takako Hosokawa, Tamako Takeda, Toshiyasu Shinmen and Ayano Endo

1   Introduction

The Bukhara Oasis is located in Transoxiana, Uzbekistan, the region between two large rivers, the Amu Darya and the Syr Darya. This region was the centre of Sogdiana, although it was also influenced by Persian culture until the Islamic invasion.

Under the direction of Rocco Rante and Djamal Mirzaakhmedov, since 2009 the Louvre Museum has undertaken joint excavations and research projects with the Archaeological Institute of Samarkand at some sites: Paykend (2010–17), Ramitan (2012), Iskijkat (2014–15), Kakishtuvan (2016), site 250 (2017) and Bukhara (2017).

Mirzaakhmedov has created a summary of the excavated glass items in Uzbekistan and concluded that it was not until the 9th century, after the Islamic dynasty, that glassware production commenced in this area (Mirzaakhmedov 2011).

In all of the sites mentioned above, fragments of glassware were unearthed. We have participated in the excavation project at the Bukhara Oasis since 2014. We have analysed the excavated glass items from various angles using the following means: arrangement and registration of the articles; classification of styles (typology); drawing figures; photographing artifacts; and chemical analysis.

In this chapter, in an attempt to evaluate glass from the Bukhara Oasis in the historical context of Islamic glass, we examine the glass artifacts unearthed in the following six sites: Paykend, Ramitan, Iskijkat, Kakishtuvan, site 250 and Bukhara.[1] The approach used stems from the viewpoint of archaeology, glass typology and chemical analysis, and it specifically focuses on the site of Paykend, where the largest amount of glassware was found.

2   Study of Early Islamic Glass Excavated at the Site of Paykend[2]

Yoko Shindo

2.1   *Finding Spots of Glass*

The site of Paykend is a massive tell that includes settlements from the ancient period as well as the Middle Ages. The site contains a citadel (trench D), a lower city (shahrestan 1: trench A, B, J; shahrestan 2: trench F), the north rampart of the shahrestan (trench C), the south rampart of the shahrestan (trench H), a pottery quarter along the canal (trench E) and several suburban areas, including a caravansary and necropolis (rabad: trench G, I, K).[3]

As a result of the 2010–17 excavations, we have registered 290 pieces of glass vessels, consisting of portions of the rim, neck, base or handle, some with decoration, and artifacts related to glass production (Fig. 9.1).

2.1.1   Citadel
The citadel is situated on the top of the tell and was the centre of the city of Paykend. Our mission performed an excavation in a section of the tell (trench D). From this area, we registered 11 sherds of glass vessels, including seven rim, base or neck fragments belonging to beakers or bottles and four pieces of glass cullet and slag, which are related to glass production.

2.1.2   Lower City (Shahrestan)
Below the citadel, is a settlement designated as a shahrestan. It is divided into two sections: shahrestan 1 and shahrestan 2. Although the shahrestan had been inhabited since before the Islamic invasion of the 8th century, and despite it being an important city for the Sogdians, we have only discovered Islamic glass. Further, almost all the glass found dates from the 9th to the 11th centuries.

---

1   The arrangement of excavated items has not been completed for the site of Bukhara, where excavation began in 2017. This data will be further discussed after the arrangement has been completed.

2   Sections 2 and 5 of the chapter has been written by Yoko Shindo. For publishing, some revisions have been added by Rante and Hosokawa, as the author passed away suddenly in September 2018.

3   The excavated area of the site has been designated as a "trench" by the director of the Louvre mission, Rante, and areas A to K, excavated up to 2016, are shown in map fig. 9.1.

In total, 193 (about 66% of the total) fragments of glass vessels were unearthed in these two areas, which include trench A, B and J in shahrestan 1 and trench F in shahrestan 2. We registered 11 pieces from trench A (fig. 9.2), 156 from trench B (figs. 9.3–8), four from trench J (fig. 9.8) in shahrestan 1 and 22 from trench F in shahrestan 2 (fig. 9.9).

It is worth noting that the 156 pieces uncovered in trench B in shahrestan 1 comprise more than 50% of the total registered pieces. Moreover, around 18% of the registered glass was excavated in strata 3736 and 3792, the garbage layers, which are located in the courtyard in trench B. A Samanid coin, which was issued in Binkent in 918–19, was also found there; thus, these two strata can be dated to the 10th century.

2.1.3 North Rampart and South Rampart of the Shahrestan

The north rampart (trench C) and the south rampart (trench H) of the shahrestan were excavated by our team. As a result, we found eight pieces of glass in trench C in the north rampart and 39 pieces in trench H in the south rampart (fig. 9.10 and fig. 9.11). From these data, it can be determined that cupping vessels were concentrated in trench H.

2.1.4 Pottery Quarter

Significant building features were found in trench E along the canal. The buildings were determined to be pottery workshops, including some kilns for unglazed and green-glazed pottery. The total number of glass fragments unearthed was 31 (fig. 9.12), among which four sherds of glass had threaded decoration, three had moulded decoration and the remaining were coarse fragments. The remains of glass debris or glaze articles used in the manufacture process were also found here; as such, it is interesting that not only waste from pottery kilns but also glass-works articles were included. It is necessary to investigate if glass manufacturing existed in this pottery quarter or if these artifacts were merely waste from other areas.

2.1.5 Suburban Areas (Rabad)

In trench G, I and K in the suburban areas (rabad), as well as in a test trench, only eight fragments of glass vessels and glass debris have been found. However, the quantities are only useful for reference purposes, as they cannot be accurately compared otherwise due to differences in the excavation methods used in these and other areas.[4]

From the data discussed, and keeping the unearthed areas in mind, it can be concluded that the proportion of discovered glass vessels is high in the shahrestan. In particular, glass products are heavily concentrated in chantier B, comprising more than 50% of the total sherds unearthed; on the other hand, the proportion of discovered artifacts related to glass production is high in areas other than the shahrestan.

2.2 Material

Analysis of the glass materials[5] should consider such factors as transparency, colour, hardness, bubbles and surface conditions, including weathering. However, the surfaces of the Paykend glass are extremely damaged due to weathering. Therefore, it is difficult to accurately determine the original glass material through either an examination with the naked eye or the results of the chemical analysis.

Under these circumstances, we have classified the glass materials based on colour tones. When glass artisans add plant ash or natron to sand during the production of glass material,[6] the raw material contains impurities. As a result, the glass contains natural tones of pale green or pale blue. Alternatively, they may add metallic oxide pigments for colouring or decolouring. We have classified Paykend glass into the following three groups: 1) natural coloured glass, 2) decolourised colourless glass, and 3) intentionally coloured glass (fig. 9.13).

2.2.1 Natural Coloured glass (fig. 9.14)

The unearthed natural coloured glass consists of tones of pale purple, pale bluish green, pale green and pale yellowish brown. Green and blue colours result from the presence of iron oxide or copper oxide, which exists in sand as impurities. The differences in the shades of the colour and colour tones are due to the thickness of the glass or the redox state during firing. At the site of Paykend natural coloured glass with a green tone is popular. The glass vessels made from this material have some characteristic manufacturing techniques, including the unique pontil mark seen on the base; this is further explained below. It is thought that this natural coloured glass was manufactured in Paykend or in the neighbouring Bukhara Oasis.

---

4   Regarding the remains of the caravanserai in the rabad, excavations were conducted under the direction of Mirzaakhmedov of the Uzbek mission before the joint survey with the French mission began. Each mission has different methods for excavating. Additionally, there is no comparison between this trench and other areas of excavation in terms of the quantity of unearthed items.
5   Regarding the chemical composition, see section 9.4 by Shinmen and Endo.
6   There are two stages for manufacturing glass: the first stage is glass-making, which refers to manufacturing glass material, and the second is glasswork, which refers to the manufacture of glass products using artificially created materials.

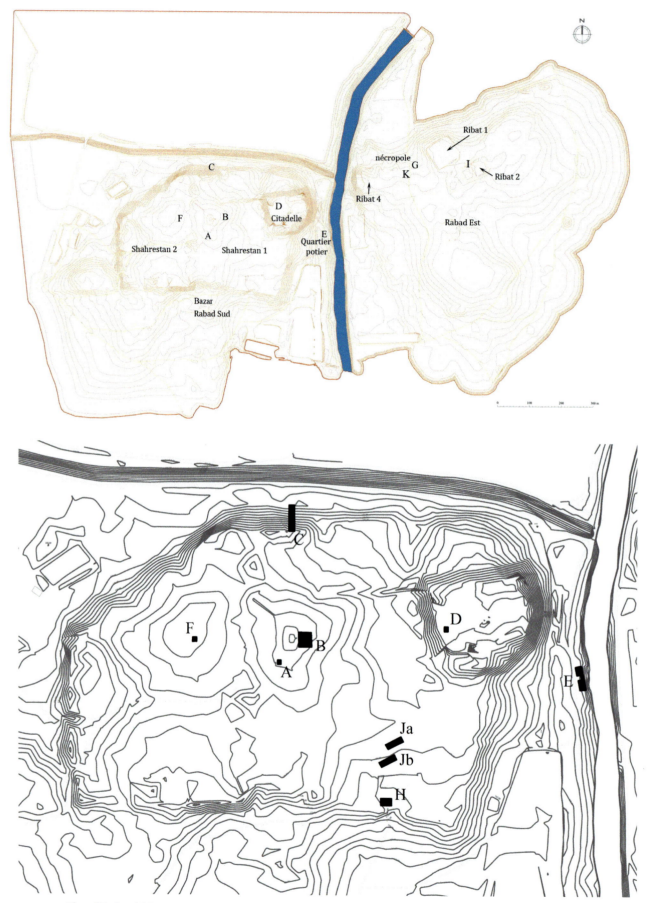

FIGURE 9.1   Plan of Paykend. Maps MAFOUB

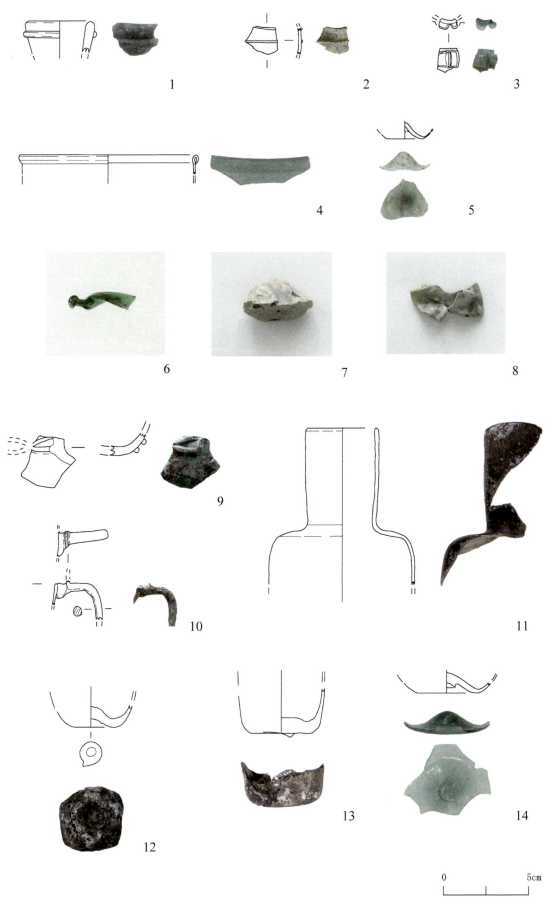

FIGURE 9.2 Paykend, trench A&D. Fragments of glass vessels. Drawings Yoko Shindo and Noriko Horiuchi: Photos Yoshie Abe, Tamako Takeda and Tami Ishida

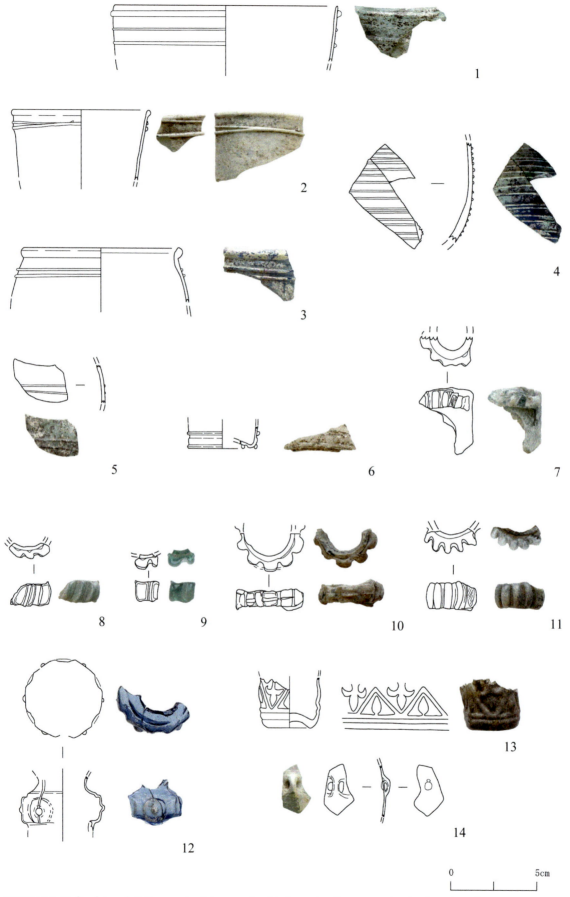

FIGURE 9.3 Paykend, trench B. Fragments of glass vessels with decoration. Drawings Yoko Shindo and Noriko Horiuchi: Photos Yoshie Abe, Tamako Takeda and Tami Ishida

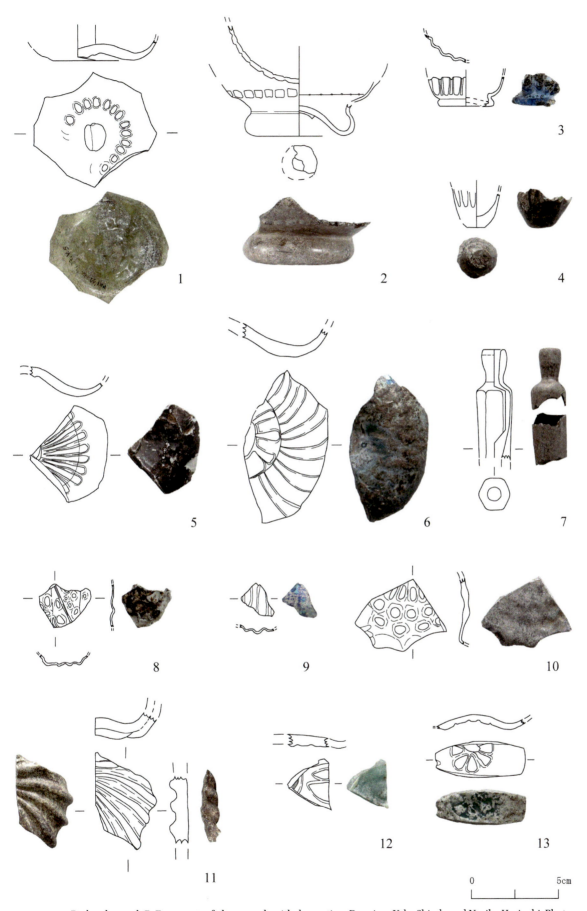

FIGURE 9.4 Paykend, trench B. Fragments of glass vessels with decoration. Drawings Yoko Shindo and Noriko Horiuchi; Photos Yoshie Abe, Tamako Takeda and Tami Ishida

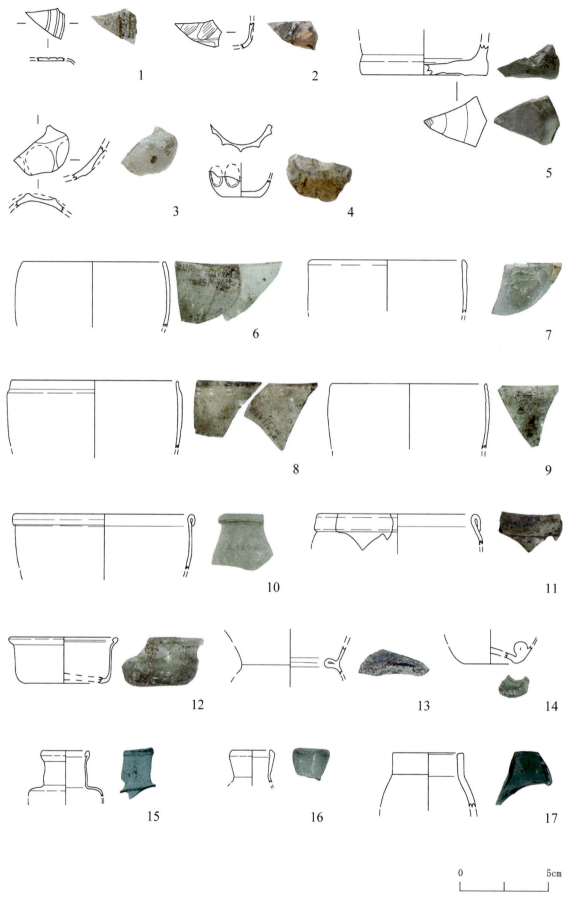

FIGURE 9.5 Paykend, trench B. Fragments of glass vessels. Drawings Yoko Shindo and Noriko Horiuchi: Photos Yoshie Abe, Tamako Takeda and Tami Ishida

GLASS IN THE BUKHARA OASIS, UZBEKISTAN

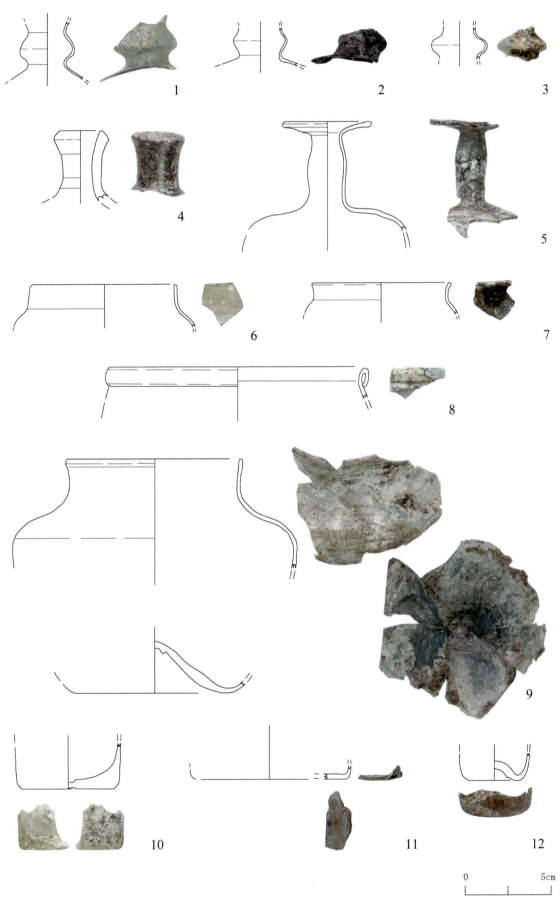

FIGURE 9.6 Paykend, trench B. Fragments of glass vessels. Drawings Yoko Shindo and Noriko Horiuchi: Photos Yoshie Abe, Tamako Takeda and Tami Ishida

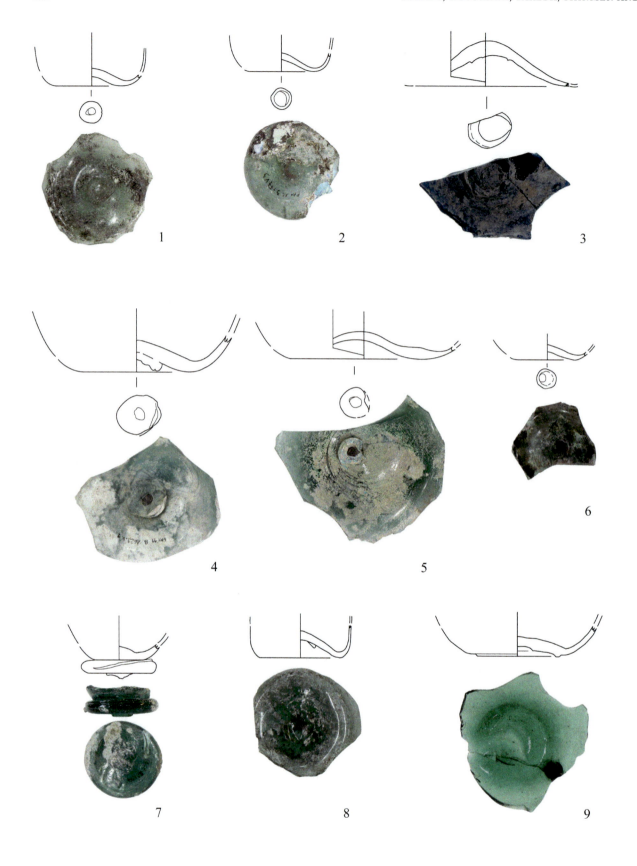

FIGURE 9.7 Paykend, trench B. Fragments of glass vessels. Drawings Yoko Shindo and Noriko Horiuchi: Photos Yoshie Abe, Tamako Takeda and Tami Ishida

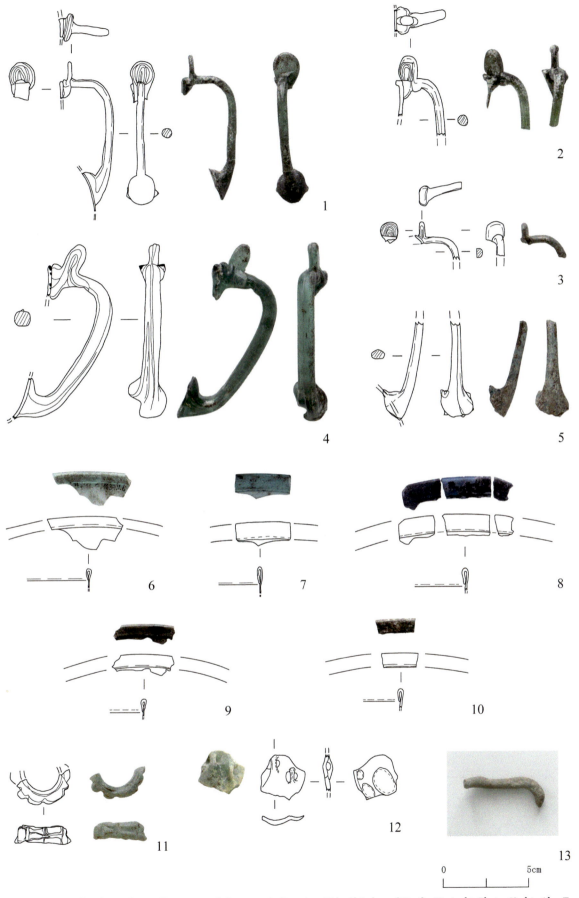

FIGURE 9.8 Paykend, trench B&J. Fragments of glass vessels. Drawings Yoko Shindo and Noriko Horiuchi: Photos Yoshie Abe, Tamako Takeda and Tami Ishida

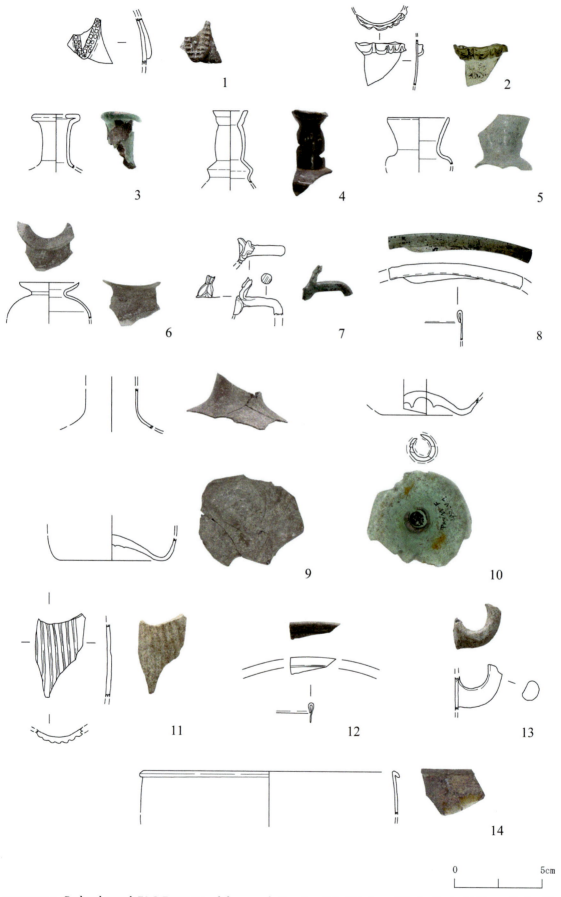

FIGURE 9.9 Paykend, trench F&C. Fragments of glass vessels. Drawings Yoko Shindo and Noriko Horiuchi: Photos Yoshie Abe, Tamako Takeda and Tami Ishida

FIGURE 9.10　Paykend, trench H. Fragments of glass vessels. Drawings Yoko Shindo and Noriko Horiuchi: Photos Yoshie Abe, Tamako Takeda and Tami Ishida

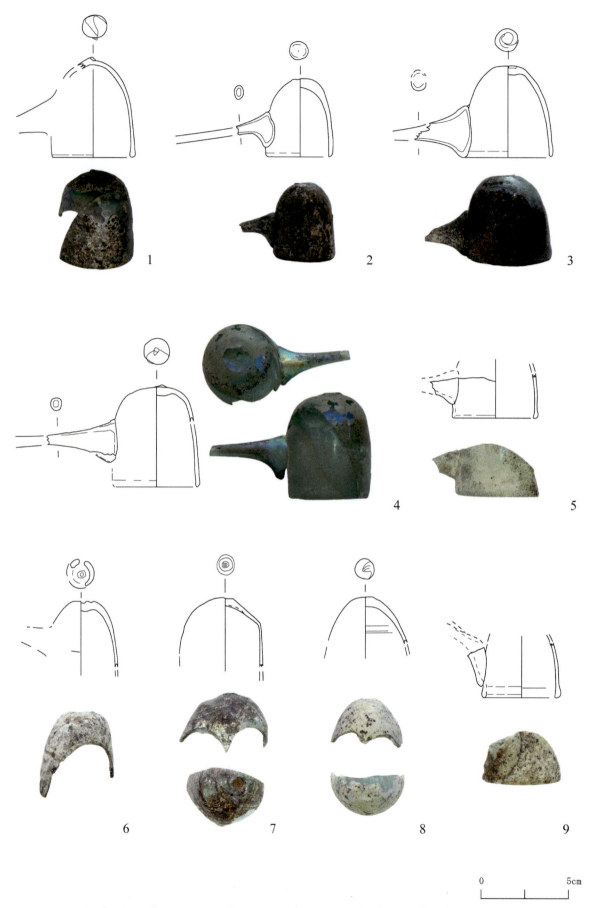

FIGURE 9.11   Paykend, trench H. Fragments of cupping vessels. Drawings Yoko Shindo and Noriko Horiuchi: Photos Yoshie Abe, Tamako Takeda and Tami Ishida

FIGURE 9.12 Trench E. Fragments of glass vessels and glass cullet and slags. Drawings Yoko Shindo and Noriko Horiuchi: Photos Yoshie Abe, Tamako Takeda and Tami Ishida

FIGURE 9.13
Three colour groups of glass materials. Photo Yoshie Abe

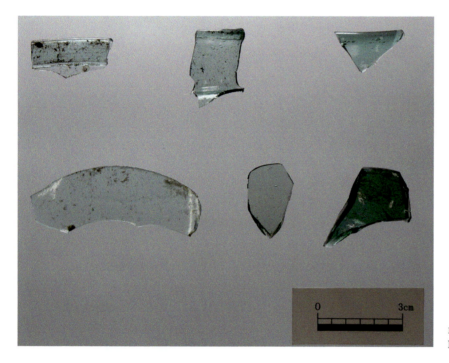

FIGURE 9.14
Natural coloured glass. Photo Yoshie Abe

Chemical analysis reveals that the natural bluish-green materials used in the vessels and artifacts related to glass production have a high potassium and magnesium value characteristic of the products made in the Bukhara Oasis; however, chemical analysis indicates that one example of olive-green glass contains a different element (fig. 9.15).[7]

2.2.2 Decolourised Colourless glass (fig. 9.16)

Decolourised colourless glass can be divided broadly into high quality and low quality. Seven examples are regarded as high-quality glass, and five of them have cut decoration. Glass of this type is almost completely decolourised, and white spots and thin layers are the result of weathering.

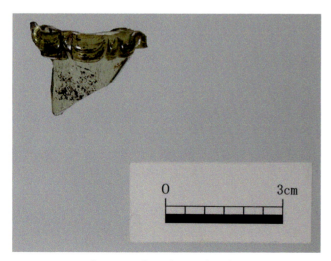

FIGURE 9.15 Olive-green glass. Photo Yoshie Abe

7 See section 9.4 by Shinmen and Endo.

FIGURE 9.16
Decolourised colourless glass. Photo Yoshie Abe

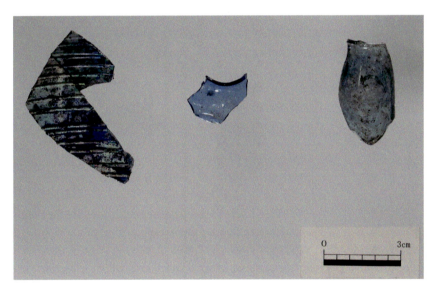

FIGURE 9.17
Coloured glass. Photo Yoshie Abe

The conditions of colourless glass of low quality are apt to deteriorate in quality. Most fragments of this type have surface covered with thick black layers, which indicate severe weathering. As a result of chemical analysis, it has been clarified that the composition of high-quality and low-quality types is different. In particular, high-quality colourless material seems to be closely related to the composition of the most commonly found Islamic glass in Iran, unlike the local products, which have high levels of potassium and magnesium. The details of this analytical study are dealt with in section 9.4.

2.2.3 Coloured Glass (fig. 9.17)

Five examples from the unearthed glass are thought to belong to this category. Blue glass was made by intentionally adding copper oxide and cobalt oxide. Two of the fragments have moulded decoration. The unearthed cullet and slag related to glass production in Paykend are green coloured. Therefore, there is a possibility that blue glass made with colouring agents was not manufactured in this city.

2.3 Manufacturing Techniques

The manufacturing techniques for glass vessels include two stages: shaping the vessel and the shaping processes for the rim and base. Both stages are performed while the glass material is hot. Vessels are shaped using the blowing technique (using a blowpipe), and a mould is used along with this. In the shaping processes for the rim or base parts, the characteristics of the periods during which and

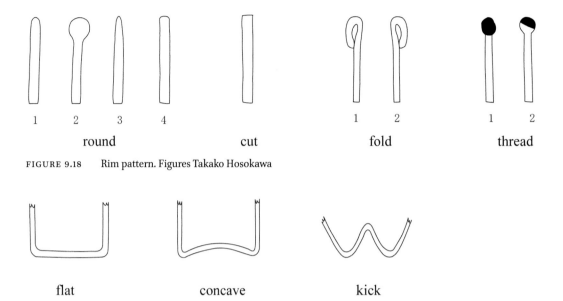

FIGURE 9.18   Rim pattern. Figures Takako Hosokawa

FIGURE 9.19   Base pattern. Figures Takako Hosokawa

regions where the glass products were manufactured are clearly shown. This section focuses on the rims, bases and handles of the Paykend glass.

A variety of techniques are seen in the glass vessels found by the Japanese mission in their excavations of the site of Fustat in Egypt, which is notable for the amount of Islamic glass it contains. In contrast, the glass vessels found in the Bukhara region, including the site of Paykend, are less skillfully made products and were made utilising only a few techniques. This observation indicates the local characteristics of the Paykend glass.

2.3.1   Rim

The rims reveal several patterns. The first pattern is a round rim with surface tension, which was fabricated by reheating the edge after cutting the vessel from the blowpipe. This is the most popular rim pattern in Paykend. This pattern can be categorised based on its detailed processing: simple (round 1), bulging (round 2), tapering (round 3) or flattened by pressing the top (round 4) (see fig. 9.18).

The next pattern is an unworked rim, which is created by cutting the vessel from the blowpipe after the glass has cooled; however, this pattern is rare.

The third pattern is an inward or outward folded rim, which is observed in beakers and small bottles found at Paykend.

The fourth pattern is a threaded rim, which resembles stringing a glass thread on the edge. The thread either covers the edge entirely (thread 1) or is only partially applied to the round rim (thread 2).

In addition to these patterns, some other variations are found. For example, the edge of the rim is bent by strongly pressing it; however, this is not categorised as a folded rim.[8] In comparison to the rim patterns of the Fustat glass or other general examples of Islamic glass, fewer and less complicated variations exist.

2.3.2   Base

The types of and techniques for the bases are closely related to the shapes of the vessels. Simple flat, concave and thick types are the most frequently seen. The kick type consists of a cone-shaped base created by pushing up the centre of the base, while the concave type includes a gently rising base (see fig. 9.19).

There are fewer base variations compared to the examples unearthed in other archaeological sites

A pontil mark can be seen on the backside of these vessels. It was made using a pontil rod, which is a glassmaking tool. The rod, tipped with a bit of hot glass, is attached to the base of the vessel and then removed, leaving a scar on the base. This characteristic double ringed pontil mark, which was popular in Paykend glass, was generally rare in Islamic glass; thus, it is worth mentioning as a special, local characteristic of the Paykend site.

2.3.3   Handles

There are a variety of handle shapes and sizes found on vessels. The method of attaching the handle to the vessel is part of the shaping process. After the softened glass

---

8   A "folded rim" is a rim that is folded intentionally so as to double it, while a "bent rim" is a rim that is bent by pressing the edge strongly and is unintentional.

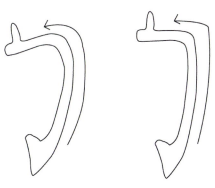

FIGURE 9.20   Handle pattern. Figures Takako Hosokawa

FIGURE 9.21   Thread decoration glass from trench H. Photo Yasuko Fujii

cane is attached to the lower part of the vessel, it is pulled upward and attached to the upper part of the vessel.

Although the handle is usually smooth and rounded, the handles of Paykend glass vessels are not upwardly rounded to form a gentle line but rather are horizontally extended and bent, as shown in fig. 9.20. This is characteristic of the vessel handles made in this area. There is a possibility that the loop-like handle was attached to a cylindrical cup and used as a mug.

2.4   Decoration

Paykend glass is mainly dated to the 9th–11th centuries, when decorated glass developed significantly in Syria, Egypt, Iraq and Iran. Three typical kinds of decoration belonging to this period – namely, lustre stained, impressed, and scratched – have not been found in our excavations thus far.

Threaded and moulded decoration was used widely before the 9th century; thus, these two decoration types are the most common in Paykend. Among the 61 examples of decorated glass, there are 27 pieces with threaded decoration and 23 pieces with moulded decoration.

2.4.1   Threaded Decoration

A total of 27 fragments with threaded decoration have been unearthed. This includes three in trench D of the citadel; one in trench A of shahrestan 1; 12 in trench B of shahrestan 1; one in trench J of shahrestan 1; three in trench F of shahrestan 2; three in trench H of the rampart; and four in trench E of pottery quarter. The types of threaded decoration are classified as such: a thin trail winding around the rim or a spiral around the body; a thick wavy belt, mainly around the neck; a snake-like winding or zigzag pattern making a special shape; and others.

Five examples have a thin trail coiled around the rim. One example found in trench H (fig. 9.21) has a colourless

FIGURE 9.22   Thread decoration glass from trench A. Photo Yasuko Fujii

body and bluish-green threads. The second, found in trench E, has a pale bluish-green body and blue threads. The third example, also from trench E, has a pale-brown body and dark-brown threads.

Regarding the two examples found in trench A and E, the thread is thicker and has a decorative winding pattern; these feature supposedly date to the period before the 9th century (fig. 9.22).[9]

Nine fragments with thick wavy threaded decoration have been unearthed: five in trench B, and one each in

---

9 Regarding the examples unearthed in Nishapur in Iran, see Kröger 1995: 106–107, no. 151; for Otrar in Kazakhstan, see Baypakov 2011: 55, ill. 35.

FIGURE 9.23 Thread decoration glass from trench B. Photo Yasuko Fujii

FIGURE 9.24 Thread decoration glass from trench F. Photo Yasuko Fujii

trench D, E, F and J (fig. 9.23). Most of them are of the bluish-green colour that is characteristic of Paykend glass, but one unearthed in trench F is olive green. Since this sole piece's chemical composition is different and the wavy thread belt is narrow, it can be assumed that it was produced in a different location.

Bottles with a wide wavy threaded decoration around the neck are distributed around Transoxiana and also in the area west of the Amu Darya River,[10] for example, in Suse in Iran (Kervran and Raugeulle 1984: fig. 7–15). As for the neck fragments with wavy threaded decoration unearthed in Paykend, their colour ranges from a bluish-green to an olive-green tinge. They include thin white layers due to weathering.

The glass piece, which comes from trench F, has a wavy threaded decoration with stamped dots on it (fig. 9.24). It was unearthed in the lower part of the burnt stratum dated to 796, so it can be dated to before the 8th century. This type of threaded decoration is similar to that on a small bottle from Dal'verzin Tepe in southern Uzbekistan, which was excavated in 1999 by the Japanese mission (Tanabe and Hori et al. 1999: 150–51) and has a human face stamped on the body.

2.4.2 Moulded Decoration

A total of 23 fragments with moulded decoration have been unearthed. Among them, 17 are from trench B, one from trench J, one from trench C, one from trench H and three from trench E. Most of the unearthed glass fragments with moulded decoration consist of simple patterns such as rib, honeycomb and flowers (Mirzaakhmedov 2011: 98, figs. 3–4,5 and 11, and 111, figs. 12–4, 5, 7, 8, 9 and 16).[11] The following two examples unearthed in trench B deserve special mention.

The first example is composed of two fragments of blue glass that were joined together, and it has a continuous pattern of a dot inside a circle (fig. 9.25). It was found in stratum 3736 of trench B, which is dated to the 10th century, as mentioned above. It is a blue hexahedron bottle decorated with a motif of a dot inside a circle on each side of the body using the mould-blowing technique. One small bottle and two pitchers with a similar motif are reported in the finds of Afrasiab (Old Samarkand),[12] so it is more likely that this type of vessel was produced in Afrasiab rather than in Paykend.

The glass fragment found in trench B has a moulded decorative pattern of trefoils in zigzag panels (fig. 9.26). Two similar examples have been found in Nishapur, Iran,

---

10 Regarding the examples unearthed in Afrasiab, see Shishkina 1986: pls. 2-14 and 21, pl. 3-3, pl. 4-7, pl. 5-4, pl. 6-5 and 9, and pl. 7; for Arch Akhsiket in Uzbekistan, see Mirzaakhmedov 2011: 108, fig. 11-7; for Otrar in Kazakhstan, see Baypakov 2011: 15, fig. 2-2 and 54-55, ills. 23 and 24; for Taraz in Kazakhstan, see Baypakov 2011: 17, figs. 3-1-3 and 29, fig. 11-11; for Kulbuk in Tajikistan, see Yakuvov 2011: 76, fig. 17 (the upper row) and 63, ill. 8.

11 Good quality honeycomb moulded glass is kept in the Paykend Historical Museum, and Mirzaakhmedov refers to it. I was permitted to see the glass in the museum through the kindness of the director of the museum.

12 For the small bottle, see Shishkina 1986: pl. 6–16; for the pitchers, see Khakimov 2004: 139, fig. 241. In addition to this, one blue glass example with a similar pattern is displayed in the Afrasiab Museum.

FIGURE 9.25 Moulded decoration glass from trench B. Photo Yasuko Fujii

FIGURE 9.26 Moulded decoration glass from trench B. Photo Yasuko Fujii

FIGURE 9.27 Pinched decoration glass from trench B. Photo Yasuko Fujii

FIGURE 9.28 Facet-cut decoration glass from trench B. Photo Yasuko Fujii

which are reported in the catalogue compiled by Jens Kröger (1995: 93–94, nos. 131 and 132).

2.4.3 Tooled and Pinched Decoration

There are five pieces with tooled decoration.

As for pinched decoration, one was unearthed in trench B, and another was unearthed in trench J (fig. 9.27). Their colours are unclear because their entire surfaces are covered with white layers due to weathering, but they are presumably pale bluish green. The decoration is made in the way that the body is pinched while the glass material is hot. This technique was also used in glass from the late Roman period and in Sasanian glass. It was not frequently used in Islamic glass in and after the 9th century, so it is possible that these products date to before the 9th century.

One fragment found in trench E has an uneven ridge-like decoration around the neck of a small bottle, which was worked sideways with a tool. The other two do not have this decoration but have a tube-like ridge inside the vessel. They are included in the count since work with a tool was performed.

2.4.4 Cut Decoration

There are five pieces with cut decoration among the glass found in Paykend. Most of them were excavated in layers dated to the 9th and 10th centuries. Two types of cut decoration techniques are seen. One is a facet-cut decoration consisting of a pattern of circles, which is an extension of Sasanian glass decoration. There are four fragments with facet-cut techniques (fig. 9.28), and one fragment with a

TABLE 9.1 Unearthed glass by district and classification

	Number of registered items	Vessel fragment	Item related to production	Decoration*	Threaded	Molded	Tooled	Cut	Others	Cupping vessels*
Citadel										
Trench D	11	7	4	3	3					
Shahrestan 1										
Trench A	11	12	0	1	1					
Trench B	156	155	1	38	12	17	3	5	1	
Trench J	4	3	1	3	1	1	1			
Shahrestan 2										
Trench F	22	22	0	3	3					
Rampart										
Trench C	8	8	0	1		1				
Trench H	39	38	1	4	3	1				25
Pottery Quarter										
Trench E	31	22	9	8	4	3	1			1
Suburb										
Trench G										
Trench I										
Trench K	2	1	1							
Ribat4	1		1							
T3	4	4								4
TB Nord	1	1								
	290	272	18	61	27	23	5	5	1	30

linear-cut technique. In the former four fragments, the walls are thinner, and the cutting is less, in comparison to Sasanian glass. A continuous circle pattern is arranged on the entire surface, which is a smaller circle than those seen in Sasanian glass. All of the facet-cut and linear-cut glass was found in trench B. They were all made from high-quality material that was completely colourless. Since the artifacts related to the high-quality colourless material have not been found in Paykend and the decoration was widely favoured in the Persian area, they are thought to have been imported from the area west of Amu Darya.

2.5 Shapes

Since almost all the artifacts that have been found are small fragments, with the exception of the cupping vessels, we cannot completely restore their shapes. Accordingly, I will give rough analogies of the fragments' shapes using artifacts excavated by the Uzbek and other missions as a reference.[13]

Mirzaakhmedov presents the multiple types of glass tableware unearthed in concentrated quantities in shahrestan 1 in the site of Paykend that date to the 10th century (Mirzaakhmedov 2011: 100–102); thus, I would like to briefly examine them here (see figs. 9.29 and 9.30).[14]

When it comes to the shapes, he mentions two types of small cups: cylindrical and flaring. The colours include clear green, yellow and blue. In addition to the cups, there are mugs, which have a cylindrical body with moulded decoration and a loop-like handle, a moulded decorated bottle with a small handle and various kinds of small bottles.

Moreover, his excavations yielded a large bottle believed to be a decanter,[15] a pot-like jar, pitchers with handles

---

13 Since the Soviet era, the Paykend site has attracted the attention of archaeologists, and the excavations by the Russian and the Uzbekistan teams were conducted after this era. Some of the excavated artifacts are now exhibited in a museum located next to the site.

14 Figs. 3 and 12 in Mirzaakhmedov 2011 are retraced.

15 The measuring result shows us that the capacity of the same type of bottle is approximately one litre. See Abdullaev 1981: ill. 1:1, 2.

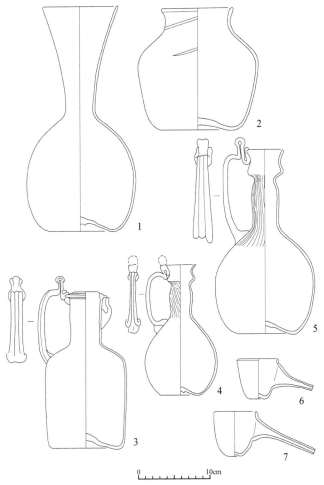

FIGURE 9.29 Artifacts excavated by the Uzbek mission (Mirzaakhmedov 2011: 98, Fig.3)

used as tableware and cupping vessels[16] used for medical purposes (Vaudour 1996). Various kinds of daily glassware were also found in the general residences dating from the 10th to the early 11th centuries in Paykend. Some of them have moulded or threaded decoration (Mirzaakhmedov 2011: 102).

Artifacts found during our excavations indicate that shapes similar to those of the abovementioned cups, bottles of various sizes, jars, pitchers and cupping vessels also existed. Based on the overall distribution of the glass objects unearthed, it is clear that a large number were from the shahrestan, as mentioned by Mirzaakhmedov, and were particularly concentrated in layers 3736 and 3792.

As for cups, only rims or base parts have been found; however, it can be assumed that small cups existed that were similar to the cylindrical and flaring types mentioned by Mirzaakhmedov. Regarding the small cup unearthed in trench B (fig. 9.31), a fragment from the rim to the base remains intact, and it is similar to the cylindrical type mentioned by Mirzaakhmedov.

It can be inferred that the fragments whose necks remain were parts of bottles. They are divided into large bottles and small bottles based on the size of the neck. From the fact that a wavy, belt-like threaded decoration was applied near the rim part of a large-sized bottle, fragments with this type of decoration can be inferred to have belonged to a large-sized bottle. There is also a hexahedron bottle among the small-sized bottles (fig. 9.32).

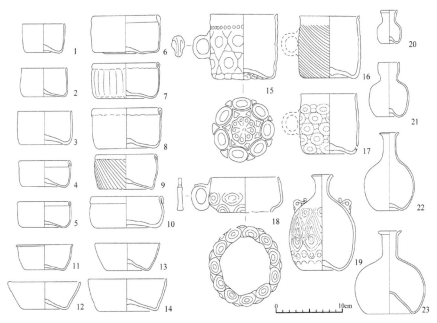

FIGURE 9.30 Artifacts excavated by the Uzbek mission (Mirzaakhmedov 2011: 111, Fig.12)

---

16 Mirzaakhmedov regards this as an alembic.

FIGURE 9.31 Fragment of small cup. Photo Yasuko Fujii

FIGURE 9.32 Fragment of bottle. Photo Yasuko Fujii

FIGURE 9.33 Fragment of large pot. Photo Yasuko Fujii

FIGURE 9.34 Handle. Photo Yasuko Fujii

For pots, a rim fragment and a base fragment were excavated from the same location in trench B, and they are supposedly part of the same object, although the body is missing (fig. 9.33). The estimated rim diameter is 10.0 cm. Small-sized bottles with an estimated rim diameter of 3.4 cm have also been unearthed.

Handles believed to have been attached to pitchers mostly consist of fragments. They are not rounded to form a gentle line but are extended horizontally and bent, as mentioned above (fig. 9.34). There is a possibility that one loop-like handle belonged to a mug.

Many cupping vessels were unearthed, particularly in trench H (fig. 9.35). There is a possibility that they were dumped there by doctors and others who used these special vessels. Additionally, there are four examples whose shapes are clearly recognisable.

Although there is no mention of the Paykend glass in the report by Mirzaakhmedov, panes have been excavated here, as shown in the reports from other archaeological sites (fig. 9.36). It is believed that these panes would have fit into the wall as window glass,[17] and there are some large examples, which have a diameter of around 40 cm, and these large-sized panes are considered to have had other uses.

---

17 In Afrasiab, window glass attached to stucco was found. Shishkina 1986: pls. 12 and 13.

FIGURE 9.35
Cupping vessel. Photo Yasuko Fujii

FIGURE 9.36
Fragment of window pane. Photo Yasuko Fujii

2.6   Artifacts Related to Glass Production

Large amounts of raw glass material and glass waste unearthed indicate the production of glass products in Paykend.[18] This clearly indicates that glass production was carried out in Paykend. Additional examples were also excavated in areas other than inside the shahrestan (see table 9.1), which indicates that the production sites were not in the ordinary residential area of the town but in the extended neighbourhood.

I previously presented a paper at the congress of the 20th AIHV (International Association for the History of Glass) related to the probability of glass production and production sites in Paykend, including the examples found in the Paykend Historical Museum (Shindo 2017). After this, the chemical analysis of the artifacts related to production verified that the chemical composition of their raw materials was different from that of common Islamic glass. A chemical analysis of the glass products was also performed, but a more detailed examination will be needed to reveal the connection between the artifacts related to glass production and the glass products.[19]

---

18   Although the examples in fig. 9.12 have turned into glass, it is not believed that they were produced in the process of making glassware; rather they were likely melted glaze and the like from pottery kilns.

19   See section 9.4 by Shinmen and Endo.

In the abovementioned presentation, I indicated that there were high-quality colourless-glass and cut-glass products at the site of Paykend that were similar in style to the Islamic glass made in Iran. In addition, the fact that those products were different from other local products in terms of chemical composition enhanced the probability that they were imports from Iran.

In conclusion, there is no doubt that glasswork was performed at Paykend; however, further studies are needed to reveal whether glassmaking, the process of compounding glass materials, was performed. At present, a study of glass materials such as sand and plant ash is in progress.

3 Other Main Sites in the Bukhara Oasis

Takako Hosokawa and Tamako Takeda

Since 2012, Ramitan, Iskijkat, Kakishtuvan, site 250 and Bukhara have been excavated in an attempt to identify each site's functions and determine the relationships among them within the Bukhara Oasis.

In this section, we discuss the remarkable glass objects uncovered in the abovementioned five sites and examine the artifacts through glass chronology and typology.

3.1 Ramitan

The site of Ramitan contains a citadel (trenches A, B, D and E), a lower city (shahrestan 1: trench C), a suburban areas (rabad: trenches F, G and H), and the Islamic city[20] (fig. 9.37). Settlement at the site of Ramitan is divided into two periods; before the Islamic invasion of the 8th century, known as the pre-Islamic period, and after the Islamic invasion, known as the Islamic period.

People had lived in the citadel and shahrestan since the 3rd century BCE. After the Islamic invasion, the urban functions of the site declined. However, the rabad and the Islamic city had been developing since the 5th century. The site expanded to the west and south and was occupied until the 15th century.

As a result of our work from 2012 to 2018, 42 glass vessel pieces were registered, including rim, neck and base fragments, some of which contained decoration.

3.1.1 Citadel and Lower City (Shahrestan)

In total, five pieces of glass articles were unearthed in the citadel and the shahrestan. They were found in the surface layers, and therefore, they likely cannot be categorised as Islamic glass.

3.1.2 Suburban Area (Rabad)

Sections of the rabad were excavated, and 37 pieces from glass objects were registered from trench F, G and H (figs. 9.38 and 9.39). It should be mentioned that one piece of facet-cut decoration glass was discovered in trench F.

The facet-cut glass was found in the layer thought to belong to the period between the 6th and 7th centuries. This layer is located just above the lowest layer, which includes fragments of pottery dates to the 5th and 6th centuries by Carbon 14 Dating.

This glass article is colourless with a blue tinge. A continuous circle pattern is arranged on the entire face. The wall is thicker and the cutting is deeper in comparison to Islamic facet-cut glass.[21] As a result, we assume that the glass is an example of Sasanian facet-cut glass.[22]

Aside from this piece of facet-cut glass, most of glass fragments belong to the period between the 9th and 11th centuries.

Additionally, we registered three fragments with threaded decoration. Two of them are classified as having a thick wavy belt around the neck; this is characteristic of pieces from Transoxiana. There are panes that are thought to have fit into the wall as window glass. One neck of a small bottle, one base fragment and one base of a lamp were also unearthed.

In trench G, most of the glass fragments were from the upper layers. One glass piece with moulded decoration, which has a simple rib pattern, and one glass piece with tooled decoration were uncovered. The latter piece has an uneven ridge-like decoration around the neck, which appears to be from a small bottle, that was worked sideways with a tool. There are also fragments of glass pane, a neck from a small bottle and the handle of a vessel. The glass with moulded decoration and the handle belong to the strata dating to the 14th–15th centuries; the panes and the neck of the bottle were unearthed in the layer dating to the 18th–19th centuries.

---

20   "Islamic city" is the term designated by Rante.
21   Regarding the examples, see Fukai 1968: 20–35, figs. 11-19; Simpson 2005: 148, figs. 2-1 to 3; Simpson 2015: 80, figs. 3-1 and 3-2; Shikaku 2013: 255, figs. 6-10.
22   Shindo pointed out that this fragment belongs to the Sasanian facet-cut glass, depending on the thickness of the fragment and the technique of cutting.

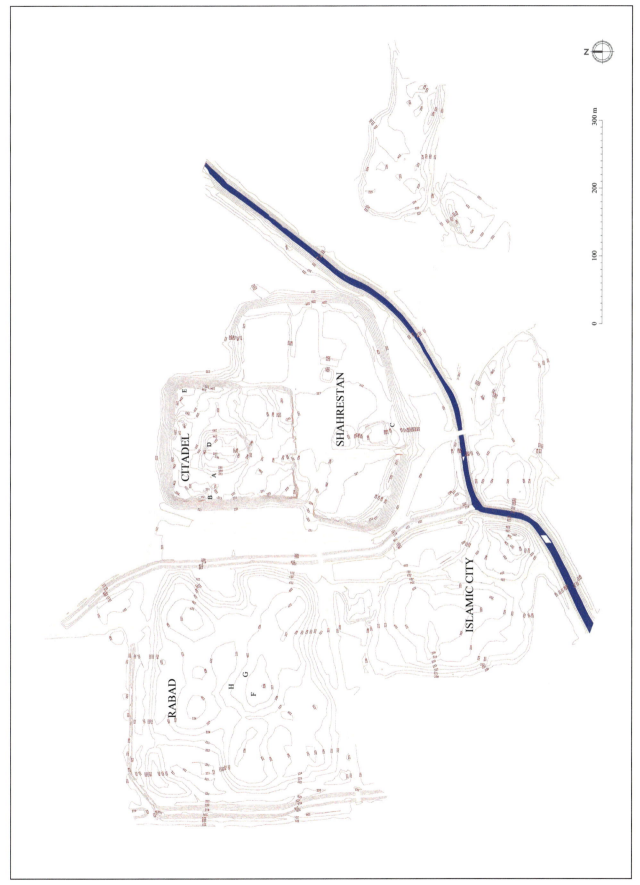

FIGURE 9.37   Plan of Ramitan. Map MAFOUB

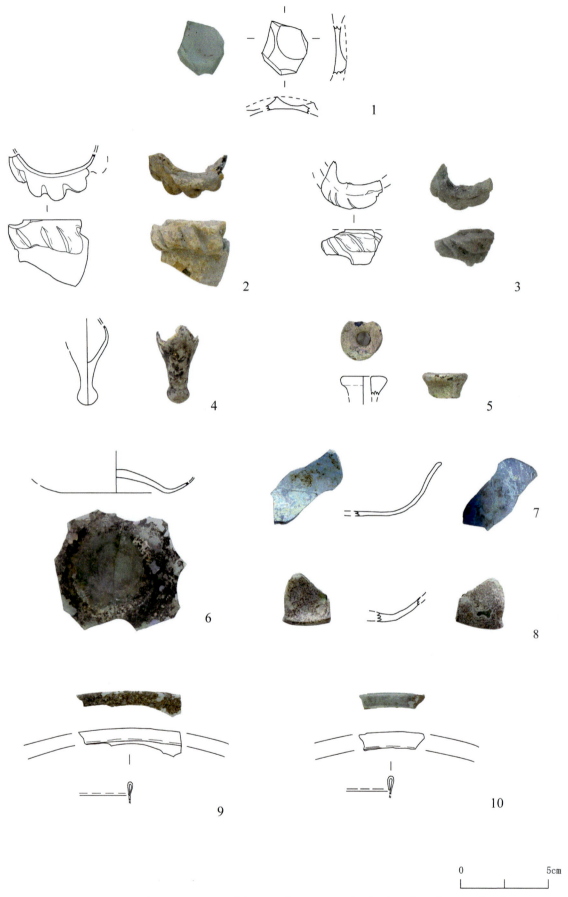

FIGURE 9.38 Ramitan, trench D&F. Fragments of glass vessels. Drawings Yoko Shindo and Noriko Horiuchi: Photos Yoshie Abe

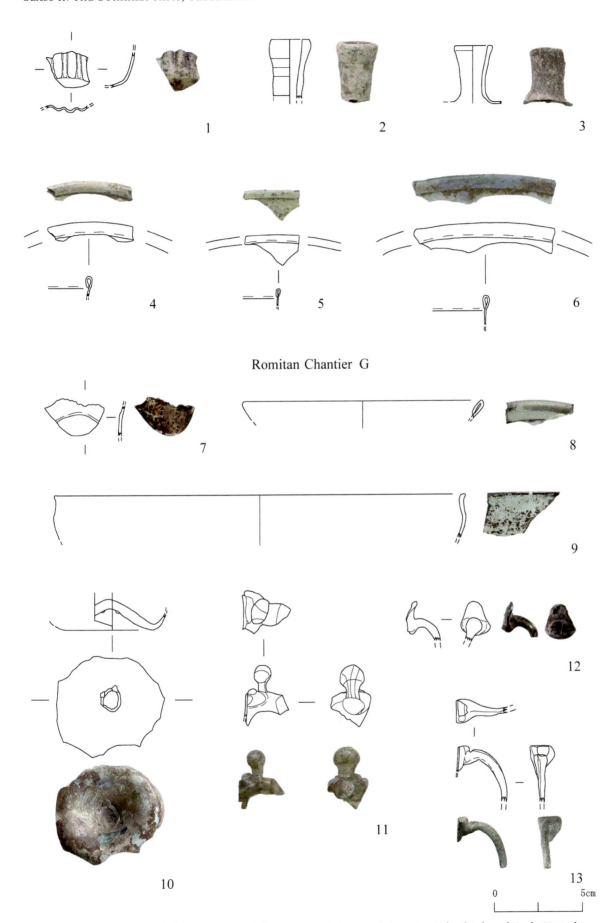

FIGURE 9.39 Ramitan, trench G & Site250, trench A. Fragments of glass vessels. Drawings Yoko Shindo and Noriko Horiuchi: Photos Yoshie Abe

3.2 Site 250

Site 250 is situated near the site of Ramitan and is believed to have contained settlements from the 1st to the 13th centuries.

In total, we registered 14 glass vessel pieces in trench A. Of these, seven glass fragments were unearthed in stratum US156, which is dated to the 10th century. The artifacts include one bowl rim, one base fragment, handles from vessels and panes. The base fragment exhibits a double ringed pontil mark that is generally rare in Islamic glass but is popular in the Bukhara Oasis (Shindo 2017: 194, fig. 2–7).

3.3 Iskijkat

The site of Iskijkat consists of a citadel and a lower city (shahrestan). The citadel is situated in the centre of the site, and the shahrestan surrounds the citadel (fig. 9.40). The site is located at the entrance of the Bukhara Oasis and on the caravan route to Samarkand. As a result of our research in 2014 and 2015, the remains of settlements dating to the period from the 3rd century BCE to the 14th or 15th centuries CE have been uncovered.

At the site, we registered 16 glass vessel pieces (fig. 9.41). We found 11 pieces containing rims, one base of a bottle and panes in the part of the citadel designated as trench A. Most of the glass fragments were unearthed in the strata dated from the 13th to 15th centuries.

A total of five glass vessel pieces were found in the northern rampart of the shahrestan designated as trench B. They include one rim of a moulded beaker and panes. All of the glass articles belong to the strata dated to the 12th century.

3.4 Kakishtuvan

The site of Kakishtuvan is a tell that consists of a citadel and a lower city (shahrestan). The citadel is situated in the centre of the site, and the shahrestan extends to the south of the citadel (fig. 9.42). The site is located at the entrance

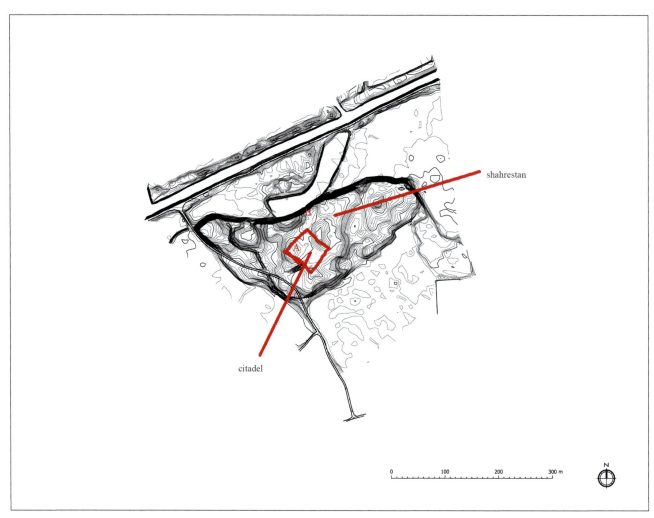

FIGURE 9.40   Plan of Iskijkat. Map MAFOUB

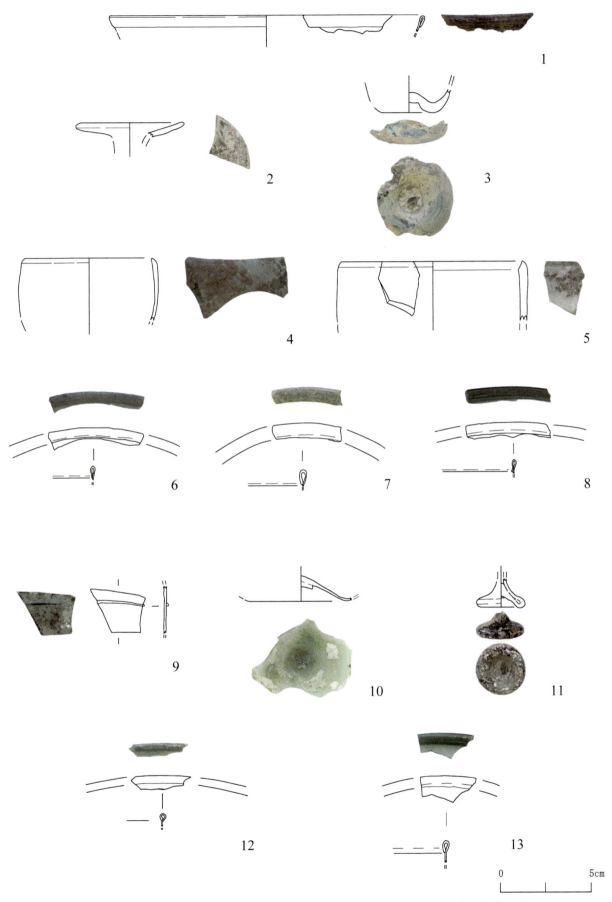

FIGURE 9.41 Iskijkat, trench A&B & Kakishtuvan, trench A. Fragments of glass vessels. Drawings Yoko Shindo and Noriko Horiuchi; Photos Yoshie Abe

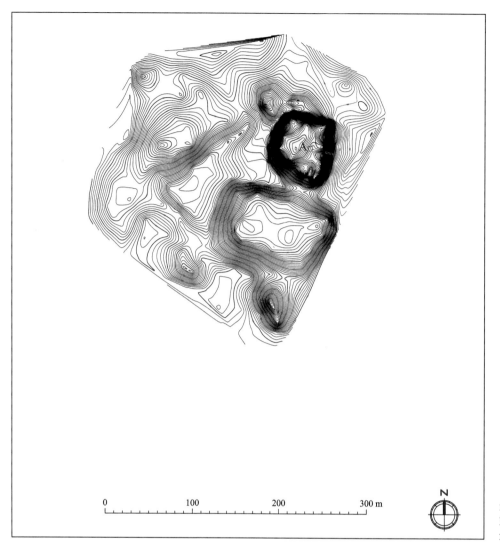

FIGURE 9.42
Plan of Kakishtuvan. Map
MAFOUB

of the Bukhara Oasis and along the caravan route to Khorezm. People had lived there since the 1st century and continued to settle there until the 14th century.

In 2016 we registered seven glass vessel pieces in trench A, which is part of the citadel. One fragment with threaded decoration was uncovered in the strata dating to the 11th to 13th centuries. The base of a goblet and panes were also unearthed.

3.5 *Bukhara*

The site of Bukhara consists of a citadel (ark; trench A) and a lower city (shahrestan; trench B).

It is assumed that habitation started around the 3rd century BCE. Around the 7th century, the city of Bukhara became the centre of Western Sogdiana. In the 10th century, Bukhara was the capital of the Samanid dynasty and served as its political, economic and cultural centre. The Mongol Empire invaded and destroyed it in the 13th century; however, Bukhara played an important role in political and economic development until the modern period (Rante and Mirzaakhmedov 2019, 252–260).

The excavation mission has been conducted since 2017, and it reveals that some buildings were constructed during an extremely productive period in the 10th and 11th centuries. Additionally, many fragments of glass and pottery were uncovered among remains from the Samanid and early Karakhanid dynasties.

3.5.1 Citadel

In total, we have registered 207 glass vessel pieces (170 pieces of sherds that could be joined together).[23] The garbage pit discovered in stratum US230 is from the 10th

---

23 After registering the 207 pieces of glass unearthed in the site of Bukhara, it was discovered that some of them could be joined together, or they were identified to be from the same vessel. Therefore, we study glass from Bukhara based on the 170 pieces of joined sherds that have been temporally mended.

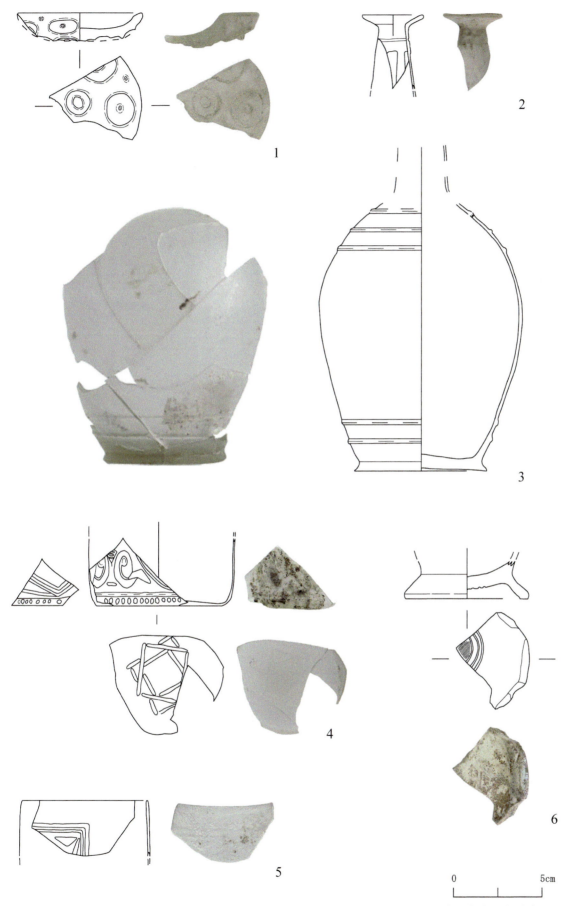

FIGURE 9.43 Bukhara, trench A. Fragments of glass vessels with cut decoration. Drawings Tamako Takeda and Takako Hosokawa: Photos Tamako Takeda and Ayano Endo

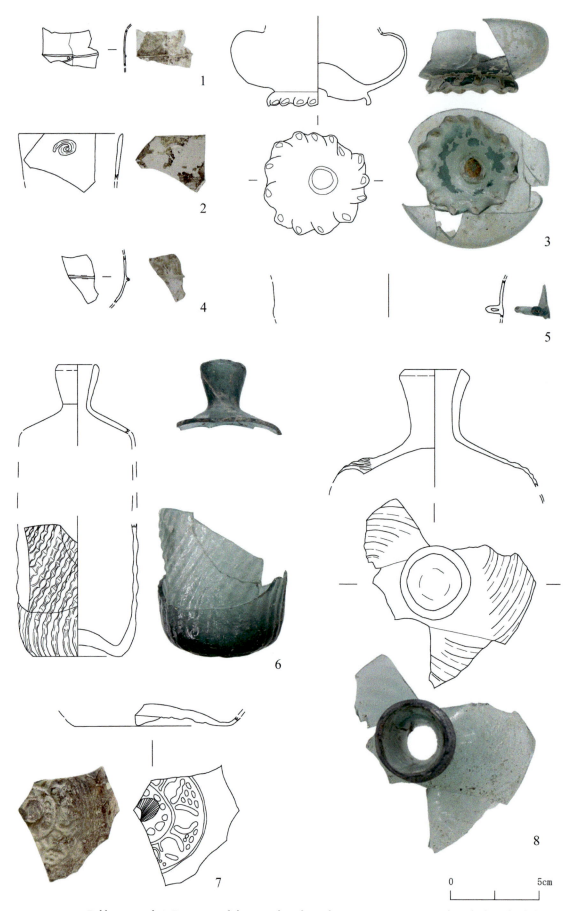

FIGURE 9.44 Bukhara, trench A. Fragments of glass vessels with cut decoration. Drawings Tamako Takeda and Takako Hosokawa: Photos Tamako Takeda and Ayano Endo

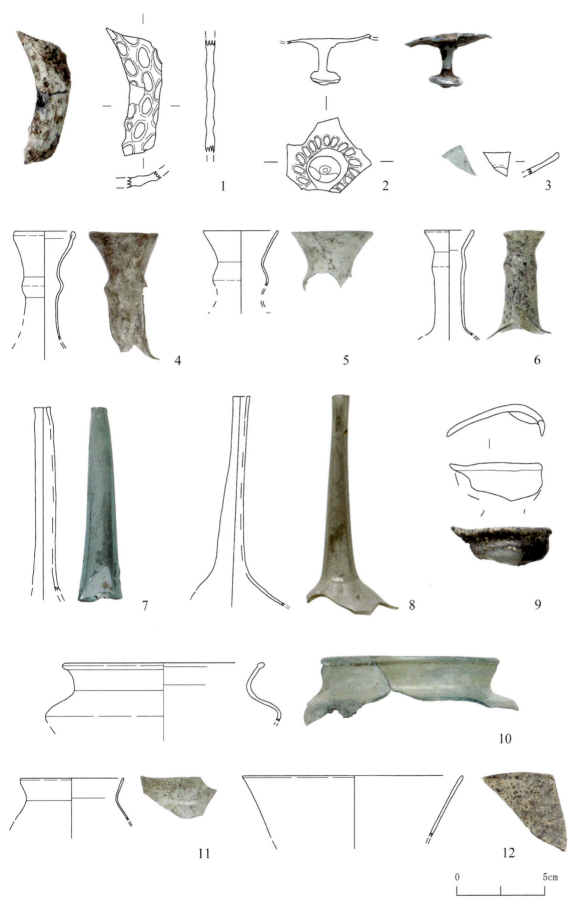

FIGURE 9.45 Bukhara, trench A. Fragments of glass vessels with cut decoration. Drawings Tamako Takeda and Takako Hosokawa: Photos Tamako Takeda and Ayano Endo

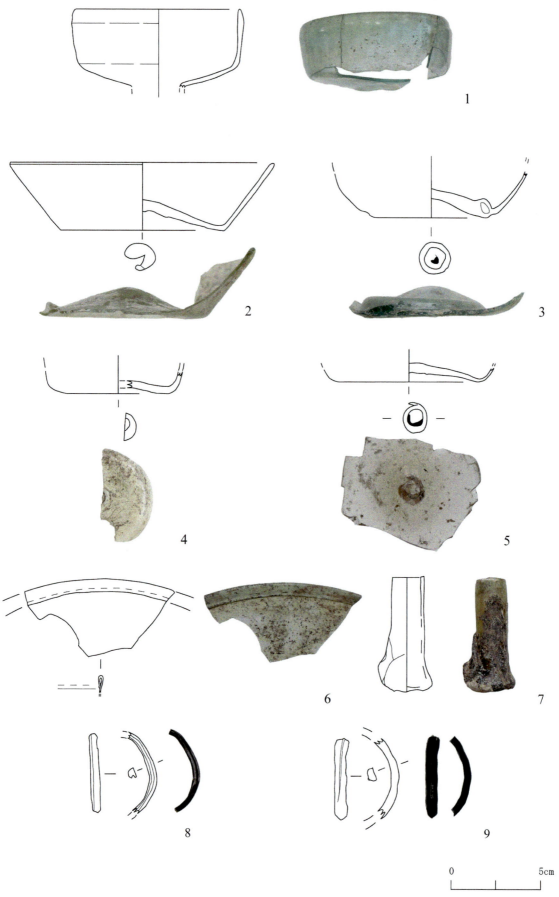

FIGURE 9.46 Bukhara, trench A. Fragments of glass vessels with cut decoration. Drawings Tamako Takeda and Takako Hosokawa: Photos Tamako Takeda and Ayano Endo

century, and it includes 91 fragments of glass articles. We examined the glass in the site of Bukhara, focusing on decoration, shape and colour.

3.5.1.1 Decoration

There are ten pieces of glass articles with cut decoration (fig. 9.43). These consist of two pieces of relief-cut decoration, one piece of facet-cut decoration and seven pieces of liner-cut decoration. They are completely colourless and made from high-quality material. Most of the articles were excavated from a pit that that belongs to stratum US230.

A small bowl has relief-cut decorations composed of circles with centred boss and double circle patterns. Relief-cut decoration is a technique in which the circumferences of a motif are removed in an attempt to emphasise the line of the motif. The traditional Sasanian technique is frequently applied to this technique. A similar small bowl was unearthed in Nishapur and Samarra.[24]

A large bottle with relief-cut decorations has an oval body and horizontal ribs on the shoulder and near the base. Similar bottles were found in the Cirebon shipwreck that sunk in the 10th century (Liebner 2014: 5–6).[25] These bottles are thought to have been imported from the region of Iran (Guillot 2012: inv. nos. 127160, 7276 and 7277).[26]

The fragments of a bottle have liner-cut decoration composed of a row of small circles and a horizontal groove near the base. The body has geometrical patterns combined with a double lozenge and a spiral. The base has a geometric motif featuring a combination of squares and a triangle pattern. A pattern of cut decoration in which small circles or ovals are carved on the shoulder and near the base is widely used on a long-necked bottle with an out-splayed rim and squared shoulder.[27] Similar bottles were unearthed in the Tomb of Princess Chenguo, who died in 1018, and the Dule Temple, where many treasures were dedicated in 1058.[28]

One fragment of beaker has a liner-cut decoration with a pattern composed of double rectangles and triangles.[29]

A neck fragment has facet-cut decorations consisting of a continuous rectangular pattern.[30] A slightly tapering neck with out-splayed rim is thought to be the upper part of cylindrical bottle with a squared shoulder.

There are five fragments of glass with tooled decoration (fig.9.44).

One glass fragment has an impressed decoration. This is a method in which the wall of glass is pinched by tools in attempt to create a motif. The tool is thought to be a tong that has a square and an oval at the end. The impressed decoration was popular in Egypt during the 9th and the 10th centuries.[31]

There is also a bottle with a unique shape and tooled decoration on the base. The bottom wall is thick, and it is pinched, twisted and shaped into a footed base by a tool. The body is horizontally expanded. Similar fragments of bases are reported in the Afrasiab Museum.[32]

The other three articles have a tube-like ridge inside and outside the vessel.

In total, there are 19 glass fragments with moulded decoration (fig. 9.44). The decoration consists of simple patterns such as rib, petal and honeycomb. Two bottles have a simple rib pattern on the shoulder, body and base. Similar examples were uncovered in Afrasiab, Kulbuk and Nishapur.[33]

Only one fragment of glass with a thread decoration was found in the site of Bukhara. Thread decoration is the most common glass decoration in the site of Paykend. In

---

24   For Nishapur, see Kröger 1995: 133, fig. 180; for Samarra, see Lamm 1928: 75, figs. 228 and 229.

25   Based on the coins and graffiti on a ceramic fragment, the ship is considered to have sunk around 970 CE.

26   The Corning Museum of Glass has a similar example. See Whitehouse 2010: fig. 269.

27   Regarding the examples unearthed in Nishapur, see Kröger 1995: 126–28, figs. 171 and 172; for Binkat-Tashkent, see Mirzaakhmedov 2011: 104, fig. 9-2; for Raya, see Shindo 2007a and b; for Barus, see Guillot (ed.) 2003: 252, fig. 32. The Corning Museum of Glass has a similar example. See Whitehouse 2010: fig. 273.

28   For the Tomb of Princess Chenguo and the Dule Temple in China, see An 1991: 131, fig. 12 and 133, fig. 16.

29   Regarding the examples unearthed in Fustat, see Shindo 1992: 583, fig.VI-6-6-14; and Scanlon and Pinder-Wilson 1993: 84, fig. 40c; for Raya, see Shindo 2008: 62, pl. 3-1-12; for Nishapur, see Kröger 1995: 151–52, fig. 202.

30   Regarding the examples unearthed in Fustat, see Shindo 1992: 583, fig. VI-6-11-1; and Scanlon and Pinder-Wilson 1993: 86–89, fig. 41i–n; for Raya, see Shindo 2008: 66, pl. 3-3-5; for Samarra, see Lamm 1928: 72, nos. 206 and 207; for Nishapur, see Kröger 1995: 126–28, figs. 171, 172 and 173.

31   Regarding the examples unearthed in Fustat, see Shindo 1992: 577, fig.VI-6-3-22 and 23; and Scanlon and Pinder-Wilson 1993: 79–82, fig. 38-a-j; for Raya, see Shindo 2007a: 107, pl. 2-8-10; for Bet Shean, see Hadad 2005: 151, pl. 31-608-122; for Nishapur, see Kröger 1995: 96–99, figs. 136–40; for Susa, see Kervran 1984: 219, fig. 8-22-25.

32   A similar example of a base with tooled decoration is displayed in the Afrasiab Museum of Samarkand.

33   Regarding the examples unearthed in Nishapur, see Kröger 1995: 89–90, figs. 120 and 121; for Afrasiab, Uzbekistan, see Shishkina 1986: pl. 8-5 ;and Mirzaakhmedov 2011: 134, ill. 5; for Kulbuk in Tajikistan, see Yakuvov 2011: 63, ill. 8. In addition, similar bottle shapes with moulded decoration are displayed in the Ark Museum in Bukhara.

addition, it is noted that a wide wavy threaded decoration around the neck has not been unearthed in the site of Bukhara thus far. This decoration is one of most popular techniques for thread decoration in Transoxiana and has been uncovered in each site in the Bukhara Oasis.

3.5.1.2 Shape

There are various tableware shapes, such as bowls, beakers, goblets, bottles, pitchers, panes and jars. In addition to this crockery, we excavated fragments of bottles with tubular necks, ewer and a lamp; this has rarely been seen in other sites in the Bukhara Oasis (figs. 9.45 and 9.46).

Two bottles with tubular necks have been uncovered in stratum US230 and are thought to be perfume sprinklers. They have long necks with a narrow opening so that contents such as rose water would not spill out. Although the body was not attached, it is thought that it had globular or flat body.[34]

Regarding the manufacturing technique, there are double ringed pontil marks on the bases of the Bukhara glass. We excavated 36 base fragments with a pontil mark, 15 fragments of which have a double ringed pontil mark.

3.5.1.3 Colour

The majority of glass articles are a natural colour with a tone of pale bluish green, pale green and pale yellowish brown. Additionally, 56 pieces of colourless glass have been unearthed, and they account for at least 30% of the total amount of pieces found. Colourless glass is heavily concentrated in stratum US230, comprising 50% of the total number of glass articles from this stratum. In other sites in the Bukhara Oasis, colourless glass accounts for about 20% of all the glass.

Colourless glass can be divided into high quality and low quality. High-quality glass is clearly decolourised and made from high-quality material. On the other hand, there is colourless pale-blown and pale-green tinged glass. The surfaces of these glass articles are normally covered with a thick black or white layer due to weathering.

Chemical analysis also indicates that the colourless glass in the site of Bukhara is divided into two groups: those discoloured with manganese, possibly made in the site or the surrounding locality, and those using a purified silica component, possibly imported from the area west of Amu Darya.[35] Furthermore, raw materials for glass production were found in the shahrestan, and there is the possibility that low-quality colourless glass was manufactured at the site of Bukhara.

3.5.2 Lower City (Shahrestan)

The shahrestan is a residential area that extends below the citadel. Excavation began in 2019. Raw material for glass and glass waste, as well as fragments of glass-vessel decoration, including moulded, thread and cut decoration, have been unearthed.

4 Chemical Analysis of Early Islamic Glass from Sites in the Bukhara Oasis, Uzbekistan

Toshiyasu Shinmen and Ayano Endo

4.1 Introduction

The archaeological studies of the glass artifacts unearthed from the main sites in the Bukhara Oasis are outlined in the previous section. The glass artifacts, dated as early Islamic glass from the 9th to 11th centuries, are mostly greenish or blueish naturally coloured ordinary wares. Only a few high-quality glasswares, such as colourless glass and coloured glass, were found. Cullet and slag were unearthed from some sites, suggesting the existence of some glass production activities.

After the appearance of the Islamic cultural sphere in the 8th century, glass manufacturing technology was developed and the use of glass products began. It is believed that glass production and use spread as along with other Islamic cultural practices. Therefore, it is important to discover where the glass manufacturing technology in the Bukhara Oasis originated and where the unearthed glass was produced. Identification of the glass's provenance can provide basic information that gives insight into trade routes, production, use and recycling, etc.

Glass provenance research requires scientific excavation of glass production sites (e.g., workshops and factories), but very few sites have actually been investigated. It is necessary to select regional glass from all glass artifacts unearthed from settlement sites and to compare them with those found in other regions. However, glass manufactured in a region dominated by Islamic culture is relatively similar to those in other regions, and it is difficult to determine regionality based on the glass fragments. Therefore, composition analysis of the glass is used to

---

34 Bottles with tubular necks used for sprinklers were found in a shipwreck in Serçe Limanı. The shipwreck is considered to have sunk in the 11th century. See Bass, Brill, Lledó, and Matthews 2009: 255, fig. 21-2, TN1–4.

35 See section 9.4 by Shinmen and Endo.

TABLE 9.2 List of analytical samples from the Bukhara Oasis

No.	C.A.No	Reg.No.	Fig.No.	site	Trench	Stratum	Part	Form	Decoration	Reg.color
1	Py001	BPG-40	Fig.9.2/12	Paykend	A (2010)	US 709	base	uncertain	-	blue
2	Py002	BPG-123·133	Fig.9.3/4	Paykend	B (2012)	US 3736	body?	uncertain	thread (straight)	pale blue (cobalt)
3	Py003	BPG-210·211	Fig.9.3/12	Paykend	B (2012)	US 3736	neck-body	bottle	mold(double circle)	pale blue (cobalt)
4	Py004	BPG-126	Fig.9.5/13	Paykend	B (2012)	US 3736	body	uncertain	ridge	pale blue (cobalt)
5	Py005	BPG-124	Fig.9.7/3	Paykend	B (2012)	US 3736	base	bottle	-	blue
6	Py006	BPG-213	no fig.	Paykend	B (2012)	US 3736	neck	bottle	-	pale blue (cobalt)
7	Py007	BPO-3	Fig.9.46/8	Paykend	uncertain (2010)	231	-	bangle	-	black
8	Py008	BPO-13	Fig.9.46/9	Paykend	B (2012)	B3815	-	bangle	-	black
9	Py009	BPG-96	Fig.9.9/2	Paykend	F (2011)	US 439	neck?	botlle?	thread (wavy)	pale olive green
10	Py010	BPG-279	Fig.9.5/2	Paykend	B (2010)	US 125	body	uncertain	facet cut (oval)	colorless
11	Py011	BPG-107	Fig.9.5/3	Paykend	B (2011)	US 657	shoulder	bottle	facet cut (circle)	colorless
12	Py012	BPG-16	Fig.9.5/4	Paykend	B (2010)	US 223	base	bottle	facet cut (circle)	colorless
13	Py013	BPG-255	Fig.9.5/5	Paykend	B (2012)	US 3736	base	uncertain	facet cut	colorless
14	Py014	BPG-125	Fig.9.6/10	Paykend	B (2012)	US 3736	base	uncertain	-	colorless
15	Py015	BPG-222	Fig.9.6/11	Paykend	B (2012)	US 3736	base	uncertain	-	colorless
16	Py016	BPG-116·120	Fig.9.6/9	Paykend	B (2012)	US 3787	rim-shoulder, base	jar	-	pale bluish green
17	Py017	BPG-214	Fig.9.5/15	Paykend	B (2012)	US 3736	rim-shoulder	bottle	-	pale bluish green
18	Py018	BPG-257	Fig.9.5/17	Paykend	B (2012)	US 3736	rim-shoulder	bottle or jar	-	pale bluish green
19	Py019	BPG-139	Fig.9.7/1	Paykend	B (2012)	US 3736	base	uncertain	-	pale bluish green
20	Py020	BPG-145	Fig.9.7/2	Paykend	B (2012)	US 3787	base	uncertain	-	pale bluish green
21	Py021	BPG-8	Fig.9.7/6	Paykend	B (2010)	US 163	base	uncertain	-	pale bluish green
22	Py022	BPG-59	Fig.9.7/4	Paykend	B (2011)	US 1629	base	botlle	-	pale bluish green
23	Py023	BPG-62	Fig.9.7/5	Paykend	B (2011)	US 1637	base	uncertain	-	pale bluish green
24	Py024	BPG-17	Fig.9.7/8	Paykend	B (2010)	US 231	base	bottle	-	pale green
25	Py025	BPG-221·252	Fig.9.7/9	Paykend	B (2012)	US 3736	base	uncertain	-	bluish green
26	Py026	BPG-224	Fig.9.8/7	Paykend	B (2012)	US 3736	rim	pane	-	pale blue
27	Py027	BPG-87	Fig.9.9/10	Paykend	F (2011)	US 432	base	bottle	-	pale bluish green
28	Py028	BPG-95	Fig.9.9/8	Paykend	F (2011)	US 437	rim	pane	-	pale bluish green
29	Py029	BPG-179	Fig.9.10/4	Paykend	H (2012)	US 4004	neck-body	bottle	-	pale blue
30	Py030	BPG-165	Fig.9.10/6	Paykend	H (2012)	US 4004	rim	bowl	-	pale bluish green
31	Py031	BPG-263	Fig.9.12/9	Paykend	E (2014)	US 4620	handle	uncertain	-	pale bluish green
32	Py032	BPG-130	no fig.	Paykend	B (2012)	US 3736	base	uncertain	-	green
33	Py033	BPG-28	Fig.9.2/7	Paykend	D (2010)	US 501	-	cullet	-	pale bluish green
34	Py034	BPG-283	Fig.9.12/18	Paykend	Ribat4 (2016)			cullet	-	pale green
35	Py035	BPG-283	Fig.9.12/18	Paykend	Ribat4 (2016)			cullet	-	pale green
36	Py036	BPG-30	Fig.9.2/6	Paykend	D (2010)	US 504	-	slag (rod)	-	pale green
37	Py037	BPG-232	Fig.9.8/13	Paykend	JB (2012)	US 4314	-	slag (rod)	-	pale bluish green
38	Py038	BPG-114	Fig.9.12/16	Paykend	E (2011)	US 974	-	slag (rod)	-	pale green
39	Py039	BPG-264	Fig.9.12/17	Paykend	E (2014)	US 4267	-	slag (block)	-	yellow green
40	Py040	BPG-54	Fig.9.12/13	Paykend	E (2010)	US 925	-	slag (block)	-	pale green
41	Py041	BPG-262	Fig.9.12/14	Paykend	E (2014)	US 1017	-	slag (block)	-	yellow green
42	Py042	BPG-275	Fig.9.12/15	Paykend	E (2014)	US 9612c	-	slag (block)	-	pale brown + pale yellowish green
43	Rm001	BRG-46	Fig.9.38/8	Romitan	D (2018)	-	body	uncertain	-	pale bluish green
44	Rm002	BRG-14	Fig.9.38/1	Romitan	F (2014)	US 1137	body	bowl?	facet cut (oval)	colorless (bluish)
45	Is001	BIG-14	Fig.9.41/5	Iskijkat	B (2015)	US 470	rim	beaker	-	colorless
46	Is002	BIG-13	Fig.9.41/8	Iskijkat	B (2015)	US 483	rim	pane	-	pale bluish green
47	Kk001	BKG-2	Fig.9.41/10	Kakishtuvan	A (2016)	US 116	base	uncertain	-	colorless (greenish)
48	Kk002	BKG-6	Fig.9.41/13	Kakishtuvan	A (2016)	US 105	rim	pane	-	pale bluish green
49	Kk003	BKG-1	no fig.	Kakishtuvan	A (2016)	US 131	base of handle	handle	-	pale bluish green
50	Bk001	BBG-80	Fig.9.43/1	Bukhara	A (2018)	US230	rim-base	bowl	relief cut (circle)	colorless
51	Bk002	BBG-83	Fig.9.43/3	Bukhara	A (2018)	US230	body-base	bottle	relief cut	colorless
52	Bk003	BBG-101·170	Fig.9.43/4	Bukhara	A (2018)	US230	body-base	bottle	liner cut	colorless
53	Bk004	BBG-163	Fig.9.43/5	Bukhara	A (2018)	US230	rim	beaker	liner cut	colorless
54	Bk005	BBG-87	Fig.9.44/2	Bukhara	A (2018)	US230	rim	beaker	impress	colorless
55	Bk006	BBG-89	no fig.	Bukhara	A (2018)	US230	base	uncertain	-	colorless
56	Bk007	BBG-104	Fig.9.45/12	Bukhara	A (2018)	US230	rim-body	beaker	-	colorless
57	Bk008	BBG-95	Fig.9.45/4	Bukhara	A (2018)	US230	rim-shoulder	bottle	buldge	colorless
58	Bk009	BBG-183	Fig.9.46/4	Bukhara	A (2018)	US230	base	uncertain	-	colorless
59	Bk010	BBG-199	no fig.	Bukhara	A (2018)	US230	body	jar	ridge	colorless
60	Bk011	BBG-121	Fig.9.44/5	Bukhara	A (2018)	US230	body	uncertain	ridge	pale bluish green
61	Bk012	BBG-164	Fig.9.45/11	Bukhara	A (2018)	US230	rim-shoulder	jar	-	pale bluish green
62	Bk013	BBG-94	Fig.9.45/5	Bukhara	A (2018)	US230	rim	botlle	buldge	pale bluish green
63	Bk014	BBG-193	Fig.9.45/3	Bukhara	A (2018)	US230	rim	uncertain	mold (circle)	pale bluish green
64	Bk015	BBG-190	Fig.9.46/1	Bukhara	A (2018)	US230	rim-body	goblet	-	pale bluish green

identify the provenance (Brill 1999; Henderson 2013). Chemical analyses of the Islamic glass from archaeological sites in Iran, Iraq, Syria and Egypt have been carried out (Brill 1995; Henderson, McLoughlin, and McPhail 2004; Freestone 2006; Kato, Nakai, and Shindo 2010.). In Uzbekistan, chemical analysis of the Islamic glass has been carried out in recent years (Abdurazakov 2009; Rehren, Osorio, and Anarbaev 2010), but very little progress has been made on the glass from the Bukhara Oasis.

In this section, we elaborate on the chemical analysis of early Islamic glass from the 9th to 11th centuries unearthed from the main sites in the Bukhara Oasis. The aim was to acquire basic information on the chemical compositions of glass in the oasis during this period.

When considering the provenance of the glass excavated from the Bukhara Oasis, it is necessary to consider three main types of glass. The first type was manufactured in the Bukhara Oasis, the second type was manufactured in neighbouring cities such as Samarkand and the third type was manufactured in foreign countries such as Iran. The first type is the ordinary ware used in the oasis. The second type are goods imported through medium-distance trade, and the glass may have been brought in as containers for luxury grocery items. The third type was imported through long-distance trade as luxury items. The glass artifacts produced in the Bukhara Oasis and the glass imported from distant areas outside the oasis were differentiated based on the chemical composition of the glass. However, as the glass artifacts unearthed from neighbouring cities such as Samarkand were not analysed, it was not possible to accurately identify the provenance of the transported glass.

4.2 *Samples*

The analytical samples consisted of 64 glass artifact fragments from the main sites in the Bukhara Oasis (table 9.2). The samples were categorised based on three parameters: archaeological site, glass colour and glass-production material. Table 9.2 shows the count for each category.

4.2.1 Archaeological Site

The bulk of the glass samples was unearthed in Paykend. Previous archaeological excavations found different types of glass in different districts within Paykend. However, this tendency was not clear when the chemical analysis was carried out, so the samples were not selected to verify the tendency. The other samples are two fragments from Ramitan, two fragments from Iskijkat, three fragments from Kakishtuvan and 15 fragments from Bukhara. There are only a few glasswares from Ramitan, Iskijkat and Kakishtuvan. A Sasanian cut glass (Rm002) was excavated from Ramitan.

4.2.2 Glass Colour

The glass artifacts were broadly classified into coloured glass, colourless glass and naturally coloured glass, and the colouring elements contained in this glass were verified.

Coloured glass is defined as glass that has intentionally been coloured by the manufacturer using certain elements, typically Mn, Fe, Co, Cu and Sb, which impart colour of different intensities to glass depending on the amount and valence of the elements. A total of nine coloured glass samples were analysed: six blue glass samples, two black glass samples and one olive-green glass sample from Paykend.

Colourless glass is formed by either using raw materials with low impurities or removing impurities such as iron from the raw material using decolourising agents such as Sb and Mn. Nineteen fragments of colourless glass were used as analytical samples (table 9.3). Many of colourless glasses were broken into small pieces and the types and parts are unknown. Some samples are slightly bluish, possibly due to the effect of impurities. Among the colourless glass, Iranian glass was unearthed from US230

TABLE 9.3 Classification of analytical samples

Site	Colored glass		Colorless glass		Naturally colored glass		Total	Note
	Product	Glass production material	Product	Glass production material	Product	Glass production material		
Paykend	9*		6		17	10	42	*blue, black, olive-green
Romitan			1		1		2	
Iskijkat			1		1		2	
Kakishtuvan			1		2		3	
Bukhara			10**		5		15	**Iran:4
total	9		19		36		64	

in Bukhara, and four samples (Bk001–004) were analysed. The provenance of the remaining six samples could not be identified.

Naturally coloured glass is coloured green unintentionally by impurities (mainly iron) in the raw materials. The colours vary from light green to dark green or bluish green, depending on the amount of impurities. The colour also changes depending on the thickness of the glass, with thin glass being nearly colourless and thicker glass having a more intense colour. Thirty-three fragments of naturally coloured glass were used as analytical samples (table 9.3).

4.2.3 Glass-Production Material

In the general glass production process, manufacturing glass materials from raw materials such as sand and ash is termed "glassmaking", and forming glassware from glass materials is termed "glassworking". In the Bukhara Oasis, it is unknown what kind of glass production process was performed as the glass workshop and furnace have not been excavated. Glass-production materials such as cullet and slag were unearthed from Paykend, so it is certain that at least the "glassworking" process was conducted. There are several glass-production materials in the naturally coloured glass mentioned above. These are evidence of glass-manufacturing activities at Paykend, and the analytical data from these samples serve as criteria for the glass in the oasis. Therefore, we compared the glass-production materials to other glass products. The analytical samples were three cullet and six slag from Paykend.

Cullet is a glass material obtained by melting a raw material in a glass furnace to form glass, cooling it and pulverising it to an appropriate size. Cullet may refer to waste glass. The cullet is a dark green and has an irregular form.

Slag is glass waste generated during glass manufacturing. There are various types, such as waste that is produced when the raw materials and cullet are melted in a crucible and that produced when forming or decorating a product. The slag excavated from Paykend is classified into rod shaped and block shaped.

4.3 *Method*

First, a non-destructive qualitative analysis of samples was carried out by energy dispersive X-ray fluorescence spectrometry (ED-XRF), and the basic glass substance, colouring elements and minor elements were revealed. Based on the results of qualitative analysis by ED-XRF, several elements were determined, and quantitative analysis of the glass was performed by inductively coupled plasma-optical emission spectrometry (ICP-OES).

4.3.1 Qualitative Analysis by ED-XRF

X-ray fluorescence analysis is an analytical method that can be used without any special pretreatment, is easy to measure and provides rapid analytical data. Depending on the performance of the equipment, a wide range of elemental analysis is possible, from light to heavy elements. For the XRF analysis, an ED-XRF analyzer SEA5120S (Hitachi High-Tech Science Corp.) was used. The analysis conditions were: tube voltage: 45 kV; collimator diameter: φ1.8 mm; sample chamber atmosphere: air; measurement time: 300 seconds. The X-ray tube was Mo and the detector was a Si (Li) type semiconductor detector. The XRF analysis was carried out using a completely non-destructive method, using a glass part with no weathering.

4.3.2 Quantitative Analysis by ICP-OES

ICP-OES was used for quantitative analysis of the materials. ICP-OES is characterised by: (1) being able to perform highly sensitive and precise analyses of trace amounts of almost all elements; (2) being able to analyse a wide range of quantitative concentrations; (3) being able to perform simultaneous determinations of multiple elements; and (4) being less affected by matrices (coexistent element). For the analysis, it was necessary to solubilise the sample, and although it is not a completely non-destructive analysis method, only a few tens of milligrams were used.

The analytical sample was solubilised with an acid decomposition method using a Teflon pressure decomposition vessel. Diamond cutters were used to separate small pieces of material from which there would be no problems conducting archaeological observations in the future, and weathering products and deteriorated layers were removed using a rotary tool. The separated pieces were pulverised with a stainless steel hammer. Approximately 10–30 mg of the powder sample was accurately weighed, 0.5 ml of aqua regia (Hydrochloric acid: Nitric acid = 1: 3) and 3 ml of hydrofluoric acid (110° C for one hour) were added to the mixture, which was placed in a Teflon pressure decomposition vessel (made of stainless steel jackets) and heated in an electric furnace. After cooling to room temperature, the mixture was transferred from the container to a Teflon beaker with about 20 ml of pure water and evaporated dry on a hot plate. Then, 5 ml of pure water was added to 3.5 ml of nitric acid and heated. After the residue was dissolved, the solution was made 100 ml in a volumetric flask.

The analytical instruments were ICP-OES 720 SE and 5100 UbV from Agilent Technologies. The 14 analytical elements were made up of 9 major elements (Ti, Al, Fe, Mn, Mg, Ca Na, K, P) and 5 minor elements (Ba, Co, Cu,

Sr, Zn). Silicon (SiO_2) could not be measured because it is volatilised when the sample is solubilised. However, as the value obtained by subtracting the total value of the main component elements from 100 wt% is substantially silicon, this value is taken as the silicon content. The measurement was carried out by simultaneous multielement analysis using a semiconductor detector. It was confirmed that the emission lines of other elements did not affect the measured element, and a wavelength with excellent sensitivity was selected.

For the quantitative analysis, a reagent manufactured by FUJIFILM Wako Pure Chemical Industries, Ltd. was used, the concentration of the main component element was adjusted to 100 ppm, and that of the minor component element was adjusted to 1 ppm, and these were used as the standard sample solution. A two-point method was used to prepare a calibration curve from a blank solution and a standard sample solution. Quantitative values are expressed as oxide (wt%).

4.3.3 Data Analysis by Cluster Analysis

In order to reveal the characteristics of the chemical composition of the analytical data and to examine the differences in the analytical data, cluster analysis using IBM SPSS Statistics 23.0 multivariate analysis software was performed. The cluster analysis is a general method of classifying objects by collecting similar objects from a mixed population (target) and forming a group (cluster). The standardised Euclidean squared distance was chosen for the distance scale, and the Ward method was chosen as the classification technique, and it was standardised by Z score. Twelve elements, excluding CoO and CuO, were used as analytical variables.

4.4 Results

Table 9.4 shows the results of the ICP-OES analysis of the glass samples. In this section, we refer to the basic glass substance of all samples. The colouring elements detected in the coloured glass are also mentioned.

4.4.1 Basic Glass Substance

Table 9.5 summarises the average and standard deviation of the chemical compositions of all samples and each site. Samples from Paykend show almost the same as the overall average for major elements. None of the other samples show significantly different average compositions, and there are no samples with completely different chemical compositions. As a result of the analysis, it was concluded that all samples were soda-lime silica glass. The maximum and minimum values of Si, Ca and Na, which are the main components of soda-lime-silica glass, are 54.6~73.9 wt% for SiO_2, 3.47~10.1 wt% for CaO and 10.8~18.5 wt% for Na_2O, indicating a large variation in the data. Therefore, plots in two graphs, MgO and K_2O AND Na_2O and CaO, are shown in order to examine the characteristics of the analytical data (figs. 9.47 and 9.48). Among the sites, the distribution range of the Paykend products, the Bukhara products and the glass-production materials are arbitrarily circled. From these figures, it can be seen that the products from Paykend with a large number of analysis points are widely distributed, and the samples from other sites are distributed so as to overlap with them. In particular, the samples from Bukhara are concentrated in one area, indicating similarities in chemical composition. In addition, the glass-production materials from Paykend are concentrated in the high K_2O range in figure 9.47 and in the high Na_2O range in figure 9.48, although their distribution areas almost overlap with the products from Paykend.

The MgO vs. K_2O graphs in figure 9.47 are used to classify soda-lime silica glass based on the type of alkali raw material used. In Islamic glass, there are two types of soda-lime silica glass made from different soda materials. One was made from natron (sodium carbonate) and the other was made from plant ash. Natron glass has low concentrations of magnesium and potassium, whereas plant ash glass has high concentrations of both elements. These glasses are plotted approximately within each frame in figure 9.47 (Brill 2001). Brill estimates that glass from Central Asia fits in the high K_2O range. According to this figure, there was no natron glass in the analytical samples, and all of them were high magnesia and high potash glass. The content of MgO was within the range of 2~5 wt% plant ash, but there were many samples with a high K_2O content of 4 wt% or more. These glass types are considered to be basically plant-ash glass based on their high MgO and high K_2O concentrations. In figure 9.47, the concentration of K_2O is divided into two groups, one group concentrated within the framework of the plant ash and the other group with a higher concentration of K_2O. It may indicate a different provenance area.

The Na_2O-CaO graph in figure 9.48 compares the concentrations of Na and Ca, which are the main components of soda-lime silica glass, and generally is also a diagram used for the classification of soda-lime silica glass. This figure shows that the concentrations of Na_2O and CaO are concentrated in the range of about 11~18 wt% and 5~8 wt%, respectively, although there are some data showing that some of them are not concentrated. A closer look at the figure reveals the tendency for Na_2O to fall between 11~13 wt% and 13~16 wt%. The Paykend products and the Bukhara products are separated, and the reason for this will be examined in a future study.

TABLE 9.4 Chemical composition by ICP-OES (wt%)

No.	C.A.No	site	Form	Color	SiO_2	TiO_2	Al_2O_3	Fe_2O_3	MgO	MnO	CaO	Na_2O	K_2O	P_2O_5	BaO	CoO	CuO	SrO	ZnO
1	Py001	Paykend	uncertain	blue	62.60	0.08	4.14	0.65	3.92	0.38	7.86	14.95	5.09	0.32	0.045	n.d.	1.77	0.066	0.008
2	Py002	Paykend	uncertain	blue	63.75	0.10	4.13	1.23	3.78	0.26	7.03	14.61	4.26	0.46	0.045	0.046	0.234	0.060	0.019
3	Py003	Paykend	botlle	blue	62.96	0.09	4.48	0.76	3.88	0.23	6.88	15.48	4.56	0.42	0.040	0.037	0.072	0.055	0.034
4	Py004	Paykend	uncertain	blue	64.32	0.09	4.09	0.74	3.53	0.20	7.28	14.02	5.13	0.43	0.038	0.014	0.033	0.068	0.011
5	Py005	Paykend	botlle	blue	57.34	0.09	4.46	0.83	4.70	0.11	7.63	18.54	5.52	0.45	0.035	0.060	0.182	0.057	0.010
6	Py006	Paykend	botlle	blue	63.33	0.14	3.25	0.96	4.56	0.42	7.72	15.73	3.38	0.36	0.043	0.012	0.031	0.051	0.017
7	Py007	Paykend	bangle	black	62.77	0.16	5.03	5.13	3.85	0.11	5.75	14.37	2.31	0.38	0.026	n.d.	0.067	0.030	0.008
8	Py008	Paykend	bangle	black	65.22	0.15	4.89	2.88	3.63	0.13	5.62	14.50	2.38	0.44	0.029	n.d.	0.074	0.036	0.007
9	Py009	Paykend	botlle?	olive-green	60.03	0.13	4.35	1.14	4.02	2.18	7.81	14.67	4.96	0.47	0.113	n.d.	0.046	0.077	0.010
10	Py010	Paykend	uncertain	colorless	72.95	0.06	1.64	0.42	5.65	0.44	4.04	12.05	2.62	0.07	0.012	n.d.	0.002	0.038	0.004
11	Py011	Paykend	botlle	colorless	73.11	0.04	1.01	0.31	5.01	0.34	6.46	11.38	2.16	0.10	0.011	n.d.	0.002	0.053	0.004
12	Py012	Paykend	botlle	colorless	73.19	0.06	1.18	0.39	5.11	0.32	5.73	11.74	2.16	0.07	0.010	n.d.	0.002	0.042	0.003
13	Py013	Paykend	uncertain	colorless	72.26	0.04	0.90	0.26	4.67	0.07	5.80	13.90	1.96	0.08	0.010	n.d.	0.001	0.040	0.002
14	Py014	Paykend	uncertain	colorless	72.76	0.04	1.00	0.33	5.26	0.34	6.33	11.70	2.09	0.09	0.016	n.d.	0.004	0.053	0.008
15	Py015	Paykend	uncertain	colorless	72.20	0.04	0.91	0.29	4.75	0.41	6.20	12.59	2.29	0.25	0.015	n.d.	0.002	0.044	0.004
16	Py016	Paykend	jar	natural	60.45	0.08	3.98	0.45	4.93	0.06	7.58	15.30	6.70	0.39	0.029	n.d.	0.004	0.060	0.006
17	Py017	Paykend	botlle	natural	62.50	0.21	5.30	1.58	4.17	0.11	6.66	15.56	3.41	0.36	0.059	n.d.	0.006	0.052	0.008
18	Py018	Paykend	botlle or jar	natural	64.62	0.22	5.36	1.64	3.24	0.06	6.55	14.71	3.12	0.37	0.037	n.d.	0.004	0.046	0.012
19	Py019	Paykend	uncertain	natural	62.36	0.12	3.86	0.93	4.69	1.07	7.69	14.55	4.18	0.41	0.061	n.d.	0.012	0.057	0.008
20	Py020	Paykend	uncertain	natural	66.75	0.09	2.22	0.86	4.78	0.42	6.98	13.41	4.08	0.33	0.027	n.d.	0.003	0.043	0.009
21	Py021	Paykend	uncertain	natural	62.92	0.13	4.06	0.97	4.17	0.72	7.56	14.53	4.32	0.45	0.056	n.d.	0.034	0.058	0.009
22	Py022	Paykend	botlle	natural	63.52	0.08	1.84	0.76	5.35	0.04	6.78	16.71	4.38	0.48	0.020	n.d.	0.006	0.041	0.008
23	Py023	Paykend	uncertain	natural	62.92	0.21	5.30	1.41	3.81	0.05	6.37	15.61	3.72	0.50	0.038	n.d.	0.004	0.044	0.007
24	Py024	Paykend	botlle	natural	56.08	0.16	4.44	1.15	5.16	0.39	10.14	15.37	6.52	0.59	0.066	n.d.	0.013	0.079	0.007
25	Py025	Paykend	uncertain	natural	63.42	0.23	5.58	1.71	3.47	0.06	6.77	15.12	3.15	0.38	0.039	n.d.	0.003	0.047	0.012
26	Py026	Paykend	pane	natural	61.08	0.10	4.32	0.78	4.13	0.61	7.57	15.97	4.90	0.39	0.051	n.d.	0.023	0.064	0.007
27	Py027	Paykend	botlle	natural	58.09	0.18	4.56	1.15	5.25	0.03	8.89	15.75	5.46	0.50	0.054	n.d.	0.003	0.069	0.006
28	Py028	Paykend	pane	natural	61.34	0.12	4.37	0.86	4.10	0.61	8.09	14.73	5.16	0.45	0.058	n.d.	0.043	0.070	0.007
29	Py029	Paykend	botlle	natural	67.88	0.10	2.37	0.85	3.31	0.13	6.04	15.59	3.20	0.45	0.025	n.d.	0.004	0.047	0.007
30	Py030	Paykend	bowl	natural	63.80	0.18	4.82	1.38	3.67	0.26	6.66	14.20	4.40	0.51	0.044	n.d.	0.011	0.056	0.008
31	Py031	Paykend	uncertain	natural	64.96	0.09	3.45	0.70	4.01	0.59	6.61	13.81	5.25	0.41	0.042	n.d.	0.021	0.054	0.010
32	Py032	Paykend	uncertain	natural	63.02	0.15	4.96	1.06	3.79	1.11	6.24	15.06	4.06	0.40	0.072	n.d.	0.022	0.055	0.007
33	Py033	Paykend	cullet	natural	60.29	0.13	3.65	0.91	5.27	0.02	7.39	16.80	5.04	0.41	0.039	n.d.	0.003	0.046	0.007
34	Py034	Paykend	cullet	natural	59.80	0.13	3.70	0.92	5.40	0.03	7.70	16.61	5.30	0.41	0.045	n.d.	0.005	0.054	0.006
35	Py035	Paykend	cullet	natural	59.81	0.13	3.76	0.97	5.21	0.03	7.40	16.96	5.30	0.42	0.046	n.d.	0.005	0.053	0.006
36	Py036	Paykend	slag (rod)	natural	59.74	0.20	4.86	1.33	4.99	0.04	7.20	16.03	5.11	0.41	0.050	n.d.	0.003	0.025	0.008
37	Py037	Paykend	slag (rod)	natural	60.45	0.12	3.80	0.97	5.03	0.02	6.20	17.62	5.34	0.37	0.045	n.d.	0.002	0.032	0.007
38	Py038	Paykend	slag (rod)	natural	54.64	0.23	6.93	1.60	4.74	0.04	7.94	15.63	7.67	0.47	0.041	n.d.	0.003	0.055	0.005
39	Py039	Paykend	slag (block)	natural	56.86	0.23	6.93	1.63	4.77	0.04	8.24	14.06	6.76	0.36	0.041	n.d.	0.003	0.057	0.006
40	Py040	Paykend	slag (block)	natural	55.84	0.23	7.08	1.68	5.05	0.04	8.67	14.35	6.62	0.34	0.038	n.d.	0.003	0.048	0.007
41	Py041	Paykend	slag (block)	natural	55.63	0.23	7.29	1.66	4.90	0.04	8.50	14.39	6.84	0.40	0.042	n.d.	0.004	0.057	0.008
42	Py042	Paykend	slag (block)	natural	60.62	0.15	4.39	1.10	4.34	0.03	6.25	16.89	5.51	0.65	0.028	n.d.	0.004	0.033	0.008
43	Rm001	Romitan	uncertain	natural	61.43	0.39	3.77	1.08	5.68	0.09	7.36	14.99	4.78	0.43	0.047	n.d.	0.006	0.045	0.008
44	Rm002	Romitan	bowl?	colorless	68.43	0.10	1.46	0.54	4.44	0.17	7.65	14.16	2.15	0.83	0.012	n.d.	0.002	0.052	0.003
45	Is001	Iskijkat	beaker	colorless	73.85	0.05	1.09	0.37	4.92	0.36	6.40	10.84	2.04	0.07	0.011	n.d.	0.003	0.043	0.003
46	Is002	Iskijkat	pane	natural	61.81	0.23	5.31	1.43	4.08	0.05	9.72	12.54	4.48	0.35	0.068	n.d.	0.006	0.068	0.008
47	Kk001	Kakishtuvan	uncertain	colorless	59.11	0.19	4.73	1.31	6.19	0.05	8.30	15.30	4.34	0.49	0.042	n.d.	0.014	0.058	0.009
48	Kk002	Kakishtuvan	pane	natural	65.36	0.07	3.07	0.71	4.83	0.16	7.12	13.65	4.80	0.34	0.023	n.d.	0.005	0.058	0.007
49	Kk003	Kakishtuvan	handle	natural	62.18	0.19	4.51	1.42	4.90	0.03	8.23	14.03	4.13	0.36	0.051	n.d.	0.004	0.054	0.007
50	Bk001	Bukhara	bowl	colorless	71.66	0.06	0.94	0.97	4.90	0.28	6.09	12.67	2.10	0.26	0.022	n.d.	0.007	0.039	0.005
51	Bk002	Bukhara	bottle	colorless	72.62	0.03	0.81	0.21	5.15	0.45	5.57	12.32	2.57	0.20	0.011	n.d.	0.004	0.039	0.008
52	Bk003	Bukhara	bottle	colorless	70.26	0.04	1.00	0.36	5.09	0.71	6.82	12.39	2.93	0.31	0.042	n.d.	0.003	0.049	0.005
53	Bk004	Bukhara	beaker	colorless	70.65	0.04	0.99	0.36	5.00	0.73	6.70	12.23	2.94	0.30	0.016	n.d.	0.004	0.048	0.004
54	Bk005	Bukhara	beaker	colorless	62.14	0.08	4.73	0.54	3.65	1.51	7.51	13.71	5.24	0.75	0.067	n.d.	0.005	0.067	0.007
55	Bk006	Bukhara	uncertain	colorless	60.32	0.08	4.89	1.76	3.63	1.57	7.59	13.86	5.37	0.76	0.069	n.d.	0.015	0.067	0.007
56	Bk007	Bukhara	beaker	colorless	65.68	0.08	1.80	0.91	4.35	1.81	7.34	13.99	3.12	0.79	0.054	n.d.	0.010	0.053	0.024
57	Bk008	Bukhara	bottle	colorless	62.76	0.08	4.11	0.75	3.57	1.65	7.52	14.31	4.42	0.70	0.058	n.d.	0.011	0.056	0.008
58	Bk009	Bukhara	uncertain	colorless	70.17	0.11	2.39	0.73	3.45	0.74	3.47	16.45	1.85	0.55	0.053	n.d.	0.012	0.021	0.009
59	Bk010	Bukhara	jar	colorless	65.63	0.07	1.69	0.63	4.48	1.46	7.25	13.64	4.09	0.88	0.083	n.d.	0.005	0.051	0.015
60	Bk011	Bukhara	uncertain	natural	65.50	0.06	3.62	1.34	3.31	0.08	6.80	13.59	4.77	0.81	0.031	n.d.	0.013	0.060	0.005
61	Bk012	Bukhara	jar	natural	66.22	0.09	3.54	0.71	3.71	0.59	6.82	13.38	4.03	0.77	0.040	n.d.	0.015	0.069	0.007
62	Bk013	Bukhara	botlle	natural	65.11	0.06	4.18	0.49	3.44	0.32	6.96	13.88	4.76	0.69	0.037	n.d.	0.006	0.051	0.006
63	Bk014	Bukhara	uncertain	natural	65.60	0.06	3.78	0.53	3.42	0.05	6.97	13.78	4.87	0.83	0.032	n.d.	0.007	0.062	0.003
64	Bk015	Bukhara	goblet	natural	66.16	0.08	3.94	0.74	3.49	0.09	6.24	14.17	4.24	0.76	0.032	n.d.	0.009	0.043	0.005

TABLE 9.5 Average chemical compositions of glass samples excavated from the Bukhara Oasis (wt%)

Site	All samples n=64		Paykend n=42		Ramitan n=2		Iskijkat n=2		Kakishtuvan n=3		Bukhara n=15	
	Mean	SD	Mean	SD	Mean	SD	Mean	SD	Mean	SD	Mean	SD
SiO_2	64.08	4.88	63.05	4.97	64.93	4.95	67.83	8.51	62.22	3.12	66.70	3.63
TiO_2	0.12	0.07	0.13	0.06	0.25	0.21	0.14	0.12	0.15	0.07	0.07	0.02
Al_2O_3	3.67	1.68	4.02	1.66	2.62	1.64	3.20	2.98	4.10	0.90	2.83	1.50
Fe_2O_3	1.02	0.71	1.13	0.81	0.81	0.38	0.90	0.75	1.15	0.38	0.74	0.40
MgO	4.43	0.72	4.48	0.66	5.06	0.88	4.50	0.60	5.31	0.77	4.04	0.70
MnO	0.40	0.50	0.30	0.40	0.13	0.06	0.21	0.22	0.05	0.01	0.80	0.63
CaO	7.05	1.10	7.07	1.07	7.50	0.20	8.06	2.35	7.88	0.66	6.64	1.05
Na_2O	14.46	1.55	14.89	1.56	14.57	0.58	11.69	1.20	14.33	0.87	13.63	1.04
K_2O	4.22	1.40	4.44	1.49	3.47	1.87	3.26	1.73	4.42	0.34	3.82	1.15
P_2O_5	0.44	0.20	0.38	0.13	0.63	0.28	0.21	0.20	0.40	0.08	0.62	0.24
BaO	0.040	0.019	0.040	0.019	0.029	0.025	0.039	0.040	0.039	0.014	0.043	0.021
CoO	0.034	0.021	0.034	0.021	n.d.		n.d.		n.d.		n.d.	
CuO	0.046	0.222	0.066	0.273	0.004	0.003	0.004	0.002	0.008	0.005	0.008	0.004
SrO	0.052	0.012	0.052	0.012	0.049	0.005	0.056	0.017	0.057	0.002	0.052	0.013
ZnO	0.008	0.005	0.008	0.005	0.005	0.004	0.006	0.004	0.007	0.001	0.008	0.005

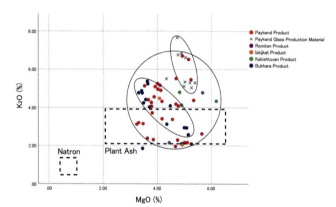

FIGURE 9.47 Plots of MgO vs. K_2O concentrations in all the samples

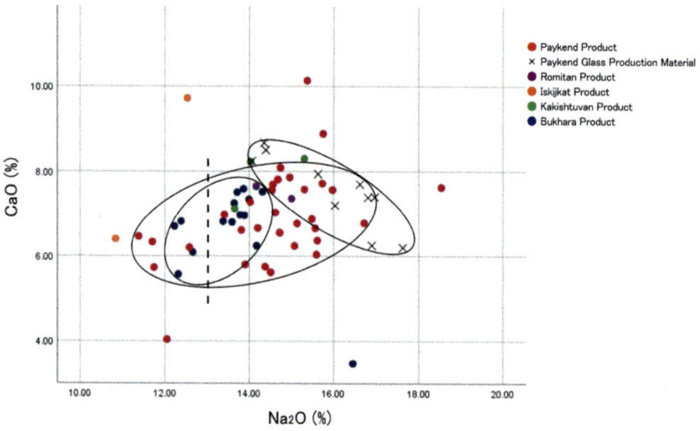

FIGURE 9.48 Plots of Na_2O vs. CaO concentrations in all the samples

The chemical composition of the glass unearthed from the Bukhara Oasis is outlined above. These glass artifacts are basically soda-lime silica glass made from plant ash.

4.4.2 Colouring Elements in the Coloured Glass

The coloured glass was examined by XRF spectrum (figs. 9.49–53) for the colouring elements of blue, black and olive glass. All the coloured glass was unearthed in Paykend.

As a result of X-ray fluorescence analysis, the blue glass was classified into Co coloured and Cu coloured. Py002 ~ 006 are Co-coloured glass. Among them, Cu, Zn and Pb were detected in accordance with Co in Py002, 003, 004 and 006 (fig. 9.49). It can be assumed that the same colouring material was used. The concentrations of CoO by ICP-OES is 0.012~0.046 wt%. In Py005, As, Ni, Cu, Zn and Pb were detected together with Co (fig. 9.50). The presence of As and Ni suggests the use of cobalt minerals such as Smaltite ((Co, Fe, Ni) As2) and Langisite ((Co, Ni) As). The concentration of CoO by ICP-OES is 0.060 wt%. As differences were observed in the types of coexisting Co, different cobalt sources were likely used. It has become clear that the use of raw cobalt materials reflects regional and historical characteristics, and production sites and production periods may differ (Gratuze 2013). Co was not detected in Py001, and high Cu was detected (fig. 9.51). Only Py001 was Cu-coloured glass.

As Fe was detected in two black glass samples from Py007 and Py008, the glasses were Fe-coloured glass (fig. 9.52). As for the Fe_2O_3 concentration, Py007 is 5.13

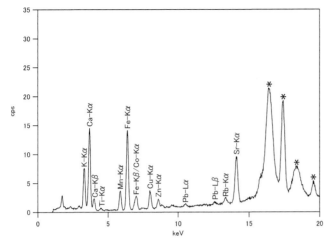

FIGURE 9.49   XRF spectra of blue glass (Py003)

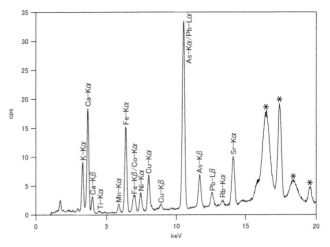

FIGURE 9.50   XRF spectra of blue glass (Py005)

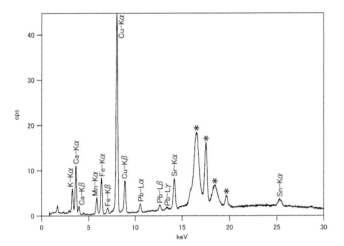

FIGURE 9.51   XRF spectra of blue glass (Py001)

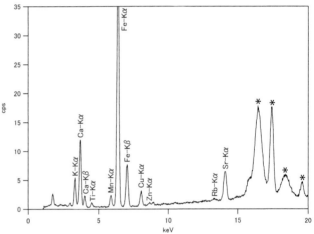

FIGURE 9.52   XRF spectra of black glass (Py008)

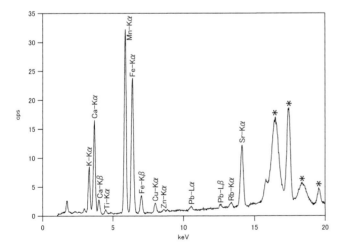

FIGURE 9.53   XRF spectra of olive-green glass (Py009)

wt%, Py008 is 2.88 wt% and the average in all samples except the coloured glass is about 0.93 wt%. These black glass samples tend to have higher CuO concentrations. The CuO concentration of black glass is 0.07 wt% on average, which is remarkable considering that the average value of the CuO concentration of all samples except the coloured glass is about 0.01 wt%. Considering that the other chemical compositions are similar, Cu likely coexists with iron colourants.

Py008 is an olive-green glass. Mn was detected in significant amounts in this sample (fig. 9.53), and the MnO concentration is 2.27 wt%. The average value of MnO in all samples except coloured glass is 0.39 wt%, indicating that P008 contained large amounts. There was only one glass in this sample with this colour tone, but the chemical composition of other elements is not much different from other samples.

From these results, it was possible to identify the colouring elements of the coloured glass excavated from Paykend. The chemical analysis data on coloured glass excavated from the Central Asian region are lacking, and it is difficult to interpret regional characteristics from this information.

4.5 Discussion

In this section, we compare the colourless glass and the naturally coloured glass and discuss the relationship between the glass-production materials and the products excavated from Paykend.

4.5.1 Comparison of the Colourless Glass and the Naturally Coloured Glass

The colourless glass and the naturally coloured glass were examined using an element concentration distribution diagram. To compare them, plotting graphs of Al_2O_3 vs. Fe_2O_3, SiO_2 vs. Al_2O_3, K_2O vs. MgO, and CaO vs. Na_2O were prepared (figs. 9.54–57). The ranges in which the colourless glass and the naturally coloured glass were distributed were bounded, respectively. These ranges are used for visualisation purposes and are not statistically significant. Table 9.6 shows the averages and standard deviation.

It can be seen from the four figures that the colourless glass and the naturally coloured glass are concentrated in different ranges. These figures show that the colourless glass has low Al_2O_3, Fe_2O_3, MgO and Na_2O concentrations and tends to have high SiO_2 concentrations. The naturally coloured glass is the opposite. This tendency can be seen from the average value in table 9.6.

In the Al_2O_3 vs. Fe_2O_3 plotting graph in figure 9.54, a strong positive correlation is observed in the colourless glass group, and the Al_2O_3 concentration is also low in the samples with a low Fe_2O_3 concentration. In the SiO_2 vs. Al_2O_3 graph in figure 9.55, a negative correlation is observed throughout the points, and both SiO_2 and Al_2O_3 show low concentrations in the colourless glass group. These results suggest that the differences in chemical composition reflect the differences in the raw materials used. As a result of using raw materials low in impurities such as silica stone as a silica source, the SiO_2 concentration is high and the Al_2O_3 and Fe_2O_3 concentrations are low. It is possible that a purified raw silica material with a low iron content was used. On the other hand, the naturally coloured glass is thought to have been made of silica containing various minerals, such as river sand.

The colourless glass group in figures 9.54 and 9.55 can be separated into ranges where the distribution is more concentrated and ranges where the distribution is slightly different. It is expected that there are various types of colourless glass with different raw materials. In addition, there were samples of colourless glass that were plotted in the range of the naturally coloured glass group. Among the colourless glass, it can be judged that the same raw material as the naturally coloured glass is used as raw silica material. These contain more than 1 wt% of MnO and are considered to be discoloured by Mn. Figure 9.58 shows the distribution of MnO vs. Fe_2O_3 concentration. In this figure, the distribution range of the colourless glass is roughly summarised. It can be seen from the figure that there is a group in which the MnO concentration is distributed in a high concentration range of about 1.5~1.8 wt%. All of these samples were unearthed in Bukhara (Bk 005~008, 010) and are features not found in the colourless glass from Paykend. It may also be the colourless glass type made in Bukhara. Other colourless glass also contained less than 1 wt% (about 0.3~0.5 wt%) MnO, but it could not be judged whether this was added as a decolourising material or was the result of impurities.

In figures 9.54 and 9.55, the naturally coloured glass Py020, Py022 and Py029 were within the colourless glass group. Py020 and Py022 are clearly green glass types that are thought to be naturally coloured. They are the bottoms of the bottles with thick walls. However, if the walls of glass are thinner, the glass colour may appear colourless. Py029 is a bottle whose surface is weathering, and the glass has a colour tone that is somewhat difficult to distinguish. The distribution of Fe_2O_3 concentration is in the range of less than 0.5~1 wt%, and the distribution overlaps between the colourless glass and the naturally coloured glass. It is considered to be a delicate concentration range in which the changes in colour tone can be visually observed depending on the firing atmosphere in the furnace and the size of the vessel during manufacturing.

Figures 9.56 and 9.57 show the difference between raw alkali materials that used glass utilising plant ash. The difference between the K_2O and Na_2O concentrations can be seen in both figures, especially in the colourless glass, where the K_2O and Na_2O graph are concentrated in the low range. The Mn decolourising glass excavated from Bukhara is distributed in the range of the naturally coloured glass group in these figures. It can be suggested that the glass was decolourised by Mn using raw materials similar to naturally coloured glass. On the other hand, the Iranian glass (Bk 001~004) excavated from Bukhara was plotted in the colourless glass zone. If this result is considered valid, it may be that other colourless glass in the same range may also come from Iran.

Based on the above results, the colourless glass was divided into two types:
(a) colourless glass using a purified silica component
(b) colourless glass discoloured with Mn.

It can be surmised that type (a) is imported from Iran, and type (b) is from the site of Bukhara or the surrounding

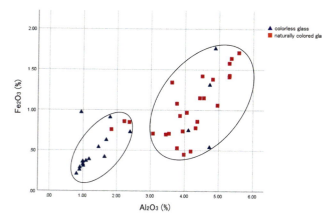

FIGURE 9.54 Plots of Al_2O_3 vs. Fe_2O_3 concentrations in the colourless glass and the naturally coloured glass

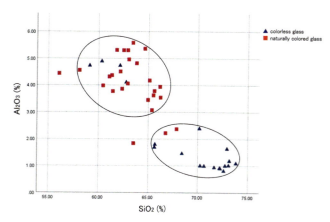

FIGURE 9.55 Plots of SiO_2 vs. Al_2O_3 concentrations in the colourless glass and the naturally coloured glass

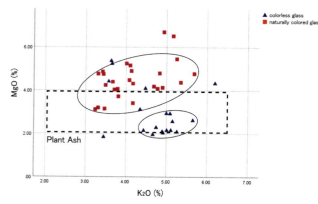

FIGURE 9.56 Plots of K_2O vs. MgO concentrations in the colourless glass and the naturally coloured glass

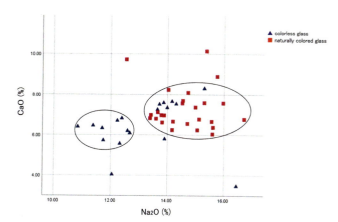

FIGURE 9.57 Plots of CaO vs. Na_2O concentrations in the colourless glass and the naturally coloured glass

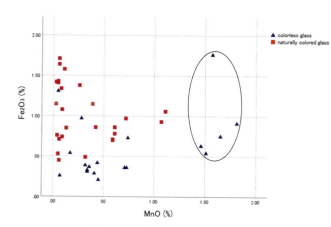

FIGURE 9.58 Plots of MnO vs. Fe_2O_3 concentrations in the colourless glass and the naturally coloured glass

TABLE 9.6 Average chemical compositions of the colourless glass and naturally coloured glass (wt%)

	Colorless glass $n=19$		Naturally colored glass $n=36$	
	Mean	SD	Mean	SD
SiO_2	68.93	4.81	61.91	3.38
TiO_2	0.07	0.04	0.15	0.07
Al_2O_3	1.96	1.47	4.41	1.27
Fe_2O_3	0.60	0.40	1.10	0.37
MgO	4.70	0.73	4.41	0.73
MnO	0.71	0.58	0.22	0.30
CaO	6.46	1.22	7.36	0.97
Na_2O	13.12	1.43	14.98	1.21
K_2O	2.97	1.14	4.90	1.10
P_2O_5	0.40	0.30	0.47	0.14
BaO	0.032	0.025	0.043	0.013
CoO	n.d.		n.d.	
CuO	0.006	0.005	0.009	0.009
SrO	0.048	0.011	0.053	0.011
ZnO	0.007	0.005	0.007	0.002

4.6 Conclusion

The investigation yielded the following conclusions:

(1) The glass artifacts unearthed in the Bukhara Oasis were soda-lime silica glass made from plant ash, and no other glass types were found.
(2) The blue glass is of two types, Co-coloured glass and Cu-coloured glass (the Co type is further subdivided), the black glass is Fe coloured and the olive-green glass is Mn coloured. In Central Asia, coloured glass has not been studied, and future investigations are necessary.
(3) The difference in chemical composition between the colourless glass and the naturally coloured glass may reflect the difference in raw silica and sodium materials.
(4) Two types of techniques were recognised: the glass was decolourised using raw materials with few impurities, and the glass was decolourised using Mn. The former may be Iranian glass, and the latter may have used raw materials similar to naturally coloured glass.
(5) After classifying glass-production materials and glass products by cluster analysis, the glass was broadly divided into four groups. The glass-production materials were divided into two chemical compositions (groups A and D). No products with the same chemical composition were found except for Py016. It can be assumed that group B glass was made in the site of Paykend site, and group C-1 glass was made in the site of Bukhara.

This study presents the chemical composition of glass from the Bukhara Oasis, especially from the sites of Paykend and Bukhara. However, there is a limit to the results that can be derived from the analysis of these samples alone. In the future, it is necessary to identify and compare the chemical composition of glass artifacts from neighbouring areas.

5 Conclusion

Yoko Shindo

We have mainly considered the glass and artifacts related to glass unearthed in the Bukhara Oasis (see table 9.8–9.17). The following discusses the findings.

At the site of Paykend, many glass vessels were unearthed in the shahrestan. They were concentrated in trench B where more than 50% of the total number of unearthed glass was found. Particularly, around 18% of all registered glass was excavated in strata 3736 and 3792, the garbage layers, which yielded coins from Binkent dated to 918–19 and thus can be dated to the 10th century. From these facts, Paykend was an important city within Sogdiana; however, it is thought that the discovered Islamic glass belongs to the period from 9th to 11th century.

At the site of Ramitan, glass vessels were rarely seen in the shahrestan and citadel, which had served as the centre of Sogdiana before the Islamic invasion. In the suburban area (rabad), most of the glass fragments were excavated from the stratum dating to the 9th century and later, except for the Sasanian cut glass.

Furthermore, at the site of Bukhara, many of the glass artifacts were unearthed in the citadel. They were especially concentrated in stratum US230, a garbage pit, which yielded the high-quality cut glass from the Persian area and is assumed to be dated from the 10th to 11th centuries, the height of the Samanid dynasty's prosperity.

This all indicates that in the Bukhara Oasis, while glass vessels were hardly used in the pre-Islamic period, they came to be used daily from the Islamic period onwards. However, most of the glass vessels were unearthed in only two of the sites, Paykend and Bukhara, and there are few examples of uncovered glasses from other sites.

Situated to the south of the Bukhara Oasis, the site of Paykend is the first commercial hub and the cultural gateway from the area west of the Amu Darya River. The site of Bukhara was the centre of politics and economics during the Samanid dynasty. The glass vessels were popular in such characteristic sites as Bukhara and Paykend; however, they were rarely used as daily tableware in Ramitan, Iskijkat, site 250 and Kakishtuvan.

A large amount of pottery was unearthed in every site in the Bukhara Oasis, and it reveals that this area was culturally earthenware centred. In contrast, quantitatively, daily glass items such as bowls and bottles are few in number and limited with regard to shape and function.

Although there are only a few types of glass articles in the Bukhara Oasis, it clearly shows that they have local characteristics in terms of styles, technique and chemical composition.

Examining their characteristics in more detail, the bottle with a wide wavy threaded decoration around the neck was popular in Paykend and would have been distributed around Transoxiana and the area west of the Amu Darya River. In addition, the bottle or beaker with simple rib-moulded decorations was also specific to Transoxiana.

Additionally, the chemical analysis of the glass vessels and artifacts related to production clarifies that the chemical composition of their raw materials was different from that of general Islamic glass. They have a high potassium and magnesium value characteristic of products made in the Bukhara Oasis.

Thus, it can be considered that glass production occurred in this area due to the fact that the glass artifacts contain characteristics – in terms of styles, technique and chemical composition – connected to artifacts related to glass production unearthed in the Bukhara Oasis.

On the other hand, colourless glass vessels with high-quality materials other than local products were uncovered in the sites of Paykend and Bukhara. Chemical analysis reveals that the colourless glass can be divided in two groups: those possibly made in the Bukhara sites or the surrounding locality, and those possibly made somewhere other than the Bukhara Oasis.

Although they are few in number, there are products that are assumed to have been imported from the area west of Amu Darya River due to the following characteristics: the high-quality colourless type, chemical composition and cut decoration. Therefore, it is concluded that in the Bukhara Oasis there are two types of glassware: those manufactured in the Bukhara Oasis around the sites of Paykend and Bukhara, and those imported from the Persian area.

Provided that the glass objects manufactured under the Islamic dynasties are called Islamic glass, the glass articles unearthed in the Bukhara Oasis should also be referred to as Islamic glass. However, glass articles from the Bukhara Oasis quite clearly show their local characteristics and lack the distinctive features of Islamic culture in terms of the shape and/or decoration typical of the 9th and 10th centuries, as seen in Fustat and other main sites of that period.[36]

Furthermore, the excavations in the Bukhara Oasis have not yet yielded glass articles adorned with the various kinds of known Islamic decoration for that period, such as lustre-painted, scratched and impressed decoration.[37] Such articles were found in many port city sites located on the sea-trade route;[38] however, they were rarely imported into the Bukhara Oasis, a hinterland of Central Asia.

On the other hand, high-quality cut glass vessels that are thought to have been made in the Persian area were unearthed. There are many cupping vessels, which were thought to be influenced by Islamic culture and used for Arabic medicinal practices. These indicate the possibility that glass articles and production techniques might have been transported along the land route.

As mentioned above, the glass from the Bukhara Oasis shows different features than the glass articles unearthed in the main Islamic sites. Thus, it can be concluded that the Bukhara Oasis enjoyed Arabic culture and custom by establishing a close relationship with the Persian area and developed its unique glass production.

In the future we expect to excavate layers dating to the pre-Islamic period, which are, of course, located lower than those already unearthed. This will enable us to determine more clearly, through an examination of the glass articles, how the material culture transformed from the pre-Islamic to the Islamic period.

Moreover, through the glass articles we will be able clarify the issue of glass production in the Bukhara Oasis using more detailed chemical analysis and examine both the relationship between each site in the Bukhara Oasis and the trade with the neighbouring oasis.

Acknowledgements

We would like to express our gratitude to Yasuko Fujii and Tami Ishida for their cooperation in our glass study, to Shuji Ninomiya, Asuka Kanto and Akiko Matsumoto for their advice and cooperation with the chemical analysis, to Noriko Horiuchi and Yoshie Abe for their cooperation in the drawings and photos, and to Satoko Mizuno and Kazue Kobayashi for their translations. This work was supported by JSPS Kakenhi (Japan Society for the Promotion of Science, Grant-in-Aid for Scientific Research) Grant Number 16H03470.

---

36 For Fustat, see Shindo 1992; Shindo 2001; Scanlon and Pinder-Wilson 2001; for Samarra, see Lamm 1928; for Suse, see Kervran 1984; Kervran and Raugeulle 1984; for Nishapur, see Kröger 1995; for Bet Shean, see Hadad 2005, etc.

37 These types of decoration have been found in Islamic glass excavated at the site of the port city of Raya on the Sinai Peninsula (Shindo 2004b, 2005, 2007b, 2008, 2012, 2015). They have also been found at various port sites in the Malay Peninsula (An 1996), Indonesia (Guillot 2011), Vietnam (Shindo 2000b), and China (An 1991; Shindo 2001).

38 In the same way, although a large quantity of Chinese ware, which was an important item in East–West trade, has been found in the port city sites on the sea route, it has not been found in the oasis cities, including Paykend and Bukhara, which were the main staging posts located along the land route.

TABLE 9.8 List of objects unearthed from Paykend 1

Fig.	Chan.	Strat.	Part	Form	Deco.	Color	Condition	Rim	Base	Reg.No.	Note
9.2/1	D (2010)	US 500	rim	uncertain	thread	pale green	thin weathering	round 1		BPG-26	
9.2/2	D (2010)	US 501	body	uncertain	thread	colorless (greenish)	thin weathering			BPG-272	
9.2/3	D (2010)	US 503	neck	botlle	thread (wavy)	pale bluish green	thin weathering			BPG-29	
9.2/4	D (2010)	US 509	rim	beaker	-	pale bluish green	thin weathering	fold 2		BPG-33	
9.2/5	D (2010)	US 509	base	botlle	-	pale bluish green	thin weathering		kick	BPG-31	pontil mark
9.2/6	D (2010)	US 504	-	slag	-	pale green	-	-	-	BPG-30	C.A. Py036
9.2/7	D (2010)	US 501	-	cullet	-	pale bluish green	-	-	-	BPG-28	C.A. Py033
9.2/8	D (2010)	US 514	-	slag	-	pale bluish green	-	-	-	BPG-34	
9.2/9	A (2010)	US 709	body-base	botlle?	thread	pale bluish green	thin weathering			BPG-41	
9.2/10	A (2010)	US 700 surface	rim+ handle	botlle?	-	pale bluish green	thick weathering	round 1		BPG-36	
9.2/11	A (2010)	US 713	rim-shoulder	botlle	-	colorless	thick weathering	round 1		BPG-42	
		US 720								BPG-44	
9.2/12	A (2010)	US 709	base	uncertain	-	blue	thick weathering		concave	BPG-40	pontil mark C.A. Py001
9.2/13	A (2010)	US 747	base	uncertain	-	colorless	thick weathering		flat	BPG-45	pontil mark
9.2/14	A (2010)	US 708	base	uncertain	-	pale bluish green	partial weathering		concave	BPG-39	pontil mark
9.3/1	B (2012)	US 3815	rim	beaker?	thread (straight)	pale bluish green	dot weathering	round 1		BPG-196	
9.3/2	B (2012)	US 3851	rim	beaker?	thread (straight)	uncertain	thick weathering	round 2		BPG-199	
9.3/3	B (2012)	US 3815	rim	Jar?	thread (straight)	pale blue (cobalt)	thin weathering	round 2		BPG-247	
9.3/4	B (2012)	US 3736	body?	uncertain	thread (straight)	pale blue (cobalt)	thin weathering			BPG-123	C.A. Py002
										BPG-133	
9.3/5	B (2010)	US 223	body?	uncertain	thread (straight)	pale bluish green	dot weathering	-	-	BPG-15	
9.3/6	B (2011)	US 1624	base	uncertain	thread (straight)	colorless	thick weathering		concave + thread	BPG-277	
9.3/7	B (2012)	US 3810	neck	botlle	thread (wavy)	pale bluish green	thin weathering			BPG-154	
9.3/8	B (2010)	US 130	neck	botlle	thread (wavy)	pale bluish green	thin weathering			BPG-3	
9.3/9	B (2010)	US 223	neck	botlle	thread (wavy)	pale bluish green	-	-	-	BPG-14	
9.3/10	B (2011)	US 622	neck	botlle	thread (wavy)	uncertain	thick weathering			BPG-103	
9.3/11	B (2011)	US 664	neck	botlle	thread (wavy)	pale green	thin weathering			BPG-109	

* Chan. : Chantier, Strat. : Stratum, Deco. : Decoration, Reg.No. : Registration Number, C.A. : Chemical Analysis

TABLE 9.9 List of objects unearthed from Paykend 2

Fig.	Trench	Strat.	Part	Form	Deco.	Color	Condition	Rim	Base	Reg.No.	Note
9.3/12	B (2012)	US 3736	neck-body	botlle	mold (double circle)	pale blue (cobalt)	partial weathering	-	-	BPG-210 BPG-211	C.A. Py003
9.3/13	B (2012)	US 3878	body-base	botlle	mold (trefoils)	colorless	thick wethering	-	concave	BPG-207	
9.3/14	B (2011)	US 1692	body	botlle?	pinch	pale bluish green	thick weathering	-	-	BPG-79	
9.4/1	B (2011)	US 1637	base	uncertain	mold (honeycomb)	colorless (greenish)	dot weathering	-	concave	BPG-63	pontil mark
9.4/2	B (2012)	US 3815	base	uncertain	mold	colorless	thin wethering	-	concave	BPG-248	pontil mark
9.4/3	B (2012)	US 3792	base	uncertain	mold (facet)	pale blue (cobalt)	partial weathering	-	concave	BPG-151	
9.4/4	B (2012)	US 3876	body-base	botlle?	mold (facet)	colorless	thick weathering	-	point	BPG-225	pontil mark
9.4/5	B (2011)	US 1680	base	uncertain	mold (petal)	uncertain	thick weathering	-	concave+mold	BPG-74	pontil mark
9.4/6	B (2012)	US 3900	base	uncertain	mold (petal)	pale bluish green	thick weathering	-	concave+mold	BPG-226	pontil mark
9.4/7	B (2011)	US 1635	rim-body	botlle (hexagonal)	mold (facet)	colorless	thick weathering	round 1	-	BPG-61	
9.4/8	B (2010)	US 149	body?	uncertain	mold (petal)	colorless	thick weathering	-	-	BPG-6	
9.4/9	B (2012)	US 3736	neck	uncertain	mold (facet)	pale blue (cobalt)	thin wethering	-	-	BPG-142	
9.4/10	B (2012)	US 3792	base	uncertain	mold (honeycomb)	colorless	thick weathering	-	concave+mold	BPG-150	
9.4/11	B (2012)	US 3808	base	uncertain	mold (petal)	uncertain	thick weathering	-	concave+mold	BPG-152	
9.4/12	B (2012)	US 3878	base	uncertain	mold (petal)	pale bluish green	thin wethering	-	concave+mold	BPG-205	
9.4/13	B (2012)	US 3851	base	uncertain	mold (petal)	pale bluish green	thick weathering	-	concave+mold	BPG-250	
9.5/1	B (2012)	US 3815	shoulder?	botlle?	liner cut (line)	colorless	thick weathering	-	-	BPG-249	
9.5/2	B (2010)	US 125	body	uncertain	facet cut (oval)	colorless	thick weathering	-	-	BPG-279	C.A. Py010
9.5/3	B (2011)	US 657	shoulder	botlle	facet cut (circle)	colorless	thick weathering	-	-	BPG-107	C.A. Py011
9.5/4	B (2010)	US 223	base	botlle	facet cut (circle)	colorless	thick weathering	-	flat	BPG-16	C.A. Py012
9.5/5	B (2012)	US 3736	base	uncertain	facet cut	colorless	thin weathering	-	flat	BPG-255	C.A. Py013
9.5/6	B (2012)	US 3736	rim	beaker	-	pale bluish green	dot weathering	round 1	-	BPG-216	
9.5/7	B (2012)	US 3825	rim	beaker	-	pale bluish green	thick weathering	round 4	-	BPG-198	
9.5/8	B (2011)	US 1682	rim	beaker	-	colorless (greenish)	dot weathering	round 3	-	BPG-76	
	B (2012)	US 3736								BPG-218	

* Strat. : Stratum, Deco. : Decoration,
Reg.No. : Registration Number, C.A. : Chemical Analysis

TABLE 9.10 List of objects unearthed from Paykend 3

Fig.	Trench	Strat.	Part	Form	Deco.	Color	Condition	Rim	Base	Reg.No.	Note
9.5/9	B (2012)	US 3736	rim	beaker	-	pale bluish green	dot weathering	round 1	-	BPG-217	
9.5/10	B (2011)	US 618	rim	beaker?	-	pale bluish green	partial weathering	fold 2	-	BPG-102	
9.5/11	B (2011)	US 1692	rim	beaker?	-	uncertain	thick weathering	fold 2	-	BPG-78	
9.5/12	B (2012)	US 3736	rim-base	small cup	-	pale bluish green	dot weathering	bent in	-	BPG-122	
9.5/13	B (2012)	US 3736	body	uncertain	ridge	pale blue (cobalt)	dot weathering	-	-	BPG-126	C.A. Py004
9.5/14	B (2012)	US 3736	base	uncertain	ridge	pale bluish green	thin weathering	-	concave	BPG-127	
9.5/15	B (2012)	US 3736	rim-shoulder	botlle	-	pale blue	-	fold 1	-	BPG-214	C.A. Py017
9.5/16	B (2012)	US 3736	rim-neck	botlle	-	pale bluish green	-	round 4	-	BPG-253	
9.5/17	B (2012)	US 3736	rim-shoulder	botlle or jar	-	pale bluish green	-	round 4	-	BPG-257	C.A. Py018
9.6/1	B (2011)	US 1637	neck - shoulder	botlle	bulge	pale bluish green	thin weathering	-	-	BPG-68	
9.6/2	B (2011)	US 1637	neck-shoulder	botlle	bulge	pale blue	thick weathering	-	-	BPG-65	
9.6/3	B (2012)	US 3862	neck	botlle	bulge	pale bluish green	thick weathering	-	-	BPG-202	
9.6/4	B (2012)	US 3776	rim-neck	botlle	-	pale blue	thick weathering	round 4	-	BPG-144	
9.6/5	B (2012)	US 3815	rim-neck	botlle	-	pale blue	thick weathering	round 1	-	BPG-194 BPG-195	
9.6/6	B (2011)	US 1624	rim-shoulder	jar	-	colorless	-	round 1	-	BPG-278	
9.6/7	B (2012)	US 3736	rim	jar	-	pale bluish green	thin weathering	round 1	-	BPG-128	
9.6/8	B (2012)	US 3907	rim	jar?	-	pale blue	thick weathering	fold 2	-	BPG-227	
9.6/9	B (2012)	US 3787	rim-base	jar	-	pale bluish green	thin weathering	round 1	- kick	BPG-116 BPG-120	C.A. Py016
9.6/10	B (2012)	US 3736	base	uncertain	-	colorless	thick weathering	-	flat	BPG-125	pontil mark C.A. Py014
9.6/11	B (2012)	US 3736	base	uncertain	-	colorless	thick weathering	-	flat?	BPG-222	C.A. Py015
9.6/12	B (2010)	US 231	base	botlle	-	colorless	thick weathering	-	concave	BPG-18	pontil mark
9.7/1	B (2012)	US 3736	base	uncertain	-	pale bluish green	partial weathering	-	concave	BPG-139	pontil mark C.A. Py019
9.7/2	B (2012)	US 3787	base	uncertain	-	pale bluish green	partial weathering	-	concave	BPG-145	pontil mark C.A. Py020
9.7/3	B (2012)	US 3736	base	botlle	-	blue	thin weathering	-	kick	BPG-124	pontil mark C.A. Py005
9.7/4	B (2011)	US 1629	base	botlle	-	pale bluish green	thin weathering	-	concave	BPG-59	pontil mark C.A. Py022
9.7/5	B (2011)	US 1637	base	uncertain	-	pale bluish green	partial weathering	-	concave	BPG-62	pontil mark C.A. Py023
9.7/6	B (2010)	US 163	base	uncertain	-	pale bluish green	partial weathering	-	concave	BPG-8	pontil mark C.A. Py021

* Strat. : Stratum, Deco. : Decoration,
   Reg.No. : Registration Number, C.A. : Chemical Analysis

TABLE 9.11 List of objects unearthed from Paykend 4

Fig.	Trench	Strat.	Part	Form	Deco.	Color	Condition	Rim	Base	Reg.No.	Note
9.7/7	B (2012)	US 3787	base	uncertain	-	pale bluish green	partial weathering	-	button	BPG-146	
9.7/8	B (2010)	US 231	base	botlle	-	pale green	partial weathering	-	concave	BPG-17	pontil mark C.A. Py024
9.7/9	B (2012)	US 3736	base	uncertain	-	bluish green	-	-	concave + short foot	BPG-221 BPG-252	C.A. Py025
9.8/1	B (2011)	US 1672 / US 1682	handle + rim	botlle?	-	pale bluish green	dot weathering	round 1		BPG-69 / BPG-77	
9.8/2	B (2012)	US 3736	handle + rim	botlle?	-	pale green	dot weathering	round 4		BPG-137	
9.8/3	B (2010)	US 201	handle	botlle?	-	colorless (greenish)	thin weathering	-		BPG-12	
9.8/4	B (2012)	US 3736	handle + rim	jug?	thread	pale green + blue	partial weathering	thread 2	-	BPG-135	
9.8/5	B (2010)	US 165	handle	botlle	-	pale blue	thin weathering	-		BPG-9	
9.8/6	B (2011)	US 1637	rim	pane	-	pale bluish green	dot weathering	fold	-	BPG-66	
9.8/7	B (2012)	US 3736	rim	pane	-	pale blue	dot weathering	fold	-	BPG-224	C.A. Py026
9.8/8	B (2012)	US 3736	rim	pane	-	pale blue	thick weathering	fold	-	BPG-134	
9.8/9	B (2010)	US 127	rim	pane	-	uncertain	thick weathering	fold	-	BPG-2	
9.8/10	B (2011)	US 645	rim	pane	-	colorless	thick weathering	fold	-	BPG-106	
9.8/11	J (2012)	US 4220	neck	botlle	thread (wavy)	pale bluish green	thin weathering	-	-	BPG-229	
9.8/12	JB (2012)	US 4308	body	uncertain	pinch	pale bluish green	thin weathering	-	-	BPG-231	
9.8/13	JB (2012)	US 4314	-	slag	-	pale bluish green	-	-	-	BPG-232	C.A. Py037
no fig.	B (2012)	US 3736	neck	botlle	-	pale blue (cobalt)	partial weathering	-	-	BPG-213	C.A. Py006
no fig.	B (2012)	US 3736	base	uncertain	-	green	-	-	uncertain	BPG-130	C.A. Py031
9.9/1	F (2011)	US 494	body	botlle	thread (zigzag) +	uncertain	thick weathering	-	-	BPG-99	
9.9/2	F (2011)	US 439	neck?	botlle?	thread (wavy)	pale olive green	dot weathering	-	-	BPG-96	C.A. Py009
9.9/3	F (2011)	US 485	rim-neck	botlle	-	pale green	thick weathering	fold 1	-	BPG-98	
9.9/4	F (2011)	US 432	rim-shoulder	botlle	-	uncertain	thick weathering	round 4	-	BPG-84	
9.9/5	F (2011)	US 435	rim-shoulder	botlle	-	pale bluish green	thin weathering	round 1	-	BPG-92	
9.9/6	F (2011)	US 413	rim - shoulder	jar	-	colorless	thin weathering	round 3	-	BPG-82	

* Strat. : Stratum, Deco. : Decoration,
  Reg.No. : Registration Number, C.A. : Chemical Analysis

TABLE 9.12 List of objects unearthed from Paykend 5

Fig.	Trench	Strat.	Part	Form	Deco.	Color	Condition	Rim	Base	Reg.No.	Note
9.9/7	F (2011)	US 432	handle + rim	bottle?	-	pale bluish green	dot weathering	round	-	BPG-85	
9.9/8	F (2011)	US 437	rim	pane	-	pale bluish green	dot weathering	fold	-	BPG-95	C.A. Py028
9.9/9	F (2011)	US 432	neck-shoulder	bottle	-	uncertain	thick weathering	-	-	BPG-90	
			base						concave	BPG-91	pontil mark
9.9/10	F (2011)	US 432	base	bottle	-	pale bluish green	partial weathering	-	concave	BPG-87	pontil mark C.A.Py027
9.9/11	C (2010)	US 305	neck or body	uncertain	mold	pale bluish green	thick weathering	-	-	BPG-21	
9.9/12	C (2010)	US 309	rim	pane	-	colorless	thick weathering	fold	-	BPG-22	
9.9/13	C (2010)	US 305	handle	cup?	-	uncertain	thick weathering	-	-	BPG-20	
9.9/14	C (2010)	US 300	rim	beaker	-	colorless	thick weathering	bent out	-	BPG-19	
9.10/1	H (2012)	US 4101	rim	beaker	thread (straight)	colorless (greenish) + bluish green	thin weathering	thread 2	-	BPG-188	
9.10/2	H (2012)	US 4045	rim	beaker	thread (straight)	colorless	thick weathering	thread 2	-	BPG-192	
9.10/3	H (2012)	US 4006	base	bottle?	thread	uncertain	thick weathering	-	round + thread	BPG-184	pontil mark
9.10/4	H (2012)	US 4004	neck- body	bottle	-	pale blue	thick weathering	-	-	BPG-179	C.A. Py029
9.10/5	H (2012)	US 4004	rim	beaker	-	colorless	thick weathering	round 1	-	BPG-186	
9.10/6	H (2012)	US 4004	rim	bowl	-	pale blue	-	round 1	-	BPG-165	C.A. Py030
9.10/7	H (2012)	US 4008	rim-shoulder	bottle	mold	colorless	thick weathering	cut	-	BPG-185	
9.10/8	H (2012)	US 4004	rim	pane	-	pale bluish green	thick weathering	fold	-	BPG-178	
9.11/1	H (2012)	US 4004	rim - base	cupping	-	pale bluish green	thick weathering	round 1	round	BPG-M2	pontil mark Ark museum
9.11/2	H (2012)	US 4004	rim - base	cupping	-	pale bluish green	thick weathering	round 1	round	BPG-M3	pontil mark Ark museum
9.11/3	H (2012)	US 4004	rim - base	cupping	-	pale bluish green	thick weathering	round 1	round	BPG-M4	pontil mark Ark museum
9.11/4	H (2012)	US 4004	rim - base	cupping	-	pale bluish green	thin weathering	round 1	round	BPG-M5	pontil mark Ark museum
9.11/5	H (2012)	US 4004	rim + spaut	cupping	-	pale bluish green	thin weathering	round 2	-	BPG-174	
9.11/6	H (2012)	US 4004	base-body	cupping	-	uncertain	thick weathering	-	round	BPG-169	pontil mark
9.11/7	H (2012)	US 4004	base	cupping	-	pale bluish green	thick weathering	-	round	BPG-170	pontil mark
9.11/8	H (2012)	US 4004	base	cupping	-	pale bluish green	thick weathering	-	round	BPG-171	pontil mark
9.11/9	H (2012)	US 4004	rim + spaut	cupping	-	uncertain	thick weathering	round 2	-	BPG-173	

* Strat. : Stratum, Deco. : Decoration,
Reg.No. : Registration Number, C.A. : Chemical Analysis

TABLE 9.13 List of objects unearthed from Paykend 6

Fig.	Trench	Strat.	Part	Form	Deco.	Color	Condition	Rim	Base	Reg.No.	Note
9.12/1	E (2014)	US 4637N	rim	beaker	thread (straight)	pale bluish green + deep blue	thin weathering	thread 2	-	BPG-276	
9.12/2	E (2014)	US 9612b	rim	uncertain	thread (straight)	pale brown + dark brown	thin weathering	thread 2	-	BPG-270	
9.12/3	E (2013)	US 4482	neck	botlle	thread (wavy)	pale green	thin weathering			BPG-235	
9.12/4	E (2013)	US 4519	-	botlle?	thread (zigzag) + stamp	uncertain	thick weathering	-	-	BPG-281	
9.12/5	E (2014)	US 9600	neck-shoulder	botlle?	mold (facet)	colorless (greenish)	thin weathering	-	-	BPG-261	
9.12/6	E (2010)	US 901	body	uncertain	mold (rib)	pale bluish green	thin weathering			BPG-48	
9.12/7	E (2010)	US 903e	base	botlle	mold (petal)	colorless (greenish)	thin weathering	-	concave+ mold	BPG-52	pontil mark
9.12/8	E (2013)	US 4418N	rim-neck	botlle	tool	colorless (greenish)	partial weathering	round 4	-	BPG-234	
9.12/9	E (2014)	US 4620	handle	uncertain	-	pale bluish green	dot weathering			BPG-263	C.A. Py031
9.12/10	E (2010)	US 902a	-	slag	-	uncertain	-	-	-	BPG-49	
9.12/11	E (2010)	US 903b	-	slag	-	uncertain	-			BPG-51	
9.12/12	E (2010)	US 910	-	slag	-	uncertain	-			BPG-53	
9.12/13	E (2010)	US 925	-	slag	-	pale green	-			BPG-54	C.A. Py040
9.12/14	E (2014)	US 1017	-	slag	-	yellow green	-			BPG-262	C.A.Py041
9.12/15	E (2014)	US 9612c	-	slag	-	pale brown	-			BPG-275	C.A.Py042
9.12/16	E (2011)	US 974	-	slag	-	pale green	-			BPG-114	C.A. Py038
9.12/17	E (2014)	US 4267	-	slag	-	yellow green	-			BPG-264	C.A. Py039
9.12/18	Ribat4 (2016)		-	cullet	-		-			BPG-283	C.A.Py034 & Py035

* Strat. : Stratum, Deco. : Decoration,
  Reg.No. : Registration Number, C.A. : Chemical Analysis

TABLE 9.14 List of objects unearthed from Ramitan and Site 250

Fig.	Trench	Strat.	Part	Form	Deco.	Color	Condition	Rim	Base	Reg.No.	Note
9.38/1	F (2014)	US 1137	body	bowl?	facet cut (oval)	colorless (bluish)	thin weathering	-	-	BRG-14	C.A. Rm002
9.38/2	F (2014)	US 1059	rim-neck	bottle	thread (weavy)	pale bluish green	thick weathering	uncertain	-	BRG-11	
9.38/3	F (2014)	US 1000	neck	bottle	thread (weavy)	pale bluish green	thin weathering	uncertain	-	BRG-4	
9.38/4	F (2014)	US 1088	base	bottle	-	uncertain	thick weathering	-	pointed base	BRG-13	
9.38/5	F (2014)	US 1036	rim-neck	bottle	-	pale bluish green	thick weathering	round 4	-	BRG-8	
9.38/6	F (2014)	US 1033	base	uncertain	-	colorless	thick weathering	-	concave	BRG-7	
9.38/7	F (2014)	US 1063	body-base	uncertain	-	pale blue	thin weathering	-	flat	BRG-45	
9.38/8	D (2018)	-	body	uncertain	-	pale bluish green	weathering	-	-	BRG-46	C.A. Rm001
9.38/9	F (2014)	US 1104	rim	pane	-	pale bluish green	thick weathering	fold	-	BRG-16	
9.38/10	F (2014)	US 1108	rim	pane	-	pale bluish green	thick weathering	fold	-	BRG-17	
9.39/1	G (2017)	US 6042	body-base	uncertain	mold (rib)	uncertain	thick weathering	-	-	BRG-43	
9.39/2	G (2017)	US 6010	rim-neck	bottle	tool	uncertain	thick weathering	round 4	-	BRG-37	
9.39/3	G (2016)	top soil	rim-neck	bottle	-	colorless	thick weathering	round 4	-	BRG-29	
9.39/4	G (2016)	top soil	rim	pane	-	uncertain	thick weathering	fold	-	BRG-30	
9.39/5	G (2017)	US 6010	rim	pane	-	uncertain	thick weathering	fold	-	BRG-38	
9.39/6	G (2017)	US 6007	rim	pane	-	pale bluish green	thick weathering	fold	-	BRG-42	

Site250

Fig.	Trench	Str.	Part	Form	Dec.	Color	Condition	Rim	Base	Reg.No.	Note
9.39/7	A (2017)	US 140	body	uncertain	mold (circle)	colorless	thick weathering	-	-	BSG-11	
9.39/8	A (2017)	US 156	rim	bowl	-	pale bluish green	thin weathering	fold 1	-	BSG-15	
9.39/9	A (2017)	US 159	rim	bowl	-	pale bluish green	dot weathering	round 1	-	BSG-3	
9.39/10	A (2017)	US 156	base	bottle	-	pale bluish green	thick weathering	-	kick	BSG-1	pontil mark
9.39/11	A (2017)	US 156	rim + handle	uncertain	-	pale bluish green	thin weathering	round 1	-	BSG-13	
9.39/12	A (2017)	US 156	handle	uncertain	-	pale bluish green	thick weathering	-	-	BSG-8	
9.39/13	A (2017)	US 102	rim + handle	uncertain	-	pale bluish green	thin weathering	round 1	-	BSG-2	

* Strat. : Stratum, Deco. : Decoration,
  Reg.No. : Registration Number, C.A. : Chemical Analysis

TABLE 9.15 List of objects unearthed from Iskijkat and Kakistuvan

Fig.	Trench	Strat.	Part	Form	Deco.	Color	Condition	Rim	Base	Reg.No.	Note
9.41/1	A (2014)	US 201	rim	uncertain		colorless	thick weathering	fould 2	-	BIG-8	
9.41/2	A (2014)	US 209	rim	bottle	-	colorless	thick weathering	round 1	-	BIG-10	
9.41/3	A (2014)	US 231	base	bottle	-	pale bluish green	thick weathering	-	concave	BIG-11	pontil mark
9.41/4	B (2015)	unstratfied find	rim	beaker	mold	pale bluish green	thick weathering	round 4	-	BIG-15	
9.41/5	B (2015)	US 470	rim	beaker	-	colorless	thick weathering	round + cut (inside)	-	BIG-14	C.A. Is001
9.41/6	B (2015)	US 405	rim	pane	-	pale bluish green	thick weathering	fold	-	BIG-16	
9.41/7	B (2015)	US 467	rim	pane	-	pale bluish green	thick weathering	fold	-	BIG-12	
9.41/8	B (2015)	US 483	rim	pane	-	pale bluish green	-	fold	-	BIG-13	C.A. Is002

Kakishtuvan

Fig.	Trench	Str.	Part	Form	Dec.	Color	Condition	Rim	Base	Reg.No.	Note
9.41/9	A (2016)	US 116	body	uncertain	thread (straight)	colorless	dot weathering	-	-	BKG-3	
9.41/10	A (2016)	US 116	base	uncertain		colorless (greenish)	dot weathering	-	concave	BKG-2	pontil mark C.A. Kk001
9.41/11	A (2016)	HORS Strat. Surface	base	goblet?		colorless	thick weathering	-	concave	BKG-5	
9.41/12	A (2016)	US 111b	rim	pane	-	pale bluish green	dot weathering	fold	-	BKG-4	
9.41/13	A (2016)	US 105	rim	pane	-	pale bluish green	-	fold	-	BKG-6	C.A. Kk002
no fig.	A (2016)	US 131	base of handle	handle	-	pale bluish green	thin weathering	-	-	BKG-1	C.A. Kk003

* Strat. : Stratum, Deco. : Decoration, Hors Strat. : Unstratified Stratum,
  Reg.No. : Registration Number, C.A. : Chemical Analysis

TABLE 9.16 List of objects unearthed from Bukhara 1

Fig.	Trench	Strat.	Part	Form	Deco.	Color	Condition	Rim	Base	Reg.No.	Note
9.43/1	A (2018)	US 230	rim-base	bowl	relief cut (circle)	colorless	-	round 1	-	BBG-80	C.A. Bk001
9.43/2	A (2018)	US 230	rim	bottle	facet cut	colorless	-	round 1	-	BBG-140	
9.43/3	A (2018)	US 230	body-base	bottle	relief cut	colorless	partial weathering	-	flat	BBG-82	
										BBG-83	C.A. Bk002
										BBG-84	
										BBG-85	
										BBG100	
										BBG-137	
										BBG-169	
										BBG-171	
										BBG-207	
9.43/4	A (2018)	US 230	body-base	bottle	liner cut	colorless	partial weathering	-	flat+cut	BBG-81	
										BBG-101	C.A. Bk003
										BBG-170	
9.43/5	A (2018)	US 230	rim	beaker	liner cut	colorless	thin weathering	round 1	-	BBG-163	C.A. Bk004
9.43/6	A (2017)	US 183	base	uncertain	liner cut	colorless	thin weathering	-	foot+cut	BBG-68	
9.44/1	A (2018)	US 230	body	-	thread	colorless	thin weathering	-	-	BBG-96	
										BBG-147	
9.44/2	A (2018)	US 230	rim	beaker	impress	colorless	partial weathering	round 1	-	BBG-87	C.A. Bk005
9.44/3	A (2018)	US 230	shoulder-base	botlle	tool	pale bluish green	thin weathering	-	concave+tool	BBG-136	
										BBG-146	
9.44/4	A (2018)	US 230	body	?	ridge	colorless	partial weathering	-	-	BBG-110	
9.44/5	A (2018)	US 230	bidy	?	ridge	pale bluish green	-	-	-	BBG-121	C.A. Bk011
9.44/6	A (2018)	US 230	rim+body+base	bottle	mold (rib)	pale bluish green	-	round 4	concave	BBG-112	
										BBG-139	
										BBG-155	
										BBG-156	
										BBG-191	
9.44/7	A (2017)	US 152	base	uncertain	mold	pale bluish green	thick weathering	-	concave+mold	BBG-31	
9.44/8	A (2018)	US 230	rim-shoulder	bottle	mold (rib)	pale bluish green	-	round 4	-	BBG-167	
										BBG-176	
										BBG-198	
9.45/1	A (2017)	US 151	body	uncertain	mold (honeycomb)	pele brown	thick weathering	-	-	BPG-30	
9.45/2	A (2017)	US 170	base+ foot	goblet	mold (petal)	colorless	thick weathering	-	foot	BBG-48	
9.45/3	A (2018)	US 230	rim	uncertain	mold (circle)	pale bluish green	-	round 1	-	BBG-193	C.A.Bk014
9.45/4	A (2018)	US 230	rim-shoulder	bottle	buldge	colorless	thin weathering	fold 1	-	BBG-91	
										BBG-95	C.A. Bk008
										BBG-108	
9.45/5	A (2018)	US 230	rim	botlle	buldge	pale bluish green	thin weathering	round 1	-	BBG-94	C.A.Bk013
9.45/6	A (2018)	US 230	rim-shoulder	botlle	buldge	pale bluish green	thick weathering	round 1	-	BBG-165	
										BBG-205	

* Strat. : Stratum, Deco. : Decoration,
  Reg.No. : Registration Number, C.A. : Chemical Analysis

TABLE 9.17 List of objects unearthed from Bukhara 2

Fig.	Trench	Str.	Part	Form	Dec.	Color	Condition	Rim	Base	Reg.No.	Note
9.45/7	A (2018)	US 230	rim-neck	bottle	-	pale bluish green	-	cut	-	BBG-157	
9.45/8	A (2018)	US 230	rim-neck	bottle	-	colorless	-	cut	-	BBG-158	
9.45/9	A (2018)	US 230	rim	ewer	-	colorless	thick weathering	round 1	-	BBG-203	
9.45/10	A (2018)	US 230	rim-shoulder	jar	-	pale bluish green	thin weathering	round 2	-	BBG-160 / BBG-161	
9.45/11	A (2018)	US 230	rim-shoulder	jar	-	pale bluish green	dot weathering	round 1	-	BBG-164	C.A. Bk012
9.45/12	A (2018)	US 230	rim-body	beaker	-	colorless	thick weathering	round 1	-	BBG-104	C.A. Bk007
9.46/1	A (2018)	US 230	rim-body	goblet	-	pale bluish green	partial weathering	round 3	-	BBG-127 / BBG-133 / BBG-149 / BBG-190	C.A.Bk015
9.46/2	A (2018)	US 230	rim-base	bowl	-	colorless	partial weathering	round 1	concave	BBG-152 / BBG-153	pontil mark
9.46/3	A (2018)	US 230	base	uncertain	-	pale bluish green	thin weathering	-	concave + ring	BBG-148	pontil mark
9.46/4	A (2018)	US 230	base	uncertain	-	colorless	thick weathering	-	concave	BBG-183	pontil mark C.A. Bk009
9.46/5	A (2018)	US 230	base	uncertain	-	colorless	partial weathering	-	concave	BBG-145	pontil mark
9.46/6	A (2018)	US 230	rim	pane	-	pale bluish green	dot wethering	fold	-	BBG-109	
9.46/7	A (2018)	US 230	core	lamp	-	colorless	thick weathering	-	-	BBG-168	
no fig.	A (2018)	US 230	body	jar	ridge	colorless	thick weathering	-	-	BBG-196 / BBG-199 / BBG-200 / BBG-201 / BBG-202	C.A. Bk010
no fig.	A (2018)	US 230	base	uncertain	-	colorless	partial weathering	-	flat	BBG-89	C.A.Bk006
9.46/8	uncertain (2010)	231	-	bangle	-	black	-	-	-	BPO-3	C.A. Py007
9.46/9	B (2012)	B3815	-	bangle	-	black	-	-	-	BPO-13	C.A. Py008

* Strat. : Stratum, Deco. : Decoration,
  Reg.No. : Registration Number, C.A. : Chemical Analysis

CHAPTER 10

Animal Remains in the Oasis of Bukhara: Preliminary Results

Decruyenaere Delphine, Rocco Rante, Manon Vuillien and Marjan Mashkour

The last few years have seen an increase in bioarchaeological research in southern Central Asia. This research has obviously played a significant role in our understanding of the subsistence economies and animal resource management of southern Eurasian communities. However, scholars have undoubtedly focused on specific topics of research and neglected others. Recent research focused on the ancient periods, in particular the Bronze and Iron Ages (Doll 2003; Joglekar 1998; Lecomte and Mashkour 2013; Lhuillier and Mashkour 2017; Lhuillier et al. 2018; MAFTUR 2013; Moore 1993a and b; Moore et al. 1994; Rouse and Cerasetti 2014; Sataev 2020; Wu, Miller, and Crabtree 2015) and inherent issues of pastoral nomadism (Frachetti and Maksudov 2014; Frachetti et al. 2017; Taylor et al. 2018 and 2019). The least documented area is probably the subsistence economies in the urban centres established in the oases along the major routes of the Silk Road during the historical periods we are treating.

While there are some studies on Turkmenistan, Northeast Iran and Afghanistan during the medieval periods (Bocherens et al. 2006; Lecomte and Mashkour 1998; Mashkour 1998; Mashkour 2013; Mashkour, Radu and Thomas 2013; Mashkour et al. 2017; Monchot et al. 2019; Smith 1997 and 1998), there are only two published studies on Uzbekistan during this time. The first one concerns the Kara-Tepe faunal remains (4th–5th century CE) in the Khorezm Oasis (Brite et al. 2017), and the second one is about the biological material discovered in a kiln in Termez that is dated to the 9th century CE (Portero et al. 2021). It is also important to mention the unpublished work of E. Serrone on the faunal material in Samarkand that led to two conferences (ASWA 2017; ICAZ 2018); another significant study looks at isotopic niches to establish connections between urban and pastoral diets during medieval times (Hermes et al. 2018).

In light of this sparse data, we are planning to carry out an archaeozoological study of sites in the Bukhara Oasis (Iskijkat, Bukhara, Paykend, Ramitan, Kakishtuvan and site 250) which should enhance our understanding of the subsistence economy and animal resource management in both urban and rural contexts. These sites, undergoing excavation by MAFOUB since 2009, have been selected to represent the various settlements and spatial organisations within the oasis (centre vs. periphery, waterways and trade routes). The populations outside the towns are composed of either sedentary villages or mobile pastoralists. Within this framework it is important to take into account the environmental, socio-political and cultural aspects of the various powers that succeeded each other in the oasis (3rd century BCE–15th century CE).

The nearly 2,000 years represented in the archaeological faunal material will document: 1) the natural environment of the oasis and the human impact, based on the spectra of wild vertebrates; 2) the evolution of the diet, described using the faunal composition in correlation with the chronological periods, the geographic position within the oasis and a site's function, 3) the animal management patterns in urban consumer sites versus peripheral producer sites, based on the slaughtering and skeletal profiles of domesticated animals. We will also analyse pack animals, camels and equines in order to track long-distance mobility.

This paper dealt with the faunal remains recovered at Iskijkat and studied during the first archaeozoological mission that took place this spring 2021. It is not exhaustive since the material is still under study, but the current research provides some clues about the dietary practices of the human communities that inhabited the site and their relationships with the numerous types of animals present at the site.

1   Iskijkat

The town of Iskijkat was founded in the 3rd century BCE on the bank of one of the meanders of the Zerafshan River at the eastern edge of the oasis and on the road linking Samarkand and Bukhara (Rante and Mirzaakhmedov 2019: 231–39). This strategic location at an important axis led to its demographic expansion and encouraged trade and the exchange of goods during the antiquity and the Middle Ages. In the 10th century CE, the historian al-Narshakhī, who lived during the Samanid period, describes a large city mainly inhabited by merchants. He specifies that the wealth and prosperity of the city did not come from its agricultural activity but from trade (al-Narshakhī ca. 940 CE; English translation: Frye 2007; Rante, Schwarz, and Tronca 2022). Today, the urban landscape has been replaced with small agricultural villages and a canal has replaced the old waterway.

The settlement consists of a large citadel forming a perfect square (70 m on each side) that is fortified with four towers at the corners. A large rampart surrounds the citadel and separates it from the shahrestan,[1] which is directly connected to the river. To the south, the area is currently covered with vineyards, but the survey material suggests that it was once a suburb of the city. Suburbs usually include a commercial and/or a manufacturing area as well as settlements. This tripartite organisation of the town and suburban areas is only clearly established from the 5th century CE onwards, although this dynamic began earlier (Rante and Mirzaakhmedov 2019: 231–39).

2   Faunal Assemblages

The assemblages briefly discussed here represent 2,154 faunal remains and weigh a total of 30,291.5 grams. They were systematically collected by hand in the two stratigraphic soundings that were carried out at the site. The first one (chantier A) was dug in the citadel in 2014; the second one (chantier B) in the shahrestan in 2015.

The faunal remains are unequally distributed between the two soundings, with the shahrestan being the most significant area in terms of the number of remains (NR). However, while the citadel yielded remains throughout the whole chronological sequence (from the 3rd century BCE to the 15th century CE), the remains unearthed in the shahrestan only appear between the 1st century BCE and the end of the 10th century CE, with the majority coming from the levels dated to the 1st century CE (fig. 10.1).

It should be noted that some of the bones are embedded in the building's walls. The contents of the clay collected for the walls was disregarded and, therefore, it contains heterogeneous objects (bones, pot sherds, etc.). Obviously, these bones cannot be dated.

Climatic and pedologic conditions in the Bukhara Oasis allowed animal bones to be preserved relatively intact. This facilitated the anatomic and taxonomic identifications carried out in the field with the help of osteological anatomic atlases (Barone 1986; Hilson 1986; Schmid 1972; Steiger 1990). Some bones specimens could not be identified in Bukhara due to the lack of reference material and were sent to the National Museum of Natural History in Paris (MNHN) with the authorisation of the Uzbek Ministry of Culture. They are currently being thoroughly analysed at the archaeozoological laboratory of the AASPE (Archéozoologie et Archéobotanique – Sociétés, pratiques et environnements) using the lab's reference collections as well as those of the main patrimonial collections of the National Museum of Natural History and also other documentation techniques, such as 3D imagery.

The external appearance of the bone bears many information on the history of the animal deposits and their

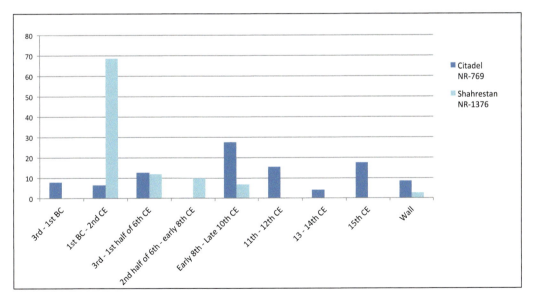

FIGURE 10.1   Percentage of Number of Remains (NR) by chantier and period

---

1   The term shahrestan is employed here as defined by Rante and Mirzaakhmedov 1 (2019: 27), i.e., as the part of the city around the citadel (qohandez). It is also identified as a kind of village dependent on the central political part of the city.

FIGURE 10.2 Traces of rodent, small ruminant metatarsal, citadel, 10th century CE, Iskijkat
© DECRUYENAERE DELPHINE

interactions with humans and the natural environment. The taphonomic observations of the bone remains indicate only a few occurrences of concretion and some traces of weathering (cracks and desquamations) due to prolonged sun exposure. In contrast, a large portion of the bones shows traces of of human modification, including numerous butchery marks (fractures, incisions, cut marks, etc.) and fire traces (heating, burning) relating to processing and/or consumption activities. Gnawing and biting traces observed on some of the bones suggest that they must have been left in open areas before being buried; evidence that carnivores were present at the site. Rodents also made their presence known (fig. 10.2). Finally, bluish traces, the result of contact with metal objects objects (oxidation), were noted on several bones.

3 Livestock

The archaeozoological study reveals a subsistence economy based mainly on domesticated animal husbandry (ca. 90% of the assemblage). Among domesticate animals, caprines (*Capra hircus* and *Ovis aries*) are predominant. Distinguishing these two species is not always easy, either because diagnostic skeletal parts are missing or damaged, or because the morphological characteristics described in the literature do not apply to all ancient populations probably due to the diversity of breeds (Boessneck 1969; Fernandez 2001; Halstead and Collins 2002; Helmer and Rocheteau 1994; Zeder and Pillar 2010; Zeder and Lapham 2010). In addition, the presence of small wild ruminants (gazelle – *Gazella subgutturosa*, roe deer – *Capreolus capreolus* and possibly saiga – *Saiga tatarica*) makes osteological differentiation even more difficult; not to mention the presence of large specimens that could be either large domestic males or wild caprines (figs. 10.3 and 10.4). A more detailed osteometrical and morphometrical study will allow us to categorise some of these bones further.

Where it was possible to distinguish sheep from goats, the majority were sheep. This is not surprising for Central Asia; this is also found to be the case in the archaeozoological studies of neighboring sites at various periods (Brite et al. 2017; Wu, Miller, and Crabtree 2015).

The management and use of the herds still needs to be studied. Demographic, skeletal and slaughtering profiles will help us determine human dietary habits and dairy product management, while isotopic studies will refine our understanding of the relationships between pastoral nomads and urban communities. Points worth considering in future investigations are the questions of how and when specialised sheep breeds emerged and what are the origins of Karakul sheep, whose fetal wool until recently was used in Astrakhan manufacturing and was highly prized.

Cattle (*Bos* sp.) is the second most common species in the faunal spectrum, just behind caprines. The numerous traces of butchery on the bones do not leave any doubts about its consumption. They must also have been used for their milk or their skin as well as for traction and draught. The muscular insertion marks, which are clearly visible on some of the bones, suggest that at least some of the herd may have been robust animals.

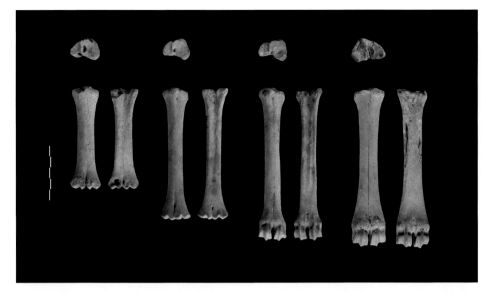

FIGURE 10.3
Metacarpals illustrating the similarity of small ruminant bones. From left to right: *Capra hircus* (juvenile), *Ovis aries* (juvenile), *Ovis aries*, large domestic or wild Caprinae
© DECRUYENAERE DELPHINE

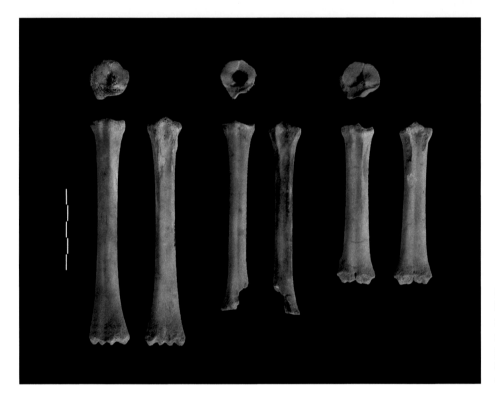

FIGURE 10.4
Metatarsals illustrating the similarity of small ruminant bones. From left to right: *Ovis aries*, a small ruminant possibly *Gazella subgutturosa* (tool), *Capra hircus*
© DECRUYENAERE DELPHINE

4 Pack Animals

Cattle was also among the pack animals that played a major role on caravan routes during the antique and medieval periods, as were camelids (either the Bactrian or dromedary camel and their hybrids) and equids (the horse, the donkey, and the mule). In a grave at Turfan (in modern-day China), archaeologists discovered a piece of writing paper that had been reused as a burial garment. It was the testimony of an Iranian merchant before a Chinese court that was recorded around 670 CE. The merchant was asking the court for help recovering a bolt of silk owed by his brother, owed him and who had disappeared and probably perished on a commercial trip into the desert with four cattle, two camels and a donkey (Recycled piece of paper found at Turfan, Xinjiang Museum. Quoted in Hansen 2017: 4).

In recent years, there has been an increasing number of biological studies of camelids (Camelus bactrianus, C. dromedarius and hybrids) – both morphological and genetic (Agut-Labordère and Redon 2020; Burger 2016; Berthon et al. 2020; Çakırlar and Berthon 2014; Dioli 2020; Francfort 2020; Mashkour and Beech 2014; Potts 2005; Ruiz et al. 2015; Steiger 1990). In the collective imagination, camelids have become the emblematic figure of the Silk Roads: they accompanied merchants, diplomatic

FIGURE 10.5A Sogdian musicians on a Bactrian camel, glazed earthenware, Tang Dynasty, National Museum of Beijing
© NATIONAL MUSEUM OF CHINA, BEIJING

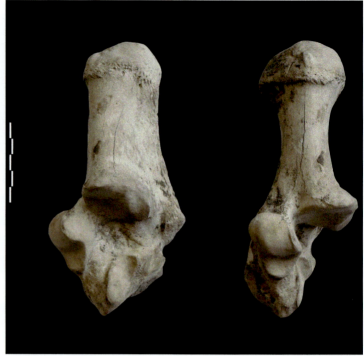

FIGURE 10.5B Right calcaneus, *Camelus* sp., shahrestan, 7th–8th centuries CE, Iskijkat
© DECRUYENAERE DELPHINE

envoys and travellers across the deserts and steppes of Central Asia. They were extensively represented especially by artists of the Tang Dynasty (7th–9th century CE), among others (fig. 10.5a).

Indeed, camelids are well adapted to carrying loads and riders – especially hybrids, whose main advantage is their significantly greater size, strength and load capacity (Tapper 2010). However, as we have just seen, they were not the only animals to escort the caravans. As with cattle, camelids could also be used for their dairy, skin or wool.

At Iskijkat, about 10 camelid remains were discovered. With the exception of a distal metatarsal from the 2nd–3rd century CE that was discovered in the citadel, they all come from the shahrestan and date from the 1st to the 10th century CE (fig. 10.5b).

It is sometimes difficult to distinguish between the various species of equids (*Equus caballus*, *E. asinus*, *E. hemionus* and the hybrids). The bones and dental remains found at Iskijkat are still being studied, but the presence of donkeys and horses has already been established. The latter played a fundamental role in transregional trade as well as in the postal network.

We know, for example, that they were used in postal relays or Yam[2] that seems to have been borrowed from the Chinese system and spread throughout the Mongol Empire as it expanded (Gazagnadou 2005 and 2017). In addition, the abundance of butchery marks associated with consumption activities found on equid bones from Iskijkat provide evidence that they could also have been eaten.

5 Other Domesticated Animals: Pigs and Chickens

Pigs and chickens were two species originating from China, were also part of the diet of the inhabitants of Iskijkat. Pigs (*Sus scrofa domesticus*) are represented by only about 25 remains, all of them discovered in the levels dated between the 1st century BCE and the 10th century CE, both in the sharestan and the citadel areas.

According to the morphology observed with the help of atlases (Cohen and Serjeantson 1996; Erbersdobler 1968), most of the bird remains collected at the site belong to the Phasianidae family (Cohen and Serjeantson 1996; Erbersdobler 1968). Some complete bones were identified as the specie *Gallus gallus domesticus* (domestic chicken).

---

2 According to Gazagnadou (2005): "*Yam* is the Arabic or Persian transcription of the Mongolian term *jam* (*djam*), originally denoting 'road, routes or direction.' In the 13th century, the term *yam* also signifies the postal service of the Mongol Khan and sometimes a postal relay."

FIGURE 10.6   Tarso-metatarsus, *Gallus gallus domesticus*, shahrestan, 1st century CE, Iskijkat
© DECRUYENAERE DELPHINE

Figure 10.6 shows a chicken's tarsometatarsus that has distinct ergot: it is either an old female or a male. It should be noted that the remains attributed to this specie are quite thin compared to present-day specimens. Hens were also raised for their eggs.

6   Wild Animals

Alongside domestic animals there is also evidence of wild species. Hunted game is mainly represented by a few bones of gazella (*Gazella subgutturosa*) and cervids. It should be noted that an especially suid large femur raises the question of whether it belonged to a wild boar. There are also uncertainties about the identification of several caprine bones that seem to belong to wild animals (see fig. 10.3). The small number of remains suggests that hunting was not a major component of the subsistence economy. In a prosperous urban context, hunting likely had social and symbolic meanings that are difficult to ascertain.

The three remains identified as belonging to a hare (*Lepus* sp.) might have come from hunts, although we did not find any evidence of processing for dietary purposes or for fur (fig. 10.7; follow the link in QR for the online 3D imagery).

7   Commensal Animals

Besides the taxa described above, there were some remains of carnivores and rodents present in the faunal assemblage. Only three remains are identified as dog (*Canis familiaris*), but their presence is well attested by the traces of gnawing and biting observed on some bones. This suggests that dogs were allowed to roam freely within the city.

A smal number of rat (*Rattus* sp.) remains are present, including two mandibles. They come from levels in the citadel dated to the 15th century.

8   Bones as Raw Material

Bones were also used as raw material for the manufacture of artifacts, as evidenced by some pre-cut pieces of bone (fig. 10.8a) and more than 20 objects coming mainly from the shahrestan. Among the latter, there are numerous metapodials from small ruminants (Caprinae or *Gazella*), and sometimes from cattle, with a vertical perforation in the proximal part of the bone. This perforation was used

FIGURE 10.7A   Pre-cut raw material, shahrestan, 1st century CE, Iskijkat
© DECRUYENAERE DELPHINE

FIGURE 10.7B   Polished cow's mandible, *Bos* sp., citadel, 2nd–3rd centuries CE, Iskijkat
© DECRUYENAERE DELPHINE

to insert a point or a sharp tool that was usually made of metal. The assemblage also yielded a large quantity of polished talus used for playing games. Some of them had holes and must have been used as pendants. The presence of four toothless and polished cow mandibles is intriguing (fig. 10.8b). Their function has not yet been determined.

9 Conclusion

In conclusion, the preliminary study of the Iskijkat animal-bone assemblage has highlighted some of the ways animals were used in the Bukhara Oasis from antiquity to the Middle Ages. Taxa represented in the faunal spectra reveal a subsistence economy based mainly on caprine and, to a lesser extent, bovine husbandry. Caprine played a major role, with a greater number of sheep present than goats. Their representation across all periods indicates that there is no major difference between the chrono-cultural periods. Animals were also used for their by-products: milk, wool, fat, etc. Pigs and chickens also played a role in the population's diet. The contribution of hunting is rather limited and primarily relates to the gazelle and cervids. Pack animals include cattles, camelids, horses, donkeys and possibly mules. Dogs and rodents are not well documented in number of remains, however, traces of gnawing and bites on the bones are abundant.

The collection method lacked systematic sieving, and this has introduced a bias in the faunal list: heavier bones belonging to larger animals are more comprehensively represented than smaller taxa. During the 2022 campaign, the samples that were collected in a few specific contexts will be sieved. This should allow us to expand the faunal list to include other taxa, such as rodents, birds, mollusks or fish. Thus, we cannot comment on the role of fishing, but given what has been found at Paykend, a neighbouring site that is currently being studied by the first author, it can be assumed that fishing was practised. Fish are also documented in Termez (Portero et al. 2021).

CHAPTER 11

Radiocarbon Dating in the Oasis of Bukhara

Pascale Richardin and Rocco Rante

In 2009 the Louvre Museum, in collaboration with the Archaeological Institute of Samarkand and the Tashkent Academy of Sciences started a program (Franco-Uzbek Archaeological Mission in the Bukhara Oasis; MAFOUB) to study the Bukhara region. The aim of this program is to study the region's territorial and historical context by investigating its human occupations, from antiquity to the Islamic period, focusing on the dynamic of the occupations, the evolution of human behaviour and the urban and cultural evolution. One major interest is to reconsider the urban development through the relations between these urban entities and western and eastern Iranian cities. It is also interested in a detailed study of local productions and imports in order to conduct an in-depth investigation of the dynamics of trade between the eastern Mediterranean and eastern Asia.

The program has several research axes. The archaeological excavation is complemented by different activities, in order to revisit and construct the historical and cultural framework of the region. Among these activities, the study of material culture occupies an important place. Moreover, in order to clarify and better determine the historical and cultural framework, the study of the excavated objects is accompanied by a solid archaeometric study.

For this purpose, the archaeological excavation has been conducted with the objective to determine an absolute chronology as concretely as possible through regular sampling of different materials that can be analysed and give absolute dates. Since the numismatic study, which has been conducted everywhere, cannot be regularly considered as solid method for dating layers, radiocarbon dates have been methodically gleaned. In this context, each archaeological trench has been studied using several C^{14} measurements.

Between 2010 and 2016, 163 measures were conducted by the Research and Restoration Centre of French Museums (C2RMF) in Paris. Between 2016 and 2018, 20 measures were conducted by the BETA Analytic laboratory in the United States.

The aim of this article is to publish the most important measures, which have been already mentioned in the first volume of *The Oasis of Bukhara* (Rante and Mirzaakhmedov 2019). For this, a coherent lot of samples, coming from every site and locus we studied within the oasis, have been organised to clearly show the entire chronological framework.

1 Methodology

There are four steps required for preparing samples for carbon 14 (C^{14}) dating:
– physical pretreatment (cleaning);
– chemical pretreatment (or extraction of carbonaceous materials), which depends on the nature of the sample being dated;
– combustion (or extraction of CO_2);
– and graphitisation (transformation of CO_2 into graphite carbon).

Only the first three stages are carried out at C2RMF; the graphitisation is carried out at the carbon 14 measurement laboratory (LMC14) at the Atomic Energy Commission (CEA) in Saclay.

1.1 Vegetal Samples: Acid / Base / Acid Wash

The charcoal or wood fragment is first washed in ultrapure water in an ultrasonic bath. Then, it undergoes a succession of extractions or washes that alternated with rinses with ultrapure water. This is the AAA protocol (acid, alkali, acid). The first acid wash removes exogenous carbonates (limestone) or others minerals and low molecular weight fulvic acids from the sample. The alkali treatment removes humic acids, and finally, the last acid wash removes the fulvic acids and CO_2 formed during the alkali rinsing.

1.2 Bone Samples and Elemental Analysis Results

The method applied for C^{14} dating bones is the Longin method (Longin 1971), the so-called "method of extracting soluble collagen". Bones are powdered and demineralised in order to recover the organic fraction. The detailed protocol has been described previously (Richardin, Porcier, Ikram, Louarn, and Berthet 2017).

Beforehand, an elementary analysis is carried out on the bone powder (~10 mg) to determine the carbon (C%) and nitrogen (N%) percentages. This makes it possible to evaluate the amount of collagen and exogenous carbon contamination in the sample.

1.3 Combustion of Samples

The dried organic fraction is then combusted under a high vacuum where the organic matter will transform into CO_2 and water. These gases are separated by cryogenic purification and the CO_2 is collected in a sealed tube. In order to control the protocols, for each series of four samples to be dated we install a standard, alternative "intercalibration sample", a reference with a known age (FIRI H, dated 2232 ± 5 BP), or a "white", South African charcoal of infinite age.

1.4 Graphitisation and Carbon 14 Measurement

The graphitisation is achieved through a direct catalytic reduction of the CO_2 with hydrogen, using Fe powder at 600° C and an excess of H_2. During the process, the carbon is deposited on the iron and the powder is pressed into a flat pellet. Radiocarbon measurements were performed at the Artemis AMS (Accelerator Mass Spectrometry) facility in Saclay (France) (Moreau et al. 2013).

Radiocarbon age measurements and the calculation of the samples' calendar dates (after calibration) are collected in tables 11.1–6. Calendar dates were determined using OxCal software v4.3.2 (Bronk Ramsey 1994 and 2017; Bronk Ramsey and Lee 2013) and the most recent calibration curve data for the Northern Hemisphere, IntCal13 (Reimer, Bard, and Bayliss 2013).

Calibration age ranges correspond to 95.4% probability (2Σ) and expressed in years cal BCE or cal CE (before or after J.-C.).

2 Ramitan

2.1 Trench A

The measures (table 11.1) presented here (Richardin and Gandolfo 2013 and 2014) depict the whole stratigraphy of this trench, which has been excavated above the citadel of Ramitan, at the foot of the palace, on its western part. Figure 11.1 (Ramitan, trench A) shows the homogeneous chronology span, which goes from the 1st century CE until the 4th–early 5th century CE. The regular occupation found in this trench is not surprising because of the excavation of the entire rampart of the earliest city. Moreover, the trench has been situated at a cross between the rampart and the square tower, in the outer side and the inner side, thus giving two different but coherent chronological situations, clearly showing the dynamic the city's abandonment.

Concerning the earliest phase, stratigraphical evidence crossed with the C^{14} dates show the rampart's foundation as occurring during the first part of the 1st century CE, which is taken into consideration in the date of the USM 212 (21–170 CE). The abandonment of the rampart in the 3rd century CE can be observed through the dates of the layers US 139 and US 153. The latest phases are dated between the 4th and the 6th centuries CE, chronologically

TABLE 11.1 Radiocarbon ages and calibrated dates of the samples from Ramitan (trench A, C, F, G and D)

Sample	Lab. code	^{14}C age (BP)	Calibrated date – 2σ (95.4 %)
Romitan – Trench A			
US 131	SacA 36156	1790 ± 30	133 cal AD (68.6%) 264 cal AD
			274 cal AD (26.8%) 330 cal AD
US 139	SacA 35827	1855 ± 30	82 cal AD (95.4%) 234 cal AD
US 148	SacA 35455	1855 ± 30	82 cal AD (95.4%) 234 cal AD
US 149	SacA 36157	1770 ± 30	138 cal AD (95.4%) 345 cal AD
US 152	SacA 35828	1835 ± 30	86 cal AD (95.4%) 246 cal AD
US 153	SacA 35456	1740 ± 30	236 cal AD (95.4%) 386 cal AD
US 173	SacA 35829	1865 ± 30	76 cal AD (95.4%) 230 cal AD
USM 212	SacA 35459	1910 ± 30	21 cal AD (93.6%) 170 cal AD
			194 cal AD (1.8%) 209 cal AD
RM2012A_108	SacA 32300	1735 ± 30	240 cal AD (95.4%) 385 cal AD
RM2012A_115	SacA 32301	1630 ± 30	346 cal AD (5.9%) 371 cal AD
			376 cal AD (64.6%) 474 cal AD
			484 cal AD (24.9%) 536 cal AD
Romitan – Trench C			
US 538	SacA 35819	1755 ± 30	180 cal AD (0.4%) 185 cal AD
			214 cal AD (95.0%) 384 cal AD
US 540	SacA 35457	1755 ± 30	180 cal AD (0.4%) 185 cal AD
			214 cal AD (95.0%) 384 cal AD
US 542	SacA 35821	1755 ± 30	180 cal AD (0.4%) 185 cal AD
			214 cal AD (95.0%) 384 cal AD

TABLE 11.1 Radiocarbon ages and calibrated dates of the samples from Ramitan (*cont.*)

Sample	Lab. code	¹⁴C age (BP)	Calibrated date – 2σ (95.4 %)
US 544	SacA 35962	1820 ± 30	90 cal AD (1.0%) 100 cal AD
			124 cal AD (90.7%) 257 cal AD
			296 cal AD (3.7%) 320 cal AD
US 552	SacA 35822	1765 ± 30	142 cal AD (2.0%) 160 cal AD
			165 cal AD (4.1%) 196 cal AD
			209 cal AD (87.9%) 354 cal AD
			367 cal AD (1.5%) 379 cal AD
US 553	SacA 35823	1905 ± 30	25 cal AD (92.4%) 175 cal AD
			191 cal AD (3.0%) 211 cal AD
US 554	SacA 35826	1790 ± 30	133 cal AD (68.6%) 264 cal AD
			274 cal AD (26.8%) 330 cal AD
Romitan – Trench F			
US 1015	SacA 45112	1140 ± 30	776 cal AD (5.5%) 792 cal AD
			802 cal AD (11.3%) 848 cal AD
			854 cal AD (78.6%) 981 cal AD
US 1036	SacA 45113	1030 ± 30	901 cal AD (2.8%) 920 cal AD
			962 cal AD (91.9%) 1040 cal AD
			1108 cal AD (0.7%) 1116 cal AD
US 1137	SacA 45115	1670 ± 30	258 cal AD (6.0%) 284 cal AD
			290 cal AD (0.4%) 295 cal AD
			321 cal AD (89.0%) 428 cal AD
US 1140	SacA 41752	1550 ± 30	422 cal AD (95.4%) 574 cal AD
US 1148	SacA 41754	1630 ± 40	338 cal AD (95.4%) 538 cal AD
US 1150	SacA 43343	1580 ± 30	410 cal AD (95.4%) 546 cal AD
US 1144	SacA 45116	1605 ± 30	396 cal AD (95.4%) 538 cal AD
USM 1203	SacA 45121	1380 ± 30	606 cal AD (95.4%) 680 cal AD
US 1209	SacA 45117	1600 ± 30	398 cal AD (95.4%) 539 cal AD
USM 1207	SacA 45122	1325 ± 30	650 cal AD (75.4%) 722 cal AD
			740 cal AD (20.0%) 768 cal AD
USM 1210	SacA 45123	1345 ± 30	640 cal AD (86.4%) 714 cal AD
			744 cal AD (9.0%) 765 cal AD
US 1215	SacA 45118	1620 ± 30	382 cal AD (95.4%) 538 cal AD
Romitan – Trench G			
US 1967	Beta-462635	1560 ± 30	420 cal AD (95.4%) 564 cal AD
US 1742	Beta-462638	1550 ± 30	422 cal AD (95.4%) 574 cal AD
US 1828	Beta-462636	680 ± 30	1270 cal AD (60.4%) 1316 cal AD
			1354 cal AD (35%) 1390 cal AD
US 1653	Beta-462634	610 ± 30	1295 cal AD (95.4%) 1404 cal AD
Romitan – The Royal Palace (Trench D)			
US 605	SacA 36152	165 ± 30	1662AD (16.9%) 1706AD
			1720AD (49.3%) 1819AD
			1832AD (10.0%) 1880AD
			1915AD (19.2%) …
US 613	SacA 35967	1590 ± 30	406AD (95.4%) 542AD
US 631	SacA 36151	85 ± 30	1688AD (25.4%) 1730AD
			1808AD (70.0%) 1926AD …
US 652	SacA 36147	1445 ± 30	564AD (95.4%) 653AD
US 2030	Beta 462637	1530 ± 30	428 cal AD (95.4%) 598 cal AD

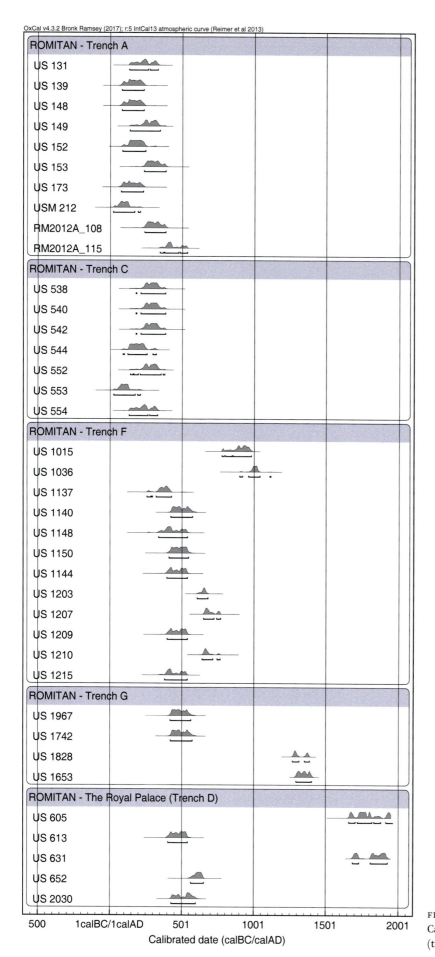

FIGURE 11.1
Calibrated dates of the samples from Ramitan (trench A, C, F, G and D)

linked to the palace constructed during this period just a few metres east.

2.2 Trench C

This trench was opened in the southern part of the shahrestan of Ramitan. It is located only a few metres from the rampart in order to gather the whole stratigraphy of this urban entity and, at the same time, the chronological phases of the rampart.

The dates (Richardin and Gandolfo 2014) from this trench (see fig. 11.1) show a homogeneous span between the 2nd and the 4th century CE. The upper layers were not dated through C^{14} but through a study of ceramic typologies. However, the wall USM 609 has been dated, in order to have a chronological indicator, to the early 7th century, which corresponds with these upper phases.

The general chronological span shows the earliest occupation occurring within the 2nd century CE, which is followed by progressive occupation until the 4th century, a period when the ceramic and architectural evidence shows increased occupation, corresponding to the fortification of the shahrestan.

2.3 Trench F

This trench is located in the upper part of the suburb of Ramitan, around which today there is a cemetery. Here, the intent was to understand the entire chronology of this part of the city. The dates (see fig. 11.1) clearly show an earliest, homogenous occupation in the 5th century CE, which continues until the first half of the 6th century (Richardin et al. 2016) and then again from the 7th century to the 11th century. The upper layers of this trench were heavily disturbed. Thus, no precise contexts have been brought to light that would allow accurate sampling. However, the ceramics helped complete the chronology of the trench. The following phases can be better observed in trench G, located only a few metres away, where these later occupations were well preserved.

2.4 Trench G

The extensive excavation called trench G was opened, as previously mentioned, close to the stratigraphical trench F. Here, a huge building has been partially brought to light (Rante and Mirzaakhmedov 2019: 183–92).

Radiocarbon dating has been conducted by BETA Analytic (see fig. 11.1).[1] Four measures have been obtained: two concerning the earliest occupations of the site, and two concerning one of the latest phases of occupation. The ancient samples were collected in 2015 (US 1742) and 2016 (US 1967) from the same archaeological phase. Both are dated between the early 5th century and the 6th century CE. By comparing them with nearby trench F, a first occupation in this suburban area can definitely be dated to the 5th century CE. The other two samples were also collected in 2015 (US 1653) and 2016 (US 1828). The former measure dated the phase to the 14th century CE and the second one to the 13th–14th centuries CE, thus showing this area was occupied for a long span of time.

2.5 The Royal Palace (Trench D)

Trench D concerns the excavation of the Royal Palace found in the central part of the square citadel. Radiocarbon dating has been obtained by C2RMF (Richardin and Gandolfo 2014) and BETA Analytic.[2] Three main chronological areas can be observed from these dates: the first concerns its origin, which can be detected from the latest dates of trench A at the foot of the palace, dating the substrate the palace was constructed above to not before the 4th century CE; the dates of US 613 and US 652 show that it was in use during the 5th and 6th centuries CE (see fig. 11.1); and the abandonment of the palace, which took place in the middle of the 6th century, as shown by the measure of ashes found above a fire altar and is confirmed by the upper destruction dated also to that period by a coin.

It is important to stress that the dated US 613 and 652 are from the material collected from many wall painting fragments of a white and red colour, attesting to the existence of wall paintings in the palace during that period.

The other measures date the latest layers related to the present occupations in the 19th and 20th centuries.

3 Paykend

3.1 The Potters' Quarter (Trench E)

Although the ceramics were brought to light in this large excavation, some C^{14} dates have also been conducted as chronological guide and to have terminus *post* and *ante* for dating the other layers. The dates identified helped clarify and add precision to the whole chronology. Here we are presenting a selection of the dated layers (Richardin and Gandolfo 2014; Richardin et al. 2016).

One of the first excavated sectors (sector B) showed it was built directly above the natural substrate. The layers and structures associated with kiln 4472 and kiln 909 (US 918, US 4505, US 4533, US 4478) are dated (table 11.2) to the end of the 8th century and the 9th century (fig. 11.2). The TL dating of the fragments belonging to the substrate layer (US 952) has also been dated to the early 8th century, thus confirming the earliest occupation of this area by the

---

1 Sample numbers: 462635, 462638, 462636, 462634.

2 Sample number: 462637.

potters' quarter as occurring as early as the end of the 8th or the beginning of the 9th centuries CE.

The ancient potter's wheel axis, consisting of a big camel bone (see fig. 11.2), also belongs to this chronological span, which correspond to the first phase of the potters' quarter. The C¹⁴ date of Axe 1021 is from the 9th to the early 11th century. By correlation with the other layers, the chronology can be confirmed and corresponds to the 9th century. The stratigraphic sequence of the other potter's wheel axis is provided by the two dates of the later Axes 4521 and 4631, both dated between the 11th and the 12th centuries.

Another group concerns the following period, dated to the 9th and 10th centuries (see fig. 11.2). The dated layers correspond to the filling (US 4529e) of the large, and several times reused, kiln 4424 and the ashtray US 4536. In the same context, but slightly later (10th century), US 4542N corresponds to a ground layer leading to part of this kiln.

The latest phase of the activity observed in this potters' quarter has to be in the 14th century, as shown by the activity of the rectangular oven 9609 (US 9612).

To conclude, samples were collected at the end of the excavation of the southern part of the potters' quarter, above the natural substrate. These two samples (US 4654 and US 4657B) are dated to the 3rd–1st centuries BCE, confirming that the earliest occupation of the site was during this period.

TABLE 11.2   Radiocarbon ages and calibrated dates of the samples from Paykend (trench E)

Sample	Lab. code	¹⁴C age (BP)	Calibrated date – 2σ (95.4%)
Paykend – Trench E			
Axe 1021	SacA 43338	1100 ± 30	886 cal AD (95.4%) 1013 cal AD
Axe 4521	SacA 43339	930 ± 30	1025 cal AD (95.4%) 1165 cal AD
Axe 4631	SacA 43340	940 ± 30	1025 cal AD (95.4%) 1160 cal AD
E 4654	SacA 45127	2080 ± 30	191 cal BC (94.5%) 38 cal BC
			9 cal BC (0.9%) 3 cal BC
E 4657B	SacA 45128	2115 ± 30	341 cal BC (1.9%) 328 cal BC
			204 cal BC (93.5%) 48 cal BC
EB3 9612A	SacA 45130	650 ± 30	1280 cal AD (43.5%) 1326 cal AD
			1343 cal AD (51.9%) 1394 cal AD
EB3 9612A	SacA 45131	575 ± 30	1302 cal AD (61.0%) 1366 cal AD
			1382 cal AD (34.4%) 1420 cal AD
EB3 9612B	SacA 45132	615 ± 30	1294 cal AD (95.4%) 1400 cal AD
EB3 9612B	SacA 45133	640 ± 30	1282 cal AD (41.0%) 1329 cal AD
			1340 cal AD (54.4%) 1396 cal AD
E 4478	SacA 36153	1180 ± 30	730 cal AD (0.7%) 736 cal AD
			768 cal AD (87.5%) 900 cal AD
			722 cal AD (2.9%) 740 cal AD
E 4505	SacA 36493	1225 ± 30	690 cal AD (26.5%) 750 cal AD
			760 cal AD (68.9%) 885 cal AD
E 4529E	SacA36149	1060 ± 30	897 cal AD (14.4%) 925 cal AD
			943 cal AD (81.0%) 1024 cal AD
E 4529e	SacA36148	1190 ± 30	722 cal AD (2.9%) 740 cal AD
			766 cal AD (89.0%) 898 cal AD
			924 cal AD (3.5%) 945 cal AD
E 4533	SacA 35817	1260 ± 30	668 cal AD (85.3%) 778 cal AD
			790 cal AD (5.9%) 828 cal AD
			838 cal AD (4.2%) 864 cal AD
E 4536	SacA36146	1145 ± 30	776 cal AD (7.0%) 794 cal AD
			800 cal AD (88.4%) 975 cal AD
E 4542N	SacA 35965	1115 ± 30	778 cal AD (1.2%) 789 cal AD
			868 cal AD (94.2%) 1013 cal AD

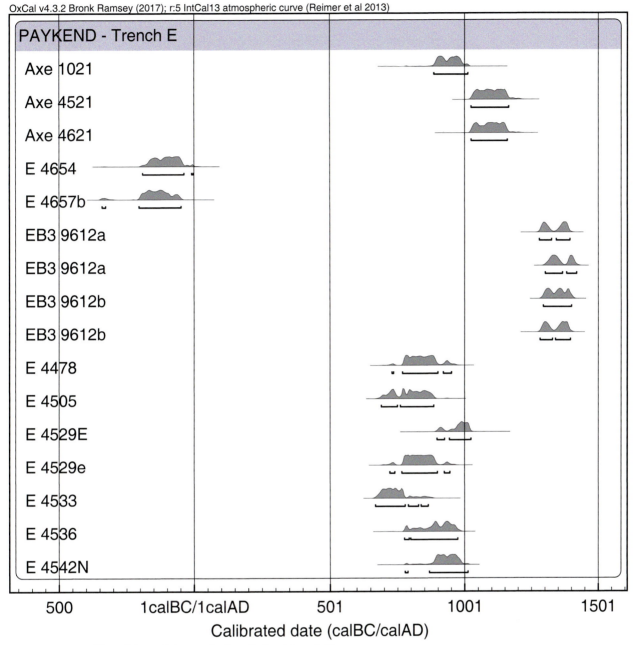

FIGURE 11.2   Calibrated dates of the samples from Paykend (trench E)

4 Iskijkat

4.1 Trench A

Trench A has been opened in the central part of a vast tepe, today called Pushmon tepe, but after some research we now know it would have corresponded with the historical site of Iskijkat (Rante, Schwarz and Tronce 2022: 231–239). More precisely, the trench has been excavated in the centre of the square citadel. The stratigraphic trench delivered a precise chronological sequence, allowing us to have an accurate scale from which to conduct comparisons.

The C^{14} dates (Richardin et al. 2016) clearly show three large chronologic areas (table 11.3 and fig. 11.3): the first one includes a chronology from the 3rd century BCE to the 1st century CE; the second, longer one includes a chronology from the 2nd to the 6th century CE; and the third one from the 7th to the 12th century. The survey of the mound around it has shown that pottery continued to be produced there until the 15th century.

USM 108 corresponds to a wall dated to the 5th–6th centuries CE, which has been reused as a foundation for the walls USM 105 and USM 100.

Concerning the origin of the site (US 392 and US 394), the study of the ceramics and stratigraphical sequence narrows the chronological span to the 2nd–3rd centuries CE. Globally, the site presents a continuity of occupation, which is observable from the C^{14} dates as well as from the archaeological sequence of layers.

TABLE 11.3   Radiocarbon ages and calibrated dates of the samples from Iskijkat (trenches A and B)

Sample	Lab. code	^{14}C age (BP)	Calibrated date 2σ (95.4%)
Iskijkat – Trench A			
USM 108	SacA 41751	1545 ± 30	424 cal AD (95.4%) 578 cal AD
US 235	SacA 44175	940 ± 30	1025 cal AD (95.4%) 1160 cal AD
US 259	SacA 44176	945 ± 30	1025 cal AD (95.4%) 1156 cal AD
US 266	SacA 44177	970 ± 30	1016 cal AD (95.4%) 1154 cal AD
US 305	SacA 44345	1255 ± 30	672 cal AD (80.3%) 779 cal AD
			790 cal AD (15.1%) 868 cal AD
US 320	SacA 44346	1610 ± 30	392 cal AD (95.4%) 538 cal AD
US 334	SacA 44347	1710 ± 30	251 cal AD (95.4%) 397 cal AD
344	SacA 44174	1725 ± 30	244 cal AD (95.4%) 388 cal AD
US 351	SacA 45110	1795 ± 30	132 cal AD (74.2%) 262 cal AD
			277 cal AD (21.2%) 328 cal AD
US 370	SacA 41749	1795 ± 30	132 cal AD (74.2%) 262 cal AD
			277 cal AD (21.2%) 328 cal AD
US 392	SacA 41750	2050 ± 30	166 cal BC (95.4%) 20 cal AD
US 394	SacA 45111	2195 ± 30	363 cal BC (95.4%) 183 cal BC
Iskijkat – Trench B			
US 446	Beta 462639	1280 ± 30	662 cal AD (95.4%) 774 cal AD
US 613	Beta 462640	1960 ± 30	40 cal BC (91.9%) 87 cal AD
			104 cal AD (3.5%) 120 cal AD
US 537	Beta 462960	1950 ± 30	21 cal BC (2.6%) 10 cal BC
			2 cal BC (92.8%) 125 cal AD

4.2   Trench B

Trench B was excavated at the northern limit of the large mound, outside the citadel and in the shahrestan. Although the first observations led to a restrained chronology in comparison to that of the citadel, the excavation and dates shown here also present a complete chronological sequence similar to the citadel. Here, only two C^{14} measures have been obtained (BETA Analytic),[3] considering the dates of the other layers were comparable to those already observed and dated within the citadel (trench A).

The shahrestan shows an interesting chronological sequence (see fig. 11.3). The C^{14} date of the lower readable layers (US 613) corresponds to the 1st century BCE to the 1st century CE, with an upper limit of the early 2nd century CE, a span that has been recorded until US 526. The second C^{14} date was obtained from the upper layer, US 537, and dated to the 1st century BCE to the 2nd century CE. The stratigraphical and ceramic analyses definitely date this phase to the 2nd century CE. The third measure was obtained for US 446, which dated to the 7th–8th centuries CE.[4]

5   Kakishtuvan

5.1   Trench A

The excavation was opened in the central highest part of the large fortified mound of Kakishtuvan, which corresponds to the citadel. The deep trench has been studied using two C^{14} dates[5] (table 11.4) and many comparisons with the previous well-dated excavations, as has been shown previously.

It has been possible to get samples dating to the 2nd–3rd centuries CE from the lower layer (fig. 11.4). No lower samples have been found, but the material found below attested to earlier occupations. The study of ceramics confirms this hypothesis and dates the earliest phase of occupation to the 1st century CE.

The next C^{14} date was obtained on a sample coming from the upper layers of the trench, US 174, and corresponds to the 5th–6th centuries CE. The stratigraphical and ceramic studies definitely date this phase to the 6th century. The high quantity of burnt material found in these layers led us to considering it as a moment when several destructions took place at Kakishtuvan.

---

3 Sample numbers: 462639, 462640.
4 The stratigraphical and ceramics studies (Rante and Mirzaakhmedov 2019: 236–39) completed this framework which otherwise would appear fragmented.

5 The C^{14} measures conducted by BETA Analytic: sample numbers 462641 and 462642.

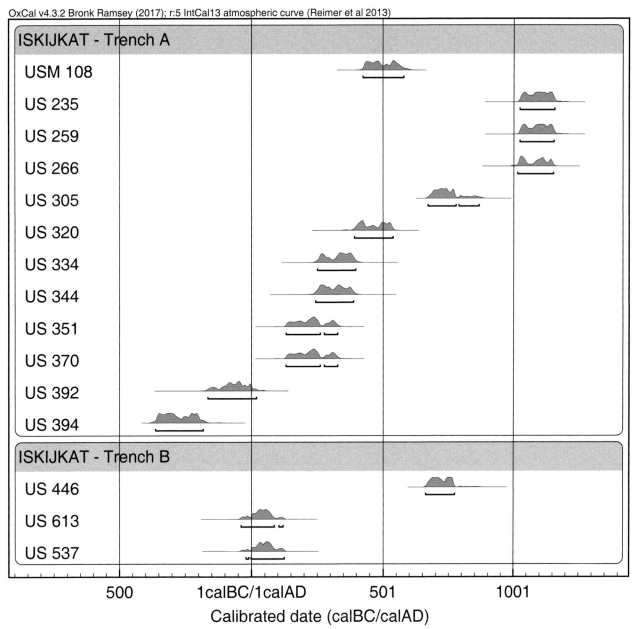

FIGURE 11.3 Calibrated dates of the samples from Iskijkat (trenches A and B)

TABLE 11.4 Radiocarbon ages and calibrated dates of the samples from Kakishtuvan (trench A)

Sample	Lab. code	^{14}C age (BP)	Calibrated date 2σ (95.4 %)
Kakishtuvan – Trench A			
US 174	Beta 462641	1590 ± 30	406 cal AD (95.4%) 542 cal AD
US 297	Beta 462642	1820 ± 30	90 cal AD (1.0%) 100 cal AD
			124 cal AD (90.7%) 257 cal AD
			296 cal AD (3.7%) 320 cal AD

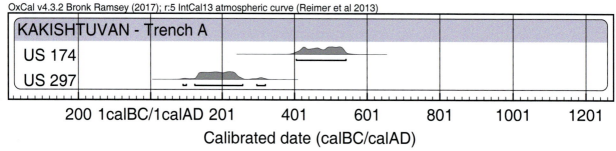

FIGURE 11.4 Calibrated dates of the samples from Kakishtuvan (trench A)

TABLE 11.5 Radiocarbon ages and calibrated dates of the samples from site 250 (trench A)

Sample	Lab. code	¹⁴C age (BP)	Calibrated date 2σ (95.4 %)
Site 250 – Trench A			
US 177	Beta 468801	1490 ± 30	436 cal AD (1.2%) 446 cal AD
			472 cal AD (2.0%) 486 cal AD
			534 cal AD (92.2%) 644 cal AD
US 230	Beta 468800	1980 ± 30	45 cal BC (95.4%) 77 cal AD

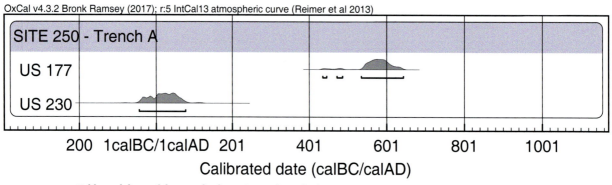

FIGURE 11.5 Calibrated dates of the samples from site 250 (trench A)

6   Site 250

6.1   Trench A

Site 250 is a bipartite site, consisting of a citadel and a small shahrestan, which is located in the centre of the oasis, only 4 km from Ramitan, thus belonging to its socio-economic sphere.

Two dates have been obtained in this trench (table 11.5);[6] the first one from the lower phase US 230 and the second one from an interesting upper phase, US 177 (fig. 10.5). The oldest date, US 230, corresponds to the 1st century BCE to the 1st century CE. The ceramics studied led us to give a later date, the 1st century CE. The second one, US 177, gives a span from the 5th to the 6th century CE. Here, as for other trenches, the 5th–6th-century phase shows several interesting archaeological observations, which led us to focus on this epoch that is marked by important unrest.

7   Bukhara

7.1   Trench A

The huge site of Bukhara, consisting of a large citadel, a large shahrestan and a suburb, whose limits are still hard to precisely define today, has been systematically excavated since 2017 by MAFOUB (Rante and Mirzaakhmedov 2019: 252–60). Trench A has been opened on the top of the huge mound that rises up in the central western part of modern Bukhara. The layers and material brought to light were

---

6 The C¹⁴ measures obtained by BETA Analytic: sample numbers 468800 and 468801.

TABLE 11.6 Radiocarbon ages and calibrated dates of the samples from Bukhara (trench A)

Sample	Lab. code	¹⁴C age (BP)	Calibrated date 2σ (95.4 %)
Bukhara – Trench A			
US 257	Beta 496820	1820 ± 30	90AD (1.0%) 100AD
			124AD (90.7%) 257AD
			296AD (3.7%) 320AD
US 275	Beta 496819	2220 ± 30	375BC (95.4%) 203BC

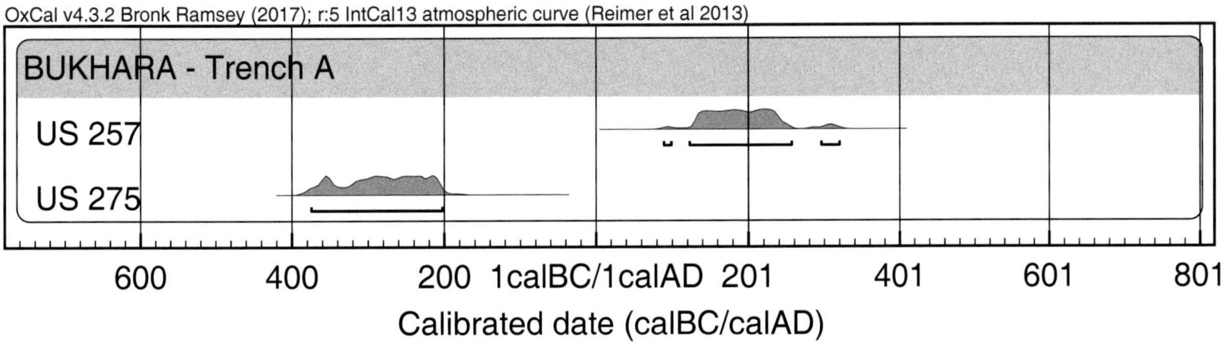

FIGURE 11.6 Calibrated dates of the samples from Bukhara (trench A)

close to that of the other excavated sites, so only two measures were provided for this excavation.[7]

The lowest layer has been dated by C¹⁴ (table 11.6), US 275, which gives the date to the 4th–3rd centuries BCE (fig. 11.6). Several comparisons with the other excavations, not only studying the pottery and the stratigraphy but also the measured radiocarbon age without Σ¹³C correction (2210 ± 30 BP) lead us to date it toward the 3rd century BCE. However, this does not excluded that this layer, and thus the earliest occupations, could be dated to the end of the 4th century BCE.

The second C¹⁴ date concerns an upper layer, US 257, which dates to the 2nd–3rd centuries CE, thus marking the beginning of an important moment characterised by several or one massive occupation within the oasis. One of the most important elements of this migration of new people was the introduction of a typical baked brick (Rante and Mirzaakhmedov 2019: 254).

8 Conclusion

For different reasons, the radiocarbon dating was not discussed in the first volume of this series on the oasis of Bukhara. Therefore, it was decided to include it in this third volume, dedicated to different activities around the oasis, in an article focusing on all the radiocarbon work completed for this research program. As stressed in the introduction, the intent of this article is not to give all the measures obtained, the total number of 183 being too large to discuss here. This article gives a selection of 75 measures that characterise the most important phases of the excavations and are able to give absolute dates that together cover the chronology of the whole oasis, from its earliest occupations until the 19th century.

The absolute dates have been sometime crossed with the study of ceramics, stratigraphy and the other elements at our disposal when completing this large chronological framework.

Acknowledgments

The authors want to thank Nathalie Gandolfo, Gaëtan Louarn, Solenne Mussard and Diane Vouriot for the sample preparation at the C2RMF. The authors also want thank the LMC14 (Laboratory of Radiocarbon Measurement) staff for their contributions to the analytical work (graphitisation and C¹⁴ measurements).

---

7 The C¹⁴ measures obtained by BETA Analytic: sample numbers 496819 and 496820.

CHAPTER 12

Luminescence Dating of Archaeological Sites from the Oasis of Bukhara

Antoine Zink, Elisa Porto and Rocco Rante

1 Introduction

This article is limited to the dating of archaeological sites. We will not discuss the chronology of the Zerafshan's paleochannels here, as they are the subject of other publications (Fouache et al. 2016; Zink et al. 2017). Moreover, we will also not discuss the contributions luminescence dating has made to the typo-chronology of Central Asian ceramics (see the chapters devoted to ceramics in this volume). Finally, we have excluded the study of the potter's quarter of Paykend, whose measurements are still in progress, from this chapter.

After an introduction to the general principles and methodology of luminescence dating, this chapter describes how the basic chronologies of the different sites were established based on material obtained from the stratigraphic excavations. We then discuss what the dating of mud bricks contributes to the chronology of the building using the example of the site of Ramitan and the strengths and weaknesses of this dating.

2 General Principles of Physical Dating

The necessary condition for dating is to start from a remarkable event, which will be the moment we seek to date. The simplest method is to establish a chronology by linking successive events, which is referred to as relative dating.

In some cases, the remarkable event is part of a physical clock. This is defined as a physical phenomenon with a remarkable moment, and it evolves with time. The evolution over time makes it possible to measure the remarkable event independent from other events. This condition, if it defines a physical date, does not in itself make it possible to define an absolute dating. Indeed, the evolution over time can be more or less fast depending on the environment. It is only if this evolution is independent of the environment that it is possible to speak of absolute dating.

3 Principle of Luminescence Dating

Luminescence dating methods use the dosimetric properties of minerals (Aitken 1985, 1998). Indeed, minerals accumulate energy from ambient radioactivity over time. After heating to 500 °C, or being exposed to sunlight for a whole day, this energy will be released in luminous form. The light intensity is proportional to the accumulated dose since the last reset and therefore is indirectly proportional to the age.

However, dating is not limited to measuring the dose accumulated by the object. In fact, the age is obtained by dividing this accumulated dose, or archaeological dose, by the dose rate, or annual dose. We define the age equation as: Age = Accumulated Dose / Annual Dose (Equation 1).

This equation always gives a calendar age. We can divide the age equation on the one hand, the numerator corresponding to the physical clock, and on the other hand, the denominator, which plays the role of corrective factor of the error introduced by the environment. From a physical point of view, the denominator represents what is known about the environment of the object: the clock speeds up or slows down depending on the radioactivity of the environment. This depends on many parameters: the radionuclide (uranium, thorium and potassium) content of the sample and its environment; the cosmic radiation measured today; and the water content. Indeed, the water in the terracotta absorbs some of the radioactivity, and thus, the dose is more important in dry ceramics than in wet ones.

The influence of the environment is thus directly integrated into the calculation at the level of the denominator (equation 1). In this sense, it is indeed a method of absolute dating. However, the multiple parameters to be taken into account leads to significant imprecision in aging. This dating method is not as precise as C^{14}. In order to minimise this uncertainty, it is important to calculate each of the parameters as precisely as possible. This leads to a preference for the direct measurement of the different parameters over the use of average values.

To determine the archaeological dose, there are various techniques, each giving its name to a dating method. Luminescence can be produced by releasing energy when heating the sample, which is called is thermoluminescence (TL), or by illuminating it, which is called optically stimulated luminescence (OSL). To switch from the amount of light from sample to the palaeodose, the sample is irradiated again in the laboratory, allowing the intensity of light to be calibrated in a unit dose (Gray – Gy).

The annual dose (mGy / a) reflects the conservation conditions of the object over time. It is calculated from measurements made in the field, for the environmental component, and in the laboratory, for the contribution from the sample itself.

4 Methodology

4.1 *Luminescence*

4.1.1 Sampling and Sample Preparation

Samples were collected during field missions in collaboration with archaeologists and ceramologists. The samples were sherds as well as architectural elements (kiln walls and bricks). Powder was sampled from these elements after removing 2 mm from the surface (to eliminate the contribution of beta from the soil; Aitken 1985) with a 1.8 mm diameter tungsten carbide drill bit. Around 100 mg of powder was collected for luminescence, alpha counting and elemental X-ray measurements. The powder was cleaned with 10% hydrochloric acid and rinsed with water, ethanol and acetone. The polymineral fraction of 4–11 μm was selected by sedimentation in 6 cm of acetone (a sedimentation time of 2 and 20 minutes repeated four times) and then deposited on the entire surface of stainless steel discs with a 9.8 mm diameter. All operations, excluding the hydrochloric acid attack, were automated. Sixteen discs were prepared for thermoluminescence and four for optically stimulated luminescence.

4.1.2 Measurements

The luminescence measurements were made with a Risø TL / OSL DA-15 reader, including a 90Sr / 90Y source delivering 6.1 Gy / min (as of 1 June 2012) and an EMI 9235QA photomultiplier. Irradiations were also conducted using a Daybreak 801 multisample irradiator equipped with a 90Sr / 90Y beta source (3.25 Gy / min on 1 January 2009) and an alpha source 238Pu (7.39 μm-2 / min on 1 January 2009).

Thermoluminescence was done by heating at 5 °C / sec and detected through a combination of Corning 7–59 (4 mm) and Chance-Pilkington HA-3 (4 mm) filters. The protocol used is based on Zimmerman's additive technique (Zimmerman 1971).

OSL was stimulated successively by an infrared laser diode (830 +/- 10 nm, 225 mW / cm2) at 60° C for 100 s then a set of 21 pairs of blue diodes (470 +/- 30 nm; 9 mW / cm 2) at 120° C for 100 s and detected through a 7.5 mm thick U-340 filter.

The fading rate was measured according to the regeneration protocol described by Zink (2008). The samples being "young" (<< 10 ka), we used Huntley and Lamothe's correction (Huntley and Lamothe 2001).

4.2 *Dosimetry*

4.2.1 Internal Dosimetry

The uranium and thorium contents of the sherds were measured by alpha counting using a Daybreak 582/583 counter using 12 mm diameter cells. We assumed the activities of the uranium and thorium series were at an equilibrium. The potassium content was measured on pellets metallised by a carbon layer using X-ray analysis in energy dispersion with a Philips XL30CP microscope coupled to an Oxford Link ISIS 3000 spectrometer, and the measurements were corrected using a ZAF quantization algorithm (SEMQuant software). The moisture content was estimated at 5%.

4.2.2 External Dosimetry

Measurements of soil gamma contribution were made using a NanoSpec (Target Gmbh) gamma spectrometer using a 2 "× 2" NaI:Tl probe. The probe was sunk 30 cm into the ground to measure the gamma contribution of the entire volume (Aitken 1985). The probe was calibrated with LSCE reference blocks (U-Th and KCl), Gif s/Yvette (Mercier et al. 1994).[1] The energy spectrum was recorded on 512 channels. The precision of the probe makes it possible to observe three peaks corresponding to natural radionuclides, potassium (K40 at 1.46 MeV), uranium (Bi214 at 1.76 MeV) and thorium (Tl208 at 2.61 MeV). The peaks of potassium and thorium are used to calibrate the energy spectrum. The third calibration point is set arbitrarily by associating channel 19 with 80 keV. We used three calculation methods: the region of interest (ROI) method (Aitken 1985) based on the three windows centred on potassium (1.38 MeV–1.53 MeV), uranium (1.69 MeV–1.84 MeV) and thorium (2.50 MeV–2.71 MeV); the 500 keV threshold method (500–2780 keV; Mercier and Falguères 2007) and the 50 keV threshold method (50–2,780 keV). The ROI method gave us an idea of the concentration of radionuclides. All of our measurements show a thorium-to-uranium ratio of 3.13 (0.45). We can therefore assume that the thorium/uranium equilibrium is globally respected (theoretical value 3.18), even if occasional imbalances may be present.

The threshold methods register more counts, and the counting uncertainty is lower with these methods than with the ROI method. Natural radionuclides emit beyond

---

1 The calibrations of the gamma spectrometer took place on 4 April 2012 and 25 June 2015 at the reference blocks of the LSCE, Gif s / Yvette (France) thanks to the kindness of H. Valladas and G. Guérin.

5.1.1 Paykend

TABLE 12.1A Paykend, luminescence analysis

Sample	Localization			IR-OSL		
	Workplace	Unit of stratification	Depth (m)	De	a-value	g-value
Surface pied	Citadel	N/A	2.0*	4.5(7)	0.099(4)	4.4(5)
Surface tesson	Citadel	N/A	2.0*	4.9(9)	0.116(7)	3.2(9)
557-1	Citadel	US557	2.0	5.9(7)	0.118(5)	4.9(2)
558-8	Citadel	US558	3.0	6.5(3)	0.153(3)	5.6(1.2)
560-2	Citadel	US560	2.5	7.0(6)	0.167(6)	4.1(1.1)
768-2	Sharestan I	US768	4.0	7.6(4)	0.180(5)	4.5(5)
PAY2012-1	Citadel	?	4.0	9.7(9)	0.147(9)	4.7(9)
PAY2012-2	Citadel	?	4.0	8.2(8)	0.138(4)	8.1(7)
PAY2012-3a	Sharestan JII	US4313	2.0	6.5(3)	0.155(3)	4.7(6)
PAY2012-3b	Sharestan JII	US4313	2.0	4.7(2)	0.154(1)	4.2(3)
PAY2012-3c	Sharestan JII	US4313	2.0	5.5(2)	0.177(3)	4.9(3)
PAY2012-4a	Sharestan JII	US4312	1.5	6.5(5)	0.199(8)	7.5(1.0)
PAY2012-4b	Sharestan JII	US4312	1.5	6.1(2)	0.253(5)	4.8(3)
PAY2012-4c	Sharestan JII	US4312	1.5	4.9(3)	0.176(5)	3.7(1.1)
PAY2012-6a	Sharestan JII	US4323	1.0	5.2(3)	0.158(3)	4.5(6)
PAY2012-6b	Sharestan JII	US4323	1.0	4.7(2)	0.157(3)	4.2(1.0)
PAY2012-6c	Sharestan JII	US4323	1.0	5.0(3)	0.152(4)	3.8(4)
PAY2012-8a	Sharestan I – secteur H	USM4007	1.0	5.6(2)	0.225(6)	8.6(1.6)
PAY2012-8b	Sharestan I – secteur H	USM4007	1.0	7.3(0.9)	0.142(14)	6.4(0.4)
PAY2012-8c	Sharestan I – secteur H	USM4007	1.0	4.3(1)	0.212(2)	5.7(5)
PAY2012-9a	Sharestan I – secteur B	US3736	0.5	4.9(5)	0.204(17)	7.0(8)
PAY2012-9b	Sharestan I – secteur B	US3736	0.5	6.2(4)	0.207(11)	41(3)
PAY2012-9c	Sharestan I – secteur B	US3736	0.5	6.0(3)	0.196(7)	4.3(5)
PAY2012-10a-1	Rabad	US4621	1.0	5.3(2)	0.163(5)	4.8(4)
PAY2012-10a-2	Rabad	US4621	1.0	5.7(5)	0.214(10)	3.8(1.4)
PAY2012-10a-3	Rabad	US4621	1.0	5.2(5)	0.196(13)	4.4(1.0)
PAY2012-10-2b-1	Rabad	US4611	1.0	–	–	–
PAY2012-10-2b-2	Rabad	US4611	1.0	5.7(1)	–	5.6(4)
PAY2012-10-2b-3	Rabad	US4611	1.0	5.6(1)	–	6.0(3)

Notes:
Unit of stratification – US
Depth – mean depth of the layer where was found the sample.
De – beta equivalent dose to the archaeological dose received by the sample since its last solar exposure – unit Gray – Gy
a-value – alpha efficiency
g-value – fading rate – correction factor due to anomalous fading – unit percent per decade – % / decade.
The number in parentheses is the numerical value of the standard uncertainty referred to the corresponding last digits of the quoted result.
*For shards collected on the surface. given that the depth of burial has necessarily varied over time. we took an average depth of 2m.

BL-OSL			Thermoluminescence					
De	a-value	g-value	Q	I	De	a-value	g-value
2.9(6)	0.090(4)	0.9(9)	2.9(5)	3.3(8)	6.2(94)	0.133(2)	0.9(2)
4.2(6)	0.068(4)	0.9(8)	4.7(5)	3.4(8)	8.1(94)	0.147(3)	0.8(2)
5.2(6)	0.068(4)	0.4(1)	5.7(4)	2.6(7)	8.3(81)	0.103(1)	0.9(2)
5.7(1)	0.057(1)	0.7(2)	4.8(4)	2.0(5)	6.8(64)	0.115(1)	0.6(2)
3.2(8)	0.106(5)	0.9(9)	6.4(4)	1.8(6)	8.2(72)	0.154(2)	0.0(3)
3.0(7)	0.056(4)	2.0(5)	3.70(1.89)	1.35(27)	5.05(1.91)	0.052(1)	0.0(4)
3.1(9)	0.052(4)	2.1(3)	7.0(8)	3.02(1.39)	10.02(1.60)	0.100(2)	1.3(1)
7.6(2)	0.056(2)	1.1(4)	5.09(1.45)	1.78(2.08)	6.87(2.54)	0.123(2)	1.3(1)
5.0(5)	0.145(5)	4.3(3)	5.01(11)	1.58(17)	6.59(20)	0.117(1)	1.4(2)
5.5(1)	0.063(1)	1.0(6)	5.14(41)	0.68(58)	5.82(71)	0.145(1)	1.1(2)
5.4(1)	0.067(1)	0.4(2)	5.23(34)	0.53(47)	5.76(58)	0.172(1)	0.0(6)
5.1(6)	0.129(6)	1.2(1.1)	4.71(32)	2.23(50)	6.94(59)	0.110(10)	0.5(1)
5.1(2)	0.177(5)	0.0(5)	7.40(20)	1.78(1.28)	9.18(1.30)	0.098(1)	0.1(1)
4.2(4)	0.149(7)	2.7(2.3)	5.47(86)	1.71(1.30)	7.18(1.56)	0.104(2)	0.9(1)
5.1(6)	0.123(4)	0.5(9)	4.08(19)	0.44(26)	4.52(32)	0.158(2)	0.0(3)
3.2(6)	0.125(11)	0.0(3.0)	3.29(12)	0.90(16)	4.19(20)	0.138(1)	0.0(3)
4.6(6)	0.120(8)	1.5(9)	3.30(34)	2.12(54)	5.42(64)	0.142(1)	0.0(6)
5.0(4)	0.168(6)	0.5(8)	4.50(39)	2.45(64)	6.95(75)	0.076(1)	1.2(3)
7.9(0.2)	0.081(0.003)	0.0(1.6)	3.46(31)	1.98(49)	5.44(58)	0.105(1)	2.1(4)
7.4(3)	0.165(5)	2.7(1.1)	3.69(42)	1.92(64)	5.61(77)	0.062(1)	1.5(1)
4.8(2)	0.176(2)	2.0(4)	5.00(59)	0.39(48)	5.39(76)	0.128(2)	1.7(3)
5.5(2)	0.183(2)	1.3(4)	3.73(39)	0.14(4)	3.87(39)	0.106(1)	0.0(4)
5.4(2)	0.174(2)	1.0(4)	2.90(55)	1.00(29)	3.90(62)	0.071(1)	0.0(1)
5.2(2)	0.117(3)	1.4(4)	3.56(19)	−0.33(24)	3.23(31)	0.091(1)	0.6(3)
4.6(4)	0.155(8)	0.9(4)	8.62(22)	−0.02(26)	8.60(34)	0.176(2)	1.6(4)
4.7(2)	0.151(3)	0.3(4)	2.58(19)	0.27(25)	2.85(31)	–	0.0(6)
3.3(4)	–	11(7)	6.15(37)	−1.14(45)	5.01(58)	–	2.2(4)
5.4(2)	–	3.4(7)	3.96(44)	0.79(56)	4.75(71)	–	0.0(8)
5.9(3)	–	1.9(4)	4.96(33)	1.01(44)	5.97(55)	–	0.3(2)

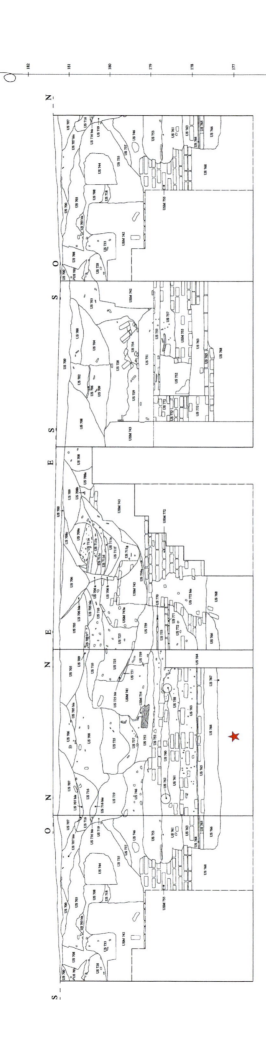

FIGURE 12.4   Paykend, shahrestan 1, trench A

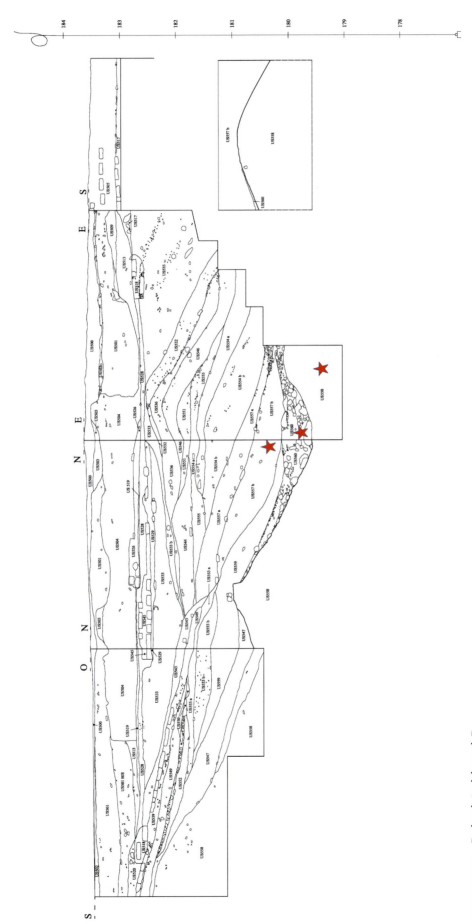

FIGURE 12.5   Paykend citadel trench D

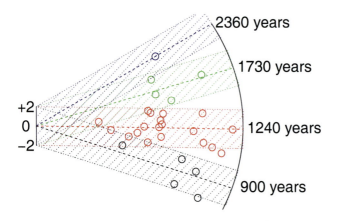

FIGURE 12.6A Ages of the sherds from Paykend: radial plot. The individual ages are read by extrapolating the radius (isochron) to the circular logarithmic scale. Precision is indicated on x-axis. The y-axis represents unit standard uncertainty. Points within coloured bands are consistent with the central age within two standard uncertainties (95% interval of confidence)

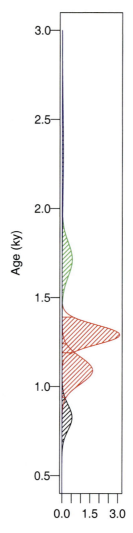

FIGURE 12.6B Ages of the sherds from Paykend: finite mixture model (five components). The different Gaussian distributions contributing to the distribution of ages based on a finite mixture model with five components

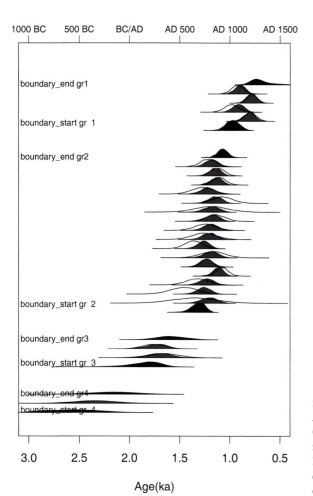

FIGURE 12.7 Age model for Paykend. For each age, two distributions have been plotted: One in the outline, which is the raw age; and a solid one based on the model assuming the groups: Paykend 1 < Paykend 2 < Paykend 3 < Paykend 4 < Paykend 5 ("<" meaning "younger than"). Other plotted distributions correspond to the estimated date of the beginning and end of the different groups

5.1.2 Ramitan

We sampled 13 sherds from the palace, the eastern wall of the square citadel (trench E), the south gate of the shahrestan and the suburb, or Islamic rabad (trench F). Like with Paykend, we were able to classify these sherds into different age groups, with a clear agreement between the graphical analyse (fig. 12.8a) and the FMM (table 12.7 and fig. 12.8b), Ramitan 1 (dating to the 11th–12th centuries), Ramitan 2 (6th–7th centuries), Ramitan 3 (3rd–5th centuries) and Ramitan 4 (1st century BCE–4th century CE). According to the age model (fig. 12.9 and fig. 12.12), the hiatus obtained between the various periods are well identified during the periods between the 1st century BCE and 1st century CE and the 6th and 9th centuries.

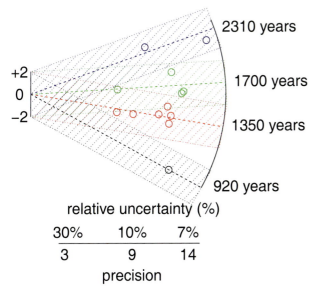

FIGURE 12.8A Age of the sherds from Ramitan: radial plot

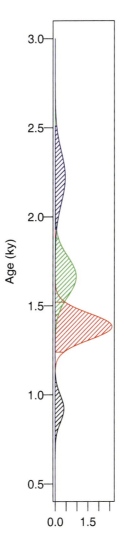

FIGURE 12.8B
Age of the sherds from Ramitan: finite mixture model (four components)

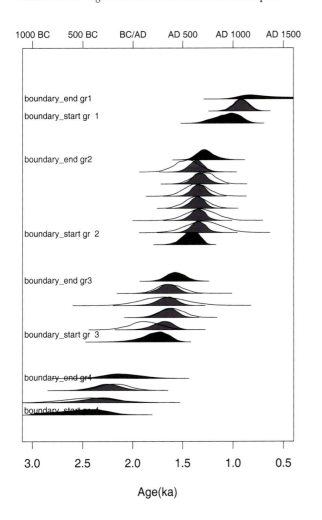

FIGURE 12.9
Age model Ramitan

TABLE 12.3A Luminescence analysis

Sample	Localization		Depth (m)	IR-OSL		
	Workplace	Unit of stratification		De	a-value	g-value
ROM14-811	Citadel	USM811	1.0	10.1(3)	0.162(2)	7.5(4)
ROM14-Shar2sud	South gate	n/a	1.0	7.8(5)	0.158(2)	3.8(2.9)
ROM14-905A	Chantier E	USM905A	8.0	–	–	–
ROM14-1121-1	Chantier F	US1121	4.0	3.9(2)	0.162(3)	4.4(5)
ROM14-1121-2	Chantier F	US1121	4.0	5.6(3)	0.163(2)	4.5(4)
ROM14-1121-3	Chantier F	US1121	4.0	6.1(2)	0.164(3)	5.7(6)
ROM14-1218-1	Chantier F	USM1218	6.5	7.1(2)	0.155(3)	5.9(2)
ROM14-1218-2	Chantier F	USM1218	6.5	–	–	–
ROM16-3	Citadel	USM2509	2.0	7.3(3)	–	6.6(7)
ROM16-4	Citadel	USM2509	1.0	5.6(1.1)	–	8.7(1.4)
ROM16-5	Chantier E	USM905	1.0	6.3(4)	–	6.1(6)
ROM16-6	Chantier E	USM905	1.0	7.6(4)	–	5.7(3)
ROM16-7	Chantier E	USM907	1.0	7.0(5)	–	5.7(5)

Notes:
Unit of stratification – US
Depth – mean depth of the layer where was found the sample.
De – beta equivalent dose to the archaeological dose received by the sample since its last solar exposure – unit Gray – Gy
a-value – alpha efficiency
g-value – fading rate – correction factor due to anomalous fading – unit percent per decade – % / decade.
The number in parentheses is the numerical value of the standard uncertainty referred to the corresponding last digits of the quoted result.

TABLE 12.3B Dosimetry analysis

Sample	U (ppm)	Th (ppm)	K2O (%)	Dα (mGy/a)	Dβ (mGy/a)	Dγ (mGy/a)	Dcos (mGy/a)	Age (ka)	Date
ROM14-811	3.1(3)	10.0(9)	4.31()	12.0	2.0	1.387(39)	0.183	2185(140)	[450BC / AD110]
ROM14-Shar2sud	3.3(3)	10.4(1.0)	3.94(6)	12.5	2.6	1.438(18)	0.183	1460(120)	[AD315 / AD795]
ROM14-905A	2.6(2)	8.2(8)	3.35()	9.8	2.8	1.288(11)	0.078	1875(150)	[160BC / AD440]
ROM14-1121-1	3.4(3)	10.8(1.0)	3.20()	13.0	2.0	1.233(33)	0.124	920(75)	[AD945 / AD1245]
ROM14-1121-2	4.1(4)	13.1(1.2)	3.33()	15.7	3.2	1.233(33)	0.124	1290(105)	[AD515 / AD935]
ROM14-1121-3	4.9(4)	15.4(1.4)	3.15()	18.6	2.9	1.233(33)	0.124	1365(120)	[AD410 / AD890]
ROM14-1218-1	3.3(3)	10.5(1.0)	3.74()	12.6	2.0	1.231(5)	0.092	1630(120)	[AD145 / AD625]
ROM14-1218-2	4.4(4)	13.9(1.3)	2.47()	16.8	2.8	1.231(5)	0.092	1295(170)	[AD380 / AD1060]
ROM16-3	4.2(3)	13.2(1.2)	3.39(4)	13.9	2.3	1.318(18)	0.183	1370(110)	[AD425 / AD865]
ROM16-4	2.8(3)	9.0(1.0)	4.94(18)	13.4	2.2	1.318(18)	0.183	1315(145)	[AD410 / AD990]
ROM16-5	3.4(4)	10.7(1.0)	4.14(11)	17.9	2.9	1.281(52)	0.183	1690(220)	[115BC / AD765]

L-OSL			Thermoluminescence				
e	a-value	g-value	Q	I	De	a-value	g-value
0.6(5)	0.113(4)	1.2(2)	9.86(54)	1.02(69)	10.87(88)	0.108(1)	0.1(1)
0.8(7)	0.120(7)	1.2(1.7)	8.90(56)	-0.54(66)	8.36(87)	0.150(2)	0.0(6)
7.9(1)	0.057(1)	0.5(2)	–	–	–	–	–
4.6(2)	0.126(2)	0.8(9)	5.88(66)	-0.25(83)	5.63(1.06)	0.099(1)	0.3(5)
4.6(8)	0.109(5)	2.0(3)	9.09(62)	1.67(89)	10.75(1.09)	0.146(2)	0.0(5)
4.6(2)	0.143(4)	2.5(9)	8.94(75)	-0.26(98)	8.69(1.23)	0.097(1)	0.0(3)
7.0(1)	0.052(1)	0.5(1)	7.86(79)	0.28(77)	8.14(97)	0.103(1)	0.0(3)
6.1(7)	0.082(6)	1.2(2)	–	–	–	–	–
8.3(1)	–	0.8(2)	6.53(23)	-0.33(29)	6.20(37)	–	0.0(1)
6.8(2)	–	1.1(3)	8.59(85)	-2.12(1.01)	6.47(1.32)	–	0.7(1)
8.7(5)	–	2.4(1.6)	–	–	–	–	–
0.7(5)	–	1.5(1.1)	–	–	–	–	–
7.3(1)	–	0.9(2)	–	–	–	–	–

TABLE 12.3B   Dosimetry analysis (cont.)

Sample	U (ppm)	Th (ppm)	K2O (%)	Dα (mGy/a)	Dβ (mGy/a)	Dγ (mGy/a)	Dcos (mGy/a)	Age (ka)	Date
ROM16-6	3.8(3)	12.1(1.4)	4.06(12)	12.3	2.0	1.281(52)	0.183	2430(240)	[895BC / AD65]
ROM16-7	4.2(2)	13.4(1.0)	3.21(7)	9.3	1.5	1.284(5)	0.183	1610(120)	[AD165 / AD645]

Notes:

Laboratory measurements

U. Th – radionuclide contents based on windows count-rate (Aitken. 1985) – Unit ppm.

K2O – radionuclide contents based on windows count-rate (Aitken. 1985) – Unit %.

Dα – alpha dose rate Dα = 0.12 (2.31 U + 0.611 Th) / (1 + 1.5 WF) – mGy/a

Dβ – beta dose rate Dβ = (0.86*0.146 U + 0.81* 0.0273 Th + 0.94*0.649 K2O) / (1 + 1.25 WF) – mGy/a

(WF – moisture content 5.0(3.0) %)

Dγ – gamma dose rate based on threshold count-rate – mGy/a

Dcos – cosmic dose rate – as a function of the depth d. based on Pescott and Hutton's (1994) formula Dcos (d) = Dcos(0) exp(-0.15d + 0.002d^2) – mGy/a. Dcos(0) cosmic dose rate at the geomagnetic latitude and altitude of sampling site (Prescott and Hutton. 1994. Appendix)

Da – annual dose rate – mGy/a

Age – Age from the resetting exposure. based on Bayesian numerical stimulation (Zink. 2013). The mean and uncertainty are rounded to 5 years.

Date – the dates in bracket define an interval estimated to have a level of confidence of 95 percent.

The number in parentheses is the numerical value of the standard uncertainty referred to the corresponding last digits of the quoted result.

TABLE 12.4 Distribution of the sherds of the different levels according to the Romitan groups. Question marks indicate that a shard can be assigned to different groups

Unit of stratification	Romitan#1	Romitan#2	Romitan#3	Romitan#4
US1121	1	2		
USM2509		2		
South gate		?------	------?	
USM1218	1	1		
USM907			1	
USM905A			1	
USM905		?------	------?	1
USM811				1

Two sherds belong to Ramitan 4. The oldest sherd (ROM16-6) comes from the north-east tower of the citadel (USM905). As the other sherds from the eastern enclosure (USM905, USM905A, USM907) are attached to the Ramitan 3 group (table 11.4), it is likely a residual fragment from a previous occupation of the site.

The second sherd in Ramitan 4 comes from USM811, one of the older walls of the palace. Although no other sherd was sampled in this wall, along with Rom16-6, it is more likely a residual fragment than a contemporaneous sherd of the wall's building. The two other sherds from the palace (wall USM2509, south of palace) belong to Ramitan 2, showing the palace's occupation during the 6th–7th centuries. Due to the scarceness of sherds from the palace, it is difficult to establish a more detailed chronology of the palace building.

The same limit is observed for the shahrestan with only one sherd (ROM14-Shar2sud) coming from the south gate. It is likely that this sherd belongs to Ramitan 2, although a link to Ramitan 3 cannot be rejected statistically. It seems difficult to extrapolate a date for the building of the shahrestan from this single sample.

It seems that the square citadel dates from around the 3rd century. Due to the limited number of sherds, it is not possible to date other places in the main town (palace and shahrestan). Early settlements are dated from the last centuries BCE (Ramitan 4). On the other hand, evidence (Ramitan 2) show that the site was occupied in the pre-Islamic period.

We analysed the trench F, located approximately at the centre of the western suburb. Two layers have been dated. The lower (USM1218) corresponds to the older wall of a structure where two sherds were collected. The two sherds belong to the pre-Islamic period; the oldest (ROM14-1218-1), in a position of re-employment, shows the presence of a settlement as early as the 2nd century.[2] These dates indicate that this area was built as early as the pre-Islamic period. The upper layer (US1121) corresponds to an occupation floor. Three sherds were sampled within it. The latest sherd (ROM14-1121-1) dates the occupation floor to the Islamic period. The other two sherds whose ages are very similar to the latest sherd from USM1218 are obviously in an intrusive position and confirm that the site was occupied during the pre-Islamic period.

5.1.3 Iskijkat

Again, it is possible to split the sherds into several groups (four groups based on radial plot, fig. 12.10a and FMM analysis, table 12.7 and fig. 12.10b): Iskijkat 1 (10th–11th centuries), Iskijkat 2 (5th–6th centuries), Iskijkat 3 (2nd–3rd centuries) and Iskijkat 4 (6th–7th centuries BCE). One sample (ISK14-249-2) belongs to either Iskijkat 1 or Iskijkat 2. The hiatuses observed by the age model (figs. 12.11 and 12.12) are in the 8th–9th centuries (Iskijkat 2 -> Iskijkat 1), during the 4th–5th centuries (Iskijkat 3 -> Iskijkat 2) and between the 1st and 3rd centuries BCE (Iskijkat 4 -> Iskijkat 3).

We intervened at the dig opened in 2014 (trench A; table 12.6), where four stratigraphic units were taken. The lower sampled stratigraphic unit we selected (US356) is leaning against the wall (USM117) and below the base (USM116) of the wall (USM110). It would date no later than the 5th–6th centuries, as shown by one of the sherds. The other two sherds belong to 2nd–3rd centuries and must therefore come from lower layers. US297 is a layer between two floors above the USM110 wall and leaning against the USM108 wall. Surprisingly, the sampled sherds partially predate those from US356, two of which belong to Iskijkat 4. The third (ISK14-297-2) has a similar age as the oldest of the US356 sherds (ISK14-356-2). Here, from an archaeological point of view, we have the reuse of waste from former layers of destruction, dating in part from the last millennium BCE. US249 is a layer of tiling associated with the USM106 wall. Of the three sherds sampled, two have similar ages

---

2 For a more detailed chronology, see the article on C^{14} in this volume.

TABLE 12.5A Luminescence analysis

Sample	Localization		IR-OSL			BL-OSL			Thermoluminescence				
	Unit of stratifi-cation	Depth (m)	De	a-value	g-value	De	a-value	g-value	Q	I	De	a-value	g-value
ISK14-297-1	US297	3.3	10.3(1.5)	0.162(10)	6.9(4)	10.2(3)	0.120(2)	2.1(6)	11.96(36)	1.96(50)	13.92(61)	0.110(1)	0.8(2)
ISK14-297-2	US297	3.3	9.8(7)	0.156(6)	6.5(6)	10.9(2)	0.056(1)	0.6(1)	12.75(55)	-1.85(67)	10.90(87)	0.112(1)	1.2(1)
ISK14-297-3	US297	3.3	10.8(1.2)	0.190(13)	4.7(1.4)	7.6(7)	0.104(7)	1.7(3)	14.16(42)	2.87(58)	17.03(72)	0.135(2)	0.7(2)
ISK14-356-1	US356	5.5	–	–	–	9.0(3)	0.046(2)	0.4(3)	6.18(73)	-1.09(88)	5.09(1.14)	0.074(2)	0.0(4)
ISK14-356-2	US356	5.5	9.1(0.9)	0.198(7)	4.1(1.5)	10.2(3)	0.059(1)	1.6(3)	7.80(57)	0.07(74)	7.87(93)	0.090(2)	0.0(2)
ISK14-356-3	US356	5.5	8.2(1.0)	0.132(5)	4.5(5)	8.0(2)	0.136(2)	3.7(8)	9.81(38)	-0.15(49)	9.66(62)	0.137(2)	1.5(2)
ISK14-249-1	US249	2.45	5.7(3)	0.137(3)	4.7(6)	6.9(2)	0.071(2)	0.9(1)	3.98(45)	-0.19(53)	3.80(70)	0.055(1)	0.4(1)
ISK14-249-2	US249	2.45	8.3(1.2)	0.171(9)	8.1(4)	4.4(1.0)	0.175(2)	3.9(5)	8.82(1.21)	1.19(1.51)	7.64(1.93)	0.200(3)	4.1(1)
ISK14-249-3	US249	2.45	10.7(2.2)	0.164(4)	5.2(2.5)	10.7(2)	0.090(2)	0.7(4)	10.78(79)	0.17(1.05)	10.95(1.31)	0.066(1)	0.3(1)
ISK14-222-1	US222	1.0	4.7(4)	0.155(3)	9.7(2.0)	5.9(2)	0.091(2)	1.8(3)	4.87(17)	-0.75(20)	4.11(26)	0.085(1)	0.8(1)
ISK14-222-2	US222	1.0	4.0(2)	0.163(2)	7.2(3)	5.1(3)	0.124(4)	2.2(6)	4.06(35)	-1.09(40)	2.98(53)	0.054(1)	0.0(1)
ISK14-222-3	US222	1.0	5.1(1)	0.164(3)	5.1(3)	4.2(2)	0.063(2)	0.7(2)	3.91(53)	1.06(67)	4.97(85)	0.054(1)	0.3(2)

Notes:
Unit of stratification – US
Depth – mean depth of the layer where was found the sample.
De – beta equivalent dose to the archaeological dose received by the sample since its last solar exposure – unit Gray – Gy
a-value – alpha efficiency
g-value – fading rate – correction factor due to anomalous fading – unit percent per decade – % / decade.
The number in parentheses is the numerical value of the standard uncertainty referred to the corresponding last digits of the quoted result.

TABLE 12.5B Dosimetry analysis

Sample	U (ppm)	Th (ppm)	K2O (%)	Dα (mGy/a)	Dβ (mGy/a)	Dγ (mGy/a)	Dcos (mGy/a)	Age (ka)	Date
ISK14-297-1	3.5(3)	11.0(1.0)	3.19(13)	13.3	2.7	1.268(7)	0.135	2475(155)	[770BC / 150BC]
ISK14-297-2	3.5(3)	11.2(1.0)	5.14(50)	13.4	3.9	1.268(7)	0.135	1965(135)	[220BC / AD320]
ISK14-297-3	2.8(3)	8.8(8)	3.30(30)	10.6	2.6	1.268(7)	0.135	2730(165)	[1045BC / 385BC]
ISK14-356-1	3.3(3)	10.5(1.0)	4.35(40)	12.6	3.4	1.248(24)	0.103	1730(125)	[35BC / AD535]
ISK14-356-2	3.7(3)	11.8(1.1)	4.56(50)	14.2	3.6	1.248(24)	0.103	1900(140)	[165BC / AD395]
ISK14-356-3	4.6(4)	14.7(1.3)	4.20(40)	17.7	3.6	1.248(24)	0.103	1510(120)	[AD265 / AD745]
ISK14-249-1	3.1(3)	9.9(9)	3.24(42)	11.9	2.7	1.278(18)	0.151	1495(100)	[AD320 / AD720]
ISK14-249-2	4.2(4)	13.4(1.2)	3.56(7)	16.1	3.1	1.278(18)	0.151	1265(180)	[AD390 / AD1110]
ISK14-249-3	4.4(4)	13.9(1.3)	4.46(4)	16.8	3.7	1.278(18)	0.151	1755(95)	[AD70 / AD450]
ISK14-222-1	4.7(4)	14.9(1.4)	3.31(10)	17.9	3.0	1.330(15)	0.183	895(50)	[AD1020 / AD1220]

TABLE 12.5B   Dosimetry analysis (cont.)

Sample	U (ppm)	Th (ppm)	K2O (%)	Dα (mGy/a)	Dβ (mGy/a)	Dγ (mGy/a)	Dcos (mGy/a)	Age (ka)	Date
ISK14-222-2	3.3(3)	10.5(1.0)	3.49(12)	12.6	2.8	1.330(15)	0.183	1075(65)	[AD810 / AD1070]
ISK14-222-3	2.8(3)	8.9(8)	4.09(15)	10.7	3.1	1.330(15)	0.183	1085(50)	[AD830 / AD1030]

Notes:

Laboratory measurements

U. Th – radionuclide contents based on windows count-rate (Aitken. 1985) – Unit ppm.

K2O – radionuclide contents based on windows count-rate (Aitken. 1985) – Unit %.

Dα – alpha dose rate Dα = 0.12 (2.31 U + 0.611 Th) / (1 + 1.5 WF) – mGy/a

Dβ – beta dose rate Dβ = (86*0.146 U + 0.81* 0.0273 Th + 0.94*0.649 K2O) / (1 + 1.25 WF) – mGy/a

(WF – moisture content 5.0 ± 3.0 %)

Dγ – gamma dose rate based on threshold count-rate – mGy/a

Dcos – cosmic dose rate – as a function of the depth d. based on Pescott and Hutton's (1994) formula Dcos (d) = Dcos(0) exp(−0.15d + 0.002d^2) – mGy/a. Dcos(0) cosmic dose rate at the geomagnetic latitude and altitude of sampling site (Prescott and Hutton. 1994. Appendix)

Da – annual dose rate – mGy/a

Age – Age from the resetting exposure. based on Bayesian numerical stimulation (Zink.2013). The mean and uncertainty are rounded to 5 years.

Date – the dates in bracket define an interval estimated to have a level of confidence of 95 percent.

The number in parentheses is the numerical value of the standard uncertainty referred to the corresponding last digits of the quoted result.

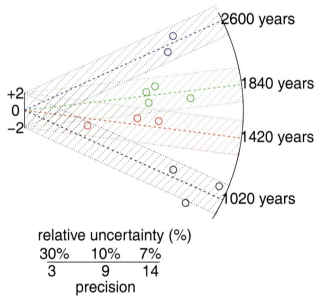

FIGURE 12.10A   Ages of the sherds from Iskijkat: radial plot

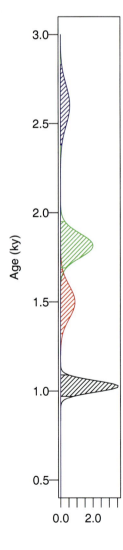

FIGURE 12.10B   Ages of the sherds from Iskijkat: finite mixture model (four components)

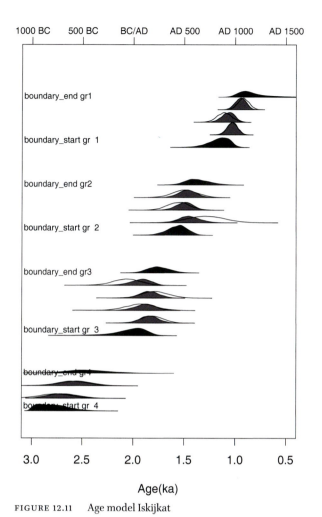

FIGURE 12.11 Age model Iskijkat

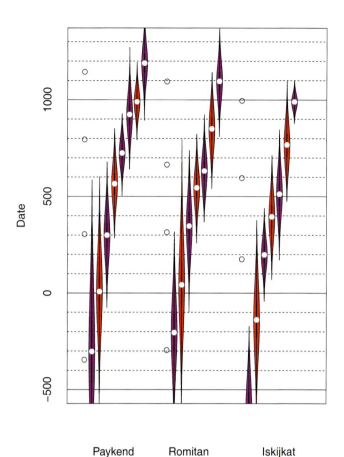

FIGURE 12.12 Summary of the chronologies of the different sites. Open circles: average dates of the groups in radial plot. Grey violin: dates of the groups following the finite mixture model. Pink violin: dates of the hiatus following the age model

TABLE 12.6 Distribution of the sherds of the different levels according to the Iskijkat groups. Question marks indicate that a shard can be assigned to different groups

Unit of stratification	Iskijkat #1	Iskijkat #2	Iskijkat #3	Iskijkat #4
US222	3			
US249	?------	-----? + 1	1	
US297			1	2
US356		1	2	

as sherds found at US356. The latest sherd is also the least accurate; it can belong to Iskijkat 2 or to Iskijkat 1. The last stratigraphic unit collected (US222) is a layer covering the USM106 wall. The three sherds clearly date from the medieval period.

We therefore have the presence of ancient occupations at the site that could correspond to the first archaeological layers of the dig, or even to a pre-urban settlement. Then, several sherds date to a pre-Islamic occupation around the 2nd–3rd centuries CE, corresponding to the basement of the stratigraphy. US356 would correspond to the pre-Islamic period (5th–6th centuries) according to the most recent sherd found in it, while US222 corresponds to the medieval period (10th–11th centuries). The date of US297 is less clear given the low precision of the most recent fragment.

5.2 Summary

At all our sites, the traces of settlements from the first millennium BCE is evidenced by a few sherds in reworked layers that precede the development of urban sites. We then observe a pre-Islamic phase between the 2nd and 4th centuries CE at our three sites. They are connected with the lower layers of the citadel and shahrestan 1 of Paykend, with the enclosure of the square citadel of Ramitan and with the lowest architectural layer of Iskijkat. The 6th century is characterised by a hiatus in Paykend and Ramitan, while Iskijkat presents activity during this time. In the

bricks, although there may be a lag of a few years between manufacturing and use after drying (Vitruvius 11: 3.2). On the other hand, if bleaching b is not effective, the dating will correspond to the sedimentation of the soil, which can not only be recent (Fodde 2009) but also date from several centuries, or even millenniums, before the use of the earth in the manufacture of the bricks; both could explain the discrepancies between the scant studies on the subject. In the layers at Tell Meggido (Israel), Porat et al. (2012) observed that the cycles of destruction and reuse of raw earth constructions are too fast to allow effective bleaching. On the other hand, Sanjurjo and Monteros Fenollós (2012) were able to date the destruction layers of Tell Qubr Abu al-'Atiq (Syria). More recently, Sanjurjo (2016) showed significant agreement between the OSL dating of mud bricks and radiocarbon and luminescence dating at two archaeological sites in the Syrian Middle Euphrates Valley.

6.2 Results

Our tests were mainly conducted at the site of Ramitan, more recently some tests were made in Kakishtuvan. The first measurements made on samples at the base of the western rampart of the square citadel gave dates from the first millennium BCE (Rom14-400, Rom14-400B). This result was encouraging, showing that there is a partial reset of the signal: we do not date the geological age of the minerals. However, the error between luminescence dating (first millennium BCE) and architectural dating (2nd–4th centuries BCE) is unacceptable. Looking in more detail, our measurements were made on the fine polymineral fraction (2–10 μm). The most important mineral in our samples is feldspar, which bleaches relatively slowly compared with quartz. For the following samples, we decided to work on the quartz extracted from the fine fraction.

Two samples come from tower A (fig. 12.17), which leads to the rampart where the two previous samples were extracted. While the brick from USM404 (Rom14-404) is in accordance with a 2nd-century dating, the brick from USM403 appears too old.

Concerning the south gate of the shahrestan enclosure, a mud brick from the western side was dated (ROM14-Shar2sud-Bri (340 BCE–210 CE)), as well as a sherd inside the structure (Rom14-Shar2sud (315–795 CE); table 12.3, b). A second brick sampled in 2016 could not be dated due to the lack of sufficient amounts of quartz. The sherd that must give a *terminus post quem* is dated later than the mud brick, suggesting that the age of the brick is overestimated by one or two centuries.

The eastern wall of the square citadel (fig. 12.18) is characterised by the presence of the unique fired brick of the site inside the structure. Nothing allows us to say that this is a restoration after the construction of the rampart. This brick is located just above the ruins of the north-east tower (USM905) which is believed to be contemporary. As noted above, the sherds found in the eastern wall (USM905, USM905A and USM907; table 11.3, b), excluding ROM16-6, belong to Ramitan 3. The dating of the fired brick (Rom14-905 (5–205 CE)) support this chronology. Two mud bricks were sampled from the eastern wall: Rom16-2 coming from the north-east tower and Rom14-907Bri from the east tower. Rom14-907Bri is slightly older than the fired brick and the sherds. The dating obtained from Rom16-2 (table 12.8, b) oddly appears much younger than the other samples and the archaeological age of rampart. It shows the limits of the method.

These results show that the dates from mud bricks are, if we remove the Rom16-2 brick, close to the archaeological dating. However, the substantial range of uncertainty could mask a systematic bias of one or two centuries. This bias may be related to partial bleaching during brick

Rom 14-404 [35BC - AD285]

Rom 14-403 [530BC - AD1]

FIGURE 12.17   Tower A

TABLE 12.7 Finite mixture model of ages

Site	Number of components	Comp#1		Comp#2		Comp#3		Comp#4		Comp#5	
Paykend	5	825(70)y	10%	1090(75)y	31%	1290(55)y	42%	1715(95)y	13%	2315(240)	4%
Romitan	4	920(75)y	8%	1385(75)y	48%	1665(110)y	27%	2220(145)y	17%		
Iskijkat	4	1025(30)y	29%	1500(90)y	20%	1815(65)y	34%	2605(115)y	17%		

Notes:
Finite mixture model (FMM) obtained using the function calc_FiniteMixture from Luminescence R package (Burow, 2017).
Age – the mean and uncertainty are rounded to 5 years.
Date – the dates in bracket define an interval estimated to have a level of confidence of 95 percent.
The number in parentheses is the numerical value of the standard uncertainty referred to the corresponding last digits of the quoted result.

TABLE 12.8A Luminescence analysis

Sample	Localization		Depth (m)	IR-OSL			BL-OSL		
	Workplace	Unit of stratification		De	a-value	g-value	De	a-value	g-value
ROM14-400	West wall	USM400	2.0	9,6(4)	0.139(5)	5,0(4)	10,7(4)	0.106(4)	1,9(1)
ROM14-400B	West wall	USM400B	8.0	9,3(3)	0,173(4)	3,5(5)	11,4(5)	0.134(6)	4,3(6)
ROM14-404	West wall	USM404	0.5	7,5(5)	0,168(6)	4,5(1,0)	8,5(2)	0.062(1)	0.4(4)
ROM14-Shar2sud	South gate	South gate	1.0	–	–	–	8,9(7)	0.046(3)	0,3(9)
ROM14-905	Nord-East tower	USM905	8.0	8,9(5)	0.185(2)	5.6(4)	8,7(3)	0.109(3)	1,2(2)
ROM14-907Bri	East tower	USM907	8.0	6,6(2)	0.115(1)	4,6(4)	7,9(1)	0.043(2)	0,9(6)
ROM14-403	West wall	USM403	1,0	7.1(3)	0.155(4)	5.9(6)	7.0(2)	0.052(5)	0.5(4)
ROM16-2	Nord-East tower	USM905	8.0	–	–	–	4,2(3)	–	0.8(5)

Notes:
Unit of stratification – US
Depth – mean depth of the layer where was found the sample.
De – beta equivalent dose to the archaeological dose received by the sample since its last solar exposure – unit Gray – Gy
a-value – alpha efficiency
g-value – fading rate – correction factor due to anomalous fading – unit percent per decade – % / decade.
The number in parentheses is the numerical value of the standard uncertainty referred to the corresponding last digits of the quoted result.

TABLE 12.8B Dosimetry analysis

Sample	U (ppm)	Th (ppm)	K2O (%)	Dα (mGy/a)	Dβ (mGy/a)	Dγ (mGy/a)	Dcos (mGy/a)	Age (ka)	Date
ROM14-400	2,9(3)	9,3(9)	4.31(19)	11,2	2,3	1.174(13)	0.160	3260(265)	[1510BC / 980BC]
ROM14-400B	3,2(3)	10,2(1.1)	3.94(33)	12,3	2,3	1.229(15)	0.078	2330(190)	[505BC / 125BC]
ROM14-404	3,3(3)	10,3(1,0)	3.35()	12,5	2,3	1.398(18)	0.196	1890(160)	[35BC / AD285]
ROM14-Shar2sud	2,9(3)	9,1(9)	3.20()	11,0	2,4	1.438(18)	0.183	2080(275)	[340BC / AD210]
ROM14-905	3,1(3)	10,0(1,0)	3,12()	12,0	2,6	1,209(12)	0,078	1910(100)	[AD5 / AD205]
ROM14-907Bri	3,1(3)	10,0(9)	2,50()	12,0	2,2	1.209(5)	0.078	2095(195)	[275BC / AD115]

TABLE 12.8B Dosimetry analysis (cont.)

Sample	U (ppm)	Th (ppm)	K2O (%)	Dα (mGy/a)	Dβ (mGy/a)	Dγ (mGy/a)	Dcos (mGy/a)	Age (ka)	Date
ROM14-403	3,2(3)	10,2(1,0)	3,04()	12,3	2,6	1.233(26)	0.160	2280(265)	[530BC / AD1]
ROM16-2	3,9(3)	12,2(1,1)	3,65(9)	14,7	3,1	1.281(52)	0.078	750(110)	[AD1155 / AD1375]

Notes:
Laboratory measurements
U. Th – radionuclide contents based on windows count-rate (Aitken. 1985) – Unit ppm.
K2O – radionuclide contents based on windows count-rate (Aitken. 1985) – Unit %.
Dα – alpha dose rate Dα = 0.12 (2.31 U + 0.611 Th) / (1 + 1.5 WF) – mGy/a
Dβ – beta dose rate Dβ = (0.86*0.146 U + 0.81* 0.0273 Th + 0.94*0.649 K2O) / (1 + 1.25 WF) – mGy/a
(WF – moisture content 5.0(3.0) %)
Dγ – gamma dose rate based on threshold count-rate – mGy/a
Dcos – cosmic dose rate – as a function of the depth d. based on Pescott and Hutton's (1994) formula Dcos (d) = Dcos(0) exp(-0.15d + 0.002d²) – mGy/a. Dcos(0) cosmic dose rate at the geomagnetic latitude and altitude of sampling site (Prescott and Hutton. 1994. Appendix)
Da – annual dose rate – mGy/a
Age – Age from the resetting exposure. based on Bayesian numerical stimulation (Zink. 2013). The mean and uncertainty are rounded to 5 years.
Date – the dates in bracket define an interval estimated to have a level of confidence of 95 percent.
The number in parentheses is the numerical value of the standard uncertainty referred to the corresponding last digits of the quoted result.

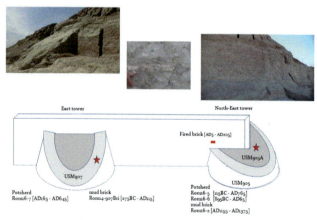

FIGURE 12.18 East wall

kneading. Improvement of the preparation protocol could reduce this error. But it is possible that the bleaching during the kneading is very weak, and in fact what we measure is the resetting due to the earth's sedimentation before its removal for the manufacture of the bricks. In this case, the dated moment is disconnected from the construction phase and would remain *a post quem* dating. The brick manufacturing process, especially the origin of the clay and the kneading step, needs to be better understood before further utilising this method.

7 Conclusion

By combining a graphical analysis (radial plot) and numerical models (finite mixture model and age model), we were able to propose a chronology of the potteries found at each site. These can be divided into four or five groups according to the sites. The majority of pottery date from the first millennium CE. Some are earlier (first millennium BCE) and would be traces of pre-urban settlements. On the contrary, some potsherds date back to the eleventh or twelfth centuries, mainly at the site of Paykend. At all sites, a group of ceramics can be dated to around the 3rd–4th centuries. The sites of Ramitan and Iskijkat show hiatuses in the 8th–9th centuries, thus clearly separating the pre-Islamic and Islamic layers. On the contrary, Paykend presents continuous occupation activity during this period.

However, the pottery can only give *post quem* dating of the archaeological layers. In order to directly date these layers, we decided to test the dating of the mud bricks. The ages obtained seem slightly older – by a few centuries – than expected. We still need to understand the exact manufacturing process at the time the mud bricks were created to formally identify the dated event and thus get an idea of the bias between it and the construction of the walls.

Conclusion

The trilogy *The Oasis of Bukhara*, of which this volume is the last, is consecrated to a huge geographical territory covering an area of 5100 km². It covers issues from the paleoenvironmental transformations linked to climatic phenomena and human behaviours since Neanderthals crossed and inhabited these regions, to the evolution of these human behaviours; and from the distribution of such social characteristics – especially over the last two thousand years (from the 3rd century BCE to the 15th–16th centuries CE) – to historical events, through the analysis of written sources, and to the natural substrate and its evolution, through the study of animals and whatever constituted life within the oasis.[1]

This trilogy provides the key to apprehending the global history of this region, while at the same time comparing it within the wider territory and history of Central Asia. In this large historical framework, one of the keys to understanding the history of the oasis of Bukhara concerns the significance of its earlier life, compared to the other oases of Central Asia, *de facto* inextricably linked to natural and climatic phenomena. Beyond the earliest populations settling around the Zerafshan delta since the Kel'teminar,[2] taking advantage of slow flows and stagnant water, the earliest well-structured occupations within the oasis itself do not appear before the 4th century BCE, by which time other oases of Central Asia such as Samarkand, Balkh or Khorezm had already been inhabited for centuries. The OSL analyses made for the geomorphological study of the oasis and their sample locations present a sort of indicator through which the climatic troubles must be understood. This means that, within the oasis, irrigation still existed after the OSL date, sometimes continuing to the present time, sometimes not. To better understand the issue, in the western part of the area of Varakhsha, located at the border of the irrigated space, we extracted a sample indicating, according to the OSL measurement, dryness troubles during the Neolithic and Bronze Age (see fig. 14, Volume 1). The territory to the east from this point, towards the oasis, is the site of later occupations. This is the case for Bash tepe (1st century CE), but also for the area of Varakhsha, where there is a possibility of earlier occupations dating to the Iron Age.

This trilogy also stresses how important the relationships between the socio-political entities scattered around Central Asia have been: in our case, how the Bukhara oasis was apprehended by those of Samarkand or Merv and how this contributed to the development of the oasis of Bukhara. The development of this oasis, as well as that of the others, was interdependent on the relationships between them. The oasis of Merv, for example, modified its economic and political policies once the oasis of Bukhara appeared and started to develop. A change in perspective is necessary to better understand the history and evolution of the territory and its human occupations. Although this trilogy lacks any in-depth comparisons with other territorial and historical entities, this methodology has been employed to study the oasis of Bukhara itself.

The history of the oasis of Bukhara is mostly characterised by an important urbanisation, and subsequently an urban evolution.[3] Urban culture profoundly transformed the history of this oasis, and, more broadly, that of the whole of Central Asia. This phenomenon is also important because nomadism formed the ancestral culture of these territories. Sedentary cultures, and then urban cultures, established and developed in this historical framework. As this trilogy shows, the case of the Bukhara oasis is emblematic in illustrating the speed and extent of urban development. From around the 1st century BCE and 1st century CE until the 3rd to 4th centuries CE, the distribution and increase of settlements within the oasis grew significantly. The 10th century CE was the apex of this huge development, reaching a total of 628 established urban entities (cities, villages and isolated forms of settlement mostly discussed in the first chapter of this volume) in addition to the other hundreds of non-urban scattered human occupations within the oasis.

This development characterised a specific distribution of settlements and a specific urban culture mostly linked to the water and to the caravan routes crossing the oasis since the first centuries of our era. Water and caravans were the main economic locomotives of the oasis, its economy being supported by agriculture and trade.

In this framework, the material culture developed in different ways. If we look at the earliest periods, globally,

---

1 Archaeobotanical aspects will be published separately.
2 On this topic see Frédérique Brunet 2005, 2011 and more recently Muhiddin Khudzhanazarov, Frédérique Brunet, Hikmatulla Hoshimov, Gourguène Davtian. Ўзбекистон-Франция "Зарафшон Неолит даври" экспедициясининг 2018–2019 йилларда олиб борган археологик изланишлари (Archaeological work of the Franco-Uzbek mission on the Neolithic in Zeravshan in 2018–2019). Ўзбекистонда археологик тадқиқотлар 2018–2019 йиллар, 2020, 12: 329–335.
3 These aspects are highlighted in Volumes 1 and 2, as well as in the first chapter of this volume.

ceramic production seems to find comparisons with the cultures established in the north/north-eastern regions, but also with Parthian and Tocharian territories. From the first centuries of the Common Era, although some ceramic typologies are still comparable with the surrounding oases, some specific Bukharian types can be observed, showing a rise in the mastery of pottery production and a liberty with typologies and styles. The following pre-Islamic centuries are characterised by fairly homogenous ceramic production, observable from south Kazakhstan to the Amou Daria. This homogeneity in pottery production is also identifiable during the early Islamic period. The 10th century and the Samanid leadership marks the apex in terms of quality and technology.

Beyond the main, most interesting discoveries related to pottery, published in this third volume (Chapter 4), the observations on ceramic production and consumption illustrate the degree of the evolution of civilisation within the oasis of Bukhara. In a different way, Chapter 9's study of glass will also show how cultures within the oasis developed through the centuries.

The study of material culture also shows how the oasis of Bukhara depended sometimes on external expertise, and sometimes produced its own technologies and methods, which were then reproduced elsewhere. Certain aspects of this study have brought up unknown and surprising issues, leading specialists to reconsider former interpretations. The so-called "Achaemenian ceramics" can be considered one of the most interesting examples. In this case, "Achaemenian ceramics" share similarities of forms and functions, but do not necessarily indicate a concrete Achaemenian occupation, at least in this area of the oasis. Often these similar characteristics appeared later. Further research on the area of Varakhsha, located on the border of the irrigated space, could perhaps clarify the presence of earlier occupations. As explained in Volume 1, while the inner oasis was still swampy and marshy for inhabitants until roughly the 4th century BCE, settlements around the irrigated spaces have been observed; it is therefore possible that it was also occupied during the Iron Age, specifically in the area of Varakhsha.[4]

In this context, this third volume is a collection of the activities we conducted in the oasis of Bukhara within the framework of the research programme MAFOUB (Mission Archéologique Franco-Ouzbèke dans l'Oasis de Bukhara, www.mafoub.com), as well as some other studies conducted by colleagues working on topics linked to this region, or working in the same area. It is therefore dedicated to different studies on the oasis of Bukhara that support, confirm and complete the archaeological work, thus rendering the results more robust. The aim is to give to the reader all possible data and perspectives issued from this territory.[5]

In an attempt to summarise this volume, one can extrapolate four axes. The first concerns the studies on territorial policy and their evolution over the centuries; Chapter 1 therefore focuses on settlements and social features within the oasis. These social features are seen throughout the evolution of the settlements, from the earliest stage of human occupation; the single tepe was a feature of all the urban areas that developed within the oasis. In the same context, following the investigation of the main territory and its urbanisation, Vardana and its surrounding territory were studied, as was Paykend. In the former site, through a detailed case study, the author focuses on medieval policy in this area, supporting previous interpretations and also proposing new ones. Vardana and its territory (Chapter 2) was an important region within the oasis, especially during the medieval period, disputing the leadership of the whole area with Bukhara. The article on Paykend (Chapter 3) is a very useful and complete synthesis of the site seen through the forty years of the Hermitage Museum's activities in the region.[6]

This first section completes the analysis published in the previous two volumes, integrating the study of two main sites in the oasis, Paykend and Vardana, and giving the authors a broad framework for their analyses and interpretations. It also completes the study of the urban distribution within the oasis, investigating in the first chapter the so-called "single tepe" – isolated monuments or very small agglomerations often located around a dwelling or residence. In this context, the distribution of the 628 urban sites within the oasis represents the highest degree of urbanisation, observed in the 10th century, the period of maximal urban increase. This outcome gives us a compelling knowledge of society and the relationships between urban entities; nothing similar has been published in the context of other sites in the region. Moreover, this also opens the field to interdisciplinary works as

---

4 An in-depth archaeological study on Varakhsha is currently in progress; the results will be published after its conclusion.

5 As announced in Volume 1, some of the archaeometric results are only published in this third volume for reasons linked to excavation, financial and administrative schedules. Other results were known previously, however, and appear in the analysis section in Volume 1.

6 Paykend has been studied in several zones except the citadel (only one partial trench was dug in 2010 to investigate the stratigraphy of the most recent layers, which was absent in the Russian publications), and has been explored by the Hermitage Museum for many years.

socio-archaeology and archaeo-economy,[7] through which we study the distribution of settlements and populations within the oasis in order to observe how these different sites differed in terms of their socio-economic aspects. Socio-political systems agglomerated in order to have a well-distributed political control within the whole oasis, earlier without any observable unique main centre, later with two main centres disputing control over the oasis, and finally with a single urban centre that became the "metropolis", Bukhara.

The second axis concerns material culture. The studies of ceramics and glass included in this volume form the new benchmark with which future studies of these periods will be compared. It is inevitable. The modern techniques and methods employed here to treat these cultural vectors of ancient humanity renders the results robust and changes the previous understanding of the timeline, opening up new chronological horizons. This generates new assemblages, new related information explaining human behaviours and their evolution, and new factors to explain migrations. It also opens the doors to new hypotheses. From the methodological point of view, they open the door to new approaches, specifically in these geographical areas.

In Chapter 4 of this volume, after a detailed and solid analysis on the huge quantity of pottery, the authors give an extensive and useful presentation of the pottery, categorised by function, identifying its characteristics and the evolution through the periods, from the earliest "Hellenistic" productions to those of the 15th century. Pottery for drinking, eating or storage, amongst other uses, is analysed and explained with reference the evolution of behaviours, giving the reader an excellent overview of the traditions of those epochs in the region. The resulting chrono-typology presents and explains the evolution of human practices and behaviours in daily life.

Glass is studied in the same analytical way in Chapter 9. The authors of this study have brought to light detailed characteristics of glasses produced within the oasis, which were sometimes exported, and of those imported from Iran or China. The study highlights proven imports through the knowledge of their chemical composition, also giving the reader and specialist the tools to recognise these characteristics without any technological support, with the naked eye.

In Chapters 7 and 8, other authors give an overview of former interpretations of later periods: the 15th–16th centuries. These interpretations are, in some cases, still accepted. They also presenting some material that was hitherto unpublished, or published only in earlier Russian reviews.

The third axis concerns the wide archaeometric work. This has not only served to support the research, whether on stratigraphy, pottery or glass studies, but has also been employed to study how these techniques work in this specific part of the world. These analyses give the study of material culture such solid support that further studies will emulate them and take them as a foundation, especially in a region where these disciplines are still under-developed and seen with suspicion. Scholars will understand the utility and the necessity of continuing along this path, and this volume will be an essential point of reference.

The analyses presented in Chapters 5 and 6 show intriguing different techniques of production of ceramics and glazed material that remain poorly known today, such as, for example, the so-called Ishkornaya production, even though the number of samples is low. These results also led to the production of "lustreware", which is rather an imitation of the Iranian lustreware produced at Bukhara. Petrographic analyses also shed a light on the raw material for producing the pottery, which admittedly is very homogenous across the whole oasis but which sometimes presents surprising differences, as in the case of the analysed material from Vardana.

The radiocarbon study presented in Chapter 11 groups an important series of dates, giving specialists the opportunity to look at their sequencing and archaeologists a larger panel of dates on which to base their chronology. The thermoluminescence analyses (OSL and TL) in Chapter 12 are a useful support to studying the material in the stratigraphical context. Although the traditional use of these analyses presents wider chronological spans, this study has been an ideal field to adopt other methods to reduce this span and provide a more exact date, as is more appropriate for these historical periods.

The last axis, which is constituted by a single paper – Chapter 10– discusses fauna. This study illustrates a wide panorama, showing the evolution of fauna over nineteen centuries, and also showing human behaviours correlated to animals throughout this vast chronology. This overview of the region's fauna will be integrated in the already established paleoenvironmental context and its evolution, providing tools to better understand how it developed and how human behaviour followed these transformations. The chapter also gives details of forthcoming studies and

---

7 On the issue of socio-archaeology, see the first chapter in Volume 2 of this trilogy (Rante and Tronca). On archaeo-economy, see Rante and Trionfetti, 2021 (Cambridge Archaeological Journal 31:4, 581–596).

Barthold, W. 2007. *Turkestan Down to the Mongol Invasion*. London.

Bartold, V.V. 1963. *Turkestan v epoxu mongolskogo nashestviya*. Sobr. soch. Vol. 1. Moscow.

Bartold, V.V. 1965. *Sob. coch*. Vol. 3. Moscow.

Bass, G.F., R.H. Brill, B. Lledó, and S.D. Matthews. 2009. *Serçe Limani: The Glass of an Eleventh-century Shipwreck*. Vol. 2. College Station, TX.

Baypakov, K. 2011. "Kazakhstan." In *The Artistic Culture of Central Asia and Azerbaijan in the 9th–15th Centuries*, edited by K. Baypakov, Sh. Pidayev, and A. Khakimov, 2: 12–64. Samarkand and Tashkent.

Baypakov, K.M. 1990. *Po sledam drevnih gorodov Kazahstana*. Alma-Ata.

Beal, S. 1884. *Si-Yu-Ki, Buddhist Records of the Western World, Translated from the Chinese of Hiuen Tsiang (A.D. 629)*. Vol. 1. London.

Beal, S. 1914. *The Life of Hiuen-Tsiang by the Shaman Hwui Li*. London.

Beleniskij, A.M., I.B. Bentovich, and O.G. Bolshakov. 1973. *Srednevekoviy gorod Sredney Azii*. Leningrad.

Berthon, R., M. Mashkour, P. Burger, and C. Çakırlar. 2020. Domestication, Diffusion and Hybridization of the Bactrian Camel: A Zooarchaeological Perspective. In *Les vaisseaux du désert et des steppes. Les camélidés dans l'Antiquité (Camelus dromedarius et Camelus bactrianus)*, edited by D. Agut-Labordère and B. Redon B., 21–26. Archéologie(s) 2. MOM Éditions. Lyon.

Bichurin, N.Ya. 1950. *Sobranie svedeniy o narodax obitavshix v Sredney Azii v drevnie vremena*. Vol. 2. Moscow and Leningrad.

Bocherens, H., M. Mashkour, D.G. Drucke, I. Moussa, and D. Billiou. 2006. "Stable Isotope Evidence for Palaeodiets in Southern Turkmenistan during Historical Period and Iron Age." *Journal of Archaeological Science* 33: 253–64.

Boessneck, J. 1969. Osteological Differences between Sheep (*Ovis aries* Linné) and Goat (Capra hircus Linné). In *Science in Archaeology: A Survey of Progress and Research*, edited by D. Brothwell and E.S. Higgs, 331–58. London.

Bolelov, S. 2000. "K voprosu o sootnoshenii tipov i ornamentov v keramike (po materialam Kalaly-gyr 2 v Levoberezhnom Khorezme)." In *Srednaya Aziya. Arkheologiya, Istoriya, Kul'tura*, 26–32. Moscow.

Bonzani, R.M. 1992. "Territorial Boundaries, Buffer Zones and Sociopolitical Complexity: A Case Study of the Nuraghi on Sardinia." In *Sardinia in the Mediterranean: A Footprint in the Sea*, edited by R.H. Tykot and T.K. Andrews, 210–20. Sheffield.

Borovkova, L.A. 1989. *Zapad Central'noj Azii (II v. do n.e.–VII v. n.e.)*. Moscow.

Bouquillon A., M. Aucouturier, and D. Chabanne. 2008. "Analyse des céramiques lustrées au laboratoire du Centre de Recherche et de Restauration des Musées de France." In *Catalogue de l'exposition Reflets d'Or – D'orient en Occident – La céramique lustrée IXe–XVe siècle*, 112–15. RMN, Paris.

Bouquillon, A., Y. Coquinot, and C. Doublet. 2013. "Pottery Study and Analysis." In *Nishapur Revisited: Stratigraphy and Ceramics of Qohandez*, edited by R. Rante and A. Collinet A, 101–35. Oxford.

Brill, R.H. 1995. "Chemical Analyses of Some Glass Fragments from Nishapur in the Corning Museum of Glass." In *Nishapur: The Early Islamic Glass*, edited by J. Kröger, 211–33. New York.

Brill, R.H. 1999. *Chemical Analyses of Early Glasses*. Vol. 2: *Tables of Analyses*. Corning.

Brill, R.H. 2001. "Some Thoughts on the Chemistry and Technology of Islamic Glass." In *Glass of the Sultans*, edited by S. Carboni and D. Whitehouse, 25–25. New York.

Brite, E.B., G. Khozhaniyazov, J.M. Marston, M.N. Cleary, and F.J. Kidd. 2017. "Kara-tepe, Karakalpakstan: Agropastoralism in a Central Eurasian Oasis in the 4th/5th century A.D. Transition." *Journal of Field Archaeology* 42 (6): 514–29.

Broglia de Moura, S. 2013. "La Fouille à Romitan. Chantier A." In *Mission Archéologique Franco-Ouzbèke dans l'Oasis de Boukhara. Rapport de fouille*, 29–35. Paris.

Brongniart A. 1877. *Traité des arts céramiques ou Des poteries considérées dans leur histoire, leur pratique et leur théorie*. Fac-similé publié en 1977 par Dessain et Tolra, Paris. 2 vols. and 1 atlas. Paris.

Bronk Ramsey, C. 1994. "Analysis of Chronological Information and Radiocarbon Calibration: The Program OxCal." *Archaeological Computing Newsletter* 41: 11–16.

Bronk Ramsey, C. 2017. "Methods for Summarizing Radiocarbon Datasets." *Radiocarbon* 59, 2: 809–33.

Bronk Ramsey, C., and S. Lee. 2013. "Recent and Planned Developments of the Program OxCal." *Radiocarbon* 55 (2–3): 720–30.

Bruno, J. and G. Puschnigg. 2022. "Bukhara and Its Neighborhood. Reassessing the Cultural Links of the Oasis from New Ceramic Evidence", *Archaeological Research in Asia*, Volume 31. https://doi.org/10.1016/j.ara.2022.100372

Brusenko, L.G., and Z.S. Galieva. 1982. "Materialy raskopov kvartala X–nachala XI vv. na gorodishche Kanka." *IMKU* 17: 124–36.

Bryune, F. 2014. "O novom issledovanii neoliticheskoy Kel'teminarskoy kul'tury (Uzbekistan)." In *Arkheologiya i istoriya Tsentral'noy Azii v trudakh frantsuzskikh uchenykh*, vol. 1, 38–62. Samarkand.

Burger, P.A. 2016. "The History of Old World Camelids in the Light of Molecular Genetics." *Trop. Anim. Health Prod.* 48: 905–13.

Burow, C. 2019. "Calc_FiniteMixture(): Apply the Finite Mixture Model (FMM) after Galbraith (2005) to a Given De Distribution. Function Version 0.4.1." In *Luminescence: Comprehensive Luminescence Dating Data AnalysisR Package*

Version 0.9.3, by S. Kreutzer, C. Burow, M. Dietze, M.C. Fuchs, C. Schmidt, M. Fischer, and J. Friedrich. Available online at: https://CRAN.R-project.org/package=Luminescence.

Buryakov, Yu., and G.A. Koshelenko. 1985. "Srednjaja Azia v antichnuju epokhu. Tashkentskij oasis (Chach)." In *Drevnejshie gosudarstva Kavkaza i Srednei Azii*, edited by G.A. Koshelenko, 297–303. Moscow.

Buryakov, YU.F. 1990. *Masterskaya torefta XIV v. v Samarkande. Kul'tura Srednevekovogo Vostoka: Izobrazitel'noe i prikladnoe iskusstvo*. Tashkent.

Cadeddu, F. 2012. *Modalità insediative e strategie di controllo della Sardegna durante l'età del Bronzo: il caso studio della Gallura*. Tesi di dottorato di Ricerca in Scienze dell'Antichità, ciclo XXIV. Università degli Studi di Udine.

Çakırlar, C., and R. Berthon. 2014. "Caravans, Camel Wrestling and Cowrie Shells: Towards a Social Zooarchaeology of Camel Hybridization in Anatolia and Adjacent Regions." *Anthropozoologica* 49: 237–52.

Campbell, D. 1926. *Arabian medicine and its influence on the middle ages*. Vol. 1. London.

Campbell, J.L., N.I. Boyd, N. Grassi, P. Bonnick, and J.A. Maxwell. 2010. "The Guelph PIXE Software Package IV." In *Nuclear Instruments and Methods B268*, 3356–63.

Cerasuolo, O. "Indagine topografica nel territorio di Varakhsha." In *Gli Scavi di Uch Kulakh (Oasi di Bukhara): Rapporto preliminare, 1997–2007*. Edited by C. Silvi Antonini and D. Mirazaakhmedov, 189–210. Pisa.

Chavannes, E. 1903. *Documents sur les Tou – Kiue (Turks) Occidentaux*. Paris.

Chisholm, M. 1968. *Rural Settlement and Land Use: An Essay in Location*. London.

Cohen, A., and D. Serjeantson. 1996. *A Manual for the Identification of Bird Bones from Archaeological Sites*, London.

Collins, A.B. 1994. *Al-Muqaddasi, The Best Division for Knowledge of the Regions: A Translation of Ahsan al-Taqasim fi Marifat al-Aqalim*. Garnet.

Compareti, M. 2003. "Rapporto delle campagne di scavo 2002 in Uzbekistan. C. Note sul toponimo Vardāna-Vardānzī." *Rivista degli Studi Orientali* 76: 39–47.

Darkevich, V.P. 1976. *Hudozhestvennyiy metall Vostoka*. Moscow.

Davidovich, E.A. 1953. *Cvetnoe okonnoe steklo XV v. iz Samarkanda: Trudyi Sredneaziatskogo Gosudarstvennogo Universiteta*. Novaya seriya. Vyip. 61. Gumanitarnyie nauki, kniga 6. Tashkent.

Davison, S. 2003. *Conservation and Restoration of Glass*. 2nd ed. Oxford.

De Goeje, M.J. 1927. *Viae Regnorum: descriptio ditionis moslemicae, auctore Abu Ishak al-Farisi al-Istakhri*. Brill.

de la Vaissière, É. 2005. *Sogdian Traders: A History*. Handbuch der Orientalistik 10. Leiden. (English translation of the 2nd edition).

Di Cosmo, Nicola. 2000. "Ancient City-States of the Tarim Basin." In *A Comparative Study of Thirty City-State Cultures: An Investigation*, edited by M.H. Hansen, 393–409. Copenhagen.

Dioli, M. 2020. "Dromedary (Camelus dromedarius) and Bactrian Camel (Camelus bactrianus) CrossbreedingHusbandry Practices in Turkey and Kazakhstan: An In-depth Review." *Pastoralism* 10, 6. DOI: 10.1186/s13570-020-0159-3.

Doll, M. 2003. "Animals and Men in Mines: The Bone Assemblages from Karnab and Mušiston." In *Man and Mining: Mensch und Bergbau*, edited by T. Stöller, G. Körlin, G. Steffens, and J. Cierny, 113–25, Deutsches Bergbau Museum.

Dye, T.S., and C.E. Buck. 2015. "Archaeological Sequence Diagrams and Bayesian Chronological Models." *Journal of Archaeological Science* 63: 84–93.

Dytchkovwskyj, D., S. Aagesen, and A. Costopoulos. 2005. "The Use of Thiessen Polygons and Viewshed Analysis to Create Hypotheses about Prehistoric Territories and Political Systems: A Test Case from the Iron Age of Spains's Alcoy Valley." *Archaeological Computing Newsletter* 62: 1–5.

Erbersdobler, K. 1968. *Vergleichend morphologische Untersuchungen an Einzelknochen des postcranialen Skeletts in Mitteleuropa vorkommender mittelgrosser Hünnervögel*. München.

Fernandez, H. 2001. "Ostéologie comparée des petits ruminants eurasiatiques sauvages et domestiques (Rupicapra, Ovis, Capra et Capreolus): Diagnose différentielle du squelette appendiculaire." PhD diss., Genève, Muséum d'Histoire Naturelle.

Filanovich, M.I. 1983. *Kul'tura Drevnebukharskogo Oazisa 3.–4. vv. n. e*. Tashkent.

Fodde, E. 2009. "Traditional Earthen Building Techniques in Central Asia." *International Journal of Architectural Heritage* 3, 2: 145–68.

Forte, M. 2002. *I sistemi informativi geografici in archeologia*. Roma.

Fouache, E., R. Rante, Dj. Mirzaakhmedov, R. Ragala, M. Dupays, C. Vella, J. Fleury, V. Andrieu-Ponnel, A. Zink, E. Porto, et al. 2016. "The Role of Catastrophic Floods Generated by Collapse of Natural Dams Since the Neolithic in the Oases of Bukhara and Qaraqöl: Preliminary Results." *International Journal of Geohazards and Environment* 2 (3): 150–65.

Fouache, E., R. Rante, M. Dupays, C. Vella, J. Fleury, R. Ragala, V. Andrieu-Ponel, A. Zink, E. Porto, and F. Brunet. 2016. "The Role of Catastrophic Floods Generated by Collapse of Natural Dams Since the Neolithic in the Oases of Bukhara and Qaraqöl: Preliminary Results." *International Journal of Geohazards and Environment* 2 (3): 150–65.

Frachetti, M.D., and F.A. Maksudov. 2014. "The Landscape of Ancient Mobile Pastoralism in the Highlands of Uzbekistan, 2000 B.C.–A.D. 1400." *Journal of Field Archaeology* 39: 195–212.

Frachetti, M.D., E. Smith, C. Traub, and W. Williams. 2017. "Nomadic Ecology Shaped the Highland Geography of Asia's Silk Roads." *Nature* 543: 193–98.

Francfort, H.-P. 2020. "Les vestiges et les représentations du Camelus dromaderiusen Asie Centrale entre le IIIe et le 1er millénaire." In *Les vaisseaux du désert et des steppes: Les camélidés dans l'Antiquité (Camelus dromedarius et Camelus bactrianus)*, edited by D.J.C. Agut-Labordère and B. Redon, 27–54. Archéologie(s) 2. MOM Éditions. Lyon.

Freestone, I.C. 2006. "Glass Production in Late Antiquity and the Early Islamic Period: A Geochemical Perspective." In *Geomaterials in Cultural Heritage*, edited by M. Maggetti and B. Messiga, 201–16. London.

Frye, R. 2007. *The History of Bukhara, by al-Narshakhi*. Princeton, NJ.

Frye, R.N. 1954. *The History of Bukhara, Translated from a Persian Abridgement of the Arabic Original by Narshakhī*. Cambridge, MA.

Fukai, S. 1968. *Study of Iranian Art and Archaeology: Glass and Metalwork*. Tokyo. (In Japanese.)

Galbraith, R.F. 1990. "The Radial Plot: Graphical Assessment of Spread in Ages." *Nuclear Tracks and Radiation Measurements* 17 (3): 207–17.

Galbraith, R.F., and R.G. Roberts. 2012. "Statistical Aspects of Equivalent Dose and Error Calculation and Display in OSL Dating: An Overview and Some Recommendations." *Quaternary Geochronology* 11: 1–27.

Gangler, A., H. Gaube, and A. Petruccioli. 2004. *Bukhara: The Eastern Dome of Islam. Urban Development, Urban Space, Architecture and Population*. London.

Gazagnadou, D. 2017. *The Diffusion of a Postal Relay System in Premodern Eurasia*. Paris.

Gazagnadou, D. 2005. "Yâm." *Encyclopédie de l'Islam*, vol. 11, E.-J. Brill. Leiden.

Genito, B., J.M. Deon, L.M. Rendina, and B. Nunziata. 2003. "Preliminary Notes on the 'Archaeological Topography in the Bukhara Oasis' Project." In *Italo-Uzbek Scientific Cooperation in Archaeology and Islamic Studies: An Overview (Rome, January 30, 2001)*, edited by S. Pagani, 55–79. Rome.

Gintzburger, G., K.M. Toderich, B.K. Mardonov, and M.M. Mahmudov. 2003. *Rangelands of the Arid and Semi-arid Zones in Uzbekistan*. Montpellier and Aleppo.

Golombek, Lisa, Robert B. Masson, and Gauvin Bailey. 1994. *Tamerlane's Tableware: A New Approach to the Chinoiserie Ceramics of Fifteenth- and Sixteenth-Century Iran*. London.

Gratuze, B. 2013. "Provenance Analysis of Glass Artefacts." In *Modern Methods for Analysing Archaeological and Historical Glass*, edited by K. Janssens, 311–34. Online.

Grenet, F., and E. de la Vaissière. 2002. "The Last Days of Panjikent." *Journal of the Institute of Silk Road Studies* 8: 155–96.

Grenet, F., and E. de la Vaissière. 2002. "The Last Days of Panjikent." *Silk Road Art and Archaeology*, 8: 155–96.

Grenet. F. 2020. "The Wooden Panels from Kafir-kala: A Group Portrait of the Samarkand *nāf* (Civic Body)." *Acta Asiatica* 119 (2): 1–22.

Grube. E.J. 2013. *Some Thoughts on the Longevitiof Sogdian Iconographyinthe Muslim World: Sogdiycyi, ih predshestvenniki, sovremenniki i nasledniki. Trudyi Gosudarstvennogo E'rmitazha*. Vol. 62. St. Petersburg.

Guillot, C. 2011. "Le Verre Ancien dans le Monde Malais." In *Introduction to Islamic Archaeology and Art: Egypt/ Iran/ Southeast Asia*, edited by Y. Shindo, 19–26. Tokyo.

Guillot, C. (ed.). 2003. *Historie de Barus: Le site de Lobu Tua, Ètudie archaéologyque et documents*. Vol. 2. Paris.

Guillot, C. 2012. "Epave de Cirebon." The cargo from the Cirebon shipwreck, available online at: http://cirebon.musee-mariemont.be/Upload_Mariemont/Etudes/Guillot_ Cire-bon.pdf.

Guionova, G., and M. Bouquet. 2017. "Ischkornaïa: de l'usage de la soude végétale dans les revêtements céramiques (Paykend, oasis de Boukhara, IXe–XIXe siècles)." In *Glazed Pottery of the Mediterranean and the Black Sea Region, 10th–18th Centuries*, vol. 2, edited by Kazan-Kishinev, 767–77 Kazan.

Guionova, G., G. Dieulefet, and C.F. Mangiaracina. 2014. "Rapport Préliminaire Sur Les Ensembles de Consommation Potière Du Chantier B." In *Mission Archéologique Franco-Ouzbèke Dans l'Oasis de Boukhara. Rapport de fouille, campagne 2014*, 98–101. Paris.

Guionova, G., M. Bouquet, S. Aubert, Th. Jullien, and N. Attia. 2013. "La Céramique." In *Mission Archéologique Franco-Ouzbèke dans l'Oasis de Boukhara. Rapport de fouille, campagne 2013*, 81–107. Paris.

Gulmini, M., R. Giannini, A.M. Lega, G. Manna, and P. Mirti 2013. "Technology of Production of Ghazanavid Glazed Pottery from Bust and Lashkar-i Bazar (Afghanistan)." *Archaeometry* 55, 4: 569–90.

Hadad, S. 2005. "Islamic Glass Vessels from the Hebrew University Excavations at Bet Shean." In *Qedem Reports 8*. Vol. 2: *Excavations at Bet Shean*, 111–201. Jerusalem.

Halstead, P., and P. Collins. 2002. "Sorting the Sheep from the Goats: Morphological Distinctions between the Mandibles and Mandibular Teeth of Adult *Ovis* and *Capra*." *Journal of Archaeological Science* 29: 545–53.

Hansen, Mogens H. 2006. *Polis: An Introduction to the Ancient Greek City-State*. Oxford.

Hansen, V. 2017. *The Silk Road: A New History with Documents*. New York and Oxford.

Helmer, D., and M. Rocheteau. 1994. "Atlas du squelette appendiculaire des principaux genres Holocènes de petits ruminants du Nord de la Méditerranée et du Proche-Orient (*Capra*,

Ovis, Rupicapra, Capreolus, Gazella)." *Fiche d'ostéologie animale pour l'archéologie, série B: Mammifères*: 1–21.

Henderson, J. 2013. *Ancient Glass: An Interdisciplinary Exploration*. New York.

Henderson, J., S. McLoughlin, and D. McPhail. 2004. "Radical Changes in Islamic Glass Technology: Evidence for Conservatism and Experimentation with New Glass Recipes from Early and Middle Islamic Raqqa, Syria." *Archaeometry* 46: 439–68.

Henning, W.B. 1948. "The Date of the Sogdian Ancient Letters." *BSOAS* 12 (3–4): 601–15.

Hermes, T.R., M.D. Frachetti, E.A. Bullion, F. Maksudov, S. Mustafokulov, and C.A. Makarewicz. 2018. "Urban and Nomadic Isotopic Niches Reveal Dietary Connectivities along Central Asia's Silk Roads." *Scientific Report* 8: 51–77.

Hilal al-Sabi. 1983. *Ustanovleniya i obyichai dvora halifov*. Moscow.

Hilson, S. 1986. *Teeth*. Cambridge.

Hinds, M. 1990. *The Zenith of Marwānid House: The Last Years of 'Abd al-Malik and the Caliphate of al-Walīd A.D. 700–715*. Volume 23 of *The History of al-Ṭabarī*. Albany, NY.

Houal, J.-B., and S. Le Maguer. 2013. "La céramique de Termez des époques antique et médiévale." In *25 ans d'archéologie française en Asie Centrale: Nouvelles méthodes, nouvelles perspectives*, edited by Julio Bendezu-Sarmiento, 423–42. Paris.

Huntley, D.J., and M. Lamothe. 2001. "Ubiquity of Anomalous Fading in K-feldspars and the Measurement and Correction for It in Optical Dating." *Canadian Journal of Earth Sciences* 38: 1093–106.

Ibn Hawqal, Abu 'l-Kasîm. 1964. *Configuration de la Terre: Kitab Surat al-Ardh*. Edited and translated by J.H. Kramers and G. Wiet. Paris.

Ibn Hawqal, Abu 'l-Kasîm. 1964. *Configuration de la Terre: Kitab Surat al-Ardh*. Edited and translated by J.H. Kramers and G. Wiet. Paris.

Ibn Sina. 1956. *Kanon vrachebnoy nauki*. Kn. II. O prostyih lekarstvah. Tashkent.

Ibn Sina. 1985. *Kanon vrachebnoy nauki*. Tashkent.

Ibragimov, N., trans. 1988. *Ibn Battuta i ego puteshestviya po Sredney Azii*. Moscow.

Ilyasov, Jangar. 2006. "Zametki o nekotorykh sredneaziatskikh tamgakh." *Zapiski vostoch- nogo otdeleniia Rossiiskogo arkheologicheskogo obshchestva* 2: 99–122.

Iskusstvo islama. Katalog vyistavki. 1990. Leningrad.

Islamische Kunst. 1984. *Loseblattkatalog unpublizierter Werke aus deutschen Museen*. Band 1. Glas. Mainz and Rhein.

Islamische Kunst. 1984. *Loseblattkatalog unpublizierter Werke aus deutschen Museen*. Band 1. Glas. Mainz and Rhein.

Itina, M.A. 1961. *Raskopki mogilnika Tazabagyabskoy kulturi Kokcha-3: Materiali Xorezmskoy ekspedicii*. Vol. 5. Moscow.

Janpoladyan, R.M. 1960. *Novyie dannyie o steklodelii Dvina*. KSIMK 120. Moscow.

Janpoladyan, R.M. 1965. *Laboratornaya posuda armyanskogo alhimika*. SA 2. Moscow.

Joglekar, P.P. 1998. "A Preliminary Report on the Faunal Remains at Takhirbai 1, Turkmenistan." In *The Archaeological Map of the Murghab Delta*, edited by A. Gubaev, G.A. Koshelenko, and M. Tosi, 115–18. Rome.

Kabanov, S.K. 1955. *Arheologicheskaya razvedka v verhney chasti dolinyi Kashka Dar'i: Trudyi Instituta istorii i arheologii. Vyip*. 7. Tashkent.

Kabanov, S.K. 1956. *Raskopki zhilogo kvartala X veka v zapadnoy chasti gorodishha Varahsha: Trudyi Instituta istorii i arheologii AN UzSSR. Vyip. VIII*. Tashkent.

Kamoliddin, Sh.S. 2011. *Muhammad An-Narshaki*. Tashkent.

Karimov, U.I. 1957. *Neizvestnoe sochinenie Ar-Razi "Kniga taynyi tayn."* Tashkent.

Kato, N., I. Nakai, and Y. Shindo. 2010. "Transitions in Islamic Plant-ash Glass Vessels: On-site Chemical Analyses Conducted at the Raya/al-Tur Area on the Sinai Peninsula in Egypt." *Journal of Archaeological Science* 37: 1381–1395.

Kazanjyan, T.T. 1955. *Ocherki po istorii himii v Armenii*. Erevan.

Kervran, M. 1984. "Les Niveaux islamique du Secteuer oriental du Tepe de l'Apadana III: Les Objets en Verre, en Pierre et en Métal." *Cahiers de la Délégation Archéologique Française en Iran* 14: 211–35.

Kervran, M., and A. Rougeulle. 1984. "Recherche sur les Niveaux islamique de la Ville des Artisans, Suse 1976–1978." *Cahiers de la Délégation Archéologique Française en Iran* 14: 50–93.

Khakimov, A. 2004. *Masterpieces of the Samarkand Museum*. Tashkent.

Khmel'nitskiy, S. 1996. *Mezhdu Samanidami i mongolami. Arkhitektura Sredney Azii ya – nachala 13 veka, 1*. Berlin and Riga.

Khmel'nitskiy, S. 2000. *Mezhdu kushanami i arabami. Arkhitektura Sredney Azii 5–8 vv*. Berlin and Riga.

Koshelenko, G.A. 1985. *Drevnejshie gosudarstva Kavkaza i Srednei Azii*. Moscow.

Kröger, J. 1995. *Nishapur: The Early Islamic Glass*. New York.

Kügelgen, A. von. 2009. "Bukhara VIII. Historiography of the Khanate 1500–1920." Originally published 15 July 2009. http://www.iranicaonline.org/articles/bukhara-viii.

Kuleshov Vyach, S., and N.Zh. Saparov. 2016. "Paykendskiy klad 2014 goda." In *MBAE* 13, 65–67. St. Petersburg.

Kulish, A.V., and S.Kh. Khuzhamov. 2019. "Klad s imitatsiyami abbasidskikh monet iz Paykenda." In *XX Vserossiyskaya numizmaticheskaya konferentsiya. Tezisy dokladov i soobshcheniy*, edited by P.G. Gaydukov et al., 42–44. Moscow.

Kultura i iskusstvo drevnego Uzbekistana. 1991. Katalog vistavki. Kniga 2. Moscow.

Kunina, N. 1997. *Antichnoe steklo v sobranii E'rmitazha*. St. Petersburg.

Kuzmina, E.E. 1958. *Mogilnik Zaman-Baba*. SE 2. Tashkent.

Lamm, C.J. 1928. *Das Glas von Samarra*. Berlin.

Lamm, G.J. 1930. *Mittelalterliche Glaser und Steinschnittarbaiten aus den Nahen Osten*. Berlin.

Lamm, G.J. 1935. *Glass from Iran in the National Museum Stockholm*. Upsala.

Lebedeva, T.I. 1990. "Keramika Afrasiaba V–VI vv. n. è." *IMKU* 23: 160–68.

Lecomte, O., and M. Mashkour. 1998. "Hyrcanie et Dehistan, de l'âge du fer à la période islamique (13e s. av.–8e s. apr. J.-C.) [*Bastan Shinasi va Tarikh*]." *Iranian Journal of Archaeology and History* 26: 9–21.

Lecomte, O., and M. Mashkour. 2013. "La cigogne, la chèvre et les renards." In *Animals, Gods and Men from East to West*, edited by A. Peruzzetto, F.D. Metzger, and L. Dirven, 27–46. BAR International Series 2516, United Kingdom.

Leriche, P. 2013. "L'apport de la Mission archéologique franco-ouzbèque (MAFouz) de Bactriane du Nord à l'histoire de l'Asie centrale." In *25 ans d'archéologie française en Asie Centrale: Nouvelles méthodes, nouvelles perspectives*, edited by Julio Bendezu-Sarmiento, 135–64. Paris.

Levina, L.M. 1971. *Keramika Nizhnej i Srednej Syrdar'i v I tysjacheletii n. e.* Moscow.

Lhuillier, J., and M. Mashkour. 2017. "Animal Exploitation in the Oases: An Archaeozoological View of Iron Age Sites in Southern Central Asia." *Antiquity* 91 (357): 655–73.

Lhuillier, J., J. Bendezu-Sarmiento, and S. Mustafakulov et al. 2018. "The Early Iron Age Occupation in Southern Central Asia: Excavation at Dzharkutan in Uzbekistan." In *A Millennium of History: The Iron Age in Southern Central Asia (2nd and 1st Millennia BC)*, edited by J. Lhuillier and N. Boroffka, 31–50. Archäologie in Iran und Turan 17, Berlin.

Liebner, H.H. 2014. "The Siren of Cirebon: A Tenth-Century Trading Vessel Lost in the Java Sea." PhD diss., University of Leeds.

Litvinsky, B.A. 2001. *Khram Oksa v Baktrii (Iuzhnii Tadzhikistan) 2: Baktriiskoe vooruzhenie v drevnevostochnom i grecheskom kontekste*. Moscow.

Litvinsky, B.A., and I.R. Pichikyan. 2000. *Ellinisticheskii khram Oksa v Baktrii (Iuzhnii Tadzhikistan) 1: Raskopki, arkhitektura, religioznaia zhizn*. Moscow.

Livshits, V.A. 1962. *Yuridicheskie dokumenty i pis'ma*. Sogdiĭskie dokumenty s gory Mug 2. Moscow.

Livshits, V.A. 2015. *Sogdian Epigraphy of Central Asia and Semirech'e*. London.

Livshits, V.A. 2015. *Sogdian Epigraphy of Central Asia and Semirech'e*. Corpus Inscriptionum iranicarum. Part 2, Inscriptions of the Seleucid and Parthian Periods and of Eastern Iran and Central Asia. Vol. 3, Sogdian. London.

Lo Muzio, C. 2009. "An Archaeological Outline of the Bukhara Oasis." *Journal of Inner Asian Art and Archaeology* 4, edited by J.A. Lerner, and L. Russell-Smith, 43–68. Turnhout.

Longin, R. 1971. "New Method of Collagen Extraction for Radiocarbon Dating." *Nature* 230: 241–42.

Lurje, P.B. 2006. "'Shapur's Will' in Bukhara." In *Ērān ud Anērān. Studies Presented to Boris Il'ich Marshak on the Occasion of His 70th Birthday*, edited by M. Compareti, P. Raffetta, and G. Scarcia, 407–18. Venice.

Lyonnet, B. 2000. "Grecheskaya okupatsiya sogdiany. Rezultaty sravnitel'nogo analiza keramiki Afrasiaba i Ai-Khanum." In *Srednyaya Aziya. Arkheologiya. Istoriya. Kul'tura. (Central Asia. Archaeology. History. Culture. Papers presented to the International Conference dedicated to the 50th anniversary of G.V. Shishkina's scholarly activity.)*, 75–80. Moscow: Gosudarstvennji musej vostoka.

Lyonnet, B. 2012. "Questions on the Date of the Hellenistic Pottery from Central Asia (Ai Khanoum, Marakanda and Koktepe)." *Ancient Civilizations from Scythia to Siberia* 18: 143–73.

Lyonnet, B. 2013. "La Céramique Hellénistique En Asie Centrale." In *Networks in the Hellenistic World: According to the Pottery in the Eastern Mediterranean and Beyond*, edited by Nina Fenn and Christiane Römer-Strehl, 351–68. Vol. 2539. BAR International Series. Oxford.

MAFTUR. 2013. *Ulug Depe: A Forgotten City in Central Asia*, Paris.

Mantellini, S. 2015. "Irrigation Systems in Samarkand." In *Encyclopaedia of History of Science, Technology, and Medicine in Non-Western Cultures*, edited by H. Seline, 1–14. Dordrech.

Mantellini, S. 2017. "A City and Its Landscape Across Time: Samarkand in the Ancient Sogdiana (Uzbekistan)." in *Proceedings of the KAINUA 2017, International Conference in Honour of Professor Giuseppe Sassatelli's 70th Birthday (Bologna, 18–21 April 2017)*, edited by S. Garagnani and A. Gaucci, 332–42. Florence.

Marquart, J. 1898. *Die Chronologie der alttükischen Inschriften*. Leipzig.

Markwart, J. 1938. Wehrot und Arang: Untersuchungen zur myth- ischen und geschichtlichen Landeskunde von Ostiran. Edited by Hans Heinrich Schaeder. Leiden; Pers. tr. by Davoud Monchi-Zadeh, Tehran (1989).

Marshak, B.I. 2012. *Keramika Sogda V–VII vekov kak istoriko-kul'turnyj pamjatnik*. St. Petersburg.

Mashkour, M. 1998. "The Subsistence Economy in the Rural Community of Geoktchik Depe in Southern Turkmenistan: Preliminary Results of the Faunal Analysis." In *Archaeozoology of the Near East III*, edited by H. Buitenhuis, L. Bartosiewicz, and A.M. Choyke, 200–20. Groningen.

Mashkour, M. 2013. "Sociétés pastorales et économies de subsistance au Nord Est de l'Iran et au Sud du Turkménistan. Archéologie française en Asie centrale. Nouvelles recherches et enjeux socioculturels." *Cahiers d'Asie Centrale* 21/22: 533–44.

Mashkour, M., and M.J. Beech (eds.). 2014. "Ancient Camelids in the Old World: Between Arabia and Europe." Proceeding of a special session on Camelids inthe Old World held at the ICAZ 2010 conference, Anthropozoologica 49. Paris.

Mashkour, M., R. Khazaeli, H. Fathi, S. Amiri, D. Decruyenaere, A. Mohaseb, H. Davoudi, S. Sheikhi, and E.W. Sauer. 2017. "Animal Exploitation and Subsistence on the Borderlines of the Sasanian Empire: A View from the Gates of the Alans (Georgia) and the Gorgan Wall (Iran)." In *Sasanian Persia between Rome and the Steppes of Eurasia*, edited by E. Sauer, 74–95. Edinburgh.

Mashkour, M., V. Radu, and R. Thomas. 2013. "Animal Exploitation during the Iron Age to Achaemenid, Sasanian and Early Islamic Periods along the Gorgan Wall." In *Persia's Imperial Power in Late Antiquity: The Great Gorgan Wall and the Frontier Landscapes of Sasanian Iran*, edited by E. Sauer, H. Rekavandi, T. Wilkinson and J. Nokandeh, 548–80. British Institute of Persian Studies, Archaeological monographs Series II, Oxbow Books, Oxford and Oakville.

Maslenitsa, S. 1975. *Iskusstvo Irana v sobranii Gosudarstvennogo muzeya iskusstva narodov Vostoka*. Leningrad.

Maslenitsyna, S. 1975. *Iskusstvo Irana v sobranii gosudarstvennogo muzeya iskusstva narodov Vostoka*. Leningrad.

Mason, R., and A. Tite. 1997. "The Beginnings of the Tin-opacification of Pottery Glazes." *Archaeometry* 39: 41–58.

Matin, M., M. Tite, and O. Watson. 2018. "On the Origins of Tin-opacified Ceramic Glazes: New Evidence from Early Islamic Egypt, the Levant, Mesopotamia, Iran, and Central Asia." *Journal of Archaeological Science* 97: 42–66.

Mercier, N., and C. Falguères. 2007. "Field Gamma Dose-rate Measurement with a NaI(Tl) Detector: Re-evaluation of the 'Threshold' Technique." *Ancient TL* 25: 1–4.

Mercier, N., H. Valladas, G. Valladas, J.L. Reyss, and J.L. Joron. 1994. "A New Dosimetric Calibration Tool." *Radiation Measurements* 23 (2–3): 507–508.

Metz, A. 1966. *Musul'manskiy Renessans*. Moscow.

Miniatyuryi k proizvedeniyam Alishera Navoi. 1982. Tashkent.

Mirzaakhmedov, Dj. 2008. *La Production Céramique du Maverannahr du IX au debut du XIII siecle: Islamisation del Asie Centrale*. Studia Iranica 39. Paris.

Mirzaakhmedov, Dj. 2011. "Uzbekistan." In *The Artistic Culture of Central Asia and Azerbaijan in the 9th–15thCenturies*. Vol. 2: *Glass*, edited by K. Baypakov, Sh. Pidayev, and A. Khakimov, 96–161. Samarkand and Tashkent.

Mirzaakhmedov, Dj., S. Pozzi, Sh.T. Adylov, M. Sultanova, and S. Mirzaakhmedov. 2016b. "Gorodishe Vardanze: Dinamika obživanija citadeli po materialam keramicheskih kompleksov sredenevekov'ja." *Istorija i archeologija Turana*, 3 (posvjashennyy yubileyu Djamaladdina Kamalovicha Mirzaakhmedova): 336–50.

Mirzaakhmedov, Dj., S. Pozzi, Sh.T. Adylov, M. Sultanova, and S. Mirzaakhmedov. 2019. "Kurgan Vardanzeh: The Dynamics of Settlement on the Citadel, Based on the Materials from Medieval Pottery Complexes." In *Urban Cultures of Central Asia from the Bronze Age to the Karakhanids: Learnings and Conclusions from New Archaeological Investigations and Discoveries, 4–6 February 2016, Bern, Switzerland*, 247–60. Harrassowitz Verlag (Schriften zur vorderasiatischen Archäologie 12). Wiesbaden.

Mirzaakhmedov, Dj., Sh.T. Adylov, S. Pozzi, S. Mirzaakhmedov, and M. Sultanova. 2013. "Issledovanija v Vardanze v 2012 g." *Archeologicheskie issledovanija v Uzbekistane 2012 g.* 9: 129–36.

Mirzaakhmedov, Dj., Sh.T. Adylov, S. Pozzi, S. Mirzaakhmedov, and M. Sultanova. 2016a. "Kurgan Vardanze: dinamika obshivanija po materialam keramicheskich complexov citadeli." *Arheologiya Uzbekistana v gody nezavisimosti: dostiženija i perspectivy*: 141–44.

Mirzaakhmedov, Dj.K. 1981. "Glazurovannaya keramika Bukhary vtoroy poloviny XVII–pervoy poloviny XVIII vv." *IMKU* 16. Tashkent.

Mirzaakhmedov, Dj.K. 1992. "Glazurovannaya keramika Tashkenta kontsa XV–nachala XVI vv." *IMKU* 26. Tashkent.

Mirzaakhmedov, Dj.K. 1998. *Eshhyo raz k voprosu o keramike s zelyonoy polivoy iz Paykenda*. IMKU 29. Samarkand.

Mirzaakhmedov, Dj.K. 2000. "Komleks Keramiki X v. iz Prigoroda Pajkenda." In *Materialy Mejdunarodnoj Konferencii Posvâšennoj 50-Letiû Naučnoj Deâtel'nosti G.B. Šiškinoj*, edited by T.G. Alpatkina, S. Bolelov, O.N. Inevatkina, and T.K. Mkrtyčev, 87–88. Moscow.

Mirzaakhmedov, Dj.K. 2004. "Novyye pozdnesrednevekovyye arkheologicheskiye kompleksy po materialam Bukhary." In *Drevnyaya i srednevekovaya kul'tura Bukharskogo oazisa*. Samarkand and Rim.

Mirzaakhmedov, Dj.K. 2007. *Kompleks materialov k sobyitiyam mongol'skogo zavoevaniya Samarkanda (Afrasiaba): Samarkand shahrining umumbashariy madaniy taraqiyot tarihida tutgan urni (Samarkand shahrining 2750 yillik yubileiga bagishlangan halkaro ilmiy simpozium materiallari)*. Tashkent and Samarkand.

Mirzaakhmedov, Dj.K. 1990. "Glazurovannaya keramika Tashkenta XVII v." In *Arkheologicheskiye raboty na novostroykakh Uzbekistana*. Tashkent.

Mirzaakhmedov, Dj.K., A.V. Omelchenko, D.O. Kholov, R.M. Toirov, D.V. Sadofeev, N.D. Sobirov, A.N. Gorin, N.J. Saparov, and A.I. Torgoev. 2013. "Otchet o raskopkah v Paykend e v 2011–12 gg." *MBAE* 12. St. Petersburg.

Mirzaakhmedov, Dj.K., A.V. Omelchenko, A.N. Gorin, V.V. Mokroborodov, G.P. Ivanov, D.O. Kholov, N.D. Sobirov, R.M.

Toirov, A.I. Torgoev, N.J. Saparov, L.O. Smirnova, and A.V. Kulish. 2016. "Otchet o raskopkah v Paykend e v 2013–14 gg." MBAE 13. St. Petersburg.

Mirzaakhmedov, Dj.K., and U. Alimov. 2006. "Novyye nakhodki pozdnesrednevekovoy polivnoy keramiki Shakhrukhii." IMKU 35. Tashkent.

Mirzaakhmedov, Dj.K., S. Ilyasova, and Sh.T. Adylov. 1999. *Srednevekovoe steklo i keramika Binkata – Tashkenta IX–XI vv. Razdel 1. Steklyannyie izdeliya.* IMKU 30. Samarkand.

Mirzaakhmedov, Dj.K., S. Pozzi, Sh.T. Adylov, S. Mirzaakhmedov, M. Niyazova, and M. Sultanova. 2016c. "Issledovanija v Vardanze v 2013 g." *Archeologicheskie issledovanija v Uzbekistane 2013–2014 goda* 10: 207–16.

Mirzaakhmedov, Dj.K., S. Stark, B.M. Abdullaev, and S.D. Mirzaakhmedov. 2013. "Raskopki Pogranichnoi Kreposti Ganchtepa Uzbeksko-Amerikanskoi Ekspeditsiei v 2012g." *Arkheologicheskie Issledovanija v Uzbekistane 2012 god* 9: 101–10.

Mirzaakhmedov, Dj.K., S. Stark, B.M. Abdullaev, M. Kenigsdorfer, S. Mirzaakhmedov, and A. Iskanderova. 2016. "Issledovanija Pamyatnikov Vostochnoi Okrainy Kampyr-Duvala v Bukharskom Sogde v 2013–14gg." *Arkheologicheskie Issledovanija v Uzbekistane 2013–14 gg* 10: 217–32.

Mirzaakhmedov, Dj.K., Sh.T. Adylov, and A.R. Mukhamedjanov. 1990. *Steklyannyie izdeliya iz Paykenda: Iz istorii kul'turnogo naslediya Buharyi*. Tashkent.

Mirzaakhmedov, Dj.K., Sh.T. Adylov, and B.H. Matbabaev. 2008. *Rezul'tatyi arheologicheskih issledovaniy na o"ekte R5b gorodishha Kuva*. IMKU 36. Tashkent.

Monchot, H., T. Lorain, and J. Bendezu-Sarmiento. 2019. "From Bone Broth to Kebab: The Importance of Caprine in the Economy of the Medieval Site of Shahr-e Gholgholah (Bâmiyân, Afghanistan)." In *Hommes et caprinés: de la montagne à la steppe, de la chasse à l'élevage: XXXIX rencontres internationales d'archéologie et d'histoire d'Antibes*, edited by L. Gourichon, C. Daujeard, and J.-P. Brugal, 285–296. Éditions APDCA. Antibes.

Moore, K.M. 1993a. "Animal Use at Bronze Age Gonur Depe." *Information Bulletin of the International Association for the Study of the Cultures of Central Asia* 19: 164–76.

Moore, K.M. 1993b. "Bone Tool Technology at Gonur Depe." *Information Bulletin of the International Association for the Study of the Cultures of Central Asia* 19: 218–27.

Moore, K.M., N.F. Miller, F.T. Hiebert, and R.H. Meadow. 1994. "Agriculture and Herding in the Early Oasis Settlements of the Oxus Civilization." *Antiquity* 68: 418–27.

Moreau, C., I. Caffy, C. Comby, E. Delqué-Količ, J.-P. Dumoulin, S. Hain, A. Quiles, V. Setti, C. Souprayen, B. Thellier, and J. Vincent. 2013. "Research and Development of the Artemis 14CAMS Facility: Status Report." *Radiocarbon* 55 (2–3): 331–37.

Morony, M.G. 1987. *Between Civil Wars: The Caliphate of Mucawiyah*. Vol. 18: *The History of al-Ṭabarī*. Albany, NY.

Mukhamedjanov, A.R. 1983. "Stratigraficheskii raskop na tsitadeli Bukhary." *Istorija Material'noj Kul'tury Uzbekistana* 18: 57–64.

Mukhamedjanov, A.R. 1994. "Economy and Social System in Central Asia in the Kushan Age." In *History and Civilisations of Central Asia*, vol. 2: 256–82. Paris.

Mukhamedjanov, A.R. 1978. *Istorija oroshenija Bucharskogo Oazisa*. Tashkent.

Mukhamedjanov, A.R., and G.L. Semyonov. 1984. *Himicheskaya laboratoriya VIII v. v Paykende*. ONU 3. Tashkent.

Mukhamedjanov, A.R., and G.L. Semyonov. 1988. *O rabotah na Central'nom raskope: Gorodishhe Paykend*. Tashkent.

Mukhamedjanov, A.R., and G.L. Semenov. 1984. "Semenov Khimicheskaya laboratoriya VIII veka v Paykende." In *Obshchestvennyye nauki v Uzbekistane* 3, 37–38. Tashkent.

Mukhamedjanov, A.R., Dj. Mirzaakhmedov, and Sh.T. Adylov. 1984. "Novye Dannue k Istorii Gorodisha Pajkend (Po Materialam Raskopok 1981 g.)." IMKU 19: 95–107.

Mukhamedjanov, A.R., Dj.K. Mirzaakhmedov, and Sh.T. Adylov. 1982. "Keramika Nizhnikh Sloev Bukhary. (Opyt Predvaritel'noj Periodizatsij)." *Istoriya Material'noj Kul'tury Uzbekistana* 17: 81–97.

Mukhamedjanov, A.R., Dj.K. Mirzaakhmedov, Sh.T. Adylov, and E.F. Vulfert. 1990. "Rezul'taty issledovanija arheologicheskih pamjatnikov Varahshinskogo massiva (po materialam rabot 1985 g." In *Arheologicheskie raboty na novostrojkah Uzbekistana*, edited by M.I. Filanovich, 141–62. Tashkent.

Mukhamedjanov, A.R., Sh.T. Adylov, Dj.K. Mirzaakhmedov, and G.L. Semenov. 1988. *Gorodishche Paykend: K probleme izucheniia srednevekovogo goroda Srednei Azii*. Leningrad and Tashkent.

Naymark, A. 2001. "Sogdiana, Its Christians and Byzantium: A Study of Artistic and Cultural Connections in Late Antiquity and Early Middle Ages." Unpublished PhD diss. Bloomington, Indiana University.

Naymark, A.I. 1995. "O nachale chekanki mednoi moneti v Bukharskom Sogde." In *Numizmatika Tsentralnoi Azii* 1, 29–50. Tashkent.

Naymark, A. 2010. "Les villes sogdiennes après les Grecs." In *Samarcande, cité mythique au coeur de l'Asie*. Edited by C. Rapin, 44–46. Dossiers d'archéologie 341. Dijon.

Negro-Ponzzi, M.M. 2005. "Mesopotamian Glassware of The Parthian and Sasanian Period: Some Note." *Annales du 16e congrés de l'Associarion Internationale pour l'Histoire du Verre, London 2003*, 141–45. London.

Nekrasova, E.G. 1999. "La citadelle de Bukhara de la fin du 9e siècle au début du 13e siècle." *Archéologie Islamique* 8–9: 37–54.

Nerazik, E.E. 1981. *Arheologicheskoe opisanie pamyatnika: Gorodishhe Toprak kala (raskopki 1965–1975 gg.)*. Moscow.

Omelchenko, A.V. 2013. "Tsitadel' Paykenda v III–V vv." In *Rossiyskaya arkheologiya* 2, 105–18. Moscow.

Omelchenko, A.V. 2012. "On the Question of Sasanian Presence in Sogdiana: Recent Results of Excavations at Paykand." *JIAAA* 7: 79–107.

Omelchenko, A.V., and V.V. Mokroborodov. Forthcoming. "Keramicheskiye kompleksy ellinisticheskogo vremeni iz Paykenda: novyye dannyye." In *Istoriya material'noy kul'tury Uzbekistana* 40.

Omelchenko, A.V. 2016. "On the Question of Sasanian Presence in Sogdiana. Recent Results of Excavations at Paykand." *Journal of Inner Asian Art and Archaeology* 7, edited by J.A. Lerner, S. Stark, and A.L. Juliano, 79–107. Turnhout.

Omelchenko, A.V. 2019. "New Excavations in the Paykend City-Site. The Sogdian Pottery Assemblage of the Hellenistic Period." In *Urban Cultures of Central Asia from the Bronze Age to the Karakhanids: Learnings and Conclusions from New Archaeological Investigations and Discoveries*, edited by Ch. Baumer and M. Novák, 203–25. Wiesbaden.

Omelchenko, A.V. 2020. "Botrosy i favissa Paykenda. Predvaritel'noye soobshcheniye." In *Istoriya i arkheologiya Turana* 5, 378–98. Samarkand.

Omelchenko, A.V., and D.O. Kholov. 2018. "Shahristan 2. Ulitsa 'A.'" In *MBAE* 14, 51–54. St. Petersburg.

Omelchenko, A.V., D.O. Kholov, A.N. Gorin, and N.D. Sobirov. 2018. "Citadel." In *MBAE* 14, 5–29. St. Petersburg.

Orton, C., and M. Hughes. 2013. *Pottery in Archaeology*. 2nd ed. Cambridge Manuals in Archaeology. Cambridge and New York.

Ouseley, W. 1800. *The Oriental Geography of Ebn Haukal, an Arabian Traveller of the Tenth Century*. London.

Papakhristu, O., and I. Akhrarov. 1981. *Steklo iz raskopa v Arke domongol'skogo gorodishha Ahsikent*. IMKU 16. Tashkent.

Parviz Holakooeia, P., J-F.de Lapérouse, F. Caròc, S. Röhrs, U. Franke, M. Müller-Wiener, and I. Reiche. 2019. "Non-invasive Scientific Studies on the Provenance and Technology of Early Islamic Ceramics from Afrasiyab and Nishapur." *Journal of Archaeological Science: Reports* 24: 759–72.

Pelliot, P. 1905. "Thomas Watters: On Yuan Chwang's Travels in India, 629–645 A.D." *Bullettin de l'Ecole Française d'Extrême-Orient* 5 (1): 423–57.

Petrushevsky, I.P. 1960. *Zemledelie i agrarnyie otnosheniya v Irane XIII–XIV vekov*. Moscow and Leningrad.

Pichon, L., B. Moignard, Q. Lemasson, C. Pacheco, and P. Walter. 2014. "Development of a Multi-detector and a Systematic Imaging System on the AGLAE External Beam." In *Nuclear Instruments and Methods in Physics Research B318, Part A*, 27–31.

Pichon, L., L. Beck, Ph. Walter, B. Moignard, and T. Guillou. 2010. "A New Mapping Acquisition and Processing System for Simultaneous PIXE-RBS Analysis with External Beam." In *Nuclear Instruments and Methods B268*, 2028–33.

Podushkin, A., F. Grenet, and N. Sims-Williams. 2007. "Les plus anciens monuments de la langue sogdienne: Les inscriptions de Kultobe au Kazakhstan." *Comptes Rendus des Séances de l'Académie des Inscriptions et des Belles Lettres*: 1005–34.

Porat, N., G.A.T. Duller, H.M. Roberts, E. Piasetzky, and I. Finkelstein. 2012. "OSL Dating in Multi-strata Tel: Megiddo (Israel) as a Case Study." *Quaternary Geochronology* 10: 359–66.

Portero, R., A. Fusaro, R. Pique, J.M. Gurt, M. Elorza, S. Gabriel, and S.R. Pidaev. 2021. "The Environment in Termez (Uzbekistan): Zooarchaeology and Anthracology of a 9th Century Tannur." *Journal of Islamic Archaeology* 8 (1): 1–21.

Potts, D. 2005. "Bactrian Camels and Bactrian Dromedary Hybrids." *The Silk Road* 3 (1): 49–58.

Powell, R.A. 2000. "Animal Home Ranges and Territories and Home Range Estimators." In *Research Techniques in Animal Ecology: Controversies and Consequences*, edited by L. Boitani and T.K. Fuller, 65–110. New York.

Pozzi, S. 2014a. "Ancient Vardāna: Results of the Last Archaeological Investigations." In *Central Asia in Antiquity. Interdisciplinary Approaches*, edited by B. Antela-Bernárdez and J. Vidal, 61–66. British Archaeological Reports, Int. Ser. Oxford.

Pozzi, S. 2014b. "Sasanian-style Sealstones from Bukhara Oasis (Uzbekistan)." *Rivista di Studi Orientali* 87 (fasc. 1–4): 135–51.

Pozzi, S. 2016. "Tamga-Nishan on the Pre-Islamic Pottery from Vardāna (Bukhara Oasis, Uzbekistan)." *Istorija i arheologija Turana* (3) (posvjashennyy yubileyu Djamaladdina Kamalovicha Mirzaakhmedova): 242–48.

Pozzi, S., S. Mirzaakhmedov, and M. Sultanova. 2019. "Preliminary Results of Archaeological Investigations at Vardana. A Focus on the Early Medieval Period." In *Urban Cultures of Central Asia from the Bronze Age to the Karakhanids.*, edited by C. Baumer and M. Novak, vol. 12: 227–46. Schriften Zur Vorderasiatischen Archäologie. Wiesbaden.

Prescott, J.R., and J.T. Hutton. 1994. "Cosmic Ray Contributions to Dose Rates for Luminescence and ESR Dating: Large Depths and Long-term Time Variations." *Radiation Measurements* 23: 497–500.

Priestman, S. 2013, "Sasanian Ceramics from the Gorgan wall and other sites on the Gorgan Plain." In *Persia's Imperial Power in Late Antiquity: The Great Wall of Gorgan and Frontier Landscapes of Sasanian Iran*, edited by E.W. Sauer, H.O Rekavandi, T.J. Wilkinson et al., 447–534. British Institute of Persian Studies Archaeological Monograph Series 11. Oxford.

Ptashnikova, I.V. 1952. *Busyi drevnego i rannesrednevekovogo Horezma*. Trudyi Horezmskoy arheologo-e'tnograficheskoy e'kspedicii. Vol. 1. Moscow.

Pugachenkova, G.A. 1948. "Samarkandskaya keramika XV v." Trudy Sredneaziatskogo gosudarstvennogo universiteta. New series. Vol. 2. Gumanitarnyie nauki, kn. 3. Tashkent.

Pugachenkova, G.A. 1949. "Glazurovannaya keramika Nisy XV–XVI vv." Trudy YUTAKE. Vol. 1. Ashkhabad.

Pugachenkova, G.A. 1989. *Drevnosti Miankalya. Iz rabot Uzbekistanskoj iskusstbobedcheskoj ekspeditsii.* Tashkent.

Puschnigg, G. 2006. *Ceramics of the Merv Oasis: Recycling the City.* Publications of the Institute of Archaeology. Walnut Creek, CA.

Puschnigg, G., and J.-B. Houal. 2019. "Regions and Regional Variations in Hellenistic Central Asia: What Pottery Assemblages Can Tell Us." *Afghanistan* 2 (1): 115–40.

Rante, R., and A. Collinet. 2013. *Nishapur Revisited: Stratigraphy and Ceramics of the Qohandez.* Oxford.

Rante, R., and Dj. Mirzaakhmedov. 2019. *The Oasis of Bukhara.* Vol. 1: *Population, Depopulation and Settlement Evolution.* Leiden.

Rante, R., and F. Trionfetti. 2021. "Economic Aspects of Settlement in the Oasis of Bukhara, Uzbekistan: An Archaeo-Economic Approach." In *Cambridge Archaeological Journal*: 581–96.

Rante, R., E. Fouache, and Dj. Mirzaakhmedov. 2016. "Dynamics of Human Settlements Ensuing from River Transformation and Changes in Commercial Behavior: The Birth of the 'North-eastern Silk Road.'" *Journal of Archaeological Science: Reports* 9: 437–47.

Rante, R., F. Schwarz, and L. Tronca. 2022. *The Oasis of Bukhara.* Vol. 2: *Archaeological Pluridisciplinary Activities and Historical Study.* Leiden.

Rapin, C., and M. Isamiddinov. 2013. "Entre sédentaires et nomades: les recherches de la archéologique franco-ouzbèke (MAFOuz) de Sogdiane sur le site de Koktepe." In *L'archéologie française en Asie centrale. Nouvelles recherches et enjeux Socioculturels. Cahiers d'Asie Centrale,* edited by J. Bendezu-Sarmiento, 21–22, 113–33. Paris.

Raspopova, V.I. 1980. *Metallicheskie izdeliya rannesrednevekovogo Sogda.* Leningrad.

Raspopova, V.I. 2010. *Steklyannyie sosudyi iz Pendzhikenta (nahodki 1950–1999 gg).* St. Petersburg.

Rehren, T., A. Osorio, and A. Anarbaev. 2010. "Some Notes on Early Islamic Glass in Eastern Uzbekistan." In *Glass Along the Silk Road from 200 BC to AD 1000,* edited by B. Zorn and A. Hilgner, 93–103. Mainz.

Reimer, P.J., E. Bard, and A. Bayliss et al. 2013. "IntCal13 and Marine13 Radiocarbon Age Calibration Curves 0–50,000 Years cal BP." *Radiocarbon* 55 (4): 1869–87.

Rhodes, E.J. 2011. "Optically Stimulated Luminescence Dating of Sediments over the Past 200,000 Years." *Annual Review of Earth and Planetary Sciences* 39 (1): 461–88.

Rice, P.M. 1987, *Pottery Analysis: A Sourcebook.* Chicago and London.

Richardin, P., and N. Gandolfo. 2013. *C2RMF Report N. 25121.* Unpublished results.

Richardin, P., and N. Gandolfo. 2014. *C2RMF Report N. 27177.* Unpublished results.

Richardin, P., D. Vouriot, G. Louarn, C. Saint-Raymond, and S. Mussard. 2016. *C2RMF Report N. 30082.* Unpublished results.

Richardin, P., S. Porcier, S. Ikram, G. Louarn, and D. Berthet. 2017. "Cats, Crocodiles, Cattle, and More: Initial Steps toward Establishing a Chronology of Ancient Egyptian Animal Mummies." *Radiocarbon* 59 (2): 595–607.

Ritter, C. 1845. *Das Buch Der Länder von Schech Ebu Ishak el Farsi el Isztachri.* Hamburg.

Roemer, H.R. 1986. "The Successors of Timur." In *Cambridge History of Iran* 6, edited by P. Jackson and L. Lockhart, 98–146. Cambridge.

Roisine, G. 2018. "Céramiques Glaçurées de Bernard Palissy: A La Recherche Des Secrets d'un Maître de la Renaissance." PhD diss., Paris Sciences et Lettres (PSL Research University). Paris.

Rouse, L.M., and B. Cerasetti. 2014. "Ojakly: A Late Bronze Age Mobile Pastoralist Site in the Murghab Region, Turkmenistan." *Journal of Field Archaeology* 39 (1): 32–50.

Rtveladze, E. 1997. *Catalogue of Antique and Medieval Coins of Central Asia.* Vol. 1. Tashkent.

Rtveladze, E. 1999. "Coins of Ancient Bukhara." In *Bukhara: The Myth and the Architecture,* edited by A. Petruccioli, 29–37. Cambridge, MA.

Ruiz, E., E. Mohandesan, R.R. Fitak, and P.A. Burger. 2015. "Diagnostic Single Nucleotide Polymorphism Markers to Identify Hybridization between Dromedary and Bactrian Camels." Conserv. Genet. Resour. 7 (2): 329–32.

Sadyik-i -Kashkari, Muhammed. 1992. *Kodeks prilichiy na Vostoke.* Tashkent.

Sanjurjo-Sánchez, J. 2016. "An Overview of the Use of Absolute Dating Techniques in Ancient Construction Materials." *Geosciences* 6 (2): 22.

Sanjurjo-Sánchez, J., and J.L. Montero Fenollós. 2012. "Chronology during the Bronze Age in the Archaeological Site Tell Qubr Abu al-'Atiq, Syria." *Journal of Archaeological Science* 39 (1): 163–74.

Saparov, N.J. 2018. "Shahristan 2. Dom VIIIa." In MBAE 14, 44–49. St. Petersburg.

Saparov, N.Zh., A.I. Torgoev. 2013. "Keramika i voprosy khronologii zhilogo kvartala Paykenda VII–VIII vv." In *Rossiyskaya arkheologiya* 3, 66–75. Moscow.

Saparov, N.Zh., and A.V. Omelchenko. 2017. "Gostinitsy Paykenda." In *Istoriya i arkheologiya Turana* 3, edited by A.E. Berdimuradov, 281–93. Samarkand.

Sataev, R. 2020. "Animal Exploitation at Gonur Tepe." In *The World of Oxus Civilization,* edited by B. Lyonnet and N. Dubova, 438–456, London – New-York.

Sayfullayev, B.K. 2007. "Novyye nakhodki kamennykh orudiy na gorodishche Paykend." In MBAE 8, 48–52. St. Petersburg.

Scanlon, G.T., and R. Pinder-Wilson. 2001. *Fustat Glass of the Early Islamic Period*. London.

Scerrato, I.E. 2014. "Report on Ethnographic Research Carried Out in the Oasis of Bukhara – May 2014." In *Mission archéologique dans l'oasis de Boukhara: Rapport préliminaire (campagne 2014)*, edited by R. Rante and Dj. Mirzaakhmedov. [Place/city of publication needed].

Schmid, E. 1972. *Atlas of Animal Bones: For Prehistorians, Archaeologists and Quaternary Geologists*, Amsterdam, London, New-York.

Schwarz, F. 2022. "Land behind Bukhara: Materials for a Landscape History of the Bukhara Oasis in the Long First Millennium." In *The Oasis of Bukhara*. Vol. 2: *Archaeological Pluridisciplinary Activities and Historical Study*, edited by R. Rante, F. Schwarz, and L. Tronca, 60–144. Leiden.

Semenov, G., and Dj. Mirzaakhmedov. 1996. *La Parmacie De Paykend: La medicine au temps des Califes*. Paris.

Semenov, G.L. 1996a. "Nardi v Irane i Srednei Azii." In *Ermitaznye chteniia pamiati V.G. Lukonina 1986–1994 gg.*, edited by E.V. Zeimal, 44–49. St. Petersburg.

Semenov, G.L. 1996b. *Sogdiiskaiia fortifikatsiia V–VIII vekov*. St. Petersburg.

Semenov, G.L. 1996c. *Studen zur sogdischen kultur an Seidnstraße*. Studies in Oriental Religions 36. Wiesbaden.

Semenov, G.L. 1996d. "Sviatilishche v Paykend e." In *Ermitaznye chteniia pamiati V.G. Lukonina 1986–1994 gg.*, edited by E.V. Zeimal, 171–78. St. Petersburg.

Semenov, G.L. 2006. "Dwelling Houses of Bukhara in the Early Middle Ages." In *Ērān ud Anērān: Studies Presented to Boris Il'ič Maršak on the Occasion of His 70th Birthday*, edited by M. Compareti, P. Raffetta, and G. Scarcia, 555–69. Venice.

Semenov, G.L., and Dj.K. Mirzaakhmedov with the participation of Sh.T. Adylov, I.K. Malkiel', and A.V. Bekhter. 2000. "Raskopki v Paykend e v 1999 g." MBAE 1. St. Petersburg.

Semenov, G.L., and Dj.K. Mirzaakhmedov. 2007. "Materialy Bukharskoj Arkheologicheskoj Ekspeditsii." *Arkheologicheskie Ekspeditsii Gosudarstvennogo Ermitazha* 8. St. Petersburg.

Semenov, G.L., and Sh.T. Adylov. 2006. "Arsenal na tsitadeli Paykend a." In *Ancient and Medieval Culture of the Bukhara Oasis*, edited by Ch.S. Antonini and Dj.K. Mirzaakhmedov, 36–43, 140–45. Samarkand and Rome.

Semenov, G.L., Dj.K. Mirzaakhmedov, B.M. Abdullaev, A.V. Bekhter, I.K. Malkiel', N.J. Saparov, N.D. Sobirov, and A.I. Torgoev. 2003. "Raskopki v Paykend e v 2002 g." MBAE 4. St. Petersburg.

Semenov, G.L., Dj.K. Mirzaakhmedov, B.M. Abdullaev, A.V. Omelchenko, N.J. Saparov, and N.D. Sobirov. 2005. "Raskopki v Paykend e v 2004 g." MBAE 6. St. Petersburg.

Semenov, G.L., Dj.K. Mirzaakhmedov, B.M. Abdullaev, A.V. Omelchenko, N.J. Saparov, A.I. Torgoev, and N.D. Sobirov. 2007. "Otchet o raskopkah v Paykend e v 2006 g." MBAE 8. St. Petersburg.

Semenov, G.L., Dj.K. Mirzaakhmedov, B.M. Abdullaev, I.K. Malkiel', N.D. Sobirov, and A.I. Torgoev. 2004. "Raskopki v Paykend e v 2003 g." MBAE 5. St. Petersburg.

Semenov, G.L., Dj.K. Mirzaakhmedov, B.M. Abdullaev, N.J. Saparov, A.I. Torgoev, and N.D. Sobirov. 2006. "Otchet o raskopkah v Paykend e v 2005 g." MBAE 7. St. Petersburg.

Semenov, G.L., Dj.K. Mirzaakhmedov, Sh.T. Adylov, A.V. Bekhter, E.F. Vulfert, I.K. Malkiel', P.B. Lurje, and A.I. Torgoev. 2001. "Raskopki v Paykend e v 2000 g." MBAE 2. St. Petersburg.

Serrone, E., E. Maini, A. Curci, S. Mantellini, and A.E. Berdimuradov. 2022. "Animal Exploitation in the Samarkand Oasis (Uzbekistan) at the Time of the Arab Conquest: Zooarchaeological Evidence from the Excavation at Kafir Kala." In *Archaeozoology of Southwest Asia and Adjacent Areas (ASWA), Proceeding of the XIIIe International Symposium University of Cyprus, Nicosia, Cyprus, 7–10 June 2017*, edited by J. Daujat, A. Hadjikoumis, R. Berthon, J. Chahoud, V. Kassianidou and J.-D. Vigne, 221–231, United State.

Serrone, E., S. Mantellini, and A. Curci. (In press). "Shepherds and Farmers in Central Asia: New Clues about Animal Exploitation from the Samarkand Oasis from the Hellenistic to the Islamic Period." In *Proceeding 13^{e}ICAZ International Conference, 2nd–7th September 2018, Ankara, Turkey*.

Sharakhimov, Sh. 1973. *Novyie steklyannyie sosudyi s Afrasiaba*. Afrasiab 2. Tashkent.

Shenkar, M. 2020. "The Origin of the Sogdian Community (*nāf*)." *Journal of the Economic and Social History of the Orient* 63: 357–88.

Shikaku, R. 2013. "Sasanian Glass and the Silk Road." In *Ancient Glass: Feast of Color*, edited by T. Taniichi, H. Azuma, and R. Shikaku, 354–57. Koka.

Shindo, Y. 1992. "Glassware." In *Excavation of al-Fustat 1978–1985*, edited by K. Sakurai and M. Kawatoko, vol. 1: 304–305 and vol. 2: 572–617. Tokyo. (In Japanese.)

Shindo, Y. 2000a. "The Early Islamic Glass from al-Fustāt, Egypt." In *Annales du 14e Congrès de l'Association Internationale pour l'Histoire du Verre, Italia / Venezia-Milano 1998*, 233–37. Lochem.

Shindo, Y. 2000b. "Glass Trade between the East and West in the 9th–10th Centuries: Islamic Glass Excavated in Ku Lao Cham, Vietnam." *Archaeological Journal* 464: 12–15. (In Japanese.)

Shindo, Y. 2003. "The Islamic Glass Finds from Rāya, Southern Sinai." In *Annales du 15e Congrès de l'Association Internationale pour l'Histoire du Verre, New York-Corning 2001*, 180–84. Nottingham.

Shindo, Y. 2004a. "Glassware from the Rāya Site." In *Archaeological Survey of the Rāya/al-Ṭūr Area on the Sinai Peninsula, Egypt, 2003*, edited by M. Kawatoko, 51–53. Tokyo.

Shindo, Y. 2004b. "The Islamic Glass Beaker with Wheel-cut Decoration from Rāya, South Sinai." *Orient: Report of the Society for Near Eastern Studies in Japan* 39: 18–38.

Shindo, Y. 2007a. "Islamic Glass of the 8th Century in Rāya." In *Archaeological Survey of the Rāya/al-Ṭūr Area on the Sinai Peninsula, Egypt, 2005 and 2006*, vol. 1 of *Islamic Archaeology and Culture*, edited by M. Kawatoko, 97–107. Tokyo.

Shindo, Y. 2008. "Various Aspects of Cut Decoration Glass Unearthed in the Rāya Site." In *Archaeological Survey of the Rāya/al-Ṭūr Area on the Sinai Peninsula, Egypt 2007*, vol. 2 of *Islamic Archaeology and Culture*, edited by M. Kawatoko, 55–68. Tokyo.

Shindo, Y. 2009. "The Islamic Glass Excavated in Egypt: Fusṭāṭ, Rāya and al-Ṭūr al-Kīlānī." In *Annales du 17ᵉ Congrès de l'Association Internationale pour l'Histoire du Verre, Anvers 2006, Brussels*, 308–13, 668. Anvers.

Shindo, Y. 2012. "Consideration about Glass with Impressed Decoration in the Islamic Period: Comparison between the Artifacts Excavated at the Rāya Site in Egypt and the Cup on Tenri Sankoukan." *Bulletin of Tenri University Sankokan Museum* 25: 79–93. (In Japanese.)

Shindo, Y. 2015. "Islamic Glass with Impressed Decoration:The Problem of Dating and Production." In *Annales du 19ᵉ congrés de l'Associarion Internationale pour l'Histoire du Verre, Piran 2012*, 455–61. Koper.

Shindo, Y. 2017. "Study on the Early Islamic Glass Excavated in Paykend in the Bukhara Oasis, Uzbekistan." In *Annales du 20e congrés de l'Associarion Internationale pour l'Histoire du Verre, Fribourg / Romont 2015*, 293–99. Rahden/Westf.

Shindo, Y. 2001. "Islamic Glass Trade by the Sea-route between the 9th–10th Centuries: Problem of Dish with Incised Decoration." *Journal of West Asian Archaeology* 2: 69–82. (In Japanese.)

Shindo, Y. 2005. "The Islamic Luster-Stained Glass between the 9th and 10th Century." In *Annales du 16ᵉ Congrès de l'Association Internationale pour l'Histoire du Verre, London 2003*, 174–77. Nottingham.

Shindo, Y. 2007b. "Lead Glass Found from Rāya and Monastery of Wādi al-Tūr Site." In *Archaeological Survey of the Rāya/al-Ṭūr Area on the Sinai Peninsula, Egypt, 2005 and 2006*, vol. 1 of *Islamic Archaeology and Culture*, edited by M. Kawatoko, 109–16. Tokyo.

Shindo, Y. 2011. "Social Change and Development as Seen in the 8th Century Islamic Glass from al- Fusṭāṭ and al-Rāya, Egypt." *Kodai (Journal of the Archaeological Society of Waseda University)* 125: 97–118. (In Japanese.)

Shirinov, T.Sh., B.H. Matboboev, and G.P. Ivanov. 1998. *Ahmad Al-Fargoniy davrida Kubo shahri*. Tashkent.

Shishkin, V.A. 1963, *Varakhsha*. Moskva.

Shishkin, V.A. 1940. *Arheologicheskie raboty 1937 g. v zapadnoj chasti Buharskogo oazisa*. Tashkent.

Shishkina, G.V. 1979. *Glazurovannaja keramika Sogda (vtaraja polovina VIII–nachalo XIII b.)*. Tashkent.

Shishkina, G.V. 1986. *Remeslennaya Produktiya Srednevekovogo Sogda Steklo Afrasiaba*. Tashkent.

Shishkina, G.V., R.Kh. Sulejmanov, and G.A. Koshelenko. 1985. "'Srednjaja Azija v antichnuju epokhu. Sogd.'" In *Drevnejshie gosudarstva Kavkasa i Srednei Azii*, edited by G.A. Koshelenko, 273–92. Moscow.

Shtark, S., and Dj.K. Mirzaakhmedov. 2015. "Pervye rezul'taty novyh issledovanij oazisnoj steny bucharskogo Sogda 'Devor-I Kampirak.'" In *Bucharskij Oazis I ego sosedi v drevnosti i Srednevekov'e*, edited by A.V. Omelchenko and Dj.K. Mirzaakhmedov, 77–99. St. Petersburg.

Shukrat, A. 2017, "L'étude de l'Arc de Boukhara." In *Mission Archéologique dans l'Oasis de Boukhara Rapport Préliminaire, Campagne 2017*, edited by R. Rante and Dj. Mirzaakhmedov, 38–45. Paris.

Silvi Antonini, C. 2009. "La ceramica e altri reperti." In *Gli scavi di Uch Kulakh (Oasis di Bukhara), Rapporto Preliminare 1997–2007*, edited by C. Silvi Antonini and Dj.K. Mirzaakhmedov, 82 Supplemento 1: 137–64. Rivista degli Studi Orientali. Pisa and Rome.

Siméon, P. 2009. *Étude du matériel de Hulbuk, de la conquête islamique jusqu'au milieu du XIᵉ siècle (90–712–441/1050). Contribution à l'étude de la céramique islamique d'Asie Centrale*. BAR International series 1945. Oxford.

Simpson, St.J. 2005. "Sasanian Glass from Nineveh." In *Annales du 16ᵉ congrés de l'Associarion Internationale pour l'Histoire du Verre, London 2003*, 146–51. Nottingham.

Simpson, St.J. 2015. "Sasanian Glassware from Mesopotamia, Gilan and the Caucasus." *Journal of Glass Study* 57: 77–96.

Sitnjakovskij, N.F. 1899. "Zametki o Bucharskoj chasti doliny Zeravshana." *Izvestija Turkenstanskago Otdela Imperatorskogo Russkogo Geograficheskogo Obshestva* 1 (2): 121–78.

Smagulov, E.A. 2015. "Nahodki iz kyzyl-kyra i rannesrednevekovye keramicheskie kurilnisty Srednej Syrdary: Buharskij Oazis i ego sosedi v drevnosti i srednevekove." Trydy Gosudarstvennogo Ermitaza. Vol. 75. St. Petersburg.

Smagulov, Ye.A. 1992. "Kompleks keramiki iz badraba gorodishcha Eski – Turkestan." *IMKU* 26. Tashkent.

Smirnova, O.I. 1970. *Ocberki iz istorii Sogda*. Moscow.

Smith, I. 1997. "Preliminary Report on the Animal Bones." In The International Merv Project. Preliminary Report of the Fifth Season (1996), edited by G. Hermann, K. Kurbansakhatov, St.J. Simpson et al. In *IRAN* 35: 31–32.

Smith, I. 1998. "A Middle Sassanian Residential Quarter: Gyaur Kala Area 5.3. The Zooarchaeological Analyses." In The International Merv Project. Preliminary Report of the Sixth Season (1997), edited by G. Hermann, K. Kurbansakhatov, St.J. Simpson et al. In *IRAN* 36: 57, 72–73.

Sobirov, I.N. 2018. "Yujnaya krepostnaya stena." In *MBAE* 14, 49–50. St. Petersburg.

Sogdijskij sbornik, Sbornik statej o pamjatnikah sogdijskovo jazyka I kul'tury najdennyx na gore Mug v Tadjikoj SSR. 1934. Leningrad.

Stark, S, F. Kidd, Dj. Mirzaakhmedov, S. Zachary, S. Mirzaakhmedov, and M. Evers. 2016. "Bashtepa 2016: Preliminary Report of the First Season of Excavations." *Archäologische Mitteilungen Aus Iran Und Turan* 48: 219–64.

Stark, S., and Dj.K. Mirzaakhmedov. 2015. "Pervye rezul'taty novykh issledovanii oazisnoi steny bukharskogo sogda 'Devor-i Kampirak.'" In *Bukharskii Oazis i ego Sosedi v Drevnosti i Srednevekov'e, na osnove materialov nauchnykh konferentsii 2010 i 2011 gg.*, edited by A.V. Omelchenko and Dj.K. Mirzaakhmedov, 77–99. Trudy Gosudarstvennogo Ėrmitaža 75. St. Petersburg.

Stark, S., F. Kidd, Dj. Mirzaakhmedov, S. Zachary, S. Mirzaakhmedov, and M. Evers. With an appendix by A. Naymark. 2019. "Bashtepa 2016: Preliminary Report of the First Season of Excavations." *Archäologische Mitteilungen aus Iran und Turan* 48: 219–64.

Staviskiy, B.YA. 1960. *Samarkandskie chernil'nyie priboryi IX–X vv. v sobranii E'rmitazha*. SA 1. Leningrad.

Steiger, C. 1990. *Vergleichend morphologische untersuchungen an einzelknochen des postkranialen skeletts der altwelkamele*. München.

Stronach, D. 1985. "On the Evolution of the Early Iranian Fire Temple." In *Acta Iranica 25: Papers in Honour of Professor Mary Boyce II*, edited by H.W. Bailey, A.D.H. Bivar, J. Duchesne-Guillemin, and J.R. Hinnells, 605–27. Leiden.

Sulejmanov, R.Kh. 1984. Rezul'taty predvaritel'nogo izuchenija gorodishcha Romitan. *IMKU* 19, 118–129.

Sulejmanov, R.H. 2000. *Drevnii Nakhshab. Problemi tsivilizacii Uzbekistana: VII v. do n.e.–VII v. n.e.* Tashkent and Samarkand.

Sulejmanov, R.Kh., and B. Urakov. 1977. "Rezul'taty Predvaritel'nogo Issledovanija Antichnogo Gorodishcha Selenija Ramish." *IMKU* 13: 55–64.

Syharev, I.A. 1948. *Dva bljuda XV v. iz Samarkanda. Trudy instituta istorii I arheologii*. Vol. 1. Tashkent.

Tanabe, K., and A. Hori et al. 1999. "Excavation at Dal'verzin Tepe, 1999." *Bulletin of the Ancient Orient Museum* 20: 101–62.

Tapper, R.S.D. 2010. "One Hump or Two? Hybrid Camels and Pastoral Cultures: An Update." https://www.soas.ac.uk/camelconference2011/file74604.pdf.

Taylor, W., S. Shnaider, R. Spengler III, L. Orlando, A. Abdykanova, and A. Krivoshapkin. 2019. "Investigating Ancient Animal Economies and Exchange in Kyrgyzstan's Alay Valley." *Antiquity* 93: 1–5.

Taylor, W., S. Shnaider, A. Abdykanova, A. Fages, F. Welker, F. Irmer, A. Seguin-Orlando, N. Khan, K. Douka, K. Kolobova, L. Orlando, A. Krivoshapkin, and N. Boivin. 2018. "Early Pastoral Economies along the Ancient Silk Road: Biomolecular Evidence from the Alay Valley, Kyrgyzstan." *PLoS ONE* 13 (10). DOI: 10.1371/journal.pone.0205646.

Terenozhkin, A.I. 1950. *Sogd i Chach*. KSIIMK 33. Moscow and Leningrad.

Terres secretes de Samarcande: Céramiques du VIII–au XIII siecle. 1993. Paris.

Tomaschek, W. 1877. *Centralasiatische Studien I, Sogdiana*. Wien.

Torgoev, A. 2007. *Shahristan II. Kompleks lavok vdol' ulicyi "A": Materialyi Buharskoy arheologicheskoy e'kspedicii*. Vol. 8. St. Petersburg.

Torgoev, A.I. 2008. "Tabiby Paykenda v proshlom i nastoyashchem." In *Rakhmat-name. Sbornik statey k 70-letiyu R.R. Rakhimova*, edited by M.Ye. Rezvan, 381–93. St. Petersburg.

Torgoev, A.I. 2018. "Shahristan 1. Dom 1." In *MBAE* 14, 39–43. St. Petersburg.

Torgoev, A.I., Dj.K. Mirzaakhmedov, A.V. Omelchenko, N.D. Sobirov, D.O. Kholov, R.M. Toirov, A.N. Gorin, and N.J. Saparov. 2011. "Otchet o raskopkah v Paykend e v 2009–10 gg." *MBAE* 11. St. Petersburg.

Torgoev, A.I., Dj.K. Mirzaakhmedov, A.V. Omelchenko, N.J. Saparov, and N.D. Sobirov. 2008. "Otchet o raskopkah v Paykend e v 2007 g." *MBAE* 9. St. Petersburg.

Torgoev, A.I., Dj.K. Mirzaakhmedov, A.V. Omelchenko, N.J. Saparov, R.M. Toirov, and N.D. Sobirov. 2009. "Otchet o raskopkah v Paykend e v 2008 g." *MBAE* 10. St. Petersburg.

Torgoev, A.I., Dj.K. Mirzaakhmedov, and A.V. Kulish. 2014. "Predvaritel'nyye dannyye po kladu mednykh monet iz Paykenda." In *Arkheologiya Uzbekistana, 1(8)*, edited by T.Sh. Shirinov, 98–108. Samarkand.

Trudnovskaya, S.A. 1952. *Ukrasheniya pozdneantichnogo Horezma po materialam raskopok Toprak-kala: Trudyi Horezmskoy arheologo-e'tnograficheskoy e'kspedicii*. Vol. 1. Moscow.

Trudnovskaya, S.A. 1981. *Predmetyi vooruzheniya i byita. Ukrasheniya: Gorodishhe Toprak kala (raskopki 1965–1975 gg.)*. Moscow.

Tskitishvili, O. 1971. "Two Questions Connected with the Topography of the Oriental City in the Early Middle Ages." Journal of the Economic and Social History of the Orient 14 (3): 311–20.

US Department of the Army. 1958. Soviet Topographic Map Symbol Technical Manual n. 30–548. Headquarters, Department of the Army, Washington, DC.

Vaudour, C. (ed.). 1996. *La médecine au temps des califes, à l'ombre d'Avicenne: Exposition*. Institute le Monde Arabe.

Vishnevskaya, N.Yu. 2001. *Remeslennye Izdelija Dzhigerbenta (IV b. do n.e.–nachalo XIII b. n.e)*. Moscow.

Vitruvius, Pollion. 2009. *De Architectura*. Translated by C. Saliou. Paris.

Voronina, V.L. 1977. *Bronzyi Ahsiketa iz kollekcii A.I. Smirnova: Srednyaya Aziya v drevnosti i srednevekov'e*. Moscow.

Vyatkin, V.L. 1926. *Afrasiab-gorodishhe byilogo Samarkanda*. Tashkent.

Watson, O. 2004. *Ceramics from Islamic Lands*. London.

Weimarn, B.V. 1974. *Iskusstvo arabskih stran i Vostoka VII–XVII vv*. Moscow.

Whitehouse, D. 2010. *Islamic Glass in The Corning Museum of Glass*. Vol. 1. Corning and New York.

Wilkinson, E. 2000. *Chinese History: A Manual*. Cambridge and London.

Wordsworth, P., 2015. Merv on Khorasanian trade routes from the 10th–13th centuries. In: Rante, R. (Ed.), Greater Khorasan. History, Geography, Archaeology and Material Culture. De Gruyter, Berlin: 51–62.

Wu, X., N.F. Miller, and P. Crabtree. 2015. "Agro-pastoral Strategies and Food Production on the Achaemenid Frontier in Central Asia: A Case Study of Kyzyltepa in Southern Uzbekistan." *Iran* 53: 93–117.

Xinjiang, R., and L. Feng. 2016. *Sogdians in China: New Evidence in Archaeological Finds and Unearthed Texts (II)*. Beijing.

Yakuvov, Y. 2011. "Tajikistan." In *The Artistic Culture of Central Asia and Azerbaijan in the 9th–15th Centuries*. Vol. 2: *Glass*, edited by K. Baypakov, Sh. Pidayev, and A. Khakimov, 65–80. Samarkand and Tashkent.

Zavyalov, V.A. 2008. *Kushanshahr pri Sasanidakh. Po materialam raskopok gorodishcha Zartepa*. St. Petersburg.

Zeder, M., and H. Lapham. 2010. "Assessing the Reliability of Criteria Used to Identify Postcranial Bones in Sheep, *Ovis*, and Goats." *Capra: Journal of Archaeological Science* 37/11: 2887–2905.

Zeder, M., and S.E. Pillar. 2010. "Assessing the Reliability of Criteria Used to Identify Mandibles and Mandibular Teeth in Sheep, *Ovis*, and Goats." *Capra: Journal of Archaeological Science* 37: 225–42.

Zhukov, V.D. 1945. *Arheologicheskoe obsledovanie v 1937 g. dvorca Termezskih praviteley: Trudyi Akademii Nauk Uz.SSR. Seriya I. Istoriya. Arheologiya. Termezskaya arheologicheskaya e'kspediciya*. Tom II. Tashkent.

Zimin, L.A. 1915a. "Otcet o letnix raskopkax v razvalini starogo Paikenda." In *Protokoly Turkestandkogo Kruzhka Liubitelei Arkheologii. Tashkent*. Tashkent.

Zimin, L.A. 1915b. "Otcet o vesennikh raskopkakh v Razvalini starogo Paykend." In *Protokoly Turkestandkogo Kruzhka Liubitelei Arkheologii*. Tashkent.

Zimmerman, D.W. 1971. "Thermoluminescent Dating Using Fine Grains from Pottery." *Archaeometry* 13: 29–52.

Zink, A. 2008. "Uncertainties on the Luminescence Ages and Anomalous Fading." *Geochronometria* 32: 47–50.

Zink, A., E. Porto, P. Richardin, N. Gandolfo, and R. Rante. 2015. "Le Grand Khorasan: Datation par des méthodes physico-chimiques (carbone 14 et luminescence)." In *Greater Khorasan*, edited by R. Rante, 161–76. Berlin, München, and Boston.

Zink, A.J.C., E. Porto, E. Fouache, and R. Rante. 2017. "Paléocours du delta du Zerafshan (oasis de Boukhara, Ouzbékistan): Premières datations par luminescence." *L'Anthropologie* 121 (1–2): 46–54.

Index

2D X-ray Fluorescence   249, 251, 259

abandonment (of settlements)   55, 107, 372, 375
Achaemenid period/records   58
administrative districts/entities (*tūmān*s)   19–21, 25, 35, 48, 69, 76, 86
    boundaries   18
Afghanistan   2*n*3, 5, 62, 264, 364
Afrasiab   158, 267, 278–279, 291–293, 300, 322, 328*n*17, 339
Akhsiket (Ferghana)   289, 298, 300
Ak tepe   21*n*17
Alai   6, 19
Alexander the Great   58
alkaline   265, 284
aluminum   252, 254, 264
Ambēr   57
amphibole/pyroxene   243–244
Amul/Amol   43
Amu Darya (Oxus River/Valley)   5, 43, 48, 322, 324, 340, 352–353
Amu Darya (river)   43, 304
    See also Oxus (river)
apatite   243
archaeozoology   2
Ark   58, 289, 334, 339*n*33
Arslān Khān Muḥammad b. Sulaymān (Western Qarakhanid)   45, 53
artifact   3, 59–62, 71, 93, 304–305, 318, 324–325, 327–328, 332, 340, 342, 346, 353–353, 369
assemblage   2, 58, 62, 63*n*32, 86, 94–97, 104, 107–109, 113–117, 119–122, 124–126, 129–130, 133–134, 136–137, 139–140, 143, 145, 147–148, 152–158, 161–166, 168–173, 228, 302, 365–166, 369–370, 407

Bactra   2*n*5, 405
Bactria/Bactriana (region)   62, 63*n*28, 147, 278, 367
Badrab   145, 165, 174–175, 280, 287–1289, 294, 296–301
Baghdad   280, 282–283, 300
Balkh. *See* Bactra
Barkad (site 0944)   20
base   11, 27, 30, 34, 48, 53, 55, 79, 86, 96, 104, 107–109, 11, 113, 115, 117–122, 124–126, 129–130, 132–137, 140, 143, 145, 147–148, 153, 156, 158–159, 164, 172, 174, 176–179, 181–185, 190, 207, 216, 219, 222, 266, 270, 273, 275–276, 280–281, 283–285, 288, 296–300, 304–305, 319–320, 325–326, 328, 332, 334, 339–340, 371, 385, 400, 402, 407
Bash tepe   1, 11, 14, 16, 23, 405
beaker   194, 304, 320, 332, 339–340, 343, 352
bevelled profile   180

Bi/Paykend   43
bipartite sites   2, 8, 10, 11, 15–16, 20–24, 380
al-Bīrūnī, Abū l-Raiḥān (d. 1048 CE)   63, 287, 290
Binkat   287, 339*n*27
Black River/Black Swamp (Sām Khwāsh, wetlands of Lower Zarafshan)   6, 19, 36–37, 43, 244, 283, 364
black-slip pottery   31, 108–109, 111, 113–117, 135, 139–140, 147–148, 152, 158, 171
body   86, 98–103, 106–107, 109, 111, 116–117, 122, 124, 129, 137, 143, 145, 153*n**, 158, 163–165, 172, 176, 192, 216, 219, 249, 267–268, 282–283, 287–288, 292–292, 295–300, 321–324, 326, 329, 340
bone   3, 53, 57, 62–63, 71, 135, 283, 365–371, 376
Bos   366, 369
bottle   57, 117, 222, 278, 285, 287, 289, 291–292, 296, 298, 301, 304, 320, 322–326, 328, 332, 339–340, 348, 352
bowl   63*n*29, , 105, 109113, 122, 124–125, 129, 132–137, 140, 145, 147–148, 152, 154–159, 171–173, 184–191, 193–196, 201, 207, 210–212, 214, 218–219, 221, 234, 266–278, 291, 293–296, 298–301, 332, 339–340, 352
brick, mud/baked   4, 30, 62, 140, 381–382, 389, 400–402, 404
Bronze Age   1, 14, 43, 278, 405
Buhe   38
Bukhara (site 0097)   22
Bukhara (oasis)   1–3, 5–6, 8–12, 14–16, 18–26, 35, 37–39, 41–43, 45, 58, 63, 69, 86, 93–95, 97–98, 107, 109, 115, 156, 158–159, 161–165, 168–171, 175, 236, 241, 244, 263, 265, 278, 286, 304–305, 318, 328, 332, 334, 340, 342–343, 346, 350, 352–353, 364–365, 370–371, 381, 400, 405–408
burnish/burnished/burnishing   109, 133, 136, 155
butchery   366, 368
BUXA   249–250, 253, 259, 261–264

calcite   98–100, 102–103, 240, 242, 244
calcium   240, 252, 256, 259
camel   4, 364, 367–368, 370, 376
camelid   367–368, 370
Camelus bactrianus   367
Camelus dromedarius   367
canals
    natural   1, 6, 19, 23, 26–27, 35–39, 41, 45, 304–305, 365
    See also water channels/water network; watercourses
Canis familiaris   369
Capra hircus   366–367
Capreolus capreolus   366

Caprinae   367, 369
caprine   366, 369–370
caravan   2*n*5, 9, 11, 22, 24, 43, 332, 334, 367–368, 405
caravan routes Silk Road; trade routes   2*n*5, 332, 334, 367, 405
caravans
    caravan roads   11, 22
carination   109, 113, 155–156, 183, 187, 190, 207
carnivore   366, 369
Cassiterite   254–257, 259
castle   11–12, 14, 27, 48
cattle   55, 366–367–370
cemeterie   11, 39*n*19
Central Asia   1, 5, 45, 48, 53, 57*n*21, 58, 62, 86, 93, 109, 136, 158–159, 173–174, 264, 266, 270, 277–279, 294, 298–301, 344, 348, 350, 352–353, 364, 366, 368, 382, 405
ceramics/pottery
    chronological sequence/dating   104, 172–173, 228, 236, 365, 377–378
    decorative motifs   171
    production/firing techniques   96–97, 353
cervid   369–370
Chach/Chāch (mod. Tashkent)   19, 43, 69, 86, 164, 169, 171, 265
chemical   3, 98, 236, 238–240, 244, 246, 249, 252, 254, 262–265, 280, 282, 287–290, 301–302, 304–305, 318–319, 322, 327–328, 340, 342, 344–353, 371, 407
chicken   135, 368–370
China   43, 45, 62, 278, 339*n*28, 353*n*37, 367–368, 407
Chorasmia. *See* Khorezm
citadels   5, 8, 10, 12, 21, 27, 29–30, 43, 45, 48, 53–54, 57–58, 62–63, 69, 76, 86, 93–95, 104–106, 116, 124–125, 130, 140, 156, 159, 161, 249, 278, 299, 304, 321, 328, 332, 334, 340, 352, 365, 368–369, 372, 375, 377–378, 380, 389, 393, 396, 399, 402, 406*n*6
cities   5, 9, 15*n*6, 18–19, 36, 58, 249, 266, 279, 291, 301–302, 342, 350, 353*n*38, 371, 405
city-states   10–11, 19–20, 22, 24
clay   3, 48, 53–56, 63, 169, 173, 236, 238, 240–241, 244, 246, 249, 251–252–253, 264, 287, 289, 365, 400, 404
climate/climatic changes   1, 6, 14, 365, 385, 405
closed form   107–108, 114, 117, 129, 137, 143, 153–155, 171
coarse   3, 102–104, 107–109, 111, 118–119, 122, 126, 130, 132, 137, 147–148, 152, 155, 158–159, 162–164, 166, 168, 172–173, 175, 241, 305
cobalt   256, 259, 262–263, 265–267, 269–270, 273, 276, 319, 346

coccio-pesto (layer of pottery fragments in floors or walls)   145
coins/coins production   19, 21, 48, 54, 56–57, 86, 93, 249
commercial   1, 22, 124–125, 140, 249, 352, 365, 367
conquest, Arab conquest   31, 35, 45, 56–57, 115
cooking vessels   120, 152, 162, 173, 175
copper   57, 62–63, 65, 69, 76, 86, 88, 91, 256, 259, 262, 265, 279, 282, 284, 302, 305, 319
courtyard   30, 48, 53, 56–58, 62–63, 249, 305
culture   1–2, 11, 45, 58, 63, 93, 153, 175, 236, 266, 277, 300, 302, 304, 340, 353, 371, 405–408
cup   57, 62, 63n29, 122, 155–156, 184–185, 266–267, 269–270, 278–280, 282–285, 294, 296, 301, 321, 324–326
cylindrical pedestal   182

decoration   3, 77, 96, 108–109, 111, 113, 115, 118, 121–122, 124, 130, 132, 135, 137, 139–140, 143, 145, 148, 152, 156–157, 164–166, 168–169, 170nn13–14, 171, 173–174, 220, 234, 251–252, 254, 257, 259, 261–265, 269, 271, 273, 289, 297, 299, 302, 304–305, 308–309, 318–319, 321
defensive walls   45
demographic   12, 21, 25, 364, 366
depopulation/abandonment   1–3, 22n19, 55, 107, 372, 375
deposit   55, 63, 95–96, 104–125, 128–130, 132–139, 143–148, 153n^{**}, 155, 158–159, 161–164, 169, 175, 240, 262, 365, 401
desertification   14, 41
desiccation   1
Dewashtich   19, 35–36
*dihqān*s (local lords)   36, 45, 300
disk   183
distribution of population. *See* population/depopulation
dog   369–370
domestic   120, 156, 162, 249, 366, 369, 400
domestic chicken   368
donkey   367–368, 370
dromedary   367
dwelling   10, 12, 23, 56, 76, 120–122, 406

Eastern Iran   5, 371
economic   2–3, 5, 11, 18, 21–24, 41–42, 94, 174, 266, 277, 300, 302, 334, 352, 405
ED-XRF Analysis   343
edge   25, 54, 58, 62, 86, 165–166, 168, 173, 180–183, 191, 207–208, 210, 217, 220, 238, 266–267, 270, 287, 320, 364
Egypt   320–321, 339, 342
elite   266, 291
empires   19, 69, 266, 270, 301
epidote   243
equid   367–368
Equus caballus   368
Equus asinus   368

Equus hemionus   368
Erkurgan/Yerkurgan   58, 172
Euphrates Valley   402
evolution   1, 5, 22, 364, 371, 382, 401, 405–408
excavation   2–5, 11–12, 21, 27, 29, 37, 41, 45, 48, 53–58, 62–63, 69, 76, 86, 93–97, 104, 116, 120, 124–125, 130, 133–134, 136, 140, 148, 152, 156–157, 159, 161, 164, 166, 168–169, 171–174, 249, 263, 266, 270, 273, 278, 283, 294, 296, 298–300, 303–305, 320–321, 324–325, 334, 340, 342, 350, 353, 364, 371–372, 375–376, 378, 381–382, 389, 400

Fa-ti   38
fabrics   3, 36, 96, 98, 104, 108–109, 111, 115–119, 121–122, 124, 126, 130, 132n11, 139, 148, 162–164, 168–169, 173, 236, 238, 240–241, 244, 249, 252, 265
Farab/Chärjew Oasis   38, 43
fauna   3, 364–366, 369–370, 407
feldspath   242
Fergana (region)   43, 298
fire place/temples   43, 48, 53–54, 62–63, 69
flared neck   221, 224
flask   57, 109, 117, 133, 140, 197, 205, 219, 222, 234, 285, 287–289, 291–292, 298, 300–301, 343
flat-base   172
fork   57
fortification/ramparts   11, 21, 23, 36, 48, 53–58, 62, 69, 76, 86, 124, 375
fortresses   11, 14, 23–24, 48, 53–55, 57, 63, 69, 76, 86, 93
forts   8, 41
Franco-Uzbek Archaeological Mission in the Oasis of Bukhara. *See* MAFOUB

Gazella subgutturosa   366–367, 369
Gallus gallus domesticus   368–369
genetic   367
geographers, Muslim   35, 43
Gijduvān/Ghijduwān/G'ijduvon (administrative district)   25, 38
Gijduvan (oblast/province)   16, 23, 26, 37, 39, 41
Gijduvan (site 0002)   16
glass/glass production   2–3, 56–57, 63, 69, 172, 175, 255–256, 268, 278–305, 318–328, 331–335, 339–344, 346–348, 350, 352–353, 406–407
glassworking   343, 350
glaze   57, 115, 124, 139–140, 148, 155, 172, 234, 249, 251–259, 262, 264–269, 271–277, 305, 327n18
glazed pottery   104, 129, 174
globular shape   190
goat   366, 370
goblet   62, 63n29, 65, 104–106–108, 113, 147, 155, 171–172, 185, 192, 195, 211, 278, 334, 340
goblets, stem-foot   62, 107, 172

gourd   109, 197
Greco-Bactrian Kingdom   278
gres   243

handle   63, 96, 104n5, 114–116–120, 124, 130, 132–133, 136–137, 139–140, 143, 145, 148, 153n^*, 159, 161–162, 164, 173, 214, 216, 219, 225–227, 233, 286, 292–293, 295, 304, 320–321, 324, 326, 328, 332
hand-shaped   104, 132–133, 164–166, 171, 173
Hellenistic   50, 58, 93, 159, 407
Hephthalite Empire/Hephthalites   45
Hermitage Museum (St. Petersburg)   2, 49, 156–157, 406
historical   ix, 1, 3–5, 8, 18, 21, 25, 27, 31, 35, 38, 43n2, 44–45, 55, 94, 236, 249, 282–283, 290, 302, 304, 322n11, 327, 346, 364, 371, 377, 405, 407
horse   86, 275, 367–368, 370
Hudud al-Alam (anonymous)   43
Hulbuk/Khulbuk   289
human occupation/settlements   1, 5–6, 8, 19, 125n10, 236, 371, 405–406
hybrid   367–368
hydrography/hydrographic   6–10, 12, 16, 26, 43
See also watercourses

Ibn Hawqal   19, 35–38
Ibn Sīnā (Avicenna)   280, 286
incised   34, 108–109, 111, 113, 115, 118, 121–122, 124, 130, 132–133, 139–140, 143, 148, 164, 166, 192
ICP-OES Analysis   344
India   43, 264
inhabitants   10, 45, 56–57, 278, 368, 406
inscriptions   18–19, 23, 55, 57, 86–87, 269
Iran   4–5, 43, 45, 48, 62, 86, 262, 280, 298, 319, 321–322, 328, 339, 342, 348, 350, 364, 407
iron   30, 53, 56–57, 62, 71, 91, 93, 249, 252, 259, 262, 305, 342–343, 347–348, 364, 372
Iron Age   14, 364, 405–406
irrigation   6, 19, 23–25, 36–37, 405
Ishtikhān canal   37
ishkornaia   249, 264–265
Iskijkat (site 0847)   3–4, 12, 94–95, 97–98, 104–117, 125, 143, 147, 152, 156–157, 165–166, 169–172, 176–181, 184–186, 188–192, 197–202, 206, 210–211, 213, 215–217, 224–225, 236–237, 239–242, 244, 246, 304, 328, 332–333, 342, 352, 361, 364, 366, 368–370, 377–379, 396, 398–400, 403–404
Islamic period   2–3, 5, 8, 18–20, 22n19, 23, 57n21, 94–95, 104, 107, 137, 143, 145, 154–155, 158, 161–164, 166, 168, 172, 174–175, 236, 328, 352–353, 371, 389, 396, 406
Islamisation   45
al-Iṣṭakhrī   35–38, 43, 278

jar   30, 34, 55, 57, 62, 63n31, 107–109, 114, 116–117, 119–121, 124–125, 129–130, 132–134, 136–137, 140, 143, 145, 147–148, 155, 159, 161–171, 173–174, 197–207, 209–215, 217–218, 223–224, 233–234, 291–292, 295, 324–325, 340

jug   34, 57, 63n29, 114, 117–121, 124, 132–133, 136, 140, 143, 145, 148, 152, 155, 159, 161–162, 164, 169, 170n13, 174, 197–198, 200–202, 204–206, 212–218, 221–224, 233, 278, 285, 292, 295–296, 301–302

Kakishtuvan/Kakhishtuvan (site 0317, Karaul tepa, mod.   3, 16, 22, 94, 95, 97–98, 116–119, 129–130, 132, 152, 156, 169, 171, 177–178, 186, 194, 197, 202, 204–205, 225, 325, 328, 332–333–334, 342, 352, 364, 378–380, 402

Kam-i Abu Muslim   16
Kampir Duval (oasis wall)   42, 43n1, 45
Kangju (state and people)   62, 93, 171
Kara Kum (desert)   5
Karmana (site 0104)   14
Karshi (Nasaf)   15
Kashkadarya (or Kashka Darya)   43, 58
Kaththa (site 0320)   16, 20, 23
Kaunchi (type of pottery)   158, 169, 170n13, 171
Kazakhstan   321n9, 322n10, 406
Kharghāna   38
Kharqāna   38
Khitfar (hydronym)   14, 16
Khorasan/Khurasan   11, 15–16, 22, 43, 45, 55, 249
Khorezm (Chorasmia)   15–16, 22, 43, 63n28, 69, 86, 164, 171, 278–279, 299, 302, 334, 364, 405
khum (large storage jars)   175
khuv/xūv (local lord, Sogdian title)   11n5, 18–19, 21, 23–24
kilns   58, 120, 168, 265, 305, 327n18, 350
Koktepe   58
Kultobe inscriptions   18–19, 23
kurgans (burial mounds)   5, 8, 11
Kushan Empire/Kushans   63, 147
Kyzyl Kum   5, 25
Kyzylkyr   109, 158–159, 161–162, 164–165, 168

lead   57, 86, 252–253–255, 264–265, 297, 400–401
Lepus   369
lid   72, 108–109, 121, 124–125, 134, 140, 143, 148, 154–155, 158, 161, 166, 168, 171, 173, 186, 189, 192, 208, 218, 234, 287, 289, 295, 301
lid domed   220
lid-seated   109, 120–121, 163–164, 166, 173, 212–213, 215, 234
loop-, side-, vertical-, strap handle   225–227
lower cities. See shahrestans
lustre   104–105, 249, 251, 258–259, 261–262, 264–265, 321

Madrasah   266, 270, 273, 283
  See also 10-verst' map; 100K map; Markov map; SRTM map
manganese   259, 262, 340
al-Maqdisī/al-Muqaddasī   35–36, 43, 53
  See also Aḥsan al-taqāsīm
marble   63
Margiana   147
markets   15
Marzangon (site 0089)   16
mausoleum   302
MEB   251
merchants   11, 18, 22, 45, 57, 364, 367
Merv   2n5, 43, 45, 154, 405
metal   56, 63, 175, 283, 290, 295–296, 298, 300, 302, 366, 370
migration/emigration   278, 301, 381, 407
military   2n5, 12, 16, 21, 26n4, 62, 69, 249
mills   5, 8, 19, 23–24, 36
minarets   53
Mongol   302, 334, 368
monochrome   115, 124, 137, 172, 234, 269–270, 273, 276
mosque   46, 53–54, 57–58, 79, 85–86, 91, 93, 303
mould-made   124, 126–127, 158, 160, 168, 234
mounds   8, 11, 63
Mount Mug(h)   11n5, 18–19, 23, 35–36, 38
mule   367, 370
Muscovite   243
Muslim   279, 301

al-Narshakhī   27, 31, 35–39, 41, 43, 45, 86n34, 364
  See also Tārīkh-i Bukhārā
Narshak (site 0457)   35
Navoi (oblast/province)   38, 244, 266
neck   109, 114, 117, 120–122, 124, 133, 136, 143, 159, 161–162, 164–166, 197–202, 204, 206, 209–210, 214–216, 218–219, 221–224, 268, 281–283, 285–289, 292–293, 295–296, 298–300, 304, 321–323, 325, 328, 339–340, 352
Neolithic   1, 43, 405
Nishapur   3–4, 262, 264, 321n9, 322, 339, 353n36, 400
Nōk Mēthan (inscription)   18–19
nomad   21, 62–63, 366

oasis   1–6, 8–12, 14–16, 19–27, 35, 37–39, 41–42, 43nn1–2, 45, 94–95, 97–98, 106–107, 117, 120, 122, 130, 137, 147, 152, 156–159, 162, 164–166, 168–169, 171–173, 175, 236, 241, 244–245, 249, 252, 263–265, 286, 342–343, 353, 364, 371, 380–381, 401, 405–408
opened form   104, 108–109, 116–117, 121, 124–125, 133, 147, 154–155, 159, 173
Ovis aries   366–367
Oxus (Amu Darya River/Valley)   1, 2n5, 11, 62
oxyde   243

pakhsa (rammed earth) constructions   55, 62, 86, 389
palace   23, 30, 32–33, 46, 53–54, 62, 64–65, 76, 83, 93, 124–125, 130, 136–137, 279, 294, 372, 375, 393, 396
paleochannel   382
Pamir   2
Panjara   292, 294, 302
Parthian   48, 406
Paykend/Paykand/Paikent/Paikand (site 0095)   ix, 2–4, 9, 11–13, 23, 36, 43, 45–48, 53–60, 62–64, 69–71, 76, 79–80, 83–84, 86–89, 92–95, 97–98, 120–125, 133, 136, 140, 152, 156–159, 161–162, 164, 166, 168–169, 173–174, 177–185, 188–189, 195–196, 198–202, 204, 206–209, 213, 215–218, 220–221, 223–227, 249–250, 254–255, 263–265, 279–286, 294, 296, 304–316, 319–329, 339, 342–344, 346–348, 350, 352–359, 364, 370, 375–377, 382, 384, 386, 388–393, 399–400, 403, 404, 406
pedestal base   109, 133, 182, 222
pelite/siltite   243
Penjikent   36, 48, 53–54, 58, 279, 284
Persian   35, 43, 45, 57, 283, 300, 304, 324, 352–353, 368n2
Peshku (district)   25, 39
petrography   ix, 238
physical   42, 301, 371, 382
pilgrim   35, 38
pig   368, 370
pipe   53, 55–56, 63, 66, 139, 174–175
Pīrmast (administrative district)   25–26, 39, 41
PIXE   239, 249, 251–252, 259, 263
Pleistocene   1, 6
plate   62, 105, 114, 126–127, 137, 158, 160, 173, 192, 196, 207, 211, 214, 241, 249, 270, 273, 343
political   2, 8–10, 12, 18–25, 31, 35, 38–39, 41–42, 249, 334, 365n1, 405, 407
population/depopulation   1–3, 9, 11, 16n8, 20–23, 25n1, 27, 36, 41, 58, 269, 277, 290, 293, 297, 301–302, 344, 364, 366, 370, 405, 407–408
pottery. See ceramics/pottery
porcelain   136, 267, 269–270, 273, 276–277, 302
potassium   240, 244, 252, 254–255, 318–319, 344, 352, 382–383, 385
pottery quarter (Paykend, Trench E)   94, 249, 304–305, 321
pottery/pottery production   ix, 2–4, 30–31, 39n21, 54–56, 58, 62, 63n32, 77, 83, 86, 91, 94–98, 104, 106–110, 112, 117–125, 129–130
principalities   42
production/artisanal areas   3, 5, 8, 10, 36, 38, 54, 57, 97, 104, 107, 113, 124, 136, 152, 156–157, 161, 169, 171–173, 175, 238, 241, 249, 251–252, 262–266, 270, 273, 275,

production/artisanal areas (*cont.*)
  278–279, 287, 291–292, 301, 303–305,
  318–319, 327, 340, 343, 346, 350,
  352–353, 371, 406–407
productivity 37
projecting profile 179
property 11, 19, 23

Qarakhanids (Muslim Turkic dynasty) 45,
  57
Qaraqöl (micro-oasis) 2n5, 5, 11
quartz 102, 241–242, 244, 253, 256, 264, 402
Qutayba b. Muslim 27, 31, 38, 45, 54n18

rabad. *See also* suburb 8, 287, 304–305, 328,
  352, 386, 393
Radiocarbon ix, 4, 371–372–373, 375–376,
  378–381, 389, 402, 407
Rāmish/Ramish/Romish tepe (site 0059) 9,
  14, 20, 156–157, 159, 161–162, 169
Ramitan/Rāmītan (mod. Romitan, site
  0074) 3, 9–10, 12, 14, 16, 19–21, 23, 94–95,
  97–98, 117, 120, 124–142, 144–146, 152,
  156–158, 160–171, 174–183, 186–189,
  191–196, 198–22, 225–227, 233–234, 304,
  328–331, 342, 352, 360, 364, 372–375,
  380, 382, 384, 393, 396, 399–400, 402,
  404
ramparts 11–12
rat 369
Rattus 369
RBS 249, 251, 259–260
red-slip pottery 105ff
resource ix, 2–3, 6, 19, 35, 42, 53, 94, 174–175,
  364
rim
  collared rim 129, 164, 205, 213, 216, 220
  dropping rim 158–159, 162, 193, 196–197,
    203, 214
  grooved rim 215, 221
  moulded rim 161, 202
  pointed rim 157, 187–189, 194, 266
  rounded rim 165, 205, 212, 214, 224
  simple rim 129–130, 155, 157, 162, 184–186,
    188–191, 195, 206–207, 210–211, 218, 222
  squared rim 202, 204, 209–210
  thickened rim 108–109, 156–159,
    163–165, 171, 186, 193, 195, 197–200, 204,
    207, 209, 215–218, 222–224, 280
  trefoil-mouthed rim 162
ring-base 130, 156, 172, 176–178, 190
rivers 9, 26, 36–37, 41–44, 304
roads/road networks 9–11, 14, 16, 22–23, 43
Royal 12, 24, 27, 36, 48, 373–375
Rūd-i Zar, river (adh-Dhar) 16, 22
ruminants 366, 369

Saiga tatarica 366
Saka (people) 62
Samanid Emirate/Samanids 18
Samanid period 19, 364
Samarra 262–263, 265, 339, 353n36

Samarkand/Samarqand 5, 16, 18–19, 21,
  27nn6–7, 35–38, 43, 58, 62, 63n28, 86,
  158, 170n13, 172, 235, 266, 269–270, 279,
  287–288, 291, 294, 300, 302, 304, 332,
  339n32, 342, 350, 364, 371, 405
Sarmatian 53, 62
Sasanian Empire/Sasanians 53, 63, 76, 86,
  147, 323–328
schiste 243
Scythian 2
SEM-EDS 249ff
Setalak 109, 158–159, 161–164, 166, 168
settlements. *See* human occupation
Shāfurkām/Shafirkam (Vardanzī/Vardana,
  district) 16
shahrestan (part of city around citadel) 8,
  10–12, 21, 29, 43, 45, 53–58, 62, 73–77,
  80–82, 86, 104n6, 107, 120, 124, 130, 133,
  157–158, 161–162, 164, 174, 249, 264, 266,
  273, 279–287, 294, 296, 304–305, 321,
  324–325, 327–328, 332, 334, 340, 352,
  365, 368–369, 375, 378, 380, 389–390,
  393, 396, 399, 402
Shahrud/Shārūd 283
shallow 109, 113–114, 155, 158, 173, 185–186,
  188–189, 191–192, 207
shape 16, 29–30, 45, 48, 86, 96–105, 107–109,
  111, 113, 115–122, 124–126, 128–130,
  132–137, 140, 143, 145, 147–150, 152–159,
  161–166, 168–174, 176–233, 267–270,
  273, 278–280, 288–289, 291–298, 300,
  320–321, 324–326, 339–340, 352–353
Shāpūr (Sasanian prince) 27, 41
sheep 34, 42, 366, 370
sherd 1, 3–4, 57, 96–104, 107, 109, 116–117,
  120–122, 124, 131, 136–137, 143, 145,
  148, 153, 155, 159, 161–162, 164–165,
  169–174, 236–241, 244, 246–247, 249,
  251–254, 258–260, 262–265, 273, 276,
  280, 304–305, 334, 365, 383, 385, 389,
  392–393, 396, 398–400, 402, 404
silica 251–253, 255, 259, 340, 344, 346, 348,
  352
silk 367
Silk Roads 364, 367
silver 21n16, 57, 62, 71, 76, 84, 88, 238, 259,
  302
sites. *See* human occupation/settlements
Sivanj/Savinj (Qal'a-yi Siminch/Suyunich,
  site 0231) 14, 16, 20, 23
slip 21, 97, 100, 105–109, 111, 113–120, 122,
  124–126, 130, 132–133, 135, 137, 139–140,
  145, 147–148, 152, 155–159, 162, 169–171,
  251–254, 264–269, 271–277
social 2, 5, 10–12, 15n6, 18, 19, 20–24, 35–36,
  120, 369, 405–406
Sogdiana (Sughd) 11n5, 18–19, 21, 35–36,
  41–42, 58, 62, 63n32, 278, 304, 334, 352
splayed profile 181
steatite 62
storage jars (*khum*) 107, 119, 145, 148, 155,
  159, 164–166, 169, 174

stratigraphic/stratigraphical 3–4, 29, 51,
  54–56, 94–97, 104, 106–108, 116, 120,
  124–125, 130, 134–135, 137, 139, 143, 145,
  147, 152, 156–157, 171, 174, 236, 249, 251,
  258, 261, 299, 365, 372, 375–378, 382,
  385, 389, 396, 399, 407
suburb (*rabad*) 5, 8–10, 12, 45, 57–58, 77,
  85–86, 91, 124, 166, 168, 365, 375, 380,
  393, 396
Sughd. *See* Sogdiana
Sulṭānābād (Ghishtī, administrative district,
  river) 16, 25–26, 37, 39, 41–42
Sus scrofa domesticus 368
Susa 262–263, 265, 339n31
Syr Darya (river/basin) 43, 63, 304
Syria 321, 342, 402

al-Ṭabarī, Muḥammad ibn Jarīr (d. 923
  CE) 18, 31, 35, 38, 43, 45
tandoor 56, 86
Tang Dynasty/period (617/18 CE) 368
Tarab (site 0043) 16
Tārīkh-i Bukhārā (al-Narshakhī) 35
Tarim basin 411
Tashkent 5, 43, 235, 269, 282, 286–288, 291,
  294, 300, 371
  See also Chach/Chāch
Tavovis/Ṭavāvīs/al-Ṭawāwīs (Khwāja Bustān,
  site 0751) 15–16
temperature 97–98, 169, 174, 343, 385
temple 12, 43, 46, 48, 53, 62–65, 69, 72, 86,
  278
tepe 1–2, 5, 8–12, 14–18, 20–24, 39n19, 377,
  405
Termez 58, 278, 294, 364, 370
tetradrachms 21
textile 166
Timurid Dynasty/period 3, 107
titanium 254
tomb 339
towns 10, 15–16, 364
trade/commerce 5, 45, 54–55, 57, 265, 271,
  279, 282, 285, 289, 340, 340, 342, 353,
  364, 368, 371, 405
tower 21, 48, 50, 52–56, 62–63, 69, 73,
  86, 125, 365, 372, 385, 396, 400,
  402–403
Transoxiana 43, 48, 53n13, 55, 69, 304, 322,
  328, 340, 352
tripartite sites 8–11, 14–16, 20–21, 24
Tūrān/Turan 43
Turfan 367
Turk 45
Turkistan/Turkestan 43, 45, 269
Turkmenistan 5, 38, 154, 364
turquoise 62, 71, 84, 256–257, 265, 303
typology 2–3, 39n21, 96, 241, 263, 298, 304,
  328

Uch Kulakh/Qulak (unique tepe) 11–14,
  21n17, 23
unique tepes (sites with unique mound) 14

urban development   12, 22, 145, 371, 405
urbanisation   18, 21–22, 405–406
Uzbekistan   ix, 3, 5, 45, 48, 57n21, 266–267, 278–279, 282, 286, 288–289, 302, 304, 322, 324n13, 339n33, 340, 342, 364

Vābkand/Vobkent (site 0116)   10, 16, 25, 38–39, 303
Varakhsha (site 0069)   14–16, 20, 22–23, 35, 53, 63, 405–406
Vardān Khudāt/Vardānkhudā (ruler of Vardāna)   25, 31, 38
Vardana/Vardanzi/Vardanzeh (site 0084)   ix, 2, 10, 16, 23, 25, 27–28, 30–33, 35–42, 134, 164–165, 236, 240, 244, 246, 406–407

villages   5, 10, 19, 25–27, 35–38, 41, 86n34, 364–365, 405
Vobkent (city)   10, 16, 25, 38–39, 303
ware   95–96, 98–105, 107–109, 111, 116, 118–119, 122, 124, 126, 130, 132, 137, 143, 147–148, 152, 155, 162–164, 168, 172–175, 233–234, 270, 297, 340, 342, 353n38
water   ix, 1–2, 6, 14, 19, 24–27, 35–39, 41–42, 45, 48, 53, 55–56, 58, 62, 66, 93, 95, 143, 155, 164, 174, 268, 280, 282, 284, 286–287, 295–296, 298, 301, 340, 343, 371, 382–383, 400–401, 405
watercourse   9–11, 14, 16, 19, 20, 22–24
wheel-made   124, 126–127

Xiongnu (tribal confederation)   62
Xuanzang (Chinese pilgrim)   35, 38

Yuezhi   21, 278

Zandanīji   38
Zerafshan/Zarafshan/Central Bukhara Collector Canal   1, 6, 14–16, 19, 25–26, 35–39, 41, 43, 45, 47, 57–58, 241, 244, 283, 364, 382, 405
Zamanbaba settlements   000
Zandana//Zandinī Zandany. *See* Zandana/Zandanī (site 0083)   16, 23, 38
Zar-i Rud (Rud-I Zar) River   16, 22
Zoroastrian   48, 58, 62, 76, 86, 300